Colorado's Thirteeners

13,800 to 13,999 Feet

From Hikes to Climbs

Gerry Roach
Jennifer Roach

Fulcrum Publishing
Golden, Colorado

To Marjorie L. Clark,
who had the courage of a hundred mountaineers

Library of Congress Cataloging-in-Publication Data

Roach, Gerry.
  Colorado's thirteeners, 13,800 to 13,999 feet : from hikes to climbs / Gerry Roach, Jennifer Roach.
     p. cm.
  Includes index.
   ISBN 1-55591-419-5 (pbk.)
   1. Hiking–Colorado–Guidebooks. 2. Mountaineering–Colorado–Guidebooks. 3. Colorado–Guidebooks. I. Roach, Jennifer. II. Title.
   GV199.42.C6 R64 2001
   796.52'2'09788–dc21   2001000091

Printed in China
0 9 8 7 6 5 4 3 2

Editorial: Daniel Forrest-Bank, Jason Cook, Amy Timms
Design: Bill Spahr
Cartography: Gerry Roach and Bill Spahr
Front cover photograph: At 13,951 feet, Ice Mountain (right) in alpenglow, Collegiate Peaks Wilderness, Sawatch Range, copyright © Eric Wunrow.
Back cover photograph: Mount Buckskin (13,865 feet) from the northeast. Photo by Gerry Roach.

Fulcrum Publishing
16100 Table Mountain Parkway, Suite 300
Golden, Colorado 80403
www.fulcrum-books.com

Contents

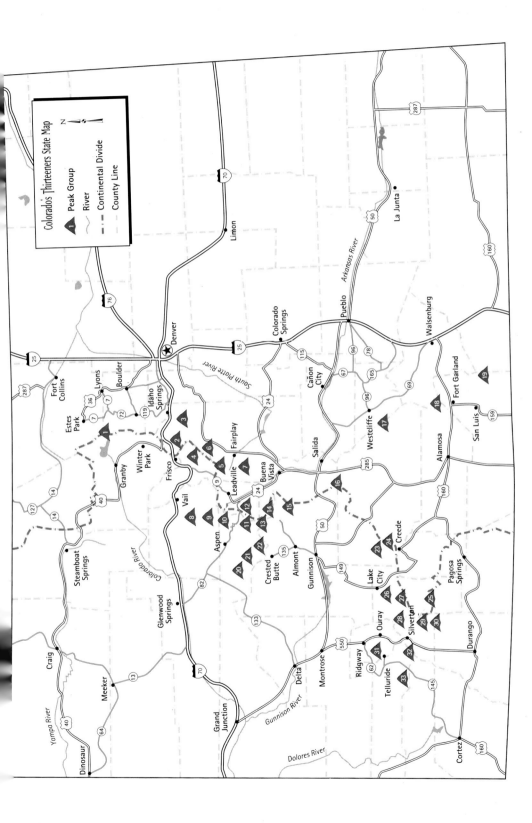

Colorados Thirteeners State Map

▲1 Peak Group
--- River
-·-·- Continental Divide
---- County Line

High above Geneva Lake on Hagerman's southwest ridge.

Preface

The elevation celebration continues. *Colorado's Thirteeners: From Hikes to Climbs* celebrates the joys that come from climbing Colorado's highest peaks. This guide is a companion volume to Gerry's previous guide, *Colorado's Fourteeners: From Hikes to Climbs,* which covers 250 routes on Colorado's 55 peaks over 14,000 feet. In this companion guide, Gerry and his wife, Jennifer, cover 205 routes on Colorado's 59 highest thirteeners, whose summits are between 13,800 and 13,999 feet.

The obvious challenge of climbing all of Colorado's fourteeners captures many people. After completing the fourteeners, many people choose to pursue the goal of climbing Colorado's 100 highest peaks. Counting schemes vary, but the fourteeners plus the thirteeners over 13,800 feet comprise Colorado's 100 highest peaks. We have coined the term *centennial thirteeners* to refer to the thirteeners between 13,800 and 13,999 feet. Climbing the 59 centennial thirteeners covered in this book is a goal commensurate in scope and difficulty to the goal of climbing Colorado's 55 fourteeners. This too is an obvious challenge.

Climbing the centennial thirteeners as an extension of the fourteener goal is only one reason to visit these great peaks. Each centennial thirteener provides a worthy outing independent of its altitude. If the large number of people climbing the fourteeners frustrates you, then you will find relief on the centennial thirteeners, which see far fewer climbers. Some people have declared that they will climb *only* the centennial thirteeners.

The San Juan Range, Colorado's largest, holds 21 centennial thirteeners. In comparison, the San Juans hold 13 fourteeners. Thus the average centennial thirteener is more remote than the average fourteener. The hardest centennial thirteeners are more difficult to climb than the hardest fourteeners. Jagged, Teakettle and Dallas, the hardest centennial thirteeners, require Class 5 climbing on their easiest routes. In comparison, no fourteener requires Class 5 climbing on its easiest route. In particular, Jagged has both Class 5 climbing and a remote position.

This book takes a broad view of Colorado's centennial thirteeners. In addition to the standard routes, we describe many alternative routes on the easier peaks and several technical routes on the harder peaks. Many routes on the centennial thirteeners are walk-ups (Class 1, Class 2, Easy Snow), but there are many wonderful scrambles (Class 3, Moderate Snow) and technical climbs (Class 4, Class 5, Steep Snow) on these peaks. We have designated the best routes, regardless of difficulty, as *Classic*. All of the routes in this guide lead to the summit of a peak.

This is a guidebook, pure and simple. It describes where to climb, but not how to climb. No book can make your judgments for you, but good instructional books can aid the process of learning the fundamentals. For an introduction to the sport of mountaineering, we recommend *Mountaineering: The Freedom of the Hills* (Mountaineers Books).

The trailheads discussed here are places passenger cars can reach. Sometimes these places are well-marked parking lots at the end of a road, and sometimes they are just points on a continuing road where the road becomes too rough for passenger cars. Four-wheel-drive vehicles can shorten many of the ascents in Colorado, but we have never felt that this aid was necessary. We need more mountain, not less.

Unlike most mountaineering guidebooks, which are a compilation of route descriptions written by many people, this book is the result of one couple's labor of love. Gerry started climbing in Colorado in 1955, and has spent parts of six decades climbing Colorado's peaks. Jennifer moved to Colorado in 1980, and has since climbed all of Colorado's 637 ranked peaks over 13,000 feet. We climbed many routes specifically for this guidebook and wrote them up immediately after each climb. Together, we have made more than 500 ascents on Colorado's 100 highest peaks.

This book is not comprehensive in its coverage of the routes on the centennial thirteeners. We could have included many more routes. For every route we climbed, we saw two more! Never lose your spirit of discovery. You should finish each workout, each climb and each book wanting more. Climb safely and have fun!

We welcome route information and constructive criticism from readers. Mail your comments to Gerry Roach and Jennifer Roach, P.O. Box 3303, Boulder, CO 80307; e-mail them at grhigh@mountains.com; or check our website at http://climb.mountains.com for recent updates.

Introduction

Safety First

Climbing is dangerous, and each individual should approach these peaks with caution. Conditions can vary tremendously depending on time of day and time of year. The route descriptions in this book assume good, summer conditions. Lightning is always a serious hazard in Colorado during the summer months. Snow conditions and cornices vary from year to year. Spring and early summer avalanches can be a function of winter storms that occurred months earlier. The previous winter's snowfall determines snow conditions in August.

Before charging forth with your city energy and competitive urges, take some time to understand the mountain environment you are about to enter. Carefully study your chosen route, and don't be afraid to retreat if conditions, yours or the mountain's, are unfavorable. Better yet, do an easier climb nearby to become familiar with the area. When both you and the mountain are ready, come back and do your dream climb.

LIGHTNING

Colorado is famous for apocalyptic lightning storms that threaten not just your life, but your soul as well. This section will have special meaning if you have ever been trapped by a storm that endures for more than an hour and leaves no gap between one peal of thunder and the next. The term *simultaneous flash-boom* has a very personal meaning for many Colorado climbers.

Dangers
- Lightning is the greatest external hazard to summer mountaineering in Colorado.
- Lightning kills people every year in Colorado's mountains.
- Direct hits are usually fatal.

Precautions
- Start early! Be off summits by noon and back in the valley by early afternoon.
- Observe thunderhead buildup carefully, noting speed and direction; towering thunderheads with black bottoms are bad.
- When lightning begins nearby, count the seconds between flash and thunder, then divide by 5 to calculate the distance to the flash in miles. Repeat to determine if lightning is approaching.

- Try to determine whether the lightning activity is cloud-to-cloud or ground strikes.
- Get off summits and ridges.

Protection
- You cannot outrun a storm; physics wins.
- When caught, seek a safe zone in the 45-degree cone around an object 5 to 10 times your height.
- Be aware of ground currents; the current from a ground strike disperses along the ground or cliff, especially in wet cracks.
- Wet items are good conductors; snow is not a good conductor.
- Separate yourself from metal objects.
- Avoid sheltering in spark gaps under boulders and trees.
- Disperse the group. Survivors can revive one who is hit.
- Crouch on boot soles, ideally on dry, insulating material such as moss or grass. Dirt is better than rock. Avoid water.
- Do not put your hands down. Put elbows on knees and hands on head. This gives current a short path through your arms rather than the longer path through your vital organs.
- Do not lie down, because current could easily go through your vital organs.

First Aid
- Know and give CPR, as CPR has revived many lightning-strike victims.
- Treat for burns; evacuate.

AVALANCHE

Hazard Forecasting
- Avalanches are the greatest external hazard to winter mountaineering in Colorado; gravity never sleeps.
- Loose-snow avalanches start at a single point and fan out downward; the danger is greatest after new snowfall.
- Slab avalanches occur when an entire snow slope starts in motion at once.
- Consistent winds of more than 15 miles per hour can build up soft slabs.
- Consistent winds of more than 25 miles per hour can build up hard slabs.
- Hard slabs develop more rapidly at low temperatures and are sensitive to temperature changes.
- Most avalanches occur on slopes of 30 to 45 degrees.
- Most avalanches that trap people are triggered by the victims themselves.
- Most avalanches that trap skiers are relatively small.
- Avalanches occur on open slopes, in gullies and in stands of open

13,870

"North Carbonate" from the northeast.

trees. Ridges, outcrops and dense stands of trees (too dense to ski through comfortably) are safer.

- Beware of avalanche danger during and after heavy winter storms. The danger factor declines with time. The rate of decrease depends strongly on temperature. Near 32 degrees Fahrenheit, the danger may persist for only a few hours. Below 0 degrees Fahrenheit, it may last for many days or even weeks.
- Deep snow smooths out terrain irregularities and promotes avalanching.
- Warm snow will bond to a warm surface much better than cold snow will bond to a cold surface. Therefore, monitor the temperature at the start of a storm.
- It generally takes a foot of new snow to produce serious avalanche danger.
- Prolonged snowfalls of an inch or more per hour should always be viewed with suspicion.
- Snowfalls that begin warm and then cool off tend to be more stable than those with the opposite trend.
- Extensive sluffing after a fresh snowfall is evidence of stability.
- Sunballs rolling down a slope are indicators of rapid changes taking place in the snow. The danger is not high if the sunballs are small and penetrate only a few inches into the surface layer. If these balls grow in size during the day and eventually achieve the form of large snow

wheels that penetrate deeply into the snow, wet-snow avalanching may be imminent.
- "Talking snow," a hollow, drumlike sound under your footsteps or skis, or a booming sound with or without a dropping jar, is a sign of serious avalanche hazard.
- Other things being equal, convex slopes offer more slab-avalanche danger than concave slopes. However, many avalanches do start on concave profiles.

Precautions
- Never travel alone.
- Avoid avalanche areas and times of high danger. The probability of being caught in an avalanche is directly proportional to the length of time you spend in the danger zone.
- Carry at least one shovel and avalanche beacons if possible.

If you must cross an avalanche slope:
- If equipped with avalanche beacons, turn to transmit mode.
- Proceed through the danger zone one person at a time. If you are buried, your rescue depends on your unburied companions.
- Remove the wrist loops of your ski poles from your wrists.
- Unhitch any ski safety straps, and loosen your pack straps.
- Put on hat and mittens, and close your parka.

If you are caught in an avalanche:
- Discard poles, skis and pack.
- Attempt to stay on the surface with a swimming motion.
- Attempt to work to the side of the avalanche.
- Grab trees.
- As the avalanche slows, close your mouth, cover your face with your hands and make an air space.
- Don't shout when buried. Sound goes into but not out of snow.

Rescue
- Don't panic. A buried person has only a 30 percent chance of survival after 30 minutes. Organized rescue in most backcountry situations is at least one hour from the scene. The lives of your buried companions depend largely on what *you* do.
- Assess any additional avalanche hazard and plan escape routes.
- Mark the last-seen point.
- If equipped with avalanche beacons, the *entire* unburied party must turn their beacons to receive. Search in a pattern that zeroes in on the strongest signal. Turn down the volume, pinpoint the victim's exact position, then dig.
- If you do not have avalanche beacons, do a quick search below the

last-seen point. Scruff around. Look for any clues and mark their location. Search likely areas near trees, on benches and near the end of the debris.
- Start a thorough search. Search the most likely area first. Use ski poles as probes if that's all you have. Do a coarse probe, with probe holes about 2 feet apart. Have all searchers form a straight line and move uphill. A coarse probe has a 70 percent chance of finding a victim buried in the probe area. Repeat a coarse probe of the most likely area several times, then move on to the next most likely area.
- Go for help. Determining when to send some of your party for additional help is a judgment call that depends on the size of your group, how far into the backcountry you are and the availability of trained rescue groups.

Leave No Trace

If you use the wilderness resource, it is your responsibility to help protect it from environmental damage. The old adage "Take nothing but pictures; leave nothing but footprints" is no longer good enough. Visitors' footprints can cause extensive damage to fragile alpine areas. The ground plants above treeline are especially vulnerable because they cling to a tenuous existence. If you destroy a patch of tundra with a careless step, it may take a hundred years for the plants to recover. In some cases, they may never recover.

The routes in this book all pass through the alpine zone. Tread lightly. Stay on the trails, and where trails do not exist, travel on durable surfaces such as rock and snow. Walk on rocks in the tundra, not on the tundra itself. If traveling over tundra is the only option, be sure to disperse use over a wide area. Let your eyes do the walking sometimes. You do not have to explore every inch on foot. Respect the environment you are entering. If you do not show respect, you are an intruder, not a visitor.

Leave No Trace (LNT), a national nonprofit organization dedicated to educating people about responsible use of the outdoors, recommends a few simple techniques for minimum-impact travel through fragile alpine environments. Learn them. Abide by them. For more information about LNT and minimum-impact outdoor ethics, visit the LNT website at www.lnt.org or call 800-332-4100. The six tenets of the LNT movement are:

1. Plan Ahead and Prepare
- Know the regulations for and special concerns about of the area you are visiting.
- Visit the backcountry in small groups.
- Avoid popular areas during times of high use.
- Choose equipment and clothing in subdued colors.
- Repackage food into reusable containers.

Mount Silverheels from the southeast.

2. Travel and Camp on Durable Surfaces

On the Trail
- Stay on designated trails. Walk in single file in the middle of the path.
- Do not shortcut switchbacks, as this can cause severe erosion problems.
- Where multiple trails exist, choose the one that is most worn.
- Where no trails exist, spread out across the terrain.
- When traveling cross-country, choose the most durable surfaces available: rock, gravel, dry grasses or snow.
- Rest on rock or in designated sites.
- Avoid wetlands and riparian areas.
- Use a map and compass to eliminate the need for rock cairns, tree scars and ribbons.
- Step to the downhill side of the trail and talk softly when encountering pack stock.

At Camp
- Choose an established, legal site that will not be damaged by your stay.
- Camping above treeline is not recommended because of damage to tundra plants.
- Restrict activities to the area where vegetation is compacted or absent.
- Keep pollutants out of water sources by camping at least 200 feet (70 adult steps) from lakes and streams.
- Move campsites frequently.

Mount Ouray from the northeast.

3. Pack It In, Pack It Out
- Pack everything that you bring into wild country back out with you.
- Protect wildlife and your food by storing rations securely.
- Pick up all spilled foods.

4. Properly Dispose of What You Can't Pack Out
- Deposit human waste in catholes dug 6 to 8 inches deep at least 200 feet from water, camp or trails. Cover and disguise the cathole when finished.
- Use toilet paper or wipes sparingly. Pack them out.
- To wash yourself or your dishes, carry water 200 feet away from streams or lakes, and use small amounts of biodegradable soap. Strain and scatter dishwater; pack out remaining particles.
- Inspect your campsite for trash and evidence of your stay. Pack out all trash: yours and others'.

5. Leave What You Find
- Treat our national heritage with respect. Leave plants, rocks and historical artifacts as you find them, for others to discover and enjoy.
- Good campsites are found, not made. Altering a site should not be necessary.
- Observe wildlife quietly from a distance; never feed wild animals.
- Let nature's sounds prevail. Keep loud voices and noises to a minimum.
- Control pets at all times. Remove dog feces.
- Do not build structures or furniture; do not dig trenches.

6. Minimize Use and Impact of Fires

- Campfires can cause lasting impacts to the backcountry. Always carry a lightweight stove for cooking. Enjoy a candle lantern instead of a fire.
- When fires are permitted, use established fire rings, fire pans or mound fires. Do not scar large rocks or overhangs.
- Gather sticks no thicker than an adult's wrist.
- Do not snap branches off live, dead or downed trees.
- Put out campfires completely.
- Remove all unburned trash from the fire ring and scatter the cool ashes over a large area far from camp.

The Rating System

We use a modified Yosemite Decimal System (YDS) to rate each route's effort and difficulty. Each route's rating has five parts: R Points, round-trip mileage, round-trip elevation gain, Class and, where snow is present, Snow Steepness. We present this information right below each route name.

R POINTS

In this book, our R Point value replaces the Yosemite Decimal System's Grade value. We feel it is a better measure of a route's overall effort and difficulty, or the route's "efferculty," as we prefer to call it. A route's R Point value expresses the route's efferculty based on the peak's elevation, the length of the approach and climb viewed in both time and distance, elevation gain and the technical difficulty of each pitch. The R Point value does *not* express the route's objective dangers and exposure, the probability of bad weather or the difficulty of retreat. You can compare the R Point numbers (abbreviated RP in each route's listing) for two routes and know which is tougher overall. You can also use the R Point number to determine how long the climb will take you. Climbers' speeds vary, but many climbers average 20 to 25 R Points per hour. For example, if you have determined that you can average 25 R Points per hour, and a route has a rating of 150 R Points, then your projected time for that route is six hours.

Here is a sampling of R Point numbers for several popular Colorado hikes and climbs:

Mount Sanitas via Dakota Ridge	26
Green Mountain via Saddle Rock	44
South Boulder Peak via Shadow Canyon	67
Mount Audubon Trail	120
Grays Peak Trail	148
Bison Peak — Southwest Ridge	157
McCurdy Mountain — South Slopes	187
Dallas Peak — East Face	337
Longs Peak — Keyhole Route	376

Pikes Peak via Barr Trail	418
Jagged Peak – North Face from Needleton	513
Vestal Peak – Wham Ridge from Elk Park	562

MILEAGE

The mileage is the round-trip hiking and climbing distance from the starting point to the summit and back to the starting point. The starting point is usually a trailhead, but we often list the mileage from four-wheel-drive parking places, lakes and other important points along the route. For harder routes, we often list the mileage incurred should you choose to descend an easier route.

ELEVATION GAIN

The elevation gain is the total elevation gain encountered from the starting point to the summit and back to the starting point. This includes any extra gain you may encounter going over passes or false summits both on the ascent and on the return.

CLASS

A route's Class is denoted by the word **Class**, followed by a number from 1 to 5.14, in ascending order of difficulty of the route's most difficult free-climbing rock pitch. Used elsewhere, a Class rating refers to a single pitch or move. Difficulties from Class 1 to Class 4 are described with a single digit only. When the difficulty reaches Class 5, the description includes decimal places. In this guide, Class 5 difficulty ranges from 5.0 to 5.7. We do not distinguish between 5.0, 5.1 and 5.2, instead indicating difficulty in this range with the rating **Class 5.0–5.2**.

We do not use adjectives such as **easy, difficult** or **severe** to rate the rock pitches. What is easy for one person may be difficult for another, and words like these only confuse the issue. In place of adjectives, we use examples to describe difficulty. The answer to the question "Just how hard is Class 3 anyway?" is "Climb Longs' Homestretch and Meeker's summit block, then you will understand the difference between easy Class 3 and hard Class 3." The list of example routes that follows includes some fourteeners and classic Front Range rock climbs for comparison. We order the routes from easiest to hardest within each Class.

Class 1:	Grays Peak – North Slopes
	Mount Edwards – East Slopes
	Mount Silverheels – South Ridge
	Mount Elbert – East Ridge
	Pikes Peak – East Slopes
	Horseshoe Mountain – Northeast Ridge
Class 2:	Mount Massive – East Slopes
	Fletcher Mountain – Southeast Ridge

Holy Cross Ridge – Halo Ridge
Handies Peak – Grizzly Gulch
Mount Hope – East Ridge

Class 2+:   Windom Peak – West Ridge
              Mount Adams – Southeast Face
              Frasco Benchmark – South Ridge
              Mount Sneffels – South Slopes
              Grizzly Peak – East Ridge

Class 3:   Longs Peak – Keyhole
              Hagerman Peak – Southwest Ridge
              Crestone Needle – South Face
              Wilson Peak – West Ridge
              "Thunder Pyramid" – West Face
              Arrow Peak – Northeast Face
              Mount Meeker – Loft

Class 4:   Sunlight Peak – South Slopes (final summit block)
              Trinity Peak – West Ridge
              Mount Wilson – North Slopes (final 150 feet)
              Pigeon Peak – Southwest Slopes
              Second Flatiron – Freeway
              "Thunder Pyramid" – South Ridge

Class 5.0–5.2: Little Bear to Blanca traverse
                Third Flatiron – Standard East Face
                Jagged Mountain – North Face
                Longs Peak – Notch Couloir

Class 5.3–5.4: Teakettle Mountain – Southeast Ridge
                Longs Peak – Kieners
                Dallas Peak – East Face
                Longs Peak – North Face
                First Flatiron – North Arête

Class 5.5:   Third Flatiron – East Face Left
              Longs Peak – Keyhole Ridge
              Boulder Canyon Dome – East Slab
              Longs Peak – Alexander's Chimney

Class 5.6:   First Flatiron – Direct East Face
              Arrow Peak – North Ridge
              Eldorado Wind Tower – Calypso
              Mount Sneffels – North Buttress

Class 5.7:	Dallas Peak – Southeast Corner
	Crestone Needle – Ellingwood Arête
	Vestal Peak – Center Shift Variation to Wham Ridge
	Boulder Canyon Castle Rock – Cussin' Crack
	Third Flatiron – Friday's Folly
	Longs Peak – Stettner's Ledges
Class 5.8:	Eldorado Bastille – The Bastille Crack
	Kit Carson – The Prow
	Crestone Needle – North Pillar
	Eldorado Bastille – West Arête

These difficulty ratings are for good, dry conditions. High-country rock rapidly becomes more difficult as it becomes wet, and a route becomes a different climb entirely when snow-covered. For example, the difficulty of Arrow Peak's Northeast Face Route can jump from Class 3 to Class 5 when it is wet or snow-covered.

We discuss descent routes only occasionally. You can descend by reversing the ascent route or by descending easier routes. When we include technical routes on a peak, we always discuss an easier route, and this is usually the logical descent route. There are often several easy routes to choose from. You must use good mountaineering judgment when selecting descent routes.

Because we have defined difficulty on rock by example, people unfamiliar with the YDS will have to do some climbs before they understand what the different Class ratings mean. This is particularly true for the more difficult ratings. The following descriptions can help.

Class 1 is trail **walking** or any hiking across open country that is no more difficult than walking on a maintained trail. The parking lot at the trailhead is easy Class 1, groomed trails are midrange Class 1 and approaching the top of Horseshoe Mountain's Northeast Ridge Route is difficult Class 1.

Class 2 is off-trail **hiking**. Class 2 usually means bushwhacking or hiking on a talus slope. You are not yet using handholds for upward movement. Almost everybody walks down Class 2 terrain facing out.

Class 2+ is a pseudo-scrambling route where you will use your hands but do not need to search very hard for handholds. We call this movement **scampering**. Most people are able to downclimb Class 2+ terrain facing out.

Class 3 is the easiest climbing category, and people usually call it **scrambling**. You are beginning to look for and use handholds for upward movement. You are now using basic climbing, not walking, movements. Though you are using handholds, you don't have to look very hard to find them. Occasionally putting your hand down for balance while crossing a talus slope does not qualify as Class 3. That is still Class 2. Many people feel the need to face in while downclimbing Class 3 terrain.

Class 4 is easy **climbing**. You are not just using handholds; you have to search for, select and test them. You are beginning to use muscle groups not involved with hiking, those of the upper body and abdominals in particular. Your movement is more focused, thoughtful and slower. Many people prefer to rappel down a serious Class 4 pitch rather than downclimb it. Many Class 3 routes in California would be rated Class 4 in Colorado.

Class 5 is **technical climbing**. You are now using a variety of climbing techniques, not just cling holds. Your movement may involve stemming with your legs, cross-pressure with your arms, pressing down on handholds as you pass them, edging on small holds, smearing, chimneying, jamming and heel hooks. A lack of flexibility will be noticeable and can hinder your movement. Your movement usually totally occupies your mind. You have come a long way from walking across the parking lot while entertaining a million thoughts. Most people choose to rappel down Class 5 pitches.

Class ratings of individual moves and pitches are solidified by the consensus of the climbing community at large and the local climbing community who are most familiar with the area. Only when there is considerable consensus for a rating can it be used as an example of that difficulty. If we are not sure of a Class rating, we add the designation (?) after the rating.

A Class rating makes no statement about how exposed a move or pitch is. Exposure is a subjective fear that varies widely from person to person. Exposure usually increases with difficulty, but there are some noticeable exceptions to this rule. Some Class 2 passages are very exposed. If exposure bothers you to the point where it impairs your movement, then increase our ratings accordingly.

We do not define difficulty in terms of equipment that you might or might not use. Historically, Class 3 meant unroped climbing and Class 4 was roped climbing. Unfortunately, there is a lot of historical momentum behind those old definitions. Under the old definition, when people say that they "Third-Classed" a pitch, all we know is that they climbed it unroped. We do not know how hard it is. After all, the Casual Route (5.10) on the Diamond of Longs Peak has been "Third-Classed." Everyone knows how hard a pitch they are willing to do unroped, but they do not know how hard a pitch someone else is willing to do unroped. There are many people who can climb every route in this guide unroped, and many more who cannot do any of the routes, with or without a rope. You are the one who must decide when to rope up.

SNOW STEEPNESS
The last part of the rating system used in this guide refers to the route's *steepest* snow or ice. The Snow Steepness rating is not part of the YDS, but we include it to provide more information about a route. If there is no snow or ice on a route, this designation is absent. Because a slope's steep-

13,898

Horseshoe Mountain from the west.

ness can be measured, this part of the rating is easier to define. The following adjectives refer to a snow slope's angle:

Easy:	0 to 30 degrees
Moderate:	30 to 45 degrees
Steep:	45 to 60 degrees
Very Steep:	60 to 80 degrees
Vertical:	80 to 90 degrees

Climbers seldom measure a slope angle accurately. They usually estimate the angle by the slope's feel, and these feelings vary widely. Even experienced climbers are notorious for guessing a slope angle to be steeper than it is. We have kept this in mind when determining the slope angles used in this guide. When a slope angle hovers around the critical junction between Moderate and Steep, we apply the Steep rating.

OTHER RATING SYSTEMS

The Yosemite Decimal System (YDS) is widely used in the United States and has evolved as the national standard. The National Climbing Classification System (NCCS) was intended to be the standard, but it has not gained wide acceptance. The difference between the YDS and NCCS numbers is confusing. We include a table that lists the correspondence between these two U.S. systems and several of the popular international systems,

YDS	NCCS	UIAA	French	British	Australian	German
Class 1	F1	I		1 (Easy)		
Class 2	F1	I		1 (Easy)		
Class 3	F2	I, II		1 (Easy)		
Class 4	F3	I, II		1 (Easy)		
Class 5.0–5.2	F4	I, II	1	2 (Moderate)	10	I
Class 5.3	F5	II	2	3a (Difficult)	11	II
Class 5.4	F5	III	3	3b (Very Difficult)	12	III
Class 5.5	F6	IV	4	4a (Severe)	12, 13	IV
Class 5.6	F6	V-	5	4b (Severe)	13	V
Class 5.7	F7	V	5	4b, 4c (JVS)	14, 15	VI
Class 5.8	F8	V+, VI-	5+	4c, 5a (VS)	15, 16, 17	VIIa, VIIb
Class 5.9	F9	VI	6a	5a, 5b (VS)	17, 18	VIIb, VIIc
Class 5.10a	F10	VI+	6a+	5b (Hard)	19	VIIc
Class 5.10b	F10	VII-	6a+, 6b	5b, 5c	20	VIIIa
Class 5.10c	F11	VII-, VII	6b	5c	20, 21	VIIIa, VIIIb
Class 5.10d	F11	VII	6b+	5c	21, 22	VIIIb, VIIIc
Class 5.11a	F12	VII+	6c	5c, 6a	22, 23	VIIIc, IXa
Class 5.11b	F12	VII+, VIII-	6c+	6a	23	IXa
Class 5.11c	F13	VIII-	7a	6a	24	IXb
Class 5.11d	F13	VIII	7a+	6a, 6b	25	IXb, IXc
Class 5.12a	F14	VIII+	7b	6b	25, 26	IXc
Class 5.12b	F14	VIII+, IX-	7b+	6b	26	Xa
Class 5.12c	F15	IX-	7b+, 7c	6b, 6c	26, 27	Xb
Class 5.12d	F15	IX	7c	6c	27	Xb, Xc
Class 5.13a	F16	IX	7c+	6c	28	Xc
Class 5.13b	F16	IX+	8a	6c, 7a	29	Xc
Class 5.13c	F17	X-	8a, 8a+	7a	30, 31	XIa
Class 5.13d	F17	X	8b, 8b+	7a	31, 32	XIb
Class 5.14a	F18	X+	8c	7b	33	XIc

including the European standard (UIAA). Note that the British system started with adjectives. It became confusing with Just Very Severe (JVS), Very Severe (VS) and Hard. These adjectives have been replaced with numbers.

You might choose to rely on the standard 10 essentials:

1. Map
2. Compass
3. Sunglasses and sunscreen
4. Extra food
5. Extra clothing
6. Headlamp/flashlight
7. First-aid supplies
8. Fire starter
9. Matches
10. Knife

Gerry relies on his Classic Commandments of Mountaineering:

Never get separated from your lunch.
Never get separated from your sleeping bag.
Never get separated from your primal urges.
Carefully consider where your primal urges are leading you.
Expect to go the wrong way some of the time.
First aid above 26,000 feet consists of getting below 26,000 feet.
Never step on the rope.
Never bivouac.
Surfer Girl is not in the mountains.
Never pass up a chance to pee.
Don't eat yellow snow.
Geologic time includes now.
Experience does not exempt you from danger; physics wins.
Have fun and remember why you started.

Update Note

Please note that since the prior edition of this book, the author has discovered that a few of the trails contained in this book are on private property. These routes are noted in the book with the disclaimer "Private Property, Permission Required." Prior to using any of these trails, the reader must get permission from the property owner; to do otherwise can be considered trespassing. The publisher and the author hereby disclaim any responsibility for utilization of any of these private trails without first obtaining permission.

Vaya con Dios!

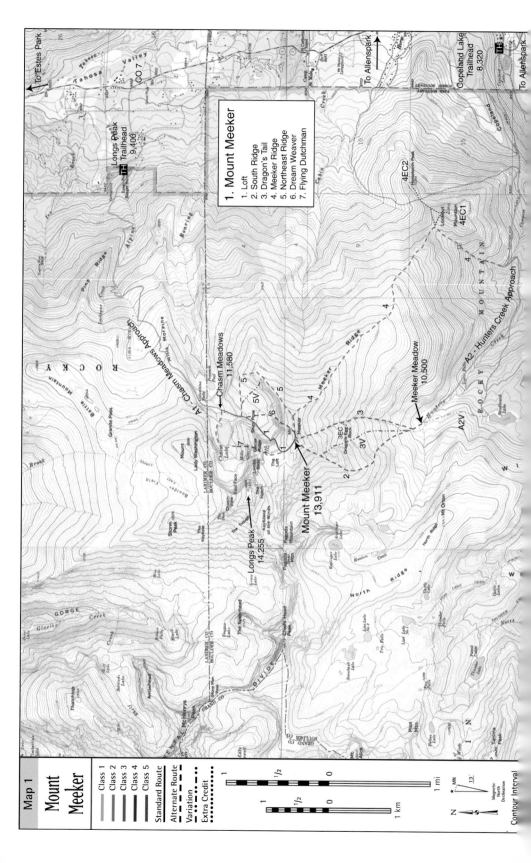

Map 1

Mount Meeker

1. Mount Meeker
1. Loft
2. South Ridge
3. Dragon's Tail
4. Meeker Ridge
5. Northeast Ridge
6. Dream Weaver
7. Flying Dutchman

Class 1
Class 2
Class 3
Class 4
Class 5
Standard Route
Alternate Route
Variation
Extra Credit

Contour Interval

Mount Meeker
13,911

Longs Peak
14,255

Chasm Meadows
11,580

Meeker Meadow
10,500

A1 - Chasm Meadows Approach

A2 - Hunters Creek Approach

Longs Peak
Trailhead
9,400

Copeland Lake
Trailhead
8,320

To Estes Park

To Allenspark

To Allenspark

Tahosa Valley

CO 7

ROCKY MOUNTAIN

ROCKY MOUNTAIN

DIVIDE

N

MN
13
Magnetic
North
Declination

1 mi
1 km

CHAPTER ONE

Front Range

Introduction

Colorado's Front Range extends from the Wyoming border southward for 175 miles to the Arkansas River Valley west of Pueblo. It is Colorado's longest range. When you approach the Rocky Mountains from the east, the Front Range provides an abrupt scenery change. The land is flat, then roars like a lion.

The Front Range contains six fourteeners and three centennial thirteeners. If you live in the urban corridor east of the Front Range, like the majority of Colorado's population, you can climb most of these peaks in one day. These three centennial thirteeners offer more than 20 routes to choose from, all of which can provide an abrupt change of pace from your office environment.

1. Mount Meeker   13,911 feet

See Map 1 on page 24

Our southward journey across Colorado starts with one of the state's best centennial thirteeners. Mount Meeker is 0.75 mile southeast of the fourteener Longs Peak, and is the second highest peak in Rocky Mountain National Park. Longs and Meeker are Colorado's northernmost fourteener and centennial thirteener, respectively. You can see Meeker's south and east slopes from the Denver metro area. Longs' summit is just visible above Meeker.

Meeker is a wonderful peak with exciting mountaineering routes, but is often overlooked because of its proximity to the much more famous Longs Peak. This should not be so. Although you can certainly test your mountaineering skills by zooming in and knocking off only the big peaks, a deeper knowledge and understanding of the mountain environment comes when you visit the lesser summits as well.

Meeker has vast east, south and west slopes that are mostly covered with large talus blocks capped by slabby cliffs. Standing in sharp contrast to these sweeping slopes is Meeker's concave north face. The steepness and size of this face are apparent from Meeker's pinpoint, exposed summit. This is one of the largest faces in Colorado, but it is just a continuation of Longs' great east face. Together, these two faces combine to form Colorado's greatest mountain cirque.

Ships Prow, a large promontory, separates Longs' east face and Meeker's north face. Ships Prow rises directly above Chasm Lake's south side to the Loft, which is the broad, 13,460-foot saddle between Longs and Meeker.

Meeker also has a 13,860-foot summit 300 yards east of the main summit. This is the summit of Meeker Ridge. Meeker has a Class 3 summit ridge and summit block; hence there is no Class 2 route up Meeker.

MAPS
Required: *Allens Park, Longs Peak, Roosevelt National Forest*
Optional: *McHenrys Peak, Isolation Peak*

TRAILHEADS

Longs Peak Trailhead
This trailhead is at 9,400 feet and provides access to Meeker's north and east sides. The trailhead is west of Colorado 7, and you can reach it from either the north or south.

If you are approaching from the north, measure from the junction of U.S. 36 and Colorado 7 east of Estes Park. Go 9.2 miles south on Colorado 7 to the signed turnoff for the Longs Peak Ranger Station. If you are approaching from the south, measure from the junction of Colorado 7 and Colorado 72 on the Peak to Peak Highway. Go 10.5 miles north on Colorado 7 to the turnoff for the Longs Peak Ranger Station. Turn west onto a dirt road and go 1.0 mile west to the Ranger Station and the trailhead. This trailhead is accessible in winter.

Copeland Lake Trailhead
This trailhead is at 8,320 feet and provides access to Meeker's east, south and west sides. The trailhead is west of Colorado 7, and you can reach it from either the north or south.

If you are approaching from the north, measure from the junction of U.S. 36 and Colorado 7 east of Estes Park. Go 13.1 miles south on Colorado 7 to the Wild Basin Road. If you are approaching from the south, measure from the junction of Colorado 7 and Colorado 72 on the Peak to Peak Highway. Go 6.6 miles north on Colorado 7 to the Wild Basin Road.

From the Wild Basin Road–Colorado 7 junction, go 0.4 mile west on the old highway to another turnoff for Wild Basin and Copeland Lake. Turn west (right) and pass through the Rocky Mountain National Park entrance fee station. The trailhead is immediately north of the entrance. This trailhead is accessible in winter.

APPROACHES

1.A1 — Chasm Meadows Approach

From Longs Peak TH at 9,400 ft: 93 RP   9.0 mi   2,180 ft   *Class 1*

You can use this approach to reach routes on Meeker's east and north sides. Start at the Longs Peak Trailhead and follow the well-marked East

Longs Peak Trail. Stay left at the Eugenia Mine–Storm Pass junction at 0.5 mile, stay left at the Jims Grove junction at 2.5 miles and reach the Chasm Lake junction after 3.5 miles. Leave the East Longs Peak Trail and hike 1.0 mile southwest (left) on the Chasm Lake Trail to Chasm Meadows at 11,580 feet. Chasm Meadows is east of and below Chasm Lake. There is an old stone cabin here, but it is locked unless a ranger is in residence. You can scramble up the gully directly west of the cabin to Chasm Lake at 11,800 feet. The postcard view from here of Longs' east face is one of the best in the Rocky Mountains.

1.A2 — Hunters Creek Approach

From Copeland Lake TH at 8,320 ft: 75 RP   8.8 mi   2,180 ft   Class 1

You can use this approach to reach routes on Meeker's south and west sides. From the Copeland Lake Trailhead, follow the Sandbeach Lake Trail as it switchbacks onto the Copeland Moraine and then climbs steadily west. Cross Campers Creek at 9,580 feet after 2.4 miles. Hike south out of the Campers Creek drainage, then continue west to Hunters Creek at 9,780 feet after 3.2 miles. Leave the Sandbeach Lake Trail on the east side of Hunters Creek and follow a faint but useful trail along the northeast side of Hunters Creek. After 1.2 miles on this trail, reach the large Meeker Meadow at 10,500 feet. The use trail ends at the meadow. This idyllic place is nestled under Meeker's huge south face, and you may marvel that such a special place can rest quietly so close to civilization.

1.A2V — Variation

From Copeland Lake TH at 8,320 ft: 81 RP   9.8 mi   2,180 ft   Class 1

From the crossing of Hunters Creek on the Sandbeach Lake Trail, do not go up Hunters Creek but continue 1.0 mile west on the Sandbeach Lake Trail to Sandbeach Lake at 10,300 feet. Find the group campsite on the lake's north side just west of a large boulder. From the group campsite's north side, follow a faint use trail 0.7 mile north to Meeker Meadow. This approach makes sense if you are camped at Sandbeach Lake.

ROUTES

1.1 — Mount Meeker — Loft *Classic*

From Longs Peak TH at 9,400 ft: 318 RP 11.4 mi 4,511 ft   Class 3   Mod Snow
From Chasm Meadows at 11,580 ft: 184 RP   2.4 mi 2,331 ft   Class 3   Mod Snow

In August this is the easiest route on Meeker's north side, and it is the standard route on Meeker. The Loft Route ascends the broad trough between Ships Prow and Meeker to the Loft. This route is dangerous when the ledges below the Loft are covered with snow. By August, the route is a Class 3 scramble.

From the Longs Peak Trailhead, follow the Chasm Meadows Approach. From Chasm Meadows, do not go to Chasm Lake but hike straight south toward Meeker's huge, concave north face. Once you are past the bottom of Ships Prow, turn southwest (right) and ascend the wide slope between Ships Prow and the western half of Meeker's north face. A moderate snow slope fills this trough in June and part of July. Climb the narrowing slope until a large, pervasive cliff blocks simple passage to the Loft.

Scramble up 100 feet of broken, Class 3 rock to the base of the cliff. Turn south (left) and climb onto a 10-foot-wide ledge angling up to the south across the cliff band. You must find this ledge if an easy ascent is to take place. Follow the ledge for 150 yards until it merges into the broken, upper part of the cliff band (Class 3). Switchback 100 feet north on a 2-foot-wide, grass-covered ledge and scramble up to the talus below the Loft (Class 3). From the switchback point, you can climb straight up, but this is more difficult. In the Loft at 13,460 feet, you are suspended high and wild between two great peaks.

From the Loft, hike 0.25 mile south then southeast up talus, and climb to the ridge above. From here you can see Meeker's dramatic summit block 50 yards to the east. Scramble east along the narrow, exposed ridge to the base of the summit block (Class 3). Meeker's summit block has stirred many souls. Climb the summit block on its northwest side via an exposed, committing, Class 3 move and revel on the highest point of one of Colorado's finest centennial thirteeners.

1.2 — Mount Meeker — South Ridge

From Copeland Lake TH at 8,320 ft: 337 RP   12.2 mi   5,591 ft   Class 3
From Meeker Meadow at 10,500 ft: 205 RP   3.4 mi   3,411 ft   Class 3

This is the easiest route to Meeker's summit, but it is seldom done because of its length. This should not be so, as this is one of Colorado's finest tours. A camp at Sandbeach Lake will shorten your summit climb considerably. Meeker's south ridge looks dubious from the east, but talus on the ridge's west side provides a Class 2+ passage. As always, you must still climb Meeker's Class 3 summit block.

From the Copeland Lake Trailhead, follow the Hunters Creek Approach. From 10,500 feet in Meeker Meadow below Meeker's south face, climb northwest and stay east (right) of some cliffs that guard the bottom of Meeker's south ridge. Continue northwest up steep talus and get onto the better-formed ridge above the cliffs. This ridge narrows at 12,200 feet, and the rocky ridge above may look intimidating. Take heart, as it all works out.

Climb steeply up large talus blocks on the ridge's west side (Class 2+), then sneak through a passage between cliffs above and cliffs below to reach 12,600 feet, where the ridge's angle relents. The views of Wild Basin and Pagoda's hidden east face are stupendous from this privileged position. Stay on the ridge's west side below the cliffs until you can climb into a

Mount Meeker from the southeast.

notch on the ridge at 13,060 feet. From here you can peer down the western couloir on Meeker's huge south face and up at Meeker's slabby summit ramparts, which look much more impressive from here than from Denver.

Stay west of the ridge crest as you climb toward the elusive summit. Scamper up a sandy section to the summit ridge, where the view of Longs and the Chasm Lake cirque will jolt your senses. Scramble east (Class 3) to Meeker's prominent summit boulder and make an airy, Class 3 move on the boulder's northwest side to reach Meeker's highest point. After decades of mountaineering, this remains one of our favorite places.

1.3 — Mount Meeker — Dragon's Tail *Classic*

From Copeland Lake TH at 8,320 ft: 429 RP 11.8 mi 5,591 ft Class 3 Mod Snow
With descent of South Ridge: 420 RP 12.0 mi 5,591 ft Class 3 Mod Snow
From Meeker Meadow at 10,500 ft: 297 RP   3.0 mi 3,411 ft Class 3 Mod Snow
With descent of South Ridge: 287 RP   3.2 mi 3,411 ft Class 3 Mod Snow

Dragon's Tail is the shallow couloir in the center of Meeker's large south face. When snow-filled, it provides an inviting route up Meeker. You can preview conditions in this couloir from Denver.

From the Copeland Lake Trailhead, follow the Hunters Creek Approach. From 10,500 feet in Meeker Meadow, climb north into the couloir's gentle beginning at 11,000 feet. Follow the tail's trail as it curves just east of Dragons Egg Rock at 12,200 feet. The couloir steepens a little before it broadens into the slope at 13,200 feet. Above the couloir, scramble up solid, down-sloping slabs to the summit ridge (Class 3). Scramble east and climb the summit boulder's northwest side to reach Meeker's highest point.

Ascending Dragon's Tail and descending the South Ridge Route makes a nice southern Tour de Meeker.

1.3V — Variation

This variation avoids the difficulties at the top of Dragon's Tail, but still allows you to climb a snow route up Meeker's south face. From 10,500 feet in Meeker Meadow, climb north and a little west into the shallow basin on the western half of Meeker's south face. Climb up gradually steepening slopes as the basin narrows into a broad couloir. Pass west of Dragons Egg Rock, then ascend a moderate snow slope to reach the 13,060-foot notch on Meeker's south ridge. Follow the upper part of the South Ridge Route to the summit.

1.3EC — Extra Credit — Dragons Egg Rock, 12,220 feet, Class 2+

At 12,100 feet, break out of your shell and scramble west like a satyr toward the safat's birthplace. Approach the summit of Dragons Egg Rock from the north.

1.4 — Mount Meeker — Meeker Ridge

From Copeland Lake TH at 8,320 ft: 406 RP   12.0 mi   5,671 ft   Class 3
With descent of South Ridge: 381 RP   12.1 mi   5,631 ft   Class 3

When you want to stretch your legs, this is a good place to do it. Meeker Ridge is Meeker's long southeast ridge, and you can see it from many Front Range cities. Though viewed by many, it is climbed by few. The ridge is 2.5 miles long, and you have to want it. Solitude will be your reward. Meeker Ridge is a named feature on the Allenspark Quadrangle, and its summit is Meeker's 13,860-foot east summit. The route is Class 2 up to Meeker's east summit, then you must traverse the narrow ridge to the main summit. This ridge is a Class 3 scramble when dry, but it is exposed and difficult to escape from, and it can be an exciting place during a thunderstorm. Start early to avoid undue excitement.

From the Copeland Lake Trailhead, follow the Hunters Creek Approach for 2.4 miles to Campers Creek at 9,580 feet. Leave the trail here and hike 0.9 mile north then northeast to the 10,420-foot saddle between Lookout Mountain and Meeker's huge mass to the northwest. Hike 0.5 mile northwest on the initially indistinct ridge to treeline at 11,000 feet, where you can see the rest of Meeker Ridge. Though long, this ridge offers a unique, sanguine position that allows you to look down on the eastern plains. Climb 2.0 miles northwest up the gentle ridge to Meeker's 13,860-foot east summit. From here you can see the main summit 300 yards to the west, and this can be a sobering view for the unprepared.

Scramble west along the exposed ridge toward the main summit (Class 3). If you eschew exposure, stay right on the ridge. If not, you can use some ledges below the ridge on its north side. This option only makes life better if the ledges are snow-free. Near the low point between the summits, there is a large block on the ridge with a small keyhole in it. Pass this block on its north side. Beyond this block, pick your way through a series of large boulders to reach the top. The last, Class 3 move onto the summit boulder finishes a fine scramble. Ascending Meeker Ridge and descending the South Ridge Route makes a comprehensive Tour de southern Meeker.

Extra Credits

1.4EC1 — Lookout Mountain, 10,715 feet, Class 4
From the 10,420-foot saddle between Lookout Mountain and Meeker, hike 0.2 mile southeast to the summit area of 10,715-foot Lookout Mountain. Locate and climb the summit boulder (Class 4). This summit boulder is harder than Meeker's.

1.4EC2 — Horsetooth Peak, 10,344 feet, Class 3
For additional fun, hike 0.4 mile northeast from Lookout Mountain to 10,344-foot Horsetooth Peak. Stay west of the peak's southwest ridge, then climb to the ridge and enjoy a Class 3 scramble to the summit.

1.5 — Mount Meeker — Northeast Ridge

From Longs Peak TH at 9,400 ft:	*303 RP*	*12.0 mi*	*4,591 ft*	*Class 3*
With descent of the Loft:	*296 RP*	*11.7 mi*	*4,561 ft*	*Class 3*
From Chasm Meadows at 11,580 ft:	*168 RP*	*3.0 mi*	*2,411 ft*	*Class 3*
With descent of the Loft:	*162 RP*	*2.7 mi*	*2,381 ft*	*Class 3*

This nifty route on Meeker gives you spectacular views of Longs. The route is Class 2 up to Meeker's east summit, then you must traverse the narrow, Class 3 ridge to Meeker's main summit. From the Longs Peak Trailhead, follow the Chasm Meadows Approach. From Chasm Meadows, do not go to Chasm Lake but hike straight south toward Meeker's sweeping north face. At 12,000 feet, turn east (left) and hike up a large talus field. Stay below all the cliffs of Meeker's north face. Once you are east of these cliffs, turn south (right) and hike up talus to reach Meeker's northeast ridge at 12,900 feet. There are spectacular views of Longs from here. Hike 0.6 mile southwest up the ridge on large talus blocks to Meeker's 13,860-foot east summit. From here, scramble west on the top part of the Meeker Ridge Route to Meeker's main summit (Class 3). Combining the Northeast Ridge Route with the Loft Route makes a nice Tour de northern Meeker.

1.5V — Variation — Iron Gates, Class 3
This is an interesting, scenic alternative between Chasm Lake and the upper part of the Northeast Ridge. Instead of staying below all the cliffs on Meeker's north face, ascend a west-facing trough between two buttresses

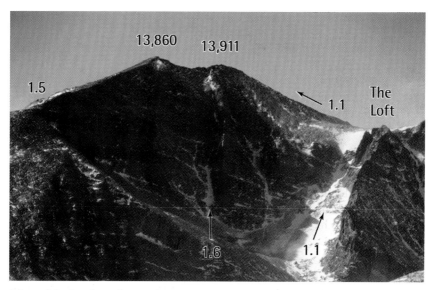

Mount Meeker from the northeast.

at the eastern edge of Meeker's north face. Ascend talus in the lower part of the trough, then enjoy some easy Class 3 scrambling as you approach a notch in the northeast ridge at 13,000 feet. The trough narrows near its top as it becomes inset between the astonishing cliffs of the flanking buttresses. The view of Longs from here is outstanding.

1.6 — Mount Meeker — Dream Weaver *Classic*

From Longs Peak TH at 9,400 ft:

465–570 RP	10.8 mi	4,511 ft	Class 4–5.6	Steep Snow/Ice

With descent of the Loft:

467–572 RP	11.1 mi	4,511 ft	Class 4–5.6	Steep Snow/Ice

From Chasm Meadows at 11,580 ft:

331–435 RP	1.8 mi	2,331 ft	Class 4–5.6	Steep Snow/Ice

With descent of the Loft:

333–437 RP	2.1 mi	2,331 ft	Class 4–5.6	Steep Snow/Ice

Dream Weaver is a narrow couloir in the center of Meeker's sweeping north face. When in good condition, Dream Weaver is one of Colorado's finest mountaineering routes. Meeker's concave north face has two large promontories protruding from it. The smaller, eastern one is called the East Arête, which you should not confuse with the Northeast Ridge. The larger, western one is a beautiful sweep of rock appropriately named the Flying Buttress. The Flying Buttress ascends directly toward Meeker's main summit. The summit of the Flying Buttress is halfway up the face.

The Dream Weaver Couloir starts on the east side of the Flying Buttress, then continues above the Flying Buttress to within 300 feet of Meeker's summit. The Dream Weaver Couloir is only 3 feet wide in places, and it is difficult to see the entire route from a single vantage. You can see the route's lower and upper portions from the trail as you approach Chasm Meadows.

This climb's nature varies a great deal depending on conditions. Parties have tried it in winter expecting an ice climb, but discovered no snow or ice in the couloir at all. In early June you can climb from Chasm Meadows to Meeker's summit on snow. As summer progresses, the snow in the route's middle portion melts, generating a nice mixed climb. In a good year the couloir's upper portion retains snow and ice into August. We recommend crampons on this route in any season. Dream Weaver can appear quite intimidating at first, but just keep going—it all works out!

From the Longs Peak Trailhead, follow the Chasm Meadows Approach. From Chasm Meadows, do not go to Chasm Lake but hike straight south toward Meeker's huge, sweeping north face. Vary not to the right or left; climb straight to the base of the Flying Buttress at 12,500 feet. The first several hundred feet on the east side of the Flying Buttress is on a wide, moderate snow slope. This snow is often present year-round.

The couloir abruptly narrows and steepens above the initial slope. In early June there is 100 feet of steep snow before the angle moderates. By mid-July, this section melts to reveal an ugly chimney with two chockstones in it. The first chockstone is Class 5.4, and the larger, upper one is Class 5.6. While casting about in the dripping cave below the second chockstone, you might wonder whether your dream is a nightmare! Take heart, as the angle moderates above this section.

Above the chockstones, ascend several hundred feet of moderate snow to reach a prominent notch between the summit of the Flying Buttress and Meeker's upper north face. When this section is snow-free, climb 200 feet of Class 5.0–5.2 rock that moderates to Class 2 scree as you approach the notch. You can escape from Dream Weaver at this notch by descending west from the notch down the basin on the west side of the Flying Buttress.

The best part of the route is above the notch, and you can see the first half of the upper part from the notch. Scramble above the notch and enter the upper couloir. Thirty feet wide at first, the couloir relentlessly narrows and steepens. Three hundred feet above the notch, the essence of the dream will be yours. The couloir narrows to 3 feet and reaches 55 degrees, becoming a veritable ribbon of snow and ice reaching for the sky. The Flying Buttress soaring beneath your front points may remind you why you started climbing in the first place.

Above the initial ribbon, the couloir widens and moderates slightly for 100 feet before reaching a second crux. Sequels are never as good, and this second crux is not quite as enjoyable as the ribbon. Above the second crux, the couloir again widens and moderates slightly before reaching a final steep section. When it is snow-filled, you can do a direct finish up the couloir. When it is snow-free, you can climb a clean, solid Class 5.0–5.2 rock pitch on the couloir's west (right) side.

The couloir deposits you on low-angle slabs, 300 feet below Meeker's main summit. For the easiest route, climb Class 3 gullies above the couloir and reach the summit ridge a short distance east of the summit. For a harder alternative, climb large blocks and slabs west of the gullies and arrive directly on the summit. As you perch on Meeker's summit boulder and look down your dream, you will be surrounded by a grand vista.

1.7 — Mount Meeker — Flying Dutchman

From Longs Peak TH at 9,400 ft:

407–430 RP	11.7 mi	4,511 ft	Class 4–5.4	Steep Snow/Ice

With descent of the Loft:

403–426 RP	11.5 mi	4,511 ft	Class 4–5.4	Steep Snow/Ice

From Chasm Meadows at 11,580 ft:

273–296 RP	2.7 mi	2,331 ft	Class 4–5.4	Steep Snow/Ice

With descent of the Loft:

269–292 RP	2.55 mi	2,331 ft	Class 4–5.4	Steep Snow/Ice

The Flying Dutchman Couloir is on the north face of Ships Prow and ends at the Loft's north side. It is east of Longs' east face and Lambs Slide. Glacier Ridge separates Lambs Slide and the Flying Dutchman.

The Flying Dutchman is a long climb, with a gain of 1,600 feet from Chasm Lake to the Loft. It is a more difficult climb than Lambs Slide but an easier climb than Dream Weaver. In June you can climb all the way from Chasm Lake to the Loft on snow and ice. In July a rock gap appears at the crux. You can see the route's upper part, including the crux, as you approach Chasm Meadows.

From the Longs Peak Trailhead, follow the Chasm Meadows Approach. From Chasm Meadows, scramble west to Chasm Lake and hike around the lake's north side. From the lake's west end, you can see the lower part of the couloir to the south. Start into the wide couloir, and climb gradually steepening, moderate snow. The couloir narrows as it turns slightly west (right), at which point you can see the crux.

The crux is a 50-foot-high, 8-foot-wide steep section. On a fine, June 14 ascent, this section was a solid, 55-degree ice slope. The water running underneath the ice spoke of its temporary nature, and by July a rock pitch had replaced the ice. Above the crux, the angle eases and snow is found again. Climb 300 feet above the crux to the top part of Lambs Slide and continue 150 feet southeast to the Loft's northern edge. Continue on the upper part of the Loft Route to Meeker's summit.

1.7EC — Extra Credit — Ships Prow, 13,340 feet, Class 4

This is an interesting scramble to an astonishing summit. From the top of Lambs Slide, scramble 100 yards east and climb the summit block's north-west side to the 13,340-foot summit of Ships Prow (Class 4).

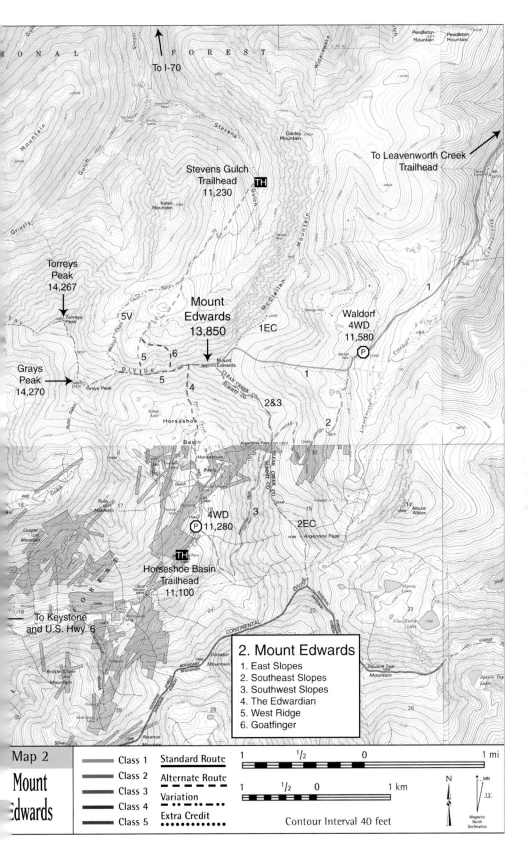

2. Mount Edwards

1. East Slopes
2. Southeast Slopes
3. Southwest Slopes
4. The Edwardian
5. West Ridge
6. Goatfinger

Map 2

Mount
Edwards

	Class 1	Standard Route
	Class 2	Alternate Route
	Class 3	Variation
	Class 4	Extra Credit
	Class 5	

Contour Interval 40 feet

2. Mount Edwards 13,850 feet

See Map 2 on page 35

Mount Edwards is 1.3 miles east of the fourteener Grays Peak, which is 4 miles south of Exit 221 on Interstate 70. Edwards' lofty summit is easy to reach, but few people climb this peak. The summit views of the fourteeners Grays and Torreys make the trek worthwhile. In August you may hear dogs barking on the Grays Peak Trail. If you turn your back on that urban adventure, you will find solitude on Edwards. Edwards also has the distinction of being on the Continental Divide.

Like most Front Range peaks, Edwards provides a variety of routes. Edwards has a rugged north face that holds some steep surprises. This face connects to Grays, and you can access it from the Stevens Gulch Trailhead. Edwards' east side has several Class 1 routes that you can access from the Leavenworth Creek and Horseshoe Basin Trailheads.

MAPS

Required: *Grays Peak, Arapaho National Forest*
Optional: *Montezuma*

TRAILHEADS

Leavenworth Creek Trailhead

This trailhead is at 9,560 feet and provides access to Edwards' east side. Take Exit 228 off Interstate 70 at Georgetown and go south through Georgetown to the beginning of the Guanella Pass Road. Go 2.6 miles south on the paved Guanella Pass Road as it climbs steeply above Georgetown to the junction with the Waldorf Road at a switchback to the south. Park cars in a parking area just north of the switchback. This is the trailhead. The Waldorf Road climbs steeply south to the west of the Guanella Pass Road. This trailhead is accessible in winter.

In summer, four-wheel-drive vehicles can go considerably farther up the dirt Waldorf Road that is FS 248.1. Measuring from the trailhead, go straight at mile 0.2, cross Leavenworth Creek at mile 0.4, switchback hard right at mile 0.9 and switchback hard left at mile 1.1. At this point, you join the old railroad grade to Waldorf, and the road gets better. Go straight (right) at mile 3.6, go straight (left) at mile 4.3 and reach the old Waldorf Mine at mile 6.2. This historic site is at 11,580 feet.

Stevens Gulch Trailhead

This trailhead is at 11,230 feet and provides access to Edwards' north side. Take Exit 221 off Interstate 70 at Bakerville. This exit is 6.3 miles west of Georgetown. Cross to the south side of Interstate 70 and find a sign for Grays Peak. Switchback 1.0 mile south up through the trees on FS 189 (dirt) to a marked junction where the Stevens Gulch and Grizzly Gulch roads split. Stay east (left) on FS 189.1 and continue for 2.0 miles to the parking lot at the well-marked trailhead. This road is steep but passable for most passenger cars.

In winter FS 189 is closed. Winter access to Stevens Gulch is from the south side of the Bakerville exit at 9,780 feet. For winter climbs above the Stevens Gulch Trailhead, add 6.0 miles and 1,460 feet.

Horseshoe Basin Trailhead

This trailhead is at 11,100 feet and provides access to Edwards' south side. Drive on U.S. 6 to the Keystone North Peak Ski Area Road. This road is 8.6 miles west of Loveland Pass and 7.8 miles east of Interstate 70, Exit 205, in Dillon. Leave U.S. 6, follow the ski area road 0.1 mile south, then turn east (left) onto Montezuma Road (paved). Go 4.7 miles east on Montezuma Road, then turn left onto the Peru Creek Road (dirt, unmarked). Follow the Peru Creek Road 4.6 miles east to the Shoe Basin Mine at 11,100 feet. Park cars here. Four-wheel-drive vehicles can continue for 0.3 mile to the start of the Argentine Pass Trail at 11,280 feet.

In winter and spring the Peru Creek Road is closed at the Montezuma– Peru Creek junction. When the Peru Creek Road is closed, add 9.2 miles and 1,100 feet to your climb.

ROUTES

2.1 — Mount Edwards — East Slopes

From Leavenworth Creek TH at 9,560 ft:	*245 RP*	*16.0 mi*	*4,290 ft*	*Class 1*
From Waldorf Mine at 11,580 ft:	*80 RP*	*3.6 mi*	*2,270 ft*	*Class 1*

This is the standard route on Edwards. In late June and July this easy hike offers a good opportunity for a wildflower clinic. The route is often used for winter ascents as well. It is a long hike from the Leavenworth Creek Trailhead on the Guanella Pass Road, but only a short stroll from the Waldorf Mine.

Start at the Leavenworth Creek Trailhead and go up the Waldorf Road that is FS 248.1. Go straight at mile 0.2, cross Leavenworth Creek at mile 0.4, switchback hard right at mile 0.9 and switchback hard left at mile 1.1. At this point, you join the old railroad grade to Waldorf. Go straight (right) at mile 3.6, go straight (left) at mile 4.3 and reach the old Waldorf Mine at mile 6.2. This historic site is at 11,580 feet. You cannot quite see Edwards' summit from here, but it is up to the west above a small basin. McClellan Mountain's rounded slopes are west-northwest of the mine.

Continue 0.25 mile south from the mine on the start of the Argentine Pass Road to the creek descending from the basin east of Edwards. Leave the road and climb 0.6 mile west up the creek's north side into the flower-strewn basin to 12,300 feet, where the basin steepens. Continue 0.3 mile west up the steeper slope above to 13,000 feet. In early summer there is an

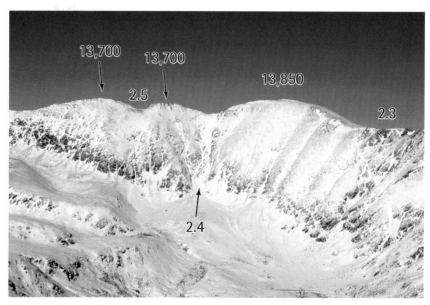

Mount Edwards from the south.

easy snow slope in the gully, which you can use or avoid. From 13,000 feet, climb 0.3 mile northwest to reach Edwards' northeast ridge at 13,440 feet just south of the 13,420-foot Edwards–McClellan saddle. Climb 0.25 mile southwest up this gentle ridge, then walk 0.1 mile west to Edwards' highest point. The views to the west of Grays and Torreys are spectacular.

2.1EC – Extra Credit – McClellan Mountain, 13,587 feet, Class 1

From the 13,420-foot Edwards–McClellan saddle, climb 0.5 mile north along the easy ridge and visit McClellan Mountain's rounded, 13,587-foot summit. McClellan is one of Colorado's 200 highest peaks, and its summit is a perfect perch for a photograph of Torreys' east face. A hundred years ago there was a railroad most of the way up McClellan Mountain so tourists could enjoy this view. Times change, but in this case the view remains the same.

2.2 – Mount Edwards – Southeast Slopes

From Leavenworth Creek TH at 9,560 ft:	*275 RP*	*19.0 mi*	*4,290 ft*	*Class 1*
With descent of East Slopes:	*260 RP*	*17.5 mi*	*4,290 ft*	*Class 1*
From Waldorf Mine at 11,580 ft:	*110 RP*	*6.6 mi*	*2,270 ft*	*Class 1*
With descent of East Slopes:	*95 RP*	*5.1 mi*	*2,270 ft*	*Class 1*

This route is longer but even gentler than the East Slopes Route. Start at the Leavenworth Creek Trailhead and follow the East Slopes Route to the Waldorf Mine at 11,580 feet. From the mine, go 0.25 mile south on the Argentine Pass Road to the creek descending from the basin east of Edwards.

Just south of the creek, take the west (right) road. This is the continuation of the Argentine Pass Road. Follow this road 0.7 mile south to another junction at 12,219 feet. Take the west (right) road again. Follow the road 1.25 miles west as it switchbacks up to Argentine Pass at 13,207 feet. Snow slopes can persist across the road until mid-July, but you can avoid them if you desire. From Argentine Pass, follow Edwards' gentle southeast ridge 0.3 mile north then 0.8 mile northwest to the summit. Ascending this route and descending the East Slopes Route makes a gentle Tour de Edwards.

2.2EC — Extra Credit — Argentine Peak, 13,738 feet, Class 1

From Argentine Pass, climb 1.0 mile south then southeast to 13,738-foot Argentine Peak, one of Colorado's 200 highest peaks.

2.3 — Mount Edwards — Southwest Slopes

From Horseshoe Basin TH at 11,100 ft:	*126 RP*	*7.2 mi*	*2,750 ft*	*Class 1*
From 4WD parking at 11,280 ft:	*116 RP*	*6.6 mi*	*2,570 ft*	*Class 1*

This is a short, easy route on Edwards, but it is only short if the Peru Creek Road is open. Start at the Horseshoe Basin Trailhead and go 0.3 mile south up the road to the start of the Argentine Pass Trail at 11,280 feet. Follow the Argentine Pass Trail 2.2 miles southeast then northeast to Argentine Pass at 13,207 feet. The Argentine Pass Trail angles across a steep slope. Several snow slopes cover the trail in winter, and some of the snow persists into July. Crossing these slopes can be tricky. If you are using this route before mid-July, consider taking an ice ax. From Argentine Pass, follow Edwards' gentle southeast ridge 0.3 mile north then 0.8 mile northwest to the summit.

2.4 — Mount Edwards — The Edwardian *Classic*

From Horseshoe Basin TH at 11,100 ft:	*209 RP*	*4.4 mi*	*2,750 ft*	*Class 2*	*Mod Snow*
From 4WD parking at 11,280 ft:	*199 RP*	*3.8 mi*	*2,570 ft*	*Class 2*	*Mod Snow*
With descent of Southwest Slopes:	*206 RP*	*5.8 mi*	*2,750 ft*	*Class 2*	*Mod Snow*
From 4WD parking at 11,280 ft:	*196 RP*	*5.2 mi*	*2,570 ft*	*Class 2*	*Mod Snow*

When the Peru Creek Road is open and snow fills the Edwardian, this is the shortest and sweetest route on Edwards. This happy combination occurs for two weeks a year in late June right after the Peru Creek Road opens. Before the Peru Creek Road opens, you will find plenty of snow and solitude. The Edwardian Couloir is on the western portion of Edwards' sweeping south face. The couloir reaches the 13,580-foot saddle between the eastern Point 13,700 on Edwards' west ridge and Edwards' summit. The Edwardian is the headwaters of Peru Creek.

Start at the Horseshoe Basin Trailhead and follow the main four-wheel-drive road 1.0 mile north into Horseshoe Basin. Continue 0.3 mile north up steepening slopes to 12,000 feet. You can see the Edwardian to the north during this approach. Leave the road and climb 0.3 mile north up easy slopes west of the creek to 12,500 feet below the 1,080-foot-high couloir. The Edwardian averages 30 degrees and reaches a maximum steepness of 33 degrees between 13,000 and 13,200 feet before it rolls regally into the 13,580-foot saddle. There is no cornice at the top. From the saddle, climb 0.2 mile east to Edwards' summit (Class 2). Ascending the Edwardian and descending the Southwest Slopes Route makes a nifty Tour de Edwards.

2.5 — Mount Edwards — West Ridge

From Stevens Gulch TH at 11,230 ft: 202 RP   7.0 mi   2,940 ft   Class 2+   Mod Snow

This is the connecting ridge between Grays Peak and Mount Edwards. In June this route provides a memorable snow climb and rough ridge ramble over two false summits. In August when the scree below the Edwards–Grays saddle is unpleasant, consider using Variation 2.5V.

Start at the Stevens Gulch Trailhead and cross to the creek's west side on a large footbridge. Hike 1.5 miles southwest on the Grays Peak Trail under Kelso Mountain's east slopes to a large trail sign at 12,020 feet. You can see Edwards' north face and the Edwards–Grays connecting ridge south of here. Leave the Grays Peak Trail before it climbs west into the basin below Torreys' east face. You can leave the Grays Peak Trail at the trail sign, cross the creek to the east and hike south up open meadows into the basin below Edwards' west ridge. You can also leave the Grays Peak Trail 200 yards beyond the sign and follow an old road south into the basin. This option gives you an easier creek crossing. Hike 1.1 miles south into the basin to 12,800 feet below the low point of the Edwards–Grays ridge.

In spring and early summer, climb a moderate snow slope to the 13,380-foot Edwards–Grays saddle. Any cornice at the top should be small and blunted by June. In August climb to the saddle on unpleasant scree. From the saddle, climb 0.2 mile east along the rough ridge to the western Point 13,700 (Class 2). The view of Grays and Torreys is spectacular from here. Descend 0.1 mile east on an easy slope to the 13,540-foot saddle between the two false summits. From here you can peer north down the Goatfinger Couloir. As you continue east, avoid cliffs east of this saddle and the eastern Point 13,700 by staying below the ridge on its south side (Class 2+). Contour into the 13,580-foot saddle between the eastern Point 13,700 and Edwards. From here you can peer south down the Edwardian Couloir. From this saddle, climb 0.2 mile east to Edwards' summit (Class 2).

2.5V — Variation

From Stevens Gulch TH at 11,230 ft: 188 RP   8.1 mi   3,380 ft   Class 2+

In late summer you can avoid the unpleasant scree below the Edwards–

Grays saddle by following the Grays Peak Trail to 13,560 feet, where it comes close to Grays' east ridge. Leave the trail, climb 100 yards southeast to Grays' east ridge at 13,600 feet and descend 0.3 mile east down Grays' east ridge to the 13,380-foot Edwards–Grays saddle. From here, continue on Edwards' West Ridge Route. Doing this variation in both directions adds 440 feet of gain to your effort. Most people will consider this an equitable trade for avoiding the scree, and the R Point rating verifies this assessment. You can also use this variation in early summer to avoid the snow climb.

2.6 — Mount Edwards — Goatfinger

From Stevens Gulch TH at 11,230 ft: 248 RP 6.8 mi 2,620 ft Class 2+ Steep Snow
With descent of West Ridge: 253 RP 6.9 mi 2,780 ft Class 2+ Steep Snow
With descent of Variation 2.5V: 265 RP 7.5 mi 3,000 ft Class 2+ Steep Snow

This is the widest and most continuous snow couloir on Edwards' broken north face. It is on the western part of the face and leads straight to the 13,540-foot saddle between the two 13,700-foot false summits on Edwards' west ridge. You can easily see Goatfinger when hiking up the first 1.5 miles of the Grays Peak Trail. The 1,000-foot-high couloir is in good shape in June, but the couloir receives more than an average amount of rockfall. The evidence of this is all the rock in the debris cone at the bottom of the couloir. In June there may also be a blunted cornice atop the couloir.

Goats hanging out at the top of the couloir exacerbate the rockfall problem. On our memorable June ascent, we noticed a goat watching us from the top of the cornice. First a little snow trickled down. Then the goat dropped down and crossed the top of the couloir at its steepest point, moments after which a bowling ball–sized rock rolled down, missing us by 15 feet. Undeterred, we carried on. Moments later a rock the size of a Ford 302 engine block cartwheeled toward us. We hot-stepped right and the block missed us by 30 feet. Shaken, we sprinted on. When we topped out, the goats were gone.

Start at the Stevens Gulch Trailhead and follow the West Ridge Route to 12,600 feet in the basin below the west ridge. Angle east from the gentler West Ridge Route and position yourself for Goatfinger. Stay to the couloir's west (right) side for the first 700 feet of moderate snow. The couloir's last 300 feet holds steep snow. Angle across to the couloir's east (left) side and finish on 55-degree snow just to the east (left) of any cornice. It's a classic finish.

From the 13,540-foot saddle at the top of the couloir, follow the upper part of the West Ridge Route to the summit. Ascending Goatfinger and descending the West Ridge Route makes a smart Tour de Edwards.

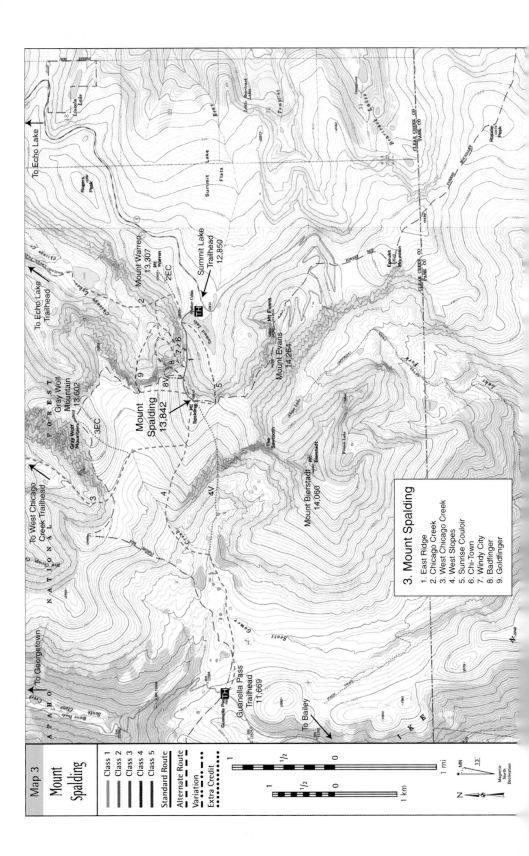

Map 3

Mount Spalding

Class 1
Class 2
Class 3
Class 4
Class 5

Standard Route
Alternate Route
Variation
Extra Credit

1 mi

1 km

N

Magnetic North Declination

3. Mount Spalding

1. East Ridge
2. Chicago Creek
3. West Chicago Creek
4. West Slopes
5. Sunrise Couloir
6. Chi-Town
7. Windy City
8. Badfinger
9. Goldfinger

To Echo Lake

To Echo Lake Trailhead

Mount Warren
13,307
2EC

Summit Lake
Trailhead
12,850

Summit Lake

Flats

Cedar Cabin

Mt Evans Campground

Mount Evans
14,264

Gray Wolf Mountain
13,602

3EC

Mount Spalding
13,842

8V

9

8 7 6

5

Mt Spalding

NATIONAL FOREST

To West Chicago Creek Trailhead

3

4

4V

The Sawtooth

Mount Bierstadt
14,060

Mt Bierstadt

Abyss Lake

Frozen Lake

Epaulet Mountain

CLEAR CREEK CO
PARK CO

Roberts Peak

CLEAR CREEK CO
PARK CO

To Georgetown

Guanella Pass
Trailhead
11,669

Scott

To Bailey

APAHO

Lincoln Lake

3. Mount Spalding   13,842 feet

See Map 3 on page 42

Mount Spalding is 1.1 miles northwest of the fourteener Mount Evans. Spalding's rounded, undistinguished summit has relegated the peak to an Extra Credit effort for those hurrying to grander goals. This should not be so. Spalding offers routes for all mountaineering appetites, and harbors many surprises along its rugged northeast face.

Spalding's northeast face can be confusing on a first visit, and it helps to use the Mount Evans Quadrangle to identify the different couloirs. The following overview may be useful. There are two moderate snow couloirs below the 12,876-foot saddle between Mount Spalding and Mount Warren. Two hundred yards west of the westernmost of these two couloirs is a very steep couloir that often has a rock barrier two-thirds of the way up. Two hundred yards west of this couloir is the Chi-Town Couloir, which is friendlier and usually has continuous snow. Two hundred yards west of Chi-Town is the Windy City Couloir, which is wide near the bottom but narrows as it approaches the ridge and usually has continuous moderate snow. Two hundred yards west of Windy City is the deeply inset Badfinger Couloir, sometimes called the Spalding Couloir, which splits the center of Spalding's northeast face. Two hundred yards northwest of Badfinger is the Black Wall, which is home to several hard rock routes. North of the Black Wall are two impressive, east-facing snow slivers that lead to the 13,020-foot saddle between Mount Spalding and Gray Wolf Mountain. The southernmost of these two couloirs is called Goldfinger. You can see Spalding's northeast face from Echo Lake's northwest corner, as well as from 12,000 feet on the Mount Evans Road just west of the saddle between Goliath Peak and Rogers Peak.

MAPS

Required: *Mount Evans, Arapaho National Forest*
Optional: *Georgetown, Harris Park, Idaho Springs, Pike National Forest*

TRAILHEADS

Echo Lake Trailhead

This trailhead is at 10,580 feet and provides access to Chicago Creek and Spalding's northeast side. Leave Interstate 70 at Exit 240 in Idaho Springs. Signs for Mount Evans mark this exit. Go 13.4 miles south on Colorado 103 to Echo Lake, which is on the highway's south side. You also can reach Echo Lake by following Colorado 103 west for 18.5 miles from the Colorado 103–Colorado 74 junction in Bergen Park. From Echo Lake's northwest side, turn west onto a dirt road with a sign for Echo Lake Park. Go 0.2 mile west then south to the trailhead.

There is also a parking lot east of Echo Lake at the junction of Colorado 103 and Colorado 5 (the Mount Evans Road). The road to Echo Lake Park is 0.6 mile west of the Colorado 103–Colorado 5 junction. This trailhead is accessible in winter.

Summit Lake Trailhead

This trailhead is at 12,850 feet and provides access to Spalding's east side. Leave Interstate 70 at Exit 240 in Idaho Springs. Go 13.4 miles south on Colorado 103 to Echo Lake. You also can reach Echo Lake by following Colorado 103 west for 18.5 miles from the Colorado 103–Colorado 74 junction in Bergen Park.

From Echo Lake's east end, follow Colorado 5 (the Mount Evans Road) for 9.1 miles as it climbs south to Summit Lake, which is on the west (right) side of the road. There are two additional parking areas on the road between Echo Lake and Summit Lake. The first is at 11,550 feet, 2.9 miles above Echo Lake. The second is at 12,150 feet, 4.8 miles above Echo Lake. Colorado 5 is closed in winter.

The Forest Service took over management of Summit Lake from the city of Denver in 1998. There is a $10 fee for driving up the Mount Evans Road. A seasonal pass costs $25. With a National Parks Golden Eagle Pass, you can get in free. Rangers collect the fee on Colorado 5 at Echo Lake. The Forest Service uses the money to improve trails and other public services, and to protect natural resources.

West Chicago Creek Trailhead

This trailhead is at 9,600 feet and provides access to the West Chicago Creek Trail and a northern approach to Spalding. Leave Interstate 70 at Exit 240 in Idaho Springs. Go 6.6 miles south on Colorado 103 to a dirt road on the south (right) side of the highway. This junction has a sign for the West Chicago Creek Campground. Leave Colorado 103 and follow the dirt road 2.8 miles southwest to the West Chicago Creek Campground and the trailhead. In winter the snowplow turns around at the start of a switchback 2.0 miles above Colorado 103. The remaining 0.8 mile to the trailhead is not plowed, but you can often drive beyond the turnaround point.

Guanella Pass Trailhead

This trailhead is at 11,669 feet and provides access to Spalding's west side. Take Exit 228 off Interstate 70 at Georgetown and go south through Georgetown to the beginning of the Guanella Pass Road. Go 10.0 miles south on the Guanella Pass Road above Georgetown, or leave U.S. 285 at Grant and go 12.2 miles north on the Guanella Pass Road. The Guanella Pass Road is mostly dirt, but is passable for passenger cars. And although it remains open in winter, keep in mind that this road is the last priority for the snowplow crew. You can see Spalding's rounded mass east of Guanella Pass to the north of the fourteener Mount Bierstadt.

ROUTES

3.1 — Mount Spalding — East Ridge *Classic*

From Summit Lake TH at 12,850 ft: *79 RP*   *2.3 mi*   *992 ft*   *Class 2+*

This short ridge walk provides a simple approach to Spalding's summit. If you are quick, you could do this hike on a summer evening after work. Start at the Summit Lake Trailhead and walk 0.25 mile north along Summit Lake's east side on a good trail to the 12,876-foot saddle between Mount Spalding and Mount Warren. Climb 0.9 mile west up Spalding's east ridge to Spalding's 13,842-foot summit. The ridge is rough in a few spots. The view of Evans' north face is spectacular from this ridge, and you can peer down several of the couloirs on Spalding's northeast face.

3.2 — Mount Spalding — Chicago Creek

From Echo Lake TH at 10,580 ft: *283 RP*   *11.7 mi*   *4,230 ft*   *Class 2+*

This route avoids the Mount Evans Road and is the normal route for mountaineers who seek a more robust ascent of Spalding. Start at the Echo Lake Trailhead and walk 0.1 mile south into the open woods near the lake's southwest corner. You also can reach this point from Echo Lake's east end by following a trail on the lake's south side.

Find the Chicago Lakes Trail near the slight ridge southwest of Echo Lake. Look for old blazes on the trees. Follow the Chicago Lakes Trail, cross to the west side of the ridge southwest of Echo Lake, descend southwest and switchback down to reach Chicago Creek at 10,300 feet. This point is south of the private property at Camp Shwayder.

Cross to Chicago Creek's west side and walk 0.55 mile southwest up the valley on an old dirt road to the Chicago Creek Reservoir at 10,600 feet. Continue on the road around the reservoir's west side and enter the Mount Evans Wilderness south of the reservoir. Hike 2.2 miles southwest on the Chicago Lakes Trail to the southernmost Chicago Lake at 11,750 feet. This is a special place, and you can marvel at Spalding's northeast face from here. From the lake's southern end, climb 0.6 mile south up a broken slope to Mount Warren's west ridge at 13,060 feet. Descend 0.25 mile west to the 12,876-foot Warren–Spalding saddle. Do not stray onto the north slopes below this saddle, as the difficulty increases rapidly in that direction. Join the East Ridge Route in the Warren–Spalding saddle and follow it to the summit.

3.2EC — Extra Credit — Mount Warren, 13,307 feet, Class 2

From 13,060 feet on Mount Warren's west ridge, climb 0.3 mile east to Mount Warren's 13,307-foot summit.

Mount Spalding from Summit Lake.

3.3 — Mount Spalding — West Chicago Creek

From West Chicago Creek TH at 9,600 ft: 341 RP   14.1 mi   4,242 ft   Class 2

Do not confuse West Chicago Creek with Chicago Creek. This long route will grant you solitude and a hefty workout. From the West Chicago Creek Trailhead, follow the West Chicago Creek Trail 3.8 miles south to its end at 11,200 feet in Hells Hole. Continue 1.5 miles southeast then south up the narrow, rocky basin under the impressive northwest face of 13,602-foot Gray Wolf Mountain. There is a huge split boulder at the top of the basin. Climb 0.25 mile south to the 12,740-foot saddle between Gray Wolf Mountain and Point 12,988. Your long approach to the high country is over. Contour 0.5 mile east, then climb 0.6 mile south to 13,400 feet on Mount Spalding's broad west ridge. Climb 0.4 mile east up talus to Spalding's summit.

3.3EC — Extra Credit — Gray Wolf Mountain, 13,602 feet, Class 2
Gray Wolf Mountain is a "Bi"—one of Colorado's 200 highest peaks. It is 0.5 mile east of the West Chicago Creek Route, and you can reach its 13,602-foot summit by hiking up grass and talus.

3.4 — Mount Spalding — West Slopes

From Guanella Pass TH at 11,669 ft: 219 RP   7.0 mi   2,511 ft   Class 2

You can climb Spalding by itself from Guanella Pass, and this is the easiest route on Spalding that avoids the Mount Evans Road. You will share the beginning of your hike with people climbing the fourteener Mount Bierstadt.

From the Guanella Pass Trailhead, follow the Colorado Fourteener Initiative (CFI) trail 0.8 mile east as it descends gently through the famous Bierstadt willows to flats at 11,500 feet near Scott Gomer Creek. The Bierstadt willows have given mountaineers fits for decades, at least until 1999 that is, when the CFI, in cooperation with the Forest Service, produced a sustainable trail through the willows complete with boardwalks to minimize environmental damage.

Just after the trail crosses Scott Gomer Creek and starts up Bierstadt's west slopes, leave the trail and hike 0.7 mile east-northeast, staying well south of the bogs along Scott Gomer Creek. Cross to Scott Gomer Creek's north side and climb 0.8 mile northeast up the slope north of upper Scott Gomer Creek. Stay north of all the cliffs that extend for a mile northwest of the Sawtooth, which is a gash in the ridge between Bierstadt and Evans. Once past the cliffs, climb 1.2 miles southeast up gentle, open slopes on Spalding's northwest side to reach the summit.

3.4V — Variation — Gomer's Gully
From Guanella Pass TH at 11,669 ft: 211 RP   6.6 mi   2,511 ft   Class 2

This significant, frequently used shortcut provides the shortest route up Spalding that does not use the Mount Evans Road. Instead of climbing around the north end of all the cliffs extending northwest from the Sawtooth, continue 0.5 mile east from 11,600 feet into a scenic basin at 11,700 feet. Ascend 0.7 mile east up the well-defined Gomer's Gully through the middle of the cliffs. Once on the slope above Gomer's Gully, climb 0.6 mile northeast to Spalding's summit. You can easily see Gomer's Gully from Guanella Pass. It rarely holds snow in winter.

3.5 — Mount Spalding — Sunrise Couloir
From Summit Lake TH at 12,850 ft: 162 RP   3.0 mi   992 ft   Class 3   Steep Snow
With descent of East Ridge: 151 RP 2.65 mi   992 ft   Class 3   Steep Snow

Sunrise Couloir rises 700 feet above Summit Lake's west end to the Evans–Spalding saddle. You can see the route from Summit Lake, where you can preview conditions from the comfort of your car. This route will gratify those looking for a technical snow challenge with a minimal approach.

To avoid trampling tundra, walk around the north side of Summit Lake and walk west to the bottom of the couloir. Although the couloir is a straightforward climb, an annoying cornice usually caps it, even in late summer. Climb the steepening couloir and find a way to overcome the cornice. In early summer you can climb a steep but smooth snow slope on the south (left) side of the cornice. In late summer you can execute a clever climb by sneaking between the rock and snow on the north (right) side of the cornice (Class 3). Mortals will appreciate crampons and an ice ax. From the Evans–Spalding saddle, hike 0.25 mile north up easy talus to Spalding's summit. Ascending the Sunrise Couloir and descending the East Ridge Route makes a terse Tour de Spalding.

3.6 — Mount Spalding — Chi-Town *Classic*

From Summit Lake TH at 12,850 ft:	271 RP	3.4 mi	2,912 ft	Class 4	Steep Snow
With descent of East Ridge:	215 RP	2.85 mi	1,952 ft	Class 4	Steep Snow
From Echo Lake TH at 10,580 ft:	337 RP	10.6 mi	3,862 ft	Class 4	Steep Snow
With descent of Chicago Creek:	349 RP	11.15 mi	4,046 ft	Class 4	Steep Snow

This is one of several couloirs on Spalding's northeast face. Refer to the peak introduction for its location. Chi-Town reaches Spalding's east ridge at 13,240 feet in a noticeable notch. Chi-Town retains its snow better than Windy City, but also is steeper than Windy City. Skiers sometimes use Chi-Town. For a short tour, you can approach Chi-Town from the Summit Lake Trailhead. For a more conventional climb, you can approach from the Echo Lake Trailhead.

From the Summit Lake Trailhead, hike 0.3 mile northeast to 13,060 feet on Mount Warren's west ridge. Descend 0.25 mile northwest down a steep but open slope to 12,100 feet, then contour 0.25 mile southwest to the base of the couloir. Do not descend from the 12,876-foot Warren–Spalding saddle, as this slope is cliffed.

From the Echo Lake Trailhead, follow the Chicago Creek Route to the southern side of the southernmost Chicago Lake at 11,750 feet. From here, hike 0.5 mile southwest to the base of the couloir at 12,100 feet.

Ascend the couloir as it narrows and steepens. The middle of the couloir holds moderate snow, and the upper 300 feet holds steep snow. The last pitch to the ridge is the steepest and may involve a few moves of Class 4 rock climbing. The feeling here is distinctly alpine. Once on the ridge at 13,240 feet, hike 0.5 mile west to Spalding's summit.

3.7 — Mount Spalding — Windy City

From Summit Lake TH at 12,850 ft:	244 RP	3.4 mi	2,912 ft	Class 2	Mod Snow
With descent of East Ridge:	186 RP	2.8 mi	1,952 ft	Class 2	Mod Snow
From Echo Lake TH at 10,580 ft:	309 RP	10.5 mi	3,862 ft	Class 2	Mod Snow
With descent of Chicago Creek:	320 RP	11.1 mi	4,046 ft	Class 2	Mod Snow

This couloir is the next big one west from Chi-Town. The upper part of the broad couloir reaches Spalding's east ridge at 13,460 feet in a flat area. The lower part of the couloir is more of an east-facing slope, and the east edge of this slope melts out first. Use either of the approaches described for Chi-Town and continue 100 yards west to Windy City. Ascend the steepening lower slopes and continue into the upper couloir for 300 feet of delightful, moderate snow climbing. Once on the ridge, hike 0.35 mile west to Spalding's summit.

Mount Spalding from the northeast.

3.8 — Mount Spalding — Badfinger

From Summit Lake TH at 12,850 ft:

444 RP	3.55 mi	2,912 ft	Class 5.7	Very Steep Snow/Ice

With descent of East Ridge:

384 RP	2.9 mi	1,952 ft	Class 5.7	Very Steep Snow/Ice

From Echo Lake TH at 10,580 ft:

504 RP	10.5 mi	3,862 ft	Class 5.7	Very Steep Snow/Ice

With descent of Chicago Creek:

515 RP	11.1 mi	4,046 ft	Class 5.7	Very Steep Snow/Ice

This couloir, sometimes called the Spalding Couloir, splits the center of Spalding's northeast face. Badfinger is deeply inset and difficult to view from a single vantage. You can see the lower couloir from Echo Lake's northwest corner, and from 12,000 feet on the Mount Evans Road just west of the saddle between Goliath Peak and Rogers Peak. To get a good view of the upper couloir, you have to be on Gray Wolf Mountain. The couloir twists like a demon, and you cannot see all of it even when climbing it.

Badfinger should be a classic but is not. The entire couloir is threatened by a long series of cornices perched on a ridge above. In May and June the disintegrating cornices thunder down the couloir at random. The large debris cone below the couloir testifies to this destruction. As the cornices stabilize, a rock band appears in the upper couloir. The rock band is difficult to see, even from the lower part of the twisting couloir. We do not recommend this route; climb it only if you feel so compelled.

Use either of the approaches described with Chi-Town and continue 0.2 mile west to the debris cone below Badfinger. Ascend the couloir as it turns east, narrows and steepens. The couloir narrows to 10 feet before it rears up in a very steep crux. This crux can be mostly rock as early as mid-June. A direct ascent up the rock band requires Class 5.7(?) climbing. The angle relents above the crux, but the upper couloir is discontinuous and is still threatened by cornices. You can move east (left) to finish on rock. The couloir ends at 13,400 feet. Hike 0.35 mile southwest to Spalding's summit.

3.8V — Variation

You can avoid the crux rock band by traversing west (right) on a 200-yard-long sloping ledge. This ledge is below the band of cornices that threaten the couloir in early summer. This variation is only reasonable in late summer once the cornices have melted and the ledge is snow-free.

3.9 — Mount Spalding — Goldfinger *Classic*

From Summit Lake TH at 12,850 ft	349 RP	4.5 mi	3,392 ft	Class 3	Steep Snow
With descent of East Ridge	274 RP	3.4 mi	2,192 ft	Class 3	Steep Snow
From Echo Lake TH at 10,580 ft	389 RP	11.4 mi	3,862 ft	Class 3	Steep Snow
With descent of Chicago Creek	383 RP	11.0 mi	4,046 ft	Class 3	Steep Snow

This couloir is the southernmost of two elegant, east-facing snow slivers that reach the 13,020-foot Spalding–Gray Wolf saddle. Goldfinger is just north of the Black Wall, and it provides the highest-quality snow climb on Spalding. You cannot see Goldfinger from the Mount Evans Road, but you can see it from the 12,876-foot Spalding–Warren saddle 0.25 mile north of the Summit Lake Trailhead. In most years Goldfinger does not have a cornice at its top.

Follow either of the approaches for Badfinger and descend to a small meadow at 11,860 feet. This is a special place ringed by ruggedness. You can see most of Goldfinger west of here. It is a good idea to hike up the hill to the north to get a full view of the couloir, to ensure that there is no cornice at the top. Climb west up steepening slopes and enter the narrow couloir at 12,400 feet. The couloir is longer than it appears. Be prepared for five rope lengths of steep snow climbing. Near the top, stay to the south (left) side of the couloir and finish on the couloir's south side. The steepness abruptly gives way to flat grass in the spacious Spalding–Gray Wolf saddle. Climb 0.7 mile south to Spalding's summit. Ascending Goldfinger and descending the East Ridge Route makes a sensible Tour de Spalding.

CHAPTER TWO

Tenmile–Mosquito Range

Introduction

This range carries the distinction and confusion of two names. The two named ranges are geographically continuous. The Continental Divide sneaks through this north–south range on an east–west line as if impatient to be elsewhere. The Tenmile Range is north of the divide, and the Mosquito Range is south of the divide.

The Tenmile Range's northern end is near Frisco on Interstate 70. The Tenmile Range has 10 numbered peaks and several imaginatively named peaks close to the Continental Divide, including 5 centennial thirteeners. The Mosquito Range has 7 centennial thirteeners close to the divide, and runs south over several lower peaks. The Mosquito Range's practical southern boundary is Trout Creek Pass on U.S. 285. Colorado 9 and U.S. 285 mark the range's east edge. Interstate 70, Colorado 91 and U.S. 24 mark the range's west edge.

These peaks can be easily accessed from both the east and the west, and the trailheads are high. In August you can ascend all 12 centennial thirteeners in the Tenmile–Mosquito Range with Class 1 or Class 2 hiking. These are some of Colorado's easiest high thirteeners, but the range hides several technical challenges. Also, remember that easy peaks do not come with a guarantee of good weather!

4. Fletcher Group

Crystal Peak	13,852 feet
Pacific Peak	13,950 feet
"Atlantic Peak"	13,841 feet
Fletcher Mountain	13,951 feet
"Drift Peak"	13,900 feet

See Map 4 on page 52

The ten numbered peaks of the Tenmile Range rise in concert south of Frisco. The first eight peaks are twelvers, Peak 9 nudges above 13,000 feet and Peak 10 leaps to 13,633 feet in preparation for one of Colorado's highest ridges. The ridge south of Peak 10 holds the Tenmile Range's five centennial thirteeners. They are all on the range crest north of the Continental Divide between Hoosier Pass and Breckenridge on Colorado 9. With a few notable exceptions, they are gentle and forgiving. These peaks are

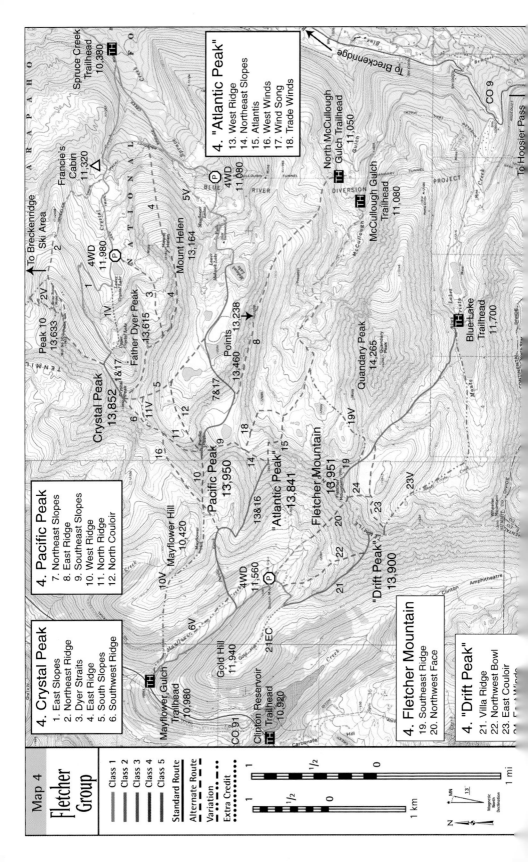

Map 4

Fletcher Group

Class 1
Class 2
Class 3
Class 4
Class 5

Standard Route
Alternate Route
Variation
Extra Credit

1 km   ½   0

1 mi   ½   0

N

MN
13°
Magnetic
North
Declination

4. Crystal Peak
1. East Slopes
2. Northeast Ridge
3. Dyer Straits
4. East Ridge
5. South Slopes
6. Southwest Ridge

4. Pacific Peak
7. Northeast Slopes
8. East Ridge
9. Southeast Slopes
10. West Ridge
11. North Ridge
12. North Couloir

4. "Atlantic Peak"
13. West Ridge
14. Northeast Slopes
15. Atlantis
16. West Winds
17. Wind Song
18. Trade Winds

4. Fletcher Mountain
19. Southeast Ridge
20. Northwest Face

4. "Drift Peak"
21. Villa Ridge
22. Northwest Bowl
23. East Couloir

To Breckenridge Ski Area

ARAPAHO

Spruce Creek
Trailhead
10,380

Francie's
Cabin
11,320

NATIONAL

FO

4WD
11,980

Peak 10
13,633

Crystal Peak
13,852

Father Dyer Peak
13,615

Mount Helen
13,164

Mayflower Hill
10,420

Mayflower Gulch
Trailhead
10,980

CO 91

Gold Hill
11,940

Clinton Reservoir
Trailhead
10,920

4WD
11,560

Pacific Peak
13,950

"Atlantic Peak"
13,841

Points
13,460

13,238

Fletcher Mountain
13,951

"Drift Peak"
13,900

Quandary Peak
14,265

Blue Lake
Trailhead
11,700

BLUE

4WD
11,080

RIVER

DIVERSION

TUNNEL

McCullough Gulch
Trailhead
11,080

North McCullough
Gulch Trailhead
11,050

PROJECT

CO 9

To Hoosier Pass

To Breckenridge

popular as training climbs, especially for residents of Summit County. There are several interesting combinations on these peaks. They are presented here in order from north to south.

MAPS
Required: *Breckenridge, Copper Mountain, White River National Forest*

TRAILHEADS

Spruce Creek Trailhead
This trailhead is at 10,380 feet and provides access to Crystal and Pacific's east sides. The trailhead is west of Colorado 9 and can be reached from either the north or south. If you are approaching from the north, go 2.5 miles south on Colorado 9 from the junction of Ski Hill Road and Lincoln and Main Streets in Breckenridge. If you are approaching from the south, go 7.6 miles north on Colorado 9 from the summit of Hoosier Pass. Turn west onto the Spruce Creek Road and follow it 1.2 miles west then southwest to the marked trailhead. This trailhead is accessible in winter.

In summer it is possible to drive farther. Three hundred yards west of the trailhead, a four-wheel-drive road climbs 2.3 miles west up Crystal Creek to Lower Crystal Lake at 11,980 feet. From the winter trailhead, the Spruce Creek Road continues 1.8 miles southwest up Spruce Creek to 11,080 feet. The Spruce Creek Road is passable for tough passenger cars with decent clearance.

McCullough Gulch Trailhead
This trailhead is at 11,080 feet and provides access to the east sides of "Atlantic," Pacific and Fletcher. The trailhead is west of Colorado 9 and can be reached from either the north or south.

If you are approaching from the north, go 7.9 miles south on Colorado 9 from the junction of Ski Hill Road and Lincoln and Main Streets in Breckenridge. If you are approaching from the south, go 2.2 miles north on Colorado 9 from the summit of Hoosier Pass. Turn west onto Summit County 850 and go 0.1 mile west. Turn north (right) onto Summit County 851 and follow it as it curves around Quandary Peak's east end and enters McCullough Gulch on Quandary's north side. Stay south (left) at mile 1.6 and park below a locked gate at mile 2.1. Summit County 851 is closed in winter.

North McCullough Gulch Trailhead
This trailhead is at 11,050 feet and provides access to Pacific's east ridge. Follow the directions for the McCullough Gulch Trailhead to the junction 1.6 miles beyond the Colorado 9–Summit County 850 junction. Turn north (right), descend, cross to McCullough Gulch's north side and climb to the end of the road at mile 2.4.

Blue Lake Trailhead

This trailhead is at 11,700 feet and provides access to "Drift" and Fletcher's east sides. From the Colorado 9–Summit County 850 junction described for the McCullough Gulch Trailhead, turn west onto Summit County 850 and go 2.2 miles west to the dam at upper Blue Lake on Monte Cristo Creek.

This is the trailhead, and there is ample parking below the dam. The winter road closure on Summit County 850 varies, but is usually 0.4 mile west of the Summit County 850–Summit County 851 junction.

Mayflower Gulch Trailhead

This trailhead is at 10,980 feet and provides access to the west sides of "Drift," Fletcher, "Atlantic," Pacific and Crystal. The trailhead is on Colorado 91 and can be approached from the north or south. If you are approaching from the north, go 6.1 miles south on Colorado 91 from the junction of Interstate 70 and Colorado 91. If you are approaching from the south, go 4.1 miles north on Colorado 91 from the summit of Fremont Pass. The trailhead is on the east side of Colorado 91. The large parking area here is plowed in winter. In summer, high-clearance vehicles can go 1.6 miles southeast to some old cabins at 11,560 feet below the Boston Mine.

4. Crystal Peak   13,852 feet

See Map 4 on page 52

Crystal is a peak for all seasons. Its easy access and gentle countenance make it inviting anytime. Crystal is 5 miles southwest of downtown Breckenridge, and can be climbed from there. The Spruce Creek Trailhead offers easy access to Crystal's many eastern routes, and you can reach the peak's west side from the Mayflower Gulch Trailhead.

ROUTES

4.1 — Crystal Peak — East Slopes *Classic*

From Spruce Creek TH at 10,380 ft:	*193 RP*	*9.4 mi*	*3,472 ft*	*Class 2*
From Lower Crystal Lake at 11,980 ft:	*116 RP*	*4.8 mi*	*1,872 ft*	*Class 2*

This charming tour up a scenic valley is the easiest route up Crystal. Start at the Spruce Creek Trailhead and go 300 yards west on the Spruce Creek Road. Leave the Spruce Creek Road, turn north (right) and follow the four-wheel-drive Crystal Creek Road as it climbs west through the forest. Cross the Burro Trail, then reach the gated Aqueduct Road at 11,200 feet. Continue west on the Crystal Creek Road and reach treeline at 11,300 feet. You will see signs for Francie's Cabin, which is tucked in the trees 200 yards north of the road. (For reservations for Francie's Cabin and other Summit Huts, call 970-925-5775 or visit their website: www.huts.org).

It is not necessary to go to Francie's Cabin. Continue west on the Crystal Creek Road, cross the Wheeler Trail at 11,400 feet, cross Crystal Creek at 11,500 feet and reach Lower Crystal Lake at 11,980 feet. If the crossing of Crystal Creek is severe, you can stay north of the creek to reach the lake. It is 2.3 miles from the Spruce Creek Trailhead to Lower Crystal Lake. When the road is dry, four-wheel-drive vehicles can reach Lower Crystal Lake.

This is an enchanting place underneath the rugged northern ramparts of 13,164-foot Mount Helen and 13,615-foot Father Dyer Peak. You can peer into the rugged cirque between Helen to the south and Father Dyer to the southwest. Crystal's high, gentle summit is to the west.

Go around Lower Crystal Lake's north side and follow the Crystal Trail 1.8 miles as it switchbacks up the slope north of the lake and then climbs west to 12,860-foot Upper Crystal Lake, nestled beneath Crystal and Father Dyer Peaks. Crystal is the peak directly west of Upper Crystal Lake. From Upper Crystal Lake's north side, climb 0.2 mile northwest up talus or snow to the 13,260-foot saddle between Peak 10 and Crystal (Class 2). Climb 0.4 mile southwest up the easy ridge to Crystal's summit. If you are lucky, the sky will be crystal clear.

4.1V – Variation

You can take a shortcut between Lower and Upper Crystal Lakes. From Lower Crystal Lake's west side, climb directly west, ascend a steep slope, then climb a small gully directly under Father Dyer's north face. Upper Crystal Lake is just beyond. This variation makes sense in winter, when snow covers the Crystal Trail.

4.2 – Crystal Peak – Northeast Ridge

From Spruce Creek TH at 10,380 ft:	*255 RP*	*9.0 mi*	*4,218 ft*	*Class 2*
With descent of East Slopes:	*22 RP*	*9.2 mi*	*3,845 ft*	*Class 2*
From Wheeler Trail at 11,400 ft:	*205 RP*	*6.0 mi*	*3,198 ft*	*Class 2*
With descent of East Slopes:	*178 RP*	*6.2 mi*	*2,825 ft*	*Class 2*

This ridge walk allows you to look down on the Crystal Lakes and climb an extra peak. Start at the Spruce Creek Trailhead and follow the East Slopes Route 1.5 miles to the Wheeler Trail at 11,400 feet. Follow the Wheeler Trail 1.0 mile north to 12,400 feet on Peak 10's east ridge. The trail is faint in this area, but is marked with large cairns. Leave the Wheeler Trail and walk 0.6 mile up Peak 10's rounded east ridge to a flat area at 13,160 feet.

From here you can look down on Lower Crystal Lake and up at Peak 10's summit. You can also look south and southwest to the ragged north faces of Mount Helen and Father Dyer Peak. Continue west, pass an electronics site at 13,400 feet and climb the upper ridge to Peak 10's 13,633-foot summit. Crystal Peak is a mile southwest.

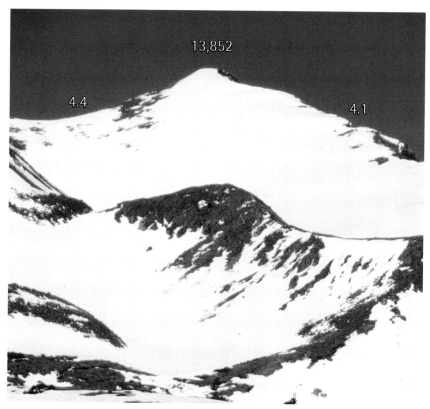

13,852

4.4

4.1

Crystal Peak from the east.

Descend 0.6 mile southwest to the 13,260-foot saddle between Peak 10 and Crystal and rejoin the East Slopes Route. You can look down on Upper Crystal Lake from here. Climb 0.4 mile southwest up the easy ridge to Crystal's summit. Ascending the Northeast Ridge Route and descending the East Slopes Route makes a nice Tour de Crystal. This loop hike eliminates the need to reclimb Peak 10 on your return.

4.2V — Variation

	RP	mi	ft	Class
From Beaver Run Resort at 9,700 ft:	287 RP	4.2 mi	4,898 ft	Class 2
From top of Mercury Super Chair at 11,460 ft:	183 RP	7.2 mi	3,138 ft	Class 2

You can approach this route from Breckenridge. From the junction of South Park Road and Main Street in Breckenridge, go 0.2 mile west on South Park Road and turn west (left) onto Village Road. Go west up Village Road to just east of (just before) the Beaver Run Resort at 9,700 feet.

In summer, go through a parking lot east of the Beaver Run Resort and get onto the dirt road south of the resort. Follow the road into the ski area west of the resort. The road starts by crossing under the Beaver Run Super Chair. This unmarked road is a Summit County road, but vehicle access may be blocked at times, particularly when the road is wet. Following the road west, stay right (straight) at mile 0.5, stay left (straight) at mile 0.6 and switchback up through the ski area to reach the Peak 9 Restaurant at 11,020 feet at mile 3.0. The road to this point, though steep, should be passable for tough passenger cars. Go 0.5 mile west on the road above the restaurant to the top of the Mercury Super Chair at 11,460 feet. This stretch of road requires high clearance. From the top of the Mercury Super Chair, climb west and get onto FS 751.

In winter you can take the Peak 9 lift or Mercury Super Chair, or ski up to this point. If you choose to ski or hike up through the ski area, the Breckenridge Ski Patrol requests that you stay to the side of the ski slopes and leash pets. Climb west above the top of the Mercury Super Chair and pass through the backcountry gate. Any winter closures will be posted there.

From the backcountry gate, go 1.3 miles southwest up FS 751 as it climbs the east shoulder of Peak 9 to reach the Wheeler Trail. Cross the Wheeler Trail, continue on the rough road 0.5 mile south-southwest through a small basin between Peaks 9 and 10 and continue 0.5 mile south on the very rough road as it climbs all the way to the electronics site at 13,400 feet on Peak 10's east ridge. Join the Northeast Ridge Route there. You may choose to leave the road in the small basin and hike southeast to reach Peak 10's east ridge at a lower elevation. This avoids the north slope below the electronics site.

4.3 — Crystal Peak — Dyer Straits *Classic*

From Spruce Creek TH at 10,380 ft:	265 RP	8.6 mi	3,702 ft	Class 2	Mod Snow
With descent of East Slopes:	246 RP	9.0 mi	3,587 ft	Class 2	Mod Snow
From Lower Crystal Lake at 11,980 ft:	188 RP	4.0 mi	2,102 ft	Class 2	Mod Snow
With descent of East Slopes:	169 RP	4.4 mi	1,987 ft	Class 2	Mod Snow

This scenic route provides a nifty spring snow climb in an alpine setting, and allows you to climb an extra peak. Start at the Spruce Creek Trailhead and follow the East Slopes Route to Lower Crystal Lake at 11,980 feet. From here, 13,164-foot Mount Helen is 0.5 mile south, and 13,615-foot Father Dyer Peak is 1.0 mile southwest. Father Dyer Peak is not named on the 1987 Breckenridge Quadrangle, but the name is official. Hike 0.2 mile around Lower Crystal Lake's south side, then climb 0.3 mile south into the small cirque formed by Helen's northwest face and Father Dyer's east and southeast ridges. Let the enchantment begin.

Climb 0.5 mile west through the cirque to 12,800 feet under Father Dyer's tiny east face. This is an exciting spot, and a yodel carries well here. Climb 0.2 mile southwest up a moderate snow slope to reach Father Dyer's southeast ridge at 13,260 feet, then scamper 0.2 mile northwest to Father Dyer's summit. Hike 0.6 mile west on rough talus to reach Crystal's summit. Ascending the Dyer Straits Route and descending the East Slopes Route makes another nice Tour de Crystal.

4.4 — Crystal Peak — East Ridge *Classic*

From Spruce Creek TH at 10,380 ft:	*356 RP*	*8.8 mi*	*4,470 ft*	*Class 3*
With descent of East Slopes:	*298 RP*	*9.1 mi*	*3,971 ft*	*Class 3*
From 4WD parking at 10,940 ft:	*321 RP*	*6.4 mi*	*3,910 ft*	*Class 3*

This sporty alternative route offers some Class 3 scrambling along an airy ridge and allows you to climb two extra peaks. Start at the Spruce Creek Trailhead, follow the Spruce Creek Road 1.2 miles west to 10,940 feet, then turn right onto the Aqueduct Road and follow it 0.2 mile north. Leave the road at 11,000 feet and climb 1.1 miles west up Mount Helen's unrelenting, steep, rounded east slopes to Helen's 13,164-foot summit. The introduction is over.

Descend 0.3 mile west on steep talus to a 12,900-foot saddle, then scramble along the rough ridge toward Father Dyer Peak. Some small towers in the middle of the traverse require routefinding and Class 3 scrambling. Scramble over Point 13,340, then descend to a 13,220-foot saddle, where the difficulty relaxes to Class 2 talus hiking. Scamper 0.4 mile northwest up to Father Dyer's 13,615-foot summit and continue 0.6 mile west to Crystal's summit. Ascending the East Ridge Route and descending the East Slopes Route makes yet another nice Tour de Crystal.

4.5 — Crystal Peak — South Slopes

From Spruce Creek TH at 10,380 ft:	*252 RP*	*10.6 mi*	*3,472 ft*	*Class 2*
With descent of East Slopes:	*230 RP*	*10.0 mi*	*3,472 ft*	*Class 2*
From 4WD parking at 11,080 ft:	*202 RP*	*7.0 mi*	*2,772 ft*	*Class 2*

This is Crystal's other standard route, and it offers you a chance to visit the lush Mohawk Lakes. Start at the Spruce Creek Trailhead and follow the Spruce Creek Road 1.8 miles southwest to the road's end at 11,080 feet. Follow the Mohawk Lake Trail for 1.3 miles as it climbs steeply west past Continental Falls to Lower Mohawk Lake and then continues on to Mohawk Lake at 12,100 feet. This is a pretty hike, and its popularity is justified.

Hike 0.1 mile around Mohawk Lake's north side on a rough use trail. Continue 1.5 miles northwest up the lush Spruce Creek valley, passing several more large lakes en route. At 12,600 feet, turn north and pick your way up a steep, rough slope for 400 feet. As the angle relaxes, continue north to Crystal's summit. You too can relax on the summit. Ascending the South Slopes Route and descending the East Slopes Route makes a comprehensive Tour de Crystal.

4.5V — Variation

To slightly shorten and vary your ascent, you can take the Mayflower Lakes Trail. This trail leaves the Spruce Creek Road 1.3 miles above the Spruce Creek Trailhead, just 0.1 mile beyond the Aqueduct Road. The trail climbs southwest past the two tiny Mayflower Lakes to join the Mohawk Lakes Trail.

4.6 — Crystal Peak — Southwest Ridge

From Mayflower Gulch TH at 10,980 ft:	*237 RP*	*7.2 mi*	*3,032 ft*	*Class 2*
From 4WD parking at 11,360 ft:	*207 RP*	*5.2 mi*	*2,652 ft*	*Class 2*

Much less popular than Crystal's east-side routes, this western route offers a higher trailhead and a unique approach to Crystal. Depending on conditions, it is a reasonably safe route for a winter ascent. Start at the Mayflower Gulch Trailhead and go 1.1 miles southeast up the road to 11,360 feet. Leave the road, head 0.2 mile northeast, cross Mayflower Creek and enter the small Pacific Creek drainage. This valley separates Pacific and "Atlantic." Climb 0.7 mile northeast up Pacific Creek. When the basin broadens and the creek turns south at 12,240 feet, leave the creek and climb 0.3 mile northeast to 12,500 feet just below the steep part of Pacific Peak's west ridge. From here you can see Crystal 1.3 miles to the northeast.

Contour 0.7 mile northeast under Pacific's impressive northwest face. When convenient, climb 0.1 mile east to the 13,220-foot Crystal–Pacific saddle. The view of Pacific's northeast face from here is impressive. Climb 0.2 mile north-northeast to Point 13,540, descend 0.1 mile northeast and continue 0.3 mile northeast up the gentle ridge to Crystal's summit. The views grow en route.

4.6V — Variation

If the crossing of Mayflower Creek is too dangerous, which it can be in June, you can avoid the ford by crossing to Mayflower Creek's north side on the concrete flow control system 200 yards southeast of the Mayflower Gulch Trailhead. Walk 1.0 mile up Mayflower Creek's north side to Pacific Creek and rejoin the route there.

4. Pacific Peak   13,950 feet

See Map 4 on page 52

Pacific Peak is on the crest of the Tenmile Range 0.9 mile southwest of Crystal Peak. With its classic pyramid shape, Pacific is the most dramatic peak in the Tenmile Range. Its rugged northeast, northwest and southwest faces give it an astonishing appearance when viewed from the north and west. Motorists on Interstate 70 have often exclaimed, "Wow! What is that?" That is Pacific. Nevertheless, there are easy routes on Pacific. The Spruce Creek and McCullough Gulch Trailheads give access to the peak's east side, and the Mayflower Gulch Trailhead gives access to the peak's west side.

ROUTES

4.7 — Pacific Peak — Northeast Slopes *Classic*

From Spruce Creek TH at 10,380 ft: 317 RP 10.6 mi 3,570 ft Class 2 Mod Snow
From 4WD parking at 11,080 ft: 266 RP 7.0 mi 2,870 ft Class 2 Mod Snow

This is the standard route up Pacific. It is a classic tour with a hike up a lake-filled valley to a nice snow climb, a chance to visit one of Colorado's highest lakes and a chance to experience Pacific's summit pyramid first-hand. If the moderate snow climb to the plateau is not to your liking and you want a snow-free route up Pacific, use the North Ridge Route.

Start at the Spruce Creek Trailhead and follow Crystal's South Slopes Route to the west end of the lake at 12,391 feet. Climb 0.6 mile southwest up a slope to the small plateau at 13,400 feet. This slope holds moderate snow into August, and you can recognize it by the ever-present ski tracks on it. An ice ax is useful on this route until late summer. Once on the plateau, hike 0.2 mile west and visit the amazing unnamed lake at 13,420 feet. Snowbound into August, this is one of the highest lakes in Colorado, if not the highest. From the lake's east end, hike 0.2 mile northwest and get onto the east ridge of Pacific's summit pyramid. Climb 0.2 mile west up steep talus to the summit. You can peer down Pacific's steep north face en route.

4.8 — Pacific Peak — East Ridge *Classic*

From North McCullough Gulch TH at 11,050 ft: 220 RP 6.8 mi 3,336 ft Class 2+
With descent of Southeast Slopes: 235 RP 8.2 mi 3,388 ft Class 2+

This is the dividing ridge between Spruce Creek to the north and McCullough Gulch to the south. With a mile of jolly scampering, this ridge gives you a chance to work on your patience and balance.

Start at the North McCullough Gulch Trailhead. From just east of the cliffs above the end of the road, bushwhack 0.2 mile north up a steep slope to reach grass slopes at 11,400 feet (Class 2). Hike 1.1 miles northwest up open slopes and reach the well-defined ridge at 12,800 feet (Class 1). Hike 0.6 mile west on rough talus along the narrowing ridge to Point 13,238 (Class 2). The introduction is over.

The second half of the ridge is more challenging. From Point 13,238, the ridge extends 0.6 mile west to the east end of Pacific's summit plateau at 13,400 feet below Pacific's summit pyramid. You can avoid difficulties on the ridge crest by staying below the ridge on its south side. If you use patience and careful routefinding, the difficulty will not exceed Class 2+. For more excitement, stay on or near the ridge crest, where you will find some Class 3 scrambling. Just as you think the difficulties should be over, you reach the tiny Point 13,460, where the ridge drops west into a notch and the rock becomes more shattered. Descend west on the ridge's south

Pacific Peak from the northeast.

side to the notch, then climb on the ridge's north side to the end of the difficulties at 13,460 feet on a small talus ridge east of the plateau.

Follow the talus ridge west, then descend slightly to reach the unnamed lake at 13,420 feet. Join the Northeast Slopes Route here for the climb up Pacific's summit pyramid. Ascending the East Ridge Route and descending the Southeast Slopes Route makes a smart Tour de Pacific. Be prepared for a snow descent. At the end of this tour, you will have 1.3 road miles between the McCullough Gulch Trailhead and the North McCullough Gulch Trailhead.

4.9 – Pacific Peak – Southeast Slopes

From McCullough Gulch TH at 11,080 ft: 24 RP 7.0 mi 2,950 ft Class 2   Mod Snow

This route up Pacific is similar to, but a little rougher than, the Northeast Slopes Route. Start at the McCullough Gulch Trailhead. Pass the road closure gate, follow the old road west, cross to Quandary Creek's north side on an aging vehicle bridge and continue west on the road. When the road switchbacks east, leave it and go west on a rough, rocky trail. Follow the trail west to a startling view of Quandary's wild Inwood Arête above a lovely cascade. Continue west on the trail to the east end of a long, narrow unnamed lake at 11,900 feet. It is 1.3 miles from the trailhead to this beautiful lake.

Follow a faint use trail around the lake's north side and hike west into the northern branch of upper McCullough Gulch. Follow this lush, scenic drainage 1.2 miles west then northwest to 12,700 feet below a wide snow slope beneath the Pacific– "Atlantic" saddle. Snow persists on this slope into August, and you cannot easily avoid it, as cliffs border it on both sides. We recommend an ice ax for this route. Choose your line, climb the moderate snow slope, then hike 0.2 mile west to the broad, 13,380-foot Pacific–"Atlantic" saddle.

From the saddle, hike 250 yards northeast to a small, 13,580-foot summit. From here you can look down on the high lake in the plateau east of Pacific's summit pyramid. Descend slightly, then climb 0.3 mile north above the lake up Pacific's south ridge to the splendid summit.

4.10 — Pacific Peak — West Ridge *Classic*

From Mayflower Gulch TH at 10,980 ft:	286 RP	5.8 mi	2,970 ft	Class 3
From 4WD parking at 11,360 ft:	256 RP	3.6 mi	2,590 ft	Class 3

This is a fine rock scramble up a high, alpine ridge. Start at the Mayflower Gulch Trailhead and follow Crystal's Southwest Ridge Route to 12,500 feet just below the steep part of Pacific's west ridge. Scramble 0.6 mile east up the steep, blocky ridge to the summit.

4.10V — Variation

From Mayflower Gulch TH at 10,980 ft:	296 RP	4.9 mi	3,090 ft	Class 3

This variation allows you to climb an extra summit en route. Start at the Mayflower Gulch Trailhead and cross to Mayflower Creek's north side on the concrete flow control system 200 yards southeast of the trailhead. Climb 200 yards southeast on an old road. When the road turns and climbs north, leave it and bushwhack 0.2 mile east to treeline at 11,400 feet. Continue 0.4 mile east up gentle slopes to 12,000 feet on the northwest ridge of Mayflower Hill. Climb 0.5 mile southeast up this gentle ridge to the summit of 12,420-foot Mayflower Hill. This suspended vantage gives you a good, head-on view of Pacific's upper west ridge and an open panorama of the area. Mayflower Hill has a small but steep north face, and large cornices form here in winter. Descend 100 yards east to a rough step in the ridge. Avoid it by descending a scree slope to the south. Hike 0.4 mile east to the bottom of Pacific's upper west ridge and join the West Ridge Route there.

4.11 — Pacific Peak — North Ridge

From Mayflower Gulch TH at 10,980 ft:	234 RP	7.2 mi	2,970 ft	Class 2
From 4WD parking at 11,360 ft:	204 RP	5.0 mi	2,590 ft	Class 2

This is an unusual but easy route on Pacific's west and north sides. It is the safest route for winter ascents of Pacific. Start at the Mayflower Gulch Trailhead and follow Crystal's Southwest Ridge Route to the 13,220-foot Crystal–Pacific saddle. Climb 0.5 mile south up Pacific's north ridge to the summit. En route, a few extra steps to the east will give you views of Pacific's impressive north face.

4.11V – Variation

From Spruce Creek TH at 10,380 ft: 295 RP   11.6 mi   3,930 ft   Class 2
From 4WD parking at 11,080 ft: 244 RP   8.0 mi   3,230 ft   Class 2

You can approach Pacific's north ridge from the east. Follow Crystal's South Slopes Route to 13,400 feet, contour 0.2 mile west and descend 0.2 mile south to the 13,220-foot Crystal–Pacific saddle. Climb 0.5 mile south up Pacific's north ridge to the summit.

4.12 – Pacific Peak – North Couloir

From Spruce Creek TH at 10,380 ft:	457 RP	10.5 mi	3,570 ft	Class 5.5	Very Steep Snow
With descent of NE Slopes:	466 RP	10.6 mi	3,570 ft	Class 5.5	Very Steep Snow
From 4WD parking at 11,080 ft:	407 RP	6.9 mi	2,870 ft	Class 5.5	Very Steep Snow
With descent of NE Slopes:	415 RP	7.0 mi	2,870 ft	Class 5.5	Very Steep Snow

This is Pacific's premier mountaineering route. When it is in good condition, this couloir is the finest snow climb in the Tenmile–Mosquito Range. The couloir is in the center of Pacific's small, steep northeast face. The 700-foot-high couloir reaches a maximum steepness of 65 degrees. For a snow climb, conditions are best in late May and June. By July, the snow in the top of the couloir melts, revealing loose rock. There is often ice in the center of the couloir before it turns into a rubble gully in late summer. You can preview conditions in this couloir from the East Ridge or South Slopes Routes on Crystal. You can also catch a distant glimpse of the upper couloir from Colorado 91 south of Interstate 70.

Start at the Spruce Creek Trailhead and follow Crystal's South Slopes Route to 12,600 feet in the basin between Crystal and Pacific. Hike 0.4 mile west-southwest to 13,200 feet below Pacific's northeast face. You can finally see the couloir from here. Climb 400 feet southwest up the lower part of the couloir to a dogleg at 13,600 feet. Turn east (left) and continue up over a 65-degree section that may be icy. The couloir's angle relents toward the top, but this section is the first to lose its snow. When it's snow-free, climb rotten Class 5.5 rock on the couloir's east (left) side. The couloir ends in a dramatic notch at 13,900 feet. Scramble 100 feet east to Pacific's summit.

4. "Atlantic Peak"   13,841 feet

See Map 4 on page 52

"Atlantic Peak" is 0.7 mile south of Pacific Peak. You cannot easily see "Atlantic" from the east, but you can see it while driving by on Colorado 91 to the west. The rounded summit of "Atlantic" is deceiving, as the

"Atlantic Peak" from the northwest.

peak's slopes are often steep and rough. "Atlantic" also has a small but mighty east face that hides some technical challenges. You can reach the peak's east side from the McCullough Gulch Trailhead and the peak's west side from the Mayflower Gulch Trailhead.

ROUTES

4.13 — "Atlantic Peak" — West Ridge

From Mayflower Gulch TH at 10,980 ft:	*206 RP*	*6.2 mi*	*2,861 ft*	*Class 2*
From 4WD parking at 11,360 ft:	*176 RP*	*4.0 mi*	*2,481 ft*	*Class 2*

This is the standard and easiest route up "Atlantic." With its easy access, it is a popular winter ascent. However, snow on this ridge increases its difficulty. The last snow passage near the summit disappears sometime in mid-July.

Start at the Mayflower Gulch Trailhead and follow Crystal's Southwest Ridge Route to 12,240 feet in Pacific Creek. Climb 0.2 mile south up a rounded slope and reach the west ridge of "Atlantic" at 12,500 feet. Climb 0.9 mile east up the increasingly narrow ridge to the summit. En route, you can peer down to the south at an old aerial tram. If there is snow on the ridge, take an ice ax, as there are some exposed traverses.

On Pacific Peak's east ridge.

4.14 — "Atlantic Peak" — Northeast Slopes

From McCullough Gulch TH at 11,080 ft: 221 RP 6.6 mi 2,761 ft Class 2 Mod Snow

This is the easiest route up "Atlantic" from the east. Start at the McCullough Gulch Trailhead and follow Pacific's Southeast Slopes Route to the 13,380-foot Pacific–"Atlantic" saddle. From here, climb 0.3 mile south up the north ridge of "Atlantic" to the summit. You can climb talus on the ridge or an easy snow slope just east of the ridge.

4.15 — "Atlantic Peak" — Atlantis *Classic*

From McCullough Gulch TH at 11,080 ft: 226 RP 6.4 mi 2,761 ft Class 2 Mod Snow
With descent of Northeast Slopes: 228 RP 6.5 mi 2,761 ft Class 2 Mod Snow

This hidden couloir has been lost for years. If you can find it, you will have a novel experience. Even though the conditions in this couloir can be previewed from Quandary's summit, few mountaineers take notice of Atlantis.

Start at the McCullough Gulch Trailhead and follow Pacific's Southeast Slopes Route to 12,700 feet. En route up the valley, you can see a pair of couloirs forming a V in the northern section of the rough east face of "Atlantic." These couloirs are not the route, but they are close to it. From

12,700 feet, hike 0.3 mile southwest until you are below these couloirs at 12,800 feet. You should now see the Atlantis Couloir north of the V couloirs. Atlantis faces southeast and holds good snow through July. There is no cornice at the top of the couloir. Climb the straight, inset couloir and reach the rounded slope above at 13,440 feet. Hike 0.2 mile west up talus to the summit.

4. CRYSTAL, PACIFIC AND "ATLANTIC" COMBINATIONS

See Map 4 on page 52

4.16 — CPA Combination — West Winds *Classic*

From Mayflower Gulch TH at 10,980 ft:	*313 RP*	*8.6 mi*	*4,263 ft*	*Class 2*
From 4WD parking at 11,360 ft:	*283 RP*	*6.4 mi*	*3,883 ft*	*Class 2*

This is the easiest way to climb Crystal, Pacific and "Atlantic" together. Start at the Mayflower Gulch Trailhead and climb Crystal's Southwest Ridge Route. From Crystal's summit, descend 0.5 mile southwest back across Point 13,540 to the 13,220-foot Crystal–Pacific saddle. Climb 0.5 mile south to Pacific's summit. Descend 0.5 mile south across tiny Point 13,580 to the 13,380-foot Pacific–"Atlantic" saddle. Climb 0.3 mile south to the summit of "Atlantic." Descend the West Ridge Route of "Atlantic" and return to the Mayflower Gulch Trailhead.

4.17 — PC Combination — Wind Song

From Spruce Creek TH at 10,380 ft: 332 RP   11.0 mi   4,282 ft   Class 2

Climbing Pacific and Crystal together from the east allows you to see both the Spruce Creek and Crystal Creek valleys. Start at the Spruce Creek Trailhead and climb Pacific's Northeast Slopes Route. From Pacific's summit, descend 0.5 mile north to the 13,220-foot Crystal–Pacific saddle. Climb 0.2 mile north-northeast to Point 13,540, descend slightly and continue 0.3 mile northeast up the gentle ridge to Crystal's summit. Descend Crystal's East Slopes Route.

4.18 — PA Combination — Trade Winds

From McCullough Gulch TH at 11,080 ft: 271 RP 7.6 mi 3,411 ft Class 2 Mod Snow

This is the traditional way to climb Pacific and "Atlantic" together. Start at the McCullough Gulch Trailhead and climb Pacific's Southeast Slopes Route. Return to the 13,380-foot Pacific–"Atlantic" saddle and climb 0.3 mile south to the summit of "Atlantic." Descend the Northeast Slopes Route of "Atlantic."

4. Fletcher Mountain   13,951 feet

See Map 4 on page 52

Fletcher Mountain, the highest and namesake peak of this group, rises 7.0 miles southwest of Breckenridge and 4.5 miles northwest of Hoosier Pass on Colorado 9. Fletcher is 0.7 mile south of "Atlantic" and 1.3 miles west of the fourteener Quandary Peak. From the east, Fletcher is hidden behind its famous parent. From the west, you can see Fletcher clearly from Colorado 91 near the Mayflower Gulch Trailhead. Fletcher is the highest thirteener in the Tenmile Range, but only by 1 foot. Sometimes that is all it takes.

Unlike the ridges between the peaks to the north, the ridge between "Atlantic" and Fletcher has many gendarmes and is too rough for comfort. Fletcher has a steep east face that holds several couloirs and a rough northwest wall. The Tenmile Range has a more alpine feeling here. You can reach Fletcher's east side from the McCullough Gulch and Blue Lake Trailheads. You can reach Fletcher's west side from the Mayflower Gulch Trailhead.

ROUTES

4.19 — Fletcher Mountain — Southeast Ridge

From Blue Lake TH at 11,700 ft: 146 RP   4.2 mi   2,251 ft   Class 2

This short, scenic route is the easiest outing on Fletcher. Start at the Blue Lake Trailhead and hike north up the slope just west of the dam at upper Blue Lake. After 200 yards, cut west and find an old mining trail through the bushes. Beyond the bushes, follow the now clear trail 0.6 mile northwest as it climbs to 12,300 feet in the hanging valley south of Fletcher and Quandary. This idyllic valley will embrace you. Quandary's rugged southwest face is above you, and Fletcher's upper slopes are to the west.

Climb 0.7 mile northwest up the valley to some tiny lakes at 13,000 feet. It is not necessary to go to the ridge above just yet. Climb 0.1 mile west up a short, steep slope and reach easy terrain at 13,240 feet. You can now see Fletcher's final summit pyramid. Hike 0.2 mile northwest and reach Fletcher's southeast ridge at 13,400 feet. Climb 0.3 mile northwest up this ridge to the summit.

4.19V — Variation

From McCullough Gulch TH at 11,080 ft: 209 RP   6.8 mi   2,871 ft   Class 2+

You can approach Fletcher's southeast ridge from McCullough Gulch on Quandary's north side. Start at the McCullough Gulch Trailhead and hike 1.3 miles west on roads and a trail to the long, unnamed lake at 11,900 feet. Hike 0.2 mile around the lake's north side and continue 1.1 miles west up McCullough Gulch to some small lakes at 12,900 feet under the

Fletcher Mountain from the northeast.

Fletcher–Quandary ridge. Climb 0.2 mile south up steep talus to reach the ridge near the 13,340-foot Fletcher–Quandary saddle. Scramble 0.3 mile west past some towers to join the upper part of Fletcher's Southeast Ridge Route at 13,400 feet.

4.20 — Fletcher Mountain — Northwest Face

From Mayflower Gulch TH at 10,980 ft: 262 RP 6.0 mi 2,971 ft Class 2 Mod Snow
From 4WD parking at 11,560 ft: 218 RP 2.8 mi 2,391 ft Class 2 Mod Snow

This route provides a refreshing late spring snow climb with a short approach. With 1,600 feet of moderate snow, the ascent is sure to augment your training program. In a normal year, snow conditions should be optimal in late May. By July, the top of the route is scree and the climb is not as attractive. The route ascends a wide couloir to the 13,620-foot saddle between Fletcher and "Drift Peak," which is 0.6 mile southwest of Fletcher.

Start at the Mayflower Gulch Trailhead and follow the dirt road southeast of Mayflower Creek for 1.6 miles to the old log cabins at 11,540 feet below the Boston Mine. The cirque above the cabins holds three summits. Directly to the east is "Atlantic Peak," which binds the cirque's northern side. Fletcher rises in the center of the cirque, and "Drift Peak" binds the cirque's south side. You can easily see the route rising to the saddle between Fletcher and "Drift Peak." It is the widest couloir in the cirque wall.

"Drift Peak" from the northwest.

From the cabins, hike 0.6 mile southeast and engage the couloir's gradually increasing steepness at 12,000 feet. Climb the 1,600-foot couloir above you. It averages 31 degrees and reaches 43 degrees near the ridge. Rockfall from the ramparts of "Drift Peak" is a possibility, but there is no cornice at the top of the couloir. When you reach the 13,620-foot saddle, you will be rewarded with expansive views to the east. Quandary dominates this view. From the saddle, climb 0.2 mile northeast up talus and easy snow slopes to Fletcher's summit.

4. "Drift Peak" 13,900 feet

See Map 4 on page 52

"Drift Peak" is 0.6 mile southwest of Fletcher. You can easily see its double-humped summit from Colorado 91 near the Mayflower Gulch Trailhead. "Drift" has attracted climbers over the years because of its easy access and distinctive shape. Although its northwest and east faces are rugged, "Drift" does have an easy route on its northwest ridge. The tiny northwest bowl has been popular with skiers for years.

There is no exact elevation given on the USGS Quadrangle for "Drift Peak." This summit rises as much as 318 feet above the Fletcher–"Drift" saddle, and this fact garners "Drift" a soft rank on the list of thirteeners. "Drift" has not appeared on earlier lists, and it is a "new" thirteener.

ROUTES

4.21 — "Drift Peak" — Villa Ridge *Classic*

From Mayflower Gulch TH at 10,980 ft:	*181 RP*	*6.8 mi*	*2,920 ft*	*Class 2*
With descent of Northwest Bowl:	*180 RP*	*6.3 mi*	*2,920 ft*	*Class 2*
From 4WD parking at 11,560 ft:	*139 RP*	*3.8 mi*	*2,340 ft*	*Class 2*
With descent of Northwest Bowl:	*138 RP*	*3.3 mi*	*2,340 ft*	*Class 2*

Villa Ridge is the northwest ridge of "Drift," and it is the easiest route on the peak. The ridge is named in memory of Henry Villa, who died in an avalanche while attempting the ridge in December 1990. The ridge does seem to harbor questionable snow in winter (Gerry backed off a winter attempt of this ridge in the early '70s). In summer the ridge offers a straight-forward hike to a unique summit.

Start at the Mayflower Gulch Trailhead and go 1.5 miles southeast up the dirt road into Mayflower Gulch to the side creek at 11,500 feet, just before reaching the log cabins below the old Boston Mine. Do not cross the side creek. Leave the main road, turn south (right) and hike up an old road. Climb 0.5 mile south up this road and reach the crest of Villa Ridge in a flower-strewn flat area at 12,000 feet. Follow the ridge 0.3 mile south-southeast across the flat area. Find and hike 0.2 mile up an old miners trail that climbs the steep slope above. At 12,500 feet, the ridge narrows, but the angle of the ridge moderates. Follow the scenic ridge 0.5 mile south-east to 13,000 feet, where the ridge merges into the tiny west face of "Drift." Continue 0.4 mile up the south edge of this face on tipsy talus to the summit. The southern summit is the highest. Ascending Villa Ridge and descending the Northwest Bowl makes a nice Tour de "Drift" and allows you to glissade on the descent.

4.21EC — Extra Credit — Gold Hill, 11,940 feet, Class 1

From 12,000 feet on lower Villa Ridge, hike 0.5 mile northwest to Gold Hill's 11,940-foot summit. This humble summit is a place for reflection. It also offers a great view of "Atlantic," Fletcher and "Drift."

4.22 — "Drift Peak" — Northwest Bowl *Classic*

From Mayflower Gulch TH at 10,980 ft:	*225 RP*	*5.8 mi*	*2,920 ft*	*Class 2*	*Mod Snow*
With descent of Villa Ridge:	*226 RP*	*6.3 mi*	*2,920 ft*	*Class 2*	*Mod Snow*
From 4WD parking at 11,560 ft:	*184 RP*	*2.8 mi*	*2,340 ft*	*Class 2*	*Mod Snow*
With descent of Villa Ridge:	*185 RP*	*3.3 mi*	*2,340 ft*	*Class 2*	*Mod Snow*

The tiny northwest bowl of "Drift" is just north of Villa Ridge. It holds a sweeping, moderate snow slope that persists well into July. This slope is a favorite for skiers, snow climbers and glissade lovers.

Start at the Mayflower Gulch Trailhead and follow the dirt road south-east of Mayflower Creek for 1.5 miles to the side creek at 11,500 feet, just before reaching the log cabins below the Boston Mine. Do not cross the side creek. Leave the main road, turn south (right) and hike up an old road. Hike 0.2 mile up this road to 11,700 feet. Leave the road and hike southeast into the intimate basin. Climb over some initial steps and reach the bottom of the sweeping snow slope at 12,400 feet. Choose your line and ascend the slope to the bottom of the small west face of "Drift" at 13,200 feet. Continue up the south edge of this face on snow or tipsy talus to the summit. Ascending the Northwest Bowl and descending Villa Ridge makes a nice Tour de "Drift" and avoids the snow on the descent.

4.23 — "Drift Peak" — East Couloir

From Blue Lake TH at 11,700 ft: 193 RP   5.5 mi   2,400 ft   Class 2+   Mod Snow

This is the easiest way to climb "Drift" from the east. Start at the Blue Lake Trailhead and follow Fletcher's Southeast Ridge Route to the easy terrain at 13,240 feet. Hike 0.5 mile west across the easy terrain to the 13,380-foot saddle between "Drift" and Point 13,515, which is 0.4 mile east of "Drift." Cross this saddle and descend 100 yards southwest to 13,280 feet. Contour 0.3 mile west-southwest under the southeast face of "Drift" to the bottom of an east-facing couloir. Climb the couloir to a 13,580-foot saddle on the south ridge of "Drift." This couloir holds moderate snow into July. From the saddle, climb 300 yards north on the rough ridge to the summit.

4.23V — Variation

From Blue Lake TH at 11,700 ft: 213 RP   5.5 mi   2,200 ft   Class 2+

You can make a rough, direct approach to the upper couloir. From the Blue Lake Trailhead, hike 0.5 mile along Blue Lake's north side, then hike 0.9 mile west on Monte Cristo Creek's north side to 12,200 feet. Hike 0.8 mile north-northwest to a tiny lake at 12,860 feet. You can see the couloir from here. Climb 0.3 mile northwest to the bottom of the couloir at 13,280 feet and join the East Couloir Route there.

4. FLETCHER AND "DRIFT" COMBINATION

See Map 4 on page 52

4.24 — FD Combination — East Winds

From Blue Lake TH at 11,700 ft: 225 RP   5.9 mi   2,971 ft   Class 2+

This is the easiest way to climb Fletcher and "Drift" together. Start at the Blue Lake Trailhead and climb Fletcher's Southeast Ridge Route. From Fletcher's summit, descend 0.2 mile southwest to the 13,620-foot Fletcher–"Drift" saddle. Descend 0.2 mile south to the 13,380-foot saddle between "Drift" and Point 13,515. Continue on the East Couloir Route of "Drift" to the peak's summit. Descend the East Couloir Route of "Drift."

Map 5
Buckskin Group

5. Clinton Peak
1. Southeast Slopes
2. Northwest Ridge

5. Traver Peak
3. East Ridge
4. South Ridge
5. Southwest Face
6. Clipper

5. Mount Buckskin
7. Northeast Slopes
8. Southeast Ridge

Legend:
Class 1
Class 2
Class 3
Class 4
Class 5
Standard Route
Alternate Route
Variation
Extra Credit

Arapaho Hooser Pass 11,539
CO 9
To Alma

Montgomery Reservoir Trailhead 10,920

Mount Lincoln 14,286

Mount Bross 14,172

Mount Cameron 14,238

Mount Democrat 14,148

4WD 11,680

Kite Lake Trailhead 12,000

Buckskin Creek Trailhead 11,340

Clinton Peak 13,857

McNamee Peak 13,780

Traver Peak 13,852

4WD 11,400

Mount Buckskin 13,865

Loveland Mountain 13,692

To Clinton Reservoir Trailhead

Fremont Pass Trailhead 11,040

Fremont Pass
CO 91

NATIONAL FOREST
ISABEL

5. Buckskin Group

Clinton Peak	13,857 feet
Traver Peak	13,852 feet
Mount Buckskin	13,865 feet

See Map 5 on page 72

These friendly peaks are east of Fremont Pass on Colorado 91 and west of Hoosier Pass on Colorado 9. Clinton and Traver are north of the fourteener Mount Democrat in the middle of the Tenmile–Mosquito Range. The range takes a small break here after all the excitement on the Fletcher Group's peaks. Clinton and Traver's east sides are gentle. These peaks are popular as training climbs, and people often climb them together. The Climax Mine on Fremont Pass blocks a direct access to Clinton and Traver's steep west sides, but there are other options for a western approach. Mount Buckskin is south of the fourteener Mount Democrat, and is usually climbed from the east.

MAPS
Required: *Alma, Climax, Pike National Forest*
Optional: *Copper Mountain*

TRAILHEADS

Montgomery Reservoir Trailhead
This trailhead is at 10,920 feet and provides access to Clinton and Traver's east sides. If you are approaching from the south, go 10.7 miles north on Colorado 9 from the U.S. 285–Colorado 9 junction in Fairplay. If you are approaching from the north, go 1.1 miles south on Colorado 9 from the summit of Hoosier Pass.

Turn west onto Park County 4. This is the northern of two Colorado 9–Park County 4 junctions. Measuring from this junction, go down the hill to the west, stay right at mile 0.8, stay right at mile 1.0, go around Montgomery Reservoir's north side and park on the reservoir's west side at mile 1.9. The road is passable for passenger cars to this point, but it rapidly turns into a rough four-wheel-drive road at the Magnolia Mine, just west of the reservoir. Four-wheel-drive vehicles can continue 2.4 miles west to 11,680 feet under Clinton and Traver's east slopes. Stock four-wheel-drive vehicles should park here. The road on up to Wheeler Lake requires specialized equipment. In winter the road is plowed to the spillway road east of Montgomery Reservoir.

Clinton Reservoir Trailhead
This trailhead is at 11,060 feet and provides access to Clinton's northwest side. The trailhead is on Colorado 91 and can be approached from the north or south. If you are approaching from the north, go 7.6 miles south

on Colorado 91 from the junction of Interstate 70 and Colorado 91. If you are approaching from the south, go 3.6 miles north on Colorado 91 from the summit of Fremont Pass. The trailhead is on the east side of Colorado 91. The parking area here is plowed in winter.

Fremont Pass Trailhead

This trailhead is at 11,040 feet and provides access to Traver's west side. If you are approaching from the south, go 12.0 miles north on Colorado 91 from Leadville. If you are approaching from the north, go 9.0 miles south on Colorado 91 from Interstate 70. The trailhead is not on top of Fremont Pass but at the lower end of the sweeping switchback 0.7 mile southeast of the pass. Park on the south side of the highway in a large pullout west of some mine buildings. This trailhead is accessible in winter.

In summer, high-clearance vehicles can go 1.4 miles southeast into the valley on a decent dirt road to a closure gate at 11,400 feet. The road ends 200 yards beyond at a mine.

Buckskin Creek Trailhead

This trailhead is at 11,340 feet and provides access to Buckskin's east side. If you are approaching from the south, go 6.0 miles north on Colorado 9 from the U.S. 285–Colorado 9 junction in Fairplay. If you are approaching from the north, go 5.8 miles south on Colorado 9 from the summit of Hoosier Pass.

Turn west onto the Kite Lake Road (dirt) in the center of Alma. Park County 10 is not the Kite Lake Road. The poorly marked Kite Lake Road is Park County 8 and it starts across the highway from a store. Follow the Kite Lake Road 4.0 miles northwest up Buckskin Gulch to the Sweet Home Mine at 11,340 feet. This is the trailhead. In winter the road is closed here and snowmobiles make heavy use of the road above this point.

Kite Lake Trailhead

This trailhead is at 12,000 feet and provides access to Buckskin's north side. From the Buckskin Creek Trailhead, continue 2.0 miles north-northeast up Park County 8 to Kite Lake at 12,000 feet. There is ample parking east of Kite Lake, and this is the trailhead. The Kite Lake Road is good most of the way, but the last mile to the lake is difficult for passenger cars. Many people choose to park their cars near a switchback 0.6 mile below the lake, or just before a side creek crossing 0.25 mile below the lake.

5. Clinton Peak   13,857 feet

See Map 5 on page 72

Clinton Peak is 2.1 miles east of Fremont Pass and 4.7 miles west of Hoosier Pass. Clinton has the distinction of being the only centennial thirteener in the Tenmile–Mosquito Range that is on the Continental Divide. Because the Continental Divide separates the Tenmile and Mosquito Ranges, Clinton is in both ranges. Clinton is a mugwump of a mountain.

You also have a choice on Clinton. You can approach Clinton's gentle east side from the Montgomery Reservoir Trailhead on the east side of the Continental Divide, or you can approach Clinton's steep northwest side from the Clinton Reservoir Trailhead on the west side of the Continental Divide.

ROUTES

5.1 — Clinton Peak — Southeast Slopes

From Montgomery Reservoir TH at 10,920 ft: 212 RP   9.2 mi   2,937 ft   Class 2
From 4WD parking at 11,680 ft: 149 RP   4.4 mi   2,177 ft   Class 2

This is the standard and easiest route up Clinton. It is one of the easiest routes on a centennial thirteener. Start at the Montgomery Reservoir Trailhead and follow the four-wheel-drive road 2.4 miles west along the Middle Fork of the South Platte to 11,680 feet. Continue 0.2 mile west on the road as it starts its steep climb to Wheeler Lake and, at 11,760 feet, cross the creek descending from Wheeler Lake. Continue on the road 0.5 mile west then north to Wheeler Lake's south side at 12,168 feet. There are some interesting, often photographed relics here, including bedsprings and an old car. When you are ready, climb 1.2 miles west-southwest from Wheeler Lake's south end to 13,300 feet in the small basin between Clinton and Traver. Climb 0.3 mile north to Clinton's summit.

5.1EC — Extra Credit — McNamee Peak, 13,780 feet, Class 2
From Clinton's summit, hike 0.5 mile southwest along the gentle ridge to McNamee Peak's 13,780-foot summit.

5.2 — Clinton Peak — Northwest Ridge

From Clinton Reservoir TH at 11,060 ft: 226 RP   8.6 mi   3,237 ft   Class 2

This alternative route up Clinton will stimulate your alpine yearnings. Start at the Clinton Reservoir Trailhead and hike 2.5 miles southeast on the Clinton Creek Trail to 11,740 feet, above Clinton Amphitheatre's north end. This trail is several hundred feet above and south of the valley. After 1.5 miles, you will have to descend 220 feet. From the end of the trail, hike 0.7 mile south-southeast to 12,000 feet at the upper end of Clinton Amphitheatre. Climb 0.6 mile west below Clinton's ragged north face to the 12,940-foot saddle between Clinton and Bartlett Mountain, which is 0.8 mile northwest of Clinton. From the saddle, climb 0.5 mile southeast up Clinton's upper northwest ridge to the summit.

5. Traver Peak   13,852 feet

See Map 5 on page 72

Traver Peak is 0.7 mile south of Clinton and 0.4 mile southeast of the Continental Divide. Poor Traver, though only 5 feet lower than Clinton, is unranked and misses all the accolades of its more famous neighbor. Nevertheless, Traver waits for you.

ROUTES

5.3 — Traver Peak — East Ridge

From Montgomery Reservoir TH at 10,920 ft: 208 RP   9.0 mi   2,932 ft   Class 2
From 4WD parking at 11,680 ft: 145 RP   4.2 mi   2,172 ft   Class 2

Splendid in its simplicity, this is a route for all seasons. Start at the Montgomery Reservoir Trailhead and follow Clinton's Southeast Slopes Route to 12,800 feet. Climb 0.3 mile south-southwest to 13,200 feet on Traver's gentle east ridge, then climb 0.5 mile west on this ridge to the summit.

5.4 — Traver Peak — South Ridge

From Montgomery Reservoir TH at 10,920 ft: 244 RP   9.6 mi   2,932 ft   Class 2
From 4WD parking at 11,680 ft: 181 RP   4.8 mi   2,172 ft   Class 2

This is a good route for a solitary summer stroll. Start at the Montgomery Reservoir Trailhead and follow the four-wheel-drive road 2.4 miles west along the Middle Fork of the South Platte. Leave this road at 11,680 feet before it crosses the creek descending from Wheeler Lake and starts the steep climb to this lake. Hike 0.3 mile southwest on another, fainter four-wheel-drive road through the bushes. When you are beyond the bushes, angle 0.7 mile southwest up to 12,400 feet on the east end of the small basin southeast of Traver. Stroll 0.8 mile southwest up this gentle basin to the 13,140-foot Traver–Democrat saddle. Climb 0.6 mile north up Traver's easy south ridge to the summit. Ascending the South Ridge Route and descending the East Ridge Route makes a tidy Tour de Traver.

5.5 — Traver Peak — Southwest Face

From Fremont Pass TH at 11,040 ft: 295 RP   5.2 mi   2,852 ft   Class 2+   Mod Snow
From 4WD parking at 11,400 ft: 259 RP   2.4 mi   2,492 ft   Class 2+   Mod Snow

When snow conditions are favorable in spring and early summer, Traver's southwest face provides a long snow climb. Avoid this face when it is snow-free. You can easily see this face from Colorado 91, and you should check conditions when going to and coming from other adventures. Be patient; then, when snow conditions are perfect, climb it.

Traver and Clinton Peaks from the southeast.

Start at the Fremont Pass Trailhead and go 1.4 miles southeast on a dirt road along the west (right) side of the valley to a road closure gate at 11,400 feet, just before a side creek crosses the road. Traver's summit is 1.0 mile northeast of you, and directly across the valley a long, straight couloir splits Traver's southwest face. This is the route. Leave the road and hike 0.4 mile north-northeast across the valley to 11,700 feet below the couloir. In June the creek crossing can be troublesome. After all, this creek is the headwaters of the mighty Arkansas River. The 2,150-foot-high couloir rises directly from 11,700 feet to the summit. The couloir averages 34 degrees. When snow conditions are good, this is an astonishing ascent. Climb it.

5. CLINTON AND TRAVER COMBINATION
See Map 5 on page 72

5.6 — CT Combination — Clipper *Classic*

From Montgomery Reservoir TH at 10,920 ft: 241 RP   10.0 mi   3,249 ft   Class 2
From 4WD parking at 11,680 ft: 177 RP   5.2 mi   2,489 ft   Class 2

This is the standard way of climbing Clinton and Traver together. The route collects McNamee Peak as well. Start at the Montgomery Reservoir Trailhead and climb Clinton's Southeast Slopes Route. From Clinton's summit, hike 0.5 mile southwest along the gentle ridge to McNamee's 13,780-foot summit. Continue 0.4 mile southeast on the still easy ridge to Traver's summit. Descend Traver's East Ridge Route.

5. Mount Buckskin   13,865 feet

See Map 5 on page 72

Mount Buckskin is 5.5 miles southwest of Hoosier Pass on Colorado 9, and 4.0 miles southeast of Fremont Pass on Colorado 91. Humble Buckskin is often overlooked, being just 1.5 miles south of the famous fourteener Mount Democrat. Remember that lesser summits often provide the best views.

ROUTES

5.7 — Mount Buckskin — Northeast Slopes

From Kite Lake TH at 12,000 ft: 102 RP   2.6 mi   1,865 ft   Class 2

This is the easiest route on Buckskin. Start at the Kite Lake Trailhead and hike 0.4 mile west-southwest on the Lake Emma Trail. Leave the trail at 12,260 feet before the trail climbs north to Lake Emma. Hike 0.1 mile south and cross to the south side of Buckskin Creek. From here, hike 0.8 mile up tundra then talus to the summit. Buckskin has a 13,860-foot northwestern summit, but the 13,865-foot southeastern summit is the mountain's high point.

5.8 — Mount Buckskin — Southeast Ridge

From Buckskin Creek TH at 11,340 ft: 178 RP   4.4 mi   2,909 ft   Class 2

This alternative route is a little longer than the Northeast Slopes Route, but it allows you to climb an extra peak. Start at the Buckskin Creek Trailhead and cross to Buckskin Creek's west side. Hike 0.4 mile west up grassy slopes to 12,000 feet, then hike 0.4 mile west-southwest up a slope to reach Loveland Mountain's east ridge at 13,000 feet. Hike 0.4 mile west up this ridge to Loveland Mountain's 13,692-foot summit, your bonus peak. Loveland Mountain is an unranked summit, but it is named and included on our list of Colorado's highest peaks. From Loveland Mountain, hike 0.9 mile north-northwest along a rocky ridge to Buckskin's summit. Ascending the Southeast Ridge Route and descending the Northeast Slopes Route makes a bountiful Tour de Buckskin.

6. Mount Silverheels   13,822 feet

See Map 6 on page 80

Mount Silverheels is a gentle giant. The massive massif is 3.5 miles southeast of Hoosier Pass on Colorado 9, and Silverheels is the only peak in this chapter that is east of Colorado 9. You can see Silverheels from the Mosquito Range, from most of South Park and from the Retirement Range to the east. Silverheels is one of the most powerful peaks in the area. Though high and mighty, Silverheels is easy to climb and has multiple routes to choose from. Silverheels is also a popular winter peak. While savoring Silverheels' gentle aspects, respect the peak's giant size and the fact that the peak is famous for high winds.

MAPS

Required: *Alma, Pike National Forest*
Optional: *Como*

TRAILHEADS

Beaver Creek Trailhead

This trailhead is at 10,740 feet and provides access to Silverheels' south side. From the famous Fairplay Hotel in the center of Fairplay, go one block north on Colorado 9, turn northeast onto Fourth Street and measure from this point. Go 0.3 mile northeast on Fourth Street to a T-junction, turn north onto Bogue Street and go one block north to a stop sign. Go straight through the stop sign and continue north on what is now Beaver Creek Lane. Turn east (right) onto FS 413 at mile 2.8 and go east to a parking area and Forest Service gate at mile 3.1. This is the winter trailhead.

From the gate, go north on FS 659 to the unmarked Beaver Creek Campground, which is just a pullout on the road's east side at mile 5.0. Continue north on FS 659 to the trailhead at mile 5.3. The trailhead is at the junction of FS 659 and FS 184. From the trailhead, you can see FS 184 climbing the hill on the northeast side of Beaver Creek. Four-wheel-drive vehicles can cross to Beaver Creek's east side and continue 1.0 mile north-northeast on FS 184 to the road's high point at 11,180 feet.

Scott Gulch Trailhead   Private Property, Permission Required

This trailhead is at 11,100 feet and provides access to Silverheels' west side. If you are approaching from the south, go 10.4 miles north on Colorado 9 from the U.S. 285–Colorado 9 junction in Fairplay. If you are approaching from the north, go 1.4 miles south on Colorado 9 from the summit of Hoosier Pass. There is a large parking area just south of Scott Gulch on the west side of Colorado 9. This trailhead is accessible in winter.

South Scott Gulch Trailhead   Private Property, Permission Required

This trailhead is at 10,920 feet and provides access to Silverheels' west side. Approaching from the south, go 9.7 miles north on Colorado 9 from the U.S. 285–Colorado 9 junction in Fairplay. Approaching from the north, go 2.1 miles south on Colorado 9 from the summit of Hoosier Pass. There is a large parking area just north of South Scott Gulch on the west side of Colorado 9. This trailhead is accessible in winter.

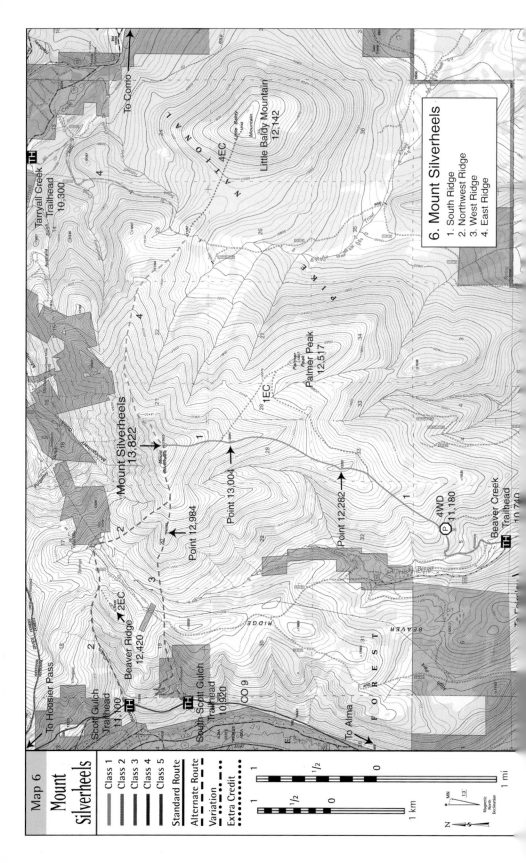

Map 6

Mount Silverheels

Legend

Class 1
Class 2
Class 3
Class 4
Class 5

Standard Route
Alternate Route
Variation
Extra Credit

Scale

1 ... 1/2 ... 0 ... 1 km
1 ... 1/2 ... 0 ... 1 mi

Magnetic North Declination 13°

6. Mount Silverheels
1. South Ridge
2. Northwest Ridge
3. West Ridge
4. East Ridge

To Como

Tarryall Creek Trailhead 10,300

Little Baldy Mountain 12,142

Mount Silverheels 13,822

Point 12,984

Point 13,004

Palmer Peak 12,517

Point 12,282

Beaver Creek Trailhead 10,740

4WD 11,180

Beaver Ridge 12,420

Scott Gulch Trailhead 11,100

South Scott Gulch Trailhead 10,920

To Hoosier Pass

To Alma

CO 9

1EC
2EC
4EC

Tarryall Creek Trailhead

This trailhead is at 10,300 feet and provides access to Silverheels' east side. Go to the small town of Como, which is 0.5 mile northwest of U.S. 285 between Fairplay and Jefferson. Measure from the historic Como Roundhouse on the southeast edge of town. Go through Como and go northwest on the Boreas Pass Road. When the Boreas Pass Road switchbacks to the east at mile 3.4, go straight onto Park County 50. Go northwest on Park County 50 through a maze of private property and reach the trailhead at mile 5.2. There is a small parking area on the road's south side and a sign for the Gold Dust Trail.

ROUTES

6.1 — Mount Silverheels — South Ridge *Classic*

From Beaver Creek TH at 10,740 ft: 156 RP 9.0 mi 3,414 ft Class 1
From 4WD parking at 11,180 ft: 127 RP 7.0 mi 2,974 ft Class 1

This is the easiest route on Silverheels, and it is the standard route for a summer ascent. Start at the Beaver Creek Trailhead and ford Beaver Creek. From Beaver Creek's east side, go 1.0 mile north up FS 184 to the road's high point at 11,160 feet. This point is just below treeline.

Leave FS 184 and hike north up an old road that is closed to vehicles. Hike 1.1 miles north-northeast on the road as it winds through some bristlecone pines at treeline. Leave the road at 12,000 feet where it starts to contour northeast, and climb 0.3 mile north to the summit of Point 12,282. You can see the rest of the route from here, but your distance to the summit is greater than it appears. Descend slightly and hike 1.0 mile north up grassy slopes to tiny Point 13,004. Descend slightly and hike 0.8 mile north up still easy slopes to the gentle giant's summit.

6.1EC — Extra Credit — Palmer Peak, 12,517 feet, Class 1+

Either going to or descending from Silverheels' summit, take the time to hike out to the 12,517-foot summit of Palmer Peak. This peak is 1.2 miles northeast of Point 12,282 on the route described above. The terrain west of Palmer is gentle, and you can configure a loop hike to suit your mood. Palmer's isolated summit sees few visitors.

6.2 — Mount Silverheels — Northwest Ridge

From Scott Gulch TH at 11,100 ft: 220 RP 6.4 mi 3,242 ft Class 2

This is a popular winter route to one of Colorado's highest peaks. Start at the Scott Gulch Trailhead and hike 1.3 miles northeast then east up Scott Gulch to the 12,180-foot saddle between Beaver Ridge and the Continental Divide. Silverheels' mighty mass will be obvious to the southeast of this saddle. Descend 0.3 mile northeast down Heartbreak Hill and cross upper Beaver Creek at 11,920 feet. You will understand this hill's name on your return trip. Duck under some power lines and climb 1.0 mile up Silverheels' rounded northwest ridge. Your views will expand as you ascend this obliging ridge to join Silverheels' west ridge at 13,320 feet. Climb 0.6 mile east across gentle terrain to Silverheels' summit. The size of Silverheels' upper slopes may fool you.

6.2EC — Extra Credit — Beaver Ridge, 12,420 feet, Class 1

From the 12,180-foot saddle, hike 0.3 mile southwest to Beaver Ridge's 12,420-foot summit. This simple summit offers great views of Silverheels and the fourteeners to the west.

6.3 — Mount Silverheels — West Ridge

From South Scott Gulch TH at 10,920 ft: *186 RP*   *5.4 mi*   *3,430 ft*   *Class 2*

This route is shorter and steeper than the Northwest Ridge Route. Start at the South Scott Gulch Trailhead and hike 0.9 mile east on some old roads up South Scott Gulch to an 11,940-foot saddle on Beaver Ridge. Descend 0.2 mile northeast down Heartless Hill and cross Beaver Creek at 11,720 feet.

Duck under some power lines and climb a steep 0.7 mile up Silverheels' west ridge to Point 12,984. You will see Silverheels' upper slopes from this vantage. From Point 12,984, descend slightly, then climb 0.9 mile east across gentle terrain to Silverheels' summit. Ascending this route and descending the Northwest Ridge Route makes a nice Tour de Silverheels. At the end of this tour, you will have 0.7 mile between the Scott Gulch and South Scott Gulch Trailheads on Colorado 9.

6.4 — Mount Silverheels — East Ridge

From Tarryall Creek TH at 10,300 ft: *168 RP*   *10.0 mi*   *3,522 ft*   *Class 1+*

This is a long, gentle hike on Silverheels' curving east ridge. Start at the Tarryall Creek Trailhead, hike 100 yards east and cross Tarryall Creek on two single log spans. During high water, these log bridges will not grant you a continuous above-water passage; you will have to ford part of the creek on spindly beaver dams.

Once you are on Tarryall Creek's south side, find the Gold Dust Trail and follow it 2.5 miles south to a small, 11,262-foot saddle near the bottom of Silverheels' east ridge. Leave the trail here and hike 0.8 mile northwest to 12,000 feet. Continue 1.7 miles west on the graceful ridge to the summit.

6.4EC — Extra Credit — Little Baldy Mountain, 12,142 feet, Class 2

From the 11,262-foot saddle, leave the Gold Dust Trail and hike 1.3 miles southeast to Little Baldy's 12,142-foot summit. Little Baldy is a significant peak, and adding it to this already arduous hike requires an additional 1,100 feet of gain.

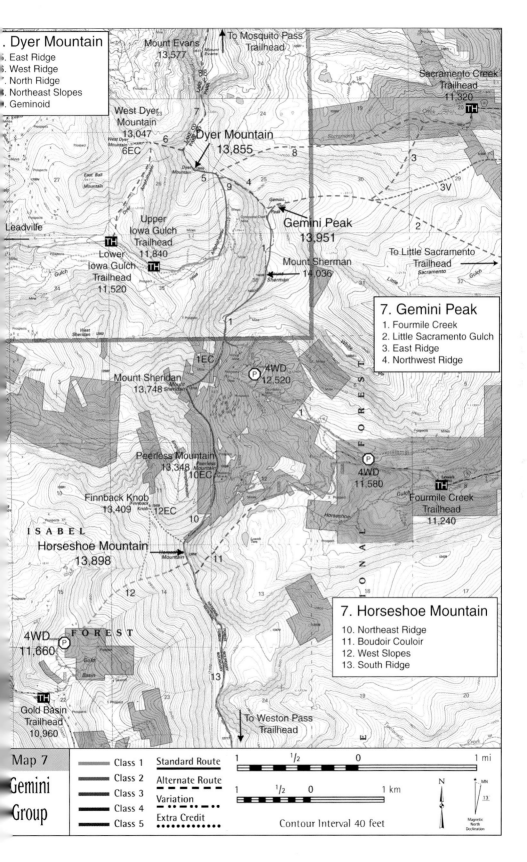

Dyer Mountain
5. East Ridge
6. West Ridge
7. North Ridge
8. Northeast Slopes
9. Geminoid

Mount Evans
13,577

To Mosquito Pass
Trailhead

Sacramento Creek
Trailhead
11,320

West Dyer
Mountain
13,047

West Dyer
Mountain
6EC

Dyer Mountain
13,855

3V

East Ball
Mountain

Leadville

Upper
Iowa Gulch
Trailhead
11,840

Gemini Peak
13,951

Lower
Iowa Gulch
Trailhead
11,520

Mount Sherman
14,036

To Little Sacramento
Trailhead

West
Sheridan

7. Gemini Peak
1. Fourmile Creek
2. Little Sacramento Gulch
3. East Ridge
4. Northwest Ridge

1EC

4WD
12,520

Mount Sheridan
13,748

Peerless Mountain
13,348
10EC

4WD
11,580

Finnback Knob
13,409   12EC

Fourmile Creek
Trailhead
11,240

ISABEL

Horseshoe Mountain
13,898

11

7. Horseshoe Mountain
10. Northeast Ridge
11. Boudoir Couloir
12. West Slopes
13. South Ridge

4WD
11,660

FOREST

Gold
Basin

13

Gold Basin
Trailhead
10,960

To Weston Pass
Trailhead

Map 7	Class 1	Standard Route
Gemini	Class 2	Alternate Route
Group	Class 3	Variation
	Class 4	Extra Credit
	Class 5	

Contour Interval 40 feet

N

MN
13
Magnetic
North
Declination

7. Gemini Group

Gemini Peak	13,951 feet
Dyer Mountain	13,855 feet
Horseshoe Mountain	13,898 feet

See Map 7 on page 83

Nine miles west of Fairplay and 8 miles east of Leadville, these friendly peaks rise in concert with their parent fourteener Mount Sherman to capture the spirit of the range. To climb beyond the fourteeners is to climb beyond the summit to a place where the essence of the place and the activity are clear.

MAPS
Required: *Mount Sherman, Pike National Forest*
Optional: *Climax, Fairplay West*

TRAILHEADS

Fourmile Creek Trailhead
This trailhead is at 11,240 feet and provides access to Gemini's south side and Horseshoe's east side. From the U.S. 285–Colorado 9 junction on Fairplay's south side, go 1.0 mile south on U.S. 285 to Park County 18. Turn west onto Park County 18 and measure from this point. Go west on Park County 18 and enter the Fourmile Creek valley and Pike National Forest at mile 4.0. Pass Fourmile Campground at mile 8.0 and park at the old Leavick townsite at mile 10.5. Leavick is not marked, but there are some old mine buildings on the road's north side; this is the trailhead for passenger cars. Four-wheel-drive vehicles can continue 2.5 miles west to 12,520 feet. In winter the road is often plowed as far as Leavick, and this is a popular place for snowmobilers.

Little Sacramento Trailhead
This trailhead is at 11,140 feet and provides access to Gemini's southeast side. From the U.S. 285–Colorado 9 junction on Fairplay's south side, go 2.1 miles north on Colorado 9 through downtown Fairplay to Park County 14. Turn west onto Park County 14 and measure from this point. Go 4.5 miles west on Park County 14 and turn down to the west (left) onto Sacramento Drive. Follow Sacramento Drive as it turns west, and reach a four-way junction at mile 5.1. Turn south (left), cross Sacramento Creek and climb back east onto the ridge south of Sacramento Gulch. Switchback twice and reach a short road heading down to the south (left) at mile 6.3. Go down this road and park at the end of the road at mile 6.4. This is the trailhead.

Upper Little Sacramento Trailhead
This trailhead is at 11,180 feet and provides access to Gemini's east side. From mile 6.3 on the route to the Little Sacramento Trailhead, continue 0.2 mile up the main road to the end of the road. This is the trailhead.

Sacramento Creek Trailhead   Private Property, Permission Required
This trailhead is at 11,320 feet and provides access to Dyer and Gemini's north sides. From the U.S. 285–Colorado 9 junction on Fairplay's south side, go 2.1 miles north on Colorado 9 through downtown Fairplay to Park County 14. Turn west onto Park County 14 and measure from this point. Go 6.6 miles west on Park County 14 up Sacramento Creek to a south (left) turn just before the road crosses to Sacramento Creek's south side. The end of the road is just beyond this crossing. Park at the turn on the creek's north side. If possible, park off the county road.

Mosquito Pass Trailhead
This trailhead is at 13,186 feet on Mosquito Pass and provides access to Dyer's north side. Mosquito Pass is Colorado's highest pass open to vehicles, and this is the highest trailhead in this book. Mosquito Pass, on the crest of the Mosquito Range, connects Alma and Leadville. A robust, high-clearance vehicle is required to reach Mosquito Pass from the east (Alma side), and a four-wheel-drive vehicle is required to reach it from the west (Leadville side). A four-wheel-drive vehicle is also recommended for the eastern approach, which is described here. Snow can persist on this road until late summer.

If you are approaching from the south, go 4.4 miles north on Colorado 9 from the U.S. 285–Colorado 9 junction in Fairplay. If you are approaching from the north, go 7.4 miles south on Colorado 9 from the summit of Hoosier Pass. Turn west onto Park County 12 and measure from this point. Go 2.7 miles west on Park County 12 to Park City. Continue west on Park County 12 up Mosquito Creek to 11,520 feet at mile 7.3. The road is good to this point. Turn west (left), cross Mosquito Creek and begin the ascent to Mosquito Pass. There is a large sign here announcing the objective. The pass is 2.7 miles from this point.

Follow the main road as it climbs south and then does an ascending traverse to the west on London Mountain's north slope. This traverse is the most likely place to find snow. Reach the 12,660-foot pass between London Mountain and the crest of the Mosquito Range at mile 9.0. Continue 1.0 mile west then southwest on the final ascending traverse to reach Mosquito Pass at mile 10.0. Park. Breathe. This is the trailhead.

Lower Iowa Gulch Trailhead
This trailhead is at 11,520 feet and provides access to Dyer's west side. Measure from the junction of U.S. 24 (Harrison Avenue) and East Third Street in downtown Leadville. Go east on East Third Street, turn south (right) onto South Toledo Street at mile 0.3, pass East Monroe Street at

mile 0.4 and continue south then east on Lake County 2 (paved). Stay north (left) at mile 4.0 on a dirt road that passes north of the active ASARCO Mine. Continue east on Iowa Gulch's north side to 11,520 feet and park at mile 5.7. The road is passable for passenger cars to this point. In winter Lake County 2 is open to the ASARCO Mine, but not beyond.

Upper Iowa Gulch Trailhead

This trailhead is at 11,840 feet and provides access to Dyer and Gemini's south sides. From the Lower Iowa Gulch Trailhead, go 0.6 mile east, pass under some large power lines and park at 11,840 feet.

Weston Pass Trailhead

This trailhead is at 11,940 feet on Weston Pass and provides access to Horseshoe's south side. You can approach Weston Pass from the east or west. The eastern approach is suitable for cars. The western approach requires a high-clearance vehicle.

If you are approaching from the east, measure from the U.S. 285–Colorado 9 junction on Fairplay's south side. Go 4.8 miles south on U.S. 285 to Park County 5, which is the east end of the Weston Pass Road. Go 16.6 miles west on the Weston Pass Road to Weston Pass and the trailhead. This road is suitable for cars.

If you are approaching from the northwest, measure from the junction of U.S. 24 (Harrison Avenue) and East Third Street in downtown Leadville. Go 7.4 miles south on U.S. 24 to Lake County 7, which is the west end of the Weston Pass Road. If you are approaching from the southwest, measure from the junction of U.S. 24 and Colorado 82, and go 7.2 miles north on U.S. 24 to the Weston Pass Road. Go 11.0 miles east on the Weston Pass Road to Weston Pass and the trailhead. A high-clearance vehicle is useful on this rocky road.

Gold Basin Trailhead

This trailhead is at 10,960 feet and provides access to Horseshoe's west side. The trailhead is on the Weston Pass Road on the west side of the pass. You can approach the trailhead from the east or west. The eastern approach is suitable for cars. The western approach requires a high-clearance vehicle.

If you are approaching from the east, descend 3.5 miles west on the Weston Pass Road from the Weston Pass Trailhead. This descent is suitable for cars.

If you are approaching from the northwest, measure from the junction of U.S. 24 (Harrison Avenue) and East Third Street in downtown Leadville. Go 7.4 miles south on U.S. 24 to Lake County 7, which is the west end of the Weston Pass Road. If you are approaching from the southwest, measure from the junction of U.S. 24 and Colorado 82, and go 7.2 miles north on U.S. 24 to the Weston Pass Road. Go 7.5 miles east on the Weston Pass Road to the trailhead. A high-clearance vehicle is useful on this rocky road. Park on the south side of the Weston Pass Road just east of a four-wheel-drive road that climbs northeast above the Weston Pass Road.

From the trailhead, four-wheel-drive vehicles can climb an additional 1.1 miles northeast on a rough road to the top of Point 11,660. The road crosses under large power lines three times in this ascent. Gold Basin east of this road is private property. Be sure to stay on the road.

7. Gemini Peak   13,951 feet

See Map 7 on page 83

Gemini Peak is 0.6 mile north of the fourteener Mount Sherman. As its name implies, Gemini has twin summits. The two summits are 250 yards apart and have almost equal elevations. The northeastern summit has the 13,951-foot elevation on the Mount Sherman Quadrangle, and this is the higher of the two summits. The high point is a distinctive stack of rocks. Gemini is not a ranked summit, but its significant height, double summit and statuesque position make it well worth climbing. In addition, Gemini is the highest centennial thirteener in the Mosquito Range and ties with Fletcher as the highest peak in this chapter.

ROUTES

7.1 — Gemini Peak — Fourmile Creek

From Fourmile Creek TH at 11,240 ft:	237 RP	10.2 mi	3,223 ft	*Class 2*
From 4WD parking at 12,520 ft:	161 RP	5.2 mi	1,943 ft	*Class 2*

This is a popular route up Gemini, but it requires traversing over Mount Sherman, a fourteener. Start at the Fourmile Creek Trailhead and go 2.5 miles northwest up the four-wheel-drive road to 12,520 feet in Fourmile Creek's upper basin. Hike 0.7 mile northwest on the continuing road and pass the old Dauntless and Hilltop mines. Climb 0.2 mile west to the 13,140-foot saddle between Sherman and 13,748-foot Mount Sheridan, which is 1.4 miles southwest of Sherman. From the saddle, climb 1.0 mile northeast up Sherman's southwest ridge on a good trail to Sherman's long, gentle, 14,036-foot summit. From Sherman's summit, hike 0.7 mile north across a ridge broad enough to be called a plateau to twin-summited Gemini Peak. Skirt or climb the southwestern summit, then climb the northeastern summit, which is the higher of the two. Return over Sherman's summit.

7.1EC — Extra Credit — Mount Sheridan, 13,748 feet, Class 2
From the 13,140-foot saddle between Sherman and Sheridan, climb 0.6

mile southwest up a broad ridge to Mount Sheridan's 13,748-foot summit. Sheridan is one of Colorado's 200 highest peaks.

7.2 — Gemini Peak — Little Sacramento Gulch

From Little Sacramento TH at 11,140 ft: 238 RP   7.0 mi   2,851 ft   Class 2

If you enjoy the way less traveled, this is a good choice. Start at the Little Sacramento Trailhead, descend to the south and hike 0.6 mile west on an old road into Little Sacramento Gulch. Leave the road before it crosses Little Sacramento Creek and climbs south to some old mines. Continue up the gulch for another 0.6 mile to 11,500 feet. Leave Little Sacramento Gulch and climb 1.3 miles northwest up broad slopes to reach Gemini Peak's east ridge at 13,000 feet. Climb 1.0 mile west up this narrowing but easy ridge to the summit.

7.3 — Gemini Peak — East Ridge

From Sacramento Creek TH at 11,320 ft: 201 RP   4.8 mi   2,631 ft   Class 2

This is the shortest route up Gemini from the east. Start at the Sacramento Creek Trailhead and walk 0.4 mile west up Sacramento Creek's south side. Leave the creek and climb 1.0 mile southwest up a shallow gulch to 13,000 feet on Gemini Peak's broad east ridge. Climb 1.0 mile west up this narrowing but easy ridge to the summit.

7.3V — Variation
From Upper Little Sacramento TH at 11,180 ft: 208 RP   7.2 mi   2,771 ft   Class 2
You can start Gemini's East Ridge Route from the Upper Little Sacramento Trailhead. This start yields a longer hike than the hike starting at the Sacramento Creek Trailhead, but it provides easier hiking. From the Upper Little Sacramento Trailhead, hike 0.8 mile west-northwest to treeline at 11,800 feet. Hike 0.6 mile northwest to reach Gemini's east ridge at 12,200 feet. Follow this gentle ridge 2.2 miles west to the summit.

7.4 — Gemini Peak — Northwest Ridge

From Upper Iowa Gulch TH at 11,840 ft: 142 RP   4.6 mi   2,211 ft   Class 2

This is a short summer climb, and Gemini's west side is most often used as a winter route. From the Upper Iowa Gulch Trailhead (or ASARCO Mine in winter), follow the road 1.1 miles northeast to 12,600 feet in Iowa Amphitheater. There can be an avalanche hazard here in winter. Climb 0.6 mile north to the 13,380-foot saddle between Gemini and Dyer. Large power lines cross this pass, so you should eat lunch somewhere else. Turn east (right) and ascend Gemini's northwest ridge for 0.6 mile to the summit.

7. Dyer Mountain   13,855 feet

See Map 7 on page 83

Dyer Mountain is 1.25 miles northwest of the fourteener Mount Sherman and 0.9 mile west-northwest of Gemini Peak. You can easily see Dyer from Leadville, which is only 6 miles to the west. Dyer is a significant, ranked peak, and you can climb it from the east or west. Dyer is a peak for all seasons.

ROUTES

7.5 — Dyer Mountain — East Ridge

From Upper Iowa Gulch TH at 11,840 ft: 126 RP   4.2 mi   2,015 ft   Class 2

This is the shortest route on Dyer. From the Upper Iowa Gulch Trailhead (summer) or ASARCO Mine (winter), follow the road 1.1 miles northeast to 12,600 feet in Iowa Amphitheater. There can be an avalanche hazard here in winter. Climb 0.6 mile north to the 13,380-foot saddle between Gemini and Dyer. Alien power lines cross this pass, so you should eat lunch elsewhere. Turn west (left) and ascend Dyer's east ridge for 0.4 mile to the summit.

7.6 — Dyer Mountain — West Ridge

From Lower Iowa Gulch TH at 11,520 ft: 220 RP   4.0 mi   2,335 ft   Class 3

This rough ridge provides a nice scramble. From the Lower Iowa Gulch Trailhead, hike 1.3 miles north-northeast through Dyer Amphitheater to the 12,780-foot saddle between Dyer Mountain and West Dyer Mountain. Turn east (right) and climb 0.4 mile up Dyer's west ridge to 13,640 feet on Dyer's north ridge. The west ridge requires some routefinding and Class 3 scrambling. Avoid the worst difficulties by staying on the ridge's south (right) side. From 13,640 feet, hike 0.3 mile south-southeast to the summit.

7.6EC — Extra Credit — West Dyer Mountain, 13,047 feet, Class 2
From the 12,780-foot saddle, hike 0.2 mile west to West Dyer Mountain's 13,047-foot summit.

7.7 — Dyer Mountain — North Ridge *Classic*

From Mosquito Pass TH at 13,186 ft: 192 RP   6.4 mi   1,629 ft   Class 2+

This high ridge walk allows you to climb an extra peak en route and remain above the trees all day. Start at the Mosquito Pass Trailhead, the highest trailhead in this book, and hike 0.3 mile south to a long, 13,300-foot summit. Continue 0.8 mile south on the undulating ridge to a saddle at 13,140 feet. Climb 0.7 mile south to the gentle, 13,577-foot summit of Mount Evans, your bonus peak. This Mount Evans bears little resemblance

Dyer Mountain from the northeast.

to the fourteener Mount Evans. From this summit, you can see your objective, Dyer Mountain, 1.2 miles to the south.

From Mount Evans' summit, hike 0.3 mile south to where the ridge narrows. Here, the plot thickens. Scamper 0.2 mile south down the narrow ridge to the 13,260-foot saddle between Mount Evans and Dyer Mountain (Class 2+). From the saddle, climb 0.2 mile south to Point 13,383. The difficulties are over. Descend slightly and hike 0.7 mile south over easy terrain to Dyer's summit.

7.8 — Dyer Mountain — Northeast Slopes

From Sacramento Creek TH at 11,320 ft: 223 RP 6.2 mi 2,535 ft Class 2

This is the shortest route on Dyer from a trailhead east of the range. Start at the Sacramento Creek Trailhead and hike 2.1 miles west up Sacramento Creek to 12,400 feet. Climb 0.6 mile southwest to the 13,380-foot saddle between Gemini and Dyer. Turn west (right) and climb 0.4 mile up Dyer's east ridge to the summit.

7. GEMINI AND DYER COMBINATION
See Map 7 on page 83

7.9 — GD Combination — Geminoid

From Upper Iowa Gulch TH at 11,840 ft: *175 RP   5.4 mi   2,586 ft   Class 2*

This is the easiest way to climb Gemini and Dyer together. Start at the Upper Iowa Gulch Trailhead and climb Gemini's Northwest Ridge Route. Return to the 13,380-foot saddle between Gemini and Dyer and climb 0.4 mile up Dyer's east ridge to Dyer's summit. Descend Dyer's East Ridge Route.

7. Horseshoe Mountain   13,898 feet
See Map 7 on page 83

Horseshoe Mountain is 3.0 miles south of the fourteener Mount Sherman and is the southernmost centennial thirteener in the Tenmile–Mosquito Range. The name *Horseshoe* comes from the distinctive cirque on the mountain's east side. You can see this cirque from U.S. 285 to the east, and climbers driving by often rediscover Horseshoe and exclaim, "Hey! That must be Horseshoe!"

Horseshoe has many charms. The mountain is easy to climb and even has a Class 1 hiking route to the summit. You can climb Horseshoe from all directions, and the namesake cirque offers a more technical challenge. However you reach it, Horseshoe's large, nearly flat summit gives you room to ponder. There is an old mine cabin on top that is worth a visit to remember life a hundred years ago. As you roam the crunchy summit scree, you can also contemplate how wildflowers poke through the rocks at this altitude.

ROUTES

7.10 — Horseshoe Mountain — Northeast Ridge

From Fourmile Creek TH at 11,240 ft: *147 RP   9.4 mi   2,658 ft   Class 1*

This is the standard route on Horseshoe, and it allows you to peer into the namesake cirque from a safe vantage. This easy hike provides a nice introduction to Colorado's high country for newcomers and a refreshing reminder for veterans.

Start at the Fourmile Creek Trailhead and go 0.9 mile northwest then west on the Fourmile Creek Road above Leavick. Leave the Fourmile Creek Road, cross to Fourmile Creek's south side on another road and follow this road as it switchbacks up the hill to the south. Stay left (straight) at a junction just before the second switchback. Follow the road as it climbs west, south and west into Horseshoe Gulch. As you climb along the gulch's north side, you can see Horseshoe's namesake cirque to the southwest. Running water often gurgles down its near-vertical walls.

Follow the road as it switchbacks up gentle slopes northeast of Horseshoe, and pass the old Peerless Mine at 13,100 feet. Follow the trail beyond the mine to the 13,180-foot saddle between Peerless and Horseshoe Mountains. It is 3.0 miles from the Fourmile Creek Road to this saddle. From the saddle, hike 0.8 mile south and southwest up Horseshoe's gentle northeast ridge to the summit. You will have an expansive view of the fourteeners Elbert and Massive to the west. The old summit mine building is 300 yards south of the highest point.

7.10EC — Extra Credit — Peerless Mountain, 13,348 feet, Class 2

From the 13,180-foot saddle, hike 0.2 mile north to Peerless Mountain's 13,348-foot summit.

7.11 — Horseshoe Mountain — Boudoir Couloir *Classic*

From Fourmile Creek TH at 11,240 ft: 253 RP 8.2 mi 2,658 ft Class 2 Mod Snow
With descent of Northeast Ridge: 236 RP 8.8 mi 2,658 ft Class 2 Mod Snow

This is a great snow climb for aspiring alpinists. The northeast-facing Boudoir Couloir ascends the namesake cirque's south side. You can see this couloir from U.S. 285 to the east. In a normal year, it will hold good snow into July.

Start at the Fourmile Creek Trailhead and follow the Northeast Ridge Route to 12,320 feet. At the switchback where the road starts climbing northwest, leave the road and hike southwest into upper Horseshoe Gulch. Pass north of two small lakes and climb to 12,800 feet in the center of the namesake cirque. This unique spot is the focal point of the mountain's energy. Near-vertical rock walls embrace you on three sides like an open-air gazebo. Appropriately, the Boudoir Couloir is the only easy egress from the embrace.

Climb south and enter the broad Boudoir Couloir. The bottom of the couloir will be talus by late June, but the upper snow should be good. Climb southwest up the shallow couloir on moderate snow to its top at 13,800 feet. Climb west up a final snow slope to reach Horseshoe's summit plateau at the old mine cabin. There is generally no cornice here. Hike 300 yards north to Horseshoe's highest point. Ascending the Boudoir Couloir and descending the Northeast Ridge Route makes a satisfying Tour de Horseshoe.

7.12 — Horseshoe Mountain — West Slopes *Classic*

From Gold Basin TH at 10,960 ft: 135 RP 5.8 mi 3,098 ft Class 2
From 4WD parking at 11,660 ft: 99 RP 3.6 mi 2,398 ft Class 2

This is an easy alternative route on Horseshoe's west side. Views of the namesake cirque are replaced with views of Elbert and Massive to the west.

Start at the Gold Basin Trailhead and go 1.1 miles up the rough four-wheel-drive road that climbs north above the Weston Pass Road. Pass under some large power lines three times and, after the third crossing, climb east to the top of Point 11,660. Gold Basin to the east of this road is private property, so avoid any temptation to cut east toward Horseshoe too soon. You can clearly see the upper part of the West Slopes Route to the northeast from the top of Point 11,660. The route ascends the rounded slope directly west of Horseshoe's summit.

From the top of Point 11,660, hike north to get around the northern end of the Gold Basin private property and descend east to a broad, 11,580-foot saddle. Get onto some old vehicle tracks and follow them northeast through the trees. Continue east on the vehicle tracks up the rounded slope above (Class 1). The grassy slopes will be flower-strewn in June and July and, to the west, you will have expansive views of Elbert and Massive in any month. At 13,400 feet, the slope steepens and the grass is replaced with talus. Continue up the talus and reach Horseshoe's summit plateau just south of the highest point (Class 2).

7.12EC — Extra Credit — Finnback Knob, 13,409 feet, Class 2
From 12,500 feet on the rounded, grassy slope, do an ascending traverse 0.8 mile north across grassy slopes to Finnback Knob's 13,409-foot summit (Class 1). This perch offers a unique view of Horseshoe, Sherman, Sheridan and Empire Gulch. From Finnback Knob, climb 0.8 mile southeast up a rough talus ridge to Horseshoe's summit (Class 2). You can include Finnback Knob after your ascent of Horseshoe by descending this route.

7.13 — Horseshoe Mountain — South Ridge *Classic*

From Weston Pass TH at 11,940 ft: *153 RP   9.0 mi   3,192 ft   Class 1*

This long ridge walk is entirely above treeline. It allows you to climb another thirteener and several ridge bumps along the way. Start at the Weston Pass Trailhead and hike 0.7 mile northeast up steep grass slopes to Point 13,380, the first ridge bump. Continue 0.8 mile north on the now gentle ridge over Point 13,525 to 13,739-foot Ptarmigan Peak, one of Colorado's 200 highest peaks. The introduction is over. Continue 3.0 miles north on the gentle, sometimes expansive ridge over Point 13,717 and Point 13,676 to reach Horseshoe's lofty summit.

7.13EC — Extra Credit — Weston Peak, 13,572 feet, Class 2
From Point 13,380 above Weston Pass, hike 0.5 mile east to Weston Peak's 13,572-foot summit. If only for a short time, this isolated summit can leave you suspended.

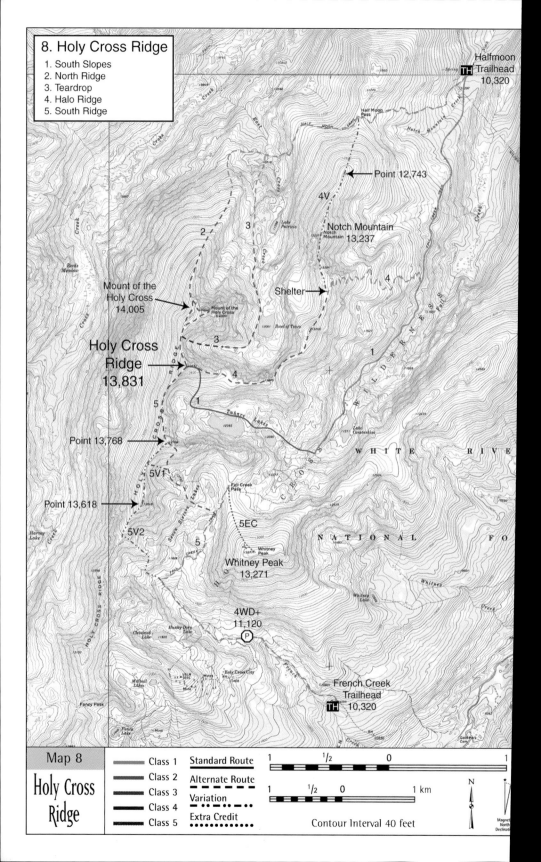

8. Holy Cross Ridge

1. South Slopes
2. North Ridge
3. Teardrop
4. Halo Ridge
5. South Ridge

Halfmoon
Trailhead
10,320

Point 12,743

4V

Notch Mountain
13,237

Mount of the
Holy Cross
14,005

Shelter

Holy Cross
Ridge
13,831

Point 13,768

5V1

Point 13,618

5V2

Fall Creek
Pass

5EC

Whitney
Peak

Whitney Peak
13,271

4WD+
11,120
Ⓟ

French Creek
Trailhead
10,320

Map 8	▬▬▬ Class 1	**Standard Route**
	▬▬▬ Class 2	**Alternate Route**
Holy Cross	▬▬▬ Class 3	**Variation**
Ridge	▬▬▬ Class 4	**Extra Credit**
	▬▬▬ Class 5	

Contour Interval 40 feet

N

Magnetic
North
Declination

CHAPTER THREE

Sawatch Range

Introduction

The Sawatch Range runs through the heartland of the Colorado Rockies. The range has 15 fourteeners, 14 centennial thirteeners, 3 county summits and Colorado's highest peak, Mount Elbert. The Sawatch Range has more fourteeners than the entire state of California or any other Colorado range, but takes second place to the San Juans for centennial thirteeners. Still, almost a third of Colorado's 100 highest peaks are in the Sawatch.

Like most Colorado ranges, the Sawatch is a linear range that runs north and south. The northern boundary is Interstate 70 west of Vail. The southern boundary is Cochetopa Pass on the Continental Divide south of Colorado 114. Between are 100 miles of mountains. Only three paved roads—Colorado 82 over Independence Pass, U.S. 50 over Monarch Pass and Colorado 114 over North Pass—cross the range. There are four wilderness areas in the Sawatch. You can climb most of the centennial thirteeners in the Sawatch with Class 2 talus hiking, but there are a few technical routes tucked away on some of these peaks.

8. Holy Cross Ridge   13,831 feet

See Map 8 on page 94

Holy Cross Ridge is 0.6 mile south-southwest of the famous fourteener Mount of the Holy Cross, and it is the Sawatch Range's northernmost centennial thirteener. Holy Cross Ridge extends 4.1 miles south-southwest from Mount of the Holy Cross to 12,380-foot Fancy Pass, and holds four 13,000-foot-plus summits. The highest of these four summits is Point 13,831—the summit of Holy Cross Ridge. People often climb Holy Cross Ridge together with Mount of the Holy Cross, but Holy Cross Ridge makes a nice outing by itself. Holy Cross Ridge is well into the Holy Cross Wilderness, and the routes to the peak are long.

MAPS

Required: *Mount of the Holy Cross, White River National Forest*
Optional: *Minturn, Mount Jackson*

TRAILHEADS

Halfmoon Trailhead

This trailhead is at 10,320 feet and provides access to the north and east sides of Holy Cross Ridge. Don't confuse this trailhead with the Halfmoon

Creek Trailhead described for Mount Oklahoma. A few miles west of Vail, take Exit 171 off Interstate 70. From the U.S. 24–Interstate 70 junction, go 2.0 miles south on U.S. 24 to the White River National Forest Ranger Station at Main and Harrison Streets in the town of Minturn.

From the White River Ranger Station, go 2.8 miles south on U.S. 24 and turn west onto the Tigiwon Road (FS 707). This turn is on the north side of a bridge over the Eagle River. Go west on the Tigiwon Road (dirt), climb steadily in long-sweeping switchbacks, pass the Tigiwon Campground at mile 6.1 and reach the Halfmoon Trailhead at mile 8.4. The Tigiwon Road is rough but passable for passenger cars. Two trails start at this trailhead. Make sure you follow the one you want. The Halfmoon Campground is just below the trailhead. The Tigiwon Road is closed in winter and usually opens in mid-June.

French Creek Trailhead

This trailhead is at 10,320 feet and provides access to the south side of Holy Cross Ridge. A few miles west of Vail, take Exit 171 off Interstate 70. From the U.S. 24–Interstate 70 junction, go 2.0 miles south on U.S. 24 to the White River National Forest Ranger Station at Main and Harrison Streets in the town of Minturn.

From the White River Ranger Station, go 10.6 miles south on U.S. 24, turn southwest (right) onto the Gold Park Road (FS 703) and measure from this point. Go southwest on the Gold Park Road up Homestake Creek, pass the Gold Park Campground at mile 7.0, pass the beginning of the Holy Cross City four-wheel-drive road (FS 759) at mile 7.6 and turn west (right) onto FS 704 at mile 8.0. Go west on FS 704 as it switchbacks up the hill, then go southwest and turn north (right) onto FS 727 at mile 10.3. Go north on FS 727, pass the Fancy Creek Trailhead, turn right (downhill) at mile 11.3, cross French Creek at mile 12.0, turn west (left) at mile 12.1 and reach the end of the road and the trailhead at a diversion dam on French Creek at mile 12.3. The road to this trailhead is passable for most passenger cars in dry conditions.

Specialized four-wheel-drive vehicles can go farther. At mile 12.1, go 50 yards north on a short spur road, turn west onto the Holy Cross City four-wheel-drive road, go 1.5 miles northwest and park at 11,120 feet before the road crosses French Creek. This so-called road is one of Colorado's roughest, and it is not suitable for stock four-wheel-drive vehicles. Vehicles attempting this road should have differential lockers, extra-high clearance and a winch.

ROUTES

8.1 — Holy Cross Ridge — South Slopes

From Halfmoon TH at 10,320 ft: 299 RP   14.2 mi   3,511 ft   Class 2

This is the easiest route on Holy Cross Ridge. It is the best route if climbing Holy Cross Ridge is your only objective, and it allows you to visit the beautiful Tuhare Lakes. Start at the Halfmoon Trailhead and hike 2.5 miles south on the Fall Creek Trail to the bottom of the Notch Mountain Trail at 11,160 feet. Continue 1.8 miles south-southwest on the Fall Creek Trail to Lake Constantine at 11,371 feet, then climb 0.6 mile southwest on the trail to Fall Creek at 11,500 feet.

Leave the Fall Creek Trail just before it crosses Fall Creek, hike 0.3 mile west to a small, unnamed lake at 11,780 feet and hike 0.3 mile northwest to Lower Tuhare Lake at 12,090 feet. Go around Lower Tuhare Lake's north side and hike 0.3 mile west-northwest to Upper Tuhare Lake at 12,365 feet. This large lake is one of Colorado's finest. Hike 0.5 mile west around Upper Tuhare Lake's north side, then hike 0.3 mile west-northwest to a tiny basin at 12,800 feet. Climb 0.4 mile north-northeast up a talus slope (Class 2), reach Halo Ridge at 13,700 feet and hike 0.1 mile west up the ridge to the summit.

8.2 — Holy Cross Ridge — North Ridge

From Halfmoon TH at 10,320 ft: 354 RP 12.5 mi 6,106 ft *Class 2*

This is a long route on Holy Cross Ridge, but it is the easiest way to climb Mount of the Holy Cross and Holy Cross Ridge together. This is a tough, one-day climb. The route crosses Halfmoon Pass and Mount of the Holy Cross to reach Holy Cross Ridge, and you must gain 1,070 feet on your return trip. Some people choose to ameliorate the route by packing in over the pass and camping near East Cross Creek. By climbing both peaks in one day, you will minimize your impact on this beautiful area, but you will maximize impact on yourself. Get in shape for this one!

Start at the Halfmoon Trailhead and hike 1.7 miles west-southwest on the Halfmoon Trail to Halfmoon Pass at 11,640 feet. Continue over the pass and descend 1.4 miles west then southwest to East Cross Creek at 10,670 feet. Cross East Cross Creek on a spindly log bridge, hike 0.4 mile west, climb north of some cliffs and reach Holy Cross' north ridge at 11,000 feet. Switchback 0.4 mile up on the ridge's west side to reach the highest trees at 11,600 feet. This is the end of the maintained trail. You cannot see Holy Cross Ridge during this approach.

From the end of the trail, climb 1.3 miles south-southwest up the long north ridge of Mount of the Holy Cross. The ridge is mostly talus interspersed with short sections of climbers trail. Stay on or west of the ridge crest and reach the upper part of the peak at 13,400 feet. From here, climb 0.4 mile southeast then east up a steep, west-facing talus slope to the 14,005-foot summit of Mount of the Holy Cross. From here you can finally see Holy Cross Ridge to the south.

Descend 0.5 mile southwest on talus to the 13,500-foot saddle between Mount of the Holy Cross and Holy Cross Ridge. Climb 0.3 mile south on the ridge's west side to the summit of Holy Cross Ridge. On your return, contour north at 13,600 feet below the summit of Mount of the Holy Cross.

Holy Cross Ridge from the north.

8.3 — Holy Cross Ridge — Teardrop

From Halfmoon TH at 10,320 ft: 433 RP   12.8 mi   5,451 ft   Class 2   Steep Snow
With descent of South Slopes: 407 RP   13.5 mi   4,481 ft   Class 2   Steep Snow
With descent of North Ridge: 419 RP   12.5 mi   5,551 ft   Class 2   Steep Snow

This long route provides an excursion into a remarkable basin. The climb out of the basin is a viable route only with good snow conditions. Start at the Halfmoon Trailhead and hike 1.7 miles west-southwest on the Halfmoon Trail to Halfmoon Pass at 11,640 feet. Continue over the pass and descend 1.4 miles west then southwest to East Cross Creek at 10,670 feet. Cross East Cross Creek on a spindly log bridge, leave the main trail 60 feet west of the creek and follow a strong side trail south to some campsites. Persevere past the campsites and locate a climbers trail in the forest. This trail is worth finding. Follow the climbers trail 0.8 mile south as it winds through rock outcrops west of East Cross Creek to reach the bench west of beautiful Lake Patricia.

Hike 1.0 mile south through the rugged, boulder-strewn basin, passing below the Cross Couloir on Mount of the Holy Cross en route, to the northwest end of the large Bowl of Tears Lake at 12,001 feet. Continue 0.4 mile south-southwest around the west side of Bowl of Tears Lake, then hike 0.3 mile west to 12,400 feet in the narrow basin between the south face of Mount of the Holy Cross and the north face of Holy Cross Ridge. Continue 0.5 mile west up steepening snow to the 13,500-foot saddle between Mount of the Holy Cross and Holy Cross Ridge. The slope's last

Holy Cross Ridge from the south.

300 feet is steep, and a cornice may guard the exit. As the snow on this slope melts, a patchwork of snow and talus appears. From the 13,500-foot saddle, climb 0.3 mile south on the ridge's west side to the summit of Holy Cross Ridge. Ascending this route and descending either the South Slopes or North Ridge Route makes a sensible Tour de Holy Cross Ridge.

8.4 — Holy Cross Ridge — Halo Ridge *Classic*

From Halfmoon TH at 10,320 ft:	*301 RP*	*14.6 mi*	*4,353 ft*	*Class 2*
With descent of South Slopes:	*301 RP*	*14.4 mi*	*4,353 ft*	*Class 2*
With descent of North Ridge:	*312 RP*	*13.4 mi*	*5,423 ft*	*Class 2*

This route circles the Bowl of Tears basin and provides excellent views of Mount of the Holy Cross. It is a long route, but you can break the distance into stages by sleeping in the Notch Mountain Shelter. This shelter is not locked, but check with the Forest Service office in Minturn for current conditions (303-827-5715).

Start at the Halfmoon Trailhead and hike 2.5 miles south on the Fall Creek Trail to the bottom of the Notch Mountain Trail at 11,160 feet. Hike 2.8 miles west up the Notch Mountain Trail to the Notch Mountain Shelter at 13,080 feet. Mount of the Holy Cross pops into view as you crest the ridge.

At the shelter, the Bowl of Tears is between you and Mount of the Holy Cross to the west. Holy Cross Ridge is 1.6 miles to the southwest. The long Halo Ridge around the basin's south end crosses two summits to reach the summit of Holy Cross Ridge. From the shelter, go 0.4 mile south-southwest to Point 13,248, a ranked thirteener, and continue 0.7 mile southwest to Point 13,373, an unranked thirteener. Turn the corner and go 0.4 mile west to a wide, flat portion of the ridge, where you can rest suspended between the summits. Continue 0.5 mile west-northwest to the summit of Holy Cross Ridge. Ascending this route and descending either the South Slopes or North Ridge Route makes a comprehensive Tour de Holy Cross Ridge.

8.4V — Variation — Notch Mountain, 13,237 feet

From Halfmoon TH at 10,320 ft:	*368 RP*	*11.4 mi*	*5,161 ft*	*Class 2+*
With descent of South Slopes:	*348 RP*	*12.8 mi*	*4,757 ft*	*Class 2+*
With descent of North Ridge:	*360 RP*	*11.8 mi*	*5,827 ft*	*Class 2+*

You can modify the beginning of the Halo Ridge Route to include a traverse of Notch Mountain. Start at the Halfmoon Trailhead and hike 1.7 miles west-southwest on the Halfmoon Trail to Halfmoon Pass at 11,640 feet. Leave the trail, hike 0.7 mile south up talus to Point 12,743, then hike 0.7 mile south-southwest on the ridge over blocky talus to the 13,237-foot summit of Notch Mountain.

The traverse across the notch between Notch Mountain's two summits requires some routefinding and Class 2+ scampering. The north face of Point 13,224—Notch Mountain's lower, southern summit—rises above the notch in a smooth sweep of rock. Getting past this cliff is the route's crux.

From Notch Mountain's 13,237-foot main summit, hike 0.1 mile south on the ridge, then descend a series of broken ledges leading down to the west side of the notch (Class 2+). Stay on the ridge's west side and scamper up broken ledges to talus slopes beyond the notch. From here, hike 0.3 mile south down talus to the Notch Mountain Shelter Cabin and continue on the Halo Ridge Route to the summit of Holy Cross Ridge.

8.5 — Holy Cross Ridge — South Ridge *Classic*

From French Creek TH at 10,320 ft: 277 RP   11.5 mi   4,019 ft   Class 2

This unique alternative route allows you to climb the southern summits of Holy Cross Ridge and avoids the crowds using the Halfmoon Trailhead. You can also visit several of the Seven Sisters Lakes. The route may give you an overdose of good tidings, as you have to reclimb some of Point 13,768 on your return trip. This extra effort and exposure keep this route from being the easiest route on Holy Cross Ridge. Still, this is the easiest way to climb Holy Cross Ridge and Point 13,768 together.

Start at the French Creek Trailhead, hike 0.1 mile north on a small trail through the trees and turn west (left) onto the Holy Cross City four-wheel-drive road. Hike 1.3 miles northwest to 11,120 feet, where the road crosses French Creek. Here, you can marvel at the so-called road that crosses the creek and observe the winch anchors in the rocks. Cross to French Creek's south side on foot, hike 50 yards west on the road and turn

right onto the beginning of the Fall Creek Trail. There is a vehicle barri-
cade at this trailhead with a pass-through for hikers.

From the beginning of the Fall Creek Trail, hike 0.5 mile west on the
trail to Hunky Dory Lake at 11,300 feet and enter the Holy Cross Wilderness en route. This well-named lake offers a petite paradise tucked in the
trees. From Hunky Dory Lake, hike 0.7 mile northwest on the Fall Creek
Trail to a small meadow at 11,700 feet where the trail heads east. You can
see Point 13,618 ahead of you during this stretch. From 11,700 feet, stay
on the trail and hike 0.3 mile northeast to the lowest of the Seven Sisters
Lakes at 11,828 feet. Stay on the trail and hike 0.5 mile northeast to another
of the Seven Sisters Lakes at 12,140 feet. From this lake, stay on the trail
and hike 0.2 mile northeast to 12,200 feet. From here, Point 13,618 is 0.8 mile
to the west and Point 13,768 is 0.9 mile to the northwest. These are the
southern summits of Holy Cross Ridge.

From 12,200 feet, leave the Fall Creek Trail and hike 0.5 mile northwest up grassy benches interspersed with rock outcrops to the highest of
the Seven Sisters Lakes at 12,750 feet. This fingered lake is a special place,
complete with an island. Scamper 0.1 mile around the lake's south side on
small ledges just above water level. From the lake's west end, hike 0.25 mile
northwest on broken ledges then talus to 13,200 feet, then hike 0.2 mile
northeast up talus and reach the east ridge of Point 13,768 at 13,500 feet.
Hike 0.1 mile northwest to the summit of Point 13,768. Point 13,768, your
bonus peak, is a "Bi"—one of Colorado's 200 highest peaks. From here you
can finally see Holy Cross Ridge and Mount of the Holy Cross to the north.

From Point 13,768, descend 0.5 mile north to the 13,380-foot saddle
between Point 13,768 and Holy Cross Ridge. From the saddle, climb 0.5 mile
north-northeast to the summit of Holy Cross Ridge. Stay on the ridge's west
side during the traverse from Point 13,768 to Holy Cross Ridge. On your
return trip, contour south at 13,500 feet west of Point 13,768. Ascending
this route and descending one of the northern routes would require a
vehicle shuttle, but would complete a grand Tour de Holy Cross Ridge.

VARIATIONS

8.5V1
From the highest of the Seven Sisters Lakes at 12,750 feet, climb 0.35 mile
west-northwest to the 13,420-foot saddle between Point 13,768 and Point
13,618. In early summer this slope holds a moderate snow slope. After the
snow melts, there is a Class 2 passage on steep talus. From the saddle,
climb 0.4 mile north-northeast to the summit of Point 13,768 and rejoin
the South Ridge Route there.

8.5V2 — Point 13,618, Class 2
You can modify the South Ridge Route to include a traverse of Point
13,618. From 11,700 feet on the Fall Creek Trail, leave the trail and hike

Mount Oklahoma from the south.

0.7 mile northwest up rough slopes to 12,940 feet on the south ridge of Point 13,618. Hike 0.5 mile north-northeast up the ridge to the summit of Point 13,618. This peak is an unranked thirteener, but it is in a unique position. Descend 0.4 mile north to the 13,420-foot saddle between Point 13,768 and Point 13,618. From the saddle, climb 0.4 mile north-northeast to the summit of Point 13,768 and rejoin the route there.

8.5EC – Extra Credit – Whitney Peak, 13,271 feet, Class 2

From 12,200 feet on the Fall Creek Trail, stay on the trail and hike 0.4 mile north-northeast to Fall Creek Pass at 12,580 feet. Leave the trail here and hike 0.8 mile south-southeast to the 13,271-foot summit of Whitney Peak, a ranked thirteener. If you include this ascent on your return trip, you can survey your work.

9. Mount Oklahoma   13,845 feet

See Map 9 on page 103

Mount Oklahoma is 1.8 miles west-southwest of Colorado's second highest peak—Mount Massive. Despite being hidden behind its famous neighbor, Mount Oklahoma is okay. Mount Oklahoma has two distinctions that Mount Massive lacks. Mount Oklahoma is on the Continental Divide and on the boundary of two wilderness areas; the Mount Massive Wilderness is to the east and the Hunter Fryingpan Wilderness is to the west.

Mount Oklahoma was officially named in 1967, so earlier editions of the Mount Champion Quadrangle do not show the name. However, maps are only a record of human attributes, such as names, and provide only a

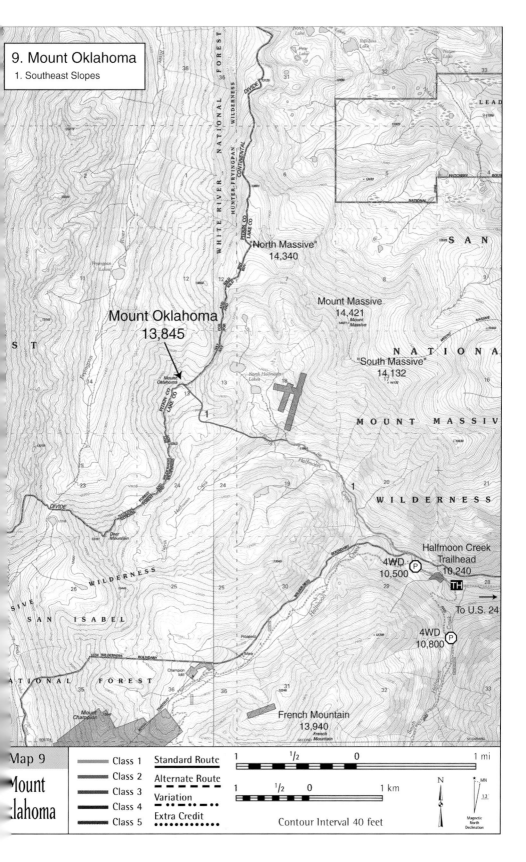

9. Mount Oklahoma
1. Southeast Slopes

WHITE RIVER NATIONAL FOREST

HUNTER-FRYINGPAN WILDERNESS

CONTINENTAL DIVIDE

LEAD

"North Massive"
14,340

SAN

Mount Massive
14,421

Mount Oklahoma
13,845

"South Massive"
14,132

NATIONA

North Halfmoon
Lake

MOUNT   MASSIV

PITKIN CO
LAKE CO

Halfmoon Creek

WILDERNESS

DIVIDE

Deer
Mountain

Halfmoon Creek
Trailhead
10,240

4WD
10,500

TH

WILDERNESS

To U.S. 24

SAN   ISABEL

4WD
10,800

ATIONAL   FOREST

Mount
Champion

French Mountain
13,940

Map 9	Class 1	Standard Route
Mount	Class 2	Alternate Route
Oklahoma	Class 3	Variation
	Class 4	
	Class 5	Extra Credit

1   1/2   0   1 mi

1   1/2   0   1 km

N

MN

13

Magnetic
North
Declination

Contour Interval 40 feet

two-dimensional representation of reality. From Mount Oklahoma's summit, you have a grand view in the midst of Colorado's highest peaks.

MAPS
Required: *Mount Champion, Mount Massive, San Isabel National Forest*

TRAILHEAD

Halfmoon Creek Trailhead
This trailhead is at 10,240 feet. It provides access to Oklahoma's south and east sides, as well as to the north and east sides of the peaks in the French Group. Don't confuse this trailhead with Halfmoon Trailhead described for Holy Cross Ridge. From Third Street and U.S. 24 (Harrison Avenue) in downtown Leadville, go 3.6 miles southwest on U.S. 24, turn west onto Colorado 300 and measure from this point. Go 0.7 mile west on Colorado 300 (paved) and turn south (left) onto Lake County 11 (dirt). Turn southwest (right) at mile 1.8 onto another dirt road marked with signs for Halfmoon Creek. Pass the San Isabel National Forest boundary at mile 3.9, pass Halfmoon Campground at mile 5.6, pass Elbert Creek Campground at mile 6.7 and reach the well-marked Mount Massive Trailhead on the road's north side at mile 7.0. Continue west to the FS 110–FS 1103A junction at mile 9.0. The trailhead is at this junction.

Four-wheel-drive vehicles can go farther. If your destination is Mount Oklahoma, go west (straight) on FS 110 (Halfmoon Road) for an additional 0.5 mile to the start of the North Halfmoon Creek Trail at 10,500 feet. If your destination is in the French Group, you can go 1.0 mile farther. From the junction of FS 110 and FS 1103A, turn south (left), drop down and ford Halfmoon Creek. Follow FS 1103A (South Halfmoon Road) as it switchbacks steeply up the hill. After 1.0 mile, park at 10,800 feet just before the road crosses South Halfmoon Creek. The bridge at this crossing is broken, and vehicle passage beyond this point is problematic. Winter road closure varies from the start of the Halfmoon Creek Road 1.8 miles from U.S. 24 to the Halfmoon Campground at mile 5.6.

ROUTE

9.1 – Mount Oklahoma – Southeast Slopes

From Halfmoon Creek TH at 10,240 ft:	*222 RP*	*8.0 mi*	*3,605 ft*	*Class 2*
From 4WD parking at 10,500 ft:	*207 RP*	*7.0 mi*	*3,345 ft*	*Class 2*

This hike starts on a good trail, and this is the easiest way to climb Mount Oklahoma. Start at the Halfmoon Creek Trailhead and go 0.5 mile west on FS 110 (Halfmoon Road) to the start of the North Halfmoon Creek Trail at 10,500 feet. Leave FS 110 and hike 1.4 miles northwest on the North Halfmoon Creek Trail into the Mount Massive Wilderness to the middle of a large meadow at 11,080 feet. Massive's large, southwest slopes and southern subpeaks are northeast of the trail, and you can see Mount Oklahoma 1.8 miles to the northwest. From the meadow, continue 0.7 mile west-northwest on the trail to 11,600 feet.

At 11,600 feet, leave the trail, hike 0.1 mile west and cross to North Halfmoon Creek's west side. Hike 0.3 mile west-northwest up a small, tree-covered ridge to treeline at 11,900 feet. Stay south of the cliffs on Mount Oklahoma's lower east ridge, and hike 0.5 mile west-northwest up a small drainage to a flat area at 12,700 feet. Climb 0.2 mile north up talus and reach Oklahoma's east ridge at 13,200 feet (Class 2). This slope is the route's crux. If you feel okay, climb 0.3 mile northwest up Oklahoma's broad, southeast slopes to the summit.

10. French Group

French Mountain	13,940 feet
Frasco Benchmark	13,876 feet
Casco Peak	13,908 feet
"Lackawanna Peak"	13,823 feet

See Map 10 on page 106

These high peaks hide west of and behind Colorado's highest peak—Mount Elbert. French Mountain is visible from U.S. 24 south of Leadville, but Casco is difficult to see from highways. Frasco Benchmark is on the ridge between French and Casco. "Lackawanna" sits by itself 1.7 miles southwest of Casco and 1.6 miles east of Colorado 82. Located near the center of Colorado's mountains, these peaks offer worthy views in all directions.

MAPS

Required: *Mount Massive, Mount Elbert, Independence Pass, San Isabel National Forest*
Optional: *Mount Champion*

TRAILHEADS

Echo Canyon Trailhead

This trailhead is at 10,000 feet and provides access to Casco's southeast side. It is not far north of Colorado 82, but the turn to this trailhead is easily missed. The turn is 12.5 miles west of the U.S. 24–Colorado 82 junction, 6.2 miles west of the town of Twin Lakes and 2.0 miles east of the Colorado 82–South Fork Lake Creek Road junction. The turn is marked with a small sign for the Echo Canyon Trail. Turn north off Colorado 82 onto a dirt road in front of a cabin and go 100 feet west to the trailhead, which has only enough parking space for one or two vehicles. Passenger cars should stop here. This trailhead is accessible in winter.

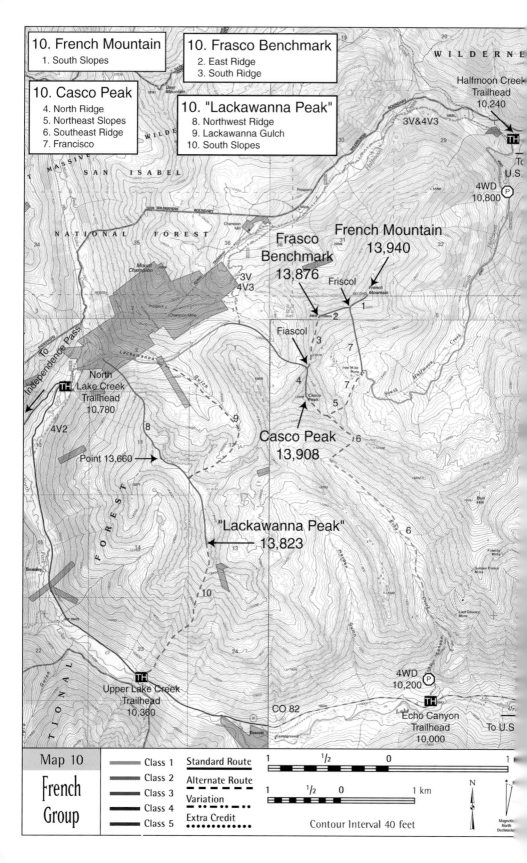

10. French Mountain
  1. South Slopes

10. Frasco Benchmark
  2. East Ridge
  3. South Ridge

10. Casco Peak
  4. North Ridge
  5. Northeast Slopes
  6. Southeast Ridge
  7. Francisco

10. "Lackawanna Peak"
  8. Northwest Ridge
  9. Lackawanna Gulch
  10. South Slopes

WILDERNE

Halfmoon Creek
Trailhead
10,240

3V&4V3

4WD
10,800 P

To
U.S.

Frasco
Benchmark
13,876

French Mountain
13,940

Friscol

3V
4V3

Fiascol

Casco Peak
13,908

North
Lake Creek
Trailhead
10,780

4V2

Point 13,660

"Lackawanna Peak"
13,823

Upper Lake Creek
Trailhead
10,360

CO 82

4WD
10,200 P

Echo Canyon
Trailhead
10,000

To U.S

Map 10

French
Group

Class 1
Class 2
Class 3
Class 4
Class 5

Standard Route

Alternate Route

Variation

Extra Credit

Contour Interval 40 feet

1   ½   0   1

1   ½   0   1 km

N

Four-wheel-drive vehicles can go a little farther. From the passenger car trailhead, go 150 feet north, turn right and go 0.25 mile north on a rough four-wheel-drive road to the end of the road at 10,200 feet. The Echo Canyon Trail starts just west of a cement foundation.

Upper Lake Creek Trailhead

This trailhead is at 10,360 feet and provides access to the south side of "Lackawanna." If you are approaching from the east, go 15.6 miles west on Colorado 82 from the U.S. 24–Colorado 82 junction. If you are approaching from the west, go 8.1 miles east on Colorado 82 from the summit of Independence Pass. Park in a pullout on the highway's south side. This trailhead is accessible in winter.

North Lake Creek Trailhead

This trailhead is at 10,780 feet and provides access to the north side of "Lackawanna" and the northwest side of Casco. If you are approaching from the east, go 19.0 miles west on Colorado 82 from the U.S. 24–Colorado 82 junction, or 3.4 miles north from the Upper Lake Creek Trailhead. If you are approaching from the west, go 4.7 miles east on Colorado 82 from the summit of Independence Pass. Turn east onto a dirt road that is 50 yards south of the first (or last, if descending) switchback of Independence Pass. Go 0.1 mile northeast on the dirt road to a parking area. The road is gated at this point, and this is the trailhead. Four-wheel-drive vehicles can ford the Lake Fork of Lake Creek and park by a road closure gate on the creek's east side. The winter road closure on Colorado 82 is 2.2 miles south of this trailhead near Graham Gulch.

10. French Mountain   13,940 feet

See Map 10 on page 106

French Mountain anchors the northern end of a ridge west of Mount Elbert. French is 2.1 miles west-northwest of Elbert and 4.1 miles south of Mount Massive. From the northeast, you can see French above Halfmoon Creek. French Mountain rests regally in the home of the giants.

ROUTE

10.1 — French Mountain — South Slopes

From Halfmoon Creek TH at 10,240 ft:	*224 RP*	*10.2 mi*	*3,700 ft*	*Class 2*
From 4WD parking at 10,800 ft:	*192 RP*	*8.2 mi*	*3,140 ft*	*Class 2*

This is the easiest route up French Mountain. Start at the Halfmoon Creek Trailhead (see Mount Oklahoma), go south on FS 1103A, drop down and cross Halfmoon Creek. Follow FS 1103A (South Halfmoon Road) 1.0 mile south as the road switchbacks steeply up the hill. At 10,800 feet, cross to South Halfmoon Creek's east side on a broken bridge. Hike 3.1 miles south-southwest then west up the continuing road to the Iron Mike Mine at 12,560 feet. Here, you are high in the basin between Elbert, Casco and French, which is 0.8 mile to the north.

Leave the road at the Iron Mike Mine, hike 0.75 mile north and climb to the 13,620-foot saddle between French and Frasco. The climb to this saddle, which carries the nickname "Friscol," is a steep hike up small talus. From Friscol, climb 0.25 mile northeast up talus on a rounded ridge to French's suspended summit.

10. Frasco Benchmark   13,876 feet

See Map 10 on page 106

Frasco Benchmark is on the ridge between French and Casco, 0.5 mile west-southwest of French and 0.8 mile north of Casco. Frasco is an unranked thirteener, but it is in an important topographic position at the intersection of three ridges. If nature had made slightly different erosional choices, Frasco might have been Colorado's highest peak.

ROUTES

10.2 — Frasco Benchmark — East Ridge

From Halfmoon Creek TH at 10,240 ft:	*224 RP*	*10.4 mi*	*3,636 ft*	*Class 2*
From 4WD parking at 10,800 ft:	*193 RP*	*8.4 mi*	*3,076 ft*	*Class 2*

This is the easiest route on Frasco Benchmark. Start at the Halfmoon Creek Trailhead (see Mount Oklahoma) and follow French's South Slopes Route to Friscol, the 13,620-foot saddle between French and Frasco. From Friscol, hike 0.35 mile west-southwest on a ridge to Frasco's summit (Class 2).

10.3 — Frasco Benchmark — South Ridge

From North Lake Creek TH at 10,780 ft:	*200 RP*	*7.5 mi*	*3,096 ft*	*Class 2+*

This harder, alternative route approaches Frasco from the west. Start at the North Lake Creek Trailhead and follow Casco's North Ridge Route to Fiascol, the 13,260-foot saddle between Casco and Frasco. From Fiascol, climb 0.55 mile north on a rough ridge to the summit of Frasco (Class 2+). Avoid some small towers by staying on the ridge's west side.

10.3V — Variation

From Halfmoon Creek TH at 10,240 ft:	*254 RP*	*11.7 mi*	*3,836 ft*	*Class 2+*
From 4WD parking at 10,500 ft:	*239 RP*	*10.7 mi*	*3,576 ft*	*Class 2+*

Let there be choices. You can approach Frasco's south ridge from the east.

Start at the Halfmoon Creek Trailhead (see Mount Oklahoma) and go 0.5 mile west on FS 110 (Halfmoon Road) to the start of the North Halfmoon Creek Trail at 10,500 feet. Continue 2.7 miles west then southwest up FS 110 to the turn for the Champion Mill at 11,540 feet. Do not enter the Champion Mill, which is private, but stay on FS 110 and cross to Halfmoon Creek's south side. Continue 1.2 miles southwest then south on FS 110 to the 12,460-foot saddle between Frasco Benchmark, which is 0.7 mile east, and Mount Champion, which is 0.8 mile west-northwest. From the saddle, descend 0.3 mile southeast on easy terrain and join the South Ridge Route in the basin at 12,260 feet.

10. Casco Peak 13,908 feet

See Map 10 on page 106

Casco Peak is 1.2 miles southwest of French and 2.6 miles west of Mount Elbert. The case for Casco is simple: you can approach this prominent peak from four different drainages. These choices let you create your own Coup de Casco.

ROUTES

10.4 — Casco Peak — North Ridge

From North Lake Creek TH at 10,780 ft: *191 RP*   *7.0 mi*   *3,128 ft*   *Class 2*

This is the shortest and easiest summer route on Casco. Start at the North Lake Creek Trailhead and walk 0.2 mile north-northeast on the beginning of the trail up the North Fork of Lake Creek. Leave this trail, hike 0.1 mile northeast on an old road and cross to the North Fork's east side. In low water you can cross the creek on rocks and keep your feet dry. This ford can be impractical in high water. For alternatives, see Variations 10.4V1 and 10.4V2.

Hike 0.4 mile east to 11,100 feet on an old road that switchbacks up through the trees on the south side of Lackawanna Gulch. Continue 0.5 mile east on a good trail on the gulch's south side to 11,500 feet. Lackawanna Gulch has two branches above this point. Cross the creek descending from the gulch's southern branch, then continue 1.0 mile northeast on the trail up the south side of the northern branch.

Leave the trail at 12,200 feet before it crosses the creek and climbs north to the saddle between Frasco Benchmark and Mount Champion. Hike 0.8 mile southeast up the upper gulch to 12,800 feet. Climb 0.2 mile east to the 13,260-foot saddle between Frasco and Casco. The climb to this saddle, which carries the nickname "Fiascol," is a short, steep hike up talus. From Fiascol, climb 0.3 mile south up Casco's well-defined north ridge to Casco's summit (Class 2). The ridge is roughest near the top.

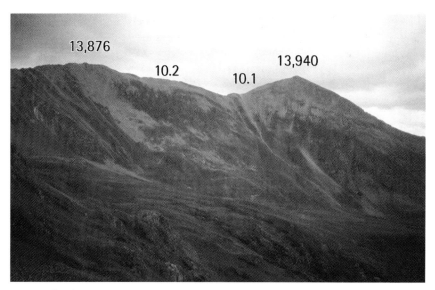

13,876
10.2
13,940
10.1

Frasco (left) and French from the south.

VARIATIONS

10.4V1
If the ford of the North Fork of Lake Creek is impractical, you can cross the creek just east of the trailhead. The creek is wider here than at the crossing 0.2 mile upstream, and this is an easier place to ford. However, even in low water, you will get your feet wet. Four-wheel-drive vehicles can cross the creek here and park at a road closure gate on the creek's east side. From the road closure gate, hike 0.3 mile north-northeast on an old road on the North Fork's east side, and join the route on Lackawanna Creek's south side near the upstream ford.

10.4V2
From North Fork bridge at 10,720 ft: 209 RP   8.6 mi   3,188 ft   Class 2
If the ford of the North Fork of Lake Creek is impractical, you also have the option of avoiding it entirely. Start on Colorado 82, 0.9 mile south of the North Lake Creek Trailhead on the south side of the highway culvert over the North Fork. Go 0.8 mile north-northwest on a four-wheel-drive road on the North Fork's east side to a road closure gate. Hike 0.3 mile north-northeast on an old road on the North Fork's east side, and join the route on Lackawanna Creek's south side near the upstream ford.

10.4V3
From Halfmoon Creek TH at 10,240 ft: 245 RP   11.2 mi   3,868 ft   Class 2
From 4WD parking at 10,500 ft: 230 RP   10.2 mi   3,608 ft   Class 2
You can approach Casco's north ridge from the east. Start at the Halfmoon

French, Frasco and Casco from the northwest.

Creek Trailhead (see Mount Oklahoma), follow Variation 10.3V and join the North Ridge Route in north Lackawanna Gulch at 12,260 feet.

10.5 — Casco Peak — Northeast Slopes

From Halfmoon Creek TH at 10,240 ft: *220 RP*   *10.3 mi*   *3,668 ft*   *Class 2*
From 4WD parking at 10,800 ft: *189 RP*   *8.3 mi*   *3,108 ft*   *Class 2*

Although longer than the North Ridge Route, this is an easy route on Casco. Start at the Halfmoon Creek Trailhead (see Mount Oklahoma) and follow the South Slopes Route on French to the Iron Mike Mine at 12,560 feet. Continue 0.1 mile southwest on the road past the mine to 12,600 feet. Leave the road here, hike 0.4 mile south-southwest to 12,800 feet, then climb 0.25 mile west up talus to reach Casco's southeast ridge at 13,300 feet. Climb 0.3 mile northwest up the ridge to Casco's summit.

10.6 — Casco Peak — Southeast Ridge

From Echo Canyon TH at 10,000 ft: *224 RP*   *8.8 mi*   *3,908 ft*   *Class 2*
From 4WD parking at 10,200 ft: *214 RP*   *8.2 mi*   *3,708 ft*   *Class 2*

This is another easy route on Casco. It is a better choice for a nonsummer ascent than either the North Ridge or Northeast Slopes Route, because the Echo Canyon Trailhead is accessible year-round and you avoid north-facing slopes.

Start this scenic tour at the Echo Canyon Trailhead, go 150 feet north, turn right and go 0.25 mile north on a four-wheel-drive road to the end of the road at 10,200 feet. The Echo Canyon Trail starts just west of a cement foundation. Hike 3.0 miles north then northwest up Echo Canyon on the Echo Canyon Trail to 12,000 feet. Above 10,800 feet, stay on the creek's northeast side. From 12,000 feet, leave the trail and climb 0.35 mile northeast to a 12,860-foot saddle on Casco's southeast ridge. Climb 0.75 mile northwest up this well-defined ridge to Casco's summit.

10. FRENCH, FRASCO AND CASCO COMBINATION

See Map 10 on page 106

10.7 — FFC Combination — Francisco *Classic*

From Halfmoon Creek TH at 10,240 ft:	*288 RP*	*11.7 mi*	*4,604 ft*	*Class 2+*
From 4WD parking at 10,800 ft:	*257 RP*	*9.7 mi*	*4,044 ft*	*Class 2+*

This is the easiest way to climb French, Frasco and Casco together. Start at the Halfmoon Creek Trailhead (see Mount Oklahoma) and climb the South Slopes Route on French. Return to 13,620-foot Friscol and hike 0.35 mile west-southwest on a ridge to the summit of Frasco (Class 2). Descend 0.55 mile southwest to 13,260-foot Fiascol between Frasco and Casco (Class 2+). This is the roughest part of the traverse, and you will need to navigate around some scruffy towers on the west side of the ridge. Fiascol is named in memory of misadventures on attempts to reach this saddle from below. Fortunately, on this traverse, you are just passing through. From Fiascol, climb 0.3 mile south up Casco's well-defined north ridge to Casco's summit (Class 2). Descend Casco's Northeast Slopes Route.

10. "Lackawanna Peak" 13,823 feet

See Map 10 on page 106

"Lackawanna" is a singular peak that sits by itself 1.8 miles southwest of Casco. Colorado 82 goes under the south and west faces of "Lackawanna" before climbing to Independence Pass, and there are good views of the peak from the highway east of the pass. "Lackawanna" is a typical Sawatch peak. It has steep lower slopes, but the terrain above treeline is gentle and forgiving. Because of the peak's proximity to Colorado 82, "Lackawanna" has a variety of routes, and you can even do it in winter.

ROUTES

10.8 — "Lackawanna Peak" — Northwest Ridge

From North Lake Creek TH at 10,780 ft:	*242 RP*	*6.2 mi*	*3,603 ft*	*Class 2*

This is the easiest route on "Lackawanna." Start at the North Lake Creek Trailhead and walk 0.2 mile north-northeast on the beginning of the trail

"Lackawanna Peak" from the southwest.

up the North Fork of Lake Creek. Leave this trail, hike 0.1 mile northeast on an old road and cross to the North Fork's east side. In low water you can cross the creek on rocks and keep your feet dry. This ford can be impractical in high water. For alternatives, see Variations 10.4V1 and 10.4V2.

Hike 0.4 mile east to 11,100 feet on an old road that switchbacks up through the trees on the south side of Lackawanna Gulch. Leave the road at 11,100 feet and climb 0.4 mile southeast up a steep hill to treeline at 12,000 feet. Climb 0.3 mile up the continuing steep hill and reach the northwest ridge of "Lackawanna" at 12,800 feet. The worst is over, and the slope angle is much gentler above this point.

From 12,800 feet, climb 0.7 mile south to the summit of Point 13,660, a thirteener with a soft rank. Descend 0.3 mile east-southeast to a 13,380-foot saddle, contour 0.3 mile southeast on the west side of Point 13,590 to a 13,540-foot saddle, then climb 0.4 mile south on an easy ridge to the summit.

10.9 — "Lackawanna Peak" — Lackawanna Gulch *Classic*

From North Lake Creek TH at 10,780 ft: 230 RP 7.0 mi 3,043 ft Class 2 Mod Snow
With descent of Northwest Ridge: 236 RP 6.6 mi 3,323 ft Class 2 Mod Snow

This is the most scenic route on "Lackawanna." Start at the North Lake Creek Trailhead and walk 0.2 mile north-northeast on the beginning of the trail up the North Fork of Lake Creek. Leave this trail, hike 0.1 mile northeast on an old road and cross to the North Fork's east side. In low water you can cross the creek on rocks and keep your feet dry. This ford can be impractical in high water. For alternatives, see Variations 10.4V1 and 10.4V2.

Hike 0.4 mile east to 11,100 feet on an old road that switchbacks up through the trees on the south side of Lackawanna Gulch. Continue 0.5 mile west on a good trail on the gulch's south side to 11,500 feet. Lackawanna Gulch has two branches above this point.

Leave the trail at 11,500 feet and hike 1.1 miles southeast up the southern (right) branch of Lackawanna Gulch to 12,400 feet. Hike 0.2 mile south to 12,600 feet, then hike 0.5 mile southwest up a small, charming basin to 13,200 feet. Climb 0.1 mile southwest up a moderate snow slope to the 13,380-foot saddle between Point 13,660 and "Lackawanna." Climb 0.4 mile south on an easy ridge to the summit. Ascending this route and descending the Northwest Ridge Route makes an obvious Tour de "Lackawanna."

10.10 — "Lackawanna Peak" — South Slopes

From Upper Lake Creek TH at 10,360 ft: 201 RP   3.4 mi   3,463 ft   Class 2

This steep climb is the shortest route on "Lackawanna." It is the best route for a winter ascent, because the Upper Lake Creek Trailhead is accessible year-round. It is also a good route when the creek crossing at the North Lake Creek Trailhead is impractical, or if you like to attack the fall line. Start at the Upper Lake Creek Trailhead and hike 0.35 mile northeast to treeline at 11,000 feet. Continue 0.5 mile northeast up the steep slope to 12,400 feet. Get onto a small ridge and climb 0.85 mile north to the summit.

11. Grizzly Peak   13,988 feet

See Map 11 on page 116

Once a fourteener, Grizzly Peak is now just Colorado's highest thirteener (and thus the highest peak in this book). It carries this honor well, being on the Continental Divide in the center of the state, and being one of the most rugged peaks in the Sawatch Range. A more obscure accolade is that this is the highest of Colorado's six 13,000-foot-plus peaks with the name *Grizzly*. It is difficult to see Grizzly from a paved highway, and this adds to its allure. Grizzly is 4.9 miles south-southwest of Independence Pass, and you can approach the peak from either the east or west side of the pass. Grizzly offers a variety of routes, none of which are trivial.

MAPS
Required: *Independence Pass, San Isabel National Forest*
Optional: *New York Peak*

TRAILHEADS

McNasser Gulch Trailhead

This trailhead is at 10,740 feet and provides access to Grizzly's east side. If you are approaching from the east, go 14.5 miles west on Colorado 82 from the U.S. 24–Colorado 82 junction. If you are approaching from the west, go 9.2 miles east on Colorado 82 from the summit of Independence Pass. Turn south onto South Fork Lake Creek Road (FS 391) and measure from this point. Go south then southwest on South Fork Lake Creek Road, go straight at mile 2.7 and reach the trailhead at mile 3.3. Park near the junction of FS 394, which climbs northwest into McNasser Gulch. Four-wheel-drive vehicles can turn northwest (right) onto FS 394 and continue 1.2 miles northwest to a locked gate at 11,360 feet in McNasser Gulch.

Grizzly Reservoir Trailhead

This trailhead is at 10,560 feet in Lincoln Gulch and provides access to Grizzly's north and west sides. If you are approaching from the east, go 9.7 miles west on Colorado 82 from the summit of Independence Pass. If you are approaching from the west, go 10.0 miles east on Colorado 82 from Aspen. Turn south onto Lincoln Creek Road (FS 106) and measure from this point. Go southeast on Lincoln Creek Road, pass the Lincoln Gulch Campground at mile 0.4, pass several designated campsites, pass the Grizzly Reservoir Dam at mile 6.2 and reach the marked trailhead on the road's east (left) side at mile 6.5. The road is rough to this point, but is passable for tough passenger cars.

The Grizzly Lake Trail goes east from this trailhead and gives access to Grizzly Peak's north side. If your destination is Grizzly's west side, you need to continue south up Lincoln Creek Road. From the trailhead, four-wheel-drive vehicles can continue 2.5 miles south on Lincoln Creek Road to 10,920 feet under Grizzly Peak's west face. The road continues beyond this point, but if your destination is Grizzly, you want to park near the stream coming from the middle of three gulches on the west face below the Grizzly–Garfield ridge.

ROUTES

11.1 — Grizzly Peak — East Ridge

From McNasser Gulch TH at 10,740 ft:	*219 RP*	*8.2 mi*	*3,248 ft*	*Class 2+*
From 4WD parking at 11,360 ft:	*182 RP*	*5.8 mi*	*2,628 ft*	*Class 2+*

This is the standard route on Grizzly. It is a rough route to a remarkable summit. Start at the McNasser Gulch Trailhead, leave FS 391 and go 1.2 miles northwest on FS 394 to a locked gate at 11,360 feet in McNasser Gulch. The road is closed to vehicles beyond this point. Hike 1.2 miles west-southwest on the continuing road, to a road junction at 11,880 feet.

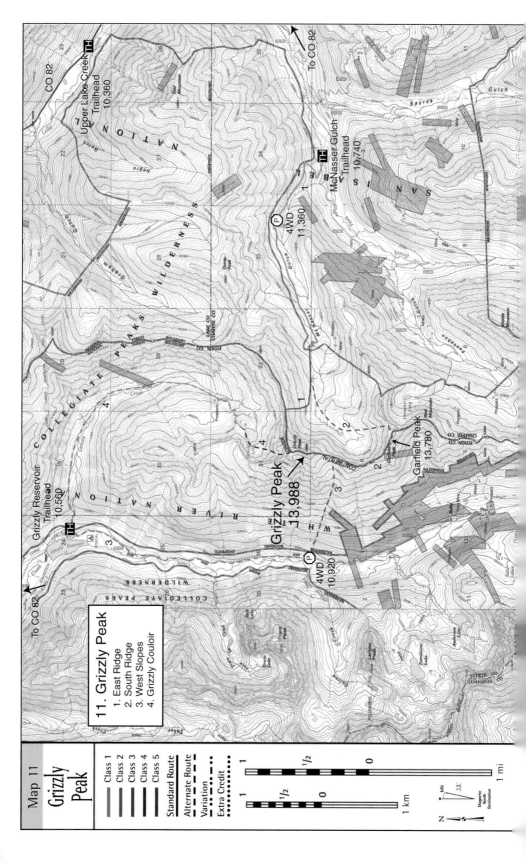

Map 11

Grizzly Peak

Class 1
Class 2
Class 3
Class 4
Class 5

Standard Route
Alternate Route
Variation
Extra Credit

1 km
1 mi

N
MN
13°
Magnetic
North
Declination

11. Grizzly Peak

1. East Ridge
2. South Ridge
3. West Slopes
4. Grizzly Couloir

Upper Lake Creek
Trailhead
10,360

CO 82

To CO 82

McNasser Gulch
Trailhead
10,740

4WD
11,360

NATIONAL

WILDERNESS

PEAKS

COLLEGIATE

Grizzly Reservoir
Trailhead
10,560

To CO 82

RIVER NATION

4WD
10,920

COLLEGIATE PEAKS WILDERNESS

Grizzly Peak
13,988

Garfield Peak
13,780

CONTINENTAL

Grizzly Peak from the northwest.

Turn north (right) and climb 0.2 mile to a mine at 12,000 feet. The road ends here.

From the end of the road at 12,000 feet, hike 0.6 mile west to 12,500 feet, entering the Collegiate Peaks Wilderness en route. Climb 0.3 mile north up a talus slope to a 13,300-foot saddle on Grizzly's east ridge (Class 2). Scamper 0.4 mile west along or on the rough ridge's south side to a minor, 13,940-foot summit (Class 2+). From here you can peer down the Grizzly Couloir to the north. Climb 0.2 mile south, then climb the summit block's west side to reach the summit (Class 2+).

11.2 — Grizzly Peak — South Ridge

From McNasser Gulch TH at 10,740 ft:	*302 RP*	*10.4 mi*	*4,208 ft*	*Class 2+*
With descent of East Ridge:	*260 RP*	*9.3 mi*	*3,728 ft*	*Class 2+*
From 4WD parking at 11,360 ft:	*265 RP*	*8.0 mi*	*3,588 ft*	*Class 2+*
With descent of East Ridge:	*223 RP*	*6.9 mi*	*3,108 ft*	*Class 2+*

This longer alternative to the East Ridge Route allows you to climb an extra peak and makes a nice circle tour possible. Start at the McNasser Gulch Trailhead and follow the East Ridge Route to 12,300 feet. Hike 0.3 mile west and get into the upper McNasser Gulch drainage. Hike 0.3 mile southwest just east of this drainage to a small lake at 12,700 feet. From here, Grizzly Peak is 0.4 mile northwest and 13,780-foot Garfield Peak is 0.5 mile south. Your initial goal is Garfield Peak.

From the lake at 12,700 feet, hike 0.3 mile south to 13,000 feet. Climb 0.2 mile south-southeast up a steep talus slope to a 13,540-foot saddle between Garfield and Point 13,740, which is 0.3 mile east-northeast of Garfield. From the saddle, climb 0.2 mile west to Garfield's summit (Class 2+). Your bonus peak is a "Bi"—one of Colorado's 200 highest peaks—and it is on the Continental Divide.

From Garfield, descend 0.3 mile west-northwest to the 13,420-foot saddle between Garfield and Grizzly (Class 2+). Climb 0.7 mile north on talus across Point 13,620 to Grizzly's summit (Class 2). Ascending this route and descending the East Ridge Route makes a circular Tour de Garfield and Grizzly, and avoids the need to reclimb Garfield on your return trip. Depending on conditions, you may choose to do this tour in the opposite direction.

11.3 — Grizzly Peak — West Slopes

From Grizzly Reservoir TH at 10,560 ft:	*237 RP*	*7.8 mi*	*3,428 ft*	*Class 2+*
From 4WD parking at 10,920 ft:	*178 RP*	*2.8 mi*	*3,068 ft*	*Class 2+*

This steep route is the easiest way to climb Grizzly from the west. Start at the Grizzly Reservoir Trailhead and go 2.5 miles south on Lincoln Creek Road (FS 106) to 10,920 feet under Grizzly Peak's west face. It is difficult to identify features on Grizzly's west face from the road. You want to leave the road at the stream coming from the middle of three gulches on the west face below the Grizzly–Garfield ridge. The middle gulch reaches the ridge mid-way between Grizzly and Garfield, which is 1.0 mile south of Grizzly.

Leave the road at 10,920 feet and hike 0.4 mile east-southeast to treeline at 11,700 feet (Class 2). From here you can see the middle gulch directly above you and a small basin high above you to the east. Climb 0.4 mile east-southeast up the gulch's south side to 12,800 feet (Class 2+). The small basin will be directly above you at this point. Climb 0.3 mile east up the center of this basin to a 13,500-foot saddle on the Continental Divide between Point 13,620 and Grizzly (Class 2). The steepest part of your ascent is over. Climb 0.3 mile north up the rounded ridge to Grizzly's summit. This is the top of the South Ridge Route.

11.4 — Grizzly Peak — Grizzly Couloir *Classic*

From Grizzly Reservoir TH at 10,560 ft:	*290 RP*	*8.0 mi*	*3,428 ft*	*Class 2+*	*Steep Snow*
With descent of West Slopes:	*289 RP*	*7.9 mi*	*3,428 ft*	*Class 2+*	*Steep Snow*

This is the premier mountaineering route on Grizzly and perhaps the best mountaineering route in the Sawatch. We prefer this couloir to the other great Sawatch couloir, Ice Mountain's Refrigerator Couloir, because the Grizzly Couloir has less rockfall. You can see the Grizzly Couloir from many high summits to the north of Grizzly Peak, and you can preview conditions from other peaks as well. Surprisingly, this couloir holds its snow long after others have gone dry. It often stays in excellent condition even into midsummer.

Start at the Grizzly Reservoir Trailhead and hike 2.0 miles east then south on the Grizzly Lake Trail to a creek crossing at 11,420 feet. Cross to Grizzly Creek's west side and hike 1.2 miles south on the Grizzly Lake Trail to Grizzly Lake at 12,500 feet. From here you can see Grizzly's impressive north face. The Grizzly Couloir is the largest and westernmost couloir on the face. The introduction is over.

Hike 0.2 mile around Grizzly Lake's north side, then hike 0.1 mile southwest to 12,800 feet. The couloir will be directly above you. Climb steepening, moderate snow and enter the wide couloir. Climb directly up the center of the couloir as it narrows. As you approach the top, climb several hundred feet of steep snow and reach the summit ridge at 13,900 feet. Hike 0.2 mile south to the summit (Class 2+). Ascending this route and descending the West Slopes Route makes a logical Tour de Grizzly.

12. Mount Hope   13,933 feet

See Map 12 on page 120

Mount Hope is 4.7 miles southwest of the small town of Twin Lakes on Colorado 82, and 2.9 miles east-southeast of the fourteener La Plata Peak. You can see Mount Hope's distinctive, round-topped shape to the southwest when driving on U.S. 24 south of Leadville. This important peak is generally gentle, but Hope does have a surprising northeast face. No matter how you approach it, you can get high on Hope.

MAPS
Required: *Mount Elbert, Winfield, San Isabel National Forest*

TRAILHEADS

Sheep Gulch Trailhead
This trailhead is at 9,860 feet and provides access to Hope's south and east sides. Turn west from U.S. 24 onto Chaffee County 390 (gravel). This junction is 14.9 miles north of the stoplight in the center of Buena Vista, 4.3 miles south of the U.S. 24–Colorado 82 junction and 19.3 miles south of the West Sixth–U.S. 24 junction in the center of Leadville. Go 9.3 miles west on Chaffee County 390 to a small dirt side road on the north side of Chaffee County 390. This side road is 100 yards west of two large beaver ponds. Do not confuse this side road with another one 0.4 mile east. Park in a pullout on the north side of Chaffee County 390 near the side road west of the beaver ponds. This is the trailhead. Four-wheel-drive vehicles can go 0.2 mile north on the side road to 9,960 feet at the beginning of the Hope Pass Trail.

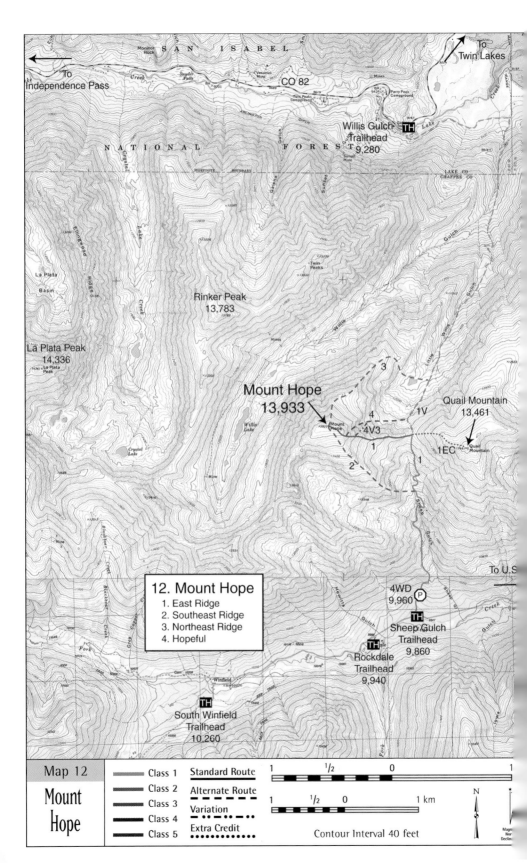

To Independence Pass

To Twin Lakes

SAN ISABEL

CO 82

Willis Gulch Trailhead
9,280

NATIONAL   FOREST

LAKE CO
CHAFFEE CO

Rinker Peak
13,783

La Plata Peak
14,336

Mount Hope
13,933

Quail Mountain
13,461

3

4

1V

4V3

1

1EC

2

To U.S

4WD
9,960 Ⓟ

12. Mount Hope
1. East Ridge
2. Southeast Ridge
3. Northeast Ridge
4. Hopeful

TH
Sheep Gulch Trailhead
9,860

TH
Rockdale Trailhead
9,940

TH
South Winfield Trailhead
10,260

Map 12		Class 1	Standard Route	1	¹/₂	0	1
Mount Hope		Class 2	Alternate Route				
		Class 3	Variation	1	¹/₂	0	1 km
		Class 4	Extra Credit				
		Class 5		Contour Interval 40 feet			

N

Magnetic North Declination

Mount Hope from the northeast.

Willis Gulch Trailhead

This trailhead is at 9,280 feet and provides access to Hope's north side. If you are approaching from the east, go 8.4 miles west on Colorado 82 from the U.S. 24–Colorado 82 junction. If you are approaching from the west, go 15.3 miles east on Colorado 82 from the summit of Independence Pass. Turn south onto a dirt road and go 120 yards southwest to the trailhead. There is ample parking here, as well as a footbridge across Lake Creek. The Willis Gulch Trail starts on the creek's south side; cross the footbridge and hike 100 yards south to the trail sign, which is on the south side of a beaver pond.

ROUTES

12.1 — Mount Hope — East Ridge *Classic*

From Sheep Gulch TH at 9,860 ft: *198 RP*   *7.2 mi*   *4,073 ft*   *Class 2*
From 4WD parking at 9,960 ft: *192 RP*   *6.8 mi*   *3,973 ft*   *Class 2*

This is the standard route on Hope. It is a short, steep stomp to a splendid summit. Start at the Sheep Gulch Trailhead and go 0.2 mile north on a small dirt road to 9,960 feet at the beginning of the Hope Pass Trail. The character of this hike will be evident in the first 100 feet of the Hope Pass Trail. It is steep. Hike north up the steep trail, pass a surprising spring after 0.7 mile, cross to the east side of Sheep Gulch after 1.3 miles, pass a cabin that is 100 yards south of the trail after 1.4 miles and reach treeline at

11,600 feet after 1.6 miles. Continue north on the still steep, still distinct trail to Hope Pass at 12,540 feet after 2.5 miles. You can see Hope's upper massif to the northwest during your ascent to the pass. At Hope Pass, expansive views open to the north and northeast.

From Hope Pass, leave the trail and hike 0.6 mile west up Hope's distinct east ridge to 13,400 feet. The ridge above looks rough, but with a little care the difficulty will not exceed Class 2. Hike 0.15 mile west on or just south of the ridge crest to the end of the difficulties at 13,800 feet. In early summer there is often a snow slope at 13,700 feet. By late summer, this snow slope will be gone. En route, you can peer into the dramatic couloir on Hope's northeast face. From 13,800 feet, hike 0.15 mile west on the now gentle slopes to Hope's highest point.

12.1V — Variation

From Willis Gulch TH at 9,280 ft: 259 RP   12.0 mi   4,653 ft   Class 2

You can approach Hope's east ridge from the north. Start at the Willis Gulch Trailhead, cross to Lake Creek's south side on a good bridge and hike 1.2 miles east on the beginning of the Willis Gulch Trail. Turn south (right) and hike 1.3 miles south to a trail junction at 10,300 feet. The western trail goes into Willis Gulch and the southern trail goes into Little Willis Gulch. Continue 2.0 miles south then southwest on the trail into Little Willis Gulch and reach a scenic lake at 11,780 feet. Continue on the trail 0.6 mile southwest to Hope Pass and join the East Ridge Route there.

12.1EC — Extra Credit — Quail Mountain, 13,461 feet, Class 2

From Hope Pass, climb 0.6 mile east to Quail Mountain's rounded, 13,461-foot summit. Quail Mountain is a "Tri"—one of Colorado's 300 highest peaks.

12.2 — Mount Hope — Southeast Ridge

From Sheep Gulch TH at 9,860 ft:	214 RP	6.2 mi	4,073 ft	Class 2
With descent of East Ridge:	215 RP	6.7 mi	4,073 ft	Class 2
From 4WD parking at 9,960 ft:	208 RP	5.8 mi	3,973 ft	Class 2
With descent of East Ridge:	209 RP	6.3 mi	3,973 ft	Class 2

This route provides an interesting alternative to Hope's East Ridge Route. In early summer you can avoid the barrier snow slope near the top of the east ridge, but you must leave the trail earlier and climb a steep, rough slope to gain this advantage. Also, the Southeast Ridge Route is shorter than the East Ridge Route. These may or may not be equitable trades, depending on your disposition.

Start at the Sheep Gulch Trailhead and follow the East Ridge Route 1.8 miles to treeline at 11,600 feet. Leave the trail here and hike 0.3 mile west up the aforementioned steep, rough slope to 12,200 feet, where the slope angle moderates. Hike 1.0 mile northwest up the ever gentling ridge to the summit. Ascending the Southeast Ridge Route and descending the East Ridge Route makes a southern Tour de Hope.

12.3 — Mount Hope — Northeast Ridge

From Willis Gulch TH at 9,280 ft: *286 RP*   *12.0 mi*   *4,653 ft*   *Class 2*
With descent of East Ridge: *280 RP*   *12.0 mi*   *4,653 ft*   *Class 2*

This is the easiest way to climb Hope from the north. Depending on conditions, it can be the easiest route on Hope. Start at the Willis Gulch Trailhead and follow the East Ridge Route's Variation 12.1V for 4.5 miles to the scenic lake at 11,780 feet. Leave the Hope Pass Trail here, hike to the lake's north side and hike 0.25 mile north-northwest up grassy slopes to 12,200 feet. Hike 0.25 mile west to reach Hope's northeast ridge at 12,500 feet. Climb 1.0 mile southwest then south up this ridge to the summit. Ascending the Northeast Ridge Route and descending the East Ridge Route makes a nice northern Tour de Hope and allows you to circumnavigate Hope's northeast face.

12.4 — Mount Hope — Hopeful *Classic*

From Sheep Gulch TH at 9,860 ft: *283 RP*   *7.6 mi*   *4,753 ft*   *Class 2*   *Mod Snow*
With descent of East Ridge: *267 RP*   *7.4 mi*   *4,413 ft*   *Class 2*   *Mod Snow*
From 4WD parking at 9,960 ft: *277 RP*   *7.2 mi*   *4,653 ft*   *Class 2*   *Mod Snow*
With descent of East Ridge: *261 RP*   *7.0 mi*   *4,313 ft*   *Class 2*   *Mod Snow*
From Willis Gulch TH at 9,280 ft: *322 RP*   *11.6 mi*   *4,653 ft*   *Class 2*   *Mod Snow*
With descent of East Ridge: *317 RP*   *11.8 mi*   *4,653 ft*   *Class 2*   *Mod Snow*

This sanguine couloir is Hope's premier mountaineering route. The couloir is in the center of Hope's small but rugged northeast face. With its crosswise ledge two-thirds of the way up, Hope's couloir resembles the Cross Couloir on Mount of the Holy Cross, but on a smaller scale. Hope's couloir is usually in good shape for climbing in June. In dry years or in other months, you can only hope that the couloir is full of snow. However, you do not have to guess. You can preview conditions in this couloir from U.S. 24 south of Leadville. A cornice usually threatens this couloir, but several variations reduce this hazard.

You can approach this climb from the south or north. If you are approaching from the south, follow the East Ridge Route to Hope Pass and descend 0.2 mile north on the trail to 12,200 feet on the north side of the pass. If you are approaching from the north, follow the East Ridge Route's Variation 12.1V to 12,200 feet on the Hope Pass Trail. Leave the Hope Pass Trail at 12,200 feet and hike 0.4 mile west to 12,600 feet in the basin below the couloir.

The couloir averages 36 degrees for 1,200 feet. It is steepest at the top. Begin your climb of the couloir, which narrows halfway up. This center section is the first to melt out. Above the center section, cross the couloir's arms and enjoy the spacious upper slope. As you approach the summit cornice, stay to the south (left) and exit the couloir to the south on a smooth slope just below the cornice at 13,700 feet. Scamper west to 13,800 feet, where you can get within a few feet of the summit cornice and peer down your climb. From 13,800 feet, hike 0.15 mile west on gentle slopes to Hope's highest point. Ascending Hopeful and descending any of the other routes makes a tremendous Tour de Hope.

VARIATIONS

12.4V1
Instead of exiting the couloir at 13,700 feet, continue up the snow and climb past the summit cornice on its south (left) side. This direct finish to 13,800 feet requires steep—and possibly very steep—snow climbing.

12.4V2
Instead of exiting the couloir at 13,700 feet, exit the couloir at 13,500 feet by climbing south (left) on the couloir's arm to reach the upper east ridge. This option reduces the time you spend underneath the cornice.

12.4V3
Instead of exiting the couloir at 13,700 feet, exit the couloir to the south (left) at 12,800 feet near the bottom of the climb. Climb 600 feet up moderate snow in another, smaller couloir and reach the east ridge at 13,400 feet. There is no cornice at the top of this side couloir. This option almost eliminates your exposure to the main couloir's cornice.

13. Emerald Group

Emerald Peak   13,904 feet
Iowa Peak   13,831 feet

See Map 13 on page 125

Emerald Peak and its companion, Iowa Peak, are on a ridge to the south of the fourteener Missouri Mountain. You cannot easily see Emerald and Iowa from paved highways, as they sit in the heartland of the Sawatch Range surrounded by six fourteeners. The fourteeners embrace these peaks as if to protect them. Emerald and Iowa are classic Sawatch peaks; they have long approaches and straightforward ascent routes. Unseen by most, they wait for the inquisitive alpinist.

MAPS
Required: *Winfield, Mount Harvard, San Isabel National Forest*
Optional: *Tincup, Harvard Lakes*

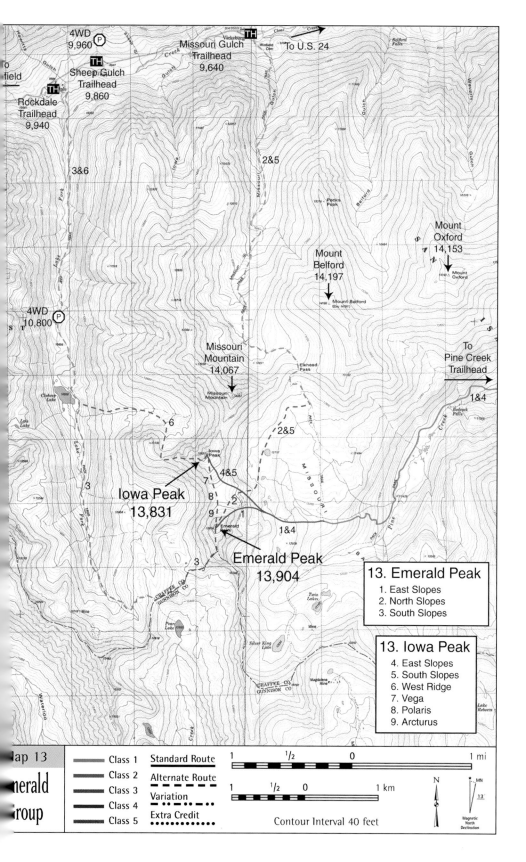

4WD
9,960 Ⓟ

Sheep Gulch
Trailhead
9,860

Missouri Gulch
Trailhead
9,640

Vicksburg

To U.S. 24

Rockdale
Trailhead
9,940

To
field

3&6

2&5

Peck's
Peak

Mount
Oxford
14,153

Mount
Oxford

Mount
Belford
14,197

Mount Belford

4WD
10,800 Ⓟ

Missouri
Mountain
14,067

Elkhead
Pass

To
Pine Creek
Trailhead

Missouri
Mountain

1&4

Clohesy
Lake

6

Iowa
Lake

2&5

Iowa
Peak

3

Iowa Peak
13,831

7 4&5

8 2

9 1

Emerald

1&4

MISSOURI

3

Emerald Peak
13,904

Twin
Lakes

Pear
Lake

13. Emerald Peak

1. East Slopes
2. North Slopes
3. South Slopes

Silver King
Lake

CHAFFEE CO
GUNNISON CO

Magdalene
Mine

13. Iowa Peak

4. East Slopes
5. South Slopes
6. West Ridge
7. Vega
8. Polaris
9. Arcturus

Waterloo

Lake
Rebecca

Creek

Map 13

merald

roup

	Class 1	Standard Route		
Class 2	Alternate Route		
Class 3	Variation		
Class 4	Extra Credit		
Class 5			

1   ½   0   1 mi

1   ½   0   1 km

N

MN

13°

Magnetic
North
Declination

Contour Interval 40 feet

TRAILHEADS

Pine Creek Trailhead

This trailhead is at 8,800 feet and provides access to the east sides of Emerald and Iowa. Turn west from U.S. 24 onto Chaffee County 388 (dirt). This junction is 12.9 miles north of the stoplight in the center of Buena Vista, 6.3 miles south of the U.S. 24–Colorado 82 junction and 21.3 miles south of the West Sixth–U.S. 24 junction in the center of Leadville. Measure from the U.S. 24–Chaffee County 388 junction. Go south on Chaffee County 388 and continue straight (left) at mile 0.3. At mile 0.6, the road makes a sharp turn up the hill to the right and becomes rougher. Passenger cars should park near the sharp turn. Four-wheel-drive vehicles can go west to the road's end at mile 0.7. Respect the private property here and, via an honor system, pay a $1-per-person fee for crossing the ranchland.

Missouri Gulch Trailhead

This trailhead is at 9,640 feet and provides access to the north sides of Emerald and Iowa. Turn west from U.S. 24 onto Chaffee County 390 (gravel). This junction is 14.9 miles north of the stoplight in the center of Buena Vista, 4.3 miles south of the U.S. 24–Colorado 82 junction and 19.3 miles south of the West Sixth–U.S. 24 junction in the center of Leadville. Go 7.7 miles west on Chaffee County 390 to Vicksburg. The trailhead is on the road's south side across from Vicksburg.

Rockdale Trailhead

This trailhead is at 9,940 feet and provides access to the west sides of Emerald and Iowa. From the Missouri Gulch Trailhead, continue 2.1 miles west on Chaffee County 390 to Rockdale, which is at an unmarked turn on the road's south side. Turn south (left), go past Rockdale's four cabins and curve down to a parking area on Clear Creek's north side. Passenger cars should park here. Four-wheel-drive vehicles can ford Clear Creek and continue 2.4 miles south toward Clohesy Lake to a signed parking area at 10,800 feet. The ford of Clear Creek is difficult for both foot and vehicle traffic in high water. Vehicles have been swept downstream in June.

13. Emerald Peak   13,904 feet

See Map 13 on page 125

Emerald Peak is 1.3 miles south of the fourteener Missouri Mountain, and sits at the junction of three significant drainages. To the east is Pine Creek, which leads down to U.S. 24 and the Arkansas River. To the west is the Lake Fork of Clear Creek, which leads down to Rockdale on the

Winfield Road. To the south is North Texas Creek, which leads down to Texas Creek and Taylor Park on the western slope. Emerald's summit is 0.2 mile north of the Continental Divide. Good tidings flow in all directions from Emerald.

ROUTES

13.1 — Emerald Peak — East Slopes

From Pine Creek TH at 8,800 ft: *413 RP   24.8 mi   5,104 ft   Class 2*

This long hike is the easiest route on Emerald. The route's near-marathon length makes it suitable for a backpacking trip. For a one-day ascent, use either the North or South Slopes Route.

Start at the Pine Creek Trailhead and go 2.2 miles west up the four-wheel-drive road to 9,200 feet, where the Pine Creek Trail starts. Hike 5.0 miles west up the Pine Creek Trail to Little Johns Cabin at 10,700 feet. Continue 3.0 miles west on the trail to the junction of the Elkhead Pass Trail and the Silver King Lake Trail at 11,520 feet. Hike 0.9 mile west on the Elkhead Pass Trail to 12,100 feet, passing treeline en route. Your 11.1-mile trail approach is over.

When the trail climbs north, leave it and hike 0.4 mile west to a small lake on a lovely bench at 12,500 feet. Climb 0.5 mile west to 13,200 feet at the base of Emerald's summit massif. Get onto Emerald's small northeast ridge and climb 0.4 mile southwest up this ridge to the summit.

13.2 — Emerald Peak — North Slopes

From Missouri Gulch TH at 9,640 ft: 289 RP   12.6 mi   5,305 ft   Class 2

This route is shorter than the East Slopes Route, but you have to cross Elkhead Pass twice en route. This keeps you high for a long time, and this can be undesirable during thunderstorm season.

Start at the Missouri Gulch Trailhead and cross to Clear Creek's south side on a good bridge. Climb 1.1 miles south up a series of memorable switchbacks on the excellent Missouri Gulch Trail and enter Missouri Gulch at 10,800 feet. Cross to the creek's east side, hike 0.3 mile south on the trail and pass an old cabin just below treeline at 11,300 feet. Hike 0.6 mile south on the trail to 11,660 feet, where the Mount Belford Trail heads southeast.

Ignore the Belford Trail, cross back to the creek's west side and continue 2.1 miles south then southeast on the Missouri Gulch Trail to Elkhead Pass at 13,220 feet. From here you can see Emerald and Iowa to the southwest. Cross Elkhead Pass and descend 0.5 mile south on the trail to 12,700 feet. Your 4.6-mile trail approach is over.

Leave the trail at 12,700 feet and contour 0.7 mile southwest to a round lake at 12,717 feet. Pass the lake and climb 0.6 mile up a northeast-

Emerald Peak from the southwest.

facing slope to the broad, 13,340-foot saddle between Emerald and Iowa. Climb 0.4 mile south up a talus slope to Emerald's summit.

13.3 — Emerald Peak — South Slopes

From Rockdale TH at 9,940 ft: *271 RP*   *14.4 mi*   *3,964 ft*   *Class 2*
From 4WD parking at 10,800 ft: *202 RP*   *9.6 mi*   *2,936 ft*   *Class 2*

This scenic alternative route is also a long hike, but you can shorten your ascent by driving to 10,800 feet in a four-wheel-drive vehicle. Start at the Rockdale Trailhead and ford Clear Creek. This difficult ford relegates this route to a late summer ascent. From Clear Creek's south side, travel 2.4 miles south up the four-wheel-drive road to a parking area at 10,800 feet. Hike 0.9 mile south to Clohesy Lake at 10,968 feet. Once private, Clohesy Lake is now public land. Hike 0.2 mile southeast around the lake's northeast side, then hike 1.7 miles south on the valley trail to treeline at 11,600 feet. Hike 1.0 mile southeast on the fading trail to a 12,500-foot saddle on the Continental Divide. From here, Emerald is 1.0 mile northeast, and you can look south down to Pear Lake, whose waters are destined for the Pacific. Your 6.2-mile approach is over.

From the 12,500-foot saddle, hike 0.6 mile northeast along the Continental Divide to 13,000 feet at the base of Emerald's summit massif near some rustic mine buildings. Climb 0.2 mile northeast up a steep scree slope to 13,600 feet. This loose slope is the route's crux, and fragments of an old mining trail may help you. From 13,600 feet, climb 0.2 mile north to Emerald's summit.

Iowa Peak from the northwest.

13. Iowa Peak   13,831 feet

See Map 13 on page 125

Iowa Peak is 0.7 mile north of Emerald Peak and 0.6 mile south-southwest of the fourteener Missouri Mountain. Named by a homesick miner a century ago, Iowa stands as a symbol of something different today. Iowa is blessed by being near the fulcrum of Colorado's mountains. Iowa can help you find your balance. Climb it.

ROUTES

13.4 — Iowa Peak — East Slopes

From Pine Creek TH at 8,800 ft: *414 RP   25.2 mi   5,031 ft   Class 2*

This is the easiest route on Iowa Peak. Start at the Pine Creek Trailhead and follow Emerald's East Slopes Route to the small lake on the lovely bench at 12,500 feet. From here, climb 0.7 mile northwest into the broad, 13,340-foot saddle between Emerald and Iowa. Climb 0.4 mile north up a talus slope to Iowa's summit.

13.5 — Iowa Peak — South Slopes

From Missouri Gulch TH at 9,640 ft: 283 RP   12.6 mi   5,231 ft   Class 2

This is a shorter but higher alternative to the East Slopes Route. Start at the Missouri Gulch Trailhead and follow Emerald's North Slopes Route to the 13,340-foot saddle between Emerald and Iowa. Climb 0.4 mile north up a talus slope to Iowa's summit. Rejoice!

13.6 — Iowa Peak — West Ridge

From Rockdale TH at 9,940 ft: *276 RP*   *10.8 mi*   *3,891 ft*   *Class 2*
From 4WD parking at 10,800 ft: *211 RP*   *6.0 mi*   *3,031 ft*   *Class 2*

Best for the balanced, this is a sporting but seldom-climbed route on Iowa. Start at the Rockdale Trailhead and follow Emerald's South Slopes Route to Clohesy Lake. Hike 0.2 mile southeast around the lake's northeast side. When you can look down on the lake, climb 0.3 mile southeast on a smaller trail to treeline at 11,600 feet and continue 0.6 mile east to 12,300 feet in the basin between Iowa and Missouri. Climb 0.5 mile south to a 13,020-foot saddle on Iowa's west ridge. Climb 0.5 mile east up this rough ridge to Iowa's summit.

13. EMERALD AND IOWA COMBINATIONS

See Map 13 on page 125

13.7 — EI Combination — Vega

From Pine Creek TH at 8,800 ft: *452 RP*   *25.8 mi*   *5,595 ft*   *Class 2*

A first-magnitude climb, this is the easiest way to climb Emerald and Iowa together from the east. Start at the Pine Creek Trailhead and climb Emerald's East Slopes Route to Emerald's summit. Descend 0.4 mile north to the 13,340-foot saddle between Emerald and Iowa, then climb 0.4 mile north up a talus slope to Iowa's summit. Descend Iowa's East Slopes Route.

13.8 — EI Combination — Polaris

From Missouri Gulch TH at 9,640 ft: *324 RP*   *13.4 mi*   *5,795 ft*   *Class 2*

This is the easiest way to climb Emerald and Iowa together from the north. Start at the Missouri Gulch Trailhead and climb Emerald's North Slopes Route to Emerald's summit. Return to the 13,340-foot saddle between Emerald and Iowa, then climb 0.4 mile north up a talus slope to Iowa's summit. Descend Iowa's North Slopes Route. If it gets dark, let Polaris guide you.

13.9 — EI Combination — Arcturus *Classic*

From Rockdale TH at 9,940 ft: *327 RP*   *13.4 mi*   *4,455 ft*   *Class 2*
From 4WD parking at 10,800 ft: *228 RP*   *8.6 mi*   *3,427 ft*   *Class 2*

This is the easiest way to climb Emerald and Iowa together from the west. Start at the Rockdale Trailhead and climb Emerald's South Slopes Route to Emerald's summit. Descend 0.4 mile north to the 13,340-foot saddle between Emerald and Iowa, then climb 0.4 mile north up a talus slope to Iowa's summit. Descend Iowa's West Ridge Route. Arcturus was the zenith star for Polynesians sailing from Tahiti to Hawaii. We hope your guiding star is visible in these mountains.

14. Ice Group

North Apostle 13,860 feet
Ice Mountain 13,951 feet

See Map 14 on page 132

Ice Mountain is on the Continental Divide, 2.1 miles south of the fourteener Huron Peak and 4.9 miles south of the town of Winfield. Ice Mountain is the central and highest peak of the Three Apostles. The 13,860-foot North Apostle is 0.4 mile northeast of Ice Mountain, and the 13,568-foot West Apostle (the noncentennial thirteener of the group) is 0.6 mile west of Ice. The Three Apostles are steeper and rougher than other Sawatch peaks, and Ice Mountain is the toughest peak in this chapter. North Apostle is easier to climb than Ice, and gives you a chance to tune up before tackling Ice. Ice Mountain and North Apostle are usually climbed together, but either peak makes a fine outing by itself.

MAPS
Required: *Winfield, San Isabel National Forest*
Optional: *Tincup, Gunnison National Forest*

TRAILHEADS
South Winfield Trailhead
This trailhead is at 10,260 feet and provides access to Ice Mountain's north side and North Apostle's west side. Turn west from U.S. 24 onto Chaffee County 390 (gravel). This junction is 14.9 miles north of the stoplight in the center of Buena Vista, 4.3 miles south of the U.S. 24–Colorado 82 junction and 19.3 miles south of the West Sixth–U.S. 24 junction in the center of Leadville. Go 11.8 miles west on Chaffee County 390 to Winfield.

From the center of Winfield, turn south (left), cross to Clear Creek's south side on a good bridge and turn west (right) onto South Fork Clear Creek Road (FS 390.2B). Go 0.3 mile west on South Fork Clear Creek Road to the trailhead; there are parking spaces on both sides of the road. Four-wheel-drive vehicles can continue 2.0 miles southwest then south-southwest on South Fork Clear Creek Road to a Forest Service road closure gate at 10,600 feet.

Texas Creek Trailhead
This trailhead is at 9,760 feet and provides access to Ice Mountain's south-

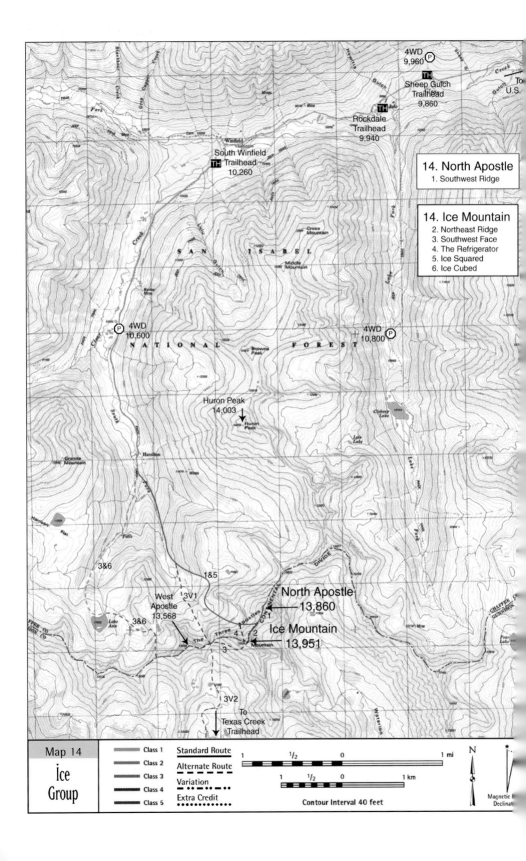

14. North Apostle
  1. Southwest Ridge

14. Ice Mountain
  2. Northeast Ridge
  3. Southwest Face
  4. The Refrigerator
  5. Ice Squared
  6. Ice Cubed

4WD
9,960

Sheep Gulch
Trailhead
9,860

To
U.S.

Rockdale
Trailhead
9,940

South Winfield
Trailhead
10,260

SAN   ISABEL

Cross
Mountain

Middle
Mountain

4WD
10,600

NATIONAL   FOREST

4WD
10,800

Browns
Peak

Clohesy
Lake

Huron Peak
14,003

Huron
Peak

Lake
Lake

Granite
Mountain

Hamilton

Lake

Mary Murphy
Flat

Falls

3&6

1&5

3V1

West
Apostle
13,568

3&6

Lake
Ann

North Apostle
13,860

The Three Apostles

4

2

Ice Mountain
13,951

3

3V2

To
Texas Creek
Trailhead

Map 14

Ice
Group

Class 1
Class 2
Class 3
Class 4
Class 5

Standard Route

Alternate Route

Variation

Extra Credit

1   1/2   0   1 mi

1   1/2   0   1 km

Contour Interval 40 feet

N

Magnetic
Declination

North Apostle from the southwest.

west side. If you are approaching from the east, go 22 miles west on Chaffee County 306 (paved) from the center of Buena Vista to Cottonwood Pass, then descend 13.9 miles west on Gunnison County 209 (dirt) to Gunnison County 742 in Taylor Park. If you are approaching from the south, go 37 miles northeast on Colorado 135 and Taylor Canyon Road (Gunnison County 742) to the Gunnison County 742–Gunnison County 209 junction on Taylor Reservoir's east side in Taylor Park. From the Gunnison County 742–Gunnison County 209 junction, go 1.2 miles north on Gunnison County 742 (now Taylor Park Road), turn east (right) onto Texas Creek Road (FS 755) and measure from this point.

Go east on Texas Creek Road, reach Texas Creek at mile 2.0, proceed east along Texas Creek's north side and reach the trailhead at mile 5.6. The unmarked trailhead is in a flat area before a steep hill, where the road becomes rougher. There are multiple versions of the road up this hill. Four-wheel-drive vehicles can continue east, pass the footbridge to Texas Lakes at mile 7.0, pass the southbound Continental Divide Trail at mile 8.1 and reach the end of the road at 9,940 feet at mile 9.0.

14. North Apostle   13,860 feet

See Map 14 on page 132

North Apostle is 0.4 mile northeast of Ice Mountain. It should really be called Northeast Apostle, but it has been called North Apostle for years. Although North Apostle has a reputation for being easy—a reputation acquired largely because of its proximity to the much harder Ice Mountain—it has steep west, north and east faces. Only the south side offers an easy ascent. Be mindful, as North Apostle has fooled many unprepared parties into trying routes other than the Southwest Ridge Route.

ROUTE

14.1 — North Apostle — Southwest Ridge

From South Winfield TH at 10,260 ft: 262 RP 11.6 mi 3,600 ft Class 2
From 4WD parking at 10,600 ft: 215 RP 7.6 mi 3,260 ft Class 2

This is the easiest way to climb North Apostle. Start at the South Winfield Trailhead and go 2.0 miles southwest then south-southwest on South Fork Clear Creek Road (FS 390.2B) to a Forest Service road closure gate at 10,600 feet. Hike 0.6 mile south on the Lake Ann Trail to the Collegiate Peaks Wilderness boundary at 10,680 feet, then continue 0.6 mile south on the trail to the Hamilton townsite and a trail junction at 10,820 feet. The Lake Ann Trail is both the Colorado Trail and the Continental Divide Trail. Pass Hamilton, cross to the west side of the South Fork of Clear Creek on the Lake Ann Trail, then leave the Lake Ann Trail and turn south (left) onto the Three Apostles Trail. Hike 0.2 mile south-southeast on the Three Apostles Trail, cross the side creek coming from Lake Ann and hike 1.0 mile south-southeast to 11,400 feet below the Three Apostles.

From 11,400 feet, hike 0.6 mile southeast to a tiny lake at 12,100 feet in the small basin between Ice Mountain's north face and North Apostle's west face. En route, skirt a cliff band on its north end. From the tiny lake, climb 0.6 mile east-southeast to the 13,460-foot saddle between Ice Mountain and North Apostle. From the saddle, climb 0.2 mile northeast up a rounded, talus-covered ridge to the summit. This perch is a great place to preview Ice's upper Northeast Ridge Route.

14. Ice Mountain   13,951 feet

See Map 14 on page 132

Steep and rough on all sides, Ice Mountain is out of character with the rest of the Sawatch peaks. In particular, Ice's north and east faces are very steep. The easiest routes on Ice require Class 3 scrambling, making Ice the toughest peak in this chapter. The center of Ice's north face holds the Refrigerator Couloir, which is the toughest mountaineering route in the Sawatch.

An unpleasant Ice Mountain reality is the peak's loose rock. Because of this, Ice Mountain is not only the most dangerous peak in this chapter, but also one of the most dangerous peaks in this book. Approach Ice with caution, wear a helmet and, if possible, pour a little ice in your veins for this one.

ROUTES

14.2 — Ice Mountain — Northeast Ridge

From South Winfield TH at 10,260 ft:	*293 RP*	*11.7 mi*	*3,731 ft*	*Class 3*
From 4WD parking at 10,600 ft:	*246 RP*	*7.7 mi*	*3,391 ft*	*Class 3*

This is the standard route on Ice Mountain. The approach to this route is straightforward, but the ridge climb to the summit is an exacting ascent on loose rock. The climb is more dangerous than it is difficult, but this ascent is not a hike. Start at the South Winfield Trailhead and follow North Apostle's Southwest Ridge Route to the 13,460-foot saddle between Ice Mountain and North Apostle. The introduction is over.

From the saddle, stay on or near the ridge crest and climb 0.1 mile southwest up Ice Mountain's northeast ridge to 13,620 feet, then descend slightly to the southwest (Class 2+). The ridge is not well defined above 13,600 feet; follow the path of least resistance as you climb a steeper stretch to 13,700 feet (Class 3). Stay on or near the ridge crest between 13,700 and 13,800 feet (Class 3). Between 13,800 feet and 13,860 feet, the ridge jumps up in a steep step that bars simple passage. To bypass this obstacle, traverse right, cross the top of a steep couloir on the ridge's west (right) side, climb around the left side of a large block (Class 3) and climb along the couloir's west (right) side and regain the ridge crest at 13,860 feet (Class 3). Even when dry, this is the route's crux. This couloir can hold snow until mid-July in a normal year, and this snow can aid or hinder your progress depending on the snow's condition and your ability to cross it. Unless you know that the route is dry, come prepared for steep snow climbing. From 13,860 feet, climb 200 feet south over easier terrain to the summit (Class 2+).

14.3 — Ice Mountain — Southwest Face

From South Winfield TH at 10,260 ft:	*413 RP*	*14.5 mi*	*4,787 ft*	*Class 3*
From 4WD parking at 10,600 ft:	*365 RP*	*10.5 mi*	*4,447 ft*	*Class 3*

This interesting alternative route on Ice Mountain is slightly easier but longer than the Northeast Ridge Route. It allows you to climb West Apostle en route. Start at the South Winfield Trailhead and follow the Northeast Ridge Route to the Hamilton townsite. Stay on the Lake Ann Trail and hike 1.8 miles south-southwest to Lake Ann at 11,509 feet.

Hike 0.2 mile east around Lake Ann's north side, then hike 0.6 mile east-southeast to a 12,380-foot saddle on a small ridge running north from the Continental Divide. From this saddle, you can look east across a small lake into the basin between Ice Mountain and North Apostle. West Apostle is 0.4 mile southeast. Climb 0.3 mile south up a rounded, rocky ridge and reach West Apostle's west ridge at 13,100 feet (Class 2+). Climb 0.25 mile east along the Continental Divide to a 13,540-foot false summit (Class 2). From the false summit, climb east on the ridge for 50 yards,

Ice Mountain from the northeast.

descend 50 feet to the south, climb east on a ledge, then climb northeast to West Apostle's 13,568-foot summit (Class 2+). West Apostle is a "Tri"— one of Colorado's 300 highest peaks. From here the view of Ice Mountain's southwest face is impressive. Study it carefully. The introduction is over.

From West Apostle, descend 50 yards south then 100 yards east on a ledge to a small rib. Scamper 0.2 mile east down a steep face to the 13,060-foot saddle between West Apostle and Ice Mountain (Class 2+). The climb from this saddle to the summit requires careful routefinding on loose rock. The climbing is mostly Class 2+ interspersed with occasional Class 3 sections.

From the saddle, climb the initial headwall (Class 3). Do an ascending traverse southeast across the lower southwest face (Class 2+). Cross a rib at two-thirds height and climb southeast (right) below the steep cliffs of Ice's dramatic 13,900-foot western false summit. Do not get too high during this long ascending traverse to the southeast. Get into a large scree gully descending from the summit ridge between Ice's 13,900-foot western false summit and the main summit. This gully is the main feature in the middle of Ice's southwest face. Climb up the gully and, when it splits, take its southeastern (right) branch. Climb up the gully's talus and small rock headwalls directly to the summit.

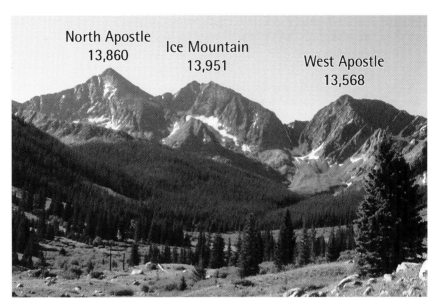

North Apostle
13,860

Ice Mountain
13,951

West Apostle
13,568

The Three Apostles from the northwest.

VARIATIONS

14.3V1 — Apostle Couloir

From South Winfield TH at 10,260 ft: 355 RP 11.4 mi 3,691 ft Class 3 Mod Snow
From 4WD parking at 10,600 ft: 307 RP   7.4 mi 3,351 ft Class 3 Mod Snow

This nice mixed climb avoids the climb over West Apostle. Follow the Northeast Ridge Route to 11,400 feet. Climb 0.6 mile south-southeast along a rock glacier's west side to 12,400 feet. Climb 0.2 mile south-southeast up a steepening but moderate snow couloir to the 13,060-foot saddle between West Apostle and Ice Mountain. This couloir is the easternmost (left) of several choices, and it normally holds snow into August. Join the Southwest Face Route in the saddle and follow it to the summit.

14.3V2 — Prospector Gulch

From Texas Creek TH at 9,760 ft: 407 RP 15.4 mi 4,191 ft   Class 3
From 4WD parking at 9,940 ft: 334 RP   8.6 mi 4,011 ft   Class 3

You can approach the Southwest Face Route from Prospector Gulch south of the peak. Start at the Texas Creek Trailhead and go 3.4 miles east on the continuing Texas Creek Road to the end of the road at 9,940 feet. Hike 0.6 mile west up the hill on the Continental Divide Trail (Timberline Trail) to 10,400 feet. Hike 0.3 mile north and reach Prospector Creek at 10,560 feet. The Trails Illustrated Map number 129 shows a trail going north from this point along Prospector Creek's east side. Only occasional remnants of this trail remain, and it is badly overgrown. It is not worth finding. Cross to Prospector Creek's west side, climb 60 yards southwest out of the creek drainage and hike 0.8 mile north-northwest on the Continental Divide Trail to a meadow at 10,960 feet. There is an unused signpost in this meadow.

Leave the trail at 10,960 feet before it starts climbing the hill west of the creek. Hike 0.8 mile north through open trees on either side of the creek to a higher meadow at 11,400 feet, where you can see Ice Mountain to the north. Hike 0.2 mile northwest then 0.7 mile north to a tiny lake at 12,220 feet. Study the southwest face of Ice as you approach up this pristine valley. From the lake at 12,220 feet, climb 0.4 mile north up steep grass to the 13,060-foot Ice–West Apostle saddle. Join the Southwest Face Route here and follow it to the summit.

14.4 – Ice Mountain – The Refrigerator *Classic*

From South Winfield TH at 10,260 ft:	*293 RP*	*10.2 mi*	*3,691 ft*	*Class 3*	*Steep Snow*
With descent of Northeast Ridge:	*246 RP*	*10.95 mi*	*3,711 ft*	*Class 3*	*Steep Snow*
From 4WD parking at 10,600 ft:	*348 RP*	*6.2 mi*	*3,351 ft*	*Class 3*	*Steep Snow*
With descent of Northeast Ridge:	*363 RP*	*6.95 mi*	*3,371 ft*	*Class 3*	*Steep Snow*

This is the premier mountaineering route on Ice Mountain, and one of the premier mountaineering routes in the Sawatch Range. The Refrigerator Couloir splits Ice Mountain's north face and rises directly toward the summit. In spite of its classic appearance and direct finish, this couloir quietly offers a dangerous ascent. Gerry almost died here in 1974 when a barrage of large rocks careened down the couloir, missing him and his party by 3 feet. Sharpen your tools, climb fast and don't climb under other people.

Start at the South Winfield Trailhead and follow the Northeast Ridge Route to 13,000 feet. The Refrigerator will be above you to the south. Climb south to the beginning of the couloir at 13,200 feet. The couloir is steep from the outset. Climb south up the couloir to 13,500 feet, where the couloir narrows, splits and steepens. The couloir's east (left) branch is the couloir you must cross near the top of the Northeast Ridge Route. This branch is not the Refrigerator. Climb the couloir's west (right) branch through a narrow, steep section to 13,600 feet. This is the steepest part of the route and the first to melt. Once past this neck, climb straight up the Refrigerator to the summit ridge at 13,900 feet. Scamper 100 feet east to the summit. Ascending the Refrigerator and descending the Northeast Ridge Route makes a smart Tour de Ice.

14. NORTH APOSTLE AND ICE COMBINATIONS
See Map 14 on page 132

14.5 – NI Combination – Ice Squared

From South Winfield TH at 10,260 ft:	*317 RP*	*12.1 mi*	*4,131 ft*	*Class 3*
From 4WD parking at 10,600 ft:	*269 RP*	*8.1 mi*	*3,791 ft*	*Class 3*

This is the standard way of climbing North Apostle and Ice Mountain together. Climbing North Apostle first gives you a good opportunity to preview the route on Ice Mountain. Start at the South Winfield Trailhead and climb North Apostle's Southwest Ridge Route. Return to the 13,460-foot saddle between Ice and North Apostle, then climb the upper part of Ice's Northeast Ridge Route. Descend Ice's Northeast Ridge Route.

14.6 — NI Combination — Ice Cubed *Classic*

From South Winfield TH at 10,260 ft:	368 RP	13.5 mi	4,659 ft	Class 3
From 4WD parking at 10,600 ft:	320 RP	9.5 mi	4,319 ft	Class 3

This is the complete traverse of the Three Apostles. The traverse works well in either direction, but is slightly easier to do from east to west because you ascend the most difficult terrain and end on the lowest peak. It is described here from east to west. Start at the South Winfield Trailhead and follow the Ice Squared Combination to Ice Mountain's summit. Descend Ice Mountain's Southwest Face Route, then thaw the ice in your veins.

15. "North Carbonate" 13,870 feet

See Map 15 on page 140

Lost in a sea of Sawatch peaks, "North Carbonate" is 2.4 miles southwest of the fourteener Mount Antero, 2.7 miles northwest of the fourteener Tabeguache Peak and 2.0 miles north of 13,663-foot Carbonate Mountain, from which it gets its nickname. Rounded and easy to climb, "North Carbonate" provides a great throne for viewing the sea of peaks.

MAPS

Required: *St. Elmo, Mount Antero, San Isabel National Forest*
Optional: *Garfield, Maysville*

TRAILHEADS

Baldwin Creek Trailhead

This trailhead is at 9,420 feet and provides access to the north and east sides of "North Carbonate." If you are approaching from the north, go 5.6 miles south on U.S. 285 from the U.S. 24–U.S. 285 junction just west of Johnsons Village, near Buena Vista. If you are approaching from the south, go 15.4 miles north on U.S. 285 from the northern U.S. 50–U.S. 285 junction in Poncha Springs. Leave U.S. 285 and go 9.6 miles west on Chaffee County 162 (paved) to the Cascade Campground. Continue 2.0 miles west on Chaffee County 162 to the Baldwin Creek Road (dirt), which is on the south side of Chaffee County 162. Park at the bottom of the Baldwin Creek Road. This is the trailhead. Four-wheel-drive vehicles can continue 3.0 miles southeast then south up the Baldwin Creek Road to a road junction at 10,840 feet. This is a good place to park four-wheel-drive vehicles.

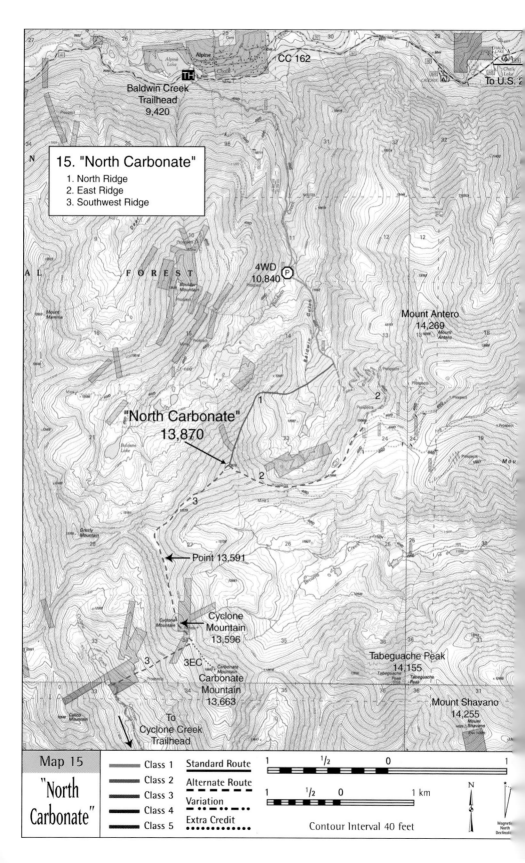

15. "North Carbonate"
1. North Ridge
2. East Ridge
3. Southwest Ridge

Baldwin Creek
Trailhead
9,420

CC 162

TH

To U.S.

4WD
10,840

P

Mount Antero
14,269

"North Carbonate"
13,870

1

2

3

Point 13,591

Cyclone
Mountain
13,596

3

3EC

Carbonate
Mountain
13,663

Tabeguache Peak
14,155

Mount Shavano
14,255

To
Cyclone Creek
Trailhead

Map 15			
"North Carbonate"	Class 1	Standard Route	
	Class 2	Alternate Route	
	Class 3	Variation	
	Class 4	Extra Credit	
	Class 5		

Contour Interval 40 feet

Magnetic
North
Declination

N

Cyclone Creek Trailhead

This trailhead is at 10,740 feet and provides access to the south side of "North Carbonate." Go 6.1 miles west on U.S. 50 from the northern U.S. 50–U.S. 285 junction in Poncha Springs. Turn north onto Chaffee County 240 and measure from this point. Go west-northwest on Chaffee County 240, pass the Angel of Shavano Campground at mile 3.8, pass the Jennings Creek Trailhead at mile 7.6 and reach the Cyclone Creek Trailhead at mile 8.2. The road is rough beyond the Angel of Shavano Campground, but is passable for tough passenger cars. Park near the old townsite of Shavano on Cyclone Creek's east side.

ROUTES

15.1 — "North Carbonate" — North Ridge

From Baldwin Creek TH at 9,420 ft:	*283 RP*	*12.0 mi*	*4,450 ft*	*Class 2*
From 4WD parking at 10,840 ft:	*195 RP*	*6.0 mi*	*3,030 ft*	*Class 2*

This direct ascent is the most popular route up "North Carbonate." Start at the Baldwin Creek Trailhead and go 3.0 miles southeast then south up the Baldwin Creek Road to a road junction at 10,840 feet. From here you can see "North Carbonate" to the south. Turn east (left) and go 1.3 miles south-southeast on the upper Baldwin Creek Road to 11,720 feet, where the road first reaches treeline. Leave the road here and contour 0.3 mile southwest through the trees to Baldwin Creek. Cross to Baldwin Creek's west side and hike 0.5 mile west up steep grass slopes to reach the north-northeast ridge of "North Carbonate" at 12,600 feet. Climb 0.9 mile south-southwest up this well-defined ridge to the summit and enjoy the views.

15.2 — "North Carbonate" — East Ridge

From Baldwin Creek TH at 9,420 ft:	*327 RP*	*16.8 mi*	*4,968 ft*	*Class 2*
With descent of North Ridge:	*292 RP*	*14.4 mi*	*4,719 ft*	*Class 2*
From 4WD parking at 10,840 ft:	*239 RP*	*10.8 mi*	*3,548 ft*	*Class 2*
With descent of North Ridge:	*204 RP*	*8.4 mi*	*3,299 ft*	*Class 2*

This route is longer but easier than the North Ridge Route. Start at the Baldwin Creek Trailhead and follow the North Ridge Route to 11,720 feet. Stay on the Baldwin Creek Road and follow it 2.3 miles southeast to 13,089 feet on Mount Antero's southwest ridge. Leave the road here and hike 0.5 mile southwest down a gentle ridge to a point near an improbable small lake. Continue 0.5 mile west-southwest down the gentle ridge to the 12,820-foot saddle between Mount Antero and "North Carbonate." This saddle is at the top of Baldwin Gulch. From the saddle, hike 0.8 mile west up talus on the east ridge of "North Carbonate" to the summit. Ascending this route and descending the North Ridge Route makes a nice Tour de "North Carbonate."

15.3 — "North Carbonate" — Southwest Ridge

From Cyclone Creek TH at 10,740 ft: 308 RP   10.0 mi   4,110 ft   Class 2

This alternative route avoids the Mount Antero–bound crowds in Baldwin Gulch and allows you to climb a bonus peak en route. Start at the Cyclone Creek Trailhead on Cyclone Creek's east side and hike 0.9 mile north-northwest to 11,180 feet. Cross to Cyclone Creek's west side and hike 0.9 mile north-northwest to a small pond at 11,440 feet. From the pond, hike 0.1 mile north, leave the trail and cross back to Cyclone Creek's east side at 11,480 feet.

From 11,480 feet, hike 0.5 mile northeast to 12,200 feet at the bottom of a talus-filled gully between 13,663-foot Carbonate Mountain and 13,596-foot Cyclone Mountain. Climb 0.5 mile northeast up this gully to the 13,260-foot saddle between Carbonate and Cyclone. From the saddle, climb 0.2 mile northwest up gentle slopes to Cyclone's summit. Cyclone, your bonus peak, is a "Bi"—one of Colorado's 200 highest peaks. From here you can see "North Carbonate" 1.6 miles to the north-northeast.

From Cyclone, hike 0.9 mile north-northwest along the gentle ridge over Point 13,591. Descend 0.3 mile northeast to a 13,229-foot saddle and climb 0.7 mile northeast to the summit of "North Carbonate." From here you have a great view of the fourteener Mount Antero.

15.3EC — Extra Credit — Carbonate Mountain, 13,663 feet, Class 2
From the 13,260-foot saddle between Carbonate and Cyclone, climb 0.4 mile southeast to the 13,663-foot summit of Carbonate Mountain, another "Bi."

16. Mount Ouray   13,971 feet
See Map 16 on page 144

Mount Ouray is the southernmost centennial thirteener in the Sawatch Range. It is 8 miles southeast of Monarch Pass on U.S. 50, and you can see it 14.0 miles southwest of Salida. Named after the great Ute Indian chief, Mount Ouray stands gentle and alone.

Mount Ouray saw more climbers a hundred years ago, when railroad trains huffed over Marshall Pass, than it sees on today's busiest summer weekend. They didn't love the mountain to death, and neither should we. There is room for everybody through the ages; all we have to do is leave no trace.

MAPS
Required: *Mount Ouray, San Isabel National Forest*
Optional: *Pahlone Peak*

TRAILHEADS

Grays Creek Trailhead
This trailhead is at 9,660 feet on the Marshall Pass Road and provides access to Ouray's east side. If you are approaching from the north, go 5.3 miles south on U.S. 285 from the southern U.S. 50–U.S. 285 junction in Poncha Springs. If you are approaching from the south, go 2.3 miles north on U.S. 285 from the summit of Poncha Pass. Turn southwest onto the Marshall Pass Road (FS 200) and measure from this point. Go southwest on the Marshall Pass Road, turn west (right) at mile 2.4 onto FS 202, turn north (right) at a four-way junction at mile 3.2 back onto FS 200 and reach the Grays Creek Trailhead at mile 7.4. Park in a small parking area on the road's north side, on the north side of Grays Creek.

Marshall Pass Trailhead
This trailhead is at 10,820 feet and provides access to Ouray's south and west sides. You can reach Marshall Pass from the east or the west.

If you are approaching from the east, go southwest from the Grays Creek Trailhead at mile 7.4, cross Tent Creek at mile 10.8 and reach the Marshall Pass Trailhead at mile 14.3.

If you are approaching from the west, go to the small community of Sargents on U.S. 50. Sargents is 10.7 miles west of Monarch Pass and 32.1 miles east of Gunnison. Turn south onto the Marshall Pass Road and go 16.6 miles east to Marshall Pass. Cross the pass and go 0.2 mile northeast to the trailhead.

The marked trailhead is on the road's east side 0.2 mile northeast of Marshall Pass. Four-wheel-drive vehicles can ascend FS 243.G, which starts on the north side of the Marshall Pass Road just across from the trailhead. This is both the Colorado Trail and the Continental Divide Trail. Switchback twice, then climb 1.4 miles northwest then north on the west side of the Continental Divide to an old mine and the end of the road at 11,400 feet.

Little Cochetopa Trailhead
This trailhead is at 8,940 feet and provides access to Ouray's northeast side and the Little Cochetopa Trail. Go 2.0 miles west on U.S. 50 from the northern U.S. 50–U.S. 285 junction in Poncha Springs. Turn south onto Chaffee County 210 and measure from this point. Go south on Chaffee County 210, go straight (left) at mile 1.3, go straight (left) at mile 2.3, turn uphill to the right at mile 4.1 and go around a ranch. Reach the trailhead at mile 4.8 just after you enter the Little Cochetopa Creek State Wildlife Management Area.

Four-wheel-drive vehicles can go 3.1 miles farther. From the two-wheel-drive trailhead, continue southwest on Chaffee County 210. Leave the State Wildlife Management Area and enter San Isabel National Forest at mile 5.5, where Chaffee County 210 changes to FS 210.3. Continue west on the increasingly rough road and reach the end of the road at 10,320 feet at mile 7.9. The Little Cochetopa Trail starts here.

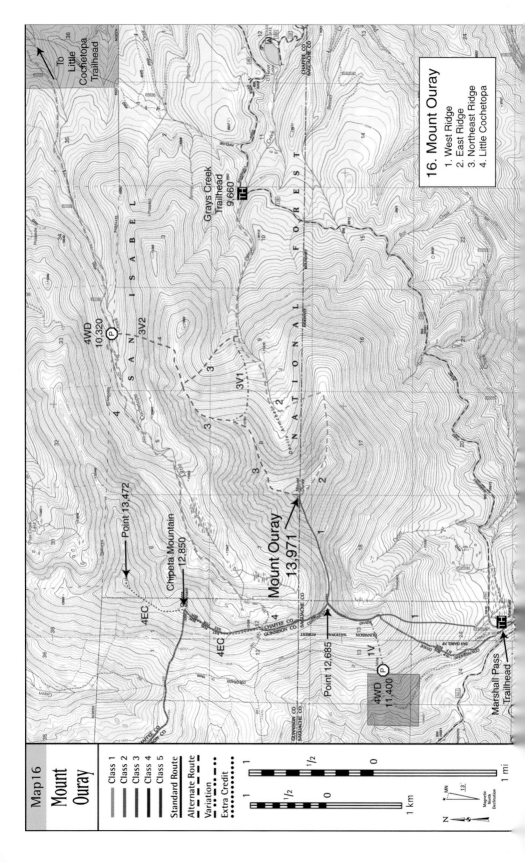

Map 16
Mount Ouray

Class 1
Class 2
Class 3
Class 4
Class 5

Standard Route
Alternate Route
Variation
Extra Credit

16. Mount Ouray
1. West Ridge
2. East Ridge
3. Northeast Ridge
4. Little Cochetopa

To Little Cochetopa Trailhead

SAN ISABEL

NATIONAL FOREST

Grays Creek Trailhead 9,660

4WD 10,320

3V2

3V1

3

3

4

2

2

Point 13,472

Chipeta Mountain 12,850

4EC

4EC

Mount Ouray 13,971

1

1

Point 12,685

1V

4WD 11,400

Marshall Pass Trailhead

CHAFFEE CO
GUNNISON CO
SAGUACHE CO

1 mi
1 km

N

Magnetic North Declination 13°

ROUTES

16.1 — Mount Ouray — West Ridge

From Marshall Pass TH at 10,820 ft: 249 RP   6.4 mi   3,241 ft   Class 2

This is the standard route on Mount Ouray. When the old railroad trains stopped on Marshall Pass, many tourists hiked up this route to savor Mount Ouray and the Colorado high country. The trains are gone, but it's still a worthy hike.

Start at the Marshall Pass Trailhead and go 0.1 mile east on the Marshall Pass Road to a dirt road heading north. This is not the four-wheel-drive road for the Colorado Trail but the next road to the east. Go 0.2 mile north then northwest on this road to the Hutchinson-Barnett cabin at 10,880 feet. This cabin is maintained and open for public use on an honor system. Please respect this historic building. From here you can see Ouray's mighty mass to the northeast.

From the cabin, hike 0.8 mile north through open trees to treeline at 11,800 feet. Continue 0.2 mile north up a slope and reach the Continental Divide at 12,200 feet. From here you can see the rest of the route along the ridge around the top of Ouray Creek. Go 0.7 mile north along the ridge of the Continental Divide to Point 12,685 and a grand view.

From Point 12,685, turn east, leave the Continental Divide, descend gently and hike 0.4 mile east along the ridge between Ouray Creek to the south and Little Cochetopa Creek to the north. You can no longer avoid Ouray's mighty mass. Climb 1,300 feet up Ouray's well-defined west ridge to the summit. On top, you can rediscover the mighty view that lured people here a hundred years ago.

16.1V — Variation

From 4WD parking at 11,400 ft: 204 RP   5.0 mi   2,601 ft   Class 2

If desired, you can shorten this already modest ascent. This is the short-est route on Mount Ouray. Start at the four-wheel-drive parking place, 1.4 miles northwest of the Marshall Pass Trailhead. From the south side of the mine at the end of the road, climb 0.3 mile east up a steep trail to reach treeline at 11,800 feet. Continue climbing 0.3 mile east up a slope and reach the Continental Divide at 12,200 feet. Join the West Ridge Route here and follow it to the summit.

16.2 — Mount Ouray — East Ridge *Classic*

From Grays Creek TH at 9,660 ft: 171 RP   8.4 mi   4,311 ft   Class 1+

This route is longer than the West Ridge Route, but it is easy and interest-ing. It gives you a chance to see Ouray's eastern cirque and sit in the Devils Armchair. Start at the Grays Creek Trailhead and find a small trail along Grays Creek's north side. This unmarked trail disappears west into the bushes from the west side of the trailhead's parking area. The trail is initially obscure, but gets better as you climb higher. Go 1.0 mile west on this trail to a side stream at 10,280 feet. The trail is good to this point. Cross the side stream and continue 0.5 mile west on the trail along Grays Creek's north side to 10,900 feet. Stick with the fading trail as it turns south (left) toward the creek. Go 0.4 mile up a small gorge that crosses the now smaller Grays Creek en route. The trail disappears near the top of this gorge.

At 11,400 feet, the gorge reaches open slopes graced with one of Colorado's finest bristlecone pine forests. Hike 0.6 mile west through this enchanted forest into the Devils Armchair at 11,840 feet. You can sit here for a while and ponder events below and Ouray's impressive eastern cirque above. When you are ready, climb 0.5 mile south up a mostly grassy slope to reach Ouray's east ridge in a flat stretch at 12,540 feet (Class 1+). Climb 1.2 miles west then northwest up Ouray's broad east ridge to the summit. There is an old trail on this ridge that is worth finding and following, as it keeps the difficulty at Class 1.

16.3 — Mount Ouray — Northeast Ridge

From Grays Creek TH at 9,660 ft:	292 RP	8.7 mi	4,311 ft	Class 2
With descent of East Ridge:	261 RP	8.55 mi	4,311 ft	Class 2

Wilder, tougher and more obscure than the East Ridge Route, this route gives you many opportunities to peer into Ouray's eastern cirque from a safe vantage. Start at the Grays Creek Trailhead and follow the East Ridge Route for 1.5 miles to 10,900 feet. Turn north (right), leave Grays Creek and bushwhack 0.25 mile north into the small drainage north of Grays Creek. Go 0.6 mile northwest up this drainage to an 11,740-foot saddle on Ouray's northeast ridge. From here you can look north down into Little Cochetopa Creek.

Climb 0.8 mile southwest then south up the gentle ridge to Point 12,761. From here you can look southeast across Ouray's eastern cirque and down into the Devils Armchair. Climb 0.8 mile west up the now rougher ridge to 13,400 feet. Midway on this stretch, you can bypass a rough stretch by staying on the ridge's north side. From 13,400 feet, climb 0.4 mile south to Ouray's summit. Ascending the Northeast Ridge Route and descending the East Ridge Route makes a perfect Tour de Ouray.

Variations

16.3V1

From Grays Creek TH at 9,660 ft:	261 RP	7.2 mi	4,311 ft	Class 2
With descent of East Ridge:	246 RP	7.8 mi	4,311 ft	Class 2

This variation shortens your ascent considerably. Follow the Northeast Ridge Route for 1.5 miles to 10,900 feet. Turn north (right), leave Grays Creek and bushwhack 0.1 mile north to the small ridge separating Grays

Creek and the unnamed creek north of Grays Creek. Turn west (left) and hike 0.4 mile up the ridge through several unique stands of bristlecone pines to treeline. Climb 0.7 mile up the steepening slope above toward Point 12,761. Near the top of the slope, angle north (right) to rejoin the Northeast Ridge Route just below Point 12,761.

16.3V2

From Little Cochetopa TH at 8,940 ft: 358 RP   12.2 mi   5,071 ft   Class 2
From 4WD parking at 10,320 ft: 268 RP   6.0 mi   3,691 ft   Class 2

You can approach Ouray's northeast ridge from Little Cochetopa Creek. From the Little Cochetopa Trailhead, go southwest on Chaffee County 210 through the Little Cochetopa Creek State Wildlife Management Area. Enter San Isabel National Forest after 0.7 mile and continue west on FS 210.3 to the end of the road after 3.1 miles.

From the end of the road at 10,320 feet, descend south, cross Little Cochetopa Creek and bushwhack 0.8 mile south then southwest up a forested slope to the 11,740-foot saddle just west of Point 11,900. Go 0.2 mile west and join the Northeast Ridge Route in a second 11,740-foot saddle.

16.4 — Mount Ouray — Little Cochetopa

From Little Cochetopa TH at 8,940 ft: 352 RP   17.4 mi   5,121 ft   Class 2
With descent of Variation 16.3V2:   336 RP   14.8 mi   5,096 ft   Class 2
From 4WD parking at 10,320 ft: 262 RP   11.2 mi   3,741 ft   Class 2
With descent of Variation 16.3V2:   245 RP   8.6 mi   3,716 ft   Class 2

This long, little-used route on Ouray allows you to see Little Cochetopa Creek and gives you a good opportunity to climb two other peaks. From the Little Cochetopa Trailhead, go southwest on Chaffee County 210 through the Little Cochetopa Creek State Wildlife Management Area. Enter San Isabel National Forest after 0.7 mile and continue west on FS 210.3 to the end of the road after 3.1 miles.

From the end of the road at 10,320 feet, hike 3.7 miles west on the Little Cochetopa Trail to a 12,300-foot saddle on the Continental Divide. Climb 0.7 mile south on the Continental Divide to Point 12,685, then join the West Ridge Route and follow it 1.2 miles east to Ouray's summit. Ascending this route and descending Variation 16.3V2 makes a northern Tour de Ouray.

16.4EC — Extra Credit — Chipeta Mountain, 12,850 feet, Class 2
Point 13,472, Class 2

From the 12,300-foot saddle, climb 0.7 mile north along the Continental Divide to 12,850-foot Chipeta Mountain. For even more credit, continue 0.8 mile north to Point 13,472, a ranked thirteener.

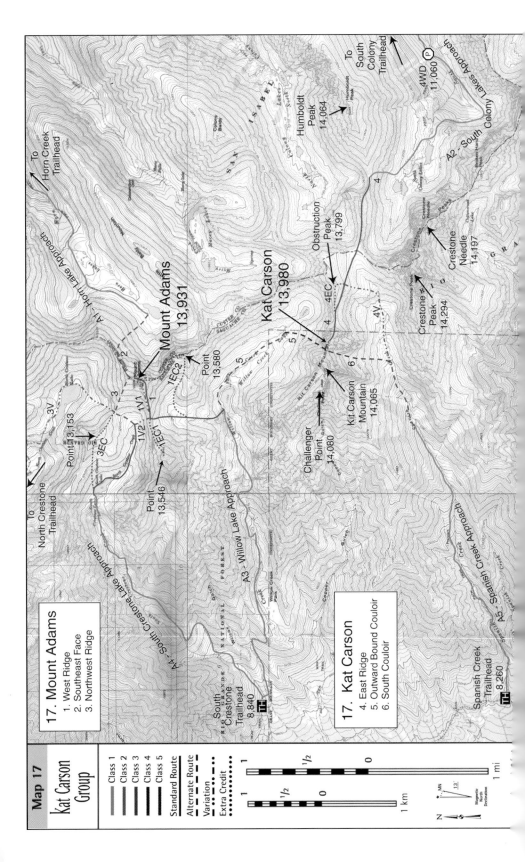

Map 17

Kat Carson
Group

Class 1 ▬▬▬▬
Class 2 ▬▬▬▬
Class 3 ▬▬▬▬
Class 4 ▬▬▬▬
Class 5 ▬▬▬▬

Standard Route ▬ ▬ ▬
Alternate Route ▬▪▬▪▬
Variation ▪▪▪▪▪
Extra Credit ▪▪▪▪▪

1 ___ ½ ___ 0 ___ 1 mi
1 ___ ½ ___ 0 ___ 1 km

N — MN
13°
Magnetic Declination

17. Mount Adams
13,931

1. West Ridge
2. Southeast Face
3. Northwest Ridge

17. Kat Carson
13,980

4. East Ridge
5. Outward Bound Couloir
6. South Couloir

To Horn Creek Trailhead
A1 - Horn Lake Approach
To North Crestone Trailhead

Point 13,153
3V
3EC
Point 13,546
1EC1
1V2 1V1
1 2
3
1EC2
Point 13,580

Mount Adams
13,931

A4 - South Crestone Lake Approach
A3 - Willow Lake Approach

Willow Creek
Willow Creek Park

NATIONAL FOREST
RIO GRANDE

South Crestone Trailhead
8,840

Kat Carson
13,980

5
5
5
4EC
Obstruction Peak
13,799
4
4
4V
Kit Carson Mountain
14,065
6
Challenger Point
14,080

Crestone Peak
14,294
Crestone Needle
14,197
Crestone Peaks

Humboldt Peak
14,064
Isabel Lake
Colony Baldy
South Colony Lakes

4WD P 11,060
To South Colony Trailhead
A2 - South Colony Lakes Approach

Spanish Creek Trailhead
8,260
A5 - Spanish Creek Approach

CHAPTER FOUR

Sangre de Cristo Range

Introduction

Sangre de Cristo means "blood of Christ" in Spanish, and the name suits this ancient place. The Sangre de Cristo Range is a long, linear range that starts where the Sawatch Range ends. The Sangres start south of Salida and run 220 miles south to Santa Fe, New Mexico. The Sangre de Cristo Range is longer than any other Colorado range. Indeed, Colorado cannot contain it!

The Wet Mountain Valley and Huerfano Park lie to the east of the northern part of the range. The large, flat San Luis Valley lies west of the range. The winds scouring this valley cannot carry their burden over the Sangres, and have left behind 700-foot-high sand dunes. The range averages only 10 to 20 miles in width, and the high peaks rise abruptly with few foothills. Approaching the Sangres is always an awesome, neck-bending experience.

The Sangres contain 10 fourteeners and five centennial thirteeners in Colorado, and all of the thirteeners in New Mexico. The fourteeners are clustered in three groups—the Crestones, the Blanca Group and the solitary Culebra Peak. Like satellites, the centennial thirteeners are close to these fourteeners. Although many of the Sangres' fourteeners are tough climbs, the Sangres' centennial thirteeners are easy to climb, and they provide some stunning views.

17. Kat Carson Group

Mount Adams   13,931 feet
"Kat Carson"   13,980 feet

See Map 17 on page 148

These peaks are the northernmost centennial thirteeners in the Sangre de Cristo Range. They are 12 miles southwest of Westcliffe in the Wet Mountain Valley and are close to the famous fourteeners, the Crestones.

The geology of the northern Sangres is different from that of other Colorado ranges, and the conglomerate rock here will come as a pleasant surprise. The rock is full of embedded knobs, and tiptoeing on these knobs can be an exciting experience. The standard routes on Mount Adams and "Kat Carson" are not technical, however, and do not require much, if any, tiptoeing.

MAPS

Required: *Crestone Peak, Horn Peak, San Isabel National Forest*
Optional: *Crestone, Rito Alto Peak, Rio Grande National Forest*

TRAILHEADS

Horn Creek Trailhead

This trailhead is on the range's east side at 9,120 feet and provides access to Mount Adams' east side. Measure from the junction of Colorado 96 and Colorado 69 in Westcliffe. Go south on Colorado 69 and turn west (right) onto Hermit Road (Custer County 160) at mile 0.4. Go west on Hermit Road and turn south (left) onto Macy Lane (Custer County 129) at mile 1.6. Go south on Macy Lane, go straight across Schoolfield Road (Custer County 140) at mile 4.7 and turn west (right) onto Horn Road (Custer County 130) at mile 6.7. Go west on Horn Road, turn south (left) at mile 10.2 and reach the signed trailhead at mile 10.6. The Horn Creek Trail goes west from the trailhead.

Four-wheel-drive vehicles can continue south for an additional 0.2 mile, but this will not improve your starting position. This trailhead is often accessible in winter.

South Colony Trailhead

This trailhead is on the range's east side at 8,780 feet and provides access to the east side of "Kat Carson." Measure from the junction of Colorado 96 and Colorado 69 in Westcliffe. Go south on Colorado 69 and turn south (right) onto Colfax Lane (Custer County 119) at mile 4.4. Go south on Colfax Lane to a T-junction and turn west (right) onto South Colony Road (Custer County 120) at mile 10.0. Go west on South Colony Road and park passenger cars on the road's north side at mile 11.5. This is the trailhead, as the road becomes a lot rougher beyond this point. This trailhead is often accessible in winter.

Four-wheel-drive vehicles can continue west for an additional 5.2 miles to 11,060 feet in the South Colony Creek Drainage. This road is one of Colorado's worst, and it becomes a little rougher every year.

South Crestone Trailhead

This trailhead is on the range's west side at 8,840 feet and provides access to the north side of "Kat Carson" and the west side of Adams. If you are approaching from the north, go 13.8 miles south on Colorado 17 from the Colorado 17–U.S. 285 junction. If you are approaching from the south, go 16.8 miles north on Colorado 17 from the Colorado 17–Colorado 112 junction in Hooper. At a point 0.5 mile south of the center of Moffat, turn east onto Saguache County Road T (paved) and go 12.5 miles east to the town of Crestone. The Crestones and Kit Carson loom higher and higher as you approach them.

Measuring from the Galena Avenue–Alder Street junction in the center of Crestone, go east on Galena Avenue, enter the Rio Grande National Forest at mile 1.1 and reach the signed trailhead at mile 2.3. The road to this popular trailhead has been improved in recent years.

North Crestone Trailhead
This trailhead is on the range's west side at 8,600 feet and provides access to Adams' northwest side. Follow the directions for the South Crestone Trailhead to the center of Crestone and measure from the Galena Avenue–Alder Street junction. Go north on Alder Street, turn northeast, cross a cattle guard and enter the Rio Grande National Forest at mile 1.2. Go northeast on FS 950, pass the North Crestone Campground's campsites and reach the signed trailhead at mile 2.1.

Spanish Creek Trailhead
This trailhead is on the range's west side at 8,260 feet and provides access to the south side of "Kat Carson." This trailhead is on private property. Please protect the permission that allows you to use it. If you are approaching from the north, go 13.8 miles south on Colorado 17 from the Colorado 17–U.S. 285 junction. If you are approaching from the south, go 16.8 miles north on Colorado 17 from the Colorado 17–Colorado 112 junction in Hooper. At a point 0.5 mile south of the center of Moffat, turn east onto Saguache County Road T (paved) and go 11.8 miles east to the entrance of the Baca Grande Chalets Grants.

Turn south (right) and measure from this point. Follow Camino Baca Grande (paved) through the subdivision, cross Crestone Creek at mile 0.8 and cross Willow Creek at mile 2.2. Continue south on a dirt road to reach Spanish Creek and the trailhead at mile 3.5. The road's crossing of Spanish creek is unsigned, so look for the creek. If possible, arrange to be dropped off at this trailhead so you can avoid parking your car on private property. If you can obtain permission, you may be able to park at the nearby ashram. The unmarked Spanish Creek Trail starts 50 yards north of the creek.

APPROACHES
17.A1 — Horn Lake Approach
From Horn Creek TH at 9,120 ft: 112 RP   10.0 mi   2,700 ft   Class 1

This approach takes you to Horn Lake, from which you can climb Adams' east side. Start at the Horn Creek Trailhead. Hike 0.3 mile southwest on the Horn Lake Trail, cross the Rainbow Trail and continue 4.7 miles southwest up Horn Creek to Horn Lake at 11,820 feet. Horses have made heavy use of the Horn Lake Trail in recent years. Mount Adams is 0.7 mile west of Horn Lake, and there are many good camping spots in this basin.

Spirit of the Sangres.

17.A2 — South Colony Lakes Approach

From South Colony TH at 8,780 ft:	*134 RP*	*13.2 mi*	*2,920 ft*	*Class 1*
From 4WD parking at 11,060 ft:	*28 RP*	*2.8 mi*	*600 ft*	*Class 1*

This is the standard approach to the South Colony Lakes and the Crestones. You can also reach "Kat Carson" from here. Measure from the South Colony Trailhead. Follow the rough four-wheel-drive road west to the boundary of San Isabel National Forest at mile 1.4. Camping is not permitted between the trailhead and the forest boundary. Continue southwest up the road, pass the Rainbow Trail at mile 2.2 and cross to South Colony Creek's north side at mile 2.7. The road becomes rougher beyond this crossing. Continue southwest up the road to 11,060 feet and a parking area at mile 5.2. The parking area is 100 yards before the road crosses back to the creek's south side.

The approach continues on the road as it crosses back to South Colony Creek's south side. There is a sturdy, double-log footbridge at this crossing. There is a second parking area 100 yards beyond this crossing, and the road is gated at this point. Continue 0.7 mile southwest on the old road. Here, there are good views of the fourteener Humboldt Peak, and the east face of Broken Hand Peak towers over you to the west. Turn north, pass the end of the road and continue on a good trail for 0.7 mile to 11,660 feet at the outlet stream below Lower South Colony Lake at mile 6.6. Although there is good camping near the lake, this is an overused area. Please leave no trace of your passage.

17.A3 — Willow Lake Approach

From South Crestone TH at 8,840 ft: 90 RP   7.4 mi   2,804 ft   Class 1

This beautiful hike takes you to Willow Lake, from which you can climb both Mount Adams and "Kat Carson." Start at the South Crestone Trailhead, go 100 yards east, turn south (right) and cross South Crestone Creek. Follow the excellent Willow Creek Trail as it climbs east then south to a ridge before descending east into the Willow Creek Drainage. The trail climbs east up this valley, crossing Willow Creek twice en route, to Willow Lake at 11,564 feet. The eastern end of this spectacular lake is ringed with cliffs and graced with a spectacular waterfall. There are camping spots below and above the lake, but camping within 300 feet of the lake is prohibited. Mount Adams is 1.0 mile northeast and "Kat Carson" is 1.3 miles southeast.

17.A4 — South Crestone Lake Approach

From South Crestone TH at 8,840 ft: 152 RP   9.0 mi   3,560 ft   Class 2

This approach takes you to 12,400 feet in the basin above South Crestone Lake, from which you can climb Adams' northwest or west ridges. Start at the South Crestone Trailhead, go 100 yards east to a trail junction and continue east (straight) on the South Crestone Lake Trail. Cross to South Crestone Creek's south side, switchback up a treeless hill away from the creek, cross back to South Crestone Creek's north side at mile 2.9 and reach South Crestone Lake at 11,780 feet at mile 3.6. The maintained trail ends here. Hike 0.3 mile southeast around either side of the lake, then hike 0.6 mile southeast up the rough valley to 12,400 feet (Class 2). There are camping places in the basin above the lake, but camping is prohibited within 300 feet of the lake.

17.A5 — Spanish Creek Approach

From Spanish Creek TH at 8,260 ft: 78 RP   7.0 mi   2,740 ft   Class 1

This difficult approach takes you to 11,000 feet in upper Spanish Creek, from which you can climb "Kat Carson." The approach starts on the deck of the San Luis Valley, so this hike can be brutally hot. Start at the Spanish Creek Trailhead. The unmarked Spanish Creek Trail starts 50 yards north of Spanish Creek, passes under (south of) a solar-powered ashram and climbs east into the Spanish Creek Drainage. The little-used Spanish Creek Trail is rough and difficult to follow in spots. The trail is mostly on the creek's north side, but it does cross to the south side twice. Between 9,600 feet and 10,600 feet, the trail climbs relentlessly through an old burn on the creek's north side. Above 10,600 feet, the angle of the valley relents, and there are good camping spots near treeline at 11,000 feet. The southern routes on "Kat Carson" are accessible from here.

17. Mount Adams   13,931 feet

See Map 17 on page 148

Mount Adams is 1.9 miles north of the fourteener Kit Carson and is the northernmost centennial thirteener in the Sangres. Compared to the majestic fourteeners of the Crestone Group, Adams offers a relatively easy ascent via a variety of routes. Remember that Adams' ease is relative to some of Colorado's hardest peaks. Adams' slopes are still steep, and a distinctive summit cap guards the summit. Adams is usually climbed with a backpack to Horn, Willow or South Crestone Lake, but, for the fit, it makes a nice day climb.

ROUTES

17.1 — Mount Adams — West Ridge *Classic*

From South Crestone TH at 8,840 ft: 275 RP   10.0 mi   5,171 ft   Class 2+
From Willow Lake at 11,564 ft: 145 RP   2.6 mi   2,367 ft   Class 2+

This is the easiest route on Mount Adams and gives you opportunity to climb other peaks en route. Start at the South Crestone Trailhead and follow the Willow Lake Approach to Willow Lake at 11,564 feet. From 100 yards east of the lake's outlet, climb 0.3 mile north up a steep, grassy slope to 12,200 feet at the southern edge of the small basin under Adams' southwest face. Climb 0.4 mile north across the basin to 12,600 feet, then climb 0.1 mile north up a steep slope to the 12,900-foot saddle west of Adams. Climb 0.1 mile east along Adams' west ridge (Class 2). When the ridge becomes rocky, climb 0.3 mile east up steep grass slopes on the ridge's south (right) side (Class 2). As you approach the summit, stay south of and below the summit block's cliffs, then climb 0.1 mile north up broken slopes on the summit block's east side to the summit (Class 2+).

VARIATIONS

17.1V1
Stay on the crest of Adams' west ridge all the way from the 12,900-foot saddle to the base of the summit block. This rocky ramble adds some Class 2+ scampering to your adventure. At the base of the summit block, traverse east below the summit block and rejoin the route for the finish on the summit block's east side.

17.1V2

From South Crestone TH at 8,840 ft:	*280 RP*	*10.4 mi*	*5,091 ft*	*Class 2+*
From South Crestone Lake at 11,780 ft:	*149 RP*	*3.2 mi*	*2,151 ft*	*Class 2+*
From 12,400 ft in basin:	*88 RP*	*1.4 mi*	*1,531 ft*	*Class 2+*

You can approach this route from South Crestone Lake. Follow the South Crestone Lake Approach to 12,400 feet in the basin above South Crestone Lake. From here, climb 0.1 mile southeast to 12,600 feet, then climb 0.1 mile south up a steep talus slope in a wide couloir to the 12,900-foot saddle below Adams' west ridge. Join the West Ridge Route there and follow it to the summit.

EXTRA CREDITS

17.1EC1 — Point 13,546, Class 2
From the 12,900-foot saddle, climb 0.5 mile west to the summit of Point 13,546. From this summit, you can look down to the northwest at South Crestone Lake. This ranked thirteener is a "Tri"—one of Colorado's 300 highest peaks.

17.1EC2 — Point 13,580, Class 2
From Adams' summit, climb 0.7 mile south then southeast to the summit of Point 13,580. This peak is a "Bi"—one of Colorado's 200 highest peaks. From this summit, you have a startling view down to Horn Lake. If you include Point 13,546 during your ascent of Adams, traverse to Point 13,580, then descend west to rejoin your ascent route, you can complete a great Tour de Adams.

17.2 — Mount Adams — Southeast Face

From Horn Creek TH at 9,120 ft:	*278 RP*	*12.0 mi*	*4,811 ft*	*Class 2+*
From Horn Lake at 11,820 ft:	*123 RP*	*2.0 mi*	*2,111 ft*	*Class 2+*

This route is slightly tougher than the West Ridge Route. Start at the Horn Creek Trailhead and follow the Horn Lake Approach to Horn Lake

Mount Adams from the northwest.

at 11,820 feet. Mount Adams is only 0.7 mile west of the lake, but a direct ascent to the summit is not practical because of cliffs on Adams' east face. From Horn Lake's north side, climb 0.7 mile west-northwest up a steep, grassy slope on Adams' southeast face, and reach Adams' northeast ridge at 13,400 feet. Climb 0.2 mile southwest to the junction of Adams' northeast and northwest ridges at 13,860 feet. From this vantage, you can look down to the north at North Crestone Lake and up the ridge to the south at

Adams' distinctive summit block. Climb 0.1 mile south to the base of the summit block. Climb to the bottom of the summit block, traverse 60 feet southeast (left) on a surprising, grass-covered ledge and climb 100 feet south up a steep, rough slope to the summit (Class 2+). From here there are unique views of the fourteeners to the south as well as "Kat Carson."

17.3 — Mount Adams — Northwest Ridge

From South Crestone TH at 8,840 ft:	*284 RP*	*10.6 mi*	*5,091 ft*	*Class 2+*
From South Crestone Lake at 11,780 ft:	*153 RP*	*3.4 mi*	*2,151 ft*	*Class 2+*
From 12,400 ft in basin:	*92 RP*	*1.6 mi*	*1,531 ft*	*Class 2+*

This alternative route gives you a chance to avoid the crowds at Willow Lake. Start at the South Crestone Trailhead and follow the South Crestone Lake Approach to 12,400 feet in the basin above South Crestone Lake. From here, climb 0.25 mile northeast up grassy slopes to the 12,780-foot saddle below Adams' northwest ridge. You can look up the ridge and wonder how you are going to climb Adams' summit block. Though not trivial, it is easier than it looks.

From the 12,780-foot saddle, climb 0.45 mile east-southeast up talus on the ridge's south (right) side, overcoming a Class 2+ rock step en route, to reach Adams' upper north ridge at 13,860 feet. Climb 0.1 mile south to the base of the summit block. Climb to the bottom of the summit block, traverse 60 feet southeast (left) on a nifty, grass-covered ledge and climb 100 feet south up a steep, rough slope to the summit (Class 2+). This is the same finish as the Southeast Face Route. Ascending this route and descending the West Ridge Route makes a wonderful Tour de Adams.

17.3V — Variation

From North Crestone TH at 8,600 ft:	*321 RP*	*14.0 mi*	*5,331 ft*	*Class 2+*
From North Crestone Lake at 11,780 ft:	*149 RP*	*3.2 mi*	*2,151 ft*	*Class 2+*

You can approach this route from North Crestone Lake. Start at the North Crestone Trailhead and hike 2.4 miles northeast up North Crestone Creek to a three-way trail junction. Turn east (right) and continue 0.5 mile east-southeast to a trail junction with the Venable Pass Trail. You do not want to go to Venable Pass. Go straight (right) and continue 2.5 miles southeast on the North Crestone Lake Trail to the large North Crestone Lake at 11,780 feet. Hike 0.5 mile southeast around the lake's north side, then climb 0.55 mile southwest to the 12,780-foot saddle below Adams' northwest ridge. Join the Northwest Ridge Route here and follow it to the summit.

17.3EC — Extra Credit — Point 13,153, Class 2

From the 12,780-foot saddle, climb 0.3 mile northwest to the summit of Point 13,153, a ranked thirteener. You can also climb to this summit from South Crestone Lake's west end across open slopes, thereby avoiding the rough hike around the lake.

17. "Kat Carson"   13,980 feet

Now officially called "Columbia Point" in memory of the *Columbia* Shuttle Crew
See Map 17 on page 148

"Kat Carson" is on the west side of the Sangres, 0.2 mile east of the fourteener Kit Carson and 1.1 miles northwest of the famous fourteener Crestone Peak. When you view the Sangres from the San Luis Valley to the west, Kit Carson is more prominent than the Crestones. The Willow Creek Drainage is north of "Kat Carson," and the Spanish Creek Drainage is south of the peak.

The complicated terrain around "Kat Carson" confuses many people on a first visit. Kit Carson Mountain is a large, complex massif comprising two summits over 14,000 feet and the thirteener "Kat Carson." The name Kit Carson *Mountain* applies to all these summits. The name Kit Carson *Peak* applies just to the massif's highest, 14,165-foot summit. Challenger Point is Kit Carson Mountain's 14,081-foot west summit. "Kat Carson" is Kit Carson Mountain's 13,980-foot east summit.

"Kat Carson" has held its nickname for many years. "Kat Carson" rises 360 feet above its connecting saddle with Kit Carson's main summit, but the separation between these two summits is only 350 yards. "Kat Carson" ranks on some lists because it rises more than 300 feet, but not on others because of its short separation. No matter how you count, "Kat Carson" is worth climbing. It is a harder climb than Mount Adams. It is the Sangres' highest centennial thirteener and the third-highest peak in this book.

ROUTES

17.4 — "Kat Carson" — East Ridge

From South Colony TH at 8,780 ft:	367 RP	18.8 mi	5,560 ft	Class 2+
From 4WD parking at 11,060 ft:	215 RP	8.4 mi	3,240 ft	Class 2+
From Lower South Colony Lake at 11,660 ft:	174 RP	5.6 mi	2,640 ft	Class 2+

This is the easiest way to climb "Kat Carson" from the east side of the range. Start at the South Colony Trailhead and follow the South Colony Lakes Approach to Lower South Colony Lake at 11,660 feet. From Lower South Colony Lake, hike 0.5 mile northwest on the continuing trail above Lower South Colony Lake's north side to Upper South Colony Lake at 12,030 feet. From here, follow the Colorado Fourteener Initiative (CFI) trail 0.5 mile north as it switchbacks up to Humboldt's west ridge. Reach the ridge just east of the 12,860-foot Humboldt–Crestone Peak saddle, then leave the trail and descend west into the saddle. Scramble 0.8 mile west on or below a ridge, pass Point 13,290 and reach the broad, 13,140-foot connecting saddle between Crestone Peak and Kit Carson (Class 2). This open area is called "Bear's Playground."

Hike 0.4 mile west-northwest across Bear's Playground to 13,460 feet. Contour 0.3 mile west below Point 13,799, alias "Obstruction Peak," to the 13,460-foot connecting saddle between "Obstruction Peak" and "Kat Carson." From this saddle, climb 0.2 mile west up steep grass and slabs (Class 2+) to the easternmost of the two summits of "Kat Carson." This summit carries the nickname "Kitty Kat Carson." Continue 0.1 mile northwest to the slightly higher, 13,980-foot summit of "Kat Carson."

17.4V — Variation

From Spanish Creek TH at 8,260 ft:	347 RP	11.8 mi	5,880 ft	Class 2+
From 11,000 ft in Spanish Creek:	221 RP	4.8 mi	3,140 ft	Class 2+

You can approach the East Ridge Route from the west side of the range. To do so, start at the Spanish Creek Trailhead and follow the Spanish Creek Approach to 11,000 feet in the upper Spanish Creek drainage. From here, hike 1.5 miles east-northeast to 12,600 feet at the western edge of Bear's Playground, then climb 0.3 mile north to 13,460 feet and join the East Ridge Route there.

17.4EC — Extra Credit — "Obstruction Peak," 13,799 feet, Class 2

Either coming or going, take time to climb Point 13,799. This ranked thirteener carries the appropriate appellation "Obstruction Peak," as it interferes with your trek between Bear's Playground and "Kat Carson." "Obstruction Peak" is a "Bi"—one of Colorado's 200 highest peaks.

17.5 — "Kat Carson" — Outward Bound Couloir

From South Crestone TH at 8,840 ft:	450 RP	12.0 mi	5,300 ft	Class 3	Steep Snow
From Willow Lake at 11,564 ft:	318 RP	4.6 mi	2,416 ft	Class 3	Steep Snow

This is an interesting mixed climb. Use the Willow Lake Approach. Go 0.4 mile east around Willow Lake's north side and hike 1.2 miles southeast up the valley to 12,200 feet. The Outward Bound Couloir is the deep couloir east of Kit Carson's North Ridge Route, and it leads directly to the 13,620-foot saddle between "Kat Carson" and Kit Carson's main, 14,165-foot summit. Climb 0.6 mile south then southwest up the gradually steepening couloir. It becomes more inset as you approach the saddle. Just below the saddle, take the couloir's eastern (left) branch. This deeply inset, north-facing couloir is often icy, and we recommend ice axes and crampons for this route. From the 13,620-foot saddle, climb 0.1 mile east up exposed, Class 3 blocks to the summit of "Kat Carson."

17.6 — "Kat Carson" — South Couloir

From Spanish Creek TH at 8,260 ft:	362 RP	10.2 mi	5,720 ft	Class 3	Mod Snow
From 11,000 ft in Spanish Creek:	237 RP	3.2 mi	2,980 ft	Class 3	Mod Snow

This is a direct route up "Kat Carson" from upper Spanish Creek. When

"Kat Carson" (Columbia Point) from the northwest.

snow conditions are good, this couloir provides a moderate snow climb and a speedy descent route. Start at the Spanish Creek Trailhead and follow the Spanish Creek Approach to 11,000 feet in the Spanish Creek drainage. From here, hike 0.7 mile east-northeast to 11,800 feet in upper Spanish Creek.

The South Couloir is the deep couloir east of the Prow—Kit Carson's sweeping south ridge. The couloir leads directly to the 13,620-foot saddle between "Kat Carson" and Kit Carson's main, 14,165-foot summit. Climb 0.8 mile north up the straight couloir to the 13,620-foot saddle. From the saddle, climb 0.1 mile east up exposed, Class 3 blocks to the summit of "Kat Carson."

18. California Group

California Peak   13,849 feet
"Huerfano Peak"   13,828 feet

See Map 18 on page 162

These peaks rise on both sides of the long Huerfano River valley less than 3 miles north of the fourteener Blanca Peak. California Peak is west of the valley and "Huerfano Peak" is east of the valley. The Huerfano valley is one of Colorado's finest, offering spectacular views of Blanca's rugged northeast face. The attendant centennial thirteeners are much easier to climb than the rugged peaks of the Blanca Group, and each offers a choice of easy routes. These routes all require an elevation gain of greater than 3,700 feet, so be prepared for a hefty hike.

MAPS
Required: *Blanca Peak, Mosca Pass, San Isabel National Forest*
Optional: *Twin Peaks, Rio Grande National Forest*

TRAILHEADS

Lower Huerfano Trailhead
This trailhead is at 10,200 feet and provides access to the north sides of California Peak and "Huerfano Peak." *Huerfano* means "orphan boy" in Spanish; as you travel to this trailhead, you will appreciate this appropriate name. Take Exit 52 from Interstate 25 north of Walsenburg and go 0.3 mile south toward Walsenburg. Turn west onto Colorado 69, go 25.1 miles northwest to Gardner and continue for an additional 0.7 mile to the far side of town. Turn west onto the Redwing spur of Colorado 69 (paved) and measure from this point. Go straight at mile 5.1, continue on the dirt road at mile 6.9 and go straight at mile 7.1. Do not turn left into Redwing. Turn left at a Y-junction at mile 12.0 and pass the entrance to the Singing River Ranch at mile 16.0. The road is plowed to this point in winter.

Public access is allowed from the Singing River Ranch to the San Isabel National Forest. Do not camp on the private land you are traveling through. The road becomes rougher at the Singing River Ranch, but is passable for most cars. Pass the entrance to the Aspen River Ranch at mile 16.9, pass a distant view of Blanca Peak at mile 19.4 and reach the boundary of San Isabel National Forest at mile 20.4. The road becomes rougher at this point, but is passable for high-clearance vehicles. Reach the trailhead at mile 21.2. The trailhead has a small sign for the Zapata Trail and Huerfano Trail. There is only enough parking space for one or two vehicles at the trailhead, but there is ample parking 100 yards beyond the trailhead. California Peak is 2.3 miles southwest of the trailhead and "Huerfano Peak" is 2.9 miles southeast of the trailhead.

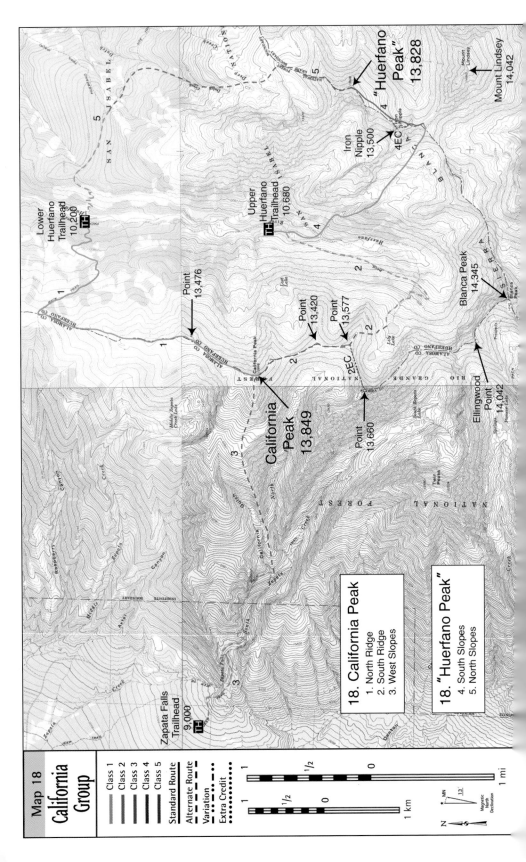

Map 18
California Group

Class 1
Class 2
Class 3
Class 4
Class 5

Standard Route
Alternate Route
Variation
Extra Credit

Lower Huerfano Trailhead 10,200

Upper Huerfano Trailhead 10,680

Iron Nipple 13,500

"Huerfano Peak" 13,828

Mount Lindsey 14,042

SAN ISABEL

SAN ISABEL

Point 13,476

Point 13,420

Point 13,577

Blanca Peak 14,345

California Peak 13,849

Point 13,660

Ellingwood Point 14,042

SIERRA

RIO GRANDE NATIONAL

ALAMOSA CO. / HUERFANO CO.

ALAMOSA CO. / HUERFANO CO.

NATIONAL FOREST

Zapata Falls Trailhead 9,000

18. California Peak
1. North Ridge
2. South Ridge
3. West Slopes

18. "Huerfano Peak"
4. South Slopes
5. North Slopes

1 mi

1 km

MN 13°
Magnetic North Declination

For an alternative approach to this trailhead, leave U.S. 160 1.9 miles west of North La Veta Pass, go 12.3 miles north on Pass Creek Road (dirt) and join the route just described 2.0 miles east of the Redwing turn.

Upper Huerfano Trailhead

This trailhead is at 10,680 feet and provides access to the south sides of California Peak and "Huerfano Peak." From the Lower Huerfano Trailhead at mile 21.2, continue south on the road and reach the trailhead at mile 22.3. The last mile to the trailhead is steep and will challenge low-power, low-clearance vehicles. The last 200 yards to the trailhead requires a four-wheel-drive vehicle, and it is best to park two-wheel-drive vehicles below this pitch. The trailhead is at the south end of a hanging meadow above the Huerfano River; there is a good view of Blanca's northeast face from the meadow. California Peak is 1.6 miles southwest of the trailhead and "Huerfano Peak" is 2.1 miles southeast of the trailhead.

Zapata Falls Trailhead

This trailhead is on the range's west side at 9,000 feet and provides access to California Peak's west side. Measure from the U.S. 160–Colorado 150 junction east of Alamosa. Go north on Colorado 150 toward Great Sand Dunes National Monument and turn east (right) onto Zapata Falls Road (dirt) at mile 10.9. Go east on Zapata Falls Road and reach the developed, marked trailhead and ample parking at mile 14.5. You can see California Peak during your approach to this trailhead.

18. California Peak 13,849 feet

See Map 18 on page 162

California Peak is 2.6 miles north-northwest of the fourteener Blanca Peak, and it guards the wilderness that surrounds its famous neighbors. You can see California Peak from the San Luis Valley to the west and from Colorado 69 to the east. The peak's slopes are gentle, and California offers a choice of long but easy hikes. California is the easiest centennial thirteener in the Sangres.

ROUTES

18.1 – California Peak – North Ridge *Classic*

From Lower Huerfano TH at 10,200 ft: 164 RP   8.4 mi   4,101 ft   Class 1

This is the easiest route on California. Start at the Lower Huerfano Trailhead and hike 1.7 miles west on the Zapata Trail to an 11,860-foot saddle on California's long, broad north ridge. The trail may be obscure in the meadows. From the saddle, hike 1.7 miles south on the broad, grassy ridge to Point 13,476. Descend 200 yards south-southwest to 13,340 feet and continue 0.7 mile south-southwest to the summit. En route, you can enjoy a view of "Huerfano Peak" to the east.

18.2 — California Peak — South Ridge

From Upper Huerfano TH at 10,680 ft: *272 RP   10.6 mi   4,203 ft   Class 2*

This alternative route allows you to visit scenic Lily Lake and climb an extra peak en route. Start at the Upper Huerfano Trailhead and walk south on the Lily Lake Trail to a trail junction. Leave the valley trail and stay west (right) on the Lily Lake Trail. Hike south then west to Lily Lake at 12,340 feet. The view of Blanca Peak is spectacular from here. An impressive wall to the west rings Lily Lake. Point 13,660 is 0.7 mile west-north-west of the lake, and Point 13,577 is 0.4 mile north-northwest of the lake.

From Lily Lake's north side, hike 0.25 mile west-northwest to 12,600 feet. Climb 0.25 mile north up a steep talus slope and reach the east ridge of Point 13,577 at 13,440 feet (Class 2). Climb 0.1 mile west-northwest to the summit of Point 13,577 and enjoy a grand vista. Point 13,577, your bonus peak, is a "Tri"—one of Colorado's 300 highest peaks. From Point 13,577, hike 0.4 mile north to Point 13,420, an unranked summit, then hike 0.8 mile north-northwest to California's summit (Class 2).

18.2EC — Extra Credit — Point 13,660, Class 2

From Point 13,577, hike 0.5 mile west-southwest along the rough ridge to Point 13,660. This peak is a "Bi"—one of Colorado's 200 highest peaks.

18.3 — California Peak — West Slopes

From Zapata Falls TH at 9,000 ft: *297 RP   9.2 mi   4,849 ft   Class 2*

This alternative route allows you to climb California Peak from the west. Done as a day trip, this hefty hike will augment your training program. Start at the Zapata Falls Trailhead and hike 2.3 miles east-southeast on the Zapata Creek Trail to California Gulch at 10,500 feet. Cross California Gulch, leave the trail and hike 1.0 mile east up the ridge just south of California Gulch to treeline at 12,000 feet (Class 2). Continue 0.3 mile east-northeast up the ridge to open slopes at 12,600 feet. Hike 1.0 mile east up gentle slopes to the summit.

18. "Huerfano Peak"   13,828 feet

See Map 18 on page 162

Often overlooked by climbers, "Huerfano Peak" rests quietly by itself 1.2 miles north of the fourteener Mount Lindsey. It is usually climbed together with Lindsey. However, this lonely peak makes a worthwhile outing by itself. You can catch distant views of "Huerfano Peak" while driving toward the Huerfano trailheads.

ROUTES

18.4 — "Huerfano Peak" — South Slopes

From Upper Huerfano TH at 10,680 ft: *189 RP*   *8.2 mi*   *3,728 ft*   *Class 2*

This is the easiest route on "Huerfano Peak." Most of the route follows the well-traveled standard route on the fourteener Mount Lindsey, and this is a rewarding scenic tour. Start at the Upper Huerfano Trailhead and walk 1.0 mile south on the Huerfano Valley Trail, which is on the Huerfano River's west side. When the Huerfano Valley Trail reaches the river in a small gorge, leave it and cross to the Huerfano River's east side. There is no bridge, and this crossing can wet your feet during high water. Once across the river, hike 0.3 mile south along the river's east side on a strong climbers trail. This trail is the beginning of the Lindsey Trail.

Continue 0.3 mile southeast on the Lindsey Trail as it climbs steeply along the right side of a talus field into a small side valley west of the dramatic Points 12,410 and 12,915. Cross the unnamed side creek at 11,300 feet and continue 0.5 mile south-southeast on the trail as it climbs a small ridge west of the drainage through the last of the trees to 11,920 feet. Descend 0.1 mile southeast and enter a small, beautiful basin. There is a spectacular view of Blanca Peak's northeast face from here. You can just see Lindsey's summit pyramid poking up above an intermediate, west-facing ridge, but you cannot yet see "Huerfano Peak." Hike 0.9 mile southeast across the basin and ascend a grassy ramp to meet the west-facing ridge at 13,000 feet. Climb 0.1 mile east up this ridge to reach Lindsey's northwest ridge at 13,140 feet. The Lindsey Trail has delivered you to the heights, and you can finally see "Huerfano Peak" 0.8 mile to the north-northeast.

Leave the Lindsey Trail at 13,140 feet and hike 0.1 mile north toward 13,500-foot Iron Nipple (Class 2). When cliffs appear to block simple passage, go over a little notch and descend 50 feet northwest into a 30-foot-wide slot between a pair of cliffs running north–south (Class 2). Hike 0.1 mile north up through this nifty slot and reach a 13,300-foot saddle between the slot cliffs and Iron Nipple's upper cliffs (Class 2). Descend 0.1 mile northeast to 13,200 feet, get below the cliffs of Iron Nipple's east face, then hike 0.2 mile north-northeast across a pesky talus slope to 13,300 feet (Class 2). The difficulties are over. Hike 0.4 mile northeast across open, semi-grassy slopes to the summit.

18.4EC — Extra Credit — Iron Nipple, 13,500 feet, Class 2+

From the small saddle at 13,300 feet, climb 0.1 mile north to Iron Nipple's 13,500-foot summit (Class 2+). This peak is unranked, but this is a fun

"Huerfano Peak" from the northwest.

scamper. You can also reach or retreat from Iron Nipple's summit via the 13,300-foot saddle between Iron Nipple and "Huerfano Peak" (Class 2+).

18.5 — "Huerfano Peak" — North Slopes

From Lower Huerfano TH at 10,200 ft: 287 RP   9.4 mi   3,908 ft   Class 2

This alternative route avoids the crowds on the standard route and takes you through a forgotten basin. Start at the Lower Huerfano Trailhead, hike 0.1 mile northeast on the Huerfano Trail and cross to Huerfano River's east side on a sturdy footbridge. Hike 0.9 mile east on the Huerfano Trail as it switchbacks up the valley's steep west face and finally levels out at 11,060 feet. Hike 0.7 mile east-southeast on the Huerfano Trail to 11,140 feet, just before the trail turns northeast. The 1967 Mosca Pass Quadrangle shows the Ute Trail heading east from this point. We do not believe the Ute Trail currently exists in this location. Perhaps it once did, but we could find no trace of it in 2000.

Leave the Huerfano Trail at 11,140 feet before it turns northeast and hike cross-country 0.2 mile east-southeast down to a meadow at 11,000 feet. Contour 0.5 mile east-southeast through mostly open trees to Dutch Creek. Hike 1.0 mile south up Dutch Creek to open slopes at 12,200 feet (Class 2). From here you can see "Huerfano Peak" 1.1 miles to the south. Hike 0.5 mile south-southeast up open, grassy slopes to a bench at 12,700 feet. Hike 0.2 mile south-southeast to the highest grass at 13,000 feet,

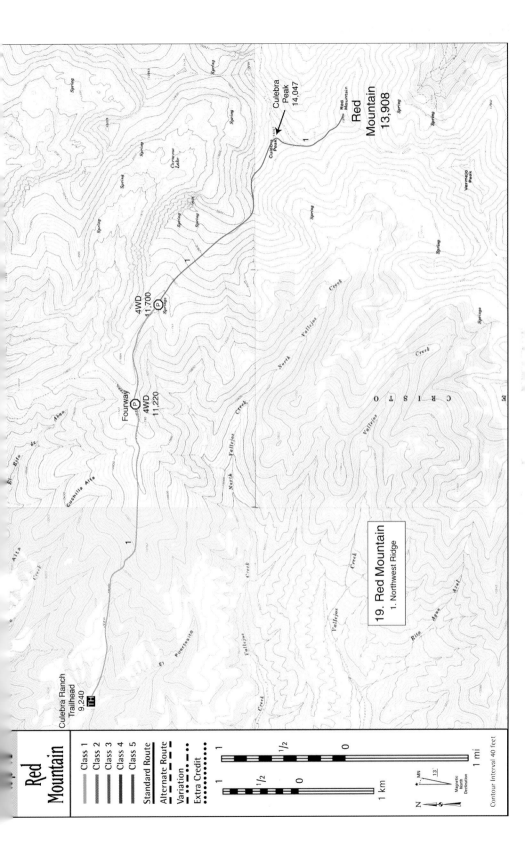

Red Mountain

- Class 1
- Class 2
- Class 3
- Class 4
- Class 5
- Standard Route
- Alternate Route
- Variation
- Extra Credit

Contour Interval 40 feet

1 mi

1 km

MN

Magnetic North Declination

13°

N

19. Red Mountain
1. Northwest Ridge

Culebra Ranch Trailhead 9,240
TH

Fourway
P 4WD 11,220

4WD 11,700 **P** Spring

Culebra Peak 14,047

Red Mountain
Red Mountain 13,908

Vermejo Peak

SANGRE DE CRISTO

North Vallejos Creek

Vallejos Creek

Vallejos Creek

Rito Azul

then climb 0.2 mile south up steep talus and reach the northeast ridge of "Huerfano Peak" at 13,400 feet (Class 2). Climb 0.2 mile southwest up the ridge to the confluence of the northeast and northwest ridges (Class 2), then climb 0.2 mile south along the rough ridge to the summit of "Huerfano Peak" (Class 2). Ascending the North Slopes Route and descending the South Slopes Route makes a great Tour de Huerfano and gives you a chance to climb Iron Nipple as well.

19. Red Mountain   13,908 feet

See Map 19 on page 167

Red Mountain is Colorado's southernmost and easternmost centennial thirteener. The peak hides in the southern end of Colorado's Sangres only 8.6 miles north of the New Mexico border. Red Mountain is 0.7 mile south-southeast of Culebra Peak, Colorado's southernmost fourteener.

All of Culebra and Red are privately owned. There is no public land near Red Mountain, and the peak is not covered on any national forest map. The ranch on the range's east side has never allowed public access. For many years, the Taylor Ranch on the range's west side allowed limited public access, but the ranch was sold in 1999, and the new owners have different ideas. After a lengthy negotiation, the Colorado Mountain Club was given permission to lead a single trip to Culebra in July 1999. Red Mountain was not included in the itinerary. We hope that there will be several legal climbs allowed each year, and that Red Mountain will be included. At the time of this writing, the ranch's new owners had not yet formulated a long-term plan. For the latest information, contact the Colorado Mountain Club's main office at 710 10th Street, Golden, CO 80401; 303-279-3080. We include the traditional route on Red Mountain here so that, when you do get permission, you will be ready to go.

MAPS
Required: *Culebra Peak, El Valle Creek*
Optional: *Taylor Ranch*

TRAILHEAD

Culebra Ranch Trailhead
This trailhead is at 9,240 feet and provides access to Red Mountain's northwest side. From the center of San Luis on Colorado 159, turn southeast onto road P.6 (Fourth Street) and measure from this point. Go southeast on road P.6 and go straight at mile 2.5 when P.6 crosses road 21. There is a stop sign at this intersection. Turn north (left) onto road L.7 at mile 4.2 at a T-junction in Chama. Go north on L.7, turn east (right) onto road 22.3 at mile 4.5 and cross Culebra Creek. Go east on road 22.3 and turn north

(left) onto road M.5 at mile 4.7. Follow road M.5 as it curves east and turns to dirt. Reach the two Culebra Ranch gates at mile 8.8.

With permission, go through the southern gate and continue south and then east to the ranch buildings at mile 10.7. Check in with ranch personnel. From the ranch, continue east and stay south (right) at mile 11.0 at a junction where the Whiskey Pass Road goes north. At mile 11.2, reach a large meadow on the road's south side. This is the trailhead.

In the past, four-wheel-drive vehicles were allowed to go beyond the trailhead when the road was dry. From the trailhead at 9,240 feet, four-wheel-drive vehicles can go 3.0 miles east up the steep road to a road junction called "Fourway" at 11,220 feet. From Fourway, four-wheel-drive vehicles can continue 1.0 mile east to a parking area at the end of the road at 11,700 feet.

ROUTE

19.1 — Red Mountain — Northwest Ridge

From Culebra Ranch TH at 9,240 ft:	394 RP	14.2 mi	6,040 ft	Class 2
From Fourway at 11,220 ft:	294 RP	8.2 mi	4,060 ft	Class 2
From 4WD parking at 11,700 ft:	265 RP	6.2 mi	3,580 ft	Class 2

The route to Red Mountain goes over the summit of the fourteener Culebra Peak. The route is up Culebra's long, distinguishing, snakelike ridge. People sometimes malign the ridge because of its length. Taking a more distant view in either time or distance, you can watch the ridge curving gracefully toward its source, Culebra's summit.

Start at the Culebra Ranch Trailhead and climb 3.0 miles east up the steep, straight four-wheel-drive road to Fourway, a road junction in a saddle at 11,220 feet. Continue climbing 1.0 mile east to the road's end at 11,700 feet. Cross to the creek's south side and climb 1.3 miles southeast up the shallow basin to reach Culebra's northwest ridge in a 13,220-foot saddle. From the saddle, climb the curving ridge 0.6 mile southeast then east to a 13,940-foot false summit. Continue 0.3 mile east-southeast in a gentle ascent to Culebra's 14,047-foot summit. From here, descend 0.6 mile south over tiny Point 13,599 to a 13,460-foot saddle, then climb 0.3 mile southeast to Red Mountain's summit. Return the way you came.

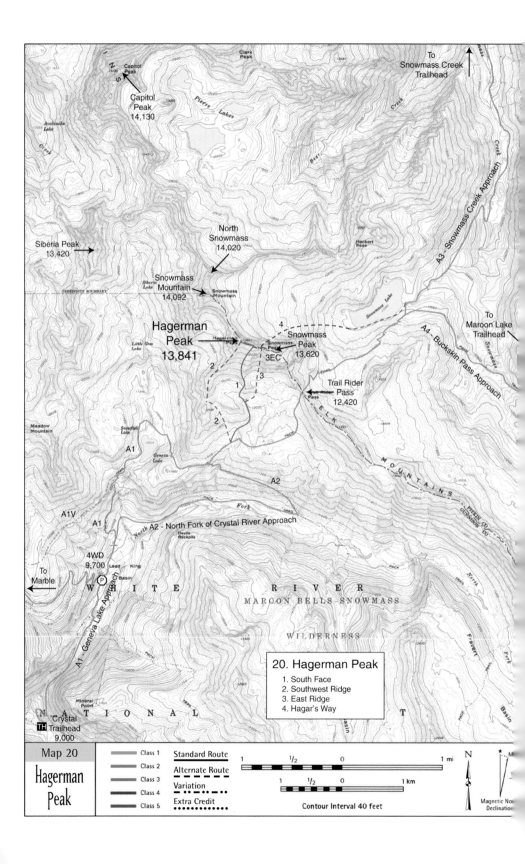

Capitol
Peak
14,130

Clark
Peak

Pierre Lakes

To
Snowmass Creek
Trailhead

Avalanche
Lake

Bear

Creek

Heckert
Pass

Siberia Peak
13,420

North
Snowmass
14,020

A3 - Snowmass Creek Approach

INDEFINITE BOUNDARY

Snowmass
Mountain
14,092

Siberia
Lake

Snowmass
Mountain

Snowmass Lake

To
Maroon Lake
Trailhead

Hagerman
Peak
13,841

Little Gem
Lake

Hagerman
Pass

4

Snowmass
Peak
13,620

A4 - Buckskin Pass Approach

2

3EC

1   3

2

Trail Rider
Pass
12,420

Trail Rider
Pass

Meadow
Mountain

A1

Snowfield
Lake

Geneva
Lake

E L K

M O U N T A I N S

PITKIN CO.
GUNNISON CO.

A2

A1V

A1

North Fork

Crystal

A2 - North Fork of Crystal River Approach

Fork

Devils
Rockpile

North

4WD
9,700

Lead   King
Basin

To
Marble

W H I T E

R I V E R

MAROON BELLS - SNOWMASS

Fravert

A1 - Geneva Lake Approach

WILDERNESS

Basin

Mineral
Point

Basin

N A   T I O N A L

T

Crystal
TH Trailhead
9,000

20. Hagerman Peak

1. South Face
2. Southwest Ridge
3. East Ridge
4. Hagar's Way

Fravert

Basin

Map 20	Class 1	Standard Route	1 ½ 0 1 mi	N
Hagerman Peak	Class 2	Alternate Route	1 ½ 0 1 km	
	Class 3	Variation		
	Class 4	Extra Credit	Contour Interval 40 feet	Magnetic North Declination
	Class 5			

CHAPTER FIVE

Elk Range

Introduction

The Elk Range lies south of Glenwood Springs and Interstate 70, and west of Aspen and Colorado 82. The Elk Range receives a lot of snow, and several major ski areas near Aspen take advantage of this fact. The Maroon Bells–Snowmass Wilderness embraces the range's beauty. In high summer the alpine valleys hold 50 shades of green and wildflower displays that can make you weep. Except for the famous views from the Maroon Lake Road, most of the Elks' high peaks are not visible from roads or towns. The Elks' exquisite beauty is reserved for those who penetrate the wilderness.

The Elk Range has six fourteeners and four centennial thirteeners. These are some of Colorado's most rugged and beautiful peaks; they will both inspire and challenge you. Although they are beautiful to look at, they are difficult and dangerous to climb. The crumbling, red sedimentary rock of the famous Maroon Bells southwest of Aspen is some of Colorado's worst rock, and it can be a nightmare to climb on for the uninitiated. "Thunder Pyramid" is made of this rock and is one of the most dangerous peaks in this book. Cathedral and "Castleabra" in the southeast end of the range also have bad rock. The rock in the northwest end of the range is better, and Hagerman offers a choice of routes. On any of these peaks, large parties increase the rockfall hazard for themselves as well as for others. Keep your party small.

20. Hagerman Peak   13,841 feet

See Map 20 on page 170

Hagerman is 0.6 mile southeast of the famous fourteener Snowmass Mountain. People rarely climb these two peaks together, though, because of the difficult ridge between them; Hagerman provides a sufficient challenge by itself. Far from paved roads, Hagerman rises between two of Colorado's most loved high-country lakes, Geneva Lake and Snowmass Lake. The climbs start with a trail hike to one of these lakes, and Hagerman offers a good opportunity for a backpack. On one visit here, we saw both an eagle and a bear at close range. From Hagerman's summit, you can survey much of the Maroon Bells–Snowmass Wilderness and further understand what this special place is all about.

MAPS

Required: *Snowmass Mtn., White River National Forest*
Optional: *Capitol Peak, Maroon Bells*

TRAILHEADS

Crystal Trailhead
This trailhead is at 9,000 feet and provides access to Lead King Basin, Geneva Lake and routes on Hagerman's south and west sides. If you are approaching from the north, go 22.0 miles south on Colorado 133 from Carbondale to the northern base of McClure Pass. If you are approaching from the south, go 3.0 miles north on Colorado 133 from the summit of McClure Pass.

Leave Colorado 133 and measure from this point. Go 6.1 miles east on a paved road to a four-way stop sign at the west end of the town of Marble. Wind through Marble with three pairs of left-then-right turns. Continue east on a dirt road that soon steepens. Go south (right) at mile 8.2, descend on a shelf road and pass Lizard Lake. Pass one of Colorado's most photographed historic mine buildings, the Crystal Mill, at mile 11.9 and continue to the town of Crystal at mile 12.1. Continue east and park in a flat area east of Crystal at mile 12.3 just before the road switchbacks up the hill. The road between Marble and Crystal will challenge low-clearance passenger cars. In winter the road is open to Marble.

Four-wheel-drive vehicles can continue for another 2.0 miles to 9,640 feet in Lead King Basin. To do this, go east from the Crystal Trailhead on the Schofield Pass Road (FS 317), switchback twice, turn north (left) at a signed junction at mile 12.65 and climb north on the rough, rocky shelf road (FS 315) into Lead King Basin. Cross to the west side of the North Fork of Crystal River on a good bridge at mile 14.0 and reach the signed four-wheel-drive trailhead on the road's east side at mile 14.3 just before the road switchbacks west up the hill and leaves Lead King Basin.

There is another, longer four-wheel-drive road to this point. It also is FS 315, and it leaves the Crystal River Road between Marble and Crystal at mile 8.2 on the approach to the Crystal Trailhead. Go 6.7 miles on this road as it switchbacks up Lost Trail Creek to 10,900 feet between Lost Trail Creek and Silver Creek, crosses Silver Creek, then descends into Lead King Basin and the four-wheel-drive trailhead. This high road is easier than the shorter approach from the Crystal Trailhead when the road is dry, but more difficult when the road is wet.

Snowmass Creek Trailhead
This trailhead is at 8,400 feet and provides access to the Snowmass Creek Approach and routes on Hagerman's north and south sides. You can reach the trailhead via one of two roads.

For the traditional approach, go 28.0 miles south on Colorado 82 from Glenwood Springs, or go 13.1 miles north on Colorado 82 from Maroon Creek Road on Aspen's north side, to the small town of Snowmass. Do not confuse the town of Snowmass with Snowmass Village. The town of Snowmass is on Colorado 82. In Snowmass, turn west onto Snowmass

Creek Road (paved) and measure from this point. Turn left at a T-junction at mile 1.7, cross Snowmass Creek at mile 10.7 and reach another T-junction at mile 10.9. Turn right at the T-junction and reach the well-marked trailhead at mile 11.3.

If you are starting in Aspen, the following alternative approach is shorter but rougher. From Maroon Lake Road on Aspen's north side, go 4.6 miles north on Colorado 82. Turn west onto Snowmass Village Road (paved) and measure from this point. Go 5.1 miles to the junction of Brush Creek Road and Divide Road in Snowmass Village, and turn right onto Divide Road (paved). At mile 6.0, turn right onto a dirt road just before you reach a lodge called "The Divide" at the Snowmass Ski Area. Descend steeply on a series of switchbacks across ski runs, go straight at mile 7.6 and reach the trailhead at mile 8.0. In winter you can usually drive to within 1.0 mile of this trailhead.

APPROACHES

20.A1 — Geneva Lake Approach

From Crystal TH at 9,000 ft:	74 RP	8.0 mi	1,960 ft	Class 1
From 4WD parking at 9,640 ft:	41 RP	4.0 mi	1,320 ft	Class 1

This is the traditional approach for climbing Hagerman. It takes you to one of Colorado's special places—Geneva Lake. Start at the Crystal Trailhead and go 0.35 mile up the four-wheel-drive road to a junction above the second switchback. Turn north (left) and follow the rough road as it climbs on the east side of the North Fork of Crystal River into Lead King Basin. Cross to the river's west side on a good bridge after 1.7 miles, pass the marked four-wheel-drive trailhead after 2.0 miles and leave the road after 2.1 miles where it starts to switchback up the hill west of the river.

Follow the Geneva Lake Trail north into the Maroon Bells–Snowmass Wilderness. Turn west (left) at a junction with the Fravert Basin Trail at 2.6 miles, switchback up the steep slope at the north end of Lead King Basin and continue north to 10,960 feet on Geneva Lake's west side at 4.0 miles. You can see Hagerman's south side during the approach, and Hagerman's west face rises east of Geneva Lake. There are several good designated camping sites near the trail above the lake's west and north sides.

20.A1V — Variation

From Lost Creek Road at 10,800 ft:	30 RP	4.4 mi	200 ft	Class 1

This unique approach to Geneva Lake requires a four-wheel-drive vehicle and minimizes your elevation gain on foot. Leave the Lost Creek–Lead King Basin Road (FS 315) at 10,800 feet just southeast of its crossing of Silver Creek. Follow an old road that soon narrows to a small trail. Contour around the grassy shoulder between Silver Creek and Lead King Basin, hike

1.7 miles northeast near the 10,800-foot level and reach the Geneva Lake Trail just south of Geneva Lake.

20.A2 — North Fork of Crystal River Approach

From Crystal TH at 9,000 ft:	108 RP	11.6 mi	2,300 ft	Class 1
From 4WD parking at 9,640 ft:	73 RP	7.6 mi	1,660 ft	Class 1

This alternative approach to Hagerman's south side works well for a day trip in which you ascend the Geneva Lake Approach and descend the North Fork of Crystal River Approach. Follow the Geneva Lake Approach to the trail junction with the Fravert Basin Trail at mile 2.6. Go 0.2 mile north (right) on the Fravert Basin Trail and cross the creek descending from Geneva Lake. There may be a rickety log bridge across the creek, situated below old supports for a nonexistent bridge. Once east of this creek, hike 1.8 miles east on the Fravert Basin Trail to a signed trail junction. Leave the Fravert Basin Trail and climb 1.2 miles northwest on a steep but good trail to reach the Trail Rider Pass Trail at 11,300 feet near a small creek descending from Hagerman's south face.

20.A3 — Snowmass Creek Approach

From Snowmass Creek TH at 8,400 ft:	133 RP	16.0 mi	2,580 ft	Class 1

This is the traditional backpacking approach to Snowmass Lake under Hagerman's north face. It is long, but worth the effort. Start at the Snowmass Creek Trailhead and walk south up Snowmass Creek's east side on the Maroon–Snowmass Trail. Pass the junction with the West Snowmass Trail after 1.2 miles and continue south on the Maroon–Snowmass Trail. After 3.7 miles, you will have an exotic view of the fourteener Snowmass Mountain above Bear Creek to the west.

After 6.0 miles, you reach a lake at 10,100 feet. Continue around the lake's east side to a second lake and the approach's crux. You must cross Snowmass Creek to reach Snowmass Lake, and there is no bridge. Either cross a 100-foot-long logjam at the upper lake's northern end, or wade the creek below the logjam. Either crossing can be dangerous in high water. Once on the creek's west side, continue 2.0 miles up the trail to Snowmass Lake at 10,980 feet. This scenic lake is a popular destination in July and August. Snowmass Peak and Hagerman Peak rise directly west of the lake; beyond, you can see Snowmass Mountain. Hagerman Peak lies between Snowmass Peak and Snowmass Mountain. Do not confuse rocky, 13,620-foot Snowmass Peak with gentler, 14,092-foot Snowmass Mountain.

You can hike from Snowmass Lake to Geneva Lake via 12,420-foot Trail Rider Pass. This pass allows you to visit both the north and south sides of Hagerman on a single visit. You can create a beautiful backcountry experience here.

Hagerman Peak from the southeast.

20.A4 — Buckskin Pass Approach

From Maroon Lake TH at 9,600 ft: *197 RP*   *15.2 mi*   *4,704 ft*   *Class 1*

With a vehicle shuttle, this route makes sense as a one-way journey. The round trip over Buckskin Pass requires more effort than the approach up Snowmass Creek, and this arduous approach is less popular than the hike up Snowmass Creek. Start at the Maroon Lake Trailhead (see "Thunder Pyramid") and follow the main trail 1.5 miles west to Crater Lake's east end. Turn right and follow the Maroon–Snowmass Trail northwest to Buckskin Pass at 12,462 feet. Descend on the trail, cross Snowmass Creek at 10,800 feet, then climb northwest to Snowmass Lake.

ROUTES

20.1 — Hagerman Peak — South Face

From Crystal TH at 9,000 ft:	*315 RP*	*14.3 mi*	*5,161 ft*	*Class 2+*
From 4WD parking at 9,640 ft:	*262 RP*	*10.3 mi*	*4,521 ft*	*Class 2+*
From Geneva Lake at 10,960 ft:	*196 RP*	*6.3 mi*	*3,201 ft*	*Class 2+*
From Snowmass Creek TH at 8,400 ft:	*464 RP*	*24.9 mi*	*7,321 ft*	*Class 2+*
From Snowmass Lake at 10,980 ft:	*252 RP*	*8.9 mi*	*4,741 ft*	*Class 2+*

This is the easiest route up Hagerman. If you have never climbed in the Elk Range, you might find the last thousand feet loose and tedious. Elk

Range veterans, though, will likely be grateful that they can climb one of the Elks' highest peaks without enduring worse rock. In any case, the approach to the upper peak is beautiful.

Use the Geneva Lake Approach, the North Fork of Crystal River Approach or the Snowmass Creek Approach. Your initial goal is to reach the point on the Trail Rider Pass Trail at 11,480 feet where the trail crosses the creek descending from the large south face of Hagerman and Snowmass Peak.

If you use the Geneva Lake Approach, hike around Geneva Lake's west side. When you are even with the lake's west end, look for an unmarked trail junction. The north (left) trail goes on up the valley to Siberia Lake. The east (right) trail goes to Trail Rider Pass. Turn east (right), hike around Geneva Lake's north end and cross the creek above the lake. In June you will have to ford the creek. By late July, you can step across on a series of well-placed stones. Hike south on the trail past a reassuring sign for Trail Rider Pass and climb above Geneva Lake's east side into the trees. There are good views to the north of 13,420-foot "Siberia Peak" from here. Follow the trail as it goes around the bottom of Hagerman's southwest ridge, turns east and climbs gently to cross the creek at 11,480 feet in the small drainage under Hagerman's south face.

If you use the North Fork of Crystal River Approach, turn east (right) when you reach the Trail Rider Pass Trail and hike 0.3 mile northeast to the same creek. If you use the Snowmass Creek Approach, hike 2.0 miles to the top of 12,420-foot Trail Rider Pass from Snowmass Lake and descend 1.2 miles on the west side of the pass to the same creek.

Leave the Trail Rider Pass Trail at 11,480 feet, hike 0.1 mile north up a small trail on the creek's west side, pass an excellent campsite and enter the narrow drainage. Stay on the creek's west side and hike 0.4 mile northeast then north up the drainage to 12,000 feet. There are two small valleys above this point. Turn west (left) and hike 0.1 mile up grass into the western valley. Turn north (right), hike 0.15 mile up rocky benches followed by a short, steep gully (Class 2+) to reach a commodious grass bench at 12,500 feet below Hagerman's south face. The introduction is over.

Hike 0.1 mile northwest up a steepening slope to 12,800 feet at the base of the face, then ascend it. The 1,100-foot climb up Hagerman's south face is consistent in angle and difficulty. There are little rock steps, which you can usually avoid at the expense of staying in looser gullies. You may choose to climb some of the rock steps to avoid the loose rock. The difficulty is consistently Class 2+. Near the top of the face, angle east (right) to avoid some cliffs and reach Hagerman's east ridge at 13,800 feet. On the ridge, you will have a stunning view of Snowmass Mountain. Turn west (left) and scamper 200 yards across a minor summit to reach Hagerman's highest point (Class 2). From here you can survey it all.

20.2 — Hagerman Peak — Southwest Ridge

From Crystal TH at 9,000 ft:	*343 RP*	*14.4 mi*	*5,201 ft*	*Class 3*
With descent of South Face:	*337 RP*	*14.35 mi*	*5,181 ft*	*Class 3*
From 4WD parking at 9,640 ft:	*290 RP*	*10.4 mi*	*4,561 ft*	*Class 3*
With descent of South Face:	*284 RP*	*10.35 mi*	*4,541 ft*	*Class 3*
From Geneva Lake at 10,960 ft:	*225 RP*	*6.4 mi*	*3,241 ft*	*Class 3*
With descent of South Face:	*218 RP*	*6.35 mi*	*3,221 ft*	*Class 3*
From Snowmass Creek TH at 8,400 ft:	*492 RP*	*25.0 mi*	*7,361 ft*	*Class 3*
With descent of South Face:	*486 RP*	*24.95 mi*	*7,341 ft*	*Class 3*
From Snowmass Lake at 10,980 ft:	*280 RP*	*9.0 mi*	*4,781 ft*	*Class 3*
With descent of South Face:	*274 RP*	*8.95 mi*	*4,761 ft*	*Class 3*

If this ridge were not in the Elk Range, it would be a classic. Large, loose blocks make the scrambling exacting, but your position is spectacular. The Southwest Ridge Route is only 0.2 mile west of the South Face Route, but is more committing, as it is difficult to retreat or escape from the southwest ridge. As with all committing adventures, when you succeed, you will have a nice feeling of accomplishment. Start early.

Follow one of the South Face Route's approaches to the creek crossing at 11,480 feet in the small drainage under Hagerman's south face. Leave the Trail Rider Pass Trail and hike 0.5 mile northwest up the drainage to a 12,380-foot pass on Hagerman's southwest ridge (Class 2). This is not the same drainage used on the South Face Route, but the next one to the west. You can see the 12,380-foot pass from the creek crossing on the Trail Rider Pass Trail at 11,480 feet.

From the pass, climb north along the ridge. The first gendarme is one of the route's cruxes. You can bypass the first set of towers on the ridge's west side. Then climb directly up the gendarme's main buttress by ascending a shallow, south-facing gully (Class 3). Once you are on top of the buttress at 12,760 feet, the ridge's steepness and difficulty ease considerably. Hike north along the amiable ridge toward the now visible upper peak (Class 2). Before reaching the upper ridge, climb into and out of a notch at 12,840 feet (Class 3). At 12,900 feet, you can escape the ridge if needed by traversing east to join the South Face Route (Class 2+).

Above 13,000 feet, you are committed to the northwest ridge on the upper part of the peak. The rock on the upper ridge is more fractured than the rock below, and large blocks are often poised above you. The difficulty is mostly Class 2+, with occasional Class 3 moves required. At 13,200 feet, stay below the ridge crest on the ridge's east (right) side. When it's easy to do so, climb back to the ridge crest. At 13,600 feet, scamper up a gully west of the ridge crest. This is your only significant excursion on the ridge's west side. Just below the summit, climb right along the exposed ridge crest for a dramatic finish to the highest point (Class 3). Ascending the Southwest Ridge Route and descending the South Slopes Route makes a good Tour de Hagerman.

20.3 — Hagerman Peak — East Ridge

From Crystal TH at 9,000 ft:	334 RP	14.5 mi	5,161 ft	Class 3
With descent of South Face:	330 RP	14.4 mi	5,161 ft	Class 3
From 4WD parking at 9,640 ft:	282 RP	10.5 mi	4,521 ft	Class 3
With descent of South Face:	277 RP	10.4 mi	4,521 ft	Class 3
From Geneva Lake at 10,960 ft:	216 RP	6.5 mi	3,201 ft	Class 3
With descent of South Face:	212 RP	6.4 mi	3,201 ft	Class 3
From Snowmass Creek TH at 8,400 ft:	483 RP	25.1 mi	7,321 ft	Class 3
With descent of South Face:	479 RP	25.0 mi	7,321 ft	Class 3
From Snowmass Lake at 10,980 ft:	272 RP	9.1 mi	4,741 ft	Class 3
With descent of South Face:	268 RP	9.0 mi	4,741 ft	Class 3

This is a more difficult route on Hagerman that also allows you to climb Snowmass Peak. Follow the South Face Route to 12,000 feet in the drainage south of Hagerman's south face. There are two small valleys above this point. Turn east (right) and hike 0.2 mile northeast then north up a talus-choked gulch. Continue 0.1 mile north to 12,600 feet at the bottom of the straight, narrow couloir below the Hagerman–Snowmass Peak saddle. This couloir is 250 yards east of the upper South Face Route.

Climb 900 feet up the couloir to the 13,500-foot, U-shaped saddle between Hagerman and Snowmass Peak (Class 2+). This couloir is snow-filled in June, but snow does not last long in this south-facing couloir. In a normal year, the couloir is snow-free by late July. When snow-free, the couloir is a bowling lane of loose rocks. There is no escape from rocks tumbling toward you in this narrow couloir. This is a ridiculous place for a large party; one or two people is plenty.

From the 13,500-foot saddle, turn west (left) and climb 300 feet up the small, narrowing, steepening face on the south side of Hagerman's east ridge (Class 3). Near the top of this face, angle south (left) and find the earliest escape from this loose, undesirable place. Once you are above this crux face, climb 200 feet northwest to reach Hagerman's east ridge at 13,800 feet (Class 2+). Scamper 200 yards west across a minor summit to reach Hagerman's highest point (Class 2). Ascending the East Ridge Route and descending the South Slopes Route makes another good Tour de Hagerman.

20.3EC — Extra Credit — Snowmass Peak, 13,620 feet, Class 2+
Snowmass Peak is a minor summit 0.3 mile east of Hagerman's highest point. Snowmass Peak is named because it is so dramatic when you view it from Snowmass Lake. However, you may not appreciate this northern drama when you approach Snowmass Peak from the south.

From the 13,500-foot saddle, scamper 150 feet east up a rubble trough on the ridge's south side. Leave the trough and climb 100 feet north to Snowmass Peak's 13,620-foot summit. This is a good perch for you to preview Hagerman's east ridge.

20.4 — Hagerman Peak — Hagar's Way

From Snowmass Creek TH at 8,400 ft: 539 RP 19.8 mi 5,441 ft Class 3 Steep Snow
With descent of South Face: 572 RP 22.4 mi 6,381 ft Class 3 Steep Snow
From Snowmass Lake at 10,980 ft: 328 RP   3.8 mi 2,861 ft Class 3 Steep Snow
With descent of South Face: 360 RP   6.4 mi 3,801 ft Class 3 Steep Snow
From Crystal TH at 9,000 ft: 494 RP 17.6 mi 6,001 ft Class 3 Steep Snow
With descent of South Face: 465 RP 16.0 mi 5,581 ft Class 3 Steep Snow
From 4WD parking at 9,640 ft: 441 RP 13.6 mi 5,361 ft Class 3 Steep Snow
With descent of South Face: 412 RP 12.0 mi 4,941 ft Class 3 Steep Snow
From Geneva Lake at 10,960 ft: 375 RP   9.6 mi 4,041 ft Class 3 Steep Snow
With descent of South Face: 346 RP   8.0 mi 3,621 ft Class 3 Steep Snow

This is the premier mountaineering route on Hagerman. It ascends the steep snow couloir that splits the large north face of Snowmass Peak and Hagerman. This couloir holds good snow through July. Use the Snowmass Creek Approach, the Geneva Lake Approach or the North Fork of Crystal River Approach.

If you use the Snowmass Creek Approach, hike 0.7 mile around Snowmass Lake's south side on a small trail. A steep, unpleasant scree slope rises above Snowmass Lake's west end and bars easy access to the gentler slopes above it. Either climb a shallow gully on the south (left) side of the scree slope (snow-filled through June) or climb grass slopes north (right) of the scree slope. Once you are above the scree slope, climb 0.3 mile west to 12,900 feet below the couloir. It is the only big couloir in this north face; you cannot miss it. From here you will fully appreciate the drama of Snowmass Peak's north face.

If you use the Geneva Lake Approach or the North Fork of Crystal River Approach, follow one of the South Face Route's approaches to the creek crossing at 11,480 feet in the small drainage under Hagerman's south face. Continue 0.4 mile east on the trail, pass a small lake at 11,700 feet and climb 0.8 mile north to 12,420-foot Trail Rider Pass. Descend 0.5 mile northeast to a switchback at 12,000 feet on the east side of the pass. Leave the trail and contour 0.5 mile north at 12,000 feet under Snowmass Peak's rugged east face. When you are past the cliffs, climb 0.3 mile west to 12,900 feet below the couloir.

Climb the 600-foot-high couloir to the 13,500-foot Hagerman–Snowmass Peak saddle. It is steep all the way. The lower part of the couloir faces northeast. Above 13,250 feet, there are two couloirs. You want to climb the north-facing, eastern (left) couloir. If there is an erosion gully in the couloir, stay to the east (left) of it. If you must cross an erosion gully, cross quickly, as this gully frequently collects debris from a large section of face surrounding the western (right) couloir. Once you are above 13,250 feet, you will be above this hazard. There is no cornice above the eastern couloir, but the last 200 feet to the notch holds the steepest snow.

Once you are in the 13,500-foot notch, breathe, climb Snowmass Peak if you wish (see Extra Credit 20.3EC) and continue on the East Ridge

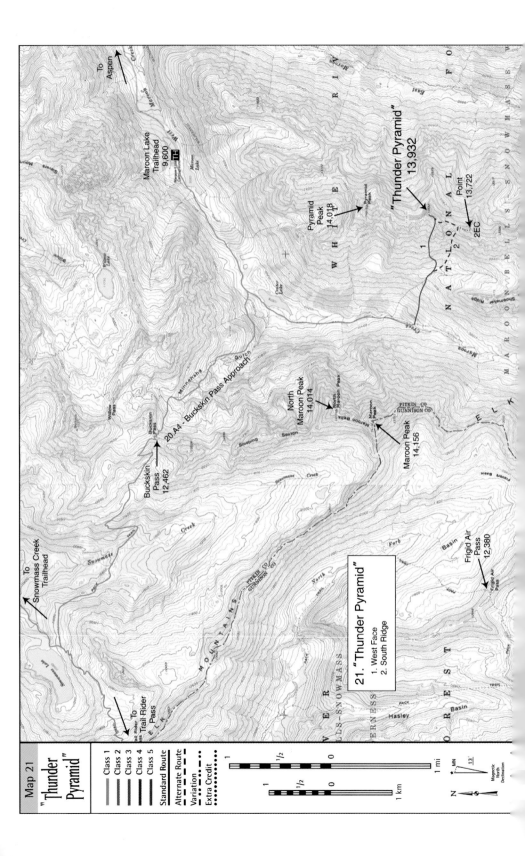

Map 21
"Thunder Pyramid"

To Aspen

Maroon Lake Trailhead 9,600

Pyramid Peak 14,018

"Thunder Pyramid" 13,932

Point 13,722

2EC

To Snowmass Creek Trailhead

Buckskin Pass 12,462

20.A4 - Buckskin Pass Approach

North Maroon Peak 14,014

Maroon Peak 14,156

PITKIN CO. GUNNISON CO.

To Trail Rider Pass

Frigid Air Pass 12,380

21. "Thunder Pyramid"
1. West Face
2. South Ridge

ELK

WILDS-SNOWMASS

WILDERNESS

FOREST

MAROON BELLS SNOWMASS

Class 1
Class 2
Class 3
Class 4
Class 5
Standard Route
Alternate Route
Variation
Extra Credit

1   1/2   0   1 mi

1   1/2   0   1 km

Magnetic North Declination   13°

N

13,932

21.2

"Thunder Pyramid" from the south.

Route to Hagerman's summit. Ascending Hagar's Way and descending the South Slopes Route makes a comprehensive Tour de Hagerman. With this circle tour, you will have to hike over Trail Rider Pass no matter which approach you use. It is an interesting choice, whether you do this hike before or after the couloir climb.

21. "Thunder Pyramid"   13,932 feet

See Map 21 on page 180

"Thunder Pyramid" is 2.5 miles south-southwest of Maroon Lake and 0.6 mile south of the fourteener Pyramid. You cannot see "Thunder Pyramid" from pedestrian vantages, and in particular, you cannot see the peak from Maroon Lake. For some, the peak's reclusive position and evocative name make it more appealing, but that opinion is often formed in a comfortable living room. After an ascent of "Thunder Pyramid," most people form the opinion that it is a hidden horror. Located in the heart of the Elk Range, this peak is steep and loose. Killer blocks lurk overhead, and handholds are literally just that: you hold them in your hand, as they are not attached to the mountain. Add a storm and your adventure can take on a fourth dimension. Approach this peak with the utmost care.

MAPS
Required: *Maroon Bells, White River National Forest*

TRAILHEAD

Maroon Lake Trailhead
This popular trailhead is at 9,600 feet and provides access to Hagerman's Buckskin Pass Approach as well as to routes on the west side of "Thunder Pyramid." From Aspen's north side, leave Colorado 82 and go 9.4 miles west on the Maroon Lake Road to the parking area east of Maroon Lake. A postcard view of the Maroon Bells greets you at the lake.

From mid-June through September, the Maroon Lake Road is closed from 8:30 A.M. to 5:00 P.M. During these hours, there is a shuttle to the lake that starts at Ruby Park in downtown Aspen. For more information, call the Roaring Fork Transportation Authority (RFTA) at 970-925-8484, or the White River National Forest at 970-925-3445. In winter the road is gated 3.0 miles from Colorado 82 at the T-Lazy-7 Guest Ranch.

ROUTES

21.1 — "Thunder Pyramid" — West Face
From Maroon Lake TH at 9,600 ft: *275 RP*   *8.8 mi*   *4,332 ft*   *Class 3*

This is the easiest route on "Thunder Pyramid." It is a dangerous climb up steep rubble gullies and poised blocks. Using a rope can increase the risk. You must be balanced on steep, loose terrain. Do not attempt this route as a large party.

Start at the Maroon Lake Trailhead and hike 1.5 miles west to Crater Lake's northeast end. Turn south (left) at a trail junction and hike 1.8 miles south along West Maroon Creek's west side. During your hike up West Maroon Creek, the Maroon Bells pass in review above you to the west and Pyramid looms to the east. Leave the trail at 10,500 feet just after it crosses to the creek's east side. "Thunder Pyramid" is only 1.1 miles east of this point, but your views of it from the valley are partial and foreshortened. The introduction is over.

Hike 0.3 mile northeast to 10,800 feet in a small drainage. Hike 0.4 mile southeast up this drainage to 11,700 feet, where the drainage flattens, opens and heads south. Leave the drainage and climb 0.25 mile east to 12,000 feet, overcoming a cliff band by climbing up a scree gully. Angle north and get into a large, white gully just above a cliff band. Finding this gully is the key to the climb. Climb along the north (left) edge of the white gully to 13,400 feet (Class 2+). Cross to the gully's south side and climb south out of the gully on very loose blocks (Class 3). Scamper up to the ridge above. This is the upper south ridge of "Thunder Pyramid."

Climb north on or just west of the ridge over two steps to the summit (Class 3). From the top of "Thunder Pyramid," you will have a unique view of the surrounding fourteeners. For a few free moments, you can let your eyes dance across the rotten ridges. Hopefully, there will be no thunder.

21.2 — "Thunder Pyramid" — South Ridge

From Maroon Lake TH at 9,600 ft:	303 RP	9.2 mi	4,332 ft	Class 4
With descent of West Face:	299 RP	9.0 mi	4,332 ft	Class 4

This route up "Thunder Pyramid" is longer and harder than the West Face Route, but it allows you to climb an additional peak and make a circle tour. Follow the West Face Route to 11,700 feet in the small drainage. Continue 0.1 mile south to 11,800 feet in the drainage. The south ridge of "Thunder Pyramid" is above you to the east. This ridge continues to Point 13,722, which is 0.4 mile south-southwest of "Thunder Pyramid."

Leave the drainage and climb east toward the gully below the 13,420-foot saddle between Point 13,722 and "Thunder Pyramid." Climb steep, loose blocks on the south (right) side of the gully (Class 4). The upper part of the gully is easier. Climb the gully all the way to the 13,420-foot saddle. Turn north (left) and contour north along narrow ledges on the east (right) side of the ridge (Class 2).

When you reach a scree gully, ascend it to regain the ridge crest at 13,740 feet (Class 2). Climb north on the ridge, then on or just west of the ridge over two steps to reach the summit (Class 3). Ascending the South Ridge Route and descending the West Face Route makes a sizable Tour de "Thunder Pyramid."

21.2EC — Extra Credit — Point 13,722, Class 2

From the 13,420-foot saddle, turn south and climb 0.15 mile south to the summit of Point 13,722 (Class 2). After making the arduous ascent to the saddle, this easy summit pitch is hard to pass up. Point 13,722 is a "Bi"—one of Colorado's 200 highest peaks. From Point 13,722, you can preview the upper South Ridge Route to "Thunder Pyramid." This is a sobering view.

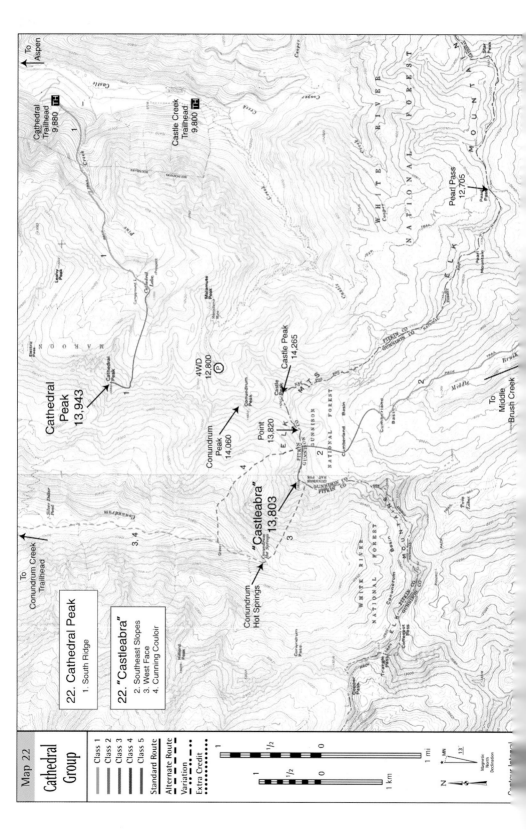

Map 22

Cathedral Group

Class 1
Class 2
Class 3
Class 4
Class 5
Standard Route
Alternate Route
Variation
Extra Credit

22. Cathedral Peak
1. South Ridge

22. "Castleabra"
2. Southeast Slopes
3. West Face
4. Cunning Couloir

To Aspen

Cathedral Trailhead 9,880

Castle Creek Trailhead 9,800

Pearl Pass 12,705

Cathedral Peak 13,943

Conundrum Peak 14,060

4WD 12,800 (P)

Castle Peak 14,265

Point 13,820

"Castleabra" 13,803

Conundrum Hot Springs

To Conundrum Creek Trailhead

To Middle Brush Creek

WHITE RIVER NATIONAL FOREST

ELK MOUNTAINS

1 mi

1 km

N

Magnetic North Declination

13,943

Cathedral Peak from the northeast.

22. Cathedral Group

Cathedral Peak   13,943 feet
"Castleabra"   13,803 feet

See Map 22 on page 184

These peaks frame the fourteener Castle, the highest peak in the Elk Range. Castle is 12.7 miles south-southwest of Aspen, and this area is well developed. Only the Maroon Bells–Snowmass Wilderness Area protects these peaks from further commercialization. Cathedral, to the north of Castle, repeats and strengthens Castle's rugged ramparts. "Castleabra," west of Castle, adds the dot to this powerful exclamation point in the southern Elks.

MAPS
Required: *Maroon Bells, Hayden Peak, Pearl Pass, White River National Forest*
Optional: *Gothic*

TRAILHEADS

Cathedral Trailhead
This trailhead is at 9,880 feet and provides access to Cathedral's east side. From Aspen's north side, leave Colorado 82 and turn west onto the Maroon Lake Road. After 30 yards, turn south (left) onto the Castle Creek

Road (paved) and measure from this point. Pass Ashcroft at mile 11.0 and turn west (right) onto a dirt road at mile 12.0. Go west on the dirt road as it switchbacks up the hill, and reach the trailhead at mile 12.5. In winter the road is open to Ashcroft.

Conundrum Creek Trailhead

This trailhead is at 8,800 feet and provides access to the west side of "Castleabra." From Aspen's north side, leave Colorado 82 and turn west onto the Maroon Lake Road. After 30 yards, turn south (left) onto the Castle Creek Road (paved) and measure from this point. Go 4.9 miles south and turn southwest (right) onto a paved road. Descend southwest, cross Castle Creek at mile 5.1 and turn south (left) onto a dirt road. Follow this road south past many private driveways to the trailhead's public parking area at mile 6.0. In winter the road is open to within 0.5 mile of the trailhead, but parking is limited. Respect private property and its owners here and park on the Castle Creek Road.

Middle Brush Creek Trailhead

This trailhead is at 9,180 feet and provides access to the southwest side of "Castleabra." From the town of Crested Butte, go 2.1 miles southeast on Colorado 135. Turn north (left) onto the Brush Creek Road, which is marked with a sign for the Country Club, and measure from this point. Follow the Brush Creek Road past the Country Club golf course, stay east (right) at mile 0.5 and turn east then north into the East River drainage. Cross the East River at mile 2.8 and cross Brush Creek at mile 4.6. Turn northeast (right) at mile 4.7 into the Brush Creek drainage on a rougher road. Turn east (right) at mile 5.7 onto the Pearl Pass Road (FS 738) and park at mile 6.0. This is the trailhead.

Beyond this point, the road narrows and crosses West Brush Creek. This ford stops most low-clearance vehicles. Four-wheel-drive vehicles can continue 6.9 miles on the Pearl Pass Road to unmarked parking at 10,820 feet. The Pearl Pass Road is well known as one of Colorado's roughest, and it can stop four-wheel-drive vehicles when it is wet. In winter the road is closed at the Cold Springs Ranch, 3.1 miles from Colorado 135.

22. Cathedral Peak   13,943 feet

See Map 22 on page 184

Cathedral is 1.7 miles north of the fourteener Castle Peak in the southeast end of the Elk Range. Even more rugged than its loftier parent, Cathedral has wild towers on its north, east and south ridges. The peak is well named. Like most Elk Range peaks, you cannot see Cathedral from highways or towns. Its majesty waits for you above the trees. Not surprisingly, Cathedral has no Class 1 or Class 2 hiking route to its summit. Because of the towers and loose rock, Cathedral does not offer a variety of routes, and we only discuss the standard route here.

ROUTE

22.1 — Cathedral Peak — South Ridge

From Cathedral TH at 9,880 ft: *277 RP   9.0 mi   4,063 ft   Class 3   Steep Snow*
From Cathedral Lake at 11,866 ft: 173 RP   2.6 mi   2,077 ft   Class 3   Steep Snow

This is the easiest route up Cathedral and has been the standard route for years. Start at the Cathedral Trailhead and hike 3.2 miles west up the Cathedral Trail to Cathedral Lake at 11,866 feet. The trail is steep and relentless in its 2,000-foot ascent. The first peak you see to the west is not Cathedral, but 13,348-foot Malamute Peak. After a set of switchbacks up a steep hill, the trail climbs southwest to reach Cathedral Lake's east edge at 11,866 feet.

From the lake, Cathedral's east ridge blocks much of your view of Cathedral's summit ramparts. However, you can see the route south of the summit. Cathedral's south ridge has two distinct towers 0.25 mile south of the summit. The route ascends the east-facing gully to the north of the northern tower. Another, more inviting gully reaches the ridge just south of the southern tower. This gully is not the route.

Hike around Cathedral Lake's north end and pick up remnants of an old miners trail as you climb west into the basin below Cathedral's south ridge. Climb to 13,200 feet below the access gully to the south ridge. This 500-foot-high gully is the route's crux. In June, the gully is solid snow. In July, only the top of the gully is snow-filled. In August, a snow remnant may remain at the top of the gully, keeping the dirt below soft. In September, the gully is snow-free and full of hard dirt.

Ascend the gully to a 13,060-foot saddle on Cathedral's south ridge. Any snow in the gully is steep. When snow-free, the gully requires Class 3 scrambling on questionable, dirt-covered rock. From the saddle, climb 0.25 mile north up the rough ridge to the summit (Class 2+).

22. "Castleabra"   13,803 feet

See Map 22 on page 184

This peak is 0.8 mile west of the fourteener Castle Peak in the southeast end of the Elk Range. Just as "Thunder Pyramid" hides behind Pyramid, "Castleabra" hides behind Castle. However, "Castleabra" is much easier to climb than "Thunder Pyramid," and "Castleabra" offers a choice of routes. "Castleabra" is the easiest of the Elks' four centennial thirteeners. If you are new to these four peaks, ease into your project and climb "Castleabra" first. Remember that the ease is relative to one of the hardest peaks in this book. Any of the long routes on "Castleabra" will challenge you.

ROUTES

22.2 — "Castleabra" — Southeast Slopes

From Middle Brush Creek TH at 9,180 ft:	429 RP	21.2 mi	4,783 ft	Class 2
From 4WD parking at 10,820 ft:	258 RP	7.4 mi	3,143 ft	Class 2

Although long and remote, this is the easiest route on "Castleabra." It has a long approach, then takes you through Cumberland Basin, one of Colorado's pristine places. A four-wheel-drive vehicle can shorten the distance considerably, but even that aid can be problematic in wet conditions. The four-wheel-drive road over Pearl Pass is well known as one of Colorado's worst. Consider using a mountain bike.

Start at the Middle Brush Creek Trailhead and go 2.5 miles up the four-wheel-drive road in Middle Brush Creek to a junction at 9,480 feet. Continue north (left) on the Pearl Pass Road in Middle Brush Creek for an additional 3.2 miles to a junction with the Twin Lakes Trail. Continue on the Pearl Pass Road, ford Middle Brush Creek twice and reach a meadow at 10,820 feet. Four-wheel-drive vehicles can park here. This point is 6.9 miles from the Middle Brush Creek Trailhead.

The old trail up Cumberland Basin is now badly overgrown. The sparse trail will speed you on your way, then desert you when you need it most. It is still worth finding, though, and will reduce your bushwhacking adventure. From the four-wheel-drive parking at 10,820 feet, walk 0.25 mile north up the road to a switchback where the road climbs southeast toward Pearl Pass. Leave the road and hike 0.1 mile west down to the trail that is visible from here. Hike 0.5 mile north on the trail into the Maroon Bells–Snowmass Wilderness. Your wilderness adventure begins shortly beyond the small sign marking the boundary.

The trail leads you down to Middle Brush Creek, where the trail appears to cross and continue on the creek's west side. The astute hiker will stop, check the map and observe that the old trail stays on the creek's east side. You will wonder where the trail is as you backtrack along a wall of bushes, but the old trail *does* stay on the creek's east side. It is buried in the bushes near the creek. Depending on your disposition, either find the trail in the bushes or hike east then north around the initial bushes and find the trail farther up the valley. Continue north and make several similar route choices as the bushes persist for 1.5 miles.

Break free from the bushes at 11,700 feet and behold Cumberland Basin. In addition to the basin, you are treated to an uninterrupted view of Castle's south ridge with its namesake turrets. Hike 1.0 mile northnorthwest into the basin on grass benches, dodging any little cliffs that intervene. Climb 0.2 mile north to the 13,380-foot saddle between 13,803-foot "Castleabra" and Point 13,820 on Castle's west ridge. The slope up to the saddle is best climbed when snow-covered, but provides reasonable passage on scree after the snow melts. Once on the ridge,

13,803

22.2

"Castleabra" from the south.

climb 0.4 mile west along the gentle ridge to the summit. Your views of
the Elk Range grow en route. In particular, the view of Castle is spectacular from here.

22.3 — "Castleabra" — West Face

From Conundrum Creek TH at 8,800 ft:	*351 RP*	*18.2 mi*	*5,003 ft*	*Class 2*
From Conundrum Hot Springs at 11,200 ft:	*144 RP*	*2.2 mi*	*2,603 ft*	*Class 2*

This arduous ascent is best done from a camp at Conundrum Hot Springs.
Start at the Conundrum Creek Trailhead and walk 8.0 miles south up the
scenic Conundrum Creek Trail to Conundrum Hot Springs at 11,200 feet.
There are marked campsites below and above the springs, and two pools
at the hot springs offer unsophisticated soaking under the northwestern
ramparts of "Castleabra."

Extract yourself from the hot springs, cross to the creek's east side
and go 100 yards south on a trail to the snout of a large rock glacier.
Leave the trail, climb east along the rock glacier's northern edge, then
climb steeply east into a tiny basin west of "Castleabra." This is a classic
wilderness position. Persevere up this tiny basin all the way to a 13,620-
foot saddle just south of the summit. Early season snow can make this
ascent easier. From the 13,620-foot saddle, climb 100 yards north up scree
to the summit.

22.4 — "Castleabra" — Cunning Couloir

From Conundrum Creek TH at 8,800 ft: 423 RP 19.0 mi 5,003 ft Class 3 Steep Snow
From Conundrum Hot Springs at 11,200 ft: 251 RP   5.0 mi 3,403 ft Class 3 Steep Snow

This hidden couloir is the premier mountaineering route on "Castleabra," and it should excite your spirit of adventure. Start at the Conundrum Creek Trailhead and walk 8.0 miles south up the scenic Conundrum Creek Trail to Conundrum Hot Springs at 11,200 feet, where you may choose to camp. For the ascent, backtrack 0.5 mile north down the trail to 10,800 feet. Leave the trail, cross Conundrum Creek and climb steeply east to 12,200 feet in an unnamed basin north of "Castleabra" and west of Castle. This basin is full of obnoxious talus, and this route is best done when the rocks are completely snow-covered.

Climb southeast to 13,000 feet and spy the crafty couloir to the south. This north-facing couloir retains snow longer than other routes on "Castleabra." Be prepared. Climb south on steep snow through embracing cliffs to the 13,380-foot saddle between "Castleabra" to the west and Castle to the east. Once on the ridge, climb 0.4 mile west along the gentle ridge to the summit. Ascending the Cunning Couloir and descending the West Face Route makes a terrific Tour de "Castleabra."

CHAPTER SIX

San Juan Range

Introduction

The San Juans are Colorado's finest range. Other Colorado ranges are linear, long and narrow. From their summits, you can almost always see civilization. The San Juans are a vast mountain area in Colorado's southwest corner covering more than 4,000 square miles! Saint John has been well represented.

The San Juans contain 11 county summits, 13 fourteeners and 21 centennial thirteeners. No other Colorado range comes close to these counts. Indeed, the San Juans contain a third of Colorado's 100 highest peaks. Not only are San Juan peaks numerous, they are rugged. Many of Colorado's most difficult peaks are in the San Juans. Six wilderness areas live here, including Colorado's largest—the Weminuche Wilderness. The San Juans are less crowded than other ranges closer to the eastern slope's metropolitan areas. It is not reasonable to climb in the San Juans on a two-day weekend from Denver, and this reduces the number of visitors. Even if you live in Durango, there are many San Juan areas that still require a multi-day backpack. The San Juans are full of jagged wilderness!

One unpleasant San Juan reality is rotten rock. If you climb a dozen San Juan peaks, you are bound to find a chip-rock slope to curse. If you climb in the San Juans long enough, you will eventually find yourself on a hard-packed dirt slope covered with ball-bearing debris at the angle of repose. If you are unlucky, there will be a cliff below you. If you keep looking, you will find diseased, knife-edge ridges with no logical means of support. Hardened San Juan veterans will run across exposed junk that can strike terror into the heart of a San Juan novice. If you stick to the standard routes on the centennial thirteeners, you will not encounter these extremes, but approach San Juan peaks with caution nevertheless.

The San Juans' large, high areas collect a lot of winter snow. The avalanche danger is often extreme in these steep mountains. The deep snow mantle takes a long time to melt, and some areas are not easily accessible until July. Many San Juan peaks carry a lot of snow into August. You should consider carrying an ice ax in any season.

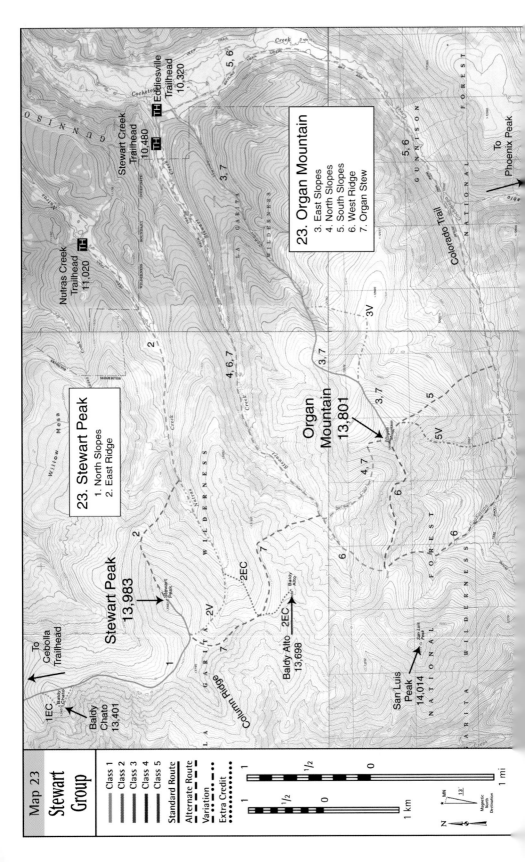

Map 23
Stewart
Group

Class 1
Class 2
Class 3
Class 4
Class 5
Standard Route
Alternate Route
Variation
Extra Credit

23. Stewart Peak
1. North Slopes
2. East Ridge

23. Organ Mountain
3. East Slopes
4. North Slopes
5. South Slopes
6. West Ridge
7. Organ Stew

Stewart Peak
13,983

Organ Mountain
13,801

Baldy Alto
13,698

Baldy Chato
13,401

San Luis Peak
14,014

Nutras Creek Trailhead 11,020

Stewart Creek Trailhead 10,480

Eddiesville Trailhead 10,320

To Cebolla Trailhead

To Phoenix Peak

GUNNISON NATIONAL FOREST

LA GARITA WILDERNESS

Colorado Trail

Column Ridge

Willow Mesa

N
MN
13°
Magnetic
North
Declination

Spirit of the San Juans.

23. Stewart Group

Stewart Peak   13,983 feet
Organ Mountain   13,801 feet

See Map 23 on page 192

These shy peaks hide in silent splendor near the fourteener San Luis in the heart of the La Garita Wilderness, 10 miles north of Creede, 20 miles east of Lake City and 40 miles south of Gunnison. The La Garita Wilderness is one of Colorado's finest. It sees few visitors compared to other wilderness areas closer to cities. It is precisely these peaks' reclusive nature that makes them well worth climbing. *Garita* means "sentry box" in Spanish, and indeed, the La Garita Mountains guard a large area halfway between the southern end of the Sawatch and the heart of the San Juans.

These peaks have their own character and provide a perfect introduction to the San Juans. They are gentler than the central San Juan peaks and are less traveled than the more accessible Sawatch peaks. Stewart, Organ and "Phoenix" compose the only trio of centennial thirteeners that have Class 1 hiking routes to their summits.

Spring Creek Pass at 10,898 feet on the Continental Divide separates the La Garitas from the rest of the San Juans. Cochetopa Pass at 10,032 feet separates the San Juans from the Sawatch. It is only because Spring Creek Pass is higher than Cochetopa Pass that the La Garitas are considered part of the San Juans. The La Garitas are really a separate range with a very unique birth.

Twenty-eight million years ago the largest volcanic eruption ever recorded in our study of Earth's history blasted forth 1,200 cubic miles of magma. That is almost 5,000 times more debris than Mount Saint Helens ejected in 1980. The result of the epic explosions is the 20-by-50-mile La Garita Caldera, which cradles today's La Garita Mountains. These gentle peaks are the remains of violence that, if it occurred today, would massively change, and perhaps destroy, human civilization. While you are hiking in the La Garitas, keep their heritage in mind and remember that intelligence does not guarantee survival.

The peace you can find on these peaks today stands in sharp contrast to their birth process. There is much to be learned here. While you are hiking, keep your eyes peeled for evidence of the ancient eruption. It left many clues. The soft, rich volcanic soils have eroded into Class 1 routes, and La Garita is replete with these soils. Many elk live here, and you may see a large elk herd. Moose also live here, having been reintroduced to Stewart Creek; they have since spread to many of the neighboring creeks.

MAPS
Required: *Stewart Peak, San Luis Peak, Halfmoon Pass, Elk Park, Gunnison National Forest, Rio Grande National Forest*

TRAILHEADS

Cebolla Trailhead
This trailhead is at 11,500 feet and provides access to Stewart's north side. *Cebolla* (pronounced "se-BOY-ah") means "onion" in Spanish. There are two routes to this trailhead, and they are both long. Winter road closures are far from this trailhead.

Route 1. From the Colorado 50–Colorado 149 junction west of Gunnison, go 45.3 miles south on Colorado 149 to Lake City. Continue south through Lake City on Colorado 149 and go another 10.0 miles southeast on Colorado 149. Just before Slumgullion Pass, turn north (left) onto Los Pinos–Cebolla Road (FS 788) and measure from this point.

Pass the Slumgullion Campground at mile 0.1, the Cannibal Plateau Trailhead at mile 1.0, the Deer Lakes Campground at mile 2.8, the Hidden Valley Campground at mile 7.3, the Spruce Campground at mile 8.4 and the Cebolla Campground at mile 9.3. Cross Mineral Creek at mile 12.1, cross Cebolla and Spring Creeks at mile 15.2 and reach a three-way junction at mile 15.3. This is Cathedral.

Turn south (right) and continue on FS 788. Go straight (left) at mile 16.4, climb east, enter Gunnison National Forest at mile 19.5, cross Los Pinos Pass at mile 21.0 and turn south (right) onto FS 790 at mile 22.1 in

Sage Park. Go south on FS 790, pass Groundhog Park at mile 24.5, turn east, cross Los Pinos Creek at mile 27.2 and reach the Cebolla Trailhead at mile 28.5. The signed trailhead is on the east side of the East Fork of Los Pinos Creek. The Cebolla Trail climbs south from here.

Route 2. If you are approaching from the north, turn south onto Colorado 114 from U.S. 50. This junction is 33.0 miles west of Monarch Pass and 7.5 miles east of Gunnison. Go 20.0 miles south on Colorado 114 and turn right onto Saguache County NN14 (BLM 3083) along Cochetopa Creek. Go 3.5 miles south on Saguache County NN14 and turn west (right) onto BLM 3084, which continues as FS 788. If you are approaching from the south, go 11.0 miles west from the summit of Cochetopa Pass. Measure from the junction of Saguache County NN14 and BLM 3084.

Go south on BLM 3084, go straight (left) at mile 8.8 and continue on FS 790, which is also called Big Meadows Road. Pass Blue Park, go straight (right) at Big Meadows at mile 19.0 and continue on FS 790. Pass Willow Park at mile 21.5 and reach the Cebolla Trailhead at mile 22.8.

Nutras Creek Trailhead
This trailhead is at 11,020 feet and provides access to Stewart's east side. There are three routes to this trailhead, and they are all long. Winter road closures are far from this trailhead.

Route 1. If you are approaching from the north, turn south onto Colorado 114 from U.S. 50. This junction is 33.0 miles west of Monarch Pass and 7.5 miles east of Gunnison. Go 20.0 miles south on Colorado 114, turn right onto Saguache County NN14 (BLM 3083) along Cochetopa Creek. Go 7.0 miles south on Saguache County NN14 to Upper Dome Reservoir's south end and turn south (right) onto Saguache County 2166, which is also called the Cochetopa Road. This junction has a sign for the Stewart Creek Trailhead. If you are approaching from the south, go 7.5 miles west from the summit of Cochetopa Pass. Measure from the junction of Saguache County NN14 and Saguache County 2166.

Go south on Saguache County 2166, go straight (right) at mile 4.3 and enter the Gunnison National Forest at mile 6.9. The road is now FS 794. Cross Pauline Creek at mile 11.3 and cross Perfecto Creek at mile 13.8. Turn west (right) at mile 14.1 and stay on FS 794. Go straight (left) at mile 16.3 and stay on FS 794. Cross Chavez Creek at mile 17.1 and reach the unsigned Nutras Creek Trailhead on Nutras Creek's north side at mile 18.6. You can see Organ Mountain southwest of the trailhead.

Route 2. Follow the Cebolla Trailhead's Route 1 to the Cebolla Trailhead. Continue east on FS 790, pass Willow Park at mile 29.6 and turn south (right) onto FS 794.28 (Perfecto Creek Road) at mile 32.1. Go south on FS 794.28, cross Pauline Creek at mile 33.0, cross Perfecto Creek at mile 34.7

and turn southwest (right) onto FS 794 at mile 36.2. Cross Chavez Creek at mile 37.0 and reach the Nutras Creek Trailhead at mile 38.5.

Route 3. Follow the Cebolla Trailhead's Route 2 to Big Meadows at mile 19.0 on FS 790. Turn south (left) onto FS 794.28 (Perfecto Creek Road). Go south on FS 794.28, cross Pauline Creek at mile 19.9, cross Perfecto Creek at mile 21.6 and turn southwest (right) onto FS 794 at mile 23.2. Cross Chavez Creek at mile 24.0 and reach the Nutras Creek Trailhead at mile 25.5.

Stewart Creek Trailhead
This trailhead is at 10,480 feet and provides access to Organ's north side. From the Nutras Creek Trailhead, continue 2.2 miles southeast on FS 794 to the Stewart Creek Trailhead. The signed trailhead is south of the road before the road crosses Stewart Creek.

Eddiesville Trailhead
This trailhead is at 10,320 feet and provides access to Organ's east and south sides, and to the north side of "Phoenix Peak." From the Stewart Creek Trailhead, continue 0.25 mile east on FS 794 to the Eddiesville Trailhead. The signed trailhead is on the road's east side where the road turns south and crosses Stewart Creek. There are two parking areas with the Eddiesville Trailhead. The main, signed northern area serves the northbound Colorado Trail. For the southbound Colorado Trail and routes on Organ and "Phoenix," go 0.1 mile south to a locked gate and a parking area at the end of the public road.

23. Stewart Peak   13,983 feet

See Map 23 on page 192

Stewart is a gentle giant of the La Garitas. Stewart used to be a fourteener, but, after a new survey, it is now just the highest centennial thirteener in the San Juans and the second-highest centennial thirteener in Colorado. You can find pyroclastic rocks here. The pile posts on Stewart's west ridge, also called Column Ridge, are reminiscent of Devils Tower in Wyoming.

ROUTES

23.1 — Stewart Peak — North Slopes *Classic*

From Cebolla TH at 11,500 ft: 134 RP   7.6 mi   2,803 ft   *Class 1*

This is the shortest and easiest route on Stewart. It is a scenic stroll that keeps you high for a long time. Start at the Cebolla Trailhead and hike 0.2 mile south on the Cebolla Trail on the east side of the East Fork of Los

Stewart Peak from the northwest.

Pinos Creek. Cross to the creek's west side and hike 0.3 mile west then south to treeline at 11,940 feet. From here you can see the large, north slopes of Baldy Chato and the sea of willows that lives here.

Hike 0.7 mile southwest on the Cebolla Trail through the willows. The trail is marked with large poles, and with a little looking you can find easy alleys between the bushes. At 12,440 feet, leave the trail and climb 0.2 mile south through more alleys in the last of the willows to the open slopes above. Hike 0.5 mile south-southeast up these grassy slopes to 13,300 feet on the rounded shoulder just east of Baldy Chato's summit. From here you can see Stewart 1.5 miles to the southeast.

Hike 0.2 mile southeast under Baldy Chato's summit and get onto the ridge between Baldy Chato and Stewart. Hike 0.8 mile south along or near this grassy, rolling ridge as Stewart looms ever larger. Leave the ridge and do a gentle, ascending traverse 0.5 mile southeast to the 13,540-foot saddle west of Stewart. Climb 0.4 mile northeast along a mostly grassy ridge to Stewart's highest point. The San Juans' highest centennial thirteener is yours.

23.1EC — Extra Credit — Baldy Chato, 13,401 feet, Class 1
Either coming or going, take time to visit Baldy Chato's 13,401-foot summit. *Chato* means "snub-nosed" or "squatty" in Spanish, and the name suits this unranked peak when you view it from afar. Nevertheless, there are dramatic views from this squatty summit.

23.2 — Stewart Peak — East Ridge

From Nutras Creek TH at 11,020 ft: *213 RP*   *8.0 mi*   *2,963 ft*   *Class 2*

Though Stewart Creek to the south sees more people headed for the fourteener San Luis, Nutras Creek has other charms. *Nutras* means "beavers" in Southern Colorado Spanish, and this creek has numerous beaver ponds; you might see foraging moose in them as well.

Start at the Nutras Creek Trailhead and hike 0.8 mile southwest on a trail along the north side of Nutras Creek to the La Garita Wilderness boundary. The 1965 Elk Park Quadrangle indicates "jeep trail" for this stretch of trail, but this old road is now closed to vehicles. Continue 0.5 mile southwest then 0.8 mile west on the increasingly sketchy trail to a side stream. After crossing this stream, you will be close to the bottom of Stewart's east ridge, but don't leave the valley just yet.

From the side stream, hike 0.5 mile west to 11,800 feet. Leave the now faint trail and valley here and climb 0.2 mile northwest through open trees to reach Stewart's east ridge at 12,200 feet. Climb 0.5 mile northwest up the well-defined ridge to a gentle area at 13,100 feet, where you can gaze down on Willow Mesa to the northeast. Turn and climb 0.7 mile southwest up Stewart's upper east ridge to the summit.

23.2V — Variation

Instead of leaving the valley at 11,800 feet, continue 1.0 mile southwest up the valley, then climb 0.8 mile west and northwest to the 13,540-foot saddle southwest of Stewart. From the saddle, climb 0.5 mile northeast on the rounded ridge to the summit. Ascending the East Ridge Route and descending this variation allows you to see all of Nutras Creek.

23.2EC — Extra Credit — Baldy Alto, 13,698 feet, Class 2

This high Baldy is 1.25 miles south of Stewart and is a "Bi"—one of Colorado's 200 highest peaks. From 11,800 feet in Nutras Creek, continue 1.0 mile southwest up the valley to 12,440 feet. Leave the main valley and climb 0.5 mile southwest to the 13,100-foot saddle between Stewart and Baldy Alto. Climb 0.5 mile southeast to Baldy Alto's 13,698-foot summit. You can include Baldy Alto when you descend Variation 23.2V.

23. Organ Mountain   13,801 feet

See Map 23 on page 192

Organ Mountain is 2.0 miles east of the fourteener San Luis. Fantastic volcanic formations give Organ Mountain its distinctive character. When seen from the south, Organ reminds you of the huge, airy instrument in a lofty cathedral. On closer inspection, you can see that some of the organ "pipes" are composed of large, rounded stones loosely embedded in ancient ash. Other parts of the volcano's complex constructions are solid, soaring dihedrals. Organ's vertical south face is a photographer's dream, but gentle north and east slopes make this an easily reached summit.

At 13,801 feet, Organ is the lowest official peak in this book. There was a time when Organ wouldn't have had this distinction, and old maps still show it as 13,799 feet. Newer surveys promoted Organ to its loftier position. Whatever the peak's altitude, it is well worth climbing. Here, you can find the heart of the La Garitas.

ROUTES

23.3 — Organ Mountain — East Slopes *Classic*

From Eddiesville TH at 10,320 ft: *150 RP*   *8.4 mi*   *3,481 ft*   *Class 1*

This is the shortest and easiest route up Organ. It offers a refreshing hike up a seldom visited valley on a reasonable trail and rolling, grassy upper slopes. Start at the southern parking area of the Eddiesville Trailhead. Hike 150 yards southwest on the Colorado Trail along the north side of a private property fence. This is also the Continental Divide Trail and the old Skyline Trail. Go south through a gate and hike 50 yards south on the trail toward a side creek, but do not cross it. The crux of the ascent is here.

The creek just south of you is Hondo Creek, which comes from Cañon Hondo, and this is where you want to go. The trail up Cañon Hondo is unsigned, and you cannot see it from the Colorado Trail. Your easy ascent depends on finding the old Cañon Hondo Trail. Fifty feet north of Hondo Creek, leave the Colorado Trail and walk west through the grass. You will find the trail within 200 feet as it enters the trees north of Hondo Creek.

Hike 2.4 miles southwest up the Cañon Hondo Trail on Hondo Creek's north side to treeline at 11,900 feet. The trail is visible for the first 1.5 miles then starts to fade. Be careful to stay on the main trail, as there are also many game trails in this area. If you lose the trail, persist up the valley, staying well north of the creek, and you will likely find it again.

From treeline at 11,900 feet, leave Cañon Hondo and do an ascending traverse 0.5 mile west up the slope to the north. Stay below a long bush barrier and, when past the willows, climb west onto Organ's rounded northeast ridge at 12,500 feet. From here you can look down into Stewart Creek to the north and see Stewart Peak to the northwest. Climb 0.4 mile southwest up the ridge to a small plateau at 13,060 feet. Stroll 0.2 mile southwest across this special, suspended space. Here, you can feel the heartbeat of the La Garitas. When you are ready, hike 0.6 mile southwest up Organ's rounded, upper northeast ridge to the summit. From here you can peer down into the pipes on Organ's south face and listen for the wind.

23.3V — Variation

From treeline at 11,900 feet, cross Hondo Creek and climb 0.6 mile south to a flat stretch on Organ's east ridge at 12,660 feet. Hike 0.5 mile west to the eastern end of the small plateau at 13,020 feet. Stroll 0.2 mile west and rejoin the route below Organ's upper northeast ridge.

23.4 — Organ Mountain — North Slopes

From Stewart Creek TH at 10,480 ft:	*184 RP*	*10.9 mi*	*3,321 ft*	*Class 2*
With descent of East Slopes:	*177 RP*	*10.2 mi*	*3,481 ft*	*Class 2*

This is another easy route on Organ. It is mostly Class 1 with a short Class 2 section near the top. Start at the Stewart Creek Trailhead and hike 4.1 miles west on the Stewart Creek Trail on the north side of Stewart Creek to treeline at 12,000 feet. This is the start of the standard route to the fourteener San Luis, so this trail sees more traffic than do others in the area.

Stewart Creek has two branches above 12,000 feet. Leave the Stewart Creek Trail, cross to Stewart Creek's south side and hike 0.4 mile south to 12,300 feet in Stewart Creek's southernmost drainage. If the ford of Stewart Creek is too difficult, continue on the Stewart Creek Trail, cross a small side stream, cross the northern branch of Stewart Creek, leave the trail and contour east at 12,300 feet into Stewart Creek's southernmost drainage.

From 12,300 feet, hike 0.3 mile southeast up Stewart Creek's southernmost drainage, then climb 0.4 mile east up a sweeping grass slope to a small, 13,460-foot saddle north of Organ's summit. Climb 0.25 mile south up a rocky slope to the summit. This is the only Class 2 climbing on the route. Ascending the North Slopes Route and descending the East Slopes Route makes a wonderful Tour de Organ that allows you to see two valleys.

23.5 — Organ Mountain — South Slopes

From Eddiesville TH at 10,320 ft:	*281 RP*	*13.6 mi*	*3,481 ft*	*Class 2*
With descent of East Slopes:	*240 RP*	*11.0 mi*	*3,481 ft*	*Class 2*
With descent of North Slopes:	*261 RP*	*12.8 mi*	*3,481 ft*	*Class 2*

This is yet another easy route up Organ. It is longer than the East and North Slopes Routes, but it takes you into one of Colorado's high, hidden valleys. Start at the southern parking area of the Eddiesville Trailhead. Hike 150 yards southwest on the Colorado Trail along the north side of a private property fence to a gate. This is also the Continental Divide Trail and the old Skyline Trail. Go south through the gate and hike 2.5 miles south then southwest around a sweeping turn into the upper Cochetopa Creek drainage. This section of the trail skirts private property, and this hidden area has been badly fouled by welfare grazing on public land.

Organ Mountain from the south.

Mercifully, after 2.5 miles, there is a cattle gate, beyond which you will only find moose and elk.

From the upper cattle gate, hike 2.7 miles west-southwest on the Colorado Trail on the north side of Cochetopa Creek past Cañon Diablo to a side stream crossing at 11,240 feet. Hike 0.1 mile west of this stream to 11,280 feet, leave the Colorado Trail and hike 0.4 mile north to treeline at 12,000 feet. Hike 1.1 miles northwest up a huge, grassy slope to the summit. Ascending the South Slopes Route and descending either the East or North Slopes Route makes a comprehensive Tour de Organ.

23.5V — Variation

Instead of leaving the Colorado Trail near the side stream crossing at 11,240 feet, continue 0.8 mile west on the Colorado Trail to another side stream. Hike 0.2 mile west of this stream, then leave the Colorado Trail. Hike 0.3 mile north through open trees to tiny Point 12,057. With the cows, moose and trail well behind you, let the mountain magic begin.

With Organ's best pipes soaring above you, hike 0.2 mile north above the side creek's west side. Contour into the side creek's drainage and go up it to 12,400 feet (Class 2). This is the heart of the La Garitas. Listen for wind above playing through the pipes. Also, remember that geologic time includes now. Climb 0.3 mile northeast up a scruffy slope to 13,300 feet on Organ's broad south ridge (Class 2). The pipes draw closer then disappear from view during this ascent. Hike 0.25 mile northwest to the summit and look back down through the pipes.

23.6 — Organ Mountain — West Ridge

From Stewart Creek TH at 10,480 ft:	*288 RP*	*12.6 mi*	*4,161 ft*	*Class 3*
With descent of East Slopes:	*226 RP*	*10.5 mi*	*3,741 ft*	*Class 3*
With descent of North Slopes:	*241 RP*	*11.75 mi*	*3,741 ft*	*Class 3*
With descent of South Slopes:	*255 RP*	*12.5 mi*	*3,741 ft*	*Class 3*
From Eddiesville TH at 10,320 ft:	*357 RP*	*19.2 mi*	*4,321 ft*	*Class 3*
With descent of East Slopes:	*262 RP*	*13.8 mi*	*3,901 ft*	*Class 3*
With descent of North Slopes:	*277 RP*	*15.05 mi*	*3,901 ft*	*Class 3*
With descent of South Slopes:	*291 RP*	*15.8 mi*	*3,901 ft*	*Class 3*

This ridge connects Organ with the fourteener San Luis. Usually, only people intent on doing both San Luis and Organ in the same day do this ridge. List-tickers beware. The crux of the route is a gap in the ridge, which you must bypass on unstable rock.

Your initial goal is to reach the 13,100-foot saddle between Organ and San Luis. You can do this by starting at either the Stewart Creek Trailhead or the Eddiesville Trailhead. From the Stewart Creek Trailhead, follow the North Slopes Route 4.1 miles to 12,000 feet in Stewart Creek. Leave the North Slopes Route here and hike 0.8 mile southwest on the continuing Stewart Creek Trail to the 13,100-foot saddle. From the Eddiesville Trailhead, follow the South Slopes Route 5.4 miles to 11,280 feet. Leave the South Slopes Route here and continue 1.4 miles west on the Colorado Trail to 11,740 feet. Just before you cross Cochetopa Creek, leave the Colorado Trail and hike 0.9 mile northwest along Cochetopa Creek's east side to 12,400 feet. Leave the creek and hike 0.5 mile north to the 13,100-foot saddle.

From the 13,100-foot saddle between Organ and San Luis, climb 0.1 mile east up a steep slope onto Organ's west ridge. Hike 0.5 mile east on the gentle ridge to Point 13,500. Organ is only 0.6 mile away and 300 feet higher, but your fun has just begun. Scamper 0.2 mile east down the increasingly rotten ridge to 13,300 feet. Now Organ is 500 feet above you. Drop down on the ridge's south side 150 yards before you reach the nasty gap. If you are not sure where this is, go east to the gap, peer into the abyss, then retreat 150 yards to the west. Descend 180 feet south below the ridge on loose rock over a crumbling mud base. Now Organ is 680 feet above you. Scramble 250 yards southwest across several shallow gullies (Class 3). Once you are past the ghastly gash, climb north to regain the ridge at 13,380 feet. Breathe.

When ready, continue 0.4 mile east up steep but solid rocks. Just below the summit, pass between some organ pipes. Perhaps your breath can fuel them. From the summit, gaze back at your accomplishment. Ascending the West Ridge Route and descending one of the easier routes makes a memorable Tour de Organ.

23. STEWART AND ORGAN COMBINATION

See Map 23 on page 192

23.7 — SO Combination — Organ Stew

From Stewart Creek TH at 10,480 ft: 372 RP   14.85 mi   5,624 ft   Class 2

This is the easiest way to climb Stewart and Organ together. Start at the Stewart Creek Trailhead and follow Organ's North Slopes Route 4.1 miles to 12,000 feet on Stewart Creek's north side. Climb 0.7 mile northwest to 13,180 feet on Baldy Alto's northeast ridge. Contour 0.7 mile west across Baldy Alto's north slopes to the 13,100-foot saddle between Baldy Alto and Stewart. Climb 0.4 mile northwest up a rough ridge to Point 13,620. Descend 0.1 mile northwest to a saddle, then contour 0.3 mile northeast to the 13,540-foot saddle southwest of Stewart. Climb 0.4 mile northeast to Stewart's summit. Return the same way to 12,000 feet in Stewart Creek. Continue on Organ's North Slopes Route to Organ's summit. Descend Organ's East Slopes Route.

24. "Phoenix Peak"   13,895 feet

See Map 24 on page 204

This gentle peak's rounded summit stands alone 7 miles northeast of Creede. "Phoenix Peak" has the distinction of being the highest peak in Mineral County. This unnamed summit has also been called "Creede Crest" and "Gwyned Peak." The most used name is "Phoenix Peak." Indeed, this ageless summit seems to rise above the ashes of time.

MAPS

Required: *Halfmoon Pass, Elk Park, Gunnison National Forest, Rio Grande National Forest*
Optional: *Creede, Mesa Mountain, San Luis Peak*

TRAILHEADS

East Willow Creek Trailhead

This trailhead is at 9,920 feet and provides access to the southwest side of "Phoenix Peak." Measure from the Mineral County Courthouse on the north side of Creede. Go 0.7 mile north, turn east (right), cross to Nelson Creek's east side on a bridge and go northeast on the gravel road up East Willow Creek. Go west (left) at mile 3.7 and reach the trailhead at mile 4.0, where the main road switchbacks to the south. Park low-clearance vehicles in a small pullout on the switchback's north side. The 1986 San Luis Peak Quadrangle shows a 10,200-foot contour line annotation 0.3 mile north of this trailhead. The elevation is wrong; it should be 10,000 feet.

Four-wheel-drive vehicles can go 1.6 miles farther to Phoenix Park. From the two-wheel-drive trailhead, go north on a rough four-wheel-drive

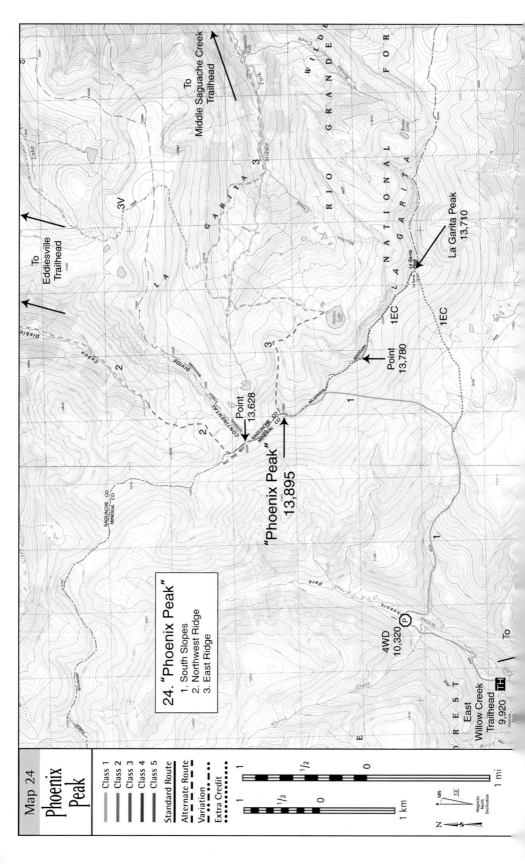

Map 24
Phoenix Peak

To Eddiesville Trailhead

To Middle Saguache Creek Trailhead

3V

WILDERNESS

LA GARITA

RIO GRANDE FOREST

LA GARITA NATIONAL FOREST

La Garita Peak 13,710

Point 13,780

1EC

1EC

CONTINENTAL DIVIDE

SAGUACHE CO
MINERAL CO

Point 13,628

3

"Phoenix Peak" 13,895

SAGUACHE CO
MINERAL CO

Diablo Canyon

2

2

1

24. "Phoenix Peak"
1. South Slopes
2. Northwest Ridge
3. East Ridge

4WD 10,320

P

EAST FOREST

East Willow Creek Trailhead 9,920

To

Legend

Class 1
Class 2
Class 3
Class 4
Class 5

Standard Route
Alternate Route
Variation
Extra Credit

1   1/2   0   1 km
1   1/2   0   1 mi

N

MN 13°
Magnetic North Declination

13,895

"Phoenix Peak" from the northwest.

road, cross a ridge and switchback down toward East Willow Creek. Turn sharply north and follow the rocky, sometimes muddy road northwest toward Phoenix Park. Cross Whited Creek at mile 5.4 and reach the Center Stock Driveway in the south end of Phoenix Park at mile 5.6. Park four-wheel-drive vehicles here at 10,320 feet. The old Center Stock Driveway goes east and crosses East Willow Creek. You can see it on the creek's east side.

Middle Saguache Creek Trailhead

This trailhead is at 10,160 feet and provides access to the east side of "Phoenix Peak." If you are approaching from the north, turn south onto Colorado 114 from U.S. 50. This junction is 33.0 miles west of Monarch

Pass and 7.5 miles east of Gunnison. Go 20.0 miles south on Colorado 114 and turn right onto Saguache County NN14 (BLM 3083) along Cochetopa Creek. Go 8.1 miles south on Saguache County NN14 to Saguache County 17FF. If you are approaching from the south, go 6.4 miles west from the summit of Cochetopa Pass. This junction has a sign for Stone Cellar. That's where you want to go. Measure from this point.

Go south on Saguache County 17FF, which is also BLM 3088. Reach the Continental Divide in the Cochetopa Hills at mile 8.4. To the east and south you have a panoramic view of the La Garita Caldera's wall. To the southwest you can see Stewart, San Luis and Organ in the center of the caldera. Here, you also cross from the Gunnison National Forest into the Rio Grande National Forest. Go south on FS 787, pass through Saguache Park and turn west (right) onto FS 744 at mile 13.3. Go west on FS 744, pass the Stone Cellar Guard Station on the south side of the road at mile 13.7, pass the Lake Fork Trail on the north side of the road at mile 15.3 and ford the Middle Fork of Saguache Creek at mile 15.4. This ford may be difficult for low-clearance vehicles in June. Continue west on the rutted dirt road, climb a steep hill and reach the end of the road and the Middle Saguache Creek Trailhead at mile 18.8. The steep hill may be difficult for two-wheel-drive vehicles when the road is muddy.

ROUTES

24.1 — "Phoenix Peak" — South Slopes

From East Willow Creek TH at 9,920 ft:	*201 RP*	*11.4 mi*	*4,395 ft*	*Class 1*
From Phoenix 4WD parking at 10,320 ft:	*154 RP*	*8.2 mi*	*3,675 ft*	*Class 1*

This is the standard and easiest route up "Phoenix Peak." This peaceful route is more likely to soothe your memories than excite your lust. Let there be time for that.

From the East Willow Creek Trailhead, go north on a rough four-wheel-drive road, cross a ridge and switchback down to the east toward East Willow Creek. Turn sharply north at 9,860 feet and follow the rocky road northwest. Cross Whited Creek on a small footbridge after 1.4 miles and reach the south end of Phoenix Park after 1.6 miles. From here you can see "Phoenix Peak" 2.3 miles to the northeast. Descend east, cross East Willow Creek and pick up the old Center Stock Driveway on the creek's east side. Hike 0.25 mile south then east on an old road to a trailhead sign and a three-log fence at 10,380 feet in an unnamed side drainage of East Willow Creek.

From the trailhead sign, hike 0.2 mile east and cross to the unnamed creek's south side. This creek crossing is incorrectly marked on the 1986 San Luis Peak Quadrangle. Do not cross the creek too soon. After the creek crossing, hike 0.2 mile east, cross a small creek and find the old Center Stock Driveway in the trees. Hike 1.4 miles east up this sometimes faint trail to treeline at 11,720 feet. You can see the summit of "Phoenix Peak" from here, but you might mistake it for the more prominent Point 13,780, which is 0.9 mile southeast of "Phoenix."

Leave the trail when you can see a small, west-facing cliff band to the northeast. Cross to the unnamed creek's north side, hike 0.2 mile northeast up grass slopes and get onto a small ridge above the cliff band. Hike 0.5 mile north up this ridge to 12,600 feet, where the ridge ends in a large, southwest-facing slope. Stay below the rocks and angle 0.7 mile north across this grassy slope to the 13,580-foot saddle between "Phoenix Peak" and Point 13,780. You will have an expansive view to the north from here, and your work is almost done. Hike 0.5 mile northwest then north to the flat summit. The highest point is graced with a large cairn, the top of which is at 13,902 feet.

24.1EC — Extra Credit — La Garita Peak, 13,710 feet, Class 2

From the summit of "Phoenix Peak," return to the 13,580-foot saddle. Hike southeast along the ridge, climbing or skirting tiny Point 13,700 as you choose. Climb over Point 13,780 (Class 2) and hike 1.0 mile southeast to 13,710-foot La Garita Peak. Before you are done with this long traverse, you may want to call this peak "La *Garunta* Peak." Nevertheless, from the summit, you will have a nice view of Machin Lake and the large basin at the head of the Middle Fork of Saguache Creek.

From La Garita's summit, descend southwest down rock then grass slopes to the large meadow below. Go southwest then west around a wet area and find the Center Stock Driveway near the point where you left it. The traverse to La Garita Peak adds 0.8 mile and 550 feet to your effort.

24.2 — "Phoenix Peak" — Northwest Ridge

From Eddiesville TH at 10,320 ft: *372 RP*   *15.0 mi*   *3,815 ft*   *Class 2*

This clever alternative route allows you to climb "Phoenix Peak" from the same trailhead area used for Organ and Stewart. It eliminates the need for the long drive to Creede. However, the route requires a ford of Cochetopa Creek that may be impractical in June.

Start at the southern parking area of the Eddiesville Trailhead. Hike 150 yards southwest on the Colorado Trail along the north side of a private property fence to a gate. This is also the Continental Divide Trail and the old Skyline Trail. Go south through the gate and hike 2.5 miles south then southwest around a sweeping turn to the west into the upper Cochetopa Creek drainage. This section of the trail skirts private property, and the area has been badly fouled by welfare grazing on public land. Mercifully, after 2.5 miles, there is a cattle gate, beyond which you will only find moose and elk.

From the upper cattle gate, hike another 1.0 mile southwest on the Colorado Trail to 10,700 feet, where you are almost even with Cañon

Diablo. During this mile you can look into the lower end of Cañon Diablo on the south side of Cochetopa Creek and gauge your position accordingly. The crux of this route is getting across Cochetopa Creek and finding the Cañon Diablo Trail. As you approach 10,700 feet, there will be a marshy area between the Colorado Trail and Cochetopa Creek. Leave the Colorado Trail at the west end of this marshy area just as the trail enters a stand of pine trees. Bushwhack 0.1 mile south, cross Cochetopa Creek, hike south through pine trees and find the Cañon Diablo Trail on the east side of Diablo Creek. The Cañon Diablo Trail does not appear on most maps, but it does exist.

Hike 2.0 miles south then southwest up the ever fainter Cañon Diablo Trail to treeline at 11,800 feet. Climb 0.5 mile south-southwest to 12,500 feet, climb 0.2 mile south-southwest up a steeper slope to 12,800 feet and climb 0.4 mile southwest to reach the Continental Divide and the northwest ridge of "Phoenix Peak" at 13,420 feet (Class 2). Hike 0.7 mile southeast over Point 13,628 to the summit of "Phoenix Peak" (Class 2). The large summit cairn will lure you on.

24.3 — "Phoenix Peak" — East Ridge *Classic*

From Middle Saguache Creek TH at 10,160 ft: 289 RP   15.8 mi   3,735 ft   Class 2

This wilderness route provides a perfect excuse for a backpack. Start at the Middle Saguache Creek Trailhead and follow the Middle Fork Trail 6.5 miles west to Machin Lake at 12,473 feet. This is an idyllic place to camp. From the north side of Machin Lake, hike 0.3 mile north-northwest to 12,700 feet on a small ridge. Cross this ridge and hike 0.2 mile northwest to 12,800 feet below the lower end of the east ridge of "Phoenix Peak." Climb 0.1 mile northwest up a steep, south-facing slope and reach the ridge at 12,940 feet. Climb 0.8 mile west up this lively ridge directly to the summit of "Phoenix Peak" (Class 2).

24.3V — Variation
From Eddiesville TH at 10,320 ft: 415 RP   24.2 mi   5,815 ft   Class 2
You can reach Machin Lake from the Eddiesville Trailhead. This is a tougher approach than the Middle Fork, but opens possibilities for extended backcountry trips. From the south parking lot at the Eddiesville Trailhead, hike 150 yards southwest on the Colorado Trail along the north side of a private property fence to a gate, then hike 0.7 mile south to a signed trail junction. Leave the Colorado Trail, hike 0.4 mile east, ford Cochetopa Creek and hike 5.8 miles southeast then southwest up the Lake Fork of Cochetopa Creek to treeline at 12,400 feet. Climb 0.9 mile southeast to the Continental Divide at 13,060 feet. Descend 1.2 miles southwest to a trail junction at 12,130 feet. Hike 1.6 miles west then south to Machin Lake. Join the East Ridge Route there and follow it to the summit.

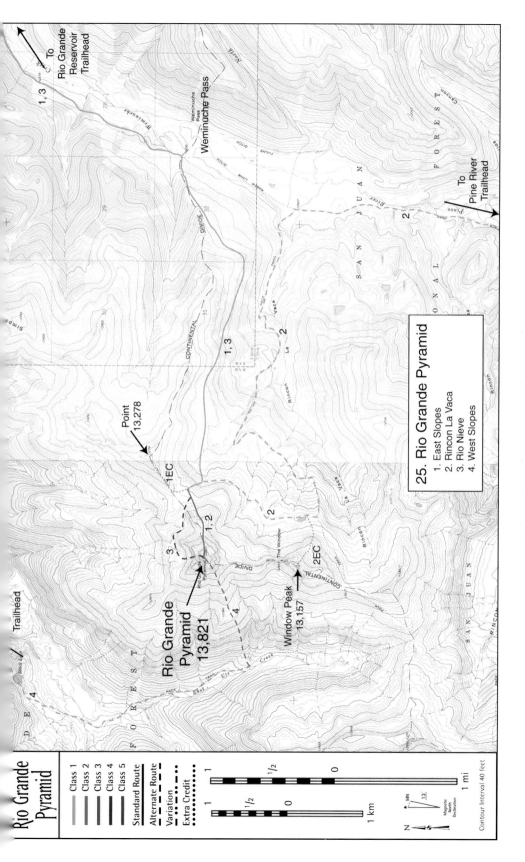

Rio Grande Pyramid

Legend:
- Class 1
- Class 2
- Class 3
- Class 4
- Class 5
- Standard Route
- Alternate Route
- Variation
- Extra Credit

Contour Interval 40 feet

Magnetic North Declination 13

25. Rio Grande Pyramid

1. East Slopes
2. Rincon La Vaca
3. Rio Nieve
4. West Slopes

Labels on map:
- To Rio Grande Reservoir Trailhead
- Weminuche Pass
- To Pine River Trailhead
- Point 13,278
- Rio Grande Pyramid 13,821
- Window Peak 13,157
- Trailhead
- SAN JUAN NATIONAL FOREST
- CONTINENTAL DIVIDE
- 1, 3
- 1, 2
- 2
- 3
- 4
- 1EC
- 2EC

25. Rio Grande Pyramid   13,821 feet

See Map 25 on page 209

Far from highways and towns, Rio Grande Pyramid is on the Continental Divide in the heart of the Weminuche Wilderness. The singular peak rises to a great height in the midst of a rolling, pastoral stretch of the Weminuche Wilderness east of the Grenadiers. An old volcanic dike runs south from the summit and frames a square-cut gap called the Window. It is difficult to see Rio Grande Pyramid from roads, but you can see it in the distance from other San Juan summits. The pyramid often floats like a siren sentinel, and you can squint through the Window at its tiny views of unknown places. Indeed, Rio Grande Pyramid has the distinction of being the centennial thirteener farthest from a fourteener. Although the campgrounds adjacent to the wilderness are well developed and well attended, the feeling soaked into the lush land surrounding this peak is one of loneliness. Rio Grande Pyramid attracts storms, then watches as they wash the embers of an ancient age.

MAPS
Required: *Rio Grande Pyramid, Weminuche Pass, Rio Grande National Forest, San Juan National Forest*
Optional: *Finger Mesa, Granite Lake, Granite Peak, Emerald Lake, Vallecito Reservoir, Uncompahgre National Forest*

TRAILHEADS

Rio Grande Reservoir Trailhead
This trailhead is at 9,340 feet and gives access to Rio Grande Pyramid's east and north sides. If you are approaching from Creede, go 20.4 miles west on Colorado 149 from the bridge on the south side of Creede to the Rio Grande Reservoir Road. If approaching from Lake City, go 32.1 miles south on Colorado 149 over Slumgullion Pass and Spring Creek Pass to the Rio Grande Reservoir Road. The well-marked Rio Grande Reservoir Road starts 1.1 miles south of the Mineral–Hinsdale county line on Colorado 149.

Measure from the junction of Colorado 149 and the Rio Grande Reservoir Road. Go west on the Rio Grande Reservoir Road (FS 520) and stay left at mile 0.5, where the road turns to dirt. Stay left at mile 3.4, reach Road Canyon Reservoir at mile 4.6, pass Road Canyon Campground at mile 5.9, go straight (left) at mile 8.2, pass River Hill Campground at mile 9.4 and reach Thirty Mile Campground at mile 10.8. Leave the Rio Grande Reservoir Road, turn south (left), cross the Rio Grande River on a good bridge, turn right, go along Thirty Mile Campground's north edge and reach the trailhead parking lot, which is on the north side of the road, at mile 11.1. The beginning of the Weminuche and Big Squaw Trails is 120 yards south of the parking area.

Ute Creek Trailhead

This trailhead is at 9,460 feet and gives access to Rio Grande Pyramid's west side. The trailhead is west of Rio Grande Reservoir. Measure from the Rio Grande Reservoir Trailhead east of the reservoir. Go west then northwest on the Rio Grande Reservoir Road (FS 520), pass a gate adjacent to the Rio Grande Reservoir Dam at mile 0.7, go along Rio Grande Reservoir's north side and turn southwest (left) onto a spur road at mile 6.0. There is a sign for the Ute Creek Trailhead at this junction. Go southwest and south on the spur road to reach the trailhead at mile 6.2. There is ample parking here.

Pine River Trailhead

This trailhead is at 7,900 feet and provides access to Rio Grande Pyramid from the south via a long trail hike up the Pine River. This trailhead provides a refreshing alternative for a long backpacking vacation. There are two approaches to this trailhead.

If you are approaching from the south or east, go to Bayfield on U.S. 160. Bayfield is 14.5 miles east of the U.S. 160–U.S. 550 junction several miles south of Durango. Turn north onto La Plata County 501 and measure from this point. Go north on La Plata County 501, go straight (right) at 8.8 miles, go straight (left) at 13.2 miles, go along Vallecito Reservoir's west side and turn east (right) at 18.5 miles. Go east on La Plata County 501 around Vallecito Reservoir's north end, cross Vallecito Creek at 19.0 miles, turn south, pass the Middle Mountain Campground, go straight (left) at mile 21.7, turn northeast into the Pine River Valley and reach the well-marked trailhead at mile 25.7.

If you are approaching from the north or west, go to Main Avenue (U.S. 550) and 32nd Street in north Durango, turn east onto 32nd Street and measure from this point. Go east on 32nd Street, turn south (right) onto La Plata County 250 (East Animas Road) at 1.3 miles and turn east (left) onto La Plata County 240 (Florida Road) after 1.5 miles. Go east on La Plata County 240, leave Durango, turn east (right) at 13.4 miles and turn north (left) onto La Plata County 501 at 16.2 miles. Go north on La Plata County 501, go straight (left) at 20.6 miles, go along Vallecito Reservoir's west side and turn east (right) at 25.9 miles. Go east on La Plata County 501 around Vallecito Reservoir's north end, cross Vallecito Creek at 26.4 miles, turn south, pass the Middle Mountain Campground, go straight (left) at mile 29.1, turn northeast into the Pine River Valley and reach the well-marked trailhead at mile 33.1.

ROUTES

25.1 — Rio Grande Pyramid — East Slopes *Classic*

From Rio Grande Reservoir TH at 9,340 ft:　319 RP　19.2 mi　4,481 ft　Class 2

This is the easiest route on Rio Grande Pyramid. The ascent requires a long trail approach followed by a short, steep ascent up rough talus. If you are fit, you can do the climb in a long day. For more comfort and time to enjoy the wilderness, you might choose to do a backpack trip.

Start at the Rio Grande Reservoir Trailhead. From the trailhead parking area, walk 120 yards south to the beginning of the Weminuche and Big Squaw Trails. Walk 80 yards south up the combined trail to a signboard where the trails diverge. You want the Weminuche Trail, which turns to the west (right) at the signboard. Hike 0.4 mile west on the Weminuche Trail, staying left on the high road en route, to a point south of and above the Rio Grande Reservoir Dam. Contour 0.7 mile west-southwest above the reservoir's south side, then begin your ascent by climbing 0.5 mile west to the edge of the Weminuche Creek drainage. Turn south, enter the drainage, hike 0.3 mile south and cross to Weminuche Creek's west side on a sturdy footbridge at 9,900 feet. Welcome to the Weminuche Wilderness.

Continue on the excellent trail as it climbs southwest well above Weminuche Creek. Cross a side creek at 10,400 feet, 1.4 miles beyond the bridge, and cross a second side creek at 10,500 feet, 2.1 miles beyond the bridge. There are good views of the lush Weminuche Creek valley in this area, but you cannot see Rio Grande Pyramid from here. Cross a third side creek at 10,640 feet, 3.1 miles beyond the bridge, just before reaching the northern edge of broad Weminuche Pass. In a dry summer there is no water available above this point. Rio Grande Pyramid remains hidden.

One hundred yards past the third side creek, leave the Weminuche Creek Trail and turn west (right) onto the Opal Lake Trail. This trail junction is marked with a weathered old sign pole that has a difficult-to-read "Skyline Trail" designation carved into it. This trail has been renamed by the Forest Service—it is now the Opal Lake Trail. The Opal Lake Trail is not marked as such on the 1964 Weminuche Pass Quadrangle, but it is marked on the Weminuche Wilderness Trails Illustrated Map number 140. The trail junction is closer to the third side creek than indicated on the Trails Illustrated Map.

Hike 1.3 miles west-southwest on the Opal Lake Trail as it climbs steeply up a rounded ridge and reaches a shoulder at 11,740 feet, where you can finally see Rio Grande Pyramid and the Window. Continue another 1.3 miles west on the Opal Lake Trail as it contours and climbs gently across a steep slope well above the Rincon La Vaca to the south. This section of trail is incorrectly marked on the Trails Illustrated Map, which shows it on the ridge above. On this traverse, you can examine Rio Grande Pyramid's upper slopes and spot the approach trail to them. From a flat area at 12,000 feet, continue on the trail 0.8 mile west then south through dense bushes to an unmarked trail junction at 12,200 feet. Leave the Opal Lake Trail and hike 0.2 mile northwest on an unnamed spur trail to 12,600 feet on the southern edge of the broad, 12,645-foot saddle 0.7 mile east-northeast of Rio Grande Pyramid. The spur trail you want is the westernmost and highest of several choices. Your 8.8-mile trail approach is over. Now all you have to do is climb the mountain.

Rio Grande Pyramid from the east.

Hike 0.4 mile west and ascend a steep scree gully with a use trail in it to a 13,120-foot shoulder just south of Point 13,185. It is not necessary to climb Point 13,185. Hike 0.15 mile west and engage the long-awaited summit pyramid at 13,200 feet. Climb 0.25 mile west up steep, unstable talus to the summit (Class 2). Stay to the south (left) of three rough sections en route. From the summit, you will have expansive views in all directions. In particular, you will have a unique view of the Needles and Grenadiers from the east. You can also return the gaze of climbers elsewhere in the San Juans who are staring at Rio Grande Pyramid in the distance.

25.1EC — Extra Credit — Point 13,278, Class 1
Either coming or going, take time to climb Point 13,278, a ranked thirteener. From the northeastern end of the broad, 12,645-foot saddle east of Rio Grande Pyramid, hike 0.5 mile northeast up a well-defined ridge to the summit of Point 13,278. From this perch, you will have a dramatic view of Rio Grande Pyramid.

25.2 — Rio Grande Pyramid — Rincon La Vaca

From Pine River TH at 7,900 ft:	721 RP	56.4 mi	5,921 ft	*Class 2*
With descent of East Slopes:	534 RP	37.8 mi	5,921 ft	*Class 2*

This route offers you an opportunity for a backpacking trip with a lofty goal. There are ample camping opportunities in the Pine River Valley and in the Rincon La Vaca. With a vehicle shuttle to the Rio Grande Reservoir

Trailhead, you can shorten the total distance and create a Grande traverse.

Start at the Pine River Trailhead and hike 6.0 miles northeast up the Pine River Trail to the junction with the Emerald Lake Trail. Continue 6.2 miles northeast on the Pine River Trail to the junction with the Flint Creek Trail. Vary not. Continue 7.5 miles northeast up the Pine River Trail to the junction with the Rincon La Osa Trail. You can now see Weminuche Pass to the north, and your goal approaches. Continue 1.7 miles north on the Pine River Trail to the junction with the Rincon La Vaca Trail. Leave the Pine River Trail here and hike 4.5 miles west and south up the Rincon La Vaca Trail to the junction with the Opal Lake Trail. The Rincon La Vaca Trail is also the Continental Divide Trail, and this is a journey through a lush land. Hike 1.3 miles north on the Opal Lake Trail to the spur trail at 12,200 feet referenced in the East Slopes Route. In this stretch of trail, you will pass east of Opal Lake and the Window. Join the East Slopes Route at the spur trail and follow that route to the summit.

25.2EC — Extra Credit — "Window Peak," 13,157 feet, Class 1

Either coming or going, climb Point 13,157, alias "Window Peak." This ranked thirteener is 0.2 mile south of the Window. From Opal Lake, hike 0.6 mile west up grass slopes to the summit. From this perch, you will have a unique view of Rio Grande Pyramid. After a short hike to the north, you can peer down into the Window. After retracing your ascent route, it is worth taking time to make a visit into the Window. This is one of Colorado's most unique positions.

25.3 — Rio Grande Pyramid — Rio Nieve *Classic*

From Rio G. Reservoir TH at 9,340 ft:	440 RP	19.6 mi	4,481 ft	Class 2	Steep Snow
With descent of East Slopes:	431 RP	19.4 mi	4,481 ft	Class 2	Steep Snow
From Pine River TH at 7,900 ft:	843 RP	56.8 mi	5,921 ft	Class 2	Steep Snow
With descent of Rincon La Vaca:	834 RP	56.6 mi	5,921 ft	Class 2	Steep Snow

The Rio Nieve Couloir splits Rio Grande Pyramid's north face. When it is in good condition, this is one of Colorado's finest wilderness snow climbs. You cannot see this couloir from the Rio Grande Reservoir Road. If you want to preview conditions, you will need to be on other San Juan summits to the north. In particular, the peaks of the Jones Group offer a distant view of this couloir. In a normal year, the couloir will be in good condition for climbing in June. In a heavy snow year, wait until early July. Avoid this couloir in a dry year.

Follow either the East Slopes Route or the Rincon La Vaca Route to the broad, 12,645-foot saddle 0.7 mile east-northeast of Rio Grande Pyramid. From here, contour 0.4 mile west-northwest to a shoulder at 12,800 feet. Go around the shoulder and contour 0.25 mile west-southwest to a point at 12,900 feet directly north of Rio Grande Pyramid's summit. You can now see your objective steeply above you to the south. The arrow-straight Rio Nieve Couloir is in the center of the face, and reaches the summit slopes just east of the summit. There is a second couloir in the western portion of the north face. If Rio Nieve is not to your liking, retreat to the 12,645-foot saddle and continue on the East Slopes Route.

If you like what you see, climb south and engage the couloir's steepness at 13,000 feet. Climb 200 feet up moderate snow, then 600 feet up steep snow. The couloir is inset, but not deeply. However, the rock on Rio Grande Pyramid is rotten, and rockfall is a possibility in this couloir. Wear a helmet. Reach talus slopes at 13,700 feet and hike 100 yards west to the summit.

25.4 — Rio Grande Pyramid — West Slopes

From Ute Creek TH at 9,460 ft: 424 RP   25.2 mi   4,821 ft   Class 2

This unique route is harder than the East Slopes Route and is seldom done. It is suitable for intrepid troubadours, but large parties should avoid this route. Start at the Ute Creek Trailhead and face your initial challenge immediately. You must ford the Rio Grande River. In June of a normal year, this will be a questionable proposition on foot. Wait until August to do this route.

Once on the south side of the Rio Grande River, hike 8.7 miles southwest up the Ute Creek Trail to the junction with the La Garita Stock Driveway at 10,900 feet. This junction is 0.2 mile beyond Black Lake. Stay on the Ute Creek Trail. Turn south-southwest (left), descend 0.6 mile southsouthwest, cross West Ute Creek at 10,670 feet and hike 0.2 mile southsouthwest to the junction with the East Ute Trail. Leave the Ute Creek Trail at this junction and turn south (left) onto the East Ute Trail. Hike 0.3 mile south, cross Middle Ute Creek at 10,720 feet and hike 1.4 miles south to a side stream crossing at 11,240 feet. Your 11.2-mile trail introduction is over. Rio Grande Pyramid's summit is only 1.4 miles away, but your fun has just begun.

Leave the comfort of the East Ute Trail and climb 0.4 mile eastnortheast to treeline at 11,800 feet. From here you can see the rest of the challenge. Climb 1.0 mile east-northeast up steep, unstable talus to the summit. You can peer through the Window en route.

26. Point 13,832 Group

Point 13,832   13,832 feet
Point 13,811   13,811 feet

See Map 26 on page 216

These peaks are on a long, high ridge running east from the fourteener Redcloud Peak, which is 10 miles southwest of Lake City. The ridge between the two peaks is easy, and these peaks are often climbed together. Though the connecting ridge is easy, getting to it is a bit of a project. These

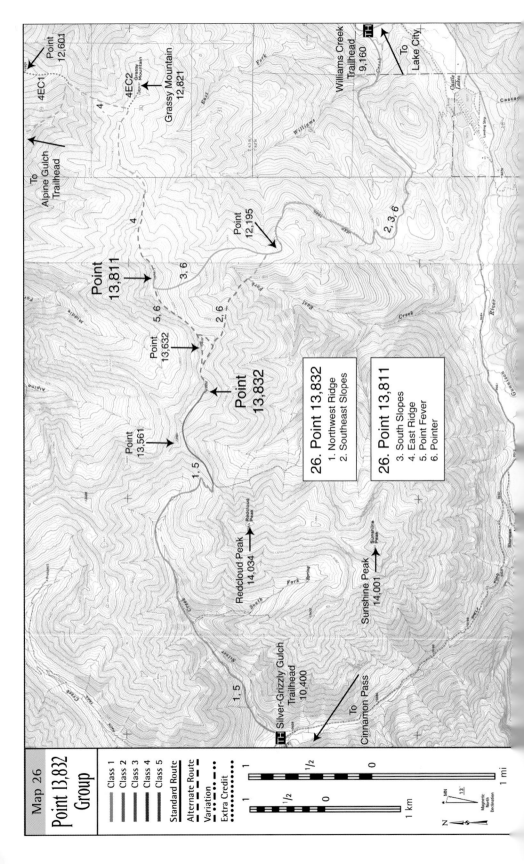

Map 26
Point 13,832
Group

Class 1
Class 2
Class 3
Class 4
Class 5
Standard Route
Alternate Route
Variation
Extra Credit

26. Point 13,832
1. Northwest Ridge
2. Southeast Slopes

26. Point 13,811
3. South Slopes
4. East Ridge
5. Point Fever
6. Pointer

Point 12,601

4EC1

4EC2

Grassy Mountain 12,821

To Alpine Gulch Trailhead

Point 12,195

Williams Creek Trailhead 9,160

To Lake City

Point 13,811

Point 13,632

Point 13,832

Point 13,561

Redcloud Peak 14,034

Sunshine Peak 14,001

Silver-Grizzly Gulch Trailhead 10,400

To Cinnamon Pass

1 mi
1 km

N
MN
13°
Magnetic North Declination

unnamed summits offer you a good workout and some time apart from the more popular places.

MAPS
Required: *Redcloud Peak, Lake San Cristobal, Gunnison National Forest*
Optional: *Lake City*

TRAILHEADS
Williams Creek Trailhead
This trailhead is at 9,160 feet and provides access to the south side of Point 13,811. From the Colorado 50–Colorado 149 junction west of Gunnison, go 45.3 miles south on Colorado 149 to Lake City. Measuring from the bridge over Henson Creek in downtown Lake City, go 2.2 miles south on Colorado 149 and turn right onto the Lake San Cristobal Road. Go around Lake San Cristobal's west side, continue up the beautiful Lake Fork of the Gunnison River and reach the trailhead at mile 8.9. The trailhead has a small parking lot on the road's north side and a sign for the Williams Creek Trail.

Silver–Grizzly Gulch Trailhead
This summer trailhead is at 10,400 feet and provides access to the Silver Creek Trail and the west side of Point 13,832. From the Williams Creek Trailhead at mile 8.9, continue west up the Lake Fork of the Gunnison River. Pass the Williams Creek Campground at mile 9.1, pass the Wager Gulch–Carson Road at mile 11.3 and reach the Mill Creek Campground at mile 13.1. Continue west on the main road and turn northwest (right) onto Cinnamon Pass Road at mile 14.3. Follow the Cinnamon Pass shelf road as it climbs northwest and reach the trailhead at mile 18.3. Park on the road's east side. The road is passable for most passenger cars to this point, and there are camping spots at or near the parking area. The Silver Creek Trail heads east from the parking area.

The other approach to this trailhead requires a four-wheel-drive vehicle. From Durango, go north on U.S. 550 to Silverton. Measuring from Silverton's north end, go northeast on the Animas River Road (Colorado 110) to Animas Forks at mile 12.3 and climb steeply east to reach Cinnamon Pass at mile 15.3. Cross the pass and descend on its east side to reach the Silver–Grizzly Gulch Trailhead at mile 21.1.

Alpine Gulch Trailhead
This trailhead is at 9,000 feet and provides access to the northeast side of Point 13,811. Measure from the junction of Second Street and Gunnison Avenue (Colorado 149) in downtown Lake City. There is a sign here for Engineer Pass. Leave Colorado 149, go two blocks west on Second Avenue to a T-junction at Bluff Street and turn south (left) onto the dirt Henson

Creek Road (Hinsdale County 20). Go 2.6 miles west on Henson Creek Road to the trailhead. There is a small sign marking the trailhead, and it is easy to miss. There is ample parking on the road's north side just east of the beginning of the Alpine Gulch Trail.

26. Point 13,832   13,832 feet

See Map 26 on page 216

Point 13,832 is 1.4 miles east-northeast of the fourteener Redcloud. If peaks could speak, this one might say nothing. It rests in peace hidden behind its famous parent. Yet the peak does seem willing to share. A visit here will grant you its peace.

ROUTES

26.1 — Point 13,832 — Northwest Ridge

From Silver–Grizzly Gulch TH at 10,400 ft: 202 RP   9.8 mi   3,432 ft   Class 2

This is the easiest route up Point 13,832. Start at the Silver–Grizzly Gulch Trailhead. Hike 1.6 miles northeast up the Silver Creek Trail to the junction with the south fork of Silver Creek that drains the basin northwest of the fourteeners Redcloud and Sunshine. Continue 1.1 miles east-northeast on the main Silver Creek Trail into the basin north of Redcloud, turn south and hike 1.1 miles up to the 13,020-foot pass between Redcloud and Point 13,832. The trail is good to this point. From the pass, climb 0.5 mile northeast up a ridge, skirt the rough Point 13,561 on its south side, then climb 0.5 mile southeast along a bumpy ridge to the summit.

26.2 — Point 13,832 — Southeast Slopes

From Williams Creek TH at 9,160 ft: 299 RP   12.6 mi   5,362 ft   Class 2

This route will test your legs and improve your routefinding skills. The route follows a good trail to treeline and then a cross-country route to the summit. One advantage to this route over the Northwest Ridge Route is that the Williams Creek Trailhead is often accessible when the Silver–Grizzly Gulch Trailhead is snowed in.

Start at the Williams Creek Trailhead and hike west on the excellent Williams Creek Trail. After 0.5 mile, cross Williams Creek's small East Fork. Hike 0.2 mile north on Williams Creek's east side, then cross to the creek's west side. The trail leaves Williams Creek here and does not return to the drainage. Hike 1.0 mile west up a small side drainage filled with old beaver dams and a few talus slopes and reach a grassy saddle at 10,000 feet. Join an old road in this saddle and follow it 0.5 mile west as it climbs up another small drainage to a large meadow in a saddle at 10,380 feet.

From here you can grab a peek at the fourteener Sunshine to the west, Half Peak to the southwest and Carson Peak to the south.

Hike 0.2 mile west to the meadow's west end, follow the road 0.4 mile north as it begins an earnest climb and switchbacks twice, then follow the road 1.0 mile northeast as it climbs through aspen trees. Consider doing this hike in September. There is a nice campsite (dry) midway along this climb at 11,100 feet. At 11,500 feet, the road reaches a broad ridge and you begin to see the heights above. Climb 0.5 mile west up the ridge, pass treeline and reach a viewpoint at 12,145 feet just south of tiny Point 12,195. From here you can see the rest of the route to Point 13,832, as well as Point 13,811, Redcloud and Sunshine. Descend 0.1 mile north on the continuing road to the 12,100-foot saddle just north of Point 12,195. From the 12,100-foot saddle, descend 0.4 mile northwest on the continuing road and cross the East Fork of Bent Creek at 11,800 feet. Your 4.8-mile trail approach is over.

Leave the road at 11,800 feet, climb 0.3 mile northwest and reach a small ridge at 12,600 feet. Climb 0.6 mile west-northwest on this ridge to gentler slopes just south of Point 13,632. Skirt 0.2 mile northwest below the summit of Point 13,632 to the 13,460-foot saddle between Point 13,632 and Point 13,832. Climb 0.4 mile west on a well-defined ridge to the summit of Point 13,832.

26. Point 13,811   13,811 feet

See Map 26 on page 216

Point 13,811 is 1.3 miles east of Point 13,832 and 2.6 miles east of the fourteener Redcloud. Point 13,811 is the easternmost thirteener on the long ridge east of Redcloud and is only 4.5 miles west of the ever popular Lake San Cristobal. The peak's suspended position at the end of the ridge gives it a stature that its gentle slopes do not suggest when you view the peak from below. The easy ridge between Point 13,832 and Point 13,811 is scenic, and many people climb these two peaks together. You can also enjoy Point 13,811 by itself on a choice of obscure routes that you are likely to have to yourself.

ROUTES

26.3 — Point 13,811 — South Slopes *Classic*

From Williams Creek TH at 9,160 ft: 212 RP   12.0 mi   4,741 ft   Class 1

This Class 1 hike is the easiest route on Point 13,811, but it is seldom used. The easy walk takes you past beaver dams, alongside enchanting meadows, through thick aspen groves and up graceful grass slopes to the summit. If you are fit, you can be on top in a few hours. If you find the length

Point 13,832 from the east.

of this hike daunting, consider using this ascent as part of a weight-loss program.

Start at the Williams Creek Trailhead and follow the Southeast Slopes Route on Point 13,832 to the 12,100 foot saddle just north of tiny Point 12,195. Leave the road here, hike north on a continuing trail, stay on the west side of Point 12,483 and start up the broad slope to the northwest. When the trail starts a long traverse to the north, leave it and hike directly up the grassy slope to a small, flat area at 13,100 feet. Do an ascending traverse up continuing grass slopes, climb to a small saddle west of the summit and go 0.1 mile east across stable rocks to the summit.

26.4 – Point 13,811 – East Ridge

From Alpine Gulch TH at 9,000 ft: *283 RP*   *14.6 mi*   *5,011 ft*   *Class 2*

This interesting route up Point 13,811 allows you to see a remote Colorado valley and climb three bonus peaks. However, you have to pay some dues. Start at the Alpine Gulch Trailhead, descend 0.1 mile south and cross Henson Creek on a sturdy footbridge at 8,900 feet. The introduction is over.

Hike 2.1 miles south on the Alpine Gulch Trail into the cool recess of Alpine Gulch. Cross Alpine Creek a discouraging five times en route. There are no bridges, and in high water these crossings will definitely wet your feet. After 2.1 miles, you will be on Alpine Creek's east side. Just before

Point 13,811 from the south.

crossing the East Fork of Alpine Creek at 9,800 feet, leave the Alpine Gulch Trail and turn south onto the Williams Creek Trail. Hike 0.8 mile south up the Williams Creek Trail to a small side creek. Cross the side creek and continue 1.0 mile south-southeast up the Williams Creek Trail to a split in the valley at 11,100 feet. Stay on the Williams Creek Trail, climb 0.6 mile southeast up the valley's eastern branch and reach an 11,820-foot saddle on the long east ridge of Point 13,811. This saddle is between Red Mountain to the northeast and Grassy Mountain to the south.

Cross to the ridge's east side and climb 0.7 mile southwest on the Williams Creek Trail to the 12,460-foot saddle between Grassy Mountain, which is now to the east, and Point 13,811, which is to the west. Stay on the trail, hike 1.0 mile west on or near the ridge crest and reach a 12,780-foot saddle. Your 6.3-mile trail approach is over. Now for the climb. Leave the trail in the 12,780-foot saddle and climb 1.0 mile west up the gentle ridge to the summit of Point 13,811 (Class 2).

EXTRA CREDITS

26.4EC1 — Point 12,601, Class 2; Red Mountain, 12,826 feet, Class 2
From the 11,820-foot saddle, climb 0.6 mile north to the summit of Point 12,601, a ranked twelver. From here, descend 0.25 mile to a 12,260-foot saddle, then climb 0.4 mile northeast to 12,826-foot Red Mountain, another ranked twelver.

26.4EC2 — Grassy Mountain, 12,821 feet, Class 2

From the 12,460-foot saddle, climb 0.3 mile southeast then east to the 12,821-foot summit of Grassy Mountain, yet another ranked twelver.

26. POINT 13,832 AND POINT 13,811 COMBINATIONS

See Map 26 on page 216

26.5 — PP Combination — Point Fever

From Silver–Grizzly Gulch TH at 10,400 ft: 312 RP   12.8 mi   4,727 ft   Class 2

This long, easy combination is the traditional way of climbing both of these peaks together. Start at the Silver–Grizzly Gulch Trailhead and follow the Northwest Ridge Route to the summit of Point 13,832. From here, descend 0.4 mile east to the 13,460-foot saddle between Point 13,832 and Point 13,632, then climb 0.1 mile east to the summit of Point 13,632. This unranked summit compensates for your extra effort by providing a stupendous view of the surprising northern flanks of both Point 13,832 and Point 13,811. Descend 0.3 mile northeast to the 13,260-foot saddle between Point 13,632 and Point 13,811, climb 0.6 mile northeast up gentle slopes to a high saddle, then walk 0.1 mile east to the summit of Point 13,811. Return via the same route. On the return, you can skirt below the summit of Point 13,632 on its south side, but you have to reclimb Point 13,832.

26.6 — PP Combination — Pointer

West-Fast from Williams Creek TH at 9,160 ft: 333 RP 13.8 mi 5,785 ft   Class 2
East-West from Williams Creek TH at 9,160 ft: 294 RP 13.8 mi 5,785 ft   Class 2

This combination, though longer than Point Fever, allows you to climb both peaks from the south. This can be an advantage when snow blocks the road to the Silver–Grizzly Gulch Trailhead. You can do the traverse in either direction, and it is slightly easier if done from east to west. However, we prefer to do the higher, harder peak first, so the traverse is described here from west to east.

Start at the Williams Creek Trailhead and climb the Southeast Slopes Route on Point 13,832. Traverse east to Point 13,811 as described in Combination 26.5. Descend the South Slopes Route of Point 13,811.

27. Half Peak   13,841 feet

See Map 27 on page 224

This unique peak is 13.3 miles southwest of Lake City and 3.8 miles southeast of the fourteener Handies Peak. The peak is surrounded by high, wild country and was once called "Wild Boy Peak." It now has the official and more descriptive name *Half Peak*. The peak is not named on the 1964 Pole Creek Mountain Quadrangle, but you can easily spot the peak's distinctive shape on the map. The peak has cliffs on three sides, and gentle south slopes interrupted by a bottleneck ridge between the lower slopes and a summit plateau. Half Peak's 800-foot-high north face truncates the gentle slopes and gives the peak its sawed-off shape. Whatever the geography, this peak will require more than half your attention.

MAPS

Required: *Pole Creek Mountain, Redcloud Peak, Gunnison National Forest*
Optional: *Howardsville, Rio Grande National Forest*

TRAILHEADS

Cataract Gulch Trailhead

This trailhead is at 9,600 feet and provides access to Half Peak's east and south sides. West of the Cataract Gulch Trailhead, the Cuba Gulch four-wheel-drive parking area at 10,700 feet provides access to Half Peak's west and south sides.

From the Colorado 50–Colorado 149 junction west of Gunnison, go 45.3 miles south on Colorado 149 to Lake City. Measuring from the bridge over Henson Creek in downtown Lake City, go 2.2 miles south on Colorado 149, turn southwest (right) onto the Lake San Cristobal Road and go around Lake San Cristobal's west side. Pass the Williams Creek Trailhead at mile 8.9, pass the Williams Creek Campground at mile 9.1, pass the Wager Gulch–Carson Road at mile 11.3, pass the Mill Creek Campground at mile 13.1 and reach the junction of the Sherman and Cinnamon Pass Roads at mile 14.3. Go west (left) on the Sherman Road (Hinsdale County 35), pass through the private property in the old Sherman townsite and reach the marked Cataract Gulch Trailhead at mile 15.5. The Cataract Gulch Trail starts on the road's south side and immediately crosses Cottonwood Creek on a log bridge. In winter the road is often open as far as the Mill Creek Campground.

From the Cataract Gulch Trailhead, four-wheel-drive vehicles can continue west on the rough road up Cottonwood Creek's north side, crossing Boulder Creek at mile 18.0, to reach the Cuba Gulch Trail at mile 18.9. There is a small sign marking the start of the Cuba Gulch Trail and a parking area on the road's south side at 10,700 feet.

Minnie Gulch Trailhead

This trailhead is at 9,820 feet and provides access to Half Peak's west side. Measuring from Silverton's north end, go northeast on the Animas River Road (Colorado 110). Go straight (left) past the Cunningham Creek Road at mile 4.1, pass Howardsville at mile 4.2, pass the Maggie Gulch four-wheel-drive road at mile 6.0 and reach the signed Minnie Gulch four-wheel-drive road at mile 6.6. This is the trailhead. Park passenger cars here.

Four-wheel-drive vehicles can continue 2.7 miles east then southeast up the Minnie Gulch Road to 11,520 feet. Measuring from the Minnie

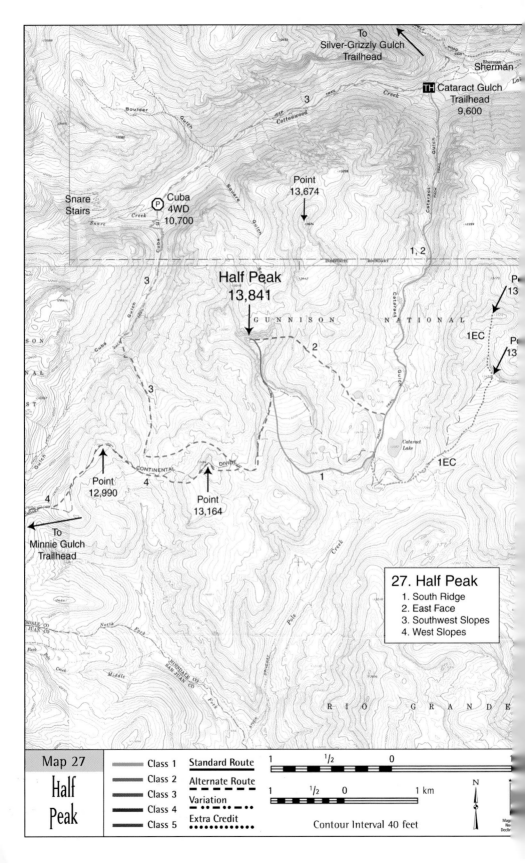

To
Silver-Grizzly Gulch
Trailhead

Sherman

TH Cataract Gulch
Trailhead
9,600

3

Boulder

Cottonwood

Snare
Stairs

Ⓟ Cuba
4WD
10,700

Point
13,674

1, 2

INDEFINITE   BOUNDARY

3

Half Peak
13,841

GUNNISON   NATIONAL

1EC

2

3

1EC

Cataract
Lake

4

CONTINENTAL   DIVIDE

Point
12,990

Point
13,164

1

4

To
Minnie Gulch
Trailhead

SAN JUAN CO.
HINSDALE CO.

SDALE CO.
JUAN CO.

North   Fork

Creek

Fork

Pole

Creek

Middle

Pole

Fork

27. Half Peak
1. South Ridge
2. East Face
3. Southwest Slopes
4. West Slopes

R I O   G R A N D E

Map 27			
Half Peak	Class 1	**Standard Route**	
	Class 2	**Alternate Route**	
	Class 3	**Variation**	
	Class 4	**Extra Credit**	
	Class 5		

1   ½   0

1   ½   0   1 km

N

Contour Interval 40 feet

13,841

Half Peak's summit plateau from the south ridge.

Gulch Trailhead, pass the foundation of an old mill on your left at mile 1.1, go straight (right) at mile 1.5, pass a waterfall on your left at mile 2.3 and reach the remains of the Esmeralda Mine at mile 2.7. Park here at 11,520 feet, as the road is blocked just beyond.

ROUTES

27.1 — Half Peak — South Ridge *Classic*

From Cataract Gulch TH at 9,600 ft: 216 RP   12.6 mi   4,241 ft   Class 2

This is the easiest route up Half Peak. It offers a long trail hike, open slopes and a narrow summit ridge. Many people choose to do this climb with a backpack to Cataract Lake. Start at the Cataract Gulch Trailhead and go south across Cottonwood Creek on a log bridge. As of 2000 there is only one log, which requires balance to walk. When the log is wet, some prefer scooting across in an ungraceful but safer position.

Once across Cottonwood Creek, hike 3.9 miles south on the trail to Cataract Lake. Continue 0.3 mile beyond to the small lake in the 12,180-foot saddle just southwest of Cataract Lake. Leave the trail and contour 0.8 mile west into a small drainage. Hike 0.9 mile north up open slopes that narrow to a ridge at 13,500 feet. Your 5.9-mile, Class 1 approach hike is over. The view of the east side of the 0.2-mile-long connecting ridge to the upper summit plateau may shock you. Take heart, as it is not as hard as it looks. If you take care to find the easiest route, the ridge's difficulty is Class 2, but there is some exposure.

Climb 150 feet along the ridge, then stay on the ridge's west (left) side. You should never be more than 80 feet below the ridge crest. In some places there is a use trail to mark the route, while in other places you must scamper across rocks. Go east across a small notch, scamper east up a scruffy slope and continue 100 yards north to the upper summit plateau at 13,660 feet. Hike 0.2 mile northwest up a remarkably smooth slope to the highest point (Class 1). The view down Half Peak's north face is dramatic, and you can marvel at the rock glacier below it.

27.1EC — Extra Credit — Point 13,450, Class 2; Point 13,524, Class 2

From the 12,180-foot saddle, continue 0.7 mile south and east on the trail, then hike 1.0 mile northeast to Point 13,450, a ranked thirteener. For even more credit, hike 0.6 mile north from Point 13,450 to Point 13,524, an even more powerful peak.

27.2 — Half Peak — East Face

From Cataract Gulch TH at 9,600 ft: 233 RP 10.8 mi 4,241 ft Class 3
With descent of South Ridge: 237 RP 11.7 mi 4,241 ft Class 3

This is a shorter but harder route up Half Peak. Follow the South Ridge Route to a small, unnamed lake 0.2 mile north of Cataract Lake. Hike 1.2 miles northwest past another unnamed lake to 12,800 feet in the basin below Half Peak's east face. Hike 0.2 mile west up the steepening slope above to 13,400 feet (Class 2), then climb 0.1 mile west up a cairned route in a shallow gully through the upper cliffs (Class 3). With careful routefinding, you will need to make only an occasional Class 3 move. Most of this ascent is Class 2+, but loose rock is a hazard. The top of this climb leaves you at 13,600 feet on the eastern edge of the summit plateau. Hike 0.2 mile west to the highest point. Ascending this route and descending the South Ridge Route makes a nifty Tour de Half.

27.3 — Half Peak — Southwest Slopes

From Cataract Gulch TH at 9,600 ft: 272 RP 17.4 mi 4,241 ft Class 2
From Cuba 4WD parking at 10,700 ft: 182 RP 10.6 mi 3,141 ft Class 2

This adventurous approach to Half Peak's upper south ridge is shorter than the Cataract Gulch approach, but only if you use a four-wheel-drive vehicle. The route is mostly Class 1, with two short Class 2 sections. Start at the Cataract Gulch Trailhead and go 3.4 miles west up the rough four-wheel-drive road to the beginning of the Cuba Gulch Trail at 10,700 feet. Go south on the Cuba Gulch Trail and immediately cross Cottonwood Creek. This ford will be difficult in June and easy in August. There may or may not be a log over the creek in June, when you most need it.

Once you are across Cottonwood Creek, hike 0.4 mile south on the trail on Cuba Gulch's west side and cross Cuba Creek on a solid bridge above a spectacular gorge. Hike 1.2 miles south on Cuba Creek's east side, crossing two small side streams en route to a third, larger stream at 11,400 feet. There is a fourth stream just beyond. The Cuba Gulch Trail soon crosses this fourth stream, goes through some bushes and continues southwest up Cuba Gulch. You want to leave the Cuba Gulch Trail between the third and fourth side streams and follow another, unsigned trail that climbs southeast. This trail is more prominent than the Cuba Gulch Trail.

Climb 0.25 mile southeast on the trail between the third and fourth streams, cross the fourth stream eventually and climb steeply toward the unnamed basin above. When the trail becomes obscure at 11,800 feet, you have a challenge and a choice. You can follow the trail as it enters the willows in the lower basin. The trail is faint, but you can find passable alleys through the bushes to reach open slopes in the basin above, where the trail is once again distinct (Class 2). The alternative is to follow faint game trails up to the southwest, get around the top of the bushes and descend back to the main trail in the basin (Class 2). Once past the bushes, hike 0.8 mile south up the basin on the resurgent trail to 12,300 feet (Class 1). There are good views of Half Peak from here.

Leave the main trail, turn east (left) and follow animal trails 1.0 mile east on grass benches below the north face of Point 13,164 to the 12,780-foot saddle between Point 13,164 and Half Peak. Climb 0.2 mile east then 0.8 mile south up open slopes to join the South Ridge Route at 13,500 feet (Class 1). Follow that route north to the summit (Class 2).

27.3EC — Extra Credit — Point 13,164, Class 2
From the 12,780-foot saddle, climb 0.3 mile west to Point 13,164, a ranked thirteener. The summit of this peak offers you a spectacular view of Half Peak.

27.4 — Half Peak — West Slopes

From Minnie Gulch TH at 9,820 ft:	*405 RP*	*20.4 mi*	*6,675 ft*	*Class 2*
From Minnie 4WD parking at 11,520 ft:	*313 RP*	*14.8 mi*	*4,875 ft*	*Class 2*

This approach to Half Peak's upper south ridge is longer than the Cuba and Cataract Gulch approaches, but it offers several advantages. If you are starting near Silverton, you can avoid the long drive to Lake City. Better, you can experience a seldom visited stretch of Colorado's Continental Divide and climb three additional peaks en route. And although a stopover is not required, this route gives you an excuse to camp in the middle of nowhere surrounded by wildflowers.

Start at the Minnie Gulch Trailhead and go east then southeast up the four-wheel-drive road into Minnie Gulch. Pass the foundation of an old mill on your left at mile 1.1, go straight (right) at mile 1.5, pass a waterfall on your left at mile 2.3 and reach the remains of the Esmeralda Mine at mile 2.7. The road is blocked to vehicles at mile 2.8 at 11,520 feet. From here, hike 1.7 miles southeast on the trail into upper Minnie Gulch to 12,680 feet below the 12,740-foot saddle at the head of Minnie Gulch. Leave the valley trail that is destined for this saddle and switchback hard north (left) onto a small trail. Follow the small trail 0.8 mile north to a ridge at 12,900 feet. The introduction is over, and you can now see Half Peak 3.4 miles to the northeast.

Descend 0.3 mile east on the small trail to 12,800 feet on the crest of the Continental Divide and follow it 1.5 miles northeast to the summit of Point 12,990, a ranked twelver. Continue 1.4 miles east on the divide to Point 13,164, a ranked thirteener, then descend 0.3 mile east to the 12,780-foot saddle east of Point 13,164. Join the Southwest Slopes Route here and follow that route to the summit.

27.4EC — Extra Credit — Cuba Benchmark, 13,019 feet, Class 2

From the initial 12,900-foot ridge, climb 0.3 mile northwest to 13,019-foot Cuba Benchmark. This unique summit offers time apart.

28. Jones Group

Niagara Peak	13,807 feet
Jones Mountain	13,860 feet
"American Peak"	13,806 feet

See Map 28 on page 229

These three peaks are 10 miles northeast of Silverton and 1.5 miles southwest of the fourteener Handies Peak. They offer a wide range of routes, from flower walks in remote valleys to steep snow couloirs. You can climb them together in a blitz or enjoy them on individual expeditions.

MAPS

Required: *Handies Peak, Uncompahgre National Forest*
Optional: *Redcloud Peak, Howardsville*

TRAILHEADS

Grouse–Burns Gulch Trailhead

This trailhead is at 10,720 feet and provides access to the Grouse Creek Trail and the north side of "American Peak," as well as to the Burns Gulch four-wheel-drive road and the west sides of Jones, Niagara and "American."

Measuring from Silverton's north end, go 4.2 miles east-northeast on Colorado 110 to Howardsville, continue northeast up the Animas River valley and reach the Eureka townsite at mile 8.0. Cross to the Animas River's west side, continue up the steep shelf road and reach the Grouse–Burns

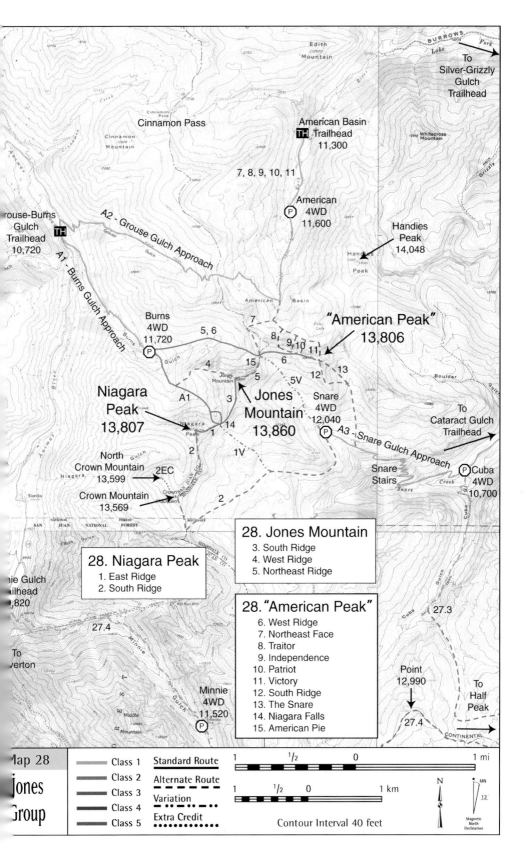

To Silver-Grizzly Gulch Trailhead

Edith Mountain

Cinnamon Pass

Cinnamon Mountain

Whitecross Mountain

American Basin
TH Trailhead
11,300

7, 8, 9, 10, 11

Grouse-Burns Gulch Trailhead 10,720

TH

A2 - Grouse Gulch Approach

American
(P) 4WD
11,600

Handies Peak 14,048

A1 - Burns Gulch Approach

American Basin

Burns 4WD 11,720
(P)

5, 6

7

"American Peak" 13,806

8
9, 10 11
6
12 13

Niagara Peak 13,807

4
15
5
5V

A1

3

Jones Mountain 13,860

Snare 4WD 12,040
(P)

Boulder

To Cataract Gulch Trailhead

A3 - Snare Gulch Approach

1
14

North Crown Mountain 13,599
2EC

2

1V

Snare Stairs

(P) Cuba 4WD 10,700

Crown Mountain 13,569

SAN JUAN NATIONAL FOREST

Eureka

27.3

28. Jones Mountain
3. South Ridge
4. West Ridge
5. Northeast Ridge

ie Gulch ailhead ,820

27.4

28. Niagara Peak
1. East Ridge
2. South Ridge

To erton

28. "American Peak"
6. West Ridge
7. Northeast Face
8. Traitor
9. Independence
10. Patriot
11. Victory
12. South Ridge
13. The Snare
14. Niagara Falls
15. American Pie

Point 12,990

To Half Peak

Minnie 4WD 11,520
(P)

27.4

CONTINENTAL

Map 28

Jones Group

—	Class 1	— Standard Route	
—	Class 2	– – Alternate Route	
—	Class 3	Variation	
—	Class 4	Extra Credit	
—	Class 5		

1   1/2   0   1 mi

1   1/2   0   1 km

N

MN
13

Magnetic North Declination

Contour Interval 40 feet

Gulch Trailhead at mile 11.1 just before the road crosses back to the river's east side. Park in a flat area on the road's west (left) side.

Several routes originate from this trailhead. Make sure you get onto the one you want. The Grouse Gulch Trail is closed to vehicles and switchbacks east above the Animas River Road 100 yards after the road crosses back to the Animas River's east side. There are two ways to start up the Burns Gulch four-wheel-drive road. The first is 100 yards south of the bridge over the Animas River and requires you to ford the Animas River. The second is just north of the bridge and avoids the Animas River ford, but still requires you to cross Grouse Creek. There is no sign for the Grouse Gulch Trail, but there are small signs for both starts of the Burns Gulch four-wheel-drive road. Four-wheel-drive vehicles can go 1.8 miles southeast on a shelf road into Burns Gulch to 11,720 feet.

American Basin Trailhead

This summer trailhead is at 11,300 feet and provides access to the north side of "American Peak." From the Silver–Grizzly Gulch Trailhead (see Point 13,832 Group) at mile 18.3 on the Cinnamon Pass Road, continue northwest on the Cinnamon Pass Road, pass the Cooper Creek Trailhead at mile 19.1 and reach the American Basin Trailhead at mile 21.9. The trailhead is at a steep switchback on the Cinnamon Pass Road. Park on the west side of the four-wheel-drive road heading south into American Basin. The last mile to the trailhead is steep but passable for most passenger cars. From the trailhead, four-wheel-drive vehicles can go 0.9 mile south into American Basin to the end of the road at 11,600 feet under Handies' west side.

The other approach to this trailhead requires a four-wheel-drive vehicle. Measuring from Silverton's north end, go northeast on the Animas River Road (Colorado 110) to Animas Forks at mile 12.3, climb steeply east to reach Cinnamon Pass at mile 15.3, cross the pass and descend on its east side to the American Basin Trailhead at mile 17.5.

APPROACHES

28.A1 – Burns Gulch Approach

From Grouse–Burns Gulch TH at 10,720 ft:	*144 RP*	*5.8 mi*	*2,500 ft*	*Class 2*
From Burns 4WD parking at 11,720 ft:	*93 RP*	*2.2 mi*	*1,500 ft*	*Class 2*

This approach takes you to the 13,220-foot Jones–Niagara saddle from the west. You can easily climb both Jones and Niagara from there. Start at the Grouse–Burns Gulch Trailhead and go 1.8 miles southeast on a four-wheel-drive shelf road into Burns Gulch to 11,720 feet.

Continue 0.8 mile southeast up the gulch, using or losing the road remnants as you choose. At 12,800 feet in the upper basin, you will see that a cliff blocks direct passage to the saddle, but you have a choice. If the upper basin is snow-free, turn north and follow an old trail that switchbacks up through the talus to reach the saddle's northern edge. If the trail is snow-covered, you might prefer to turn south and hike up talus or early summer snow to the base of the scruffy cliffs below the Jones–Niagara saddle. Climb through the west (right) side of the cliffs (Class 2+) and traverse east (left) into the saddle.

28.A2 — Grouse Gulch Approach

From Grouse–Burns Gulch TH at 10,720 ft: 100 RP   5.6 mi   2,920 ft   Class 1

This approach provides access to the many routes on the north side of "American Peak." It is useful if you are starting on the Silverton side of the range. Start at the Grouse–Burns Gulch Trailhead and hike 2.0 miles east up the Grouse Gulch Trail to the 13,020-foot pass at Grouse Gulch's east end. You can see Handies' west side across American Basin from the pass. Do a 0.8-mile descending traverse southeast on a trail to 12,400 feet in American Basin. You can see the north side of "American Peak" from here.

28.A3 — Snare Gulch Approach

From Cataract Gulch TH at 9,600 ft: 130 RP   12.4 mi   2,440 ft   Class 1
From Cuba 4WD parking at 10,700 ft: 62 RP   5.6 mi   1,340 ft   Class 1

This approach takes you into one of Colorado's remote valleys. You can reach the east sides of Jones, Niagara and "American" from the two branches of upper Snare Gulch. The southern branch of upper Snare Gulch is a wonderland of lakes, grassy benches and wildflowers. This approach is a long one on foot, but it can be shortened or eliminated with a four-wheel-drive vehicle.

Start at the Cataract Gulch Trailhead (see Half Peak) and go west on the rough four-wheel-drive road up Cottonwood Creek's north side. Cross Boulder Creek after 2.5 miles and pass the parking area at 10,700 feet for the Cuba Gulch Trail after 3.4 miles. Continue 0.2 mile west on the road, switchback twice and go 0.6 mile west to the beginning of a horrendous climb called the Snare Stairs. The road switchbacks 12 times up the hill to the north for 1.1 miles, gaining 640 feet in the process. Vehicles longer than 15 feet will have to back up to negotiate many of the tight turns. However, foot traffic will have no problem.

From the 12th switchback at 11,640 feet, go 0.4 mile west to an old cabin at 11,800 feet. Above the cabin, continue on the road as it switchbacks twice more, pass treeline, then go 0.5 mile west to reach North Snare Creek at 12,040 feet. If you are still driving, park here below an old mine. The narrow shelf road beyond this point climbs southeast then west around the base of Jones' east ridge to reach the southern branch of upper Snare Creek.

Niagara Peak from the northwest.

28. Niagara Peak   13,807 feet

See Map 28 on page 229

Niagara Peak is 9.0 miles northeast of downtown Silverton on the east side of the upper Animas River. You cannot see Niagara from any paved road, but its majesty comes into view as you approach Animas Forks on the Engineer Pass Road. Niagara's steep north face stands in sharp contrast to many of the rounded summits in this area. Although this north face is pretty to look at, it is rotten and undesirable as a climbing objective. Niagara offers two easy ridges and a lofty perch high above the old Eureka townsite.

ROUTES

28.1 — Niagara Peak — East Ridge

From Grouse–Burns Gulch TH at 10,720 ft:	*192 RP*	*6.4 mi*	*3,087 ft*	*Class 2+*
From Burns 4WD parking at 11,720 ft:	*136 RP*	*2.8 mi*	*2,087 ft*	*Class 2+*

This is the standard route on Niagara. Start at the Grouse–Burns Gulch Trailhead and follow the Burns Gulch Approach to the 13,220-foot Jones–Niagara saddle. From this privileged position, climb 0.3 mile west on a use trail up Niagara. Initially, stay on the north (right) side of Niagara's east ridge. At 13,540 feet, cross the ridge and finish your ascent on the ridge's south side (Class 2+). There is a use trail all the way to the summit.

28.1V — Variation

From Cataract Gulch TH at 9,600 ft:	298 RP	16.8 mi	4,207 ft	Class 2+
From Cuba 4WD parking at 10,700 ft:	208 RP	10.0 mi	3,107 ft	Class 2+
From Snare 4WD parking at 12,040 ft:	126 RP	4.4 mi	1,767 ft	Class 2+

You can reach the Jones–Niagara saddle from Snare Gulch to the east. To do this, start at the Cataract Gulch Trailhead (see Half Peak) and follow the Snare Gulch Approach to the four-wheel-drive parking spot by North Snare Creek at 12,040 feet. From here, hike 1.1 miles southeast then west on a narrow shelf road around the east end of Jones' east ridge. Pass north of a pretty lake at 12,420 feet on the east end of the southern branch of upper Snare Gulch. From here, hike 0.8 mile northwest through the lush basin to the 13,220-foot Jones–Niagara saddle. Join the East Ridge Route here and follow it to the summit.

28.2 — Niagara Peak — South Ridge

From Cataract Gulch TH at 9,600 ft:	364 RP	19.2 mi	4,665 ft	Class 2+
From Cuba 4WD parking at 10,700 ft:	274 RP	12.4 mi	3,565 ft	Class 2+
From Snare 4WD parking at 12,040 ft:	192 RP	6.8 mi	2,225 ft	Class 2+

Approached from the east, this route gives you a chance to walk across upper Snare Gulch and enjoy the lakes and flowers there. Start at the Cataract Gulch Trailhead (see Half Peak) and follow the Snare Gulch Approach. From the four-wheel-drive parking spot by North Snare Creek at 12,040 feet, cross to the creek's south side and follow the narrow shelf road south as it climbs around the base of Jones' east ridge and goes west into the large basin at the head of Snare Creek. After 1.1 miles, leave the road and go to the first large lake at 12,420 feet. Hike 1.0 mile southwest across the fairy-tale basin past several other lakes to the base of the steep slope below the 13,060-foot saddle south of Crown Mountain. Climb to this saddle via a small gully (Class 2+) or ascend a moderate snow slope.

From the 13,060-foot saddle, climb 0.4 mile north up a ridge to 13,569-foot Crown Mountain (Class 2). You can see the rest of the route to Niagara from here. Descend 0.2 mile northeast to the 13,340-foot Crown–Niagara saddle and continue 0.3 mile north along the ridge to the base of Niagara's south ridge. Climb 0.2 mile north up this ridge on loose rocks to the summit.

28.2EC — Extra Credit — "North Crown Mountain," 13,599 feet, Class 2

From the summit of Crown Mountain, climb 0.25 mile northwest on a nifty ridge to 13,599-foot "North Crown Mountain."

28. Jones Mountain   13,860 feet

See Map 28 on page 229

Jones Mountain is 1.7 miles southwest of the fourteener Handies Peak and only 0.6 mile northeast of Niagara Peak. Jones and Niagara are often climbed together. Compared to Niagara, Jones has a gentler countenance. It is the second peak you take a photograph of when driving near Animas Forks, not the first. Jones compensates by being higher than Niagara.

ROUTES

28.3 — Jones Mountain — South Ridge

From Grouse–Burns Gulch TH at 10,720 ft:	*207 RP*	*7.0 mi*	*3,140 ft*	*Class 2*
From Burns 4WD parking at 11,720 ft:	*151 RP*	*3.4 mi*	*2,140 ft*	*Class 2*
From Cataract Gulch TH at 9,600 ft:	*314 RP*	*17.4 mi*	*4,260 ft*	*Class 2*
From Cuba 4WD parking at 10,700 ft:	*224 RP*	*10.6 mi*	*3,160 ft*	*Class 2*
From Snare 4WD parking at 12,040 ft:	*141 RP*	*5.0 mi*	*1,820 ft*	*Class 2*

This is the standard route on Jones. Follow the East Ridge Route on Niagara, or that route's variation, to the 13,220-foot Jones–Niagara saddle. From the saddle, climb 0.6 mile north-northeast then north to Jones' summit. This ridge is easier than Niagara's east ridge.

28.4 — Jones Mountain — West Ridge

From Grouse–Burns Gulch TH at 10,720 ft:	*191 RP*	*6.2 mi*	*3,140 ft*	*Class 2*
From Burns 4WD parking at 11,720 ft:	*135 RP*	*2.6 mi*	*2,140 ft*	*Class 2*

This is a more direct but steeper route than the South Ridge Route. Start at the Grouse–Burns Gulch Trailhead and go 1.8 miles southeast on a four-wheel-drive shelf road into Burns Gulch to 11,720 feet. Continue 0.5 mile southeast up the gulch to 12,200 feet, using or losing the road remnants as you choose. Leave the valley, climb 0.3 mile northeast up a steep slope and reach Jones' west ridge at 12,900 feet. From this position, you have a great view of Niagara's north face. When ready, climb 0.5 mile east up the narrow but easy ridge to the summit. Ascending the West Ridge Route and descending the South Ridge Route makes a nice Tour de Jones.

28.5 — Jones Mountain — Northeast Ridge

From Grouse–Burns Gulch TH at 10,720 ft:	*211 RP*	*7.2 mi*	*3,140 ft*	*Class 2*
From Burns 4WD parking at 11,720 ft:	*155 RP*	*3.6 mi*	*2,140 ft*	*Class 2*

This alternative route takes you into a unique basin. Start at the Grouse-Burns Gulch Trailhead and go 1.8 miles southeast on a four-wheel-drive shelf road into Burns Gulch to 11,720 feet. Leave the road here and hike 0.7 mile east-northeast to a tiny lake at 12,500 feet in the northern branch of upper Burns Gulch. From here you can see Jones' ragged north face, which will augment your opinion of this peak. From the lake, climb 0.6 mile east then southeast to reach the 13,340-foot Jones–"American" saddle. The last 200 feet to the pass is up a rough talus slope.

From the Jones–"American" saddle, climb 0.5 mile south then southwest to the summit. This ridge is rougher than Jones' south ridge. Midway up the ridge, you will need to stay below the ridge on its southeast (left) side to avoid some towers.

28.5V — Variation

From Cataract Gulch TH at 9,600 ft:	*307 RP*	*15.6 mi*	*4,260 ft*	*Class 2*
From Cuba 4WD parking at 10,700 ft:	*217 RP*	*8.8 mi*	*3,160 ft*	*Class 2*
From Snare 4WD parking at 12,040 ft:	*135 RP*	*3.2 mi*	*1,820 ft*	*Class 2*

You can approach this route from Snare Gulch to the east. To do this, start at the Cataract Gulch Trailhead (see Half Peak) and follow the Snare Gulch Approach to the four-wheel-drive parking spot by North Snare Creek at 12,040 feet. Leave the road here and hike 1.1 miles northwest up North Snare Creek to reach the 13,340-foot Jones–"American" saddle. This approach to the saddle is gentler than the western approach. Join the Northeast Ridge Route in the saddle and follow it to the summit.

28. "American Peak"   13,806 feet

See Map 28 on page 229

"American Peak" is 0.8 mile east-northeast of Jones and 1.0 mile southsouthwest of the fourteener Handies Peak. Of the three peaks in the Jones Group, "American Peak" offers the most route choices. You can approach "American" from Burns Gulch to the west, American Basin to the north or Snare Gulch to the east. "American" offers a choice of easy routes, and the peak's north face holds four snow couloirs that offer spiffy, early summer snow climbs.

ROUTES

28.6 — "American Peak" — West Ridge

From Grouse–Burns Gulch TH at 10,720 ft:	*210 RP*	*7.3 mi*	*3,086 ft*	*Class 2*
From Burns 4WD parking at 11,720 ft:	*154 RP*	*3.7 mi*	*2,086 ft*	*Class 2*
From Cataract Gulch TH at 9,600 ft:	*306 RP*	*15.7 mi*	*4,206 ft*	*Class 2*
From Cuba 4WD parking at 10,700 ft:	*216 RP*	*8.9 mi*	*3,106 ft*	*Class 2*
From Snare 4WD parking at 12,040 ft:	*134 RP*	*3.3 mi*	*1,766 ft*	*Class 2*

This is the easiest route on "American Peak." Follow the Northeast Ridge Route on Jones, or that route's variation, to the 13,340-foot Jones–"American" saddle. The summit of "American Peak" is 0.5 mile

Jones Mountain from the northeast.

east of this saddle. From the saddle, follow a use trail 0.1 mile north then northeast to 13,400 feet. Continue 0.3 mile east on the use trail across a tedious talus slope south of Point 13,744 to the 13,580-foot saddle between Point 13,744 and the summit of "American." Even with the use trail, this is a rough traverse, but it is better than climbing over the top of Point 13,744. From the 13,580-foot saddle, stay just south of the ridge crest and climb 0.15 mile east to the summit of "American." From here you can wave at people climbing the standard route on the fourteener Handies.

28.7 — "American Peak" — West Face

From American Basin TH at 11,300 ft: 163 RP 6.2 mi 2,506 ft Class 2   Easy Snow
From American 4WD parking at 11,600 ft: 140 RP 4.4 mi 2,206 ft Class 2   Easy Snow

This is the easiest way to climb "American Peak" from American Basin north of the peak. Start at the American Basin Trailhead and go 0.9 mile south on the four-wheel-drive road, crossing the Lake Fork of the Gunnison River en route, to the end of the road at 11,600 feet. From here, hike 0.9 mile south on a trail to 12,400 feet in the center of American Basin. This is the beginning of the standard route on the fourteener Handies Peak, and the steep north face of "American Peak" looms to the south during this approach.

At 12,400 feet, the Handies Peak Trail climbs to the east and the Grouse Gulch Trail climbs to the west. Leave both trails at 12,400 feet and hike 0.25 mile south-southwest up the westernmost of two gullies to 12,800 feet. From here, climb 0.3 mile southwest up an easy snow slope

"American Peak" from the north.

to a 13,260-foot saddle on the northwest ridge of "American Peak." From the 13,260-foot saddle, climb 0.2 mile southeast on the northwest ridge to 13,440 feet, leave the ridge, then climb 0.1 mile south-southeast to 13,480 feet on the southwest ridge of "American" north of the Jones–"American" saddle. Join the West Ridge Route here and follow it to the summit.

28.7V — Variation
From Grouse–Burns Gulch TH at 10,720 ft: 218 RP   8.2 mi   4,326 ft   Class 2
You can approach this route and the couloirs on the north face of "American" from Grouse Gulch west of the peak. To do so, start at the Grouse–Burns Gulch Trailhead and follow the Grouse Gulch Approach to 12,400 feet in American Basin. Join the West Face Route there and follow it to the summit.

28.8 — "American Peak" — Traitor

From American Basin TH at 11,300 ft: 254 RP 5.5 mi 2,506 ft Class 2 Steep Snow
From American 4WD parking at 11,600 ft: 230 RP 3.7 mi 2,206 ft Class 2 Steep Snow
From Grouse–Burns Gulch TH at 10,720 ft: 309 RP 7.5 mi 4,326 ft Class 2 Steep Snow

Traitor is the westernmost and steepest of the four couloirs on the north face of "American Peak." Start at the American Basin Trailhead and follow the West Face Route or its variation to 12,400 feet in American Basin. Leave the Handies Peak and Grouse Gulch Trails here and hike 0.3 mile south up the easternmost of two gullies to a bench at 12,860 feet. You can see Traitor to the southwest. Climb 0.1 mile southwest to 13,000 feet directly below the couloir. There is generally no cornice at the top of Traitor, but inspect it carefully before starting.

If conditions are unfavorable, you can hike east to one of the easier couloirs or hike west to join the West Face Route. If conditions are favorable, both yours and the mountain's, climb 0.15 mile south up the steep, treacherous, inset couloir to the 13,580-foot saddle 100 yards west of Point 13,744 on the west ridge of "American." If there is melting snow on the couloir's walls, there can be rockfall in this couloir. Wear a helmet. From the saddle, climb 0.4 mile east-southeast, passing the tops of Independence and Patriot en route, to the summit of "American."

28.9 — "American Peak" — Independence *Classic*

From American Basin TH at 11,300 ft: *180 RP 5.4 mi 2,586 ft Class 2 Mod Snow*
From American 4WD parking at 11,600 ft: *156 RP 3.6 mi 2,286 ft Class 2 Mod Snow*
From Grouse–Burns Gulch TH at 10,720 ft: 235 RP 7.4 mi 4,406 ft Class 2 Mod Snow

The bottom of this couloir is 0.2 mile east of Traitor, and Independence is easier to climb than its treacherous neighbor. Follow the Traitor Route to the bench at 12,860 feet. Climb 0.15 mile southeast to a higher bench at 13,060 feet. The Independence Couloir is south of and above this point. Climb 0.2 mile south up the couloir on moderate snow to the 13,620-foot saddle 100 yards east of Point 13,744 on the west ridge of "American." From the saddle, climb 0.25 mile east-southeast, passing the top of Patriot en route, to the summit of "American."

28.10 — "American Peak" — Patriot

From American Basin TH at 11,300 ft: *170 RP 5.3 mi 2,506 ft Class 2 Mod Snow*
From American 4WD parking at 11,600 ft: 146 RP 3.5 mi 2,206 ft Class 2 Mod Snow
From Grouse–Burns Gulch TH at 10,720 ft: 225 RP 7.3 mi 4,326 ft Class 2 Mod Snow

Patriot is the easiest of the four couloirs on the north side of "American Peak." It is broad and has no cornice at its top. It is also the first of the four couloirs to melt out, and the upper few hundred feet may be scree. Follow the Independence Route to the upper bench at 13,060 feet. Hike 0.1 mile east-southeast to 13,100 feet. Patriot is south of and above this point. Climb 0.15 mile south-southwest up moderate snow to the 13,580-foot saddle between Point 13,744 and the summit of "American." Climb 0.15 mile east to the summit of "American."

28.11 — "American Peak" — Victory

From American Basin TH at 11,300 ft: *251 RP 5.5 mi 2,506 ft Class 2 Steep Snow*
From American 4WD parking at 11,600 ft: 227 RP 3.7 mi 2,206 ft Class 2 Steep Snow
From Grouse–Burns Gulch TH at 10,720 ft: 306 RP 7.5 mi 4,326 ft Class 2 Steep Snow

Victory is the easternmost of the four couloirs on the north face of "American." It is not as steep as Traitor, but it is still steep. Victory reaches a saddle east of the summit, and it is harder to see during your approach.

Follow the Patriot Route to 13,100 feet and continue 0.15 mile south-southeast to 13,200 feet. Victory is south of and above this point. Climb 0.15 mile south up the elegant, steep couloir to a small, 13,700-foot saddle east of the summit, then climb 0.1 mile west to the summit.

28.11V — Variation

Halfway up the couloir at 13,400 feet, leave the main couloir and climb a steeper branch couloir to the west (right). Reach the summit ridge at 13,760 feet just 100 feet east of the summit.

28.12 — "American Peak" — South Ridge

From Cataract Gulch TH at 9,600 ft:	*280 RP*	*14.0 mi*	*4,206 ft*	*Class 2*
From Cuba 4WD parking at 10,700 ft:	*191 RP*	*7.2 mi*	*3,106 ft*	*Class 2*
From 12,000 feet in Snare Gulch:	*117 RP*	*2.4 mi*	*1,806 ft*	*Class 2*

This is the easiest way to climb "American Peak" from Snare Gulch east of the peak. Start at the Cataract Gulch Trailhead (see Half Peak) and follow the Snare Gulch Approach to 12,000 feet near the beginning of the road's long traverse to North Snare Creek. This spot is 0.1 mile beyond treeline and 0.4 mile before the parking spot at North Snare Creek. Leave the road at 12,000 feet and hike 0.6 mile north-northwest to 12,800 feet in a small basin. Climb 0.3 mile west up scree and reach the south ridge of "American" at 13,340 feet. Climb 0.3 mile north-northwest up this easy ridge to the summit.

28.13 — "American Peak" — The Snare

From Cataract Gulch TH at 9,600 ft:	*327 RP*	*13.8 mi*	*4,206 ft*	*Class 2*	*Mod Snow*
From Cuba 4WD parking at 10,700 ft:	*237 RP*	*7.0 mi*	*3,106 ft*	*Class 2*	*Mod Snow*
From 12,000 feet in Snare Gulch:	*164 RP*	*2.2 mi*	*1,806 ft*	*Class 2*	*Mod Snow*

This is an unlikely snow climb on the southeast side of "American Peak." It is difficult to see the Snare from roads, but you can preview conditions in this hidden couloir from Half Peak to the south. Don't wait too long for this one. Follow the South Ridge Route to 12,800 feet. You will be able to see the Snare from here. Climb 0.4 mile northwest up moderate snow through a sea of rotten rock to the small, 13,700-foot saddle at the top of Victory. Climb 0.1 mile west to the summit.

28. NIAGARA, JONES AND "AMERICAN" COMBINATIONS
See Map 28 on page 229

28.14 — NJ Combination — Niagara Falls *Classic*

From Grouse–Burns Gulch TH at 10,720 ft:	*242 RP*	*7.6 mi*	*3,727 ft*	*Class 2+*
From Burns 4WD parking at 11,720 ft:	*186 RP*	*4.0 mi*	*2,727 ft*	*Class 2+*

This is the easiest way to climb Jones and Niagara together. Climb Niagara's

"American" Jones Niagara

Burns Gulch

The Jones Group from the west.

East Ridge Route and descend that route to the 13,220-foot Jones–Niagara saddle. Continue on Jones' South Ridge Route to Jones' summit. Descend Jones' South Ridge Route.

28.14V — Variation

From Cataract Gulch TH at 9,600 ft:	349 RP	17.1 mi	4,847 ft	Class 2+
From Cuba 4WD parking at 10,700 ft:	259 RP	10.3 mi	3,747 ft	Class 2+
From Snare 4WD parking at 12,040 ft:	177 RP	4.7 mi	2,407 ft	Class 2+

You can climb Jones and Niagara from Snare Gulch to the east. Climb Jones' Northeast Ridge Route, Variation 28.5V, to Jones' summit. Descend 0.6 mile south to the 13,220-foot Jones–Niagara saddle, then climb 0.3 mile west to Niagara's summit. Descend Niagara's East Ridge Route, Variation 28.1V.

28.15 — NJA Combination — American Pie

From Grouse–Burns Gulch TH at 10,720 ft:	284 RP	8.8 mi	4,193 ft	Class 2+
From Burns 4WD parking at 11,720 ft:	228 RP	5.2 mi	3,193 ft	Class 2+

This is the easiest way to climb Niagara, Jones and "American" together. Follow Niagara Falls (Combination 28.14) to Jones' summit. Descend Jones' Northeast Ridge Route to the 13,340-foot Jones–"American" saddle. Follow the West Ridge Route on "American" to the summit of "American." Descend the West Ridge Route of "American."

28.15V — Variation *Classic*

From Cataract Gulch TH at 9,600 ft:	382 RP	17.8 mi	5,353 ft	Class 2+
From Cuba 4WD parking at 10,700 ft:	292 RP	11.0 mi	4,253 ft	Class 2+
From Snare 4WD parking at 12,040 ft:	209 RP	5.4 mi	2,913 ft	Class 2+

You can climb "American," Jones and Niagara from Snare Gulch to the east. Climb the South Ridge Route on "American" to the summit of "American." Descend the West Ridge Route of "American" to the 13,340-foot Jones–"American" saddle. Continue on Niagara Falls' Variation 28.14V and return to Snare Gulch.

29. Vestal Group

Arrow Peak	13,803 feet
Vestal Peak	13,864 feet
Trinity Peak	13,805 feet

See Map 29 on page 242

At last, we have reached the heartland. The Vestal Group, combined with the Pigeon Group to the south and the fourteeners Sunlight, Eolus and Windom, comprise 10 of Colorado's 104 highest peaks. Here, Colorado's mountains take on a new dimension as peaks leap from a mold that could belong to another planet. The heartland's summits scrape the sky, grace the eye and stir the soul.

The Vestal Group holds three of Colorado's most dramatic peaks. They are only 9 miles south-southwest of Silverton, but they feel a world apart. The peaks have rugged north faces that rise in narrowing, steepening sweeps to their skyscraper summits. In particular, Vestal's north face, called Wham Ridge, is a beautiful sweep of smooth, solid rock. The Vestal Group is so singular that it has the distinction of being almost an entire range in and of itself—the Grenadier Range.

The Grenadier Range is an 8-mile-long ridge that runs east-west between the Animas River and Vallecito Creek. The range is distinct from the rest of the San Juans because it is made of quartzite. Finally, you can find a solid crack in which to anchor your rope, and indeed, you may choose to use a rope on these peaks. Although the core rock is solid, the ledges are littered with loose blocks. Set in motion, they can quickly prove fatal to anyone below you. And although the standard routes on these peaks are not extremely difficult, they are steep and dangerous. Climb here with great care.

MAPS
Required: *Snowdon Peak, Storm King Peak, San Juan National Forest*

TRAILHEADS

Elk Park Trailhead
This trailhead is at 8,860 feet and provides access to all the peaks in the Vestal Group from the west via the Durango & Silverton Narrow Gauge

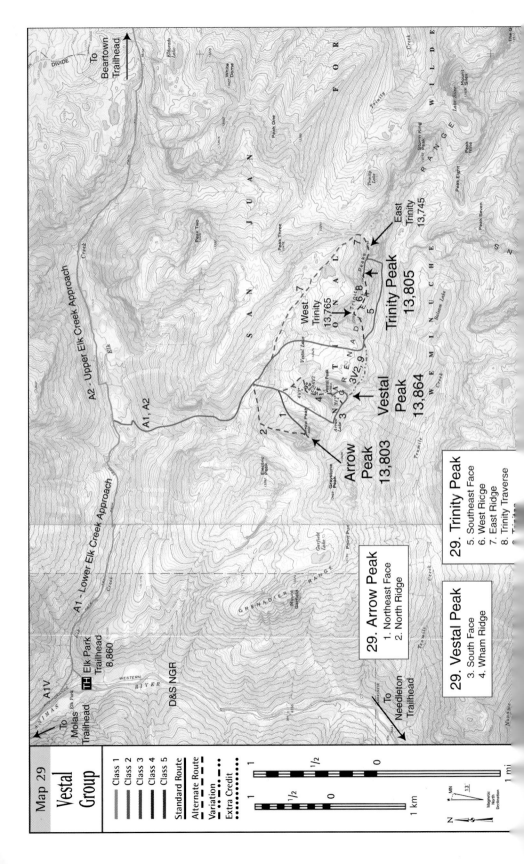

Map 29

Vestal Group

Class 1
Class 2
Class 3
Class 4
Class 5

Standard Route
Alternate Route - - - -
Variation ·········
Extra Credit ·········

29. Arrow Peak
1. Northeast Face
2. North Ridge

29. Vestal Peak
3. South Face
4. Wham Ridge

29. Trinity Peak
5. Southeast Face
6. West Ridge
7. East Ridge
8. Trinity Traverse

Arrow Peak
13,803

Vestal Peak
13,864

Trinity Peak
13,805

West Trinity
13,765

East Trinity
13,745

A1, A2

A2 - Upper Elk Creek Approach

A1, A2 - Lower Elk Creek Approach

Elk Park Trailhead
8,860

To Molas Trailhead

To Needleton Trailhead

To Beartown Trailhead

DIVIDE

SAN JUAN NATIONAL FOREST

WEMINUCHE WILDERNESS

GRENADIER RANGE

D&S NGR

WESTERN RIVER

Railroad (D&S NGR) and the Elk Creek Trail. Elk Park is in the Animas River Canyon 5.7 miles south of Silverton. You reach Elk Park by rail or foot, not by road. The D&S NGR goes through the canyon, but the gorge is too narrow to accommodate both tracks and a road. You can take a morning train from Durango and be in Elk Park in late morning, or take an afternoon train from Silverton and be in Elk Park in midafternoon. The fare to Elk Park is considerably cheaper from Silverton, and reservations are usually not needed when boarding in Silverton. A detailed table of the D&S NGR schedule and fares is included with the Needleton Trailhead in the Pigeon Group. This trailhead is not accessible in winter.

Molas Trailhead

This trailhead is at 10,620 feet and provides access to all the peaks in the Vestal Group from the west via the Molas and Elk Creek Trails. If you are approaching from the north, measure from the U.S. 550–Colorado 110 junction just south of downtown Silverton. Go south on U.S. 550 toward Durango, pass a turn to the east (left) for the Molas Country Store at mile 4.9 and turn east (left) onto a dirt road at mile 5.4. A highway sign for Molas Lake and the Molas Trail marks this turn.

If you are approaching from the south, go 40.6 miles north on U.S. 550 from the junction of 32nd Street and Main Avenue (U.S. 550) in north Durango to the summit of Molas Pass at 10,910 feet and measure from this point. From the summit of Molas Pass, continue north on U.S. 550 toward Silverton, pass a turn to the west (left) for Little Molas Lake at mile 0.4 and turn east (right) onto a dirt road at mile 1.1. A highway sign for Molas Lake and the Molas Trail marks this turn.

Go 120 yards east on the dirt road and turn north (left) into a large parking lot. This is the trailhead. The Molas Trail, part of the Colorado Trail, starts to the south of the parking lot. This trailhead is accessible in winter.

Beartown Trailhead

This trailhead is at 11,700 feet and provides access to the peaks of the Vestal Group from the east via the upper Elk Creek Trail, as well as to the peaks of the Pigeon Group from the north via Hunchback Pass and Vallecito Creek. This trailhead is at the doorstep of a mighty wilderness, and just reaching the trailhead can be an adventure. There are two approaches to the trailhead, and both require a four-wheel-drive vehicle.

If you are approaching from Silverton, you must cross Stony Pass, which is almost a thousand feet higher than the trailhead. Measure from the junction of the Cement Creek Road and the Animas River Road in the north end of Silverton. Both of these roads are Colorado 110. Turn east (right) onto the Animas River Road, go 4.2 miles east-northeast up the Animas River Valley and turn south (right) onto the Cunningham Creek Road (FS 589) in Howardsville. Go 1.7 miles south-southeast on the

Cunningham Creek Road and turn east (left) onto the Stony Pass Road (FS 737) at mile 5.9. Go 4.2 miles southeast up the Stony Pass Road and reach 12,650-foot Stony Pass at mile 10.1. At the pass, you are treated to a distant view of Rio Grande Pyramid. From Stony Pass, descend 6.5 miles southeast on what is now the Rio Grande Reservoir Road (FS 520) and turn south (right) onto the Beartown Road (FS 506) at mile 16.6. This approach meets the Rio Grande Reservoir approach (below) at this junction.

If you are approaching from Lake City or Creede, follow the directions for the Ute Creek Trailhead described for Rio Grande Pyramid. Measure from the junction of the Rio Grande Reservoir Road and the Ute Creek Trailhead spur road. Go west on the Rio Grande Reservoir Road (FS 520), pass the Lost Trail Campground at mile 0.9, pass the Lost Trail Creek Trailhead at mile 1.3, cross a side creek and stay left at mile 2.8. Pass a cattle guard at the entrance to Brewster Park at mile 4.4 and reach the bottom of Timber Hill at mile 6.6. Timber Hill has had a bad reputation among backcountry drivers for many years. If the road is wet, it can indeed present a driving challenge. Reach a gate at the top of Timber Hill at mile 8.6 and turn south (left) onto the Beartown Road (FS 506) at mile 9.6. This approach meets the Stony Pass approach (above) at this junction.

Measure anew from the junction of the Rio Grande Reservoir Road and the Beartown Road. Descend 0.4 mile south on the Beartown Road and ford the Rio Grande River. Even for vehicles, this ford can be difficult to impossible in June. Plan accordingly. Pass the Beartown site and the westbound Colorado Trail at mile 4.5. There are no buildings visible at Beartown; it is truly a ghost town. Reach the Beartown Trailhead at mile 5.6. There is a trail register and sign here, but only enough parking space for three or four vehicles. If necessary, you can park 0.4 mile below the trailhead, or you can continue up the road above the trailhead for another 0.6 mile to Kite Lake at 12,100 feet. This trailhead is not accessible in winter.

APPROACHES

29.A1 — Lower Elk Creek Approach

From Elk Park TH at 8,860 ft:	*149 RP*	*9.8 mi*	*2,780 ft*	*Class 2*
From 9,980 ft in Elk Creek:	*91 RP*	*3.8 mi*	*1,500 ft*	*Class 2*

This, the easiest approach to the Vestal Group, takes you to 11,400 feet in Vestal Creek. Take the Durango & Silverton Narrow Gauge train from either Durango or Silverton and get off at Elk Park. Walk 100 yards east along the north side of the engine turnaround spur tracks. At the wye's eastern end, hike north up the hill on a spur of the Elk Creek Trail. Hike 0.2 mile northeast, join the main Elk Creek Trail at a sign announcing your entry into the Weminuche Wilderness and hike 100 yards east to a sign and trail register. The Elk Creek Trail is also the Colorado Trail, and it is an excellent trail. Welcome to Elk Creek.

From the trail register, hike 2.7 miles east above Elk Creek's north side to a large beaver pond just south of the trail at 9,980 feet. There is a great view of Arrow Peak to the south, and there are several campsites nearby. The introduction is over.

Leave the comfort of the Elk Creek Trail and hike 120 yards south on some boulders around the beaver pond's east side. Hike 150 yards south on a faint trail, pass some flat campsites and reach the top of the Elk Creek gorge. Angle southeast down to Elk Creek on a rough trail and cross to Elk Creek's south side. There is no bridge here, and this crossing can be difficult in high water. It has given many parties fits over the years.

Once on the creek's south side, hike south up the steep hill and find the beginning of the Vestal Creek Trail. Vestal Creek and this use trail are not marked on the Storm King Peak Quadrangle. Vestal Creek drains the north faces of Arrow, Vestal and the Trinity Peaks, and finding the Vestal Creek Trail is not optional. There is an old trail along Vestal Creek, but it is seldom used and we do not recommend it. The correct trail is high on the slope above Vestal Creek's east side. Hike 0.1 mile west on the beginning of the Vestal Creek Trail, which is on a small bench 100 feet above Elk Creek. Turn south and hike 1.0 mile steeply uphill on the rough trail to 11,200 feet (Class 2). Descend slightly and reach the creek where the valley turns to the southeast. Hike 0.5 mile southeast to the east end of a meadow at 11,400 feet. This is called the "lower meadow." There are several campsites near the meadow and in the trees beyond this point. Arrow and Vestal are 0.75 mile southeast and south of this meadow, and Trinity Peak is 1.5 miles to the southeast.

29.A1V – Variation

From Molas TH at 10,620 ft: 216 RP   16.4 mi   4,460 ft   *Class 2*

This popular alternative adds 6.6 miles and 1,680 feet of elevation gain to your journey, but it avoids the train's cost and crowds. Start at the Molas Trailhead and hike 1.8 miles south then east on the Molas Trail, which soon joins the Colorado Trail. Descend gently across meadows to a viewpoint at 10,100 feet. From here you can look southeast across the Animas Canyon into Elk Creek, and beyond to the peaks of the Vestal Group. To reach them, you have to cross the canyon.

Descend 1.0 mile southeast down a series of switchbacks, cross Molas Creek, then cross the Animas River on a solid footbridge at 8,900 feet. Hike 0.1 mile south along the railroad tracks, then hike 0.7 mile southeast on the beginning of the Elk Creek Trail as it climbs above the tracks. Join the Lower Elk Creek Approach at the Weminuche Wilderness boundary.

29.A2 – Upper Elk Creek Approach

From Beartown TH at 11,700 ft: 283 RP   16.8 mi   5,220 ft   *Class 2*

This approach to the Vestal Group requires a four-wheel-drive vehicle, but it offers opportunities for an extended backcountry trip. Start at the

Beartown Trailhead and hike 0.8 mile northeast on FS Trail 833, which is the Continental Divide Trail. Merge with the Colorado Trail and hike 0.8 mile northeast then southeast to another trail junction where the Continental Divide Trail heads north and the Colorado Trail heads south. Hike 0.5 mile south on the Colorado Trail to a high point of 12,700 feet. Here, you are perched on the Continental Divide. East of you, Bear Creek flows into the Rio Grande River, which is destined for the Gulf of Mexico. West of you, Elk Creek flows into the Animas River, whose waters ultimately strive to reach the Gulf of California via the Colorado River.

When you are ready, leave your lofty perch and descend 4.4 miles west down Elk Creek to the beaver pond at 9,980 feet. Join the Lower Elk Creek Approach here and follow it to 11,400 feet in Vestal Creek.

29. Arrow Peak   13,803 feet

See Map 29 on page 242

Anchoring the Vestal Group's west end, Arrow Peak is well named. Sharp as an arrow, the peak is aimed at the sky as if poised for a launch to return to the world from which it came. From the beaver pond and as you approach up Vestal Creek, it is Arrow that first draws your attention. This siren peak points at a way for others to follow. Arrow is Colorado's extant peak. Arrow draws many and rejects some. Approach with respect.

ROUTES

29.1 — Arrow Peak — Northeast Face *Classic*

From Elk Park TH at 8,860 ft:	*409 RP*	*11.8 mi*	*5,183 ft*	*Class 3*
From Molas TH at 10,620 ft:	*507 RP*	*18.4 mi*	*6,863 ft*	*Class 3*
From Beartown TH at 11,700 ft:	*526 RP*	*18.8 mi*	*7,623 ft*	*Class 3*
From 9,980 ft in Elk Creek:	*324 RP*	*5.8 mi*	*3,903 ft*	*Class 3*
From 11,400 ft in Vestal Creek:	*190 RP*	*2.0 mi*	*2,403 ft*	*Class 3*

This is the easiest route on Arrow Peak. If you take care to follow the route as described here, the difficulty will not exceed Class 3. There is a lot of Class 2+ and Class 3 climbing on this route, and much harder climbing always lurks nearby. Even Arrow's easiest route is steep and flirts with loose rock. This is a bad route to be on in a storm.

Use one of the approaches to the lower meadow at 11,400 feet in Vestal Creek. The route is partially obscured from here. Leave the Vestal Creek Trail 150 yards west of the lower meadow's east end, hike south on a faint trail into the meadow and cross to Vestal Creek's south side. Hike 0.3 mile south up a steep slope on a strong climbers trail to 12,000 feet at the north end of the basin between Arrow and Vestal. You can see the route from here.

Arrow Peak from the northeast.

The salient feature of Arrow's northeast face is a huge, north-facing ramp that sweeps up from 12,200 feet to a saddle just north of the summit. This ramp harbors the route. There are near-vertical, east-facing cliffs above and below the ramp. There are two smaller ramps below and east of the huge ramp that are definitely not the route.

From 12,000 feet, hike 0.2 mile southwest across grass and talus to 12,200 feet at the east end of a grassy ledge system 200 feet above the bottom of the huge ramp. The grassy ledges allow you to avoid some smooth slabs that dominate the bottom of the huge ramp. Climb 150 feet west up grassy ledges and reach the outer, east edge of the huge ramp above the initial smooth slabs. At no point in the ascent do you actually climb in the gully between the ramp and the cliffs above the ramp. Climb 200 yards south up the ramp's eastern edge on solid rocks and grass steps (Class 2+). Hike 400 yards up gentler slabs and scree near the ramp's eastern edge (Class 2). As you climb, examine the upper part of the route.

The upper part of the huge ramp is broken into two ramps as it steepens and sweeps up to the southwest to end at a small saddle between Arrow's main summit and a subsummit 200 yards to the north. Don't make the mistake of staying on the huge ramp's extreme eastern edge when the ramp splits, as this will leave you on the eastern ramp higher up. Angle across scree in the middle of the huge ramp and get onto the western or higher ramp near its bottom, where egress from the lower ramp is still easy (Class 2). Before you become embroiled in Arrow's upper difficulties, take a moment to savor the view to the east of Vestal's Wham Ridge. This is one of Colorado's most unique mountain profiles.

Once you are on the western, upper ramp, climb 150 yards up its southeastern edge (Class 2+). This is the rib between the two upper ramps. Once again, do not climb in the gully between the upper ramp and the near-vertical cliffs above it. When the rib steepens and blocks simple passage, cross to the rib's southeast (left) side and climb 100 feet up blocks and ledges (Class 3). This is your only excursion on the upper rib's left side. When it's easy, traverse back to the rib and ascend it for 200 feet (Class 3).

Fifty feet before you reach Arrow's north ridge, climb 100 feet south up a chimney system (Class 3). Your ascent of the huge ramp is over. All that remains is the summit tower. Climb 250 feet south up broken ledges that are east of Arrow's upper north ridge (Class 3). This is the upper portion of Arrow's northeast face. Yodel. You are on the summit. Take a moment to look toward the sky.

29.2 — Arrow Peak — North Ridge

From Elk Park TH at 8,860 ft:	*802 RP*	*11.6 mi*	*5,183 ft*	*Class 5.6*
From Molas TH at 10,620 ft:	*900 RP*	*18.2 mi*	*6,863 ft*	*Class 5.6*
From Beartown TH at 11,700 ft:	*919 RP*	*18.6 mi*	*7,623 ft*	*Class 5.6*
From 9,980 ft in Elk Creek:	*717 RP*	*5.6 mi*	*3,903 ft*	*Class 5.6*
From 11,400 ft in Vestal Creek:	*583 RP*	*1.8 mi*	*2,403 ft*	*Class 5.6*
With descent of Northeast Face:	*573 RP*	*1.9 mi*	*2,403 ft*	*Class 5.6*

This technical route on Arrow has become popular in recent years. Use one of the approaches to the lower meadow at 11,400 feet in Vestal Creek. Cross to Vestal Creek's south side and climb 0.4 mile west-southwest up steep, tree-covered ledges to reach Arrow's north ridge at 11,800 feet (Class 4). Climb four pitches south up the slabby ridge, which is really more of a face at this point (Class 5.6). Climb two loose, Class 4 pitches, then scramble up 400 feet of steep scree on the ridge's east side. Get onto the upper, narrow ridge and follow it to Arrow's northern subsummit (Class 3). Climb south over the subsummit on loose blocks, then join the Northeast Face Route at the top of the huge ramp (Class 3) and follow it to the summit.

29. Vestal Peak   13,864 feet

See Map 29 on page 242

While Arrow aims for the stars, Vestal tends Earth's hearth. The Grenadiers' highest peak, Vestal anchors the range well. The clean sweep of rock on Vestal's north side that is called Wham Ridge is unrivaled in the San Juans. You can get a fleeting view of Vestal from near Molas Pass on U.S. 550, but, as always, the best views are reserved for the wilderness traveler.

The 1964 Storm King Peak Quadrangle originally had a significant error at Vestal's summit. The elevation was incorrectly given as 13,664 feet instead of the correct elevation of 13,864 feet. Worse, 200 feet of contour lines were missing. The mistakes were corrected in the 1975 edition of the map. The elevation now reads 13,864 feet, and the missing contour lines are crammed on top of Vestal. Even with the addition of the missing contour lines, the map still does not accurately represent Vestal's summit topography. The map suggests a wavy approach to Vestal's summit, but the reality is that the approach to Vestal's summit is uniform in steepness. Also, other maps based on the USGS maps still carry the incorrect elevation of 13,664 feet. In particular, the Trails Illustrated Weminuche Wilderness Map number 140 has the incorrect elevation for Vestal.

ROUTES

29.3 — Vestal Peak — South Face

From Elk Park TH at 8,860 ft:	*375 RP*	*12.8 mi*	*5,244 ft*	*Class 2+*
From Molas TH at 10,620 ft:	*475 RP*	*19.4 mi*	*6,924 ft*	*Class 2+*
From Beartown TH at 11,700 ft:	*493 RP*	*19.8 mi*	*7,684 ft*	*Class 2+*
From 9,980 ft in Elk Creek:	*290 RP*	*6.8 mi*	*3,964 ft*	*Class 2+*
From 11,400 ft in Vestal Creek:	*155 RP*	*3.0 mi*	*2,464 ft*	*Class 2+*

This is the easiest route on Vestal. This route is easier but looser than Arrow's Northeast Face Route. Although Vestal's north face is mostly solid, the south face is surprisingly loose, and a casual misstep can quickly launch a fatal missile. This only makes a difference if there is someone below you, but the difference is enormous. Tread lightly.

Use one of the approaches to the lower meadow at 11,400 feet in Vestal Creek. You can just see Vestal's summit 0.8 mile south of here. Leave the Vestal Creek Trail 150 yards west of the lower meadow's east end, hike south on a faint trail into the meadow and cross to Vestal Creek's south side. Hike 0.3 mile south up a steep slope on a strong climbers trail to 12,000 feet at the north end of the basin between Arrow and Vestal. Hike 0.2 mile south-southwest and, when convenient, get onto a small, red, rock glacier in the middle of the basin between Arrow and Vestal. Hike 0.4 mile south-southwest on top of this rock rib to 12,500 feet. The introduction is over.

Scramble 0.1 mile south-southwest up a steep scree slope to the 12,860-foot Arrow–Vestal saddle (Class 2+). We call this slope the "Dues Collector," as it will extract the rest of your wilderness entrance fee. From the saddle, hike 0.1 mile east-southeast on a ridge to 13,000 feet at the base of Vestal's western ramparts (Class 2). Hike 0.2 mile east-south-east to 13,200 feet on a climbers trail that does an ascending traverse underneath the cliffs of Vestal's southwest face (Class 2). Avoid any temptation to get too high during this ascending traverse. Your goal is to get around to the east side of Vestal's south ridge, which is the right skyline ahead of you during the traverse.

From 13,200 feet on the east side of Vestal's south ridge, you can see a huge gully heading north toward the summit. This is the weakness in Vestal's defenses that you have circled the peak to find. The route does not ascend the gully directly but, rather, it is on the ledges west (left) of the gully. From 13,200 feet, scamper 100 yards east up a steeper ascending traverse to within 100 feet of the gully (Class 2+). Climb 200 yards directly north up broken ledges to 13,600 feet at a point 30 feet below Vestal's upper southeast ridge (Class 2+). This is the section where loose rock lurks. If you want, take time to go to the ridge and peer down Vestal's steep, convoluted northeast face.

From 13,600 feet, climb 200 feet west on a ledge on the ridge's south side, then ascend 100 feet west up a small gully to a small notch (Class 2+). From here you can look down the top part of Vestal's southwest face. Stay south of any difficulties, climb 200 feet northwest on scree, then scamper 100 feet north to Vestal's highest point (Class 2+).

VARIATIONS

29.3V1 — Southwest Face, Class 4

At 13,100 feet, leave the ascending traverse and climb northeast directly up Vestal's southwest face (Class 4). This is a steeper, harder version of the south-face ascent. Seen from below, the ascent is easier than it looks, as there are many ledges. The Class 4 moves are on the short rock walls between the ledges. As with the south face, the ledges are littered with loose blocks.

29.3V2 — Southeast Face, Class 2+

You can approach Vestal's South Face Route from the east. Climb to the 12,860-foot Vestal–West Trinity saddle as described with Trinity Peak's South-east Face Route. Hike 0.5 mile west on an easy ridge and skirt Point 13,220 on its north side (Class 2). At the base of Vestal's southeast ramparts, descend to the south, then contour 0.1 mile west on a climbers trail to 13,000 feet at the bottom of the huge gully on Vestal's south face.

A direct ascent up the gully is possible and requires passing three Class 3 chockstones en route. We do not recommend this route, as any rock bounding down from on high is likely to end up in this gully. An easier and safer alternative is to cross to the gully's west side and climb north up broken ledges to join the South Face Route at 13,300 feet (Class 2+).

29.4 — Vestal Peak — Wham Ridge *Classic*

From Elk Park TH at 8,860 ft:	562 RP	12.0 mi	5,244 ft	Class 5.4
From Molas TH at 10,620 ft:	661 RP	18.6 mi	6,924 ft	Class 5.4
From Beartown TH at 11,700 ft:	680 RP	19.0 mi	7,684 ft	Class 5.4
From 9,980 ft in Elk Creek:	477 RP	6.0 mi	3,964 ft	Class 5.4
From 11,400 ft in Vestal Creek:	342 RP	2.2 mi	2,464 ft	Class 5.4
With descent of South Face:	342 RP	2.6 mi	2,464 ft	Class 5.4

Solid rock, a beautiful line and a wilderness setting combine to make Wham Ridge one of Colorado's best mountaineering routes. The name

Vestal Peak from the north.

Wham Ridge refers to Vestal's entire north face, so "Ridge" here is a misnomer. However, the route we describe follows the east edge of the face, which is a well-defined ridge. This is the easiest way to climb Wham Ridge.

Use one of the approaches to the lower meadow at 11,400 feet in Vestal Creek. Leave the Vestal Creek Trail 150 yards west of the lower meadow's east end, hike south on a faint trail into the meadow and cross to Vestal Creek's south side. Hike 0.3 mile south up a steep slope on a strong climbers trail to 12,000 feet at the north end of the basin between Arrow and Vestal. Depending on your disposition, Wham Ridge will be either appallingly or appealingly apparent from here. Hike 0.2 mile south to 12,200 feet on a grassy slope at the bottom of Wham Ridge. The combination of solid rock above and grass below makes this a very unique place. Don't engage the rock yet, but hike 0.1 mile southeast up the grass under Wham's rock to an open area at 12,300 feet, where you can look down on Vestal Lake to the east. The introduction is over.

Engage Wham Ridge and climb west up a grass ramp (Class 2+). Initially, stay near the east (left) edge of the face and climb up to the highest grass ramp on the lower face (Class 2+). Once on the highest ramp, climb an ascending traverse to the west all the way across Wham Ridge to 12,600 feet on the west (right) edge of the face (Class 2+). You may feel smug that you have gained so much elevation so easily.

Climb the west edge of the face as the angle steepens relentlessly. The difficulty steadily increases from Class 2+ to Class 4. Near the top of the smooth slabs, the difficulty takes another upward turn. Step east (left) and climb 100 feet up a clean, beautiful slab with a crack in it to the bottom of Wham's more broken upper face (Class 5.4). This pitch is the route's crux.

Stay near the upper face's west edge and climb another 300 feet (Class 4). Near the top of the face, traverse into the center of the face and climb a long, Class 4 pitch to Vestal's northern subsummit. From here you are perched above the technical difficulties and can see the main summit 100 yards to the south. Climb south over the subsummit and climb a scree gully up to the main summit (Class 2+). Ascending Wham Ridge and descending the South Face Route makes a tidy Tour de Vestal.

VARIATIONS

29.4V1 – Direct Start, Class 5.3 (?)
Start at Wham Ridge's low point and climb 300 feet up elegant, fractured but still solid rock to reach the grass ramps.

29.4V2 – Center Shift, Class 5.6–5.7
The center of Wham Ridge provides harder climbing. If you follow the path of least resistance, you can keep the difficulty at Class 5.6. If you take a direct line up the center of the smooth face, you can climb some delectable and protectable Class 5.7 pitches.

29. Trinity Peak   13,805 feet

See Map 29 on page 242

Trinity Peak is 0.8 mile east-southeast of Vestal and is an even more remote prize. The three Trinity Peaks rise in syzygy, and Trinity Peak, the highest of the three, is in the middle. Guarded by 13,765-foot West Trinity and 13,745-foot East Trinity, Trinity Peak, or Middle Trinity as it is sometimes called, is difficult to reach. The Trinity Peaks' north faces echo the Wham Ridge, and Trinity Peak dares Arrow to abdicate.

ROUTES

29.5 — Trinity Peak — Southeast Face

From Elk Park TH at 8,860 ft:	444 RP	15.4 mi	5,705 ft	Class 2+
From Molas TH at 10,620 ft:	542 RP	22.0 mi	7,385 ft	Class 2+
From Beartown TH at 11,700 ft:	561 RP	22.4 mi	8,145 ft	Class 2+
From 9,980 ft in Elk Creek:	359 RP	9.4 mi	4,425 ft	Class 2+
From 11,400 ft in Vestal Creek:	225 RP	5.6 mi	2,925 ft	Class 2+

This is the easiest route on Trinity Peak. Use this route if you do not care to climb West or East Trinity and climbing Trinity Peak is your only objective. Use one of the approaches to the lower meadow at 11,400 feet in Vestal Creek. Continue 0.4 mile east-southeast up the Vestal Creek Trail to the western edge of a higher meadow at 11,740 feet. This is called the "upper meadow." Cross to Vestal Creek's south side and climb 0.5 mile southeast up a steep, grassy slope on a faint climbers trail to 12,300 feet. The trail dies here, but you no longer need one. Hike 0.5 mile south up open, grassy slopes, then climb 0.1 mile southeast diagonally up a steep scree slope to the 12,860-foot Vestal–West Trinity saddle. The scree slope below this saddle supports a climbers trail and is not as difficult as the "Dues Collector" slope leading to the Arrow–Vestal saddle.

   Cross to the saddle's south side, descend a little and contour 0.2 mile southeast on talus (Class 2). Round a corner and do a descending traverse 0.7 mile east (Class 2). Drop to 12,600 feet during this traverse and stay below all the cliffs of West Trinity and Trinity Peak en route. When you reach the gully descending from the Trinity Peak–East Trinity saddle, climb 0.2 mile north up this rubble gully to 13,300 feet (Class 2+). It is not necessary to go all the way into the 13,340-foot saddle. Fifty feet below the saddle, turn west (left) and climb 0.2 mile west up a steep, rubble-filled gully to the summit of Trinity Peak (Class 2+). Use great care in this gully, as rocks set in motion rattle all the way down it.

29.6 — Trinity Peak — West Ridge

From Elk Park TH at 8,860 ft:	509 RP	15.0 mi	6,115 ft	Class 4
From Molas TH at 10,620 ft:	608 RP	21.6 mi	7,795 ft	Class 4

From Beartown TH at 11,700 ft:	626 RP	22.0 mi	8,555 ft	Class 4
From 9,980 ft in Elk Creek:	424 RP	9.0 mi	4,835 ft	Class 4
From 11,400 ft in Vestal Creek:	290 RP	5.2 mi	3,335 ft	Class 4

This is the easiest way to climb West Trinity and Trinity Peak together. Follow the Southeast Face Route to the 12,860-foot Vestal–West Trinity saddle. From the saddle, climb 0.4 mile east-northeast up West Trinity's west ridge to West Trinity's 13,765-foot summit. The first half of this ridge is Class 2+, and the upper half requires some Class 3 scrambling. Stay near but not exactly on the ridge. The view of Trinity Peak from West Trinity is both exciting and sobering.

From West Trinity, descend 0.2 mile southeast to 13,300 feet (Class 2). Contour 0.1 mile east on a wide ledge below some cliffs that form the 13,380-foot Trinity Peak–West Trinity saddle (Class 2). Climb slightly, round a corner and contour another 0.1 mile east on the same ledge below a smooth flatiron face (Class 2).

There is a vertical step in the west ridge of Trinity Peak just east of this flatiron face. When you are even with and below this vertical step, leave the ledge that you have been following. Climb a steep ascending traverse 300 feet to the northeast up little walls between ledges (Class 3). Climb to the base of a 30-foot-high, south-facing chimney. You can see this chimney's west wall from the Class 2 ledge before you begin the ascending traverse. Climb north up the 30-foot-high chimney (Class 4). This short pitch is the route's crux. Climb another 50 feet northeast to a higher ledge (Class 4). Contour 0.1 mile east on this higher ledge until it delivers you to a little basin (Class 2+). Climb 0.1 mile northeast up the little basin to Trinity Peak's summit (Class 3).

29.7 — Trinity Peak — East Ridge

From Elk Park TH at 8,860 ft:	471 RP	14.8 mi	6,075 ft	Class 3
From Molas TH at 10,620 ft:	569 RP	21.4 mi	7,755 ft	Class 3
From Beartown TH at 11,700 ft:	588 RP	21.8 mi	8,515 ft	Class 3
From 9,980 ft in Elk Creek:	386 RP	8.8 mi	4,795 ft	Class 3
From 11,400 ft in Vestal Creek:	252 RP	5.0 mi	3,295 ft	Class 3

This is the easiest way to climb East Trinity and Trinity Peak together. Use one of the approaches to the lower meadow at 11,400 feet in Vestal Creek. Continue 0.4 mile east-southeast up the Vestal Creek Trail to the western edge of a higher meadow at 11,740 feet. This is called the "upper meadow." Continue 0.3 mile east-southeast up the Vestal Creek Trail to 12,000 feet. The Vestal Creek Trail dies here, but you no longer need a trail. Continue 0.6 mile east-southeast up the valley on luxurious grass slopes to an unnamed lake at 12,396 feet. Go around the lake's north side and climb 0.5 mile southeast up grass then scree to 13,060-foot Trinity Notch. This is not the lowest point in the ridge north of East Trinity, but it is the easiest notch to reach, and it is also the notch closest to East Trinity.

The Three Trinities from the northwest.

From Trinity Notch, climb 0.1 mile south up a steep slope to a lower-angled slope at 13,300 feet (Class 2+). Climb 0.2 mile southwest up easier slopes to the 13,745-foot summit of East Trinity (Class 2).

From East Trinity, scramble 100 feet south (Class 3), then downclimb 200 feet west into a steep, west-facing gully (Class 3). This section is the route's crux. Descend 0.1 mile west down the steep gully (Class 3). Cross the south-facing gully below the 13,340-foot Trinity Peak–East Trinity saddle (Class 3). Climb 0.2 mile west up a steep, rubble-filled gully to the summit of Trinity Peak (Class 2+). Use great care in both of these gullies.

29. VESTAL GROUP COMBINATIONS

See Map 29 on page 242

29.8 — WTE Combination — Trinity Traverse *Classic*

From Elk Park TH at 8,860 ft:	*521 RP*	*14.9 mi*	*6,095 ft*	*Class 4*
From Molas TH at 10,620 ft:	*620 RP*	*21.5 mi*	*7,775 ft*	*Class 4*
From Beartown TH at 11,700 ft:	*639 RP*	*21.9 mi*	*8,535 ft*	*Class 4*
From 9,980 ft in Elk Creek:	*436 RP*	*8.9 mi*	*4,815 ft*	*Class 4*
From 11,400 ft in Vestal Creek:	*302 RP*	*5.1 mi*	*3,315 ft*	*Class 4*

This is the most common way of climbing Trinity Peak, as it allows you to collect West and East Trinity as well. The traverse can be done in either direction, but it is usually done from west to east. This allows you to upclimb both the Class 4 pitches on Trinity Peak and the Class 3 scrambling on East Trinity while limiting your downclimbing to nothing harder than Class 2+. Ascend Trinity Peak's West Ridge Route and descend Trinity Peak's East Ridge Route.

29.9 — AVWTE Combination — Trinitas *Classic*

From Elk Park TH at 8,860 ft:	723 RP	16.8 mi	8,742 ft	Class 4
From Molas TH at 10,620 ft:	822 RP	23.4 mi	10,422 ft	Class 4
From Beartown TH at 11,700 ft:	840 RP	23.8 mi	11,182 ft	Class 4
From 9,980 ft in Elk Creek:	637 RP	10.8 mi	7,462 ft	Class 4
From 11,400 ft in Vestal Creek:	503 RP	7.0 mi	5,962 ft	Class 4

For the fit, this is one of Colorado's grand tours, as it collects all the peaks in the Vestal Group, including West and East Trinity. It is best done from west to east. Climb Arrow's Northeast Face Route and descend to 12,200 feet in the basin between Arrow and Vestal. Join Vestal's South Face Route here and follow it to Vestal's summit. Descend Variation 29.3V2 to the 12,860-foot Vestal–West Trinity saddle and, from here, complete the Trinity Traverse (Combination 29.8).

30. Pigeon Group

Jupiter Mountain   13,830 feet
Pigeon Peak   13,972 feet
Turret Peak   13,835 feet
Jagged Mountain   13,824 feet

See Map 30 on page 257

These centennial thirteeners are in the Weminuche Wilderness 15 miles south of Silverton. They are part of the appropriately named Needle Mountains and are some of Colorado's most rugged and remote peaks. Surrounded by miles of wild country, they are usually done with a backpack. You can approach Jupiter on the excellent Needle Creek Trail, but Pigeon, Turret and Jagged require poor-trail and off-trail approaches. Jagged is the most remote of Colorado's centennial thirteeners and requires a multi-day effort. On top of Jagged you are in the heartland of Colorado's most remote mountains.

MAPS
Required: *Columbine Pass, Mountain View Crest, Snowdon Peak, Storm King Peak, San Juan National Forest*
Optional: *Electra Lake, Vallecito Reservoir, Rio Grande National Forest*

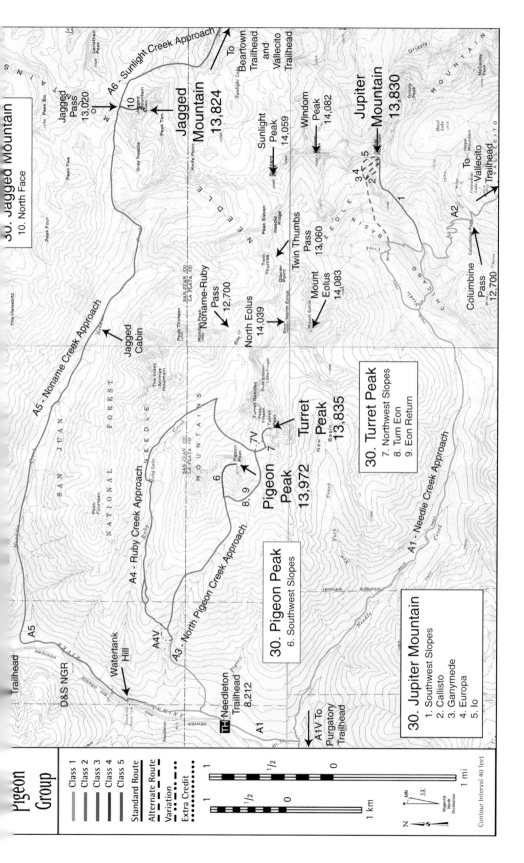

Pigeon Group

Legend:
- Class 1
- Class 2
- Class 3
- Class 4
- Class 5
- Standard Route
- Alternate Route
- Variation
- Extra Credit

Contour Interval 40 feet

Magnetic North Declination 13

30. Jagged Mountain
10. North Face

30. Turret Peak
7. Northwest Slopes
8. Turn Eon
9. Eon Return

30. Pigeon Peak
6. Southwest Slopes

30. Jupiter Mountain
1. Southwest Slopes
2. Callisto
3. Ganymede
4. Europa
5. Io

Jagged Mountain 13,824
Jagged Pass 13,020
Sunlight Peak 14,059
Windom Peak 14,082
Jupiter Mountain 13,830
Twin Thumbs Pass 13,060
Twin Thumbs 14,083
Mount Eolus 14,083
North Eolus 14,039
Noname-Ruby Pass 12,700
Columbine Pass 12,700
Pigeon Peak 13,972
Turret Peak 13,835

A1 - Needle Creek Approach
A2
A3 - North Pigeon Creek Approach
A4 - Ruby Creek Approach
A4V
A5 - Noname Creek Approach
A6 - Sunlight Creek Approach
A1V To Purgatory Trailhead

To Beartown Trailhead and Vallecito Trailhead
To Vallecito Trailhead

Needleton Trailhead 8,212
Jagged Cabin
Watertank Hill

SAN JUAN NATIONAL FOREST
NEEDLE MOUNTAINS

SAN JUAN CO / LA PLATA CO

Chicago Basin
New York Basin

TRAILHEADS

Needleton Trailhead

This trailhead is at 8,212 feet and provides access to all four centennial thirteeners in the Pigeon Group. From Needleton you can ascend Needle Creek to reach Jupiter, North Pigeon Creek or Ruby Creek to reach Pigeon and Turret, and Noname Creek to reach Jagged. Needle Creek is also the popular approach for the standard routes up the three fourteeners Sunlight, Eolus and Windom.

Needleton is deep in the Animas River Canyon 13 miles south of Silverton. You reach Needleton by rail or foot, not by road. The Durango and Silverton Narrow Gauge Railroad (D&S NGR) goes through the canyon, but the gorge is too narrow to accommodate both tracks and a road. The nearest road, U.S. 550, is many miles to the west and separated from the Animas River Canyon by the West Needle Mountains. Approaching these peaks behind a hundred-year-old steam locomotive puffing through a wild canyon is one of the trip's charms. The greatest hazard of the approach is hanging your head out the window and getting a cinder in your eye!

The privately owned D&S NGR starts operation on May 8, runs four trains a day between Durango and Silverton in the summer and continues with a reduced schedule until October 30. Backpackers can board trains in Durango or Silverton. The fare to Needleton is considerably cheaper from Silverton, and reservations are usually not needed when boarding in Silverton. The Durango train depot is at 479 Main Avenue, Durango, CO 81301, and you can make reservations by calling 970-247-2733. Make reservations for northbound trains early. Backpackers can board in Elk Park or Needleton on a space-available basis and must have a ticket or the exact fare in cash.

A schedule and table of fares follow for all trains. This information is current as of 2001.

Schedule

Durango	Needleton	Elk Park	Silverton	Operating Dates
7:30 A.M.	9:59 A.M.		11:00 A.M.	June 19–Aug. 10
8:15 A.M.	10:44 A.M.	11:18 A.M.	11:45 A.M.	May 6–June 18 and Aug. 11–Oct. 28
8:15 A.M.		11:18 A.M.	11:45 A.M.	June 19–Aug. 10
9:00 A.M.			12:30 P.M.	May 15–Oct. 14
9:45 A.M.			1:15 P.M.	June 5–Sept. 26

Silverton	Elk Park	Needleton	Durango	Operating Dates
1:15 P.M.			4:45 P.M.	June 19–Aug. 10
2:00 P.M.	2:25 P.M.		5:30 P.M.	June 19–Aug. 10
2:00 P.M.	2:25 P.M.	3:00 P.M.	5:30 P.M.	May 6–June 4 and Sept. 27–Oct. 28
2:45 P.M.			6:15 P.M.	May 15–Oct. 14
3:30 P.M.	3:55 P.M.	4:30 P.M.	7:00 P.M.	June 5–Sept. 26

Fares

As of 2004, the Durango-Silverton Railroad charged $60 roundtrip no matter where you get on or off.

Purgatory Trailhead

This trailhead is at 8,800 feet. The Purgatory Trail and Animas River Trail provide a long trail-access to Needle Creek and Needleton. For those who prefer not to take the train to Needleton, this is the best alternative. If you are approaching from the south, measure from 32nd Street and Main Avenue (U.S. 550) in north Durango and go 24.7 miles north on U.S. 550. If you are approaching from the north, go 7.7 miles south on U.S. 550 from the summit of Coal Bank Pass. The trailhead and Purgatory Campground are on the east side of U.S. 550 across from the Purgatory Resort. This trailhead is accessible in winter.

Vallecito Trailhead

This trailhead is at 7,900 feet and provides access to Jupiter from the east via a long trail hike over 12,700-foot Columbine Pass. You can also approach Jagged from this trailhead, which provides a refreshing alternative for a long backpacking vacation. There are two approaches to this trailhead.

If you are approaching from the south or east, go to Bayfield on U.S. 160. Bayfield is 14.5 miles east of the U.S. 160–U.S. 550 junction several miles south of Durango. In Bayfield, turn north onto La Plata County 501 and measure from this point. Go north on La Plata County 501, go straight (right) at mile 8.8, go straight (left) at mile 13.2, go along Vallecito Reservoir's west side and go straight (left) at mile 18.5 onto La Plata County 500. Continue north on La Plata County 500 and reach the Vallecito Campground and Trailhead at mile 21.3.

If you are approaching from the north or west, go to Main Avenue (U.S. 550) and 32nd Street in north Durango, turn east onto 32nd Street and measure from this point. Go east on 32nd Street, turn south (right) onto La Plata County 250 (East Animas Road) at mile 1.3 and turn east (left) onto La Plata County 240 (Florida Road) at mile 1.5. Go east on La Plata County 240, leave Durango, turn east (right) at mile 13.4 and turn north (left) onto La Plata County 501 at mile 16.2. Go north on La Plata County 501, go straight (left) at mile 20.6, go along Vallecito Reservoir's west side and go straight (left) at mile 25.9 onto La Plata County 500. Continue north on La Plata County 500 and reach the Vallecito Campground and Trailhead at mile 28.7.

The trailhead's parking lot is on the road's west (left) side just after you enter the San Juan National Forest. The Vallecito Trail starts here and goes around the Vallecito Campground's west side. This is the route used by horses. For backpackers, it is easier and shorter to walk north on the road through the campground and get onto the foot trail at the campground's north end. You can save 0.3 mile of walking if you are dropped off at the campground's north end; however, there is no vehicle parking there. For extended trips, you need to park in the trailhead parking lot. This trailhead is accessible in winter.

APPROACHES

30.A1 – Needle Creek Approach

From Needleton TH at 8,212 ft: *110 RP*   *12.0 mi*   *2,788 ft*   *Class 1*

This is the easiest approach to Jupiter. Take the Durango & Silverton Narrow Gauge train from either Durango or Silverton and get off at Needleton. This is the Needleton Trailhead. Cross the suspension bridge to the Animas River's east side, turn south (right) and walk 0.7 mile south along the Animas River to the start of the Needle Creek Trail at 8,300 feet. The signed Needle Creek Trail is on Needle Creek's north side.

From the junction of the Animas River Trail and the Needle Creek Trail, turn east, enter the Weminuche Wilderness and hike 5.3 miles east up the excellent Needle Creek Trail to a trail junction at 11,000 feet in Lower Chicago Basin. This unmarked trail junction is at the confluence of two creeks. The southern creek emerges from a colorful gorge. There are campsites above and below this confluence. This is a heavily used area in July and August.

30.A1V – Variation

From Purgatory TH at 8,800 ft: *233 RP*   *28.2 mi*   *4,400 ft*   *Class 1*

This alternative adds considerable distance and elevation gain to your journey, but it avoids the train's cost and crowds. Start at the Purgatory Trailhead and follow the Purgatory Trail 3.7 miles east then southeast down Cascade Creek to the Animas River at 7,700 feet. Cross to the Animas River's southeast (far) side on a footbridge 60 yards east (down-

Turret Peak from the west.

stream) of the confluence of Cascade Creek and the Animas River. Follow the excellent Animas River Trail 5.1 miles east along the Animas River's south side to Needle Creek and the Needle Creek Trail. The railroad is on the river's north side. Join the Needle Creek Approach at the beginning of the Needle Creek Trail and follow it east into Chicago Basin.

30.A2 — Johnson Creek Approach

From Vallecito TH at 7,900 ft: *367 RP*   *32.2 mi*   *5,820 ft*   *Class 1*

This seldom used approach to Jupiter requires a long backpack trip, but it avoids the train's cost and crowds. This approach is suitable for an extended trip. Consider doing a traverse and using the train only one way.

Start at the Vallecito Trailhead and follow the Vallecito Creek Trail 8.3 miles north to its junction with the Johnson Creek Trail at 9,120 feet. There are many campsites near here. Cross to Vallecito Creek's west side on a footbridge and follow the Johnson Creek Trail 6.4 miles west as it climbs steadily up Johnson Creek to 12,700-foot Columbine Pass. Johnson Creek is beautiful and rugged, and you are deep in the wilderness here. Cross Columbine Pass and descend 1.4 miles northwest into Chicago Basin to a stream crossing at 11,680 feet near the junction of two trails. There is a campsite in the trees just west of the stream crossing.

30.A3 – North Pigeon Creek Approach

From Purgatory TH at 8,800 ft: 301 RP   24.2 mi   5,140 ft   Class 2
From Needleton TH at 8,212 ft: 140 RP   5.2 mi   3,528 ft   Class 2
From Ruby Creek Trail at 9,800 ft: 94 RP   2.8 mi   1,940 ft   Class 2

This is the shortest approach to Pigeon and Turret. This rough approach uses a poor trail, then requires a steep bushwhack. The route is above the Animas River in the steep creek leading to Pigeon's southwest slopes. This creek is unnamed on the 1972 Snowdon Peak Quadrangle, but is referred to as North Pigeon Creek in this book. North Pigeon Creek is between Pigeon Creek and Ruby Creek, which are named on the 1972 Snowdon Peak Quadrangle. All of these drainages are difficult to identify from the Animas River. Take some time to understand this complicated terrain before you enter the wilderness. All trails and trail junctions on this approach are unsigned.

If you take the train, get off at Needleton and cross the suspension bridge to the Animas River's east side. If you start at the Purgatory Trailhead, follow the Purgatory Trail 3.7 miles east then southeast down Cascade Creek to the Animas River at 7,700 feet. Cross to the Animas River's southeast (far) side on a footbridge 60 yards east (downstream) of the confluence of Cascade Creek and the Animas River. Follow the Animas River Trail 5.1 miles east along the Animas River's south side to Needle Creek and the Needle Creek Trail. Do not go east up Needle Creek but continue 0.7 mile north on the Animas River Trail to the east end of the footbridge over the Animas River at Needleton.

From the east end of the Needleton footbridge, walk 260 yards north on a wide trail past several private cabins to a rickety old gate and Pigeon Creek. Cross Pigeon Creek, pass a rusty rail car and walk 0.2 mile north on the continuing Animas River Trail to a long meadow at 8,260 feet. There are several idyllic campsites here, and we call this "Camper's Meadow." The introduction is over, as one of the keys to this approach waits for you in this meadow.

Walk north as the meadow narrows and enter the meadow's 100-yard-long northern lobe. Walk around the east end of a large tree that fell into the meadow and across the trail in 2000. Twenty feet north of the fallen tree, look through the trees on the meadow's east edge and find a strong trail that angles north up the steep slope east of the meadow. This trail, the Ruby Creek Trail, does not connect to the Animas River Trail, and finding it is your key to the heights.

Leave the Animas River Trail and climb the initial steep slope on the Ruby Creek Trail. Hike 100 yards east through small trees to the southern edge of another idyllic meadow called "Upper Camper's Meadow." Look sharp and follow the faint trail as it takes a surprise turn to the south. Hike 100 yards south then 150 yards east to the bottom of a steep slope that is the beginning of the Needle Mountains. The Ruby Creek Trail can be difficult to follow to this point, but you must find it to avoid a bush-whacking disaster. When the trail angles north up the steep slope, routefinding becomes easier.

Follow the now clear Ruby Creek Trail 0.3 mile northeast to a rounded ridge at 9,200 feet. Continue 0.2 mile east on the trail as it enters the North Pigeon Creek drainage and climbs to North Pigeon Creek at 9,500 feet. Cross to North Pigeon Creek's north side and ponder this route's next mystery: there are two trails beyond this point. The obvious, main trail angles northwest across the slope. This is not the route (see Ruby Creek Approach, Variation 30.A4V). A lesser-used trail climbs steeply northeast above the creek. This is the continuation of the Ruby Creek Trail and the route. The drainage above this point is rough, and we do not recommend a direct ascent up the creek.

From North Pigeon Creek, climb 0.15 mile northeast on the brutally steep Ruby Creek Trail and follow it up a tiny ridge to yet another faint trail junction at 9,800 feet. The Ruby Creek Approach and the North Pigeon Creek Approach diverge at this junction. The continuation of the Ruby Creek Trail leaves the tiny ridge here and does an ascending traverse north-east into the tiny drainage north of the tiny ridge. At the beginning of this ascending traverse, there is an aspen tree with a columbine carved into it. This is not the route.

The North Pigeon Creek Approach leaves the Ruby Creek Trail at the 9,800-foot trail junction and continues up the tiny ridge. Climb 0.2 mile east up the tiny ridge, following a faint trail that quickly fades to a cairned route that in turn fades to Class 2 bushwhacking. At 10,200 feet, bush-whack 0.6 mile east-southeast up and across steep slopes to 11,000 feet in the upper North Pigeon Creek drainage. The drainage here is much easier, and the worst part of your approach is over. Climb 0.5 mile east-southeast through open trees in the drainage to the west end of a large, flat meadow at 11,740 feet. Stroll 0.1 mile east-southeast into the idyllic meadow.

This elusive destination is worth the effort. Camping here is easy, and views are plentiful. Pigeon rises dramatically 0.7 mile to the east. Turret is hidden, but is only 1.1 miles east-southeast. A herd of gregarious goats often stay in this basin, and they may come right into your camp. Pee in the rocks. Otherwise, the goats will dig up the tundra to get the salt.

30.A4 — Ruby Creek Approach

From Purgatory TH at 8,800 ft:	*339 RP*	*27.2 mi*	*5,200 ft*	*Class 2+*
From Needleton TH at 8,212 ft:	*181 RP*	*8.2 mi*	*3,588 ft*	*Class 2+*
From North Pigeon Approach at 9,800 ft:	*137 RP*	*5.8 mi*	*2,000 ft*	*Class 2+*

This alternative approach to Pigeon and Turret gives you access to several other high thirteeners in the Ruby Creek drainage. Also, once you are in Ruby Creek, you can cross to Needle Creek via 13,060-foot Twin Thumbs Pass and to Noname Creek via 12,700-foot Ruby–Noname Pass. These options give you many possibilities for extended trips. However, this is a very rough approach. A direct ascent up Ruby Creek from the Animas is so difficult that it has left several strong people speechless. The rough and difficult-to-follow Ruby Creek Trail is the only practical approach from the Animas. This trail climbs slopes well south of Ruby Creek before entering the Ruby Creek drainage at 10,500 feet. All trails and trail junctions on this approach are unsigned. Allow a full day for this approach.

Follow the North Pigeon Creek Approach to the faint trail junction on the tiny ridge at 9,800 feet. The Ruby Creek Approach and the North Pigeon Creek Approach diverge at this junction. The continuation of the Ruby Creek Trail leaves the tiny ridge here and does an ascending traverse northeast into the tiny drainage north of the tiny ridge. At the beginning of this ascending traverse, there is an aspen tree with a columbine carved into it. This is the route.

Climb 0.4 mile northeast on the Ruby Creek Trail as it enters then ascends the tiny drainage north of the tiny ridge, then climbs northeast to reach 10,340 feet on the main ridge separating North Pigeon Creek and Ruby Creek. Cross to the north side of this ridge and continue 0.1 mile east on the Ruby Creek Trail as it climbs to 10,480 feet. For the first time, you can hear Ruby Creek below you to the north and catch peekaboo views of Peak Fourteen above you to the northeast. Just after you climb down a 6-foot rock barrier, the trail splits and, once again, you have a challenge and a choice.

For the next 0.2 mile, you have a choice between a high and a low route. The high route goes above a cliff band and the low route goes below it. Both routes work and are equal in difficulty. The low route descends steeply at first, then contours east. The high route climbs near to a 10,500-foot saddle on the Ruby–North Pigeon Ridge, then descends to the east. We recommend the high route, which is better marked and more traveled. When the routes rejoin, contour 0.3 mile east and reach the western edge of an open avalanche swath at 10,500 feet. From here you have an unobstructed view of Peak Fourteen's rugged south face. Welcome to the Ruby Creek drainage.

Follow the rough Ruby Creek Trail 0.4 mile east on Ruby Creek's south side to a tiny lake west of Ruby Lake. There is a campsite here. Cross to Ruby Creek's north side and hike 0.1 mile east to Ruby Lake. Hike 0.25 mile around Ruby Lake's north side, then climb 0.15 mile steeply north away from the creek. Contour 0.3 mile east above some willows, then climb 0.7 mile southeast on the creek's north side to a luscious meadow at 11,600 feet. This is the traditional camping area for climbs of the surrounding peaks. Pigeon is 0.7 mile west-southwest and Turret is 0.6 mile south-southwest. Animas Mountain, Peak Thirteen and Monitor Peak loom to the northeast.

30.A4V – Variation
From the trail junction at the North Pigeon Creek crossing at 9,500 feet, follow the obvious, main trail that angles northwest across the slope instead

of the Ruby Creek Trail, which climbs north directly up the slope. Climb northwest on this easy trail, then pay your dues. Climb up an increasingly steep trail that turns into a cairned route over several rock outcrops. Persist on the rough route and rejoin the Ruby Creek Trail at 10,000 feet.

30.A5 — Noname Creek Approach

From Purgatory TH at 8,800 ft:	526 RP	37.0 mi	6,820 ft	Class 2+
From Needleton TH at 8,212 ft:	328 RP	18.0 mi	5,208 ft	Class 2+

This is the traditional approach to Jagged. The Noname Creek drainage is one of Colorado's most spectacular valleys, and an outing here will likely lodge in your memory forever. The Noname Creek Approach is longer but less rugged than the Ruby Creek Approach. Still, this hike is not for the faint-hearted. The trail is often obtuse, and every year a few more trees fall across the trail and increase the effort required to penetrate the wilderness. Mortals with a heavy pack should allow a day and a half to reach the hallowed heights above treeline. All trails and trail junctions on this approach are unsigned. Jagged is the only one of Colorado's 100 highest peaks that requires more than a day to approach, but your effort will be rewarded.

The mileages given along this approach are measured from the Needleton Bridge. If you start at the Purgatory Trailhead, add 9.5 miles to these numbers for your mileage from that trailhead. The Animas River Trail north of Needleton can be hard to find in spots. Following these directions will minimize your misadventures. Follow the North Pigeon Creek Approach to "Camper's Meadow" at mile 0.4. Walk north as the meadow narrows and enter the meadow's 100-yard-long northern lobe. Walk around the east end of a large tree that fell into the meadow and across the trail in 2000. Twenty feet north of the fallen tree, walk past the turnoff for the North Pigeon Creek and Ruby Creek Approaches. Twenty feet farther north, turn west (left) at a faint trail junction in the meadow. The stronger trail that goes straight ahead through the meadow's northern lobe is not the route. Take the fainter trail to the left.

Hike north-northwest out of Camper's Meadow, go down a little hill in the trees and enter another meadow called "Hunter's Meadow." Walk 120 yards north through Hunter's Meadow, pass some wooden camp structures and find the continuing trail at the northwest corner of Hunter's Meadow. Hike 100 yards northwest on the trail and join another version of the Animas River Trail. From here northward, there is only one version of the Animas River Trail.

Hike north on the now more distinct Animas River Trail, cross North Pigeon Creek at mile 0.5 and begin climbing above the Animas River at mile 0.7. This is the prelude to the infamous Watertank Hill. Contour 100 feet above the river, then climb a steep hill to 200 feet above the river at mile 0.9. Contour 200 feet above the river and look down on the railway's old historic watertank at mile 1.0. You are now above some cliffs that bar progress along the river's edge, even in low water. Walk north to a precipitous drop-off. The introduction is over.

Descend 200 feet west down the legendary Watertank Hill, the steepest trail in this book (Class 2+). This can be an intimidating task with a heavy pack, as an uncontrolled fall here would do far more than skin your knee. Your task is compounded by the fact that you must descend Watertank Hill at the beginning of your journey, when you are not tuned up and your pack is at its heaviest. Your task will be further compounded if the hill is wet, and some parties make good use of a rope here. Your only solace is in knowing that this is the easiest route. Other routes have been oft tried, but none are easier. When you reach the river's edge north of Watertank Hill at mile 1.1, you will have paid your initial wilderness entrance fee.

After Watertank Hill, hike northeast on the Animas River Trail, cross Ruby Creek at mile 1.4 and continue northeast to reach Noname Creek at mile 2.2. There is a lot of deadfall in this section. The trail becomes obscure in the alluvial rocks near Noname Creek. Persist across the rocks to the north, cross Noname Creek and resist any temptation to hike east up the creek. That is an error that has made strong people weep. From Noname Creek's north side at 8,460 feet, hike 80 yards north to a nice campsite distinguished with two old pipes. Hike 100 yards north under some rocks on the reemergent trail and look sharp for a trail heading steeply up the hill to the east at mile 2.3. This is the beginning of the Noname Creek Trail. If you miss this junction, you will come to another nice campsite just north of the trail junction. If you have not been backpacking in a while, you may feel like you have completed a day's work when you reach this spot. If so, consider camping here. Once you start up the Noname Creek Trail, you will not reach a reasonsble campsite with easy access to water for 3.0 miles—all of it hot and steep.

When you are ready, leave the comfort of the campsites north of Noname Creek and start up the Noname Creek Trail. The Noname Creek Trail stays on Noname Creek's north side all the way to the heights. Climb the initial embankment, hike northeast and reach an old utility pole that still has an insulator on top at mile 2.4. From this pole, hike east up the hill and take care to follow the faint trail over some rocks. The trail becomes more distinct above the rocks. Hike east then southeast on the trail as it climbs high above Noname Creek. You may feel like you are paying a second entry fee as you climb an unyielding, brutally steep hill to enter the Weminuche Wilderness. Persevere up the trail and, at 10,460 feet, reach the first decent campsite at mile 5.4. This campsite is under the southwest face of the Heisspitz.

Continue southeast up the trail, climb another steep hill and, at 10,740 feet, reach the Jagged Cabin at mile 6.1. Some people walk past this cabin without seeing it. It is at the west end of a long meadow where you have an unobstructed view of Jagged and Knife Point to the east. The Jagged Cabin, though old, is still serviceable and can provide basic shelter in bad weather. There is good camping nearby, and access to Noname Creek is 120 yards west of the cabin via a spur trail. Now you can start to get a return on your investment.

From Jagged Cabin, continue east-southeast through the meadow, enter the trees at the end of the meadow and head south toward Noname Creek. Fifty yards north of (before) Noname Creek at 10,760 feet, turn east (left) onto the continuation of the main Noname Creek Trail at mile 6.8. There is a campsite on Noname Creek's north side just beyond this trail junction. Even if you use this campsite, it is not necessary to cross Noname Creek. If you do cross Noname Creek here and hike south, you will be headed for Twin Thumbs Pass and Needle Creek. That is not the route.

Climb east up a brutally steep hill and, at 11,040 feet, reach another trail junction at mile 7.4. Turn northeast (left) onto the continuation of the main Noname Creek Trail. This trail junction is 100 yards before a campsite near the confluence with the branch of Noname Creek below the fourteener Sunlight Peak. Again, do not cross Noname Creek.

Climb northeast up another brutally steep hill, at the top of which is a great view of the surrounding peaks. At 11,800 feet, pass a campsite in the trees and reach the west end of another lush meadow at mile 7.9. The trail is sketchy beyond this point. Hike around the meadow's north edge, climb yet another brutally steep hill and pass through a narrow gap in some barrier cliffs above a nasty boulder field. Hike east on easier terrain to a small lake at 12,180 feet at mile 8.5. This is an idyllic campsite; please leave no trace of your time here. To complete this epic approach, hike around the lake's north side and climb east to reach 13,020-foot Jagged Pass at mile 9.0. At Jagged Pass, you are suspended in the heart of the wilderness and can gaze east down into Sunlight Basin and south up at the climbing route on Jagged.

30.A6 — Sunlight Creek Approach

From Vallecito TH at 7,900 ft:	*438 RP*	*29.6 mi*	*4,800 ft*	*Class 2*
From Beartown TH at 11,700 ft:	*404 RP*	*22.0 mi*	*6,706 ft*	*Class 2*

This alternative approach to Jagged from the east takes you into one of Colorado's most remote valleys. If you start at the Beartown Trailhead, hike 1.0 mile south to 12,493-foot Hunchback Pass, then hike 6.5 miles south down the Vallecito Creek Trail to 9,640 feet. If you start at the Vallecito Trailhead, hike 11.3 miles north up the Vallecito Creek Trail to 9,640 feet. Leave the Vallecito Creek Trail, hike 0.1 mile west and ford Vallecito Creek. This ford can be difficult to impossible in June, but is usually reasonable in August. Hike 0.1 mile north, get onto the north side of Sunlight Creek and find the Sunlight Creek Trail. This use trail has evolved into a reasonable trail in recent years. Hike 2.3 miles west on the

Sunlight Creek Trail to 11,500 feet near treeline. Hike 1.0 mile north-northeast under Jagged's eastern ramparts to a small, bow-shaped lake at 12,700 feet. Jagged is only 0.4 mile southwest, and you can study the route from this camp.

30. Jupiter Mountain   13,830 feet

See Map 30 on page 257

Jupiter is Colorado's mountain of mountains. It is at the head of Needle Creek 15 miles south-southeast of Silverton and 0.6 mile south of the fourteener Windom Peak. Jupiter is not Colorado's highest or even largest peak, but it is the first and largest-appearing peak you see when hiking up the Needle Creek Trail into Colorado's largest wilderness. From Jupiter's summit, you have an astonishing view of Colorado's wilderness heartland. You can easily keep track of the nearby fourteeners, then peer beyond to Monitor Peak's reclusive east face, Jagged and distant Rio Grande Pyramid. To the southwest, you can just see Shiprock in New Mexico.

ROUTES

30.1 — Jupiter Mountain — Southwest Slopes *Classic*

From Purgatory TH at 8,800 ft:	*526 RP*	*32.1 mi*	*7,270 ft*	*Class 2+*
From Needleton TH at 8,212 ft:	*331 RP*	*15.9 mi*	*5,658 ft*	*Class 2+*
From Vallecito TH at 7,900 ft:	*562 RP*	*34.3 mi*	*8,010 ft*	*Class 2+*
From 11,680 ft in Chicago Basin:	*126 RP*	*2.1 mi*	*2,190 ft*	*Class 2+*

This is the standard and easiest route on Jupiter. This is the easiest route on a centennial thirteener in the Pigeon and Vestal Groups, and when Zeus is in a hurry, he goes this way. Use either the Needle Creek Approach or the Johnson Creek Approach.

If you use the Needle Creek Approach, find the creek confluence at 11,000 feet in Lower Chicago Basin. Leave the main trail and cross Needle Creek just above the confluence. Do not cross the side creek coming down from the southeast that emerges from a red gorge. Find a trail between the two creeks and follow it 0.9 mile southeast then south along the top of the side creek's gorge. There are good views of 13,310-foot Aztec Mountain a mile to the south. When the trail crosses the side creek, leave it north of (before) the crossing, hike north up a steep hill and walk 50 yards north to the other branch of the Columbine Pass Trail at 11,680 feet. This is the end of the Johnson Creek Approach. There are several campsites in the trees west of here, and you can see Jupiter's southwest slopes above this point.

From 11,680 feet on the side creek's north side, leave the Columbine Pass Trail and hike 0.35 mile east-northeast through tall grass to 12,200 feet at the bottom of Jupiter's steep but easy southwest slopes. Climb 0.4 mile

13,830

30.1

Jupiter Mountain from the west.

northeast up steep, grassy slopes, dodging some minor cliffs en route, and reach Jupiter's west ridge at 13,400 feet. The view of the fourteener Eolus 1.5 miles to the northwest grows as you climb. From the ridge, Windom and Sunlight pop into view to the north. Climb 0.25 mile east on talus on the ridge's south (right) side to a 13,780-foot false summit.

From here the view of the summit ramparts may startle you. You are close, but not done.

The 200-foot scramble from the 13,780-foot false summit to the main summit is not as hard as it looks. Jupiter's summit is the westernmost of several towers that you can see from the false summit. From the false summit, scramble 80 feet east on the ridge or below the ridge on its north side (Class 2+). Descend 20 feet into the small saddle between the false and main summits (Class 2+). From the saddle, do an ascending traverse on the ridge's northwest (left) side and climb a small gully to a small notch just south of the highest point (Class 2). Cross to the notch's east side and climb 30 feet north up a gully to another notch (Class 2), from which you can look down Jupiter's steep north face. Climb west over an exposed block (Class 2+) and walk 20 feet north to the highest point. The view is Jovian.

30.2 — Jupiter Mountain — Callisto

From Purgatory TH at 8,800 ft:	552 RP	32.4 mi	7,270 ft	Class 2+	Mod Snow
With descent of Southwest Slopes:	556 RP	32.25 mi	7,270 ft	Class 2+	Mod Snow
From Needleton TH at 8,212 ft:	358 RP	16.2 mi	5,658 ft	Class 2+	Mod Snow
With descent of Southwest Slopes:	362 RP	16.05 mi	5,658 ft	Class 2+	Mod Snow
From Vallecito TH at 7,900 ft:	608 RP	35.5 mi	8,570 ft	Class 2+	Mod Snow
With descent of Southwest Slopes:	593 RP	34.9 mi	8,290 ft	Class 2+	Mod Snow
From 11,400 ft in Chicago Basin:	157 RP	2.4 mi	2,470 ft	Class 2+	Mod Snow
With descent of Southwest Slopes:	157 RP	2.7 mi	2,470 ft	Class 2+	Mod Snow

This short couloir is in the center of Jupiter's north face. In early summer it provides an alpine alternative to the Southwest Slopes Route. Use either the Needle Creek Approach or the Johnson Creek Approach.

If you use the Needle Creek Approach, find the creek confluence at 11,000 feet in Lower Chicago Basin. Do not cross Needle Creek here. Continue 0.7 mile northeast on the main trail, cross Needle Creek at 11,200 feet and climb 0.2 mile east on the Columbine Pass Trail to 11,400 feet, where the trail starts a long ascending traverse to the south. If you use the Johnson Creek Approach, descend 0.45 mile north from 11,680 feet on the Columbine Pass Trail to this spot.

Leave the Columbine Pass Trail at 11,400 feet and climb 0.6 mile northeast to 12,600 feet in the basin between Jupiter and Windom. Hike 0.25 mile east to 13,100 feet below Jupiter's north face. From here you can see several couloirs to the south; this is a special, seldom visited spot. Callisto is the westernmost couloir, and it faces north. Hike 0.1 mile south and get into the couloir at 13,300 feet. Climb the short couloir on moderate snow and reach Jupiter's west ridge at 13,580 feet. Join the Southwest Slopes Route here and follow that route to the summit. Ascending Callisto and descending the Southwest Slopes Route makes an obvious Tour de Jupiter.

30.3 — Jupiter Mountain — Ganymede

From Purgatory TH at 8,800 ft: 616 RP 32.4 mi 7,270 ft Class 2+ Steep Snow
With descent of Southwest Slopes: 610 RP 32.25 mi 7,270 ft Class 2+ Steep Snow
From Needleton TH at 8,212 ft: 421 RP 16.2 mi 5,658 ft Class 2+ Steep Snow
With descent of Southwest Slopes: 415 RP 16.05 mi 5,658 ft Class 2+ Steep Snow
From Vallecito TH at 7,900 ft: 672 RP 35.5 mi 7,270 ft Class 2+ Steep Snow
With descent of Southwest Slopes: 656 RP 34.9 mi 6,990 ft Class 2+ Steep Snow
From 11,400 ft in Chicago Basin: 221 RP 2.4 mi 2,470 ft Class 2+ Steep Snow
With descent of Southwest Slopes: 220 RP 2.7 mi 2,470 ft Class 2+ Steep Snow

Ganymede is a longer version of Callisto. Follow the approach to Callisto and find the northwest-facing Ganymede Couloir just east of Callisto. Ganymede does not hold snow as well as Callisto, but it does provide a nifty climb when it is in good shape. Start at the bottom of Callisto, climb southeast over a steep section and enter the northwest-facing Ganymede Couloir. Climb southeast up the narrowing, slightly twisting couloir on moderate to steep snow and reach Jupiter's west ridge at 13,700 feet. Join the Southwest Slopes Route here and follow that route to the summit.

30.4 — Jupiter Mountain — Europa

From Purgatory TH at 8,800 ft: 614 RP 32.3 mi 7,230 ft Class 2+ Steep Snow
With descent of Southwest Slopes: 610 RP 32.2 mi 7,250 ft Class 2+ Steep Snow
From Needleton TH at 8,212 ft: 420 RP 16.1 mi 5,618 ft Class 2+ Steep Snow
With descent of Southwest Slopes: 416 RP 16.0 mi 5,638 ft Class 2+ Steep Snow
From Vallecito TH at 7,900 ft: 670 RP 35.4 mi 8,530 ft Class 2+ Steep Snow
With descent of Southwest Slopes: 656 RP 34.85 mi 8,270 ft Class 2+ Steep Snow
From 11,400 ft in Chicago Basin: 220 RP 2.3 mi 2,430 ft Class 2+ Steep Snow
With descent of Southwest Slopes: 220 RP 2.65 mi 2,450 ft Class 2+ Steep Snow

This couloir provides a longer snow climb than either Callisto or Ganymede. Follow the approach to Callisto, climb 100 yards southeast on moderate snow and reach the base of Europa at 13,400 feet. Ascend the steepening, narrowing slope and climb steep snow to the saddle between Jupiter's 13,780-foot false summit and main summit. Scramble east on the last part of the Southwest Slopes Route to the summit.

30.5 — Jupiter Mountain — Io

From Purgatory TH at 8,800 ft: 656 RP 32.3 mi 7,230 ft Class 2+ Very Steep Snow
With descent of SW Slopes: 651 RP 32.2 mi 7,250 ft Class 2+ Very Steep Snow
From Needleton TH at 8,212 ft: 462 RP 16.1 mi 5,618 ft Class 2+ Very Steep Snow
With descent of SW Slopes: 457 RP 16.0 mi 5,638 ft Class 2+ Very Steep Snow
From Vallecito TH at 7,900 ft: 712 RP 35.4 mi 8,530 ft Class 2+ Very Steep Snow
With descent of SW Slopes: 697 RP 34.9 mi 8,270 ft Class 2+ Very Steep Snow
From 11,400 ft in Chicago Basin: 262 RP 2.3 mi 2,430 ft Class 2+ Very Steep Snow
With descent of SW Slopes: 261 RP 2.7 mi 2,450 ft Class 2+ Very Steep Snow

This is Jupiter's premier mountaineering route. Io is the narrow, north-facing couloir just west of the Jupiter–Windom ridge, and it goes directly to Jupiter's summit. You cannot see Io from Chicago Basin, but you can preview it from Windom's summit. Io is prone to rockfall; wear a helmet.

Follow the approach to Europa and continue 100 yards east toward the face below the Jupiter–Windom ridge. When you can see the narrow Io Couloir piercing Jupiter's north face, turn south and climb the tight defile as it steepens. Io is very steep near the top. If the snow is thin or gone, the top of the couloir requires some Class 4 climbing. Reach the tiny notch on the Southwest Slopes Route that is just east of the summit. Climb west over an exposed block (Class 2+) and walk 20 feet north to the highest point. Colorado's mountain of mountains is yours.

30. Pigeon Peak   13,972 feet

See Map 30 on page 257

Pigeon is Colorado's archetypal centennial thirteener. It is admired by many from afar but climbed by few. Climbing Pigeon takes you into the heart of the Needle Mountains, and toward the essence of the mountaineering experience as well.

Pigeon is 2.5 miles east of Needleton in the Animas River Canyon. You can see Pigeon from the railroad through the canyon, and thousands of tourists admire Pigeon every summer. You can also see Pigeon from the U.S. 550–Colorado 110 junction south of Silverton. This view allows you to preview snow conditions on the north-facing finish of the Southwest Slopes Route. Pigeon is also visible from U.S. 550 south of the Purgatory Ski Area. This view allows you to ponder the heavy mantel of snow that grips Pigeon in winter. Pigeon's wildest feature, a great east face, is hidden in these views. The best view is reserved for the wilderness traveler.

ROUTE

30.6 — Pigeon Peak — Southwest Slopes *Classic*

From Purgatory TH at 8,800 ft via N Pigeon Creek: 583 RP 26.0 mi 7,372 ft Class 4
From Needleton TH at 8,212 ft via N Pigeon Creek: 356 RP 7.0 mi 5,760 ft Class 4
From 11,740 ft in North Pigeon Creek: 158 RP 1.8 mi 2,232 ft Class 4
From Purgatory TH at 8,800 ft via Ruby Creek: 751 RP 31.1 mi 8,972 ft Class 4
From Needleton TH at 8,212 ft via Ruby Creek: 524 RP 12.1 mi 7,360 ft Class 4
From 11,600 ft in Ruby Creek: 262 RP 3.9 mi 3,772 ft Class 4

This is the standard and easiest route on Pigeon. This route's north-facing summit pitch is snow-free for only two months a year. The previous winter's snow lingers through June, and the first September storm leaves a dusting

Pigeon Peak from the southeast.

that does not melt in the fall. Climb this route in July or August. Use either the North Pigeon Creek Approach or the Ruby Creek Approach.

If you use the North Pigeon Creek Approach, start in the meadow at 11,740 feet west of Pigeon. Climb 0.4 mile northeast up steep slopes to 12,400 feet in the tiny basin between Pigeon's long northwest ridge and steep west ridge.

If you use the Ruby Creek Approach, start in the meadow at 11,600 feet in Ruby Creek. Climb 0.2 mile west to 12,000 feet, then climb 0.5 mile southwest up a blocky but easy slope to the 13,100-foot Pigeon–Turret saddle. Cross the saddle and descend 0.3 mile west-southwest to a 12,780-foot saddle south of Pigeon. Cross this saddle and descend 0.1 mile west down a steep rubble slope to 12,400 feet. Contour 0.2 mile northwest then 0.15 mile northeast under Pigeon's cliffs into the tiny basin between Pigeon's long northwest ridge and steep west ridge.

From 12,400 feet in the tiny basin, climb 0.3 mile east up the basin's steep grass slopes to 13,500 feet (Class 2). Dodge small cliffs en route. Continue 0.1 mile east up steeper, rubble gullies to the northern base of the summit pyramid at 13,700 feet (Class 2+). Climb 30 feet south up a blocky weakness in the summit pyramid (Class 3). Climb 15 feet up a steep, chimneylike slot (Class 4). This is the route's crux. Continue 80 feet south up the weakness, then climb 100 feet east to the highest point (Class 3). Pigeon's summit is the northern of two points and is capped by a cracked block.

30. Turret Peak   13,835 feet

See Map 30 on page 257

Turret is 0.5 mile southeast of Pigeon. Turret is harder to approach but easier to climb than Pigeon. Deep in the wilderness, Turret has a better summit view than Pigeon, and the bonus of a majestic view of Pigeon's great east face. You can see Turret from the same distant vantages as Pigeon, and you can easily preview conditions on this reclusive peak. Together, Pigeon and Turret are Colorado's most dynamic duo of centennial thirteeners. After investing the effort to approach Pigeon, most people elect to climb Turret as well. However, Turret by itself offers a sublime wilderness experience.

ROUTE

30.7 — Turret Peak — Northwest Slopes *Classic*

From Purgatory TH at 8,800 ft via N Pigeon Creek:	545 RP	26.6 mi	7,235 ft	Class 2+
From Needleton TH at 8,212 ft via N Pigeon Creek:	322 RP	7.6 mi	5,623 ft	Class 2+
From 11,740 ft in North Pigeon Creek:	128 RP	2.4 mi	2,095 ft	Class 2+
From Purgatory TH at 8,800 ft via Ruby Creek:	605 RP	29.2 mi	7,435 ft	Class 2+
From Needleton TH at 8,212 ft via Ruby Creek:	382 RP	10.2 mi	5,823 ft	Class 2+
From 11,600 ft in Ruby Creek:	126 RP	2.0 mi	2,235 ft	Class 2+

This is the standard and easiest route on Turret. The top of the route is north-facing and holds snow most of the year. Consider taking an ice ax. Use either the North Pigeon Creek Approach or the Ruby Creek Approach.

If you use the North Pigeon Creek Approach, start in the meadow at 11,740 feet west of Pigeon. Climb 0.6 mile east-southeast up grass then rock slopes to a 12,780-foot saddle under Pigeon's south face. This saddle is the northern of two saddles that you can see from the meadow at 11,740 feet. Turret comes into view at the 12,780-foot saddle, and you can see the rest of the route from here. From the 12,780-foot saddle, climb 0.3 mile east on an ascending traverse, crossing two rubble gullies en route, to the easy slopes just south of the 13,100-foot Pigeon–Turret saddle. It is not necessary to go into the Pigeon–Turret saddle. Climb 0.1 mile southeast up easy slopes to 13,280 feet on a southern spur of Turret's northwest ridge.

If you use the Ruby Creek Approach, start in the meadow at 11,600 feet in Ruby Creek. Climb 0.2 mile west to 12,000 feet, then climb 0.5 mile southwest up a blocky but easy slope to the 13,100-foot Pigeon–Turret saddle. Cross the saddle and climb 0.1 mile southeast on the south side of Turret's northwest ridge to 13,280 feet on a southern spur of Turret's northwest ridge.

From 13,280 feet on the southern spur of Turret's northwest ridge, you will have an astonishing view of Pigeon's east face and also of Turret's small but steep west face. Climb 100 yards northeast and reach Turret's northwest ridge at 13,360 feet. From here you can look down steeper slopes on Turret's lower north face. Climb 80 yards east toward a steep section where the ridge merges with the northern edge of Turret's west face. The route to this point is Class 2.

Climb 50 yards east through the steep section via blocks and a small V-slot (Class 2+). You are now at the bottom of Turret's upper north face. Climb 150 yards south up this broken face to Turret's summit (Class 2). If there is snow anywhere on the route, it will be on this face. Turret's summit is commodious, and the view is expansive in all directions. You can see many of Colorado's finest peaks from here. In particular, you can see Jagged.

30.7V — Variation
From the 13,100-foot Pigeon–Turret saddle, contour 100 yards east on the north side of Turret's northwest ridge. Climb a shallow, north-facing couloir and reach Turret's northwest ridge at 13,360 feet (Class 2+). Snow lingers in this couloir.

30. PIGEON AND TURRET COMBINATIONS
See Map 30 on page 257

30.8 — PT Combination — Turn Eon *Classic*

From Purgatory TH at 8,800 ft via N Pigeon Creek: 677 RP 27.85 mi 8,807 ft Class 4
From Needleton TH at 8,212 ft via N Pigeon Creek: 450 RP 8.85 mi 7,195 ft Class 4
From 11,740 ft in North Pigeon Creek: 252 RP 3.65 mi 3,667 ft Class 4

If climbing Pigeon and Turret is your only objective, this is the most expedient way of doing so. Use the North Pigeon Creek Approach. From the meadow at 11,740 feet, climb Pigeon's Southwest Slopes Route and return to 12,400 feet in the tiny basin between Pigeon's long northwest ridge and steep west ridge. Contour 0.15 mile southwest then 0.2 mile southeast under Pigeon's steep southwest face. Climb 0.1 mile east up a steep rubble slope to the 12,780-foot saddle south of Pigeon. From here, continue on Turret's Northwest Slopes Route and return to the 11,740-foot meadow.

30.9 — PT Combination — Eon Return

From Purgatory TH at 8,800 ft via Ruby Creek: 792 RP 31.7 mi 9,707 ft Class 4
From Needleton TH at 8,212 ft via Ruby Creek: 565 RP 12.7 mi 8,095 ft Class 4
From 11,600 ft in Ruby Creek: 303 RP 4.5 mi 4,507 ft Class 4

If you use the Ruby Creek Approach as part of an extended adventure, then this is the most expedient way to climb Pigeon and Turret together. From the 11,600-foot meadow in Ruby Creek, climb Turret's Northwest Slopes Route and return to the 13,100-foot Pigeon–Turret saddle. Continue on Pigeon's Southwest Slopes Route as described from Ruby Creek and return to Ruby Creek.

30. Jagged Mountain   13,824 feet

See Map 30 on page 257

Jagged is Colorado's premier centennial thirteener. Recalcitrant with its secrets, this mighty mountain surrounds itself with wilderness, and there are no good views of Jagged from civilization. Poised on the Continental Divide between the Animas River and Vallecito Creek, Jagged is 1.4 miles northeast of the fourteener Sunlight Peak. Sunlight is relatively easy to approach via Needle Creek, but most people take two days to reach a high camp near Jagged. Indeed, Jagged is the only one of Colorado's 100 highest peaks that requires a multi-day approach.

Jagged is jagged. The peak is a half-mile-long ridge festooned with summits and spires. Even identifying the main summit is a challenge. Several pioneering parties climbed to Jagged's heights only to discover that they were on a false summit. Dwight Lavender made the first ascent of Jagged in 1933 and reported that "Jagged Mountain is probably the most difficult peak yet ascended in the Colorado Rockies." Even today, traverses between the summits are not practical, and Jagged has only one reasonable route to its main summit. This route holds the essence of wilderness mountaineering. If you have never been to Jagged, make it your next outing.

ROUTE

30.10 — Jagged Mountain — North Face *Classic*

From Purgatory TH at 8,800 ft via Noname: 736 RP 37.8 mi 7,664 ft Class 5.0–5.2
From Needleton TH at 8,212 ft via Noname: 513 RP 18.8 mi 6,052 ft Class 5.0–5.2
From Vallecito TH at 7,900 ft via Sunlight: 688 RP 31.0 mi 5,964 ft Class 5.0–5.2
From Beartown TH at 11,700 ft via Sunlight: 648 RP 23.4 mi 7,870 ft Class 5.0–5.2
From 13,020 ft on Jagged Pass: 145 RP   0.8 mi   844 ft Class 5.0–5.2

This is the best route in this book and Colorado's best peak climb. It is a combination of a sublime wilderness approach and a steep, serpentine climb punctuated with three surprising cruxes. Most of the loose blocks on this route have been knocked off, and the rock on this climb is surprisingly solid. Use either the Noname Creek or Sunlight Creek Approach. If you use the Noname Creek Approach, follow it all the way to 13,020-foot Jagged Pass. If you use the Sunlight Creek Approach, climb 0.3 mile west from the bow-shaped lake at 12,700 feet to reach Jagged Pass.

From Jagged Pass, you can see most of the route on Jagged's north face. Before charging forth, take some time to inspect the route, as it is difficult to see the big picture once you are on the complex face. There is a deep snow couloir in the center of the north face. Jagged's main summit is the first summit west of the deep notch at the top of this couloir. The route on the north face is west (right) of the snow couloir and reaches a deep notch west

Jagged Mountain from the north-northeast.

Route 30.10 on Jagged's north face.

(right) of the main summit. You cannot see all the way into this notch from Jagged Pass. The route above the high notch is on Jagged's south-west face, and you cannot see this portion of the route from Jagged Pass.

When you are ready, launch! From Jagged Pass, contour 150 yards south-southwest on a use trail, then do an ascending traverse for 200 yards to the south up a steep grass slope (Class 2). Get above some lower boiler-plate slabs, but don't get too high as you approach the cliffs of Jagged's north face. Contour 100 yards southeast toward the bottom of the snow couloir (Class 2+). The beginning of the climbing route is 100 feet west of (before) the couloir.

Scamper up to the base of the face (Class 2+) and climb 10 feet up a 1-foot-wide vertical crack (Class 4). This crack is often wet. Climb up 20 feet (Class 3) and, when the rock above you gets steep, squeeze around a corner to the east (left) and climb 50 feet up an exposed, left-angling ramp (Class 4). This ramp is often wet and covered with ball bearings of decomposing granite, and it has raised many neck hairs. Nevertheless, this ramp is the key to the lower route; there is no easier way. This is the route's first crux.

From the top of the ramp, zigzag up the wall above, utilizing grass ramps. There are foot-sized platforms in the grass from all the traffic, and the climbing is surprisingly easy for such a steep wall. Sometimes you come close to the couloir, but you never enter it. The climbing is continuous Class 2+ with an occasional Class 3 move. If you find yourself making harder moves, look around for an easier way. Climb to the top of the highest grass ramp on the couloir's west (right) side. From here you can peer up at the notch at the top of the couloir, which is only 150 feet above you. This notch is not the route.

Turn west (right) away from the couloir and zigzag 100 feet up to the west to a tidy little saddle between a gendarme and the upper cliffs (Class 2+). Descend 20 feet to the west and cross the top of a gully. This gully is below a huge vertical chimney in the upper wall. This chimney is visible from Jagged Pass. The gully below the chimney can contain snow for much of the summer, and you may need an ice ax here.

After you are across the gully, avoid a direct ascent up the crack right under the upper cliffs. Descend 20 feet west, then climb 30 feet west up gravel-covered ledges. Climb west up a chute (Class 4), then turn south (left) and climb up over a rounded edge (Class 4). This is the route's second crux. Above this, zigzag 120 feet up to the west on the now familiar interlocked ledges. Scamper as high as you can until you are trapped by steep rock above. This stretch is Class 2+ with an occasional Class 3 move.

Turn south (left) and behold the route's third crux. Climb 40 feet south up one of two systems. The exposed, eastern route requires several pulls between rubble-covered ledges (Class 5.0–5.2). The western system ascends one of two parallel cracks (Class 5.0–5.2). The western route is shorter, less exposed, harder and easier to protect. Once you are above this third crux, scamper 40 feet southwest into the high notch west of the summit. From here you can look down Jagged's southwest face.

From the high notch, traverse 30 feet southwest, then climb 40 feet east up ledges (Class 3). Traverse 120 feet southeast on blocks and exposed ledges (Class 3). This dramatic traverse takes you to a large sandy ledge below a south-facing chimney. Climb 50 feet north up the chimney and step west (left) around the chockstone at its top (Class 3). Climb 100 feet northeast up blocks and ledges to the summit ridge (Class 3). There is a long step across in this section, but the rock is very clean. Once on the summit ridge, scamper 50 feet north to the highest point (Class 2+). The commodious summit area is graced with a large, flat slab suitable for serious lounging. If only for a few moments, Colorado's denizen of the wilderness is yours. You can either descend the ascent route or do a dramatic 165-foot rappel to the north, which bypasses the third crux and upper climb.

31. Teakettle Group

Teakettle Mountain	13,819 feet
Dallas Peak	13,809 feet

See Map 31 on page 280

Teakettle and Dallas are tough centennial thirteeners above Ouray and Telluride, respectively. Teakettle is 5.0 miles southwest of Ouray and Dallas is 3.4 miles north of Telluride. The easiest route on each of these peak is technical, and these are two of Colorado's hardest peaks. Of the two, Dallas is the harder peak to climb, and it is the hardest peak in this book. Bad rock is a given on these peaks. Choose your weather and partners carefully.

MAPS
Required: *Mount Sneffels, Telluride, Uncompahgre National Forest*
Optional: *Ironton*

TRAILHEADS

Yankee Boy Basin Trailhead
This trailhead is at 10,700 feet and provides access to Teakettle's south side. On U.S. 550, go 0.4 mile southwest past Ouray's south edge. Turn south (right) onto Ouray County 361 (dirt) and measure from this point. Follow Ouray County 361 (Yankee Boy Basin Road) as it turns and climbs steeply west up Canyon Creek. Stay right at mile 4.7, continue west on a spectacular shelf road, go straight at mile 6.0 and reach a short side road on the left at mile 6.7. Ample parking is available on the side road; it is best to park passenger cars here. The road beyond this point becomes rougher rapidly, but four-wheel-drive vehicles can continue for an additional 0.9 mile to a level stretch in the road at 11,300 feet. There are two

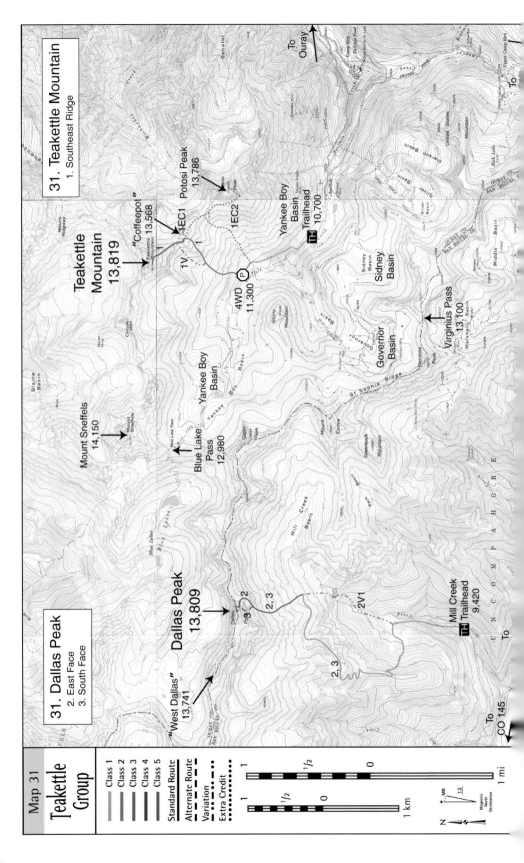

Map 31
Teakettle Group

Class 1
Class 2
Class 3
Class 4
Class 5
Standard Route
Alternate Route
Variation
Extra Credit

31. Teakettle Mountain
1. Southeast Ridge

31. Dallas Peak
2. East Face
3. South Face

Teakettle Mountain 13,819

"Coffeepot" 13,568

Potosi Peak 13,786

1EC1

1EC2

1

1V

4WD 11,300

Yankee Boy Basin Trailhead 10,700

Mount Sneffels 14,150

Blue Lake Pass 12,980

Yankee Boy Basin

Sidney Basin

Governor Basin

Virginius Pass 13,100

To Ouray

Dallas Peak 13,809

"West Dallas" 13,741

2
3
2, 3

2V1

2, 3

Mill Creek Trailhead 9,420

To CO 145

U N C O M P A H G R E

1 mi

1 km

N

MN

13°

Magnetic North Declination

13,819

31.1

Teakettle Mountain from the southeast.

parking areas on the road's south side. Amazingly, this trailhead is often accessible in winter.

Although the road into Yankee Boy Basin is a public road, the property on both sides of the road is mostly private. In 2000 the Forest Service instituted a regulated camping system in Yankee Boy Basin. The Forest Service has designated three specific campsites and collects a $12-per-day fee for their use. Detailed information is available at a kiosk on the road, or call 970-240-5300 or 970-240-5416.

Mill Creek Trailhead

This trailhead is at 9,420 feet and provides access to Dallas' west, south and east sides. If you are approaching from the west, go 1.9 miles east toward Telluride from Society Turn on Colorado 145. If you are approaching from Telluride, go 1.2 miles west from the Telluride Middle School on Telluride's west side. Turn north onto Mill Creek Road. This turn is not signed. Go 1.7 miles north, then west, then east to the Mill Creek Trailhead. The trailhead is along the road just before a locked gate for the Telluride water supply ponds. The signed Deep Creek Trail starts on the road's north side.

31. Teakettle Mountain   13,819 feet

See Map 31 on page 280

Teakettle is named for the arch and overhanging rock that flank the summit tower. The formation looks like the handle, pot and spout of a teakettle when you view it from the fourteener Mount Sneffels 1.7 miles to the west. Though a significant portion of the spout fell away during the 1998–1999 winter, diminishing the classic shape, memories and historic photographs remain.

Teakettle's namesake features are only the top of the mountain. The mountain's north and south faces are festooned with cliffs, while the east and west ridges look like an undone jigsaw puzzle. Teakettle does have alternative routes, but only the standard route is described here. Go prepared for Class 5 rock climbing. From Teakettle's tiny, flat summit, you can see all of the San Juans' fourteeners and most of the San Juans' centennial thirteeners. This sensational summit satiates both saints and satyrs.

ROUTE

31.1 — Teakettle Mountain — Southeast Ridge *Classic*

From Yankee Boy Basin TH at 10,700 ft:	275 RP	4.5 mi	3,999 ft	Class 5.3
From 4WD parking at 11,300 ft:	245 RP	2.7 mi	3,399 ft	Class 5.3

Despite a steep, grungy approach, this is a classic route. On the upper mountain, you dodge fantastic formations on your way to the unavoidable summit tower. The summit climb is classic all by itself.

Start at the Yankee Boy Basin Trailhead and go west up the Yankee Boy Basin Road. Turn north (right) after 0.2 mile and go northwest up the four-wheel-drive road. A spectacular view of Potosi Peak emerges to the north as you climb. After 0.75 mile, cross a small creek at 11,200 feet that comes from Potosi's southwest face, then continue west-northwest up to a level area in the road at 11,300 feet after 0.9 mile. Look north and admire Teakettle's summit ramparts. Also, notice the 13,568-foot rock summit called "Coffeepot," which is 0.4 mile southeast of Teakettle. If you intend to climb Potosi Peak as well as Teakettle, study Potosi's southwest face carefully. The introduction is over.

Leave the road and hike 0.2 mile north up a steep, grassy slope that takes you past an initial cliff band to 11,800 feet. Continue 0.2 mile north-northeast up still steep slopes to a less steep area and the highest grass at 12,300 feet. From here you can see Teakettle's imposing upper cliffs to the north and a rough ridge descending toward you from "Coffeepot." Stay to the east (right) of this ridge and climb 0.35 mile northeast up a very steep and loose rocky slope to the base of "Coffeepot" at 13,440 feet. The unrelenting ascent from the road to "Coffeepot" is tiring, but leaves you with a great view and poised for your summit push.

Go to a bench and viewpoint under the southwest side of "Coffeepot." You do not need to go to the bench under the northwest side of "Coffeepot." Examine the upper part of Teakettle carefully. At first glance, the route may not be obvious. The ridge crest from "Coffeepot" to Teakettle is not the route. You can see a steep, black gully that leads from the talus slopes below and southeast of the ridge to easier slopes above. That is part of the route. Take heart, as the black gully is easier than it appears from the viewpoint. The route above the black gully traverses benches and climbs gullies to reach the base of the summit pyramid. You cannot see all of the ascent gullies from the viewpoint.

When you are ready, descend 150 feet southwest from the viewpoint. Descend west around the south end of a cliff band that blocks a direct descent from the viewpoint. When you are below the cliff, contour north then northwest at 13,000 feet on loose rocks toward the base of the black gully. Do an ascending traverse into the black gully just above a steep section at its base. The gully will look easier from here. Climb 250 feet up the black gully (Class 2+). Near the top of the gully, the route steepens and there are two choices. Climb the gully's western (left) branch and exit west to the top of the gully (Class 3). The gully's eastern (right) branch is Class 4.

Surprisingly, the ascent from the top of the black gully to the base of the summit tower is only Class 2. From the top of the black gully, contour and climb gently northwest toward the summit pyramid on a climbers trail. On this traverse, you will be below the jigsaw towers and faces of Teakettle's southeast ridge. When it presents itself, climb north up a broad, sandy gully through a major cliff band. Climb northwest on the climbers trail below another cliff band, climb north up a narrower, sandy gully through the cliffs and hike northwest to the base of the summit tower. You can look through the circular, 8-foot arch just to the south of the summit tower. It is easy to climb into the arch, and this unique position provides a priceless photo. You can also climb onto the remains of the spout to the northeast of the summit tower.

For the summit climb, scramble 30 feet north up a gully to a notch at the summit tower's northeast corner (Class 2+). From here you can peer down Teakettle's ragged north face. The summit pitch is only 40 feet long, but it is steep. From the notch, climb 20 feet up two blocks and traverse left into a tiny alcove in the chimney system on the summit tower's east face (Class 5.0–5.2). Climb 20 feet up the left side of the upper chimney to the summit (Class 5.3).

Teakettle's summit is one of Colorado's finest. The high point is a flat, 5-foot-by-3-foot block with dramatic exposure to the west. Teakettle's summit is large enough for a two-person tea party—just don't drop your cookies. The view from here will swallow your best yodel. For the descent, either downclimb the summit pitch or rappel 40 feet east from a sling around a block that is just north of the flat block.

Teakettle and Potosi from the south.

31.1V — Variation

From the highest grass at 12,300 feet, go west (left) of the cliffs running south from "Coffeepot" and ascend a small basin full of unstable rocks. Rejoin the route on the traverse to the bottom of the black gully at 13,000 feet. This route saves 800 feet of climbing, but many consider this a poor trade given the unstable footing in the basin. People most often use this route on their descent. This eliminates the 400-foot climb back to the bench below "Coffeepot."

EXTRA CREDITS

31.1EC1 — "Coffeepot," 13,568 feet, Class 5.0–5.2

Either going to or returning from Teakettle, hike around to the east side of "Coffeepot." Scramble up 30 feet (Class 3) and climb a 20-foot chimney to the 13,568-foot summit of "Coffeepot" (Class 5.0–5.2). The chimney is flared and steep, but you can get a secure body position in it.

31.1EC2 — Potosi Peak, 13,786 feet, Class 2+

Potosi Peak is 1.0 mile southwest of Teakettle, and climbing it together with Teakettle makes sense after you have invested in the ascent from the road to the ridge. Potosi's extensive summit cliffs and flat summit give it a distinctive appearance rivaling that of Teakettle. *Potosi* means "great wealth" in Quechua.

From Teakettle's summit, return to the viewpoint under the southwest corner of "Coffeepot." Traverse under the south face of "Coffeepot" and descend 0.3 mile southeast to the 12,980-foot saddle between Teakettle and Potosi (Class 2). Climb 0.1 mile southwest to 13,200 feet under the cliffs of Potosi's west face. Do not go all the way to the base of the cliffs. Contour 300 yards south to a corner, then 300 yards south-southeast to a ridge. Climb 200 feet north-northeast up this ridge, then do an ascending traverse for 0.2 mile northeast under the cliffs of Potosi's southeast face to 13,400 feet. Before you reach the skyline ridge ahead of you, climb 200 feet northwest up a rough, 40-foot-wide gully system (Class 2+). Traverse east to a wider, sandy gully and ascend it to within 150 feet of its top. Leave the sandy gully and climb a 20-foot-long crack on the gully's west (left) side (Class 2+). Once above the sandy gully, climb 300 feet north up rubble-covered ledges to a corner east of Potosi's highest cliff (Class 2+). Scamper through this cliff's east end (Class 2+) and walk 100 yards west across the sandy surface to the highest point. The summit is large enough for a soccer game—just don't miss the ball.

For the descent, return to the 12,980-foot Teakettle–Potosi saddle. Descend southwest down a rubble-filled chute through a cliff band to 12,400 feet on the wide talus slope below the cliff band. Do not continue straight down below this point. Angle down to the south (left) across the slope, cross a gully and contour south to the top of a large grass slope. Descend southwest down this steep grass to a point just above the lowest grass at 11,800 feet. Look carefully to the east and find a scree-filled gully. Downclimb into the top of the gully (Class 2+), descend scree to the trees and reach the Yankee Boy Basin Road at the creek crossing at 11,200 feet. Go 0.15 mile west-northwest up the road to your starting point for Teakettle.

31. Dallas Peak   13,809 feet

See Map 31 on page 280

Dallas Peak has many moods and faces. When you view it from Colorado 145 southwest of Telluride, Dallas is undistinguished and looks easy to climb. When you view it from Mount Sneffels 2.0 miles to the northeast, Dallas looks ferocious. Set aside your Colorado-peak prejudice. Dallas is one of Colorado's hardest peaks, and is the hardest peak in this book. Climbing Dallas feels like climbing a displaced test-piece from the Canadian Rockies.

There are multiple approaches to Dallas' summit tower, and they all have long stretches of exposed, Class 2+ scampering. There are several routes up the 180-foot-high summit tower, and they all require Class 5 rock climbing. The easiest routes on the summit tower are on its cold, often snowy north face. This is not a good place to learn how to rock climb. Come prepared for the challenge.

ROUTES

31.2 — Dallas Peak — East Face *Classic*

From Mill Creek TH at 9,420 ft: *337 RP*   *9.3 mi*   *4,589 ft*   *Class 5.3*

This is the standard and easiest route on Dallas. Many people do it as a day climb, but some prefer to pack in to a basin at 11,200 feet to shorten the climb and allow more time for rope work on the summit tower. In any case, start early, as this is a bad summit to be on during an electrical storm. Snow lingers on the upper north face well into summer, and the first storm at the end of summer usually leaves snow on the upper ledges that may not be visible from below. In a monsoon summer there may be no days when the summit pitch is dry. Snow usually chokes the gully below the chockstone through summer and into fall. It is a good idea to carry an ice ax on this route at any time of year. Also, we recommend a helmet for this climb.

Start at the Mill Creek Trailhead and hike 0.4 mile northeast up the Deep Creek Trail past the Telluride water supply ponds and through two switchbacks to a signed trail junction. Turn west (left) and hike 0.7 mile north through three switchbacks to a meadow at 10,000 feet. You can see the south face of Dallas 1.6 miles north of here. From the meadow, hike 0.8 mile west on the Deep Creek Trail to a trail junction on a ridge at 10,620 feet. Leave the Deep Creek Trail here and turn north (right) onto the Sneffels Highline Trail. Hike 0.6 mile north through seven switchbacks to 11,200 feet in the Mount Sneffels Wilderness. Contour 0.6 mile northeast into the basin southwest of Dallas. There are campsites near here for backpackers. Continue 0.5 mile east on the Sneffels Highline Trail to 11,400 feet on a ridge running south from Dallas, then descend 0.2 mile northeast to 11,300 feet below Dallas' south face. You are only 0.6 mile from the summit of Dallas at this point, but your adventure has just begun.

Leave the comfort of the Sneffels Highline Trail at 11,300 feet south of Dallas' summit. Hike 0.3 mile north up steep grass toward the gully that is the weakness in the rocks below Dallas' upper south face (Class 2). Stay to the east (right) side of the gully and climb loose rocks and ball-bearing scree over hardpan up to a 30-foot-high cliff band surrounded by loose rock (Class 2+). Climb through the cliff band where it is solid (Class 3). Climb above the cliff band and find a small use trail. Angle northeast (right), climb through a second, smaller cliff band and angle northeast on scree up to a small ridge at 13,000 feet (Class 2+). You are now above a large cliff that is 0.2 mile southeast of Dallas' summit. Climb 100 yards northeast on the use trail to another ridge at 13,200 feet (Class 2). Your ascent on the south side of Dallas is over.

Cross the second ridge and climb north into Dallas' complicated and dramatic upper east face (Class 2+). Cross a gully in the center of the face, cross a small ridge north of the gully, traverse 100 feet north, climb 200 feet west up to a barrier cliff band and traverse 100 feet south (Class 2+). You are now looking down the gully in the center of the upper east face. You have not yet been on Dallas' east ridge, but you can begin to feel the air of the north face. Climb west up a 40-foot, Class 4 pitch near the south end of the barrier cliff. There may be slings at the top of this pitch. Climb 200 feet west up to the eastern base of the summit tower (Class 2+). As you approach, you can see a car-sized chockstone above a deep gully in the summit tower's lower east face. This gully may be full of snow.

For the summit tower, climb north across the deep gully, stay below the deep gully's northern wall and go 20 feet north to a smaller gully. This gully is just south of Dallas' east ridge. If you reach the east ridge and can see the north face, you have gone too far. Climb 120 feet west up the smaller, east-facing gully (Class 4). From the top of the gully, you can see the north face for the first time. Scramble 100 feet southwest to a hole at the top of the deep gully but still below the car-sized chockstone (Class 2+). Now you can really see the north face. Your ascent on the east side of Dallas is over.

Do a 20-foot, airy, Class 3 traverse to the west as north-face air rushes up your pants. Reach the top of a 20-foot-wide, sloping ramp that leads down to the west into the north face. Descend 60 feet down this ramp. Stop. The 90-foot-long summit pitch is now above you. The crux of the pitch and the route is 15 feet above the ramp. Climb 10 feet up a crack, step west (right) and climb 10 feet up to easier ground (Class 5.3). Climb 40 feet up Class 4 ramps and walls. There is a lot of loose rock in this section. Make a Class 5.0–5.2 move into an alcove. Climb the east (left) wall of the alcove (Class 5.0–5.2). Scramble 10 feet southeast up a loose gully (Class 3). Your ascent on the north side of Dallas is over. Wobble 5 feet east to the summit cairn. Bravo! The summit of Dallas is big enough for a Ping-Pong game—just don't lunge for the ball.

For the descent, go 20 feet east to the summit's northeast edge and a sling anchor around a large block. It takes 25 feet of sling to go around this block. Rappel 85 feet down the summit tower's vertical northeast corner. Finish the rappel by going through a large hole, and end the rappel below the car-sized chockstone. A doubled 165-foot rope will just suffice. If the snow under the chockstone plugs the hole, you will need to rappel over the chockstone's east face. This will lengthen the rappel to 110 feet.

VARIATIONS

31.2V1 – Stan's Shortcut, Class 2
This is the shortcut that Telluride locals use to reach the summit of Dallas in a little over three hours. Stan himself said, "Those elk know what they're doing." From the meadow at 10,000 feet, leave the Deep Creek Trail and bushwhack 0.4 mile north along Mill Creek's west side. Cross to Mill Creek's east side and bushwhack 0.2 mile northeast. The multiple game trails in this area converge into one strong trail. Follow this trail 250 yards northwest

13,809

31.2

Dallas Peak from the east-southeast.

along a ledge in the cliffs south of the waterfall below Mill Creek Basin. Hike 0.1 mile northeast, cross to Mill Creek's north side and climb 0.3 mile north up steep grass to the Sneffels Highline Trail. Cross the trail and rejoin the route where it begins the ascent up Dallas' south slopes.

31.2V2 — Chock It Up, Class 4

From the base of the summit tower, climb 100 feet up the deep gully in the summit tower's lower east face to a point below the car-sized chockstone. This gully may be full of snow. There are two holes above you. The larger, southern one is where the rappel ends. Climb 20 feet north through the smaller, northern hole to the edge of the north face and rejoin the route there. The difficulty of this climb depends on how much snow is below the chockstone. If there is a lot of snow, the climb is Class 3 or easier. If there is no snow, the climb is Class 4.

31.2V3 — Ledge Lover's Lament, Class 5.6

Parties that miss the standard summit pitch often end up doing this variation. From the bottom of the summit pitch on the sloping ramp on the north face, descend 70 feet west to the ramp's low point, then climb 50 feet west on another ramp to the edge of a crack and gully system (Class 2+). Climb up to a big crack. Either climb the crack or climb on the right edge of it. Exit the crack to the left on a ramp, climb up then right around an overhang and climb back left into a dihedral about 15 feet below the summit ridge (Class 5.5). Climb up the dihedral to the summit ridge (Class 5.6). This is the crux of the variation. Once on the summit ridge, scramble 40 feet east along the exposed ridge to the summit cairn.

31.2V4 — Southeast Corner, Class 5.7

From the base of the summit tower, scramble southwest (left) onto a 6-foot chockstone between the summit tower and a lower tower south of the summit (Class 2+). Climb north up a long pitch on small faces and in flared cracks to the summit (Class 5.7). This pitch is much harder than the standard finish, but it is in the sun.

31.2V5 — Moccasin Man, Difficulty Unknown

Our longtime friend Stewart Krebs, a Montrose native who grew up climbing in the San Juans, told us this story while we were climbing Peak C in the Gore Range. When Stu took his grown son up Dallas, they had finished the rappel and were back at the base of the summit tower. Suddenly a man appeared on the summit and asked Stu for directions down to him and his son. Stu gave the man a quick description of the standard finish on the summit tower. Within 60 seconds, the man was with them. He had long, flowing red hair, spoke with an Irish accent and wore moccasins laced up to his knees. The man asked Stu for directions down the mountain's east face. Again Stu obliged. The man immediately took off running down the steep, exposed slope. Stu, who does not exaggerate, said that his feet barely touched the rocks. In seconds he was gone. When Stu rushed down to catch a glimpse, he only heard a faint padding as the man disappeared around the corner hundreds of feet below, then silence.

Where had Moccasin Man come up? Surely from the west side. But how? Had he followed the west ridge, traversed on the summit tower's south side, then soloed the Southeast Corner? Possible, but not likely. Stu would have seen him before he made the summit. Could he have traversed on the summit tower's north face and finished with one of the north-side routes? Possible, but not likely. If he had done that, he would not have needed directions for the north-side descent. It seems likely that Moccasin Man traversed on the crest of the west ridge. We have inquired locally about Moccasin Man, but other than his brief encounter with Stu, he left no trace of his passage.

31.3 — Dallas Peak — South Face

From Mill Creek TH at 9,420 ft:	*671 RP*	*9.3 mi*	*4,589 ft*	*Class 5.6 (?)*
With descent of East Face:	*669 RP*	*9.3 mi*	*4,589 ft*	*Class 5.6 (?)*

This route is seldom done, obscure and tough. Follow the East Face Route to 13,000 feet at the bottom of the steep part of Dallas' south face. Starting in the center of the face, a large gully full of chockstones heads diagonally northeast through the cliffs. Climb it. There are three crux chockstones. At the top of the gully, scramble northeast onto the chockstone below the Southeast Corner. Ascending this route and descending the East Face Route makes an obtuse Tour de Dallas.

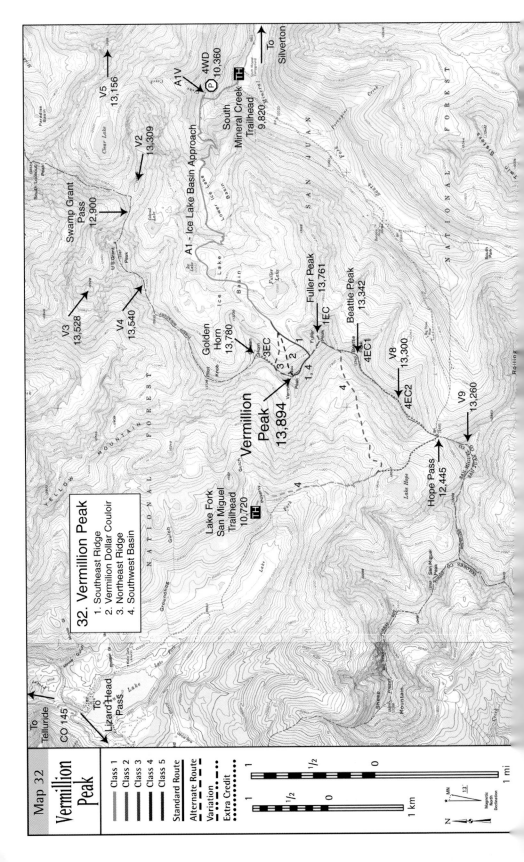

Map 32
Vermillion Peak

32. Vermillion Peak
1. Southeast Ridge
2. Vermilion Dollar Couloir
3. Northeast Ridge
4. Southwest Basin

Legend:
- Class 1
- Class 2
- Class 3
- Class 4
- Class 5
- Standard Route
- Alternate Route
- Variation
- Extra Credit

N

Magnetic North Declination
13°
MN

1 mi
1/2   0   1
1 km
1/2   0   1

To Telluride
CO 145
To Lizard Head Pass

YELLOW MOUNTAIN FOREST

Lake Fork San Miguel Trailhead 10,720 TH

Golden Horn 13,780

V3 13,528

V4 13,540

Swamp Grant Pass 12,900

V2 13,309

V5 13,156

A1V
4WD 10,360 P

South Mineral Creek Trailhead 9,820 TH

To Silverton

A1. Ice Lake Basin Approach

Ice Lake Basin

Fuller Lake

Lower Ice Lake

Clear Lake
Paradise Basin
Island Lake

3EC

Vermillion Peak 13,894

1,4
2
3
1

Fuller Peak 13,761
1EC

Beattie Peak 13,342
4EC1

V8 13,300
4EC2

Hope Pass 12,445

V9 13,260

SAN MIGUEL CO
SAN JUAN CO

San Miguel Peak

SAN JUAN NATIONAL FOREST

32. Vermillion Peak   13,894 feet

See Map 32 on page 290

This important peak is 9.0 miles west of Silverton, 4.5 miles east of Lizard Head Pass and 4.0 miles south of Ophir. Surprisingly, San Juan County, the San Juans' core county, does not contain a fourteener. It does have Vermillion Peak, however, and Vermillion is the highest peak in San Juan County. From the Silverton area to the east, Vermillion is reclusive, and you can only catch a glimpse of Vermillion when driving west on U.S. 550 from Silverton. However, from Colorado 145 near Trout Lake to the west, Vermillion and its rugged neighbors dominate the view.

Vermillion means "flame-red," and the name fits this colorful peak. Vermillion's rosy rock is pretty to look at, but rotten to climb on. Vermillion's standard routes are a reasonable tour, but you should always treat Vermillion with respect.

MAPS
Required: *Ophir, San Juan National Forest, Uncompahgre National Forest*
Optional: *Silverton, Mount Wilson*

TRAILHEADS

South Mineral Creek Trailhead
This trailhead is at 9,820 feet and provides access to Vermillion's east side. If you are approaching from the north, go 7.8 miles south on U.S. 550 from the summit of Red Mountain Pass. If you are approaching from the south, go 2.0 miles west on U.S. 550 from the Colorado 110–U.S. 550 junction on Silverton's south side. Turn south onto San Juan County 7 (South Mineral Creek Road) and measure from this point. Go west on San Juan County 7, stay straight (left) at mile 3.7 and reach the trailhead at mile 4.4. There are several informal camping areas along this road. The trailhead and a parking area are on the road's north side and the South Mineral Campground is on the road's south side. The Ice Lake Trail starts on the trailhead's west side.

High-clearance vehicles can park higher and also shorten the approach. At mile 3.7, turn north (right) onto the Clear Lake Road and climb 1.0 mile northwest to the first switchback at 10,360 feet at mile 4.7. There is limited parking on the switchback's west side. An unmarked trail starts on the switchback's west side and goes west to join the Ice Lake Trail.

Lake Fork San Miguel Trailhead
This trailhead is at 10,720 feet and provides access to Vermillion's west side. If you are approaching from the north, go 10.1 miles south on Colorado 145 from Society Turn west of Telluride. If you are approaching from the south, go 1.9 miles north on Colorado 145 from the summit of Lizard Head Pass. Turn east onto North Trout Lake Road (FS 626) and measure

from this point. Go south then southeast on North Trout Lake Road, pass a historic watertank on the road's north side at mile 0.9, enter the Uncompahgre National Forest at mile 1.4 and turn north (left) onto Hidden Lake Road (FS 627) at mile 1.7. Go southeast on Hidden Lake Road as it switchbacks up the hill southeast of Trout Lake and reach the trailhead on the east side of a switchback at mile 4.3. The popular Lake Hope Trail goes from this trailhead to Lake Hope at 11,860 feet.

APPROACH

32.A1 — Ice Lake Basin Approach

From South Mineral Creek TH at 9,820 ft: 127 RP   8.6 mi   3,080 ft   Class 1

This approach provides access to the routes on Vermillion's east side. The popular Ice Lake Basin Trail takes you to a remarkable high basin. Some people choose to backpack into Ice Lake Basin, not because of the climbs' lengths, but just because Ice Lake Basin is a wonderful place to camp.

Start at the South Mineral Creek Trailhead and hike west up the Ice Lake Trail, which starts on the trailhead's west side. In the first 1.0 mile the trail crosses to Clear Creek's west side and switchbacks 12 times up to 10,400 feet. Turn west (left) at the 12th switchback where a trail joins from the east. Hike 1.0 mile steeply west to the eastern edge of Lower Ice Lake Basin at 11,400 feet. There is nice camping in the trees near the small lake here. Continue 0.6 mile west across Lower Ice Lake Basin and enjoy a nice view of Golden Horn, one of Vermillion's neighbors. Climb 0.7 mile south then north to pass a cliff band and reach Ice Lake's eastern edge at 12,280 feet.

From Ice Lake, hike 0.5 mile south on a use trail to a tiny lake at 12,580 feet that is 0.2 mile north of Fuller Lake. Leave the use trail to Fuller Lake and hike 0.2 mile west onto a grassy bench. Pick up an old, cairned trail on this bench and hike 0.3 mile southwest to 12,900 feet. Vermillion is 0.6 mile southwest, and the peak's rugged east face dominates your view. Several routes on Vermillion are accessible from here.

32.A1V — Variation

From 4WD parking at 10,360 ft: 102 RP   6.8 mi   2,540 ft   Class 1

You can save 1.8 miles and 540 feet by starting at the first switchback on the Clear Lake Road. From the switchback, hike west on an unmarked trail and cross Clear Creek below one waterfall and above another. This ford can be exciting and dangerous in high water. Join the Ice Lake Trail after 0.1 mile.

ROUTES

32.1 — Vermillion Peak — Southeast Ridge *Classic*

From S Mineral Creek TH at 9,820 ft: 246 RP 10.2 mi 4,074 ft Class 2+ Mod Snow
From 4WD parking at 10,360 ft: 217 RP 8.4 mi 3,534 ft Class 2+ Mod Snow
From 12,900 ft in Ice Lake Basin: 98 RP 1.6 mi   994 ft Class 2+ Mod Snow

This is the standard and easiest route on Vermillion. The route avoids most of Vermillion's loose rock and provides great views in all directions. Start at the South Mineral Creek Trailhead and follow the Ice Lake Basin Approach to 12,900 feet west of and above Fuller Lake. Vermillion is imposing from here. The route is the left skyline ridge, which is easier than it looks.

Hike 0.3 mile southwest to 13,000 feet in the basin below Vermillion and Fuller Peak, which is 0.4 mile southeast of Vermillion. Climb 0.2 mile southeast up a steep slope to the 13,500-foot saddle between these two peaks. This slope holds moderate snow well into summer and, in some years, through summer. The north (right) side of the slope melts first. Carry an ice ax for this route unless you have definitive information that there is a snow-free passage up this slope. When it is snow-free, there is a use trail in the steep scree below the saddle.

From the 13,500-foot saddle, climb northwest on a use trail along the ridge toward Vermillion. Climb on the ridge initially, then move to the south (left) side of the ridge to avoid several towers (Class 2). Make a Class 2+ move out of a small saddle below a large tower that you might have noticed during your approach, then continue doing Class 2 traverses and climbs on the ridge's south side. Go around a corner where you can see the summit pyramid and traverse below the ridge toward it (Class 2). Climb 100 feet north up a dirt-filled gully into a notch in the ridge southeast of the summit pyramid (Class 2+). From here you can look down Vermillion's east face, and this is the top of the Vermillion Dollar Couloir. Climb 100 feet southwest up broken rocks to the summit (Class 2+). This is an airy perch. There are expansive views of San Juan Peaks in all directions, and you can also see into Utah.

32.1EC — Extra Credit — Fuller Peak, 13,761 feet, Class 2

Fuller Peak is 0.4 mile southeast of Vermillion and offers an easy addition to your climb. From the 13,500-foot Vermillion–Fuller saddle, hike 0.2 mile southeast up the scenic ridge to Fuller's summit. There is a good view of Vermillion from here.

32.2 — Vermillion Peak — Vermillion Dollar Couloir

From S Mineral Creek TH at 9,820 ft:	*315 RP*	*10.0 mi*	*4,074 ft*	*Class 3*	*Steep Snow*
With descent of Southeast Ridge:	*315 RP*	*10.1 mi*	*4,074 ft*	*Class 3*	*Steep Snow*
From 4WD parking at 10,360 ft:	*286 RP*	*8.2 mi*	*3,534 ft*	*Class 3*	*Steep Snow*
With descent of Southeast Ridge:	*286 RP*	*8.3 mi*	*3,534 ft*	*Class 3*	*Steep Snow*
From 12,900 ft in Ice Lake Basin:	*168 RP*	*1.4 mi*	*994 ft*	*Class 3*	*Steep Snow*
With descent of Southeast Ridge:	*168 RP*	*1.5 mi*	*994 ft*	*Class 3*	*Steep Snow*

This couloir splits Vermillion's east face and reaches a notch just to the southeast of the summit. This couloir provides a fine climb when it is filled with stable snow. Avoid this couloir when the snow is discontinuous or gone. Rockfall is a hazard in this couloir at any time. Wear a helmet.

Start at the South Mineral Creek Trailhead and follow the Ice Lake Basin Approach to 12,900 feet west of and above Fuller Lake. You can see the couloir from here. Preview it carefully. Hike 0.35 mile west-southwest to 13,000 feet at the base of Vermillion's east face. There is a steep section at the bottom of the couloir. If it is covered with solid good snow, climb it. If the lower snow is questionable, climb to the west (right) around the steep part. This may involve some Class 3 scrambling. At 13,500 feet, above the initial steep part, climb 500 feet up the now well-defined couloir into the notch southeast of the summit. The top part of the couloir is the steepest section, and this is an exciting, alpine place. From the notch, climb 100 feet southwest up broken rocks to the summit (Class 2+). Ascending the Vermillion Dollar Couloir and descending the Southeast Ridge Route makes a distinctive Tour de Vermillion.

32.3 — Vermillion Peak — Northeast Ridge

From S Mineral Creek TH at 9,820 ft:	*249 RP*	*10.2 mi*	*4,074 ft*	*Class 3*
With descent of Southeast Ridge:	*247 RP*	*10.2 mi*	*4,074 ft*	*Class 3*
From 4WD parking at 10,360 ft:	*221 RP*	*8.4 mi*	*3,534 ft*	*Class 3*
With descent of Southeast Ridge:	*219 RP*	*8.4 mi*	*3,534 ft*	*Class 3*
From 12,900 ft in Ice Lake Basin:	*102 RP*	*1.6 mi*	*994 ft*	*Class 3*
With descent of Southeast Ridge:	*100 RP*	*1.6 mi*	*994 ft*	*Class 3*

This is Vermillion's other ridge. It is a route for properly trained and equipped mountaineers, not for casual hikers. Start at the South Mineral Creek Trailhead and follow the Ice Lake Basin Approach to 12,900 feet west of and above Fuller Lake. The route is the right skyline ridge that connects Vermillion to Golden Horn, which is 0.4 mile northeast of Vermillion. You would likely do this ridge when climbing Golden Horn and Vermillion together.

Hike 0.3 mile west across the basin to 13,060 feet below the Vermillion–Golden Horn saddle. Do not climb directly to the saddle. Climb a southwest-angling ramp to 13,300 feet, then climb north through a break in the cliffs on an old trail. Reach Vermillion's northeast ridge at 13,400 feet just above the 13,380-foot Vermillion–Golden Horn saddle.

Scramble southwest toward Vermillion's summit. The initial part of the ridge is fun and requires some easy Class 3 scrambling on or near the ridge. At 13,600 feet, bypass a tower on the ridge's west (right) side (Class 3). At 13,700 feet, you will reach the base of a vertical step in the ridge. A direct ascent of this step is not reasonable. Traverse 100 yards south on a sloping ledge on the ridge's east (left) side. This airy traverse takes you halfway across Vermillion's upper east face. Snow on this ledge makes this traverse a climb, not a hike. When snow-free, the ledge is an airy, Class 2+ scree scrabble. When you reach the Vermillion Dollar Couloir, climb 120 feet southwest up the top of the couloir to the notch southeast of the summit. Be prepared for steep snow climbing. From the

13,894

32.1

Vermillion Peak from the southwest.

famous notch, climb 100 feet southwest up broken rocks to the summit (Class 2+). Ascending the Northeast Ridge Route and descending the Southeast Ridge Route allows you to climb both Golden Horn and Fuller with Vermillion.

32.3V — Variation
If Vermillion's northeast ridge is not to your liking at all, contour across Vermillion's lower east face on a bench at 13,460 feet from the 13,380-foot Vermillion–Golden Horn saddle to the 13,500-foot Vermillion–Fuller saddle (Class 2), then continue on the Southeast Ridge Route. This traverse is the easiest route for climbing Golden Horn, Vermillion and Fuller together.

32.3EC — Extra Credit — Golden Horn, 13,780 feet, Class 2+
Golden Horn is the dramatic peak 0.4 mile northeast of Vermillion. It has an astonishing appearance when you view it from Lower Ice Lake Basin. It is equally astonishing when you view it from the west. Golden Horn, not Vermillion, is the area's headline-grabbing peak. After you climb it, you will have bragging rights. Fortunately for braggers, Golden Horn is not difficult to climb.

From the 13,380-foot Vermillion–Golden Horn saddle, do an ascending traverse northeast on scree below some cliffs (Class 2+). The rock here is loose but not difficult. When you are past the cliffs, climb northwest up broken rocks to the summit (Class 2+). This is a fun finish. Golden Horn has two summits. The western one is the highest.

32.4 — Vermillion Peak — Southwest Basin

From Lake Fork San Miguel TH at 10,720 ft: 238 RP   7.4 mi   3,675 ft   Class 2+

This intriguing alternative route provides a great view of Vermillion's namesake colors and avoids the snow slopes on the routes above Ice Lake Basin. It also allows you to climb an additional peak en route and provides access to two other peaks.

Start at the Lake Fork San Miguel Trailhead and hike 0.2 mile southeast on the excellent Lake Hope Trail to Poverty Gulch. You have a view of 13,738-foot Pilot Knob from here. Cross the creek in Poverty Gulch and continue on the trail 0.9 mile south to the beginning of a steep climb at 10,920 feet. Hike 0.4 mile south up a set of short switchbacks to treeline at 11,500 feet, then continue on the trail 0.2 mile south to 11,700 feet. Lake Hope is 0.3 mile south of and above this point, but you do not need to go all the way to the lake. From 11,700 feet, there is a great view of multi-hued Vermillion 1.3 miles to the northeast. You can also see 13,761-foot Fuller Peak and 13,342-foot Beattie Peak southeast of Vermillion. Your next goal is to reach the saddle between Fuller and Beattie

At 11,700 feet, leave the Lake Hope Trail and hike across grass 0.7 mile east-northeast to 12,100 feet in the basin south of Vermillion. Hike 0.2 mile east-northeast up steep scree on the south (right) side of a scruffy cliff band, then hike 0.2 mile east-northeast to 12,700 feet at the top of the basin (Class 2). Climb 0.1 mile east up steeper scree to the 13,020-foot Fuller–Beattie saddle (Class 2).

From the Fuller–Beattie saddle, climb 0.3 mile north up a very steep scree slope to Fuller's 13,761-foot summit (Class 2+). This ornery slope will test your legs, but you will be rewarded with a good view of Vermillion from Fuller's summit. Descend 0.2 mile northwest down a scenic ridge to the 13,500-foot Vermillion–Fuller saddle. Join the Southeast Ridge Route in this saddle and follow it to the summit.

EXTRA CREDITS

32.4EC1 — Beattie Peak, 13,342 feet, Class 2
From the 13,020-foot Fuller–Beattie saddle, climb 0.2 mile south up scree to Beattie's 13,342-foot summit. Beattie is a ranked thirteener.

32.4EC2 — "V8," 13,300 feet, Class 2+
From Beattie's summit, climb 0.7 mile southwest along a rough ridge to the 13,300-foot summit of "V8"—another ranked thirteener. From here, descend 0.6 mile southwest down a rough slope to 12,445-foot Hope Pass and follow the trail 0.5 mile northwest to Hope Lake. This completes a grand circle tour that allows you to climb four peaks.

33. Gladstone Peak   13,913 feet

See Map 33 on page 298

Remote, rugged and rotten, this peak is 13.0 miles southwest of Telluride and 4.8 miles northwest of Lizard Head Pass. Standing between the fourteeners Mount Wilson and Wilson Peak, Gladstone is one of the sentinels of the San Miguel Mountains. You can see it for long distances to the east. In particular, from Vermillion's summit, Gladstone frames Lizard Head.

Gladstone is Colorado's westernmost centennial thirteener, and is the only centennial thirteener in the San Miguels. Like the rest of the San Juans, the San Miguels are loaded with rotten rock. Although Gladstone does have alternative routes, only the standard route is described here. Gladstone has a life of its own compared to its higher neighbors, and Gladstone climbers often mutter that the peak's name should be "*Sad*stone." Barely balanced blocks are poised to wipe you out, and they have proven fatal. Approach this peak with care.

MAPS

Required: *Mount Wilson, Dolores Peak, San Juan National Forest, Uncompahgre National Forest*
Optional: *Little Cone, Gray Head*

TRAILHEADS

Wilson Mesa Trailhead

This trailhead is at 10,420 feet and provides access to upper Navajo Basin and Gladstone's north side. If you are approaching from the north or west, go 6.7 miles east on Colorado 145 from the Colorado 145–Colorado 62 junction. If you are approaching from the south or east, go 6.0 miles west on Colorado 145 from Society Turn west of Telluride.

Turn south onto the Silver Pick Road (dirt) and measure from this point. Cross the San Miguel River, stay left at mile 3.3, take the middle of three roads at mile 4.0, enter the Uncompahgre National Forest at mile 6.3 and stay left at mile 6.4. Reach the trailhead near some campsites at mile 7.2 at a gate that is usually locked. The Silver Pick Road is steep and rough, but is passable for most passenger cars. If the gate at the trailhead is unlocked, high-clearance vehicles can continue 1.7 miles south up the road to the privately owned Silver Pick Mine at 10,960 feet.

Navajo Lake Trailhead

This trailhead is at 9,340 feet and provides access to Navajo Basin on Gladstone's west side. If you are approaching from the north, go 5.4 miles south on Colorado 145 from the summit of Lizard Head Pass (10,250 feet).

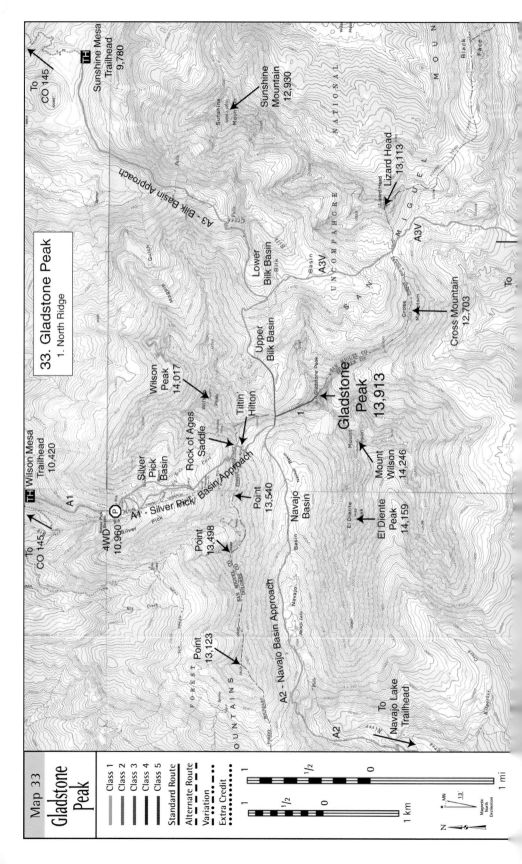

Map 33
Gladstone
Peak

33. Gladstone Peak
1. North Ridge

Legend:
Class 1
Class 2
Class 3
Class 4
Class 5
Standard Route
Alternate Route
Variation
Extra Credit

Sunshine Mesa Trailhead 9,780
Sunshine Mountain 12,930
Lizard Head 13,113
A3V
Cross Mountain 12,703
A3 - Bilk Basin Approach
Lower Bilk Basin
A3V
Upper Bilk Basin
To CO 145

Wilson Peak 14,017
Tiltin Hilton
Rock of Ages Saddle
Silver Pick Basin
Wilson Mesa Trailhead 10,420
A1
4WD 10,960
A1 - Silver Pick Basin Approach
Point 13,540
Point 13,498
Navajo Basin
Gladstone Peak 13,913
Mount Wilson 14,246
El Diente Peak 14,159

Point 13,123
A2 - Navajo Basin Approach
To Navajo Lake Trailhead
A2

To CO 145

UNCOMPAHGRE NATIONAL

MIGUEL

SAN MIGUEL CO / DOLORES CO

FOREST MOUNTAINS

N

1 mi
1 km

Magnetic North Declination 13°

Gladstone Peak from the east.

If you are approaching from the south, go 9.5 miles north on Colorado 145 from the Rico Post Office.

Turn west onto the Dunton Road (FS 535) and measure from this point. Go west on the Dunton Road (dirt) as it climbs to the meadows near Coal Creek. Go straight at mile 4.2, pass Morgan Camp (private) at mile 5.0, descend to the West Dolores River, turn hard south (left) at mile 7.2 and reach the trailhead at mile 7.3. The Dunton Road is passable for passenger cars, and there is ample parking at the well-marked trailhead. The Dunton Road is not plowed in winter.

Sunshine Mesa Trailhead

This trailhead is at 9,780 feet and provides access to Gladstone's east side. From Society Turn west of Telluride, go 2.7 miles west on Colorado 145 to South Fork Road, which is 100 yards west of milepost 71. Turn south onto South Fork Road and measure from this point. Go east on South Fork Road, cross the San Miguel River and enter the Uncompahgre National Forest at mile 1.0. Go south, turn west (right) onto Road 63J at mile 2.2 and cross to the west side of the South Fork of the San Miguel River. Climb south on Road 63J, switchback up onto Sunshine Mesa and reach the trailhead at the end of the road at mile 7.7.

Cross Mountain Trailhead

This trailhead is at 10,050 feet and provides access to Gladstone's east side. This trailhead is 0.1 mile northwest of Colorado 145, 2.0 miles southwest of the summit of Lizard Head Pass (10,250 feet). There is a small parking area here, and there are trail signs near the trees to the north. The

Cross Mountain Trail goes north from the trailhead. This trailhead is accessible in winter.

APPROACHES

33.A1 — Silver Pick Basin Approach

From Wilson Mesa TH at 10,420 ft: 118 RP   7.4 mi   3,040 ft   Class 1

You can approach Gladstone's North Ridge Route from Silver Pick Basin to the north of the peak. Start at the Wilson Mesa Trailhead and go 1.7 miles south up the road to the Silver Pick Mine at 10,960 feet.

There are two routes leading from the Silver Pick Mine to upper Silver Pick Basin. The longer, easier route follows the four-wheel-drive road above the mine, turns left at 11,200 feet and continues up a four-wheel-drive road through the rocks on the basin's west side to the remains of an old mine building at 12,140 feet. A shorter, more scenic route follows an old trail that leaves the four-wheel-drive road 300 yards above the Silver Pick Mine. The trail climbs around rocky outcrops on the basin's east side before rejoining the road at the mine building at 12,140 feet.

From 12,140 feet, switchback up a trail to the 13,020-foot saddle, called the "Rock of Ages Saddle," between the fourteener Wilson Peak and Point 13,540, which is 1.0 mile west of Wilson Peak. The trail does not climb directly to the pass but switchbacks up the scree west of the pass. You cannot easily see this trail from below, and it is not marked on the 1953 Mount Wilson Quadrangle. The trail is well worth finding, because the scree below the pass is very loose. When you reach the pass, you will see a startling view of the fourteeners Mount Wilson and El Diente across Navajo Basin. You can also see Gladstone and its north ridge to the northeast (left) of Mount Wilson. From the saddle, descend 120 yards south to the Rock of Ages Mine at 12,880 feet. There is an old shack here called the "Tiltin' Hilton." From the mine, contour 0.4 mile southeast to 12,800 feet below the 13,140-foot saddle at the base of Gladstone's north ridge.

33.A2 — Navajo Basin Approach

From Navajo Lake TH at 9,340 ft: 183 RP   14.6 mi   3,460 ft   Class 1

You can approach Gladstone's North Ridge Route from Navajo Basin west of the peak. Start at the Navajo Lake Trailhead and hike 5.0 miles north and east on the Navajo Lake Trail to Navajo Lake at 11,154 feet. There are campsites here in the trees. Hike 0.2 mile around Navajo Lake's north side, then hike 1.1 miles east up a trail through a long scree slope to reach the grassy benches in upper Navajo Basin at 12,000 feet. There are many open camping sites on these benches. Hike 1.0 mile east, then northeast, then southeast to 12,800 feet in upper Navajo Basin below the 13,140-foot saddle at the base of Gladstone's north ridge.

33.A3 — Bilk Basin Approach

From Sunshine Mesa TH at 9,780 ft: 108 RP   9.8 mi   2,280 ft   Class 1

You can approach Gladstone's North Ridge Route from Bilk Basin east of the peak. Start at the Sunshine Mesa Trailhead and contour 2.0 miles west then south on an old road to the Morning Star Mine on Bilk Creek's west side at 10,100 feet. The fourteener Wilson Peak is high above this point to the west. From the mine, hike 1.0 mile south on the Lizard Head Trail, enter the Lizard Head Wilderness and switchback above Bilk Creek. You will have views of several cascades on Bilk Creek, and you will be able to see Sunshine Mountain to the east. Hike 0.3 mile west and enter lower Bilk Basin at 11,060 feet. When you emerge from the trees, you can see Gladstone to the southwest. It is distinguished with a permanent snowfield below its north face, and the north ridge is the right skyline.

The trail above this point is incorrectly marked on the 1953 Mount Wilson Quadrangle. Continue 0.6 mile on the Lizard Head Trail as it climbs above the lower basin's north side and then climbs south to 11,400 feet at the creek descending from upper Bilk Basin. Leave the Lizard Head Trail here and hike 1.0 mile north and west on a trail that does not show on the Mount Wilson Quadrangle. Follow this trail as it switchbacks into upper Bilk Basin at 12,060 feet. There is a small lake in this enchanting place. The gray hulk of mighty Wilson Peak is 0.7 mile northwest and Gladstone with its distinctive black rock is 0.8 mile southwest.

33.A3V — Variation

From Cross Mountain TH at 10,050 ft: 138 RP   12.0 mi   3,170 ft   Class 1

You can reach Bilk Basin from the Cross Mountain Trailhead. From the trailhead, hike 3.5 miles south on the Cross Mountain Trail to the 11,980-foot saddle 0.4 mile west of 13,113-foot Lizard Head. As tough as Gladstone is, you may still feel happy that you are climbing Gladstone instead of Lizard Head. Descend 1.5 miles north on the Lizard Head Trail to the creek crossing at 11,400 feet above lower Bilk Basin. Join the Bilk Basin Approach here for the climb into upper Bilk Basin.

ROUTE

33.1 — Gladstone Peak — North Ridge

From Wilson Mesa TH at 10,420 ft:	270 RP	8.6 mi	4,153 ft	Class 3
From Navajo Lake TH at 9,340 ft:	352 RP	15.8 mi	4,573 ft	Class 3
From Sunshine Mesa TH at 9,780 ft:	338 RP	12.4 mi	4,133 ft	Class 3
From Cross Mountain TH at 10,050 ft:	377 RP	14.6 mi	5,023 ft	Class 3

This is the standard and easiest route up Gladstone Peak. Use the Silver Pick Basin Approach, the Navajo Basin Approach or the Bilk Basin Approach. The Silver Pick Basin Approach is shortest if reaching Gladstone

Gladstone Peak from the northwest.

Peak is your only objective. A camp in Navajo Basin provides easy access to Gladstone as well as to the surrounding fourteeners. The less-traveled Bilk Basin Approach will give you solitude and access to both Gladstone and Wilson Peaks.

From 12,800 feet in upper Navajo Basin, climb 0.1 mile east up a steep slope to the 13,140-foot saddle at the base of Gladstone's north ridge. From 12,060 feet in Bilk Basin, climb 0.8 mile west-southwest to reach this saddle. Once on the ridge, climb 0.5 mile south up the ridge to the summit. The upper part of the ridge harbors some large, questionable blocks. Scrambling over and around these blocks requires great care. One block the size of a grand piano wobbles as you pass over it. From the summit, you can look down on Lizard Head and beyond to Vermillion. Descend with even greater care.

Appendix

IN DEFENSE OF MOUNTAINEERING GUIDEBOOKS

By Gerry Roach

I am always amazed when I see stumps of once large trees near treeline. They are not going to grow back, at least not until a comet hits Earth and changes the balance of nature. I am equally amazed that nothing grows on mine tailings. Even a comet may not make them fertile. We are the future generation, and we have stumps and tailings to look at. Yet the mountains are not dead. We can climb them, then loll about in fields of flowers.

Ironically, we now drive up the miners' old roads in our fancy four-wheel-drive vehicles made of mined metals, hike uphill for a few hours to a summit and claim a personal victory or conquest. Miners and loggers make physical extractions from the mountains. Climbers make mental extractions from the mountains. For now, we have driven most mining and logging offshore. We no longer rush to the mountains to get the gold; we go to get their good tidings.

A debate today swirls around the opinion that even climbers' mental extractions are causing unacceptable environmental damage. We leave too many footprints. Those who choose to make an effort are being cast as pseudo-criminals who love the mountains to death. Eh? I take a longer view. Death to a mountain is when it is mined into oblivion like Bartlett Mountain. Death to a mountain is when it commits suicide like Mount Saint Helens. As violent as those actions were, we can still climb the stumps of those peaks. There are still good tidings there.

Any long view must compare the damage done by climbers' boots with that caused by monster trucks. Obviously, boots pale in comparison. Still, are boots too much? Sometimes yes. What do we do? Rather than lament the lost age when we could walk unfettered by such concerns, we should strap in and solve the problem. For a government agency to shut the door and refuse entry is not a solution. Excess footprints are easily dealt with. We need sustainable trails through the fragile alpine zone. The Colorado Fourteener Initiative is creating these trails. Their efforts are a grand example of the public's ability to strap in and solve the problem. There is no environmental problem created by climbers that cannot be solved by climbers.

Our mental extractions from the mountains are going to continue to increase. So is the positive social value of these gifts. As society creaks and groans in other arenas, we need the mountains' good tidings more than ever. The gift that mountains offer society is immense. Mountains give us an arena where we can lift not just our bodies, but our spirits. Without uplifted spirits, we devolve. Mountaineering is a great metaphor for life. It is worth fighting for. I view guidebooks as part of the solution, not part of the problem.

I started climbing in 1955 and for 20 years could not conceive of writing a guidebook. I reasoned, like a miner, that the good tidings were hidden and that, once found, they should be protected by a claim. I felt a proprietary ownership of the secrets I found with my efforts. I felt that sharing the secret would diminish it as a microscope can change the microbe. I dashed across the globe to discover secrets before they were diminished. Although I had many unique climbs and experiences, this effort left me frustrated and exhausted. I could not dash fast enough. Too many people were ahead of me. After I shared an ascent of the Matterhorn in 1973 with a hundred other people, I pointed to the heavens and started pontificating about the lost age. Then I realized no one was listening. They were just climbing the Matterhorn. Society had jumped my claim. I pondered this for many years.

Still, I did not write a guidebook. I reasoned that sharing would attract still more people and hasten the demise. I clung to this view as the population quietly doubled and mountain use increased tenfold. My pontifical finger withered. I was alone with my memories of the lost age. Then early one morning in 1981, I sat upright in bed and started writing a guidebook. It was done in a week. At the time, I could not explain it, but I knew that not sharing would hasten the demise. Finally, I just set the demise aside. I knew that what the mountains need is love.

Approached with love, the mountains can endure our mental extractions forever. Approached with malice, greed or ignorance, the mountains will indeed suffer. Worse, even with love, climbers may lose their access to other interests and opinions. The government agencies and monster trucks stand ready. The best we can do is love the mountains and share this love. Climbers as a group need to evolve. We must spread our arms wide and embrace not just the mountains, but other user groups as well. The mountains need ambassadors—loving user groups who are intimate with their secrets. I offer my guidebooks from a deep love for the mountains so that future ambassadors can also share the mountains' good tidings.

Map Information

We have written this book to be used with good maps. We recommend the USGS topographic quadrangles. They are available in many shops and at the Map Sales Office in the Denver Federal Center; call 303-202-4700 or toll-free in US 888-275-8747 for information. You can order maps from the Federal Center by mail or phone. All the quadrangles referred to in this book are 7.5-minute quadrangles, and they all use feet, not meters. The non-topographic National Forest maps and topographic Trails Illustrated maps are useful and can be obtained at quality outdoor stores. These maps give you the big picture, and they often have more current road information than the USGS quadrangles. We list the required and optional USGS quadrangles and National Forest maps with each peak or group of peaks, both in the text and in the following lists.

FRONT RANGE MAPS

1. Meeker
Required: *Allens Park, Longs Peak, Roosevelt National Forest*
Optional: *McHenrys Peak, Isolation Peak*

2. Edwards
Required: *Grays Peak, Arapaho National Forest*
Optional: *Montezuma*

3. Spalding
Required: *Mount Evans, Arapaho National Forest*
Optional: *Georgetown, Harris Park, Idaho Springs, Pike National Forest*

TENMILE–MOSQUITO RANGE MAPS

4. Crystal, Pacific, "Atlantic," Fletcher, "Drift"
Required: *Breckenridge, Copper Mountain, White River National Forest*

5. Clinton, Traver, Buckskin
Required: *Alma, Climax, Pike National Forest*
Optional: *Copper Mountain*

6. Silverheels
Required: *Alma, Pike National Forest*
Optional: *Como*

7. Gemini, Dyer, Horseshoe
Required: *Mount Sherman, Pike National Forest*
Optional: *Climax, Fairplay West*

SAWATCH RANGE MAPS

8. Holy Cross Ridge
Required: *Mount of the Holy Cross, White River National Forest*
Optional: *Minturn, Mount Jackson*

9. Oklahoma
Required: *Mount Champion, Mount Massive, San Isabel National Forest*

10. French, Frasco, Casco, "Lackawanna"
Required: *Mount Massive, Mount Elbert, Independence Pass, San Isabel National Forest*
Optional: *Mount Champion*

11. Grizzly
Required: *Independence Pass, San Isabel National Forest*
Optional: *New York Peak*

12. Hope
Required: *Mount Elbert, Winfield, San Isabel National Forest*

13. Emerald, Iowa
Required: *Winfield, Mount Harvard, San Isabel National Forest*
Optional: *Tincup, Harvard Lakes*

14. North Apostle, Ice Mountain
Required: *Winfield, San Isabel National Forest*
Optional: *Tincup, Gunnison National Forest*

15. "North Carbonate"
Required: *St. Elmo, Mount Antero, San Isabel National Forest*
Optional: *Garfield, Maysville*

16. Ouray
Required: *Mount Ouray, San Isabel National Forest*
Optional: *Pahlone Peak*

SANGRE DE CRISTO RANGE MAPS

17. Adams, "Kat Carson"
Required: *Crestone Peak, Horn Peak, San Isabel National Forest*
Optional: *Crestone, Rito Alto Peak, Rio Grande National Forest*

18. California, "Huerfano"
Required: *Blanca Peak, Mosca Pass, San Isabel National Forest*
Optional: *Twin Peaks, Rio Grande National Forest*

19. Red
Required: *Culebra Peak, El Valle Creek*
Optional: *Taylor Ranch*

ELK RANGE MAPS

20. Hagerman
Required: *Snowmass Mtn., White River National Forest*
Optional: *Capitol Peak, Maroon Bells*

21. "Thunder Pyramid"
Required: *Maroon Bells, White River National Forest*

22. Cathedral, "Castleabra"
Required: *Maroon Bells, Hayden Peak, Pearl Pass, White River National Forest*
Optional: *Gothic*

SAN JUAN RANGE MAPS

23. Stewart, Organ
Required: *Stewart Peak, San Luis Peak, Halfmoon Pass, Elk Park, Gunnison National Forest, Rio Grande National Forest*

24. "Phoenix Peak"
Required: *Halfmoon Pass, Elk Park, Gunnison National Forest*, Rio Grande National Forest
Optional: *Creede, Mesa Mountain, San Luis Peak*

25. Rio Grande Pyramid
Required: *Rio Grande Pyramid, Weminuche Pass, Rio Grande National Forest*, San Juan National Forest
Optional: *Finger Mesa, Granite Lake, Granite Peak, Emerald Lake, Vallecito Reservoir, Uncompahgre National Forest*

26. Point 13,832, Point 13,811
Required: *Redcloud Peak, Lake San Cristobal, Gunnison National Forest*
Optional: *Lake City*

27. Half Peak
Required: *Pole Creek Mountain, Redcloud Peak, Gunnison National Forest*
Optional: *Howardsville, Rio Grande National Forest*

28. Niagara, Jones, "American"
Required: *Handies Peak, Uncompahgre National Forest*
Optional: *Redcloud Peak, Howardsville*

29. Arrow, Vestal, Trinity
Required: *Snowdon Peak, Storm King Peak, San Juan National Forest*

30. Jupiter, Pigeon, Turret, Jagged
Required: *Columbine Pass, Mountain View Crest, Snowdon Peak, Storm King Peak, San Juan National Forest*
Optional: *Electra Lake, Vallecito Reservoir, Rio Grande National Forest*

31. Teakettle, Dallas
Required: *Mount Sneffels, Telluride, Uncompahgre National Forest*
Optional: *Ironton*

32. Vermillion
Required: *Ophir, San Juan National Forest, Uncompahgre National Forest*
Optional: *Silverton, Mount Wilson*

33. Gladstone
Required: *Mount Wilson, Dolores Peak, San Juan National Forest, Uncompahgre National Forest*
Optional: *Little Cone, Gray Head*

SHOPPING LIST FOR ALL USGS QUADRANGLES

Allens Park
Alma
Blanca Peak
Breckenridge
Capitol Peak
Climax
Columbine Pass
Como
Copper Mountain
Creede
Crestone
Crestone Peak
Culebra Peak
Dolores Peak
El Valle Creek
Electra Lake
Elk Park
Emerald Lake
Fairplay West
Finger Mesa
Garfield
Georgetown
Gothic
Granite Lake
Granite Peak
Gray Head
Grays Peak
Halfmoon Pass
Handies Peak
Harris Park
Harvard Lakes
Hayden Peak
Horn Peak
Howardsville

Idaho Springs
Independence Pass
Ironton
Isolation Peak
Lake City
Lake San Cristobal
Little Cone
Longs Peak
Maroon Bells
Maysville
McHenrys Peak
Mesa Mountain
Minturn
Montezuma
Mosca Pass
Mount Antero
Mount Champion
Mount Elbert
Mount Evans
Mount Harvard
Mount Jackson
Mount Massive
Mount of the Holy Cross
Mount Ouray
Mount Sherman
Mount Sneffels
Mount Wilson
Mountain View Crest
New York Peak
Ophir
Pahlone Peak
Pearl Pass
Pole Creek Mountain
Redcloud Peak

Rio Grande Pyramid
Rito Alto Peak
St. Elmo
San Luis Peak
Silverton
Snowdon Peak
Snowmass Mountain
Stewart Peak

Storm King Peak
Taylor Ranch
Telluride
Tincup
Twin Peaks
Vallecito Reservoir
Weminuche Pass
Winfield

SHOPPING LIST FOR NATIONAL FOREST MAPS

Arapaho National Forest
Gunnison National Forest
Pike National Forest
Rio Grande National Forest
Roosevelt National Forest

San Isabel National Forest
San Juan National Forest
Uncompahgre National Forest
White River National Forest

Difficulty of Easiest Routes

This list sorts Colorado's centennial thirteeners by difficulty of easiest route. The Class determines the easiest route, not the R Points. When multiple routes have the same Class, we use the R Points to break the tie. The standard route is not always the easiest route. When the standard route and easiest route differ, we list the easiest route here if we also describe it in the text. We consider Easy Snow equivalent to Class 2 difficulty, Moderate Snow equivalent to Class 3 difficulty and Steep Snow equivalent to Class 4 difficulty.

CLASS 1
Edwards – East Slopes
Silverheels – South Ridge
Horseshoe – Northeast Ridge
California – North Ridge
Stewart – North Slopes
Organ – East Slopes
"Phoenix" – South Slopes
Point 13,811 – South Slopes

CLASS 1+
Ouray – East Ridge

CLASS 2
Crystal – East Slopes
Pacific – North Ridge
"Atlantic" – West Ridge
Fletcher – Southeast Ridge

"Drift" – Villa Ridge
Clinton – Southeast Slopes
Traver – East Ridge
Buckskin – Northeast Slopes
Gemini – Northwest Ridge
Dyer – East Ridge
Holy Cross Ridge – South Slopes
Oklahoma – Southeast Slopes
French – South Slopes
Frasco – East Ridge
Casco – North Ridge
"Lackawanna" – Northwest Ridge
Hope – East Ridge
Emerald – South Slopes
Iowa – West Ridge
North Apostle – Southwest Ridge
"North Carbonate" – North Ridge
"Huerfano" – South Slopes
Red – Northwest Ridge
"Castleabra" – Southeast Slopes
Rio Grande Pyramid – East Slopes
Point 13,832 – Northwest Ridge
Half – South Ridge
Jones – South Ridge
"American" – West Ridge

CLASS 2+
Spalding – East Ridge
Grizzly – East Ridge
Adams – West Ridge
"Kat Carson" – East Ridge
Hagerman – South Face
Niagara – East Ridge
Vestal – South Face
Trinity – Southeast Face
Jupiter – Southwest Slopes
Turret – Northwest Slopes
Vermillion – Southwest Basin

CLASS 3
Meeker – Loft
Ice – Northeast Ridge
"Thunder Pyramid" – West Face
Cathedral – South Ridge
Arrow – Northeast Face
Gladstone – North Ridge

CLASS 4
Pigeon — Southwest Slopes

CLASS 5
Jagged — North Face
Teakettle — Southeast Ridge
Dallas — East Face

Classic Routes

FRONT RANGE *CLASSIC* ROUTES

Loft of Meeker	Class 3, Moderate Snow
Dragon's Tail of Meeker	Class 3, Moderate Snow
Dream Weaver of Meeker	Class 4–5.6, Steep Snow/Ice
Edwardian of Edwards	Class 2, Moderate Snow
East Ridge of Spalding	Class 2+
Chi-Town of Spalding	Class 4, Steep Snow
Goldfinger of Spalding	Class 3, Steep Snow

TENMILE–MOSQUITO RANGE *CLASSIC* ROUTES

East Slopes of Crystal	Class 2
Dyer Straits of Crystal	Class 2, Moderate Snow
East Ridge of Crystal	Class 3
Northeast Slopes of Pacific	Class 2, Moderate Snow
East Ridge of Pacific	Class 2+
West Ridge of Pacific	Class 3
Atlantis of "Atlantic"	Class 2, Moderate Snow
West Winds Combination	Class 2
Villa Ridge of "Drift"	Class 2
Northwest Bowl of "Drift"	Class 2, Moderate Snow
Clipper Combination	Class 2
South Ridge of Silverheels	Class 1
North Ridge of Dyer	Class 2+
Boudoir Couloir of Horseshoe	Class 2, Moderate Snow
West Slopes of Horseshoe	Class 2
South Ridge of Horseshoe	Class 1

SAWATCH RANGE *CLASSIC* ROUTES

Halo Ridge of Holy Cross Ridge	Class 2
South Ridge of Holy Cross Ridge	Class 2
Francisco Combination	Class 2+
Lackawanna Gulch of "Lackawanna"	Class 2, Moderate Snow

Grizzly Couloir of Grizzly	Class 2+, Steep Snow
East Ridge of Hope	Class 2
Hopeful of Hope	Class 2, Moderate Snow
Arcturus Combination	Class 2
Refrigerator of Ice	Class 3, Steep Snow
Ice Cubed Combination	Class 3
East Ridge of Ouray	Class 1+

SANGRE DE CRISTO RANGE *CLASSIC* ROUTES

West Ridge of Adams	Class 2+
North Ridge of California	Class 1

SAN JUAN RANGE *CLASSIC* ROUTES

North Slopes of Stewart	Class 1
East Slopes of Organ	Class 1
East Ridge of "Phoenix"	Class 2
East Slopes of Rio Grande Pyramid	Class 2
Rio Nieve of Rio Grande Pyramid	Class 2, Steep Snow
South Slopes of Point 13,811	Class 1
South Ridge of Half	Class 2
Independence of "American"	Class 2, Moderate Snow
Niagara Falls Combination	Class 2+
Variation 28.15V	Class 2+
Northeast Face of Arrow	Class 3
Wham Ridge of Vestal	Class 5.4
Trinity Traverse Combination	Class 4
Trinitas Combination	Class 4
Southwest Slopes of Jupiter	Class 2+
Southwest Slopes of Pigeon	Class 4
Northwest Slopes of Turret	Class 2+
Turn Eon Combination	Class 4
North Face of Jagged	Class 5.0–5.2
Southeast Ridge of Teakettle	Class 5.3
East Face of Dallas	Class 5.3
Southeast Ridge of Vermillion	Class 2+, Moderate Snow

What Is a Peak?

The question about what constitutes an official peak and what is just a false summit has plagued mountaineers for decades. Most mountaineers know all about false summits. When you reach what you think is the summit and discover that the peak you are trying to climb is still farther and higher, you are on a false summit. For many mountaineers, this is all they need to know, and the following discussion will seem banal.

The traditional list of Colorado fourteeners has varied from 52 to 55 peaks over the years, and has always been based on a healthy degree of emotionalism. Peaks have come and gone from the list of fourteeners for sentimental reasons. In this high-tech peak-bagging age, however, many climbers are interested in peak lists based on a rational system. These climbers are interested in the discussion about what constitutes a peak because the answer determines the list's contents and, hence, their climbs.

For some time in Colorado, a single, simple criterion has been used to determine if a summit is a peak or a false summit: For a summit to be a peak, it must rise at least 300 vertical feet above the saddle connecting it to its neighbor. If just one criterion is going to be used, this is a good one. There is nothing sacred about 300 feet. It is just a round number that seems to make sense in Colorado. This criterion serves most people most of the time, and the peak list that follows uses it.

When Is a Peak Climbed?

After grappling with the question of what is a peak, we need to think about the question: When is a peak climbed? Most people would squirm if you drove a vehicle to within a few feet of a summit and then walked the last few feet to the summit, and most people would squirm if you did not reach the highest point at all. Two necessary conditions seem to be that you must reach the highest point under your own power and that you must gain a certain amount of elevation. The crux question is, how much elevation?

An obvious answer is that to climb a mountain you must climb from the bottom to the top. Although the top of most mountains is well defined, the bottom is not. One definition is that the bottom of all mountains is sea level. This flip definition makes little topographic sense, and it means that few people have ever climbed anything.

In Colorado there has been a long-standing informal agreement that one should gain 3,000 feet for a "legal" ascent of a fourteener. Of course there is nothing sacred about the number 3,000. It is approximately equal to the vertical distance between treeline and summit, and it represents a nice workout, but other than that, it is just a one-number estimate for defining the bottom of a Colorado mountain. Even people who are careful to gain 3,000 feet on the first peak of the day often hike the connecting ridge to the next peak and claim a legal ascent of the second peak after an ascent of only a few hundred feet. Most people who climb Colorado peaks do this.

A good minimum criterion for climbing a peak is that you should gain a vertical height under your own power equal to the peak's rise from its highest connecting saddle with a neighbor peak. If you do less than that, you are just visiting summits, not climbing mountains. Beyond this minimum gain, you are free to gain as much altitude as your peak-bagging conscience requires. The greater your elevation gain, the greater your karmic gain. Except for ridge traverses, 3,000 feet seems to satisfy most people.

Peak List

The following list covers all of Colorado's peaks 13,000 feet and above. By the 300-foot criterion, this covers Colorado's 637 highest peaks. We present this extended list in the hope that you will be inspired to return to the high country repeatedly for more adventures.

A peak qualifies for this list if it is named or ranked. Named summits are on the list if they are ranked or unranked. The officially named summits include peaks, mounts, mountains, named ridges, named benchmarks if they do not have a peak name, named rocks and named hills. We enclose unofficial names in quotation marks. If a summit has both a peak name and a named benchmark, the peak name takes precedence.

We list ranked summits whether they are named or not. We rank a summit if it rises at least 300 feet from the highest connecting saddle to a higher ranked summit. The closest, higher, ranked summit is the **parent**. It is interesting to be on a summit and know where the nearest higher peak is. A fine point is that the parent may be a different peak from the higher ranked summit above the highest connecting saddle. In the rare case in which there are two or more connecting saddles of the same elevation leading to different, higher, ranked summits, the closest summit is the parent. Our list differs from other lists in that we search for a higher, ranked parent, not another peak on the list that may be lower and unranked. That would be a **neighbor**.

We give interpolated elevations to summits and saddles that are only shown with contour lines. Most USGS quadrangles covering Colorado's mountains have 40-foot contour intervals. Thus, we add 20 feet to the elevation of the highest closed contour for a summit without a given elevation. We give unmarked saddles an elevation halfway between the highest contour that does not go through the saddle and the lowest contour that does go through the saddle.

A summit has a **hard rank** if, using either given or interpolated elevations, the summit rises at least 300 feet from its highest connecting saddle to a higher ranked summit. Summits that do not have a hard rank but that could rank if interpolated elevations were *not* used for either the summit or connecting saddle have a **soft rank**. Summits with a soft rank have a left-justified *S* in the Rank column. A right-justified number in the Rank column means the peak has a hard rank. No number in the Rank column means that the peak is named but unranked.

The Mile column shows the straight-line map distance in miles between the peak and its parent. The Quadrangle column gives the USGS 7.5-minute quadrangle that shows the peak's summit. The parent may be on a different quadrangle. The Rg column shows the peak's range as follows: *FR* for Front, *GO* for Gore, *TM* for Tenmile-Mosquito, *SW* for Sawatch, *SC* for Sangre de Cristo, *EL* for Elk and *SJ* for San Juan. The following abbreviations are used: *Pk* for Peak, *Mt* for Mount, *Mtn* for Mountain and *BM* for Benchmark.

PEAKS SORTED BY ELEVATION
Corrections and additions to these tables are posted at:
www.climb.mountains.com/Book_Land_files/Thirteener_files/13ers_List_Fixes.htm

Rank	Elev	Peak Name	Parent	Mile	Rise	Quadrangle	Rg
1	14,433	Elbert, Mt	Whitney, Mt	667.0	9,093	Mt Elbert	SW
2	14,421	Massive, Mt	Elbert, Mt	5.1	1,961	Mt Massive	SW
3	14,420	Harvard, Mt	Elbert, Mt	15.0	2,360	Mt Harvard	SW
4	14,345	Blanca Pk	Harvard, Mt	103.0	5,326	Blanca Pk	SC
S	14,340	"North Massive"	Massive, Mt	0.9	280	Mt Massive	SW
5	14,336	La Plata Pk	Elbert, Mt	6.3	2,276	Mt Elbert	SW
6	14,309	Uncompahgre Pk	La Plata Pk	84.0	4,249	Uncompahgre Pk	SJ
	14,300	"Massive Green"	Massive, Mt	0.4	120	Mt Massive	SW
7	14,294	Crestone Pk	Blanca Pk	27.5	4,554	Crestone Pk	SC
8	14,286	Lincoln, Mt	Massive, Mt	22.3	3,866	Alma	TM
9	14,270	Grays Pk	Lincoln, Mt	25.2	2,770	Grays Pk	FR
10	14,269	Antero, Mt	Harvard, Mt	17.7	2,503	Mt Antero	SW
11	14,267	Torreys Pk	Grays Pk	0.6	560	Grays Pk	FR
12	14,265	Castle Pk	La Plata Pk	20.8	2,337	Hayden Pk	EL
13	14,265	Quandary Pk	Lincoln, Mt	3.2	1,125	Breckenridge	TM
14	14,264	Evans, Mt	Grays Pk	9.8	2,764	Mt Evans	FR
	14,260	"East Crestone"	Crestone Pk	0.1	80	Crestone Pk	SC
	14,260	"Northeast Crestone"	Crestone Pk	0.1	120	Crestone Pk	SC
	14,256	"West Evans"	Evans, Mt	0.3	116	Mt Evans	FR
15	14,255	Longs Pk	Torreys Pk	43.5	2,940	Longs Pk	FR
16	14,246	Wilson, Mt	Uncompahgre Pk	33.1	4,026	Mt Wilson	SJ
	14,238	Cameron, Mt	Lincoln, Mt	0.5	138	Alma	TM
17	14,229	Shavano, Mt	Antero, Mt	3.8	1,619	Maysville	SW
18	14,197	Belford, Mt	Harvard, Mt	3.3	1,337	Mt Harvard	SW
19	14,197	Crestone Needle	Crestone Pk	0.5	457	Crestone Pk	SC
20	14,197	Princeton, Mt	Antero, Mt	5.2	2,431	Mt Antero	SW
21	14,196	Yale, Mt	Harvard, Mt	5.6	1,896	Mt Yale	SW
	14,180	"East La Plata"	La Plata Pk	0.2	80	Mt Elbert	SW
22	14,172	Bross, Mt	Lincoln, Mt	1.1	312	Alma	TM
23	14,165	Kit Carson Mtn	Crestone Pk	1.3	1,025	Crestone Pk	SC
	14,159	El Diente	Wilson, Mt	0.8	259	Dolores Pk	SJ
24	14,156	Maroon Pk	Castle Pk	8.1	2,336	Maroon Bells	EL
25	14,155	Tabeguache Pk	Shavano, Mt	0.7	455	Saint Elmo	SW
26	14,153	Oxford, Mt	Belford, Mt	1.2	653	Mt Harvard	SW
27	14,150	Sneffels, Mt	Wilson, Mt	15.8	3,930	Mt Sneffels	SJ
28	14,148	Democrat, Mt	Lincoln, Mt	1.7	768	Climax	TM
	14,134	"South Elbert"	Elbert, Mt	1.0	234	Mt Elbert	SW
	14,132	"South Massive"	Massive, Mt	0.7	232	Mt Massive	SW
29	14,130	Capitol Pk	Maroon Pk	7.5	1,750	Capitol Pk	EL
30	14,110	Pikes Pk	Evans, Mt	60.3	5,530	Pikes Pk	FR
	14,110	"South Wilson"	Wilson, Mt	0.3	170	Mt Wilson	SJ
	14,100	"West Wilson"	Wilson, Mt	0.3	120	Mt Wilson	SJ
31	14,092	Snowmass Mtn	Capitol Pk	2.3	1,152	Snowmass Mtn	EL
32	14,083	Eolus, Mt	Wilson, Mt	25.5	3,863	Columbine Pass	SJ
33	14,082	Windom Pk	Eolus, Mt	1.7	1,022	Columbine Pass	SJ
34	14,081	Challenger Point	Kit Carson Mtn	0.2	301	Crestone Pk	SC
35	14,073	Columbia, Mt	Harvard, Mt	1.9	893	Mt Harvard	SW
36	14,067	Missouri Mtn	Belford, Mt	1.3	847	Winfield	SW
37	14,064	Humboldt Pk	Crestone Needle	1.4	1,204	Crestone Pk	SC
38	14,060	Bierstadt, Mt	Evans, Mt	1.4	720	Mt Evans	FR
	14,060	Conundrum Pk	Castle Pk	0.4	240	Hayden Pk	EL
	14,060	"Southeast Longs"	Longs Pk	0.2	240	Longs Pk	FR
39	14,059	Sunlight Pk	Windom Pk	0.5	399	Storm King Pk	SJ
40	14,048	Handies Pk	Uncompahgre Pk	11.2	2,148	Handies Pk	SJ
41	14,047	Culebra Pk	Blanca Pk	25.0	4,667	Culebra Pk	SC
42	14,042	Ellingwood Point	Blanca Pk	0.5	342	Blanca Pk	SC

Rank	Elev	Peak Name	Parent	Mile	Rise	Quadrangle	Rg
43	14,042	Lindsey, Mt	Blanca Pk	2.3	1,542	Blanca Pk	SC
	14,039	North Eolus	Eolus, Mt	0.2	179	Storm King Pk	SJ
44	14,037	Little Bear Pk	Blanca Pk	1.0	377	Blanca Pk	SC
45	14,036	Sherman, Mt	Democrat, Mt	8.1	896	Mt Sherman	TM
46	14,034	Redcloud Pk	Handies Pk	4.9	1,454	Redcloud Pk	SJ
	14,020	"North Snowmass"	Snowmass Mtn	0.2	40	Snowmass Mtn	EL
	14,020	"Northwest Lindsey"	Lindsey, Mt	0.2	40	Blanca Pk	SC
	14,020	"South Bross"	Bross, Mt	0.6	80	Alma	TM
	14,020	"South Little Bear"	Little Bear Pk	0.2	80	Blanca Pk	SC
47	14,018	Pyramid Pk	Maroon Pk	2.1	1,518	Maroon Bells	EL
48	14,017	Wilson Pk	Wilson, Mt	1.5	877	Mt Wilson	SJ
49	14,015	Wetterhorn Pk	Uncompahgre Pk	2.8	1,635	Wetterhorn Pk	SJ
	14,014	North Maroon Pk	Maroon Pk	0.4	234	Maroon Bells	EL
50	14,014	San Luis Pk	Redcloud Pk	27.1	3,116	San Luis Pk	SJ
51	14,005	Holy Cross, Mt of the	Massive, Mt	18.9	2,105	Mt of the Holy Cross	SW
52	14,003	Huron Pk	Missouri Mtn	3.2	1,503	Winfield	SW
53	14,001	Sunshine Pk	Redcloud Pk	1.3	501	Redcloud Pk	SJ
	13,995	"Sunlight Spire"	Sunlight Pk	0.2	215	Storm King Pk	SJ
54	13,988	Grizzly Pk A	La Plata Pk	6.7	1,928	Independence Pass	SW
55	13,983	Stewart Pk	San Luis Pk	2.5	883	Stewart Pk	SJ
56	13,980	"Kat Carson"	Kit Carson Mtn	0.2	360	Crestone Pk	SC
	13,980	"Kitty Kat Carson"	"Kat Carson"	0.1	80	Crestone Pk	SC
	13,980	"Prow, The"	Kit Carson Mtn	0.1	40	Crestone Pk	SC
57	13,972	Pigeon Pk	Eolus, Mt	1.5	1,152	Snowdon Pk	SJ
58	13,971	Ouray, Mt	Shavano, Mt	13.5	2,671	Mt Ouray	SW
59	13,951	Fletcher Mtn	Quandary Pk	1.2	611	Copper Mtn	TM
	13,951	Gemini Pk	Sherman, Mt	0.7	171	Mt Sherman	TM
60	13,951	Ice Mtn	Huron Pk	2.1	1,011	Winfield	SW
61	13,950	Pacific Pk	Fletcher Mtn	1.4	570	Breckenridge	TM
62	13,943	Cathedral Pk	Castle Pk	1.7	523	Hayden Pk	EL
63	13,940	French Mtn	Elbert, Mt	2.1	1,080	Mt Massive	SW
64	13,933	Hope, Mt	La Plata Pk	2.9	873	Mt Elbert	SW
65	13,932	"Thunder Pyramid"	Pyramid Pk	0.6	312	Maroon Bells	EL
66	13,931	Adams, Mt	Kit Carson Mtn	1.9	871	Horn Pk	SC
67	13,913	Gladstone Pk	Wilson, Mt	0.6	733	Mt Wilson	SJ
68	13,911	Meeker, Mt	Longs Pk	0.7	451	Allens Park	FR
69	13,908	Casco Pk	French Mtn	1.2	648	Mt Elbert	SW
70	13,908	Red Mtn A	Culebra Pk	0.7	448	Culebra Pk	SC
71	13,904	Emerald Pk	Missouri Mtn	1.3	564	Winfield	SW
S	13,900	"Drift Pk"	Fletcher Mtn	0.6	280	Copper Mtn	TM
72	13,898	Horseshoe Mtn	Sherman, Mt	2.8	758	Mt Sherman	TM
73	13,895	"Phoenix Pk"	San Luis Pk	5.0	1,515	Halfmoon Pass	SJ
74	13,894	Vermillion Pk	Gladstone Pk	9.2	3,674	Ophir	SJ
	13,876	Frasco BM	French Mtn	0.5	256	Mt Massive	SW
75	13,870	"North Carbonate"	Antero, Mt	2.4	1,050	Saint Elmo	SW
76	13,865	Buckskin, Mt	Democrat, Mt	1.5	725	Climax	TM
77	13,864	Vestal Pk	Sunlight Pk	4.3	1,124	Storm King Pk	SJ
78	13,860	Jones Mtn A	Handies Pk	1.7	520	Handies Pk	SJ
	13,860	Meeker Ridge	Meeker, Mt	0.2	40	Allens Park	FR
79	13,860	North Apostle	Ice Mtn	0.4	400	Winfield	SW
80	13,857	Clinton Pk	Democrat, Mt	2.0	517	Climax	TM
81	13,855	Dyer Mtn	Sherman, Mt	1.2	475	Mt Sherman	TM
82	13,852	Crystal Pk	Pacific Pk	0.9	632	Breckenridge	TM
	13,852	Traver Pk	Clinton Pk	0.7	232	Climax	TM
83	13,850	Edwards, Mt	Grays Pk	1.3	470	Grays Pk	FR
84	13,849	California Pk	Ellingwood Point	2.2	629	Blanca Pk	SC
85	13,845	Oklahoma, Mt	Massive, Mt	1.8	745	Mt Champion	SW
	13,842	Spalding, Mt	Evans, Mt	1.1	262	Mt Evans	FR

Rank	Elev	Peak Name	Parent	Mile	Rise	Quadrangle	Rg
86	13,841	"Atlantic Pk"	Fletcher Mtn	0.7	421	Copper Mtn	TM
87	13,841	Hagerman Pk	Snowmass Mtn	0.6	341	Snowmass Mtn	EL
88	13,841	Half Pk	Handies Pk	3.9	1,501	Pole Creek Mtn	SJ
89	13,835	Turret Pk	Pigeon Pk	0.5	735	Snowdon Pk	SJ
90	13,832	Point 13,832	Redcloud Pk	1.4	812	Redcloud Pk	SJ
91	13,831	Holy Cross Ridge	Holy Cross, Mt of the	0.6	331	Mt of the Holy Cross	SW
S	13,831	Iowa Pk	Missouri Mtn	0.6	291	Winfield	SW
92	13,830	Jupiter Mtn	Windom Pk	0.6	370	Columbine Pass	SJ
93	13,828	"Huerfano Pk"	Lindsey, Mt	1.2	688	Blanca Pk	SC
94	13,824	Jagged Mtn	Sunlight Pk	1.4	964	Storm King Pk	SJ
95	13,823	"Lackawanna Pk"	Casco Pk	1.8	883	Independence Pass	SW
96	13,822	Silverheels, Mt	Bross, Mt	5.5	2,283	Alma	TM
97	13,821	Rio Grande Pyramid	Jagged Mtn	10.8	1,881	Rio Grande Pyramid	SJ
98	13,819	Teakettle Mtn	Sneffels, Mt	1.7	759	Mt Sneffels	SJ
99	13,811	Point 13,811	Point 13,832	1.2	551	Redcloud Pk	SJ
100	13,809	Dallas Pk	Sneffels, Mt	2.0	869	Telluride	SJ
101	13,807	Niagara Pk	Jones Mtn A	0.6	587	Handies Pk	SJ
102	13,806	"American Pk"	Jones Mtn A	0.8	466	Handies Pk	SJ
103	13,805	Trinity Pk	Vestal Pk	1.2	945	Storm King Pk	SJ
104	13,803	Arrow Pk	Vestal Pk	0.5	943	Storm King Pk	SJ
105	13,803	"Castleabra"	Castle Pk	0.9	423	Maroon Bells	EL
106	13,801	Organ Mtn A	San Luis Pk	2.0	694	San Luis Pk	SJ
107	13,799	"Obstruction Pk"	"Kat Carson"	0.5	339	Crestone Pk	SC
108	13,795	Arkansas Mt	Buckskin Mt	1.9	575	Climax	TM
109	13,795	Point 13,795	Handies Pk	1.3	495	Redcloud Pk	SJ
110	13,794	Rito Alto Pk	Adams, Mt	7.3	1,134	Rito Alto Pk	SC
111	13,794	Square Top Mtn	Edwards, Mt	3.4	814	Montezuma	FR
112	13,786	Animas Mtn	Pigeon Pk	1.2	1,086	Snowdon Pk	SJ
113	13,786	Potosi Pk	Teakettle Mtn	1.0	806	Ironton	SJ
114	13,783	Rinker Pk	La Plata Pk	1.8	923	Mt Elbert	SW
115	13,781	Mosquito Pk	Buckskin, Mt	2.3	561	Climax	TM
116	13,780	Garfield Pk	Grizzly Pk A	0.8	360	Independence Pass	SW
117	13,780	Golden Horn	Vermillion Pk	0.4	400	Ophir	SJ
	13,780	McNamee Pk	Clinton Pk	0.5	80	Climax	TM
118	13,768	Point 13,768	Holy Cross Ridge	0.8	388	Mt of the Holy Cross	SW
119	13,767	US Grant Pk	Golden Horn	1.7	747	Ophir	SJ
120	13,765	Trinity Pk West	Trinity Pk	0.4	385	Storm King Pk	SJ
121	13,762	Point 13,762	Harvard, Mt	2.8	822	Mt Harvard	SW
122	13,761	Bull Hill	Elbert, Mt	1.6	421	Mt Elbert	SW
123	13,761	Deer Mt	Oklahoma, Mt	1.7	941	Mt Champion	SW
	13,761	Fuller Pk	Vermillion Pk	0.5	261	Ophir	SJ
124	13,752	San Miguel Pk	Vermillion Pk	2.4	1,307	Ophir	SJ
125	13,752	Storm King Pk	Trinity Pk	1.3	612	Storm King Pk	SJ
126	13,748	Sheridan, Mt	Sherman, Mt	1.3	608	Mt Sherman	TM
127	13,745	Aetna, Mt	Tabeguache Pk	4.7	1,245	Garfield	SW
128	13,745	Trinity Pk East	Trinity Pk	0.2	405	Storm King Pk	SJ
S	13,741	"West Dallas"	Dallas Pk	0.6	281	Telluride	SJ
S	13,740	"West Eolus"	Eolus, Mt	0.3	280	Mtn View Crest	SJ
	13,739	Ptarmigan Pk	Horseshoe Mtn	2.5	279	Mt Sherman	TM
129	13,738	Argentine Pk	Edwards, Mt	1.9	638	Montezuma	FR
130	13,738	Grizzly Pk B	San Miguel Pk	1.6	758	Ophir	SJ
131	13,738	Pilot Knob	Golden Horn	0.5	398	Ophir	SJ
132	13,738	Sayers BM	La Plata Pk	1.9	958	Mt Elbert	SW
133	13,736	Point 13,736	Deer Mtn	1.2	676	Mt Champion	SW
134	13,735	"T 0"	Dallas Pk	1.4	395	Telluride	SJ
135	13,723	Vermejo Pk	Red Mtn A	1.3	761	Culebra Pk	SC
136	13,722	"Animas Forks Mtn"	Handies Pk	3.5	1,142	Handies Pk	SJ
137	13,722	Point 13,722	"Thunder Pyramid"	0.4	302	Maroon Bells	EL

Rank	Elev	Peak Name	Parent	Mile	Rise	Quadrangle	Rg
138	13,716	Pole Creek Mtn	Half Pk	5.2	1,536	Pole Creek Mtn	SJ
139	13,714	Silver Mtn A	Uncompahgre Pk	2.5	1,054	Uncompahgre Pk	SJ
140	13,712	Point 13,712	Shavano, Mt	0.9	332	Mt Antero	SW
141	13,711	Twining Pk	Point 13,736	2.2	1,251	Mt Champion	SW
	13,710	La Garita Pk	"Phoenix Pk"	1.9	232	Halfmoon Pass	SJ
142	13,708	Grizzly Mtn	"North Carbonate"	1.7	568	Saint Elmo	SW
S	13,708	Point 13,708	"Animas Forks Mtn"	0.5	288	Handies Pk	SJ
143	13,705	Colony Baldy	Humboldt Pk	1.4	925	Crestone Pk	SC
144	13,705	Six, Pk	Jagged Mtn	1.0	685	Storm King Pk	SJ
	13,705	Thirteen, Pk	Monitor Pk	0.2	245	Storm King Pk	SJ
S	13,704	Glacier Point	Eolus, Mt	0.5	284	Storm King Pk	SJ
S	13,701	Treasurevault Mtn	Mosquito Pk	0.4	281	Climax	TM
145	13,700	Fifteen, Pk	Turret Pk	0.2	320	Snowdon Pk	SJ
146	13,700	Grizzly Pk C	Jupiter Mtn	0.7	440	Columbine Pass	SJ
147	13,698	Baldy Alto	Stewart Pk	1.2	518	Stewart Pk	SJ
148	13,695	Monitor Pk	Animas Mtn	0.5	315	Storm King Pk	SJ
149	13,694	Gilpin Pk	Dallas Pk	1.7	720	Telluride	SJ
	13,694	"Kismet"	Sneffels, Mt	0.4	194	Mt Sneffels	SJ
150	13,693	Rolling Mtn	San Miguel Pk	2.3	913	Ophir	SJ
	13,692	Loveland Mtn	Buckskin, Mt	0.8	192	Climax	TM
151	13,691	Point 13,691	Point 13,832	2.7	471	Redcloud Pk	SJ
152	13,690	Wheeler Mtn	Fletcher Mtn	1.6	310	Copper Mtn	TM
153	13,688	Point 13,688 A	Point 13,832	1.6	428	Redcloud Pk	SJ
154	13,688	Point 13,688 B	"Animas Forks Mtn"	1.1	388	Handies Pk	SJ
155	13,686	Cirque Mtn	Teakettle Mtn	0.6	546	Mt Sneffels	SJ
156	13,684	Bald Mtn	Silverheels, Mt	7.6	2,104	Boreas Pass	FR
157	13,684	Oso, Mt	Grizzly "Pk C"	4.9	1,664	Emerald Lake	SJ
	13,684	White Ridge	Sherman, Mt	1.2	184	Mt Sherman	TM
158	13,682	Seven, Pk	Six, Pk	0.8	422	Storm King Pk	SJ
159	13,681	Point 13,681	Silver Mtn A	1.0	501	Uncompahgre Pk	SJ
160	13,676	Purgatoire Pk	Vermejo Pk	1.8	849	Culebra Pk	SC
161	13,674	Point 13,674	Half Pk	1.3	374	Redcloud Pk	SJ
162	13,672	Tweto, Mt	Buckskin, Mt	1.2	412	Climax	TM
163	13,670	Jackson, Mt	Holy Cross, Mt of the	3.2	1,810	Mt Jackson	SW
164	13,667	White, Mt	Antero, Mt	1.3	847	Mt Antero	SW
	13,664	"K2"	Capitol Pk	0.5	84	Capitol Pk	EL
165	13,663	Carbonate Mtn	"North Carbonate"	2.0	434	Saint Elmo	SW
166	13,661	Lookout Pk	Gilpin Pk	8.6	841	Ophir	SJ
167	13,660	Point 13,660 A	California Pk	1.1	400	Twin Pks	SC
168	13,660	Point 13,660 B	Pole Creek Mtn	1.5	840	Pole Creek Mtn	SJ
S	13,660	Point 13,660 C	"Lackawanna Pk"	0.9	280	Independence Pass	SW
169	13,660	Wood Mtn	Point 13,688 B	0.5	320	Handies Pk	SJ
	13,658	Hamilton Pk	Blanca Pk	1.5	278	Blanca Pk	SC
170	13,657	Carson Pk	Half Pk	3.6	1,477	Pole Creek Mtn	SJ
171	13,656	Coxcomb Pk	Wetterhorn Pk	1.8	796	Wetterhorn Pk	SJ
172	13,651	Taylor Mtn	Aetna, Mt	1.2	631	Garfield	SW
173	13,646	Champion, Mt	Point 13,736	0.6	306	Mt Champion	SW
174	13,646	Point 13,646	Grizzly Mtn	1.7	546	Saint Elmo	SW
175	13,642	Redcliff	Coxcomb Pk	0.5	502	Wetterhorn Pk	SJ
176	13,641	Bard Pk	Torreys Pk	5.5	1,651	Grays Pk	FR
177	13,635	"Electric Pk"	Cathedral Pk	0.9	335	Hayden Pk	EL
178	13,633	Pk 10	Crystal Pk	0.9	373	Breckenridge	TM
179	13,631	Point 13,631 A	Garfield Pk	2.2	971	New York Pk	SW
180	13,631	Point 13,631 B	Point 13,722	0.7	331	Maroon Bells	EL
	13,630	"Esprit Point"	Shavano, Mt	0.8	250	Maysville	SW
181	13,628	Silex, Mt	Storm King Pk	0.8	808	Storm King Pk	SJ
182	13,627	White Dome	Trinity Pk East	2.2	967	Storm King Pk	SJ
183	13,626	Point 13,626	Princeton, Mt	1.4	486	Mt Yale	SW

Rank	Elev	Peak Name	Parent	Mile	Rise	Quadrangle	Rg
184	13,626	West Spanish Pk	Culebra Pk	20.4	3,685	Spanish Pks	SC
	13,620	Snowmass Pk	Hagerman Pk	0.2	120	Snowmass Mtn	EL
185	13,617	Guardian, The	Silex, Mt	0.6	557	Storm King Pk	SJ
186	13,616	Point 13,616	La Plata Pk	1.6	436	Mt Elbert	SW
	13,615	Father Dyer Pk	Crystal Pk	0.6	115	Breckenridge	TM
187	13,614	North Star Mtn	Wheeler Mtn	0.9	434	Breckenridge	TM
188	13,611	Pico Asilado	Crestone Needle	1.7	831	Crestone Pk	SC
	13,604	Jones Pk	Point 13,712	0.7	144	Mt Antero	SW
189	13,604	Tijeras Pk	Pico Asilado	1.7	744	Crestone Pk	SC
190	13,602	Gray Wolf Mtn	Evans, Mt	2.2	582	Mt Evans	FR
	13,599	"North Crown Mtn"	Niagara Pk	0.6	259	Handies Pk	SJ
191	13,598	Electric Pk A	Rito Alto Pk	6.1	938	Electric Pk	SC
192	13,596	Cyclone Mtn	Carbonate Mtn	0.5	336	Saint Elmo	SW
193	13,590	Matterhorn Pk	Wetterhorn Pk	0.9	570	Uncompahgre Pk	SJ
194	13,589	One, Pk	White Dome	0.8	409	Storm King Pk	SJ
195	13,588	Cottonwood Pk	Electric Pk A	3.7	1,128	Valley View Hot Spgs	SC
	13,587	McClellan Mtn	Edwards, Mt	0.8	167	Grays Pk	FR
196	13,581	Emma, Mt	Gilpin Pk	0.8	561	Telluride	SJ
197	13,581	Point 13,581	Carson Pk	1.5	681	Pole Creek Mtn	SJ
198	13,580	Clark Pk	Capitol Pk	1.2	440	Capitol Pk	EL
199	13,580	Point 13,580 A	Point 13,581	1.2	360	Pole Creek Mtn	SJ
200	13,580	Point 13,580 B	Adams, Mt	0.5	440	Horn Pk	SC
S	13,580	Point 13,580 C	Harvard, Mt	1.0	280	Mt Harvard	SW
201	13,580	Powell, Mt (Pk B)	Jackson, Mt	21.8	3,000	Mt Powell	GO
202	13,580	Twin Pks A	Ellingwood Point	1.6	640	Twin Pks	SC
203	13,579	Chiefs Head Pk	Longs Pk	1.4	719	Isolation Pk	FR
204	13,577	Evans B, Mt	Dyer Mt	1.2	317	Climax	TM
	13,577	Gravel Mtn	Point 13,688 B	0.4	157	Handies Pk	SJ
205	13,577	Point 13,577	Point 13,660 A	0.5	317	Blanca Pk	SC
206	13,575	Greylock Mtn	Windom Pk	1.2	555	Columbine Pass	SJ
207	13,575	Rosalie Pk	Evans A, Mt	3.0	675	Harris Park	FR
208	13,574	Parnassus, Mt	Bard Pk	1.0	537	Grays Pk	FR
209	13,573	Broken Hand Pk	Crestone Needle	0.8	673	Crestone Pk	SC
	13,572	Weston Pk	Horseshoe Mtn	3.6	272	Mt Sherman	TM
	13,569	Crown Mtn	Niagara Pk	0.6	229	Handies Pk	SJ
	13,568	"Coffeepot"	Teakettle Mtn	0.4	188	Telluride	SJ
210	13,568	West Apostle	Ice Mtn	0.6	508	Winfield	SW
211	13,566	Point 13,566	Point 13,691	1.9	746	Redcloud Pk	SJ
212	13,565	Point 13,565	Culebra Pk	1.4	545	El Valle Creek	SC
	13,561	Hayden Pk	"Electric Pk"	0.8	181	Hayden Pk	EL
213	13,560	Hagues Pk	Longs Pk	16.0	2,420	Trail Ridge	FR
214	13,555	Bartlett Mtn	Clinton Pk	0.8	615	Copper Mtn	SW
S	13,555	Point 13,555	"Huerfano Pk"	1.0	295	Blanca Pk	SC
215	13,555	Wasatch Mtn	Lookout Pk	2.1	495	Telluride	SJ
216	13,554	Fluted Pk	Adams, Mt	1.2	734	Horn Pk	SC
217	13,554	McCauley Pk	Grizzly Pk C	0.7	454	Columbine Pass	SJ
218	13,553	Gibbs Pk	Rito Alto Pk	4.2	693	Electric Pk	SC
	13,553	Mamma, Mt	Point 13,646	0.5	53	Saint Elmo	SW
219	13,553	Pettingell Pk	Torreys Pk	7.4	1,563	Loveland Pass	FR
220	13,552	Tower Mtn	Niagara Pk	5.4	1,652	Howardsville	SJ
221	13,550	Point 13,550	"Castleabra"	0.9	530	Gothic	EL
S	13,548	Point 13,548	Mosquito Pk	0.7	288	Climax	TM
222	13,546	Point 13,546	Adams, Mt	0.8	646	Horn Pk	SC
S	13,545	Point 13,545	Twining Pk	0.7	285	Mt Champion	SW
223	13,542	Whitecross Mtn	Handies Pk	1.4	562	Redcloud Pk	SJ
224	13,541	Point 13,541	Point 13,580 B	0.8	361	Crestone Pk	SC
225	13,540	Eleven, Pk	Sunlight Pk	0.6	400	Storm King Pk	SJ

Rank	Elev	Peak Name	Parent	Mile	Rise	Quadrangle	Rg
226	13,540	Point 13,540 A	Wilson Pk	1.0	520	Dolores Pk	SJ
227	13,540	Point 13,540 B	Wood Mtn	2.6	520	Redcloud Pk	SJ
228	13,540	"V 4"	US Grant Pk	0.4	320	Ophir	SJ
229	13,540	White Rock Mtn	Point 13,550	2.8	800	Gothic	EL
230	13,538	Emma Burr Mtn	Princeton, Mt	9.6	1,238	Cumberland Pass	SW
231	13,537	Point 13,537	White Rock Mtn	2.5	757	Maroon Bells	EL
232	13,535	"K49"	Deer Mtn	1.2	555	Mt Champion	SW
233	13,535	Point 13,535	Jones Mtn A	1.5	515	Handies Pk	SJ
234	13,531	Point 13,531	Hope, Mt	1.5	431	Mt Elbert	SW
235	13,530	"Epaulie"	Rosalie Pk	1.2	350	Harris Park	FR
236	13,528	Boulder Mtn	Point 13,646	1.6	588	Saint Elmo	SW
237	13,528	Leviathan Pk	Jagged Mtn	0.7	588	Storm King Pk	SJ
238	13,528	Treasure Mtn	Hagerman Pk	7.0	2,821	Snowmass Mtn	EL
239	13,528	"V 3"	US Grant Pk	0.4	388	Ophir	SJ
240	13,524	Point 13,524 A	Carson Pk	1.4	464	Pole Creek Mtn	SJ
241	13,524	Point 13,524 B	Gibbs Pk	3.3	624	Rito Alto Pk	SC
	13,523	Browns Pk	Huron Pk	0.7	183	Winfield	SW
	13,523	Epaulet Mtn	"Epaulie"	0.5	143	Mt Evans	FR
242	13,522	Milwaukee Pk	Pico Asilado	0.5	302	Crestone Pk	SC
243	13,521	Star Pk	Castle Pk	4.1	816	Pearl Pass	EL
244	13,517	Point 13,517 A	Huron Pk	1.5	457	Winfield	SW
S	13,517	Point 13,517 B	Point 13,580 B	0.4	297	Crestone Pk	SC
245	13,517	Trinchera Pk	Point 13,565	10.3	977	Trinchera Pk	SC
246	13,516	Keefe Pk	Point 13,537	1.3	496	Maroon Bells	EL
247	13,514	Ypsilon Mtn	Hagues Pk	2.6	1,116	Trail Ridge	FR
248	13,513	Point 13,513	Gibbs Pk	2.4	453	Electric Pk	SC
249	13,510	Point 13,510 A	San Luis Pk	7.8	1,570	Baldy Cinco	SJ
250	13,510	Point 13,510 B	Emma, Mt	5.0	610	Ironton	SJ
251	13,510	"T 11"	Lookout Pk	1.3	452	Telluride	SJ
S	13,509	Telluride Pk	Point 13,510 A	0.5	289	Ironton	SJ
252	13,507	Eureka Mtn	Rito Alto Pk	2.0	807	Rito Alto Pk	SC
253	13,505	Point 13,505	Point 13,631 A	1.3	525	New York Pk	SW
254	13,502	Fairchild Mtn	Ypsilon Mtn	1.2	922	Trail Ridge	FR
255	13,502	North Arapaho Pk	Chiefs Head Pk	15.4	1,665	Monarch Lake	FR
	13,500	Iron Nipple	"Huerfano Pk"	0.6	200	Blanca Pk	SC
	13,500	Needle Ridge	Sunlight Pk	0.4	200	Storm King Pk	SJ
256	13,500	Point 13,500	Twining Pk	0.7	360	Independence Pass	SW
	13,500	Red Mtn B	Garfield Pk	0.4	120	Independence Pass	SW
	13,500	Sixteen, Pk	Fifteen, Pk	0.1	80	Snowdon Pk	SJ
257	13,498	Point 13,498	Point 13,540 A	0.6	358	Dolores Pk	SJ
258	13,497	Hunter Pk	Keefe Pk	1.4	477	Maroon Bells	EL
259	13,497	Pagoda Mtn	Longs Pk	0.7	397	Isolation Pk	FR
260	13,496	Mears Pk	"T 0"	1.3	556	Mt Sneffels	SJ
261	13,492	Whitehouse Mtn	Teakettle Mtn	1.9	592	Ouray	SJ
262	13,490	Marcy, Mt	Point 13,513	1.2	430	Electric Pk	SC
263	13,490	Point 13,490	Point 13,513	1.0	990	Rito Alto Pk	SC
264	13,489	Graystone Pk	Arrow Pk	0.6	509	Storm King Pk	SJ
265	13,487	Cuatro Pk	Trinchera Pk	2.2	707	Trinchera Pk	SC
266	13,487	Storm Pk A	Tower Mtn	1.4	627	Silverton	SJ
267	13,481	Three Needles	"T 11"	1.0	421	Telluride	SJ
268	13,478	Canby Mtn	Niagara Pk	6.2	938	Howardsville	SJ
269	13,478	Three, Pk	Trinity Pk East	0.9	498	Storm King Pk	SJ
270	13,477	"T 10"	Three Needles	0.6	537	Ironton	SJ
271	13,475	Two, Pk	Three, Pk	0.8	535	Storm King Pk	SJ
272	13,475	"V 10"	Grizzly Pk B	0.7	375	Ophir	SJ
273	13,472	La Junta Pk	Wasatch Mtn	0.7	612	Telluride	SJ
	13,472	Eighteen, Pk	Windom Pk	0.5	212	Columbine Pass	SJ
274	13,472	Point 13,472 A	Ouray, Mt	1.9	1,172	Mt Ouray	SW

Rank	Elev	Peak Name	Parent	Mile	Rise	Quadrangle	Rg
S	13,472	Point 13,472 B	Point 13,517 A	0.5	292	Winfield	SW
275	13,470	Silver Mtn B	Wasatch Mtn	2.2	410	Telluride	SJ
S	13,468	Miranda Pk	Point 13,565	0.9	288	El Valle Creek	SC
276	13,468	Ridgeway, Mt	Teakettle Mtn	1.0	448	Mt Sneffels	SJ
S	13,467	"Big Blue Pk"	Silver Mtn A	0.8	287	Uncompahgre Pk	SJ
277	13,466	"Alamosito"	Vermejo Pk	1.2	557	Culebra Pk	SC
278	13,463	Point 13,463	Garfield Pk	1.8	563	Independence Pass	SW
279	13,462	Point 13,462 A	Huron Pk	1.1	322	Winfield	SW
280	13,462	Point 13,462 B	Point 13,517 A	1.6	562	Winfield	SW
281	13,462	Treasury Mtn	Treasure Mtn	1.4	522	Snowmass Mtn	EL
282	13,461	Quail Mtn	Hope, Mt	1.4	921	Mt Elbert	SW
S	13,460	"East Windom"	Windom Pk	0.6	280	Columbine Pass	SJ
283	13,460	Point 13,460	Sayers BM	1.4	440	Independence Pass	SW
284	13,460	San Joaquin Ridge	Silver Mtn B	1.3	360	Telluride	SJ
285	13,460	Sleeping Sexton	North Maroon Pk	0.6	440	Maroon Bells	EL
286	13,455	Ute Ridge	White Dome	4.9	962	Rio Grande Pyramid	SJ
287	13,454	Hanson Pk	Tower Mtn	3.6	914	Handies Pk	SJ
288	13,454	"Campbell Creek Pk"	Point 13,795	1.0	394	Redcloud Pk	SJ
289	13,451	Kendall Pk	Canby Mtn	4.1	1,311	Howardsville	SJ
290	13,450	Horn Pk	Fluted Pk	1.3	710	Horn Pk	SC
291	13,450	Point 13,450	Carson Pk	1.2	350	Pole Creek Mtn	SJ
	13,447	Hurricane Pk	Hanson Pk	0.8	267	Handies Pk	SJ
292	13,441	Apache Pk	North Arapaho Pk	2.2	1,101	Monarch Lake	FR
293	13,441	"S 6"	"T 0"	1.0	381	Mt Sneffels	SJ
294	13,436	"T 5"	Emma, Mt	1.8	416	Telluride	SJ
295	13,435	"Mascot Pk"	Yale, Mt	0.8	375	Mt Yale	SW
296	13,435	Taylor Pk A	Star Pk	1.3	815	Pearl Pass	EL
297	13,434	Point 13,434	Kendall Pk	1.2	534	Howardsville	SJ
298	13,433	Point 13,433	Jackson, Mt	0.6	413	Mt Jackson	SW
299	13,432	Jenkins Mtn	Sayres BM	4.0	692	Pieplant	SW
S	13,432	"Oscar's Pk"	Wasatch Mtn	1.0	292	Telluride	SJ
300	13,432	"Sundog"	Sunshine Pk	0.9	332	Redcloud Pk	SJ
301	13,432	Twin Sister East	Rolling Mtn	2.2	1,332	Ophir	SJ
	13,430	Gray Needle	Jagged Mtn	0.3	130	Storm King Pk	SJ
302	13,428	Vallecito Mtn	Leviathan Pk	0.5	568	Storm King Pk	SJ
303	13,427	Grizzly "Pk D"	Torreys Pk	1.5	847	Grays Pk	FR
304	13,427	Point 13,427	Wood Mtn	1.4	407	Handies Pk	SJ
305	13,425	Mummy Mtn	Hagues Pk	1.4	485	Estes Park	FR
306	13,423	Spread Eagle Pk	Point 13,524 B	0.9	443	Electric Pk	SC
307	13,420	Eagles Nest (Pk A)	Powell, Mt	1.2	640	Mt Powell	GO
	13,420	Index, The	Animas Mtn	0.2	240	Snowdon Pk	SJ
	13,420	Rowe Pk	Hagues Pk	0.4	200	Trail Ridge	FR
308	13,420	"Siberia Pk"	Snowmass Mtn	1.2	760	Snowmass Mtn	EL
S	13,420	Ten, Pk	Jagged Mtn	0.3	280	Storm King Pk	SJ
	13,420	Twin Thumbs	Eleven, Pk	0.2	120	Storm King Pk	SJ
309	13,417	"SoSo, Mt"	Oso, Mt	0.8	677	Emerald Lake	SJ
310	13,416	Little Giant Pk	Kendall Pk	1.3	556	Howardsville	SJ
311	13,414	Cleveland Pk	Tijeras Pk	1.4	434	Crestone Pk	SC
312	13,411	"Heisshorn"	Wetterhorn Pk	1.2	471	Wetterhorn Pk	SJ
313	13,410	Four, Pk	Six, Pk	1.2	510	Storm King Pk	SJ
	13,409	Finnback Knob	Horseshoe Mtn	0.6	149	Mt Sherman	TM
314	13,409	Hilliard Pk	Keefe Pk	0.6	309	Maroon Bells	EL
315	13,409	Navajo Pk	Apache Pk	0.4	309	Monarch Lake	FR
316	13,408	Wilcox, Mt	Argentine Pk	1.1	548	Montezuma	FR
317	13,405	Mariquita Pk	Cuatro Pk	1.4	385	El Valle Creek	SC
318	13,402	Nine, Pk	Storm King Pk	0.5	582	Storm King Pk	SJ
319	13,402	Point 13,402	"Phoenix Pk"	1.7	422	Halfmoon Pass	SJ
320	13,402	Rhoda, Mt	Point 13,434	0.4	302	Howardsville	SJ

Rank	Elev	Peak Name	Parent	Mile	Rise	Quadrangle	Rg
	13,401	Baldy Chato	Stewart Pk	1.5	181	Stewart Pk	SJ
321	13,401	Point 13,401	Tijeras Pk	0.9	301	Crestone Pk	SC
322	13,401	White BM	White Rock Mtn	0.5	381	Gothic	EL
	13,397	South Arapaho Pk	North Arapaho Pk	0.5	97	Monarch Lake	FR
323	13,393	Bent Pk	Carson Pk	1.2	373	Pole Creek Mtn	SJ
324	13,391	Parry Pk	North Arapaho Pk	12.5	1,720	Empire	FR
325	13,391	Rogers Pk	Evans A, Mt	2.4	515	Harris Park	FR
326	13,385	Chicago Pk	Point 13,510 B	1.8	365	Ironton	SJ
327	13,384	Point 13,384	Cleveland Pk	0.9	364	Crestone Pk	SC
328	13,384	Prize BM	Point 13,631 A	1.6	604	Pieplant	SW
329	13,383	Baldy Cinco	Point 13,510 A	1.9	843	Baldy Cinco	SJ
S	13,382	"East Pole Creek Mtn"	Pole Creek Mtn	0.8	282	Pole Creek Mtn	SJ
330	13,382	Gold Dust Pk	Jackson, Mt	3.1	922	Mt Jackson	SW
331	13,382	Williams Mtn	Twining Pk	4.1	1,682	Mt Champion	SW
332	13,380	Geissler Mtn East	Twining Pk	1.1	560	Mt Champion	SW
333	13,380	Music Mtn	Milwaukee Pk	0.9	400	Crestone Pk	SC
334	13,380	Point 13,380	White Rock Mtn	1.3	480	Gothic	EL
335	13,380	Precarious Pk	Point 13,631 B	2.1	640	Maroon Bells	EL
336	13,380	South Lookout Pk	US Grant Pk	1.2	520	Ophir	SJ
337	13,378	Italian Mtn	Star Pk	3.5	1,358	Pearl Pass	EL
338	13,377	Point 13,377	"Heisshorn"	0.5	357	Wetterhorn Pk	SJ
339	13,375	Lakes Pk	Cottonwood Pk	2.1	675	Electric Pk	SC
340	13,374	Point 13,374	Harvard, Mt	1.9	394	Mt Harvard	SW
341	13,374	Twin Sister West	Twin Sister East	0.4	394	Ophir	SJ
342	13,370	Buckskin BM	Sleeping Sexton	2.0	908	Maroon Bells	EL
343	13,370	Dome Mtn	Tower Mtn	1.3	670	Howardsville	SJ
344	13,370	Guyot, Mt	Bald Mtn	2.0	1,324	Boreas Pass	FR
345	13,369	Monumental Pk	Aetna, Mt	2.1	1,029	Garfield	SW
346	13,368	Sultan Mtn	Twin Sister East	4.6	1,868	Silverton	SJ
347	13,362	De Anza Pk A	Gibbs Pk	1.1	622	Electric Pk	SC
348	13,362	Englemann Pk	Bard Pk	1.8	542	Grays Pk	FR
349	13,362	Pearl Mtn	Castle Pk	2.5	582	Pearl Pass	EL
350	13,359	"T 7"	Point 13,510 B	1.4	499	Ironton	SJ
351	13,357	"Silverthorne, Mt"	Powell, Mt	10.9	1,097	Willow Lakes	GO
352	13,352	Hoosier Ridge	Silverheels, Mt	3.3	932	Breckenridge	TM
353	13,350	Hermit Pk	Rito Alto Pk	0.9	330	Rito Alto Pk	SC
354	13,348	Malemute Pk	Conundrum Pk	1.1	368	Hayden Pk	EL
	13,348	Peerless Mtn	Horseshoe Mtn	0.9	168	Mt Sherman	TM
355	13,346	"North Gold Dust"	Gold Dust Pk	1.3	806	Mt Jackson	SW
356	13,345	Point 13,345	Emma Burr Mtn	1.1	445	Cumberland Pass	SW
357	13,342	Beattie Pk	Vermillion Pk	0.7	322	Ophir	SJ
358	13,342	Point 13,342	Ute Ridge	1.4	726	Rio Grande Pyramid	SJ
	13,340	Glacier Ridge	Longs Pk	0.5	40	Longs Pk	FR
359	13,340	Herard, Mt	Cleveland Pk	4.7	2,040	Medano Pass	SC
360	13,340	Owen A, Mt	Point 13,490	2.0	600	Electric Pk	SC
361	13,340	Point 13,340 A	"SoSo, Mt"	1.2	440	Emerald Lake	SJ
362	13,340	Point 13,340 B	"Heisshorn"	1.7	745	Uncompahgre Pk	SJ
	13,340	Ships Prow	Longs Pk	0.5	40	Longs Pk	FR
363	13,339	Brown Mtn	Hanson Pk	1.8	639	Ironton	SJ
364	13,338	Kendall Mtn	Kendall Pk	0.7	318	Silverton	SJ
365	13,336	Point 13,336	Buckskin BM	1.1	636	Maroon Bells	EL
	13,335	Maxwell, Mt	Mariquita Pk	0.8	275	El Valle Creek	SC
366	13,334	Coney BM	Bent Pk	1.9	994	Finger Mesa	SJ
367	13,334	Venable Pk	Fluted Pk	2.7	634	Rito Alto Pk	SC
368	13,333	De Anza Pk B	Mariquita Pk	1.0	473	El Valle Creek	SC
	13,333	"East Thorn"	"Silverthorne, Mt"	0.5	233	Willow Lakes	GO
	13,333	Twin Pks B	Rinker Pk	0.9	233	Mt Elbert	SW
369	13,330	"Proposal Pk"	Hanson Pk	1.9	550	Handies Pk	SJ
370	13,328	Cinnamon Mtn	Point 13,535 B	1.1	308	Handies Pk	SJ

Rank	Elev	Peak Name	Parent	Mile	Rise	Quadrangle	Rg
371	13,327	McHenrys Pk	Chiefs Head Pk	1.2	907	McHenrys Pk	FR
	13,326	Storm Pk B	Longs Pk	0.8	186	Longs Pk	FR
372	13,326	West Buffalo Pk	Point 13,374	9.7	1,986	Marmot Pk	TM
373	13,325	Point 13,325	Storm Pk A	0.5	465	Silverton	SJ
	13,322	Leahy Pk	"Electric Pk"	0.9	142	Hayden Pk	EL
374	13,322	Point 13,322	Jenkins Mtn	2.4	902	Pieplant	SW
375	13,321	Sunshine Mtn	Point 13,540 B	2.5	1,421	Handies Pk	SJ
376	13,321	Trico Pk	Point 13,510 B	0.9	461	Ironton	SJ
	13,319	Palmyra Pk	Silver Mtn B	0.5	179	Telluride	SJ
377	13,317	Point 13,317	Point 13,626	2.3	737	Saint Elmo	SW
378	13,315	"T 8"	"T 7"	0.7	495	Ironton	SJ
379	13,313	Point 13,313	Baldy Cinco	0.7	413	Baldy Cinco	SJ
380	13,312	Point 13,312 A	Point 13,566	0.8	452	Redcloud Pk	SJ
381	13,312	Point 13,312 B	Pearl Mtn	0.6	412	Pearl Pass	EL
382	13,312	Point 13,312 C	Point 13,463	1.0	452	Pieplant	SW
383	13,312	Williams Mtn South A	Williams Mtn	1.5	572	Thimble Rock	SW
384	13,310	Alice, Mt	Chiefs Head Pk	1.4	850	Isolation Pk	FR
385	13,310	Aztec Mtn	Jupiter Mtn	1.9	610	Columbine Pass	SJ
	13,310	Emery Pk	Point 13,330	0.4	130	Handies Pk	SJ
386	13,310	Point 13,310	Point 13,340 A	0.6	330	Emerald Lake	SJ
	13,309	Echo Mtn	McCauley Mtn	0.5	209	Columbine Pass	SJ
387	13,309	"V 2"	US Grant Pk	0.8	409	Ophir	SJ
388	13,308	Point 13,308	Point 13,342	0.8	606	Rio Grande Pyramid	SJ
389	13,307	Warren, Mt	Rogers Pk	1.1	367	Mt Evans	FR
390	13,302	Point 13,302	Oso, Mt	1.7	722	Storm King Pk	SJ
391	13,301	Geissler Mtn West	Geissler Mtn East	0.6	481	Mt Champion	SW
392	13,300	Daly, Mt	Clark Pk	1.4	800	Capitol Pk	EL
393	13,300	East Buffalo Pk	West Buffalo Pk	0.9	480	Marmot Pk	TM
394	13,300	"El Punto"	Point 13,340 B	0.6	320	Uncompahgre Pk	SJ
395	13,300	Galena Mtn	Canby Mtn	2.1	360	Howardsville	SJ
396	13,300	Middle Pk	Point 13,498	5.4	1,960	Dolores Pk	SJ
397	13,300	Point 13,300 A	Point 13,505	1.4	520	New York Pk	SW
398	13,300	Point 13,300 B	Twining Pk	2.7	600	Mt Champion	SW
399	13,300	Point 13,300 C	Wetterhorn Pk	0.7	440	Wetterhorn Pk	SJ
400	13,300	Point 13,300 D	Point 13,302	0.6	560	Columbine Pass	SJ
S	13,300	Point 13,300 E	Point 13,460	0.6	280	Independence Pass	SW
S	13,300	Point 13,300 F	South Lookout Pk	0.4	280	Ophir	SJ
401	13,300	Summit Pk	"Phoenix Pk"	40.5	2,760	Summit Pk	SJ
	13,300	"Tigger Pk"	Princeton, Mt	1.1	240	Mt Antero	SW
402	13,300	"V 8"	Beattie Pk	0.6	320	Ophir	SJ
403	13,295	Point 13,295	Sayers BM	2.7	435	Pieplant	SW
404	13,294	Citadel	Pettingell Pk	1.0	314	Loveland Pass	FR
405	13,294	James Pk	Parry Pk	1.5	714	Empire	FR
406	13,292	Electric Pk B	Arrow Pk	0.6	832	Storm King Pk	SJ
407	13,292	Sheep Mtn A	Canby Mtn	1.9	632	Howardsville	SJ
	13,292	Waverly Mtn	Oxford, Mt	1.1	152	Mt Harvard	SW
408	13,290	Dolores Pk	Middle Pk	1.1	710	Dolores Pk	SJ
409	13,286	Bonita Pk	"Proposal Pk"	1.0	506	Handies Pk	SJ
410	13,285	Point 13,285	San Luis Pk	2.5	665	San Luis Pk	SJ
411	13,284	Point 13,284	Point 13,300 B	2.7	424	Mt Champion	SW
412	13,283	Five, Pk	Four, Pk	0.6	303	Storm King Pk	SJ
413	13,282	Point 13,282	Point 13,300 A	1.1	822	New York Pk	SW
414	13,282	Truro Pk	Point 13,300 A	1.3	822	New York Pk	SW
415	13,281	Grizzly Pk E	Jenkins Mtn	1.9	581	Pieplant	SW
416	13,281	Lady Washington, Mt	Longs Pk	0.7	301	Longs Pk	FR
417	13,278	Point 13,278	Rio Grande Pyramid	1.1	633	Weminuche Pass	SJ
418	13,277	Comanche Pk	Fluted Pk	1.5	497	Horn Pk	SC
419	13,277	Ruby Mtn	Grays Pk	1.2	439	Montezuma	FR

Rank	Elev	Peak Name	Parent	Mile	Rise	Quadrangle	Rg
420	13,276	Kiowa Pk	Navajo Pk	1.3	736	Ward	FR
	13,275	Mendota Pk	"T 5"	0.8	175	Telluride	SJ
421	13,274	Seigal Mtn	"Animas Forks Mtn"	1.0	374	Handies Pk	SJ
422	13,271	Whitney Pk	Point 13,768	1.4	691	Mt of the Holy Cross	SW
423	13,270	"Crestolita"	Broken Hand Pk	0.5	490	Crestone Pk	SC
	13,270	Pecks Pk	Belford, Mt	1.0	50	Mt Harvard	SW
424	13,269	Antora Pk	Ouray, Mt	6.8	2,409	Bonanza	SW
425	13,266	Geneva Pk	Argentine Pk	4.7	926	Montezuma	FR
426	13,266	Marble Mtn	Milwaukee Pk	1.1	526	Crestone Pk	SC
427	13,266	Wildhorse Pk	Seigal Mtn	4.0	966	Wetterhorn Pk	SJ
428	13,265	Knife Point	Sunlight Pk	0.8	325	Storm King Pk	SJ
429	13,262	Heisspitz, The	Four, Pk	0.9	362	Storm King Pk	SJ
430	13,261	Point 13,261	Point 13,278	0.7	321	Weminuche Pass	SJ
431	13,260	"Pk G"	Powell, Mt	2.3	1,000	Vail East	GO
432	13,260	Point 13,260 A	Seigal Mtn	2.2	520	Handies Pk	SJ
433	13,260	Point 13,260 B	Precarious Pk	0.8	440	Maroon Bells	EL
434	13,260	Point 13,260 C	Coney BM	1.2	400	Finger Mesa	SJ
435	13,260	"V 9"	Rolling Mtn	1.0	397	Ophir	SJ
	13,259	Whitehead Pk	Rhoda, Mt	0.4	119	Howardsville	SJ
436	13,256	Broken Hill	Matterhorn Pk	2.0	798	Uncompahgre Pk	SJ
437	13,255	Point 13,255	Grizzly Pk E	1.6	555	Winfield	SW
438	13,254	Henry Mtn	Point 13,345	11.0	1,674	Fairview Pk	SW
439	13,253	Point 13,253	Point 13,255	2.0	433	Winfield	SW
440	13,252	"S 8"	Mears Pk	1.6	552	Sams	SJ
	13,250	Bancroft, Mt	Parry Pk	0.7	253	Empire	FR
441	13,248	Point 13,248	Holy Cross Ridge	1.3	308	Mt of the Holy Cross	SW
442	13,245	"Pk Z"	"Pk G"	4.0	785	Willow Lakes	GO
443	13,244	Point 13,244	Point 13,336	1.1	424	Highland Pk	EL
444	13,244	Spring Mtn	Venable Pk	0.7	464	Horn Pk	SC
445	13,242	"S 4"	"S 6"	0.8	302	Mt Sneffels	SJ
446	13,241	"U 3"	Redcliff	0.7	461	Wetterhorn Pk	SJ
	13,238	Landslide Pk	Geneva Pk	0.4	138	Montezuma	FR
	13,237	Notch Mtn	Point 13,248	0.9	217	Mt of the Holy Cross	SW
447	13,235	Point 13,235	Point 13,253	0.9	375	Pieplant	SW
448	13,234	Sniktau, Mt	Grizzly Pk D	2.4	520	Grays Pk	FR
449	13,233	Belleview Mtn	Maroon Pk	1.9	693	Maroon Bells	EL
450	13,233	Turner Pk	Yale, Mt	3.9	1,173	Tincup	SW
451	13,232	Hesperus Mtn	Grizzly Pk B	24.5	2,852	La Plata	SJ
452	13,232	Point 13,232 A	Point 13,260 B	0.4	412	Maroon Bells	EL
453	13,232	Point 13,232 B	Sayres BM	1.7	332	Pieplant	SW
	13,230	"Pk F"	"Pk G"	0.4	250	Vail East	GO
454	13,230	"Pk Q"	"Pk G"	2.0	730	Vail East	GO
455	13,230	Point 13,230 A	Point 13,308	1.9	770	Rio Grande Pyramid	SJ
S	13,230	Point 13,230 B	Point 13,284	0.7	290	Mt Champion	SW
456	13,229	Point 13,229	Point 13,565	0.6	329	El Valle Creek	SC
457	13,229	Red Mtn C	Hoosier Ridge	0.7	369	Breckenridge	TM
S	13,228	Eight, Pk	Nine, Pk	0.4	288	Storm King Pk	SJ
458	13,223	Audubon, Mt	Apache Pk	3.4	843	Ward	FR
	13,222	Macomber Pk	Tower Mtn	0.7	122	Howardsville	SJ
459	13,222	Point 13,222 A	Point 13,340 B	0.6	322	Uncompahgre Pk	SJ
460	13,222	Point 13,222 B	Point 13,300 D	0.8	402	Emerald Lake	SJ
S	13,220	California Mtn	Hanson Pk	0.6	280	Handies Pk	SJ
S	13,220	Ellingwood Ridge	La Plata Pk	1.5	280	Mt Elbert	SW
461	13,220	Greenhalgh Mtn	Sheep Mtn A	0.8	400	Howardsville	SJ
462	13,220	Hagar Mtn	Point 13,294	0.5	320	Loveland Pass	FR
S	13,220	King Solomon Mtn	Little Giant Pk	0.5	280	Howardsville	SJ
463	13,220	Lavender Pk	Hesperus Mtn	0.5	400	La Plata	SJ
	13,220	Little Finger	Fifteen, Pk	0.2	120	Snowdon Pk	SJ
464	13,220	"Pk C"	"Pk G"	1.6	520	Vail East	GO

Rank	Elev	Peak Name	Parent	Mile	Rise	Quadrangle	Rg
	13,220	"Pk E"	"Pk G"	0.6	200	Vail East	GO
465	13,220	"Weminuche Pk"	"SoSo, Mt"	1.8	800	Emerald Lake	SJ
466	13,220	"S 7"	Mears Pk	1.0	400	Sams	SJ
467	13,218	Engineer Mtn	Point 13,260 A	0.9	438	Handies Pk	SJ
468	13,218	Irving Pk	Oso, Mt	1.2	638	Columbine Pass	SJ
469	13,218	Jones Mtn B	Emma Burr Mtn	3.0	638	Tincup	SW
470	13,216	Point 13,216	Point 13,380	0.7	316	Maroon Bells	EL
471	13,215	"Hassell Pk"	Pettingell Pk	1.5	395	Loveland Pass	FR
	13,215	Red Pk A	Hoosier Ridge	0.7	115	Breckenridge	TM
472	13,214	Fairview Pk	Henry Mtn	4.6	1,234	Fairview Pk	SW
	13,213	Campbell Pk	"T 0"	0.5	233	Telluride	SJ
473	13,213	"Pk L"	"Pk Q"	1.5	753	Vail East	GO
	13,213	Thirsty Pk	Lakes Pk	0.8	233	Electric Pk	SC
474	13,212	Point 13,212	Point 13,284	0.7	312	Mt Champion	SW
475	13,209	Gladstone Ridge	Jones Mtn B	2.6	949	Mt Yale	SW
476	13,209	Homestake Pk	Whitney Pk	5.5	1,459	Homestake Reservoir	SW
	13,209	Lambertson Pk	Italian Mtn	0.5	229	Pearl Pass	EL
477	13,208	Powell Pk	McHenrys Pk	0.4	388	McHenrys Pk	FR
478	13,208	Teocalli Mtn	Point 13,550	2.4	788	Gothic	EL
479	13,206	Hayden Mtn South	"T 8"	1.1	549	Ironton	SJ
480	13,206	Point 13,206	Point 13,377	0.6	306	Wetterhorn Pk	SJ
481	13,205	Eagle Pk A	Cottonwood Pk	2.0	545	Electric Pk	SC
482	13,205	Jacque Pk	Pacific Pk	4.6	2,065	Copper Mtn	TM
483	13,205	Nebo, Mt	Point 13,230 A	0.6	505	Storm King Pk	SJ
484	13,204	Lenawee Mtn	Grizzly Pk D	1.0	344	Grays Pk	FR
485	13,203	Bennett Pk	Summit Pk	17.0	1,663	Jasper	SJ
486	13,203	"Leaning South Pk"	Cuatro Pk	1.1	303	Trinchera Pk	SC
487	13,203	Tuttle Mtn	Brown Mtn	1.7	503	Handies Pk	SJ
488	13,203	Williams Mtn South B	Williams Mtn	0.5	423	Mt Champion	SW
489	13,202	Point 13,202	Twining Pk	2.0	422	Mt Champion	SW
490	13,201	Point 13,201	Point 13,300 C	1.3	661	Wetterhorn Pk	SJ
491	13,198	Point 13,198	Grizzly Pk A	2.8	658	Independence Pass	SW
492	13,195	Pk 9	Pk 10	0.6	415	Breckenridge	TM
493	13,194	London Mtn	Mosquito Pk	1.7	534	Climax	TM
494	13,192	"Fancy Pk"	Point 13,768	2.2	372	Mt Jackson	SW
S	13,192	Moss, Mt	Lavender Pk	0.3	292	La Plata	SJ
495	13,189	Red Pk B	"Silverthorne, Mt"	1.6	929	Willow Lakes	GO
	13,188	Sheep Mtn B	San Miguel Pk	1.3	128	Mt Wilson	SJ
496	13,185	Valois, Mt	Aztec Mtn	2.1	325	Columbine Pass	SJ
497	13,184	Beaubien Pk	De Anza Pk B	3.1	604	El Valle Creek	SC
	13,184	Rowe Mtn	Hagues Pk	0.9	44	Trail Ridge	FR
	13,182	Bullion Mtn	Aztec Mtn	0.8	202	Columbine Pass	SJ
498	13,180	Grand Turk	Sultan Mtn	0.6	404	Silverton	SJ
499	13,180	Point 13,180 A	Point 13,631 B	0.5	320	Maroon Bells	EL
500	13,180	Point 13,180 B	Point 13,691	2.1	524	Redcloud Pk	SJ
S	13,180	Point 13,180 C	Point 13,285	0.5	280	San Luis Pk	SJ
	13,180	Point Pun	Graystone Pk	0.6	200	Snowdon Pk	SJ
501	13,180	Santa Fe Pk	Geneva Pk	1.3	480	Montezuma	FR
502	13,180	"Valhalla, Mt"	"Silverthorne, Mt"	1.6	760	Willow Lakes	GO
	13,177	Yellow Mtn	Pilot Knob	0.6	197	Ophir	SJ
503	13,176	Copeland Mtn	Alice, Mt	4.1	1,116	Isolation Pk	FR
504	13,172	Conejos Pk	Summit Pk	8.2	1,912	Platoro	SJ
505	13,169	Point 13,169	Point 13,230 A	1.2	989	Rio Grande Pyramid	SJ
506	13,169	Sheep Mtn C	Point 13,681	2.7	592	Sheep Mtn	SJ
507	13,165	Amherst Mtn	Valois, Mt	1.5	1,225	Columbine Pass	SJ
508	13,165	"Stony Pass Pk"	Canby Mtn	0.7	577	Howardsville	SJ
	13,164	Helen, Mt	Pk 10	1.3	264	Breckenridge	TM
509	13,164	Kelso Mtn	Torreys Pk	1.6	784	Grays Pk	FR
510	13,164	Point 13,164	Half Pk	1.3	384	Pole Creek Mtn	SJ

Rank	Elev	Peak Name	Parent	Mile	Rise	Quadrangle	Rg
511	13,162	Point 13,162 A	Baldy Cinco	1.3	493	Baldy Cinco	SJ
512	13,162	Point 13,162 B	Point 13,550	0.9	382	Gothic	EL
513	13,159	Point 13,159	Lookout Pk	1.3	379	Ophir	SJ
514	13,158	Point 13,158	Uncompahgre Pk	1.8	378	Uncompahgre Pk	SJ
515	13,158	Twilight Pk	Pigeon Pk	4.9	2,338	Snowdon Pk	SJ
516	13,157	"Window Pk"	Rio Grande Pyramid	0.9	300	Rio Grande Pyramid	SJ
517	13,156	"V 5"	South Lookout Pk	1.3	616	Ophir	SJ
	13,155	Baldy Mtn	Point 13,244	0.6	175	Highland Pk	EL
518	13,155	Point 13,155	Point 13,285	1.7	415	San Luis Pk	SJ
519	13,153	Point 13,153 A	Herard Mtn	0.9	653	Medano Pass	SC
520	13,153	Point 13,153 B	Adams, Mt	0.7	373	Horn Pk	SC
521	13,153	Taylor Pk B	Powell Pk	1.0	413	McHenrys Pk	FR
522	13,151	Pomeroy Mtn	Grizzly Mtn	2.1	611	Saint Elmo	SW
523	13,150	Arikaree Pk	Kiowa Pk	0.8	570	Monarch Lake	FR
524	13,150	Montezuma Pk	Summit Pk	1.6	690	Summit Pk	SJ
525	13,149	Babcock Pk	Lavender Pk	0.9	529	La Plata	SJ
526	13,148	South River Pk	Montezuma Pk	21.3	2,228	South River Pk	SJ
527	13,147	Point 13,147	Monumental Pk	1.4	527	Garfield	SW
528	13,145	Point 13,145 A	La Junta Pk	0.6	325	Telluride	SJ
S	13,145	Point 13,145 B	Point 13,284	1.2	285	Mt Champion	SW
529	13,144	Precipice Pk	"U 3"	1.5	484	Wetterhorn Pk	SJ
530	13,143	Little Horn Pk	Fluted Pk	0.9	323	Horn Pk	SC
531	13,143	Willoughby Mtn	Point 13,336	1.8	442	Highland Pk	EL
	13,140	"Dicker's Peck"	Navajo Pk	0.1	40	Monarch Lake	FR
S	13,140	Emerson Mtn	Amherst Mtn	0.5	280	Columbine Pass	SJ
	13,140	Guyselman Mtn (Pk M)	"Pk L"	0.6	240	Mt Powell	GO
532	13,140	Point 13,140 A	Point 13,255	0.6	320	Winfield	SW
533	13,140	Point 13,140 B	Jenkins Mtn	1.1	320	Pieplant	SW
534	13,140	Point 13,140 C	Truro Pk	0.4	320	New York Pk	SW
S	13,140	Point 13,140 D	"Weminuche Pk"	0.4	280	Emerald Lake	SJ
	13,140	Robeson Pk	Bard Pk	0.9	200	Grays Pk	FR
535	13,140	Twelve, Pk	Monitor Pk	0.5	320	Storm King Pk	SJ
536	13,139	Hayden Mtn North	Hayden Mtn South	1.2	519	Ironton	SJ
537	13,139	Savage Pk	"Fancy Pk"	2.8	1,153	Mt Jackson	SW
538	13,138	Ogalalla Pk	Copeland Mtn	1.4	718	Isolation Pk	FR
539	13,136	Hunchback Mtn	White Dome	0.8	356	Storm King Pk	SJ
540	13,135	Francisco Pk	Beaubien Pk	1.0	435	El Valle Creek	SC
541	13,134	"S 9"	"S 8"	0.7	354	Sams	SJ
	13,134	Sullivan Mtn	Santa Fe Pk	0.6	274	Montezuma	FR
542	13,132	Flora, Mt	Parry Pk	2.4	686	Empire	FR
543	13,132	"Darley Mtn"	Point 13,260 A	0.9	512	Handies Pk	SJ
	13,132	Sewanee Pk	Point 13,147	0.6	232	Garfield	SW
544	13,130	Eva, Mt	Parry Pk	0.8	430	Empire	FR
545	13,130	Point 13,130	Point 13,180 A	0.8	350	Maroon Bells	EL
	13,130	"Rain Pk"	"Silverthorne, Mt"	0.6	230	Willow Lakes	GO
	13,129	Black BM	"Pk G"	0.2	29	Vail East	GO
546	13,128	Lomo Liso Mtn	Francisco Pk	0.8	308	El Valle Creek	SC
547	13,126	Pika Pk	Gold Dust Pk	0.7	506	Mt Jackson	SW
	13,125	Kennedy, Mt	Aztec Mtn	0.6	265	Mtn View Crest	SJ
548	13,123	Point 13,123 A	Point 13,498	1.1	463	Dolores Pk	SJ
549	13,123	Point 13,123 B	Cottonwood Pk	0.8	303	Electric Pk	SC
	13,123	Spiller Pk	Babcock Pk	0.5	183	La Plata	SJ
550	13,122	Peters Pk	Point 13,322 B	0.4	342	Emerald Lake	SJ
551	13,122	Point 13,122	Point 13,490	1.2	302	Rito Alto Pk	SC
552	13,121	"Pk N"	"Pk L"	1.2	421	Mt Powell	GO
553	13,121	Point 13,121	Greylock Mtn	0.5	341	Columbine Pass	SJ
554	13,118	Isolation Pk	Copeland Mtn	2.2	938	Isolation Pk	FR
555	13,117	"Cupid"	Grizzly Pk D	1.0	377	Grays Pk	FR

Rank	Elev	Peak Name	Parent	Mile	Rise	Quadrangle	Rg
556	13,113	Lizard Head	Gladstone Pk	1.9	1,113	Mt Wilson	SJ
557	13,112	Fitzpatrick Pk	Point 13,345	2.1	958	Cumberland Pass	SW
558	13,111	Cow BM	"Darley Mtn"	2.3	531	Wetterhorn Pk	SJ
559	13,111	Point 13,111	Point 13,510 A	4.6	811	San Luis Pk	SJ
560	13,110	Point 13,110	Point 13,308	1.2	450	Storm King Pk	SJ
561	13,109	Point 13,109	Rhoda, Mt	0.8	329	Howardsville	SJ
	13,108	Thunder Mtn	Greylock Mtn	1.0	248	Columbine Pass	SJ
562	13,108	Williams Mtn North	Williams Mtn	0.8	408	Mt Champion	SW
563	13,106	Point 13,106	Uncompahgre Pk	2.2	726	Uncompahgre Pk	SJ
564	13,105	Bushnell Pk	Cottonwood Pk	11.1	2,405	Bushnell Pk	SC
565	13,105	Point 13,105	Amherst Mtn	0.9	325	Columbine Pass	SJ
566	13,102	Point 13,102	Monumental Pk	1.7	482	Garfield	SW
567	13,100	"Corbett Pk"	Whitehouse Mtn	0.5	320	Ouray	SJ
	13,100	Gore Thumb	"Pk L"	0.4	200	Vail East	GO
	13,100	"Leaning North Pk"	"Leaning South Pk"	0.5	160	Trinchera Pk	SC
568	13,100	Middle Mtn A	Point 13,463	1.1	520	Independence Pass	SW
	13,100	"Pk C Prime"	"Pk C"	0.2	120	Vail East	GO
	13,100	"Pk H"	"Pk G"	0.4	140	Vail East	GO
569	13,100	Point 13,100 A	Point 13,681	1.8	480	Sheep Mtn	SJ
570	13,100	Point 13,100 B	Pika Pk	2.1	600	Mt Jackson	SW
571	13,100	Point 13,100 C	Point 13,111	1.9	400	Baldy Cinco	SJ
S	13,100	Point 13,100 D	Little Bear Pk	1.0	280	Twin Pks	SC
	13,100	South Twilight Pk	Twilight Pk	0.3	200	Snowdon Pk	SJ
572	13,095	Kreutzer, Mt	Emma Burr Mtn	1.6	355	Tincup	SW
573	13,095	"Tomboy Pk"	Chicago Pk	0.5	315	Telluride	SJ
574	13,093	Point 13,093	Sunshine Mtn	1.4	353	Handies Pk	SJ
575	13,091	Point 13,091	Point 13,106 A	1.8	591	Uncompahgre Pk	SJ
576	13,090	Point 13,090	Point 13,140 C	1.1	350	New York Pk	SW
577	13,090	"Solitude, Mt"	"Pk Z"	2.0	710	Vail East	GO
578	13,088	Paiute Pk	Audubon, Mt	0.9	468	Monarch Lake	FR
579	13,088	Virginia Pk	Point 13,140 A	0.8	428	Winfield	SW
580	13,085	Keller Mtn	"Valhalla, Mt"	2.1	745	Willow Lakes	GO
581	13,085	"Pk X"	"Pk Z"	0.8	465	Vail East	GO
582	13,085	Point 13,085	Point 13,100 B	1.0	625	Mt Jackson	SW
583	13,082	Boreas Mtn	Bald Mtn	2.9	923	Boreas Pass	FR
584	13,081	"Huerfanito"	Lindsey, Mt	1.1	501	Blanca Pk	SC
585	13,079	"North Traverse Pk"	"Valhalla, Mt"	1.3	659	Willow Lakes	GO
586	13,078	Point 13,078	Point 13,317	1.4	738	Saint Elmo	SW
587	13,078	Whale Pk	Geneva Pk	4.7	982	Jefferson	FR
588	13,077	Snowdon Pk	Twilight Pk	3.8	1,337	Snowdon Pk	SJ
	13,077	Winfield Pk	Virginia Pk	0.7	177	Winfield	SW
	13,076	Florida Mtn	Valois, Mt	0.8	176	Columbine Pass	SJ
589	13,075	North Twilight Pk	Twilight Pk	0.4	335	Snowdon Pk	SJ
	13,075	"Pk Z Prime"	"Solitude, Mt"	0.4	215	Vail East	GO
590	13,075	Point 13,075	Hanson Pk	1.0	415	Handies Pk	SJ
591	13,074	Garfield, Mt	Graystone Pk	1.0	374	Snowdon Pk	SJ
592	13,074	Point 13,074	Point 13,300 A	1.0	454	New York Pk	SW
593	13,073	Blackwall Mtn	Wildhorse Pk	1.3	453	Wetterhorn Pk	SJ
594	13,071	Hunts Pk	Bushnell Pk	4.3	891	Wellsville	SC
595	13,070	Point 13,070	Pomeroy Mtn	0.6	330	Saint Elmo	SW
596	13,070	Sheep Mtn D	Point 13,105	0.4	370	Columbine Pass	SJ
S	13,069	Chiquita, Mt	Ypsilon Mtn	1.0	283	Trail Ridge	FR
597	13,069	Point 13,069	Niagara Pk	4.1	329	Howardsville	SJ
S	13,066	Kendall BM	Kendall Mtn	0.7	286	Silverton	SJ
S	13,062	Centennial Pk	Lavender Pk	0.5	282	La Plata	SJ
598	13,062	Point 13,062 A	Hagerman Pk	2.1	642	Snowmass Mtn	EL
599	13,062	Point 13,062 B	Hermit Pk	1.9	842	Rito Alto Pk	SC
600	13,062	West Needle Mtn	Twilight Pk	1.0	562	Snowdon Pk	SJ

Rank	Elev	Peak Name	Parent	Mile	Rise	Quadrangle	Rg
S	13,060	"Igloo Pk"	Point 13,198	0.5	280	Independence Pass	SW
	13,060	Middle Mtn B	Point 13,462 A	0.6	120	Winfield	SW
601	13,060	Point 13,060 A	Clark Pk	0.5	320	Capitol Pk	EL
602	13,060	Point 13,060 B	Point 13,062 B	0.4	360	Rito Alto Pk	SC
S	13,060	Point 13,060 C	Peters Pk	0.4	280	Emerald Lake	SJ
	13,060	Saint Sophia Ridge	Emma, Mt	0.5	160	Telluride	SJ
603	13,058	Owen B, Mt	Treasury Mtn	7.5	1,358	Oh Be Joyful	EL
604	13,057	East Partner Pk	"Pk X"	1.0	557	Vail East	GO
605	13,055	Point 13,055	Kreutzer, Mt	1.6	315	Tincup	SW
606	13,054	Point 13,054	Eureka Mtn	1.6	594	Rito Alto Pk	SC
607	13,052	Houghton Mtn	Tuttle Mtn	1.5	472	Handies Pk	SJ
608	13,051	Point 13,051	Silver Mtn A	1.1	351	Uncompahgre Pk	SJ
609	13,050	"Dead Man Pk"	Point 13,384	0.8	390	Crestone Pk	SC
610	13,050	Point 13,050	Point 13,345	1.5	550	Cumberland Pass	SW
	13,049	Green Mtn	"Stony Pass Pk"	0.6	69	Howardsville	SJ
	13,047	"Pk D"	"Pk G"	1.0	267	Vail East	GO
	13,047	West Dyer Mtn	Dyer Mtn	0.7	267	Mt Sherman	TM
611	13,046	Point 13,046	Snowdon Pk	0.6	386	Snowdon Pk	SJ
	13,043	Eagle Pk B	Point 13,100 B	0.4	233	Mt Jackson	SW
612	13,042	Point 13,042	Twin Sisters East	2.1	942	Silverton	SJ
613	13,041	"Grand Traverse Pk"	"North Traverse Pk"	0.7	301	Willow Lakes	GO
614	13,041	"West Partner Pk" (Pk U)	"East Partner Pk" (Pk V)	0.9	581	Vail East	GO
	13,041	Wolcott Mtn	"S 6"	0.6	181	Mt Sneffels	SJ
615	13,039	Point 13,039	Sleeping Sexton	0.9	419	Maroon Bells	EL
616	13,038	"Old Baldy"	North Arapaho Pk	0.9	338	Monarch Lake	FR
	13,036	United States Mtn	Chicago Pk	1.0	176	Ironton	SJ
617	13,035	West Elk Pk	Owen B, Mt	13.9	3,055	West Elk Pk	EL
618	13,034	Point 13,034	Point 13,111	2.0	654	Baldy Cinco	SJ
619	13,033	Williams Mtn South C	Williams Mtn South A	1.4	493	Thimble Rock	SW
620	13,032	Organ Mtn B	Amherst Mtn	0.4	452	Columbine Pass	SJ
621	13,028	Point 13,028	Point 13,060 B	0.7	328	Rito Alto Pk	SC
622	13,026	Point 13,026	Point 13,202	1.7	326	Mt Champion	SW
623	13,024	"Snow Pk"	"Valhalla, Mt"	0.8	484	Willow Lakes	GO
S	13,024	Van Wirt Mtn	Point 13,102	0.7	284	Garfield	SW
	13,023	Niwot Ridge	Navajo Pk	0.6	163	Monarch Lake	FR
S	13,020	"North Irving"	Irving Pk	0.4	280	Columbine Pass	SJ
624	13,020	Point 13,020 A	Point 13,336	0.5	320	Maroon Bells	EL
625	13,020	Point 13,020 B	Pico Asilado	0.7	360	Crestone Pk	SC
S	13,020	Point 13,020 C	Point 13,510 A	0.9	286	Baldy Cinco	SJ
626	13,020	"S 10"	"S 9"	0.8	360	Sams	SJ
627	13,020	"Unicorn Pk"	Montezuma Pk	0.6	440	Summit Pk	SJ
	13,019	Cuba BM	Niagara Pk	3.4	119	Howardsville	SJ
628	13,017	Point 13,017	"Window Pk"	1.0	400	Rio Grande Pyramid	SJ
629	13,016	Point 13,016	Point 13,051	1.5	676	Uncompahgre Pk	SJ
630	13,015	Point 13,015	Point 13,402	1.2	315	Halfmoon Pass	SJ
631	13,014	Chief Mtn	Point 13,261	9.8	2,474	Little Squaw Creek	SJ
	13,012	Hope Mtn	Jupiter Mtn	0.9	232	Columbine Pass	SJ
632	13,012	Twin Sisters	Bushnell Pk	1.0	552	Bushnell Pk	SC
633	13,010	"Golden Bear Pk"	Hagar Mtn	1.2	350	Loveland Pass	FR
634	13,010	Point 13,010	Chief Mtn	2.9	1,790	Cimarrona Pk	SJ
635	13,006	Pennsylvania Mtn	Evans B, Mt	2.2	699	Climax	TM
	13,005	"Climber's Point"	"Solitude, Mt"	0.5	225	Vail East	GO
636	13,003	Point 13,003	Point 13,026	1.9	503	Mt Champion	SW
	13,003	Ruffner Mtn	"S 7"	0.4	23	Sams	SJ
637	13,001	Point 13,001	Point 13,202	0.9	501	Mt Champion	SW

PEAKS SORTED BY QUADRANGLE

Rank	Elev	Peak Name	Parent	Mile	Rise	Quadrangle	Rg
68	13,911	Meeker, Mt	Longs Pk	0.7	451	Allens Park	FR
	13,860	Meeker Ridge	Meeker, Mt	0.2	40	Allens Park	FR
8	14,286	Lincoln, Mt	Massive, Mt	22.3	3,866	Alma	TM
	14,238	Cameron, Mt	Lincoln, Mt	0.5	138	Alma	TM
22	14,172	Bross, Mt	Lincoln, Mt	1.1	312	Alma	TM
	14,020	"South Bross"	Bross, Mt	0.6	80	Alma	TM
96	13,822	Silverheels, Mt	Bross, Mt	5.5	2,283	Alma	TM
249	13,510	Point 13,510 A	San Luis Pk	7.8	1,570	Baldy Cinco	SJ
329	13,383	Baldy Cinco	Point 13,510 A	1.9	843	Baldy Cinco	SJ
379	13,313	Point 13,313	Baldy Cinco	0.7	413	Baldy Cinco	SJ
511	13,162	Point 13,162 A	Baldy Cinco	1.3	493	Baldy Cinco	SJ
571	13,100	Point 13,100 C	Point 13,111	1.9	400	Baldy Cinco	SJ
618	13,034	Point 13,034	Point 13,111	2.0	654	Baldy Cinco	SJ
S	13,020	Point 13,020 C	Point 13,510 A	0.9	286	Baldy Cinco	SJ
4	14,345	Blanca Pk	Harvard, Mt	103.0	5,326	Blanca Pk	SC
42	14,042	Ellingwood Point	Blanca Pk	0.5	342	Blanca Pk	SC
43	14,042	Lindsey, Mt	Blanca Pk	2.3	1,542	Blanca Pk	SC
44	14,037	Little Bear Pk	Blanca Pk	1.0	377	Blanca Pk	SC
	14,020	"Northwest Lindsey"	Lindsey, Mt	0.2	40	Blanca Pk	SC
	14,020	"South Little Bear"	Little Bear Pk	0.2	80	Blanca Pk	SC
84	13,849	California Pk	Ellingwood Point	2.2	629	Blanca Pk	SC
93	13,828	"Huerfano Pk"	Lindsey, Mt	1.2	688	Blanca Pk	SC
	13,658	Hamilton Pk	Blanca Pk	1.5	278	Blanca Pk	SC
205	13,577	Point 13,577	Point 13,660 A	0.5	317	Blanca Pk	SC
S	13,555	Point 13,555	"Huerfano Pk"	1.0	295	Blanca Pk	SC
	13,500	Iron Nipple	"Huerfano Pk"	0.6	200	Blanca Pk	SC
584	13,081	"Huerfanito"	Lindsey, Mt	1.1	501	Blanca Pk	SC
424	13,269	Antora Pk	Ouray, Mt	6.8	2,409	Bonanza	SW
156	13,684	Bald Mtn	Silverheels, Mt	7.6	2,104	Boreas Pass	FR
344	13,370	Guyot, Mt	Bald Mtn	2.0	1,324	Boreas Pass	FR
583	13,082	Boreas Mtn	Bald Mtn	2.9	923	Boreas Pass	FR
13	14,265	Quandary Pk	Lincoln, Mt	3.2	1,125	Breckenridge	TM
61	13,950	Pacific Pk	Fletcher Mtn	1.4	570	Breckenridge	TM
82	13,852	Crystal Pk	Pacific Pk	0.9	632	Breckenridge	TM
178	13,633	Pk 10	Crystal Pk	0.9	373	Breckenridge	TM
	13,615	Father Dyer Pk	Crystal Pk	0.6	115	Breckenridge	TM
187	13,614	North Star Mtn	Wheeler Mtn	0.9	434	Breckenridge	TM
352	13,352	Hoosier Ridge	Silverheels, Mt	3.3	932	Breckenridge	TM
457	13,229	Red Mtn C	Hoosier Ridge	0.7	369	Breckenridge	TM
	13,215	Red Pk A	Hoosier Ridge	0.7	115	Breckenridge	TM
492	13,195	Pk 9	Pk 10	0.6	415	Breckenridge	TM
	13,164	Helen, Mt	Pk 10	1.3	264	Breckenridge	TM
564	13,105	Bushnell Pk	Cottonwood Pk	11.1	2,405	Bushnell Pk	SC
632	13,012	Twin Sisters	Bushnell Pk	1.0	552	Bushnell Pk	SC
29	14,130	Capitol Pk	Maroon Pk	7.5	1,750	Capitol Pk	EL
	13,664	"K2"	Capitol Pk	0.5	84	Capitol Pk	EL
198	13,580	Clark Pk	Capitol Pk	1.2	440	Capitol Pk	EL
392	13,300	Daly, Mt	Clark Pk	1.4	800	Capitol Pk	EL
601	13,060	Point 13,060 A	Clark Pk	0.5	320	Capitol Pk	EL
634	13,010	Point 13,010	Chief Mtn	2.9	1,790	Cimarrona Pk	SJ
28	14,148	Democrat, Mt	Lincoln, Mt	1.7	768	Climax	TM
76	13,865	Buckskin, Mt	Democrat, Mt	1.5	725	Climax	TM
80	13,857	Clinton Pk	Democrat, Mt	2.0	517	Climax	TM
	13,852	Traver Pk	Clinton Pk	0.7	232	Climax	TM
108	13,795	Arkansas Mt	Buckskin Mt	1.9	575	Climax	TM
115	13,781	Mosquito Pk	Buckskin, Mt	2.3	561	Climax	TM

Rank	Elev	Peak Name	Parent	Mile	Rise	Quadrangle	Rg
	13,780	McNamee Pk	Clinton Pk	0.5	80	Climax	TM
S	13,701	Treasurevault Mtn	Mosquito Pk	0.4	281	Climax	TM
	13,692	Loveland Mtn	Buckskin, Mt	0.8	192	Climax	TM
162	13,672	Tweto, Mt	Buckskin, Mt	1.2	412	Climax	TM
204	13,577	Evans B, Mt	Dyer Mt	1.2	317	Climax	TM
S	13,548	Point 13,548	Mosquito Pk	0.7	288	Climax	TM
493	13,194	London Mtn	Mosquito Pk	1.7	534	Climax	TM
635	13,006	Pennsylvania Mtn	Evans B, Mt	2.2	699	Climax	TM
32	14,083	Eolus, Mt	Wilson, Mt	25.5	3,863	Columbine Pass	SJ
33	14,082	Windom Pk	Eolus, Mt	1.7	1,022	Columbine Pass	SJ
92	13,830	Jupiter Mtn	Windom Pk	0.6	370	Columbine Pass	SJ
146	13,700	Grizzly "Pk C"	Jupiter Mtn	0.7	440	Columbine Pass	SJ
206	13,575	Greylock Mtn	Windom Pk	1.2	555	Columbine Pass	SJ
217	13,554	McCauley Pk	Grizzly Pk C	0.7	454	Columbine Pass	SJ
	13,472	Eighteen, Pk	Windom Pk	0.5	212	Columbine Pass	SJ
S	13,460	"East Windom"	Windom Pk	0.6	280	Columbine Pass	SJ
385	13,310	Aztec Mtn	Jupiter Mtn	1.9	610	Columbine Pass	SJ
	13,309	Echo Mtn	McCauley Mtn	0.5	209	Columbine Pass	SJ
400	13,300	Point 13,300 D	Point 13,302	0.6	560	Columbine Pass	SJ
468	13,218	Irving Pk	Oso, Mt	1.2	638	Columbine Pass	SJ
496	13,185	Valois, Mt	Aztec Mtn	2.1	325	Columbine Pass	SJ
	13,182	Bullion Mtn	Aztec Mtn	0.8	202	Columbine Pass	SJ
507	13,165	Amherst Mtn	Valois, Mt	1.5	1,225	Columbine Pass	SJ
S	13,140	Emerson Mtn	Amherst Mtn	0.5	280	Columbine Pass	SJ
553	13,121	Point 13,121	Greylock Mtn	0.5	341	Columbine Pass	SJ
	13,108	Thunder Mtn	Greylock Mtn	1.0	248	Columbine Pass	SJ
565	13,105	Point 13,105	Amherst Mtn	0.9	325	Columbine Pass	SJ
	13,076	Florida Mtn	Valois, Mt	0.8	176	Columbine Pass	SJ
596	13,070	Sheep Mtn D	Point 13,105	0.4	370	Columbine Pass	SJ
620	13,032	Organ Mtn B	Amherst Mtn	0.4	452	Columbine Pass	SJ
S	13,020	"North Irving"	Irving Pk	0.4	280	Columbine Pass	SJ
	13,012	Hope Mtn	Jupiter Mtn	0.9	232	Columbine Pass	SJ
59	13,951	Fletcher Mtn	Quandary Pk	1.2	611	Copper Mtn	TM
S	13,900	"Drift Pk"	Fletcher Mtn	0.6	280	Copper Mtn	TM
86	13,841	"Atlantic Pk"	Fletcher Mtn	0.7	421	Copper Mtn	TM
152	13,690	Wheeler Mtn	Fletcher Mtn	1.6	310	Copper Mtn	TM
214	13,555	Bartlett Mtn	Clinton Pk	0.8	615	Copper Mtn	SW
482	13,205	Jacque Pk	Pacific Pk	4.6	2,065	Copper Mtn	TM
7	14,294	Crestone Pk	Blanca Pk	27.5	4,554	Crestone Pk	SC
	14,260	"East Crestone"	Crestone Pk	0.1	80	Crestone Pk	SC
	14,260	"Northeast Crestone"	Crestone Pk	0.1	120	Crestone Pk	SC
19	14,197	Crestone Needle	Crestone Pk	0.5	457	Crestone Pk	SC
23	14,165	Kit Carson Mtn	Crestone Pk	1.3	1,025	Crestone Pk	SC
34	14,081	Challenger Point	Kit Carson Mtn	0.2	301	Crestone Pk	SC
37	14,064	Humboldt Pk	Crestone Needle	1.4	1,204	Crestone Pk	SC
56	13,980	"Kat Carson"	Kit Carson Mtn	0.2	360	Crestone Pk	SC
	13,980	"Kitty Kat Carson"	"Kat Carson"	0.1	80	Crestone Pk	SC
	13,980	"Prow, The"	Kit Carson Mtn	0.1	40	Crestone Pk	SC
107	13,799	"Obstruction Pk"	"Kat Carson"	0.5	339	Crestone Pk	SC
143	13,705	Colony Baldy	Humboldt Pk	1.4	925	Crestone Pk	SC
188	13,611	Pico Asilado	Crestone Needle	1.7	831	Crestone Pk	SC
189	13,604	Tijeras Pk	Pico Asilado	1.7	744	Crestone Pk	SC
209	13,573	Broken Hand Pk	Crestone Needle	0.8	673	Crestone Pk	SC
224	13,541	Point 13,541	Point 13,580 B	0.8	361	Crestone Pk	SC
242	13,522	Milwaukee Pk	Pico Asilado	0.5	302	Crestone Pk	SC
S	13,517	Point 13,517 B	Point 13,580 B	0.4	297	Crestone Pk	SC
311	13,414	Cleveland Pk	Tijeras Pk	1.4	434	Crestone Pk	SC
321	13,401	Point 13,401	Tijeras Pk	0.9	301	Crestone Pk	SC

Rank	Elev	Peak Name	Parent	Mile	Rise	Quadrangle	Rg
327	13,384	Point 13,384	Cleveland Pk	0.9	364	Crestone Pk	SC
333	13,380	Music Mtn	Milwaukee Pk	0.9	400	Crestone Pk	SC
423	13,270	"Crestolita"	Broken Hand Pk	0.5	490	Crestone Pk	SC
426	13,266	Marble Mtn	Milwaukee Pk	1.1	526	Crestone Pk	SC
609	13,050	"Dead Man Pk"	Point 13,384	0.8	390	Crestone Pk	SC
625	13,020	Point 13,020 B	Pico Asilado	0.7	360	Crestone Pk	SC
41	14,047	Culebra Pk	Blanca Pk	25.0	4,667	Culebra Pk	SC
70	13,908	Red Mtn A	Culebra Pk	0.7	448	Culebra Pk	SC
135	13,723	Vermejo Pk	Red Mtn A	1.3	761	Culebra Pk	SC
160	13,676	Purgatoire Pk	Vermejo Pk	1.8	849	Culebra Pk	SC
277	13,466	"Alamosito"	Vermejo Pk	1.2	557	Culebra Pk	SC
230	13,538	Emma Burr Mtn	Princeton, Mt	9.6	1,238	Cumberland Pass	SW
356	13,345	Point 13,345	Emma Burr Mtn	1.1	445	Cumberland Pass	SW
557	13,112	Fitzpatrick Pk	Point 13,345	2.1	958	Cumberland Pass	SW
610	13,050	Point 13,050	Point 13,345	1.5	550	Cumberland Pass	SW
	14,159	El Diente	Wilson, Mt	0.8	259	Dolores Pk	SJ
226	13,540	Point 13,540 A	Wilson Pk	1.0	520	Dolores Pk	SJ
257	13,498	Point 13,498	Point 13,540 A	0.6	358	Dolores Pk	SJ
396	13,300	Middle Pk	Point 13,498	5.4	1,960	Dolores Pk	SJ
408	13,290	Dolores Pk	Middle Pk	1.1	710	Dolores Pk	SJ
548	13,123	Point 13,123 A	Point 13,498	1.1	463	Dolores Pk	SJ
212	13,565	Point 13,565	Culebra Pk	1.4	545	El Valle Creek	SC
S	13,468	Miranda Pk	Point 13,565	0.9	288	El Valle Creek	SC
317	13,405	Mariquita Pk	Cuatro Pk	1.4	385	El Valle Creek	SC
	13,335	Maxwell, Mt	Mariquita Pk	0.8	275	El Valle Creek	SC
368	13,333	De Anza Pk B	Mariquita Pk	1.0	473	El Valle Creek	SC
456	13,229	Point 13,229	Point 13,565	0.6	329	El Valle Creek	SC
497	13,184	Beaubien Pk	De Anza Pk B	3.1	604	El Valle Creek	SC
540	13,135	Francisco Pk	Beaubien Pk	1.0	435	El Valle Creek	SC
546	13,128	Lomo Liso Mtn	Francisco Pk	0.8	308	El Valle Creek	SC
191	13,598	Electric Pk A	Rito Alto Pk	6.1	938	Electric Pk	SC
218	13,553	Gibbs Pk	Rito Alto Pk	4.2	693	Electric Pk	SC
248	13,513	Point 13,513	Gibbs Pk	2.4	453	Electric Pk	SC
262	13,490	Marcy, Mt	Point 13,513	1.2	430	Electric Pk	SC
306	13,423	Spread Eagle Pk	Point 13,524 B	0.9	443	Electric Pk	SC
339	13,375	Lakes Pk	Cottonwood Pk	2.1	675	Electric Pk	SC
347	13,362	De Anza Pk A	Gibbs Pk	1.1	622	Electric Pk	SC
360	13,340	Owen A, Mt	Point 13,490	2.0	600	Electric Pk	SC
	13,213	Thirsty Pk	Lakes Pk	0.8	233	Electric Pk	SC
481	13,205	Eagle Pk A	Cottonwood Pk	2.0	545	Electric Pk	SC
549	13,123	Point 13,123 B	Cottonwood Pk	0.8	303	Electric Pk	SC
157	13,684	Oso, Mt	Grizzly "Pk C"	4.9	1,664	Emerald Lake	SJ
309	13,417	"SoSo, Mt"	Oso, Mt	0.8	677	Emerald Lake	SJ
361	13,340	Point 13,340 A	"SoSo, Mt"	1.2	440	Emerald Lake	SJ
386	13,310	Point 13,310	Point 13,340 A	0.6	330	Emerald Lake	SJ
460	13,222	Point 13,222 B	Point 13,300 D	0.8	402	Emerald Lake	SJ
465	13,220	"Weminuche Pk"	"SoSo, Mt"	1.8	800	Emerald Lake	SJ
S	13,140	Point 13,140 D	"Weminuche Pk"	0.4	280	Emerald Lake	SJ
550	13,122	Peters Pk	Point 13,322 B	0.4	342	Emerald Lake	SJ
S	13,060	Point 13,060 C	Peters Pk	0.4	280	Emerald Lake	SJ
324	13,391	Parry Pk	North Arapaho Pk	12.5	1,720	Empire	FR
405	13,294	James Pk	Parry Pk	1.5	714	Empire	FR
	13,250	Bancroft, Mt	Parry Pk	0.7	253	Empire	FR
542	13,132	Flora, Mt	Parry Pk	2.4	686	Empire	FR
544	13,130	Eva, Mt	Parry Pk	0.8	430	Empire	FR
305	13,425	Mummy Mtn	Hagues Pk	1.4	485	Estes Park	FR
438	13,254	Henry Mtn	Point 13,345	11.0	1,674	Fairview Pk	SW
472	13,214	Fairview Pk	Henry Mtn	4.6	1,234	Fairview Pk	SW

Rank	Elev	Peak Name	Parent	Mile	Rise	Quadrangle	Rg
366	13,334	Coney BM	Bent Pk	1.9	994	Finger Mesa	SJ
434	13,260	Point 13,260 C	Coney BM	1.2	400	Finger Mesa	SJ
127	13,745	Aetna, Mt	Tabeguache Pk	4.7	1,245	Garfield	SW
172	13,651	Taylor Mtn	Aetna, Mt	1.2	631	Garfield	SW
345	13,369	Monumental Pk	Aetna, Mt	2.1	1,029	Garfield	SW
527	13,147	Point 13,147	Monumental Pk	1.4	527	Garfield	SW
	13,132	Sewanee Pk	Point 13,147	0.6	232	Garfield	SW
566	13,102	Point 13,102	Monumental Pk	1.7	482	Garfield	SW
S	13,024	Van Wirt Mtn	Point 13,102	0.7	284	Garfield	SW
221	13,550	Point 13,550	"Castleabra"	0.9	530	Gothic	EL
229	13,540	White Rock Mtn	Point 13,550	2.8	800	Gothic	EL
322	13,401	White BM	White Rock Mtn	0.5	381	Gothic	EL
334	13,380	Point 13,380	White Rock Mtn	1.3	480	Gothic	EL
478	13,208	Teocalli Mtn	Point 13,550	2.4	788	Gothic	EL
512	13,162	Point 13,162 B	Point 13,550	0.9	382	Gothic	EL
9	14,270	Grays Pk	Lincoln, Mt	25.2	2,770	Grays Pk	FR
11	14,267	Torreys Pk	Grays Pk	0.6	560	Grays Pk	FR
83	13,850	Edwards, Mt	Grays Pk	1.3	470	Grays Pk	FR
176	13,641	Bard Pk	Torreys Pk	5.5	1,651	Grays Pk	FR
	13,587	McClellan Mtn	Edwards, Mt	0.8	167	Grays Pk	FR
208	13,574	Parnassus, Mt	Bard Pk	1.0	537	Grays Pk	FR
303	13,427	Grizzly Pk D	Torreys Pk	1.5	847	Grays Pk	FR
348	13,362	Englemann Pk	Bard Pk	1.8	542	Grays Pk	FR
448	13,234	Sniktau, Mt	Grizzly Pk D	2.4	520	Grays Pk	FR
484	13,204	Lenawee Mtn	Grizzly Pk D	1.0	344	Grays Pk	FR
509	13,164	Kelso Mtn	Torreys Pk	1.6	784	Grays Pk	FR
	13,140	Robeson Pk	Bard Pk	0.9	200	Grays Pk	FR
555	13,117	"Cupid"	Grizzly Pk D	1.0	377	Grays Pk	FR
73	13,895	"Phoenix Pk"	San Luis Pk	5.0	1,515	Halfmoon Pass	SJ
	13,710	La Garita Pk	"Phoenix Pk"	1.9	232	Halfmoon Pass	SJ
319	13,402	Point 13,402	"Phoenix Pk"	1.7	422	Halfmoon Pass	SJ
630	13,015	Point 13,015	Point 13,402	1.2	315	Halfmoon Pass	SJ
40	14,048	Handies Pk	Uncompahgre Pk	11.2	2,148	Handies Pk	SJ
78	13,860	Jones Mtn A	Handies Pk	1.7	520	Handies Pk	SJ
101	13,807	Niagara Pk	Jones Mtn A	0.6	587	Handies Pk	SJ
102	13,806	"American Pk"	Jones Mtn A	0.8	466	Handies Pk	SJ
136	13,722	"Animas Forks Mtn"	Handies Pk	3.5	1,142	Handies Pk	SJ
S	13,708	Point 13,708	"Animas Forks Mtn"	0.5	288	Handies Pk	SJ
154	13,688	Point 13,688 B	"Animas Forks Mtn"	1.1	388	Handies Pk	SJ
169	13,660	Wood Mtn	Point 13,688 B	0.5	320	Handies Pk	SJ
	13,599	"North Crown Mtn"	Niagara Pk	0.6	259	Handies Pk	SJ
	13,577	Gravel Mtn	Point 13,688 B	0.4	157	Handies Pk	SJ
	13,569	Crown Mtn	Niagara Pk	0.6	229	Handies Pk	SJ
233	13,535	Point 13,535	Jones Mtn A	1.5	515	Handies Pk	SJ
287	13,454	Hanson Pk	Tower Mtn	3.6	914	Handies Pk	SJ
	13,447	Hurricane Pk	Hanson Pk	0.8	267	Handies Pk	SJ
304	13,427	Point 13,427	Wood Mtn	1.4	407	Handies Pk	SJ
369	13,330	"Proposal Pk"	Hanson Pk	1.9	550	Handies Pk	SJ
370	13,328	Cinnamon Mtn	Point 13,535 B	1.1	308	Handies Pk	SJ
375	13,321	Sunshine Mtn	Point 13,540 B	2.5	1,421	Handies Pk	SJ
	13,310	Emery Pk	Point 13,330	0.4	130	Handies Pk	SJ
409	13,286	Bonita Pk	"Proposal Pk"	1.0	506	Handies Pk	SJ
421	13,274	Seigal Mtn	"Animas Forks Mtn"	1.0	374	Handies Pk	SJ
432	13,260	Point 13,260 A	Seigal Mtn	2.2	520	Handies Pk	SJ
S	13,220	California Mtn	Hanson Pk	0.6	280	Handies Pk	SJ
467	13,218	Engineer Mtn	Point 13,260 A	0.9	438	Handies Pk	SJ
487	13,203	Tuttle Mtn	Brown Mtn	1.7	503	Handies Pk	SJ
543	13,132	"Darley Mtn"	Point 13,260 A	0.9	512	Handies Pk	SJ

Rank	Elev	Peak Name	Parent	Mile	Rise	Quadrangle	Rg
574	13,093	Point 13,093	Sunshine Mtn	1.4	353	Handies Pk	SJ
590	13,075	Point 13,075	Hanson Pk	1.0	415	Handies Pk	SJ
607	13,052	Houghton Mtn	Tuttle Mtn	1.5	472	Handies Pk	SJ
207	13,575	Rosalie Pk	Evans A, Mt	3.0	675	Harris Park	FR
235	13,530	"Epaulie"	Rosalie Pk	1.2	350	Harris Park	FR
325	13,391	Rogers Pk	Evans A, Mt	2.4	515	Harris Park	FR
12	14,265	Castle Pk	La Plata Pk	20.8	2,337	Hayden Pk	EL
	14,060	Conundrum Pk	Castle Pk	0.4	240	Hayden Pk	EL
62	13,943	Cathedral Pk	Castle Pk	1.7	523	Hayden Pk	EL
177	13,635	"Electric Pk"	Cathedral Pk	0.9	335	Hayden Pk	EL
	13,561	Hayden Pk	"Electric Pk"	0.8	181	Hayden Pk	EL
354	13,348	Malemute Pk	Conundrum Pk	1.1	368	Hayden Pk	EL
	13,322	Leahy Pk	"Electric Pk"	0.9	142	Hayden Pk	EL
443	13,244	Point 13,244	Point 13,336	1.1	424	Highland Pk	EL
	13,155	Baldy Mtn	Point 13,244	0.6	175	Highland Pk	EL
531	13,143	Willoughby Mtn	Point 13,336	1.8	442	Highland Pk	EL
476	13,209	Homestake Pk	Whitney Pk	5.5	1,459	Homestake Reservoir	SW
66	13,931	Adams, Mt	Kit Carson Mtn	1.9	871	Horn Pk	SC
200	13,580	Point 13,580 B	Adams, Mt	0.5	440	Horn Pk	SC
216	13,554	Fluted Pk	Adams, Mt	1.2	734	Horn Pk	SC
222	13,546	Point 13,546	Adams, Mt	0.8	646	Horn Pk	SC
290	13,450	Horn Pk	Fluted Pk	1.3	710	Horn Pk	SC
418	13,277	Comanche Pk	Fluted Pk	1.5	497	Horn Pk	SC
444	13,244	Spring Mtn	Venable Pk	0.7	464	Horn Pk	SC
520	13,153	Point 13,153 B	Adams, Mt	0.7	373	Horn Pk	SC
530	13,143	Little Horn Pk	Fluted Pk	0.9	323	Horn Pk	SC
220	13,552	Tower Mtn	Niagara Pk	5.4	1,652	Howardsville	SJ
268	13,478	Canby Mtn	Niagara Pk	6.2	938	Howardsville	SJ
289	13,451	Kendall Pk	Canby Mtn	4.1	1,311	Howardsville	SJ
297	13,434	Point 13,434	Kendall Pk	1.2	534	Howardsville	SJ
310	13,416	Little Giant Pk	Kendall Pk	1.3	556	Howardsville	SJ
320	13,402	Rhoda, Mt	Point 13,434	0.4	302	Howardsville	SJ
343	13,370	Dome Mtn	Tower Mtn	1.3	670	Howardsville	SJ
395	13,300	Galena Mtn	Canby Mtn	2.1	360	Howardsville	SJ
407	13,292	Sheep Mtn A	Canby Mtn	1.9	632	Howardsville	SJ
	13,259	Whitehead Pk	Rhoda, Mt	0.4	119	Howardsville	SJ
	13,222	Macomber Pk	Tower Mtn	0.7	122	Howardsville	SJ
461	13,220	Greenhalgh Mtn	Sheep Mtn A	0.8	400	Howardsville	SJ
S	13,220	King Solomon Mtn	Little Giant Pk	0.5	280	Howardsville	SJ
508	13,165	"Stony Pass Pk"	Canby Mtn	0.7	577	Howardsville	SJ
561	13,109	Point 13,109	Rhoda, Mt	0.8	329	Howardsville	SJ
597	13,069	Point 13,069	Niagara Pk	4.1	329	Howardsville	SJ
	13,049	Green Mtn	"Stony Pass Pk"	0.6	69	Howardsville	SJ
	13,019	Cuba BM	Niagara Pk	3.4	119	Howardsville	SJ
54	13,988	Grizzly Pk A	La Plata Pk	6.7	1,928	Independence Pass	SW
95	13,823	"Lackawanna Pk"	Casco Pk	1.8	883	Independence Pass	SW
116	13,780	Garfield Pk	Grizzly Pk A	0.8	360	Independence Pass	SW
S	13,660	Point 13,660 C	"Lackawanna Pk"	0.9	280	Independence Pass	SW
256	13,500	Point 13,500	Twining Pk	0.7	360	Independence Pass	SW
	13,500	Red Mtn B	Garfield Pk	0.4	120	Independence Pass	SW
278	13,463	Point 13,463	Garfield Pk	1.8	563	Independence Pass	SW
283	13,460	Point 13,460	Sayers BM	1.4	440	Independence Pass	SW
S	13,300	Point 13,300 E	Point 13,460	0.6	280	Independence Pass	SW
491	13,198	Point 13,198	Grizzly Pk A	2.8	658	Independence Pass	SW
568	13,100	Middle Mtn A	Point 13,463	1.1	520	Independence Pass	SW
S	13,060	"Igloo Pk"	Point 13,198	0.5	280	Independence Pass	SW
113	13,786	Potosi Pk	Teakettle Mtn	1.0	806	Ironton	SJ
250	13,510	Point 13,510 B	Emma, Mt	5.0	610	Ironton	SJ

Rank	Elev	Peak Name	Parent	Mile	Rise	Quadrangle	Rg
S	13,509	Telluride Pk	Point 13,510 A	0.5	289	Ironton	SJ
270	13,477	"T 10"	Three Needles	0.6	537	Ironton	SJ
326	13,385	Chicago Pk	Point 13,510 B	1.8	365	Ironton	SJ
350	13,359	"T 7"	Point 13,510 B	1.4	499	Ironton	SJ
363	13,339	Brown Mtn	Hanson Pk	1.8	639	Ironton	SJ
376	13,321	Trico Pk	Point 13,510 B	0.9	461	Ironton	SJ
378	13,315	"T 8"	"T 7"	0.7	495	Ironton	SJ
479	13,206	Hayden Mtn South	"T 8"	1.1	549	Ironton	SJ
536	13,139	Hayden Mtn North	Hayden Mtn South	1.2	519	Ironton	SJ
	13,036	United States Mtn	Chicago Pk	1.0	176	Ironton	SJ
203	13,579	Chiefs Head Pk	Longs Pk	1.4	719	Isolation Pk	FR
259	13,497	Pagoda Mtn	Longs Pk	0.7	397	Isolation Pk	FR
384	13,310	Alice, Mt	Chiefs Head Pk	1.4	850	Isolation Pk	FR
503	13,176	Copeland Mtn	Alice, Mt	4.1	1,116	Isolation Pk	FR
538	13,138	Ogalalla Pk	Copeland Mtn	1.4	718	Isolation Pk	FR
554	13,118	Isolation Pk	Copeland Mtn	2.2	938	Isolation Pk	FR
485	13,203	Bennett Pk	Summit Pk	17.0	1,663	Jasper	SJ
587	13,078	Whale Pk	Geneva Pk	4.7	982	Jefferson	FR
451	13,232	Hesperus Mtn	Grizzly Pk B	24.5	2,852	La Plata	SJ
463	13,220	Lavender Pk	Hesperus Mtn	0.5	400	La Plata	SJ
S	13,192	Moss, Mt	Lavender Pk	0.3	292	La Plata	SJ
525	13,149	Babcock Pk	Lavender Pk	0.9	529	La Plata	SJ
	13,123	Spiller Pk	Babcock Pk	0.5	183	La Plata	SJ
S	13,062	Centennial Pk	Lavender Pk	0.5	282	La Plata	SJ
631	13,014	Chief Mtn	Point 13,261	9.8	2,474	Little Squaw Creek	SJ
15	14,255	Longs Pk	Torreys Pk	43.5	2,940	Longs Pk	FR
	14,060	"Southeast Longs"	Longs Pk	0.2	240	Longs Pk	FR
	13,340	Glacier Ridge	Longs Pk	0.5	40	Longs Pk	FR
	13,340	Ships Prow	Longs Pk	0.5	40	Longs Pk	FR
	13,326	Storm Pk B	Longs Pk	0.8	186	Longs Pk	FR
416	13,281	Lady Washington, Mt	Longs Pk	0.7	301	Longs Pk	FR
219	13,553	Pettingell Pk	Torreys Pk	7.4	1,563	Loveland Pass	FR
404	13,294	Citadel	Pettingell Pk	1.0	314	Loveland Pass	FR
462	13,220	Hagar Mtn	Point 13,294	0.5	320	Loveland Pass	FR
471	13,215	"Hassell Pk"	Pettingell Pk	1.5	395	Loveland Pass	FR
633	13,010	"Golden Bear Pk"	Hagar Mtn	1.2	350	Loveland Pass	FR
372	13,326	West Buffalo Pk	Point 13,374	9.7	1,986	Marmot Pk	TM
393	13,300	East Buffalo Pk	West Buffalo Pk	0.9	480	Marmot Pk	TM
24	14,156	Maroon Pk	Castle Pk	8.1	2,336	Maroon Bells	EL
47	14,018	Pyramid Pk	Maroon Pk	2.1	1,518	Maroon Bells	EL
	14,014	North Maroon Pk	Maroon Pk	0.4	234	Maroon Bells	EL
65	13,932	"Thunder Pyramid"	Pyramid Pk	0.6	312	Maroon Bells	EL
105	13,803	"Castleabra"	Castle Pk	0.9	423	Maroon Bells	EL
137	13,722	Point 13,722	"Thunder Pyramid"	0.4	302	Maroon Bells	EL
180	13,631	Point 13,631 B	Point 13,722	0.7	331	Maroon Bells	EL
231	13,537	Point 13,537	White Rock Mtn	2.5	757	Maroon Bells	EL
246	13,516	Keefe Pk	Point 13,537	1.3	496	Maroon Bells	EL
258	13,497	Hunter Pk	Keefe Pk	1.4	477	Maroon Bells	EL
285	13,460	Sleeping Sexton	North Maroon Pk	0.6	440	Maroon Bells	EL
314	13,409	Hilliard Pk	Keefe Pk	0.6	309	Maroon Bells	EL
335	13,380	Precarious Pk	Point 13,631 B	2.1	640	Maroon Bells	EL
342	13,370	Buckskin BM	Sleeping Sexton	2.0	908	Maroon Bells	EL
365	13,336	Point 13,336	Buckskin BM	1.1	636	Maroon Bells	EL
433	13,260	Point 13,260 B	Precarious Pk	0.8	440	Maroon Bells	EL
449	13,233	Belleview Mtn	Maroon Pk	1.9	693	Maroon Bells	EL
452	13,232	Point 13,232 A	Point 13,260 B	0.4	412	Maroon Bells	EL
470	13,216	Point 13,216	Point 13,380	0.7	316	Maroon Bells	EL
499	13,180	Point 13,180 A	Point 13,631 B	0.5	320	Maroon Bells	EL

Rank	Elev	Peak Name	Parent	Mile	Rise	Quadrangle	Rg
545	13,130	Point 13,130	Point 13,180 A	0.8	350	Maroon Bells	EL
615	13,039	Point 13,039	Sleeping Sexton	0.9	419	Maroon Bells	EL
624	13,020	Point 13,020 A	Point 13,336	0.5	320	Maroon Bells	EL
17	14,229	Shavano, Mt	Antero, Mt	3.8	1,619	Maysville	SW
	13,630	"Esprit Point"	Shavano, Mt	0.8	250	Maysville	SW
371	13,327	McHenrys Pk	Chiefs Head Pk	1.2	907	McHenrys Pk	FR
477	13,208	Powell Pk	McHenrys Pk	0.4	388	McHenrys Pk	FR
521	13,153	Taylor Pk B	Powell Pk	1.0	413	McHenrys Pk	FR
359	13,340	Herard, Mt	Cleveland Pk	4.7	2,040	Medano Pass	SC
519	13,153	Point 13,153 A	Herard Mtn	0.9	653	Medano Pass	SC
255	13,502	North Arapaho Pk	Chiefs Head Pk	15.4	1,665	Monarch Lake	FR
292	13,441	Apache Pk	North Arapaho Pk	2.2	1,101	Monarch Lake	FR
315	13,409	Navajo Pk	Apache Pk	0.4	309	Monarch Lake	FR
	13,397	South Arapaho Pk	North Arapaho Pk	0.5	97	Monarch Lake	FR
523	13,150	Arikaree Pk	Kiowa Pk	0.8	570	Monarch Lake	FR
	13,140	"Dicker's Peck"	Navajo Pk	0.1	40	Monarch Lake	FR
578	13,088	Paiute Pk	Audubon, Mt	0.9	468	Monarch Lake	FR
616	13,038	"Old Baldy"	North Arapaho Pk	0.9	338	Monarch Lake	FR
	13,023	Niwot Ridge	Navajo Pk	0.6	163	Monarch Lake	FR
111	13,794	Square Top Mtn	Edwards, Mt	3.4	814	Montezuma	FR
129	13,738	Argentine Pk	Edwards, Mt	1.9	638	Montezuma	FR
316	13,408	Wilcox, Mt	Argentine Pk	1.1	548	Montezuma	FR
419	13,277	Ruby Mtn	Grays Pk	1.2	439	Montezuma	FR
425	13,266	Geneva Pk	Argentine Pk	4.7	926	Montezuma	FR
	13,238	Landslide Pk	Geneva Pk	0.4	138	Montezuma	FR
501	13,180	Santa Fe Pk	Geneva Pk	1.3	480	Montezuma	FR
	13,134	Sullivan Mtn	Santa Fe Pk	0.6	274	Montezuma	FR
10	14,269	Antero, Mt	Harvard, Mt	17.7	2,503	Mt Antero	SW
20	14,197	Princeton, Mt	Antero, Mt	5.2	2,431	Mt Antero	SW
140	13,712	Point 13,712	Shavano, Mt	0.9	332	Mt Antero	SW
164	13,667	White, Mt	Antero, Mt	1.3	847	Mt Antero	SW
	13,604	Jones Pk	Point 13,712	0.7	144	Mt Antero	SW
	13,300	"Tigger Pk"	Princeton, Mt	1.1	240	Mt Antero	SW
85	13,845	Oklahoma, Mt	Massive, Mt	1.8	745	Mt Champion	SW
123	13,761	Deer Mt	Oklahoma, Mt	1.7	941	Mt Champion	SW
133	13,736	Point 13,736	Deer Mtn	1.2	676	Mt Champion	SW
141	13,711	Twining Pk	Point 13,736	2.2	1,251	Mt Champion	SW
173	13,646	Champion, Mt	Point 13,736	0.6	306	Mt Champion	SW
S	13,545	Point 13,545	Twining Pk	0.7	285	Mt Champion	SW
232	13,535	"K49"	Deer Mtn	1.2	555	Mt Champion	SW
331	13,382	Williams Mtn	Twining Pk	4.1	1,682	Mt Champion	SW
332	13,380	Geissler Mtn East	Twining Pk	1.1	560	Mt Champion	SW
391	13,301	Geissler Mtn West	Geissler Mtn East	0.6	481	Mt Champion	SW
398	13,300	Point 13,300 B	Twining Pk	2.7	600	Mt Champion	SW
411	13,284	Point 13,284	Point 13,300 B	2.7	424	Mt Champion	SW
S	13,230	Point 13,230 B	Point 13,284	0.7	290	Mt Champion	SW
474	13,212	Point 13,212	Point 13,284	0.7	312	Mt Champion	SW
488	13,203	Williams Mtn South B	Williams Mtn	0.5	423	Mt Champion	SW
489	13,202	Point 13,202	Twining Pk	2.0	422	Mt Champion	SW
S	13,145	Point 13,145 B	Point 13,284	1.2	285	Mt Champion	SW
562	13,108	Williams Mtn North	Williams Mtn	0.8	408	Mt Champion	SW
622	13,026	Point 13,026	Point 13,202	1.7	326	Mt Champion	SW
636	13,003	Point 13,003	Point 13,026	1.9	503	Mt Champion	SW
637	13,001	Point 13,001	Point 13,202	0.9	501	Mt Champion	SW
1	14,433	Elbert, Mt	Whitney, Mt	667.0	9,093	Mt Elbert	SW
5	14,336	La Plata Pk	Elbert, Mt	6.3	2,276	Mt Elbert	SW
	14,180	"East La Plata"	La Plata Pk	0.2	80	Mt Elbert	SW
	14,134	"South Elbert"	Elbert, Mt	1.0	234	Mt Elbert	SW

Rank	Elev	Peak Name	Parent	Mile	Rise	Quadrangle	Rg
64	13,933	Hope, Mt	La Plata Pk	2.9	873	Mt Elbert	SW
69	13,908	Casco Pk	French Mtn	1.2	648	Mt Elbert	SW
114	13,783	Rinker Pk	La Plata Pk	1.8	923	Mt Elbert	SW
122	13,761	Bull Hill	Elbert, Mt	1.6	421	Mt Elbert	SW
132	13,738	Sayers BM	La Plata Pk	1.9	958	Mt Elbert	SW
186	13,616	Point 13,616	La Plata Pk	1.6	436	Mt Elbert	SW
234	13,531	Point 13,531	Hope, Mt	1.5	431	Mt Elbert	SW
282	13,461	Quail Mtn	Hope, Mt	1.4	921	Mt Elbert	SW
	13,333	Twin Pks B	Rinker Pk	0.9	233	Mt Elbert	SW
S	13,220	Ellingwood Ridge	La Plata Pk	1.5	280	Mt Elbert	SW
14	14,264	Evans, Mt	Grays Pk	9.8	2,764	Mt Evans	FR
	14,256	"West Evans"	Evans, Mt	0.3	116	Mt Evans	FR
38	14,060	Bierstadt, Mt	Evans, Mt	1.4	720	Mt Evans	FR
	13,842	Spalding, Mt	Evans, Mt	1.1	262	Mt Evans	FR
190	13,602	Gray Wolf Mtn	Evans, Mt	2.2	582	Mt Evans	FR
	13,523	Epaulet Mtn	"Epaulie"	0.5	143	Mt Evans	FR
389	13,307	Warren, Mt	Rogers Pk	1.1	367	Mt Evans	FR
3	14,420	Harvard, Mt	Elbert, Mt	15.0	2,360	Mt Harvard	SW
18	14,197	Belford, Mt	Harvard, Mt	3.3	1,337	Mt Harvard	SW
26	14,153	Oxford, Mt	Belford, Mt	1.2	653	Mt Harvard	SW
35	14,073	Columbia, Mt	Harvard, Mt	1.9	893	Mt Harvard	SW
121	13,762	Point 13,762	Harvard, Mt	2.8	822	Mt Harvard	SW
S	13,580	Point 13,580 C	Harvard, Mt	1.0	280	Mt Harvard	SW
340	13,374	Point 13,374	Harvard, Mt	1.9	394	Mt Harvard	SW
	13,292	Waverly Mtn	Oxford, Mt	1.1	152	Mt Harvard	SW
	13,270	Pecks Pk	Belford, Mt	1.0	50	Mt Harvard	SW
163	13,670	Jackson, Mt	Holy Cross, Mt of the	3.2	1,810	Mt Jackson	SW
298	13,433	Point 13,433	Jackson, Mt	0.6	413	Mt Jackson	SW
330	13,382	Gold Dust Pk	Jackson, Mt	3.1	922	Mt Jackson	SW
355	13,346	"North Gold Dust"	Gold Dust Pk	1.3	806	Mt Jackson	SW
494	13,192	"Fancy Pk"	Point 13,768	2.2	372	Mt Jackson	SW
537	13,139	Savage Pk	"Fancy Pk"	2.8	1,153	Mt Jackson	SW
547	13,126	Pika Pk	Gold Dust Pk	0.7	506	Mt Jackson	SW
570	13,100	Point 13,100 B	Pika Pk	2.1	600	Mt Jackson	SW
582	13,085	Point 13,085	Point 13,100 B	1.0	625	Mt Jackson	SW
	13,043	Eagle Pk B	Point 13,100 B	0.4	233	Mt Jackson	SW
2	14,421	Massive, Mt	Elbert, Mt	5.1	1,961	Mt Massive	SW
S	14,340	"North Massive"	Massive, Mt	0.9	280	Mt Massive	SW
	14,300	"Massive Green"	Massive, Mt	0.4	120	Mt Massive	SW
	14,132	"South Massive"	Massive, Mt	0.7	232	Mt Massive	SW
63	13,940	French Mtn	Elbert, Mt	2.1	1,080	Mt Massive	SW
	13,876	Frasco BM	French Mtn	0.5	256	Mt Massive	SW
51	14,005	Holy Cross, Mt of the	Massive, Mt	18.9	2,105	Mt of the Holy Cross	SW
91	13,831	Holy Cross Ridge	Holy Cross, Mt of the	0.6	331	Mt of the Holy Cross	SW
118	13,768	Point 13,768	Holy Cross Ridge	0.8	388	Mt of the Holy Cross	SW
422	13,271	Whitney Pk	Point 13,768	1.4	691	Mt of the Holy Cross	SW
441	13,248	Point 13,248	Holy Cross Ridge	1.3	308	Mt of the Holy Cross	SW
	13,237	Notch Mtn	Point 13,248	0.9	217	Mt of the Holy Cross	SW
58	13,971	Ouray, Mt	Shavano, Mt	13.5	2,671	Mt Ouray	SW
274	13,472	Point 13,472 A	Ouray, Mt	1.9	1,172	Mt Ouray	SW
201	13,580	Powell, Mt (Pk B)	Jackson, Mt	21.8	3,000	Mt Powell	GO
307	13,420	Eagles Nest (Pk A)	Powell, Mt	1.2	640	Mt Powell	GO
	13,140	Guyselman Mtn (Pk M)	"Pk L"	0.6	240	Mt Powell	GO
552	13,121	"Pk N"	"Pk L"	1.2	421	Mt Powell	GO
45	14,036	Sherman, Mt	Democrat, Mt	8.1	896	Mt Sherman	TM
	13,951	Gemini Pk	Sherman, Mt	0.7	171	Mt Sherman	TM
72	13,898	Horseshoe Mtn	Sherman, Mt	2.8	758	Mt Sherman	TM
81	13,855	Dyer Mtn	Sherman, Mt	1.2	475	Mt Sherman	TM

Rank	Elev	Peak Name	Parent	Mile	Rise	Quadrangle	Rg
126	13,748	Sheridan, Mt	Sherman, Mt	1.3	608	Mt Sherman	TM
	13,739	Ptarmigan Pk	Horseshoe Mtn	2.5	279	Mt Sherman	TM
	13,684	White Ridge	Sherman, Mt	1.2	184	Mt Sherman	TM
	13,572	Weston Pk	Horseshoe Mtn	3.6	272	Mt Sherman	TM
	13,409	Finnback Knob	Horseshoe Mtn	0.6	149	Mt Sherman	TM
	13,348	Peerless Mtn	Horseshoe Mtn	0.9	168	Mt Sherman	TM
	13,047	West Dyer Mtn	Dyer Mtn	0.7	267	Mt Sherman	TM
27	14,150	Sneffels, Mt	Wilson, Mt	15.8	3,930	Mt Sneffels	SJ
98	13,819	Teakettle Mtn	Sneffels, Mt	1.7	759	Mt Sneffels	SJ
	13,694	"Kismet"	Sneffels, Mt	0.4	194	Mt Sneffels	SJ
155	13,686	Cirque Mtn	Teakettle Mtn	0.6	546	Mt Sneffels	SJ
260	13,496	Mears Pk	"T 0"	1.3	556	Mt Sneffels	SJ
276	13,468	Ridgeway, Mt	Teakettle Mtn	1.0	448	Mt Sneffels	SJ
293	13,441	"S 6"	"T 0"	1.0	381	Mt Sneffels	SJ
445	13,242	"S 4"	"S 6"	0.8	302	Mt Sneffels	SJ
	13,041	Wolcott Mtn	"S 6"	0.6	181	Mt Sneffels	SJ
16	14,246	Wilson, Mt	Uncompahgre Pk	33.1	4,026	Mt Wilson	SJ
	14,110	"South Wilson"	Wilson, Mt	0.3	170	Mt Wilson	SJ
	14,100	"West Wilson"	Wilson, Mt	0.3	120	Mt Wilson	SJ
48	14,017	Wilson Pk	Wilson, Mt	1.5	877	Mt Wilson	SJ
67	13,913	Gladstone Pk	Wilson, Mt	0.6	733	Mt Wilson	SJ
	13,188	Sheep Mtn B	San Miguel Pk	1.3	128	Mt Wilson	SJ
556	13,113	Lizard Head	Gladstone Pk	1.9	1,113	Mt Wilson	SJ
21	14,196	Yale, Mt	Harvard, Mt	5.6	1,896	Mt Yale	SW
183	13,626	Point 13,626	Princeton, Mt	1.4	486	Mt Yale	SW
295	13,435	"Mascot Pk"	Yale, Mt	0.8	375	Mt Yale	SW
475	13,209	Gladstone Ridge	Jones Mtn B	2.6	949	Mt Yale	SW
S	13,740	"West Eolus"	Eolus, Mt	0.3	280	Mtn View Crest	SJ
	13,125	Kennedy, Mt	Aztec Mtn	0.6	265	Mtn View Crest	SJ
179	13,631	Point 13,631 A	Garfield Pk	2.2	971	New York Pk	SW
253	13,505	Point 13,505	Point 13,631 A	1.3	525	New York Pk	SW
397	13,300	Point 13,300 A	Point 13,505	1.4	520	New York Pk	SW
413	13,282	Point 13,282	Point 13,300 A	1.1	822	New York Pk	SW
414	13,282	Truro Pk	Point 13,300 A	1.3	822	New York Pk	SW
534	13,140	Point 13,140 C	Truro Pk	0.4	320	New York Pk	SW
576	13,090	Point 13,090	Point 13,140 C	1.1	350	New York Pk	SW
592	13,074	Point 13,074	Point 13,300 A	1.0	454	New York Pk	SW
603	13,058	Owen B, Mt	Treasury Mtn	7.5	1,358	Oh Be Joyful	EL
74	13,894	Vermillion Pk	Gladstone Pk	9.2	3,674	Ophir	SJ
117	13,780	Golden Horn	Vermillion Pk	0.4	400	Ophir	SJ
119	13,767	US Grant Pk	Golden Horn	1.7	747	Ophir	SJ
	13,761	Fuller Pk	Vermillion Pk	0.5	261	Ophir	SJ
124	13,752	San Miguel Pk	Vermillion Pk	2.4	1,307	Ophir	SJ
130	13,738	Grizzly Pk B	San Miguel Pk	1.6	758	Ophir	SJ
131	13,738	Pilot Knob	Golden Horn	0.5	398	Ophir	SJ
150	13,693	Rolling Mtn	San Miguel Pk	2.3	913	Ophir	SJ
166	13,661	Lookout Pk	Gilpin Pk	8.6	841	Ophir	SJ
228	13,540	"V 4"	US Grant Pk	0.4	320	Ophir	SJ
239	13,528	"V 3"	US Grant Pk	0.4	388	Ophir	SJ
272	13,475	"V 10"	Grizzly Pk B	0.7	375	Ophir	SJ
301	13,432	Twin Sister East	Rolling Mtn	2.2	1,332	Ophir	SJ
336	13,380	South Lookout Pk	US Grant Pk	1.2	520	Ophir	SJ
341	13,374	Twin Sister West	Twin Sister East	0.4	394	Ophir	SJ
357	13,342	Beattie Pk	Vermillion Pk	0.7	322	Ophir	SJ
387	13,309	"V 2"	US Grant Pk	0.8	409	Ophir	SJ
S	13,300	Point 13,300 F	South Lookout Pk	0.4	280	Ophir	SJ
402	13,300	"V 8"	Beattie Pk	0.6	320	Ophir	SJ
435	13,260	"V 9"	Rolling Mtn	1.0	397	Ophir	SJ

Rank	Elev	Peak Name	Parent	Mile	Rise	Quadrangle	Rg
	13,177	Yellow Mtn	Pilot Knob	0.6	197	Ophir	SJ
513	13,159	Point 13,159	Lookout Pk	1.3	379	Ophir	SJ
517	13,156	"V 5"	South Lookout Pk	1.3	616	Ophir	SJ
261	13,492	Whitehouse Mtn	Teakettle Mtn	1.9	592	Ouray	SJ
567	13,100	"Corbett Pk"	Whitehouse Mtn	0.5	320	Ouray	SJ
243	13,521	Star Pk	Castle Pk	4.1	816	Pearl Pass	EL
296	13,435	Taylor Pk A	Star Pk	1.3	815	Pearl Pass	EL
337	13,378	Italian Mtn	Star Pk	3.5	1,358	Pearl Pass	EL
349	13,362	Pearl Mtn	Castle Pk	2.5	582	Pearl Pass	EL
381	13,312	Point 13,312 B	Pearl Mtn	0.6	412	Pearl Pass	EL
	13,209	Lambertson Pk	Italian Mtn	0.5	229	Pearl Pass	EL
299	13,432	Jenkins Mtn	Sayres BM	4.0	692	Pieplant	SW
328	13,384	Prize BM	Point 13,631 A	1.6	604	Pieplant	SW
374	13,322	Point 13,322	Jenkins Mtn	2.4	902	Pieplant	SW
382	13,312	Point 13,312 C	Point 13,463	1.0	452	Pieplant	SW
403	13,295	Point 13,295	Sayers BM	2.7	435	Pieplant	SW
415	13,281	Grizzly Pk E	Jenkins Mtn	1.9	581	Pieplant	SW
447	13,235	Point 13,235	Point 13,253	0.9	375	Pieplant	SW
453	13,232	Point 13,232 B	Sayres BM	1.7	332	Pieplant	SW
533	13,140	Point 13,140 B	Jenkins Mtn	1.1	320	Pieplant	SW
30	14,110	Pikes Pk	Evans, Mt	60.3	5,530	Pikes Pk	FR
504	13,172	Conejos Pk	Summit Pk	8.2	1,912	Platoro	SJ
88	13,841	Half Pk	Handies Pk	3.9	1,501	Pole Creek Mtn	SJ
138	13,716	Pole Creek Mtn	Half Pk	5.2	1,536	Pole Creek Mtn	SJ
168	13,660	Point 13,660 B	Pole Creek Mtn	1.5	840	Pole Creek Mtn	SJ
170	13,657	Carson Pk	Half Pk	3.6	1,477	Pole Creek Mtn	SJ
197	13,581	Point 13,581	Carson Pk	1.5	681	Pole Creek Mtn	SJ
199	13,580	Point 13,580 A	Point 13,581	1.2	360	Pole Creek Mtn	SJ
240	13,524	Point 13,524 A	Carson Pk	1.4	464	Pole Creek Mtn	SJ
291	13,450	Point 13,450	Carson Pk	1.2	350	Pole Creek Mtn	SJ
323	13,393	Bent Pk	Carson Pk	1.2	373	Pole Creek Mtn	SJ
S	13,382	"East Pole Creek Mtn"	Pole Creek Mtn	0.8	282	Pole Creek Mtn	SJ
510	13,164	Point 13,164	Half Pk	1.3	384	Pole Creek Mtn	SJ
46	14,034	Redcloud Pk	Handies Pk	4.9	1,454	Redcloud Pk	SJ
53	14,001	Sunshine Pk	Redcloud Pk	1.3	501	Redcloud Pk	SJ
90	13,832	Point 13,832	Redcloud Pk	1.4	812	Redcloud Pk	SJ
99	13,811	Point 13,811	Point 13,832	1.2	551	Redcloud Pk	SJ
109	13,795	Point 13,795	Handies Pk	1.3	495	Redcloud Pk	SJ
151	13,691	Point 13,691	Point 13,832	2.7	471	Redcloud Pk	SJ
153	13,688	Point 13,688 A	Point 13,832	1.6	428	Redcloud Pk	SJ
161	13,674	Point 13,674	Half Pk	1.3	374	Redcloud Pk	SJ
211	13,566	Point 13,566	Point 13,691	1.9	746	Redcloud Pk	SJ
223	13,542	Whitecross Mtn	Handies Pk	1.4	562	Redcloud Pk	SJ
227	13,540	Point 13,540 B	Wood Mtn	2.6	520	Redcloud Pk	SJ
288	13,454	"Campbell Creek Pk"	Point 13,795	1.0	394	Redcloud Pk	SJ
300	13,432	"Sundog"	Sunshine Pk	0.9	332	Redcloud Pk	SJ
380	13,312	Point 13,312 A	Point 13,566	0.8	452	Redcloud Pk	SJ
500	13,180	Point 13,180 B	Point 13,691	2.1	524	Redcloud Pk	SJ
97	13,821	Rio Grande Pyramid	Jagged Mtn	10.8	1,881	Rio Grande Pyramid	SJ
286	13,455	Ute Ridge	White Dome	4.9	962	Rio Grande Pyramid	SJ
358	13,342	Point 13,342	Ute Ridge	1.4	726	Rio Grande Pyramid	SJ
388	13,308	Point 13,308	Point 13,342	0.8	606	Rio Grande Pyramid	SJ
455	13,230	Point 13,230 A	Point 13,308	1.9	770	Rio Grande Pyramid	SJ
505	13,169	Point 13,169	Point 13,230 A	1.2	989	Rio Grande Pyramid	SJ
516	13,157	"Window Pk"	Rio Grande Pyramid	0.9	300	Rio Grande Pyramid	SJ
628	13,017	Point 13,017	"Window Pk"	1.0	400	Rio Grande Pyramid	SJ
110	13,794	Rito Alto Pk	Adams, Mt	7.3	1,134	Rito Alto Pk	SC
241	13,524	Point 13,524 B	Gibbs Pk	3.3	624	Rito Alto Pk	SC

Rank	Elev	Peak Name	Parent	Mile	Rise	Quadrangle	Rg
252	13,507	Eureka Mtn	Rito Alto Pk	2.0	807	Rito Alto Pk	SC
263	13,490	Point 13,490	Point 13,513	1.0	990	Rito Alto Pk	SC
353	13,350	Hermit Pk	Rito Alto Pk	0.9	330	Rito Alto Pk	SC
367	13,334	Venable Pk	Fluted Pk	2.7	634	Rito Alto Pk	SC
551	13,122	Point 13,122	Point 13,490	1.2	302	Rito Alto Pk	SC
599	13,062	Point 13,062 B	Hermit Pk	1.9	842	Rito Alto Pk	SC
602	13,060	Point 13,060 B	Point 13,062 B	0.4	360	Rito Alto Pk	SC
606	13,054	Point 13,054	Eureka Mtn	1.6	594	Rito Alto Pk	SC
621	13,028	Point 13,028	Point 13,060 B	0.7	328	Rito Alto Pk	SC
25	14,155	Tabeguache Pk	Shavano, Mt	0.7	455	Saint Elmo	SW
75	13,870	"North Carbonate"	Antero, Mt	2.4	1,050	Saint Elmo	SW
142	13,708	Grizzly Mtn	"North Carbonate"	1.7	568	Saint Elmo	SW
165	13,663	Carbonate Mtn	"North Carbonate"	2.0	434	Saint Elmo	SW
174	13,646	Point 13,646	Grizzly Mtn	1.7	546	Saint Elmo	SW
192	13,596	Cyclone Mtn	Carbonate Mtn	0.5	336	Saint Elmo	SW
	13,553	Mamma, Mt	Point 13,646	0.5	53	Saint Elmo	SW
236	13,528	Boulder Mtn	Point 13,646	1.6	588	Saint Elmo	SW
377	13,317	Point 13,317	Point 13,626	2.3	737	Saint Elmo	SW
522	13,151	Pomeroy Mtn	Grizzly Mtn	2.1	611	Saint Elmo	SW
586	13,078	Point 13,078	Point 13,317	1.4	738	Saint Elmo	SW
595	13,070	Point 13,070	Pomeroy Mtn	0.6	330	Saint Elmo	SW
440	13,252	"S 8"	Mears Pk	1.6	552	Sams	SJ
466	13,220	"S 7"	Mears Pk	1.0	400	Sams	SJ
541	13,134	"S 9"	"S 8"	0.7	354	Sams	SJ
626	13,020	"S 10"	"S 9"	0.8	360	Sams	SJ
	13,003	Ruffner Mtn	"S 7"	0.4	23	Sams	SJ
50	14,014	San Luis Pk	Redcloud Pk	27.1	3,116	San Luis Pk	SJ
106	13,801	Organ Mtn A	San Luis Pk	2.0	694	San Luis Pk	SJ
410	13,285	Point 13,285	San Luis Pk	2.5	665	San Luis Pk	SJ
S	13,180	Point 13,180 C	Point 13,285	0.5	280	San Luis Pk	SJ
518	13,155	Point 13,155	Point 13,285	1.7	415	San Luis Pk	SJ
559	13,111	Point 13,111	Point 13,510 A	4.6	811	San Luis Pk	SJ
506	13,168	Sheep Mtn C	Point 13,681	2.7	592	Sheep Mtn	SJ
569	13,100	Point 13,100 A	Point 13,681	1.8	480	Sheep Mtn	SJ
266	13,487	Storm Pk A	Tower Mtn	1.4	627	Silverton	SJ
346	13,368	Sultan Mtn	Twin Sister East	4.6	1,868	Silverton	SJ
364	13,338	Kendall Mtn	Kendall Pk	0.7	318	Silverton	SJ
373	13,325	Point 13,325	Storm Pk A	0.5	465	Silverton	SJ
498	13,180	Grand Turk	Sultan Mtn	0.6	404	Silverton	SJ
S	13,066	Kendall BM	Kendall Mtn	0.7	286	Silverton	SJ
612	13,042	Point 13,042	Twin Sisters East	2.1	942	Silverton	SJ
57	13,972	Pigeon Pk	Eolus, Mt	1.5	1,152	Snowdon Pk	SJ
89	13,835	Turret Pk	Pigeon Pk	0.5	735	Snowdon Pk	SJ
112	13,786	Animas Mtn	Pigeon Pk	1.2	1,086	Snowdon Pk	SJ
145	13,700	Fifteen, Pk	Turret Pk	0.2	320	Snowdon Pk	SJ
	13,500	Sixteen, Pk	Fifteen, Pk	0.1	80	Snowdon Pk	SJ
	13,420	Index, The	Animas Mtn	0.2	240	Snowdon Pk	SJ
	13,220	Little Finger	Fifteen, Pk	0.2	120	Snowdon Pk	SJ
	13,180	Point Pun	Graystone Pk	0.6	200	Snowdon Pk	SJ
515	13,158	Twilight Pk	Pigeon Pk	4.9	2,338	Snowdon Pk	SJ
	13,100	South Twilight Pk	Twilight Pk	0.3	200	Snowdon Pk	SJ
588	13,077	Snowdon Pk	Twilight Pk	3.8	1,337	Snowdon Pk	SJ
589	13,075	North Twilight Pk	Twilight Pk	0.4	335	Snowdon Pk	SJ
591	13,074	Garfield, Mt	Graystone Pk	1.0	374	Snowdon Pk	SJ
600	13,062	West Needle Mtn	Twilight Pk	1.0	562	Snowdon Pk	SJ
611	13,046	Point 13,046	Snowdon Pk	0.6	386	Snowdon Pk	SJ
31	14,092	Snowmass Mtn	Capitol Pk	2.3	1,152	Snowmass Mtn	EL
	14,020	"North Snowmass"	Snowmass Mtn	0.2	40	Snowmass Mtn	EL

Rank	Elev	Peak Name	Parent	Mile	Rise	Quadrangle	Rg
87	13,841	Hagerman Pk	Snowmass Mtn	0.6	341	Snowmass Mtn	EL
	13,620	Snowmass Pk	Hagerman Pk	0.2	120	Snowmass Mtn	EL
238	13,528	Treasure Mtn	Hagerman Pk	7.0	2,821	Snowmass Mtn	EL
281	13,462	Treasury Mtn	Treasure Mtn	1.4	522	Snowmass Mtn	EL
308	13,420	"Siberia Pk"	Snowmass Mtn	1.2	760	Snowmass Mtn	EL
598	13,062	Point 13,062 A	Hagerman Pk	2.1	642	Snowmass Mtn	EL
526	13,148	South River Pk	Montezuma Pk	21.3	2,228	South River Pk	SJ
184	13,626	West Spanish Pk	Culebra Pk	20.4	3,685	Spanish Pks	SC
55	13,983	Stewart Pk	San Luis Pk	2.5	883	Stewart Pk	SJ
147	13,698	Baldy Alto	Stewart Pk	1.2	518	Stewart Pk	SJ
	13,401	Baldy Chato	Stewart Pk	1.5	181	Stewart Pk	SJ
39	14,059	Sunlight Pk	Windom Pk	0.5	399	Storm King Pk	SJ
	14,039	North Eolus	Eolus, Mt	0.2	179	Storm King Pk	SJ
	13,995	"Sunlight Spire"	Sunlight Pk	0.2	215	Storm King Pk	SJ
77	13,864	Vestal Pk	Sunlight Pk	4.3	1,124	Storm King Pk	SJ
94	13,824	Jagged Mtn	Sunlight Pk	1.4	964	Storm King Pk	SJ
103	13,805	Trinity Pk	Vestal Pk	1.2	945	Storm King Pk	SJ
104	13,803	Arrow Pk	Vestal Pk	0.5	943	Storm King Pk	SJ
120	13,765	Trinity Pk West	Trinity Pk	0.4	385	Storm King Pk	SJ
125	13,752	Storm King Pk	Trinity Pk	1.3	612	Storm King Pk	SJ
128	13,745	Trinity Pk East	Trinity Pk	0.2	405	Storm King Pk	SJ
144	13,705	Six, Pk	Jagged Mtn	1.0	685	Storm King Pk	SJ
	13,705	Thirteen, Pk	Monitor Pk	0.2	245	Storm King Pk	SJ
S	13,704	Glacier Point	Eolus, Mt	0.5	284	Storm King Pk	SJ
148	13,695	Monitor Pk	Animas Mtn	0.5	315	Storm King Pk	SJ
158	13,682	Seven, Pk	Six, Pk	0.8	422	Storm King Pk	SJ
181	13,628	Silex, Mt	Storm King Pk	0.8	808	Storm King Pk	SJ
182	13,627	White Dome	Trinity Pk East	2.2	967	Storm King Pk	SJ
185	13,617	Guardian, The	Silex, Mt	0.6	557	Storm King Pk	SJ
194	13,589	One, Pk	White Dome	0.8	409	Storm King Pk	SJ
225	13,540	Eleven, Pk	Sunlight Pk	0.6	400	Storm King Pk	SJ
237	13,528	Leviathan Pk	Jagged Mtn	0.7	588	Storm King Pk	SJ
	13,500	Needle Ridge	Sunlight Pk	0.4	200	Storm King Pk	SJ
264	13,489	Graystone Pk	Arrow Pk	0.6	509	Storm King Pk	SJ
269	13,478	Three, Pk	Trinity Pk East	0.9	498	Storm King Pk	SJ
271	13,475	Two, Pk	Three, Pk	0.8	535	Storm King Pk	SJ
	13,430	Gray Needle	Jagged Mtn	0.3	130	Storm King Pk	SJ
302	13,428	Vallecito Mtn	Leviathan Pk	0.5	568	Storm King Pk	SJ
S	13,420	Ten, Pk	Jagged Mtn	0.3	280	Storm King Pk	SJ
	13,420	Twin Thumbs	Eleven, Pk	0.2	120	Storm King Pk	SJ
313	13,410	Four, Pk	Six, Pk	1.2	510	Storm King Pk	SJ
318	13,402	Nine, Pk	Storm King Pk	0.5	582	Storm King Pk	SJ
390	13,302	Point 13,302	Oso, Mt	1.7	722	Storm King Pk	SJ
406	13,292	Electric Pk B	Arrow Pk	0.6	832	Storm King Pk	SJ
412	13,283	Five, Pk	Four, Pk	0.6	303	Storm King Pk	SJ
428	13,265	Knife Point	Sunlight Pk	0.8	325	Storm King Pk	SJ
429	13,262	Heisspitz, The	Four, Pk	0.9	362	Storm King Pk	SJ
S	13,228	Eight, Pk	Nine, Pk	0.4	288	Storm King Pk	SJ
483	13,205	Nebo, Mt	Point 13,230 A	0.6	505	Storm King Pk	SJ
535	13,140	Twelve, Pk	Monitor Pk	0.5	320	Storm King Pk	SJ
539	13,136	Hunchback Mtn	White Dome	0.8	356	Storm King Pk	SJ
560	13,110	Point 13,110	Point 13,308	1.2	450	Storm King Pk	SJ
401	13,300	Summit Pk	"Phoenix Pk"	40.5	2,760	Summit Pk	SJ
524	13,150	Montezuma Pk	Summit Pk	1.6	690	Summit Pk	SJ
627	13,020	"Unicorn Pk"	Montezuma Pk	0.6	440	Summit Pk	SJ
100	13,809	Dallas Pk	Sneffels, Mt	2.0	869	Telluride	SJ
S	13,741	"West Dallas"	Dallas Pk	0.6	281	Telluride	SJ
134	13,735	"T 0"	Dallas Pk	1.4	395	Telluride	SJ

Rank	Elev	Peak Name	Parent	Mile	Rise	Quadrangle	Rg
149	13,694	Gilpin Pk	Dallas Pk	1.7	720	Telluride	SJ
196	13,581	Emma, Mt	Gilpin Pk	0.8	561	Telluride	SJ
	13,568	"Coffeepot"	Teakettle Mtn	0.4	188	Telluride	SJ
215	13,555	Wasatch Mtn	Lookout Pk	2.1	495	Telluride	SJ
251	13,510	"T 11"	Lookout Pk	1.3	452	Telluride	SJ
267	13,481	Three Needles	"T 11"	1.0	421	Telluride	SJ
273	13,472	La Junta Pk	Wasatch Mtn	0.7	612	Telluride	SJ
275	13,470	Silver Mtn B	Wasatch Mtn	2.2	410	Telluride	SJ
284	13,460	San Joaquin Ridge	Silver Mtn B	1.3	360	Telluride	SJ
294	13,436	"T 5"	Emma, Mt	1.8	416	Telluride	SJ
S	13,432	"Oscar's Pk"	Wasatch Mtn	1.0	292	Telluride	SJ
	13,319	Palmyra Pk	Silver Mtn B	0.5	179	Telluride	SJ
	13,275	Mendota Pk	"T 5"	0.8	175	Telluride	SJ
	13,213	Campbell Pk	"T 0"	0.5	233	Telluride	SJ
528	13,145	Point 13,145 A	La Junta Pk	0.6	325	Telluride	SJ
573	13,095	"Tomboy Pk"	Chicago Pk	0.5	315	Telluride	SJ
	13,060	Saint Sophia Ridge	Emma, Mt	0.5	160	Telluride	SJ
383	13,312	Williams Mtn South A	Williams Mtn	1.5	572	Thimble Rock	SW
619	13,033	Williams Mtn South C	Williams Mtn South A	1.4	493	Thimble Rock	SW
450	13,233	Turner Pk	Yale, Mt	3.9	1,173	Tincup	SW
469	13,218	Jones Mtn B	Emma Burr Mtn	3.0	638	Tincup	SW
572	13,095	Kreutzer, Mt	Emma Burr Mtn	1.6	355	Tincup	SW
605	13,055	Point 13,055	Kreutzer, Mt	1.6	315	Tincup	SW
213	13,560	Hagues Pk	Longs Pk	16.0	2,420	Trail Ridge	FR
247	13,514	Ypsilon Mtn	Hagues Pk	2.6	1,116	Trail Ridge	FR
254	13,502	Fairchild Mtn	Ypsilon Mtn	1.2	922	Trail Ridge	FR
	13,420	Rowe Pk	Hagues Pk	0.4	200	Trail Ridge	FR
	13,184	Rowe Mtn	Hagues Pk	0.9	44	Trail Ridge	FR
S	13,069	Chiquita, Mt	Ypsilon Mtn	1.0	283	Trail Ridge	FR
245	13,517	Trinchera Pk	Point 13,565	10.3	977	Trinchera Pk	SC
265	13,487	Cuatro Pk	Trinchera Pk	2.2	707	Trinchera Pk	SC
486	13,203	"Leaning South Pk"	Cuatro Pk	1.1	303	Trinchera Pk	SC
	13,100	"Leaning North Pk"	"Leaning South Pk"	0.5	160	Trinchera Pk	SC
167	13,660	Point 13,660 A	California Pk	1.1	400	Twin Pks	SC
202	13,580	Twin Pks A	Ellingwood Point	1.6	640	Twin Pks	SC
S	13,100	Point 13,100 D	Little Bear Pk	1.0	280	Twin Pks	SC
6	14,309	Uncompahgre Pk	La Plata Pk	84.0	4,249	Uncompahgre Pk	SJ
139	13,714	Silver Mtn A	Uncompahgre Pk	2.5	1,054	Uncompahgre Pk	SJ
159	13,681	Point 13,681	Silver Mtn A	1.0	501	Uncompahgre Pk	SJ
193	13,590	Matterhorn Pk	Wetterhorn Pk	0.9	570	Uncompahgre Pk	SJ
S	13,467	"Big Blue Pk"	Silver Mtn A	0.8	287	Uncompahgre Pk	SJ
362	13,340	Point 13,340 B	"Heisshorn"	1.7	745	Uncompahgre Pk	SJ
394	13,300	"El Punto"	Point 13,340 B	0.6	320	Uncompahgre Pk	SJ
436	13,256	Broken Hill	Matterhorn Pk	2.0	798	Uncompahgre Pk	SJ
459	13,222	Point 13,222 A	Point 13,340 B	0.6	322	Uncompahgre Pk	SJ
514	13,158	Point 13,158	Uncompahgre Pk	1.8	378	Uncompahgre Pk	SJ
563	13,106	Point 13,106	Uncompahgre Pk	2.2	726	Uncompahgre Pk	SJ
575	13,091	Point 13,091	Point 13,106 A	1.8	591	Uncompahgre Pk	SJ
608	13,051	Point 13,051	Silver Mtn A	1.1	351	Uncompahgre Pk	SJ
629	13,016	Point 13,016	Point 13,051	1.5	676	Uncompahgre Pk	SJ
431	13,260	"Pk G"	Powell, Mt	2.3	1,000	Vail East	GO
	13,230	"Pk F"	"Pk G"	0.4	250	Vail East	GO
454	13,230	"Pk Q"	"Pk G"	2.0	730	Vail East	GO
464	13,220	"Pk C"	"Pk G"	1.6	520	Vail East	GO
	13,220	"Pk E"	"Pk G"	0.6	200	Vail East	GO
473	13,213	"Pk L"	"Pk Q"	1.5	753	Vail East	GO
	13,129	Black BM	"Pk G"	0.2	29	Vail East	GO
	13,100	Gore Thumb	"Pk L"	0.4	200	Vail East	GO

Rank	Elev	Peak Name	Parent	Mile	Rise	Quadrangle	Rg
	13,100	"Pk C Prime"	"Pk C"	0.2	120	Vail East	GO
	13,100	"Pk H"	"Pk G"	0.4	140	Vail East	GO
577	13,090	"Solitude, Mt"	"Pk Z"	2.0	710	Vail East	GO
581	13,085	"Pk X"	"Pk Z"	0.8	465	Vail East	GO
	13,075	"Pk Z Prime"	"Solitude, Mt"	0.4	215	Vail East	GO
604	13,057	"East Partner Pk" (Pk V)	"Pk X"	1.0	557	Vail East	GO
	13,047	"Pk D"	"Pk G"	1.0	267	Vail East	GO
614	13,041	"West Partner Pk" (Pk U)	"East Partner Pk" (Pk V)	0.9	581	Vail East	GO
	13,005	"Climber's Point"	"Solitude, Mt"	0.5	225	Vail East	GO
195	13,588	Cottonwood Pk	Electric Pk A	3.7	1,128	Valley View Hot Spgs	SC
420	13,276	Kiowa Pk	Navajo Pk	1.3	736	Ward	FR
458	13,223	Audubon, Mt	Apache Pk	3.4	843	Ward	FR
594	13,071	Hunts Pk	Bushnell Pk	4.3	891	Wellsville	SC
417	13,278	Point 13,278	Rio Grande Pyramid	1.1	633	Weminuche Pass	SJ
430	13,261	Point 13,261	Point 13,278	0.7	321	Weminuche Pass	SJ
617	13,035	West Elk Pk	Owen B, Mt	13.9	3,055	West Elk Pk	EL
49	14,015	Wetterhorn Pk	Uncompahgre Pk	2.8	1,635	Wetterhorn Pk	SJ
171	13,656	Coxcomb Pk	Wetterhorn Pk	1.8	796	Wetterhorn Pk	SJ
175	13,642	Redcliff	Coxcomb Pk	0.5	502	Wetterhorn Pk	SJ
312	13,411	"Heisshorn"	Wetterhorn Pk	1.2	471	Wetterhorn Pk	SJ
338	13,377	Point 13,377	"Heisshorn"	0.5	357	Wetterhorn Pk	SJ
399	13,300	Point 13,300 C	Wetterhorn Pk	0.7	440	Wetterhorn Pk	SJ
427	13,266	Wildhorse Pk	Seigal Mtn	4.0	966	Wetterhorn Pk	SJ
446	13,241	"U 3"	Redcliff	0.7	461	Wetterhorn Pk	SJ
480	13,206	Point 13,206	Point 13,377	0.6	306	Wetterhorn Pk	SJ
490	13,201	Point 13,201	Point 13,300 C	1.3	661	Wetterhorn Pk	SJ
529	13,144	Precipice Pk	"U 3"	1.5	484	Wetterhorn Pk	SJ
558	13,111	Cow BM	"Darley Mtn"	2.3	531	Wetterhorn Pk	SJ
593	13,073	Blackwall Mtn	Wildhorse Pk	1.3	453	Wetterhorn Pk	SJ
351	13,357	"Silverthorne, Mt"	Powell, Mt	10.9	1,097	Willow Lakes	GO
	13,333	"East Thorn"	"Silverthorne, Mt"	0.5	233	Willow Lakes	GO
442	13,245	"Pk Z"	"Pk G"	4.0	785	Willow Lakes	GO
495	13,189	Red Pk B	"Silverthorne, Mt"	1.6	929	Willow Lakes	GO
502	13,180	"Valhalla, Mt"	"Silverthorne, Mt"	1.6	760	Willow Lakes	GO
	13,130	"Rain Pk"	"Silverthorne, Mt"	0.6	230	Willow Lakes	GO
580	13,085	Keller Mtn	"Valhalla, Mt"	2.1	745	Willow Lakes	GO
585	13,079	"North Traverse Pk"	"Valhalla, Mt"	1.3	659	Willow Lakes	GO
613	13,041	"Grand Traverse Pk"	"North Traverse Pk"	0.7	301	Willow Lakes	GO
623	13,024	"Snow Pk"	"Valhalla, Mt"	0.8	484	Willow Lakes	GO
36	14,067	Missouri Mtn	Belford, Mt	1.3	847	Winfield	SW
52	14,003	Huron Pk	Missouri Mtn	3.2	1,503	Winfield	SW
60	13,951	Ice Mtn	Huron Pk	2.1	1,011	Winfield	SW
71	13,904	Emerald Pk	Missouri Mtn	1.3	564	Winfield	SW
79	13,860	North Apostle	Ice Mtn	0.4	400	Winfield	SW
S	13,831	Iowa Pk	Missouri Mtn	0.6	291	Winfield	SW
210	13,568	West Apostle	Ice Mtn	0.6	508	Winfield	SW
	13,523	Browns Pk	Huron Pk	0.7	183	Winfield	SW
244	13,517	Point 13,517 A	Huron Pk	1.5	457	Winfield	SW
S	13,472	Point 13,472 B	Point 13,517 A	0.5	292	Winfield	SW
279	13,462	Point 13,462 A	Huron Pk	1.1	322	Winfield	SW
280	13,462	Point 13,462 B	Point 13,517 A	1.6	562	Winfield	SW
437	13,255	Point 13,255	Grizzly Pk E	1.6	555	Winfield	SW
439	13,253	Point 13,253	Point 13,255	2.0	433	Winfield	SW
579	13,088	Virginia Pk	Point 13,140 A	0.8	428	Winfield	SW
	13,077	Winfield Pk	Virginia Pk	0.7	177	Winfield	SW
	13,060	Middle Mtn B	Point 13,462 A	0.6	120	Winfield	SW
532	13,140	Point 13,140 A	Point 13,255	0.6	320	Winfield	SW

PEAKS SORTED BY NAME

Rank	Elev	Peak Name	Parent	Mile	Rise	Quadrangle	Rg
66	13,931	Adams, Mt	Kit Carson Mtn	1.9	871	Horn Pk	SC
127	13,745	Aetna, Mt	Tabeguache Pk	4.7	1,245	Garfield	SW
277	13,466	"Alamosito"	Vermejo Pk	1.2	557	Culebra Pk	SC
384	13,310	Alice, Mt	Chiefs Head Pk	1.4	850	Isolation Pk	FR
102	13,806	American Pk"	Jones Mtn A	0.8	466	Handies Pk	SJ
507	13,165	Amherst Mtn	Valois, Mt	1.5	1,225	Columbine Pass	SJ
136	13,722	"Animas Forks Mtn"	Handies Pk	3.5	1,142	Handies Pk	SJ
112	13,786	Animas Mtn	Pigeon Pk	1.2	1,086	Snowdon Pk	SJ
10	14,269	Antero, Mt	Harvard, Mt	17.7	2,503	Mt Antero	SW
424	13,269	Antora Pk	Ouray, Mt	6.8	2,409	Bonanza	SW
292	13,441	Apache Pk	North Arapaho Pk	2.2	1,101	Monarch Lake	FR
129	13,738	Argentine Pk	Edwards, Mt	1.9	638	Montezuma	FR
523	13,150	Arikaree Pk	Kiowa Pk	0.8	570	Monarch Lake	FR
108	13,795	Arkansas Mt	Buckskin Mt	1.9	575	Climax	TM
104	13,803	Arrow Pk	Vestal Pk	0.5	943	Storm King Pk	SJ
86	13,841	"Atlantic Pk"	Fletcher Mtn	0.7	421	Copper Mtn	TM
458	13,223	Audubon, Mt	Apache Pk	3.4	843	Ward	FR
385	13,310	Aztec Mtn	Jupiter Mtn	1.9	610	Columbine Pass	SJ
525	13,149	Babcock Pk	Lavender Pk	0.9	529	La Plata	SJ
156	13,684	Bald Mtn	Silverheels, Mt	7.6	2,104	Boreas Pass	FR
147	13,698	Baldy Alto	Stewart Pk	1.2	518	Stewart Pk	SJ
	13,401	Baldy Chato	Stewart Pk	1.5	181	Stewart Pk	SJ
329	13,383	Baldy Cinco	Point 13,510 A	1.9	843	Baldy Cinco	SJ
	13,155	Baldy Mtn	Point 13,244	0.6	175	Highland Pk	EL
	13,250	Bancroft, Mt	Parry Pk	0.7	253	Empire	FR
176	13,641	Bard Pk	Torreys Pk	5.5	1,651	Grays Pk	FR
214	13,555	Bartlett Mtn	Clinton Pk	0.8	615	Copper Mtn	SW
357	13,342	Beattie Pk	Vermillion Pk	0.7	322	Ophir	SJ
497	13,184	Beaubien Pk	De Anza Pk B	3.1	604	El Valle Creek	SC
18	14,197	Belford, Mt	Harvard, Mt	3.3	1,337	Mt Harvard	SW
449	13,233	Belleview Mtn	Maroon Pk	1.9	693	Maroon Bells	EL
485	13,203	Bennett Pk	Summit Pk	17.0	1,663	Jasper	SJ
323	13,393	Bent Pk	Carson Pk	1.2	373	Pole Creek Mtn	SJ
38	14,060	Bierstadt, Mt	Evans, Mt	1.4	720	Mt Evans	FR
S	13,467	"Big Blue Pk"	Silver Mtn A	0.8	287	Uncompahgre Pk	SJ
	13,129	Black BM	"Pk G"	0.2	29	Vail East	GO
593	13,073	Blackwall Mtn	Wildhorse Pk	1.3	453	Wetterhorn Pk	SJ
4	14,345	Blanca Pk	Harvard, Mt	103.0	5,326	Blanca Pk	SC
409	13,286	Bonita Pk	"Proposal Pk"	1.0	506	Handies Pk	SJ
583	13,082	Boreas Mtn	Bald Mtn	2.9	923	Boreas Pass	FR
236	13,528	Boulder Mtn	Point 13,646	1.6	588	Saint Elmo	SW
209	13,573	Broken Hand Pk	Crestone Needle	0.8	673	Crestone Pk	SC
436	13,256	Broken Hill	Matterhorn Pk	2.0	798	Uncompahgre Pk	SJ
22	14,172	Bross, Mt	Lincoln, Mt	1.1	312	Alma	TM
363	13,339	Brown Mtn	Hanson Pk	1.8	639	Ironton	SJ
	13,523	Browns Pk	Huron Pk	0.7	183	Winfield	SW
342	13,370	Buckskin BM	Sleeping Sexton	2.0	908	Maroon Bells	EL
76	13,865	Buckskin, Mt	Democrat, Mt	1.5	725	Climax	TM
122	13,761	Bull Hill	Elbert, Mt	1.6	421	Mt Elbert	SW
	13,182	Bullion Mtn	Aztec Mtn	0.8	202	Columbine Pass	SJ

Rank	Elev	Peak Name	Parent	Mile	Rise	Quadrangle	Rg
564	13,105	Bushnell Pk	Cottonwood Pk	11.1	2,405	Bushnell Pk	SC
S	13,220	California Mtn	Hanson Pk	0.6	280	Handies Pk	SJ
84	13,849	California Pk	Ellingwood Point	2.2	629	Blanca Pk	SC
	14,238	Cameron, Mt	Lincoln, Mt	0.5	138	Alma	TM
288	13,454	"Campbell Creek Pk"	Point 13,795	1.0	394	Redcloud Pk	SJ
	13,213	Campbell Pk	"T 0"	0.5	233	Telluride	SJ
268	13,478	Canby Mtn	Niagara Pk	6.2	938	Howardsville	SJ
29	14,130	Capitol Pk	Maroon Pk	7.5	1,750	Capitol Pk	EL
165	13,663	Carbonate Mtn	"North Carbonate"	2.0	434	Saint Elmo	SW
170	13,657	Carson Pk	Half Pk	3.6	1,477	Pole Creek Mtn	SJ
69	13,908	Casco Pk	French Mtn	1.2	648	Mt Elbert	SW
12	14,265	Castle Pk	La Plata Pk	20.8	2,337	Hayden Pk	EL
105	13,803	"Castleabra"	Castle Pk	0.9	423	Maroon Bells	EL
62	13,943	Cathedral Pk	Castle Pk	1.7	523	Hayden Pk	EL
S	13,062	Centennial Pk	Lavender Pk	0.5	282	La Plata	SJ
34	14,081	Challenger Point	Kit Carson Mtn	0.2	301	Crestone Pk	SC
173	13,646	Champion, Mt	Point 13,736	0.6	306	Mt Champion	SW
326	13,385	Chicago Pk	Point 13,510 B	1.8	365	Ironton	SJ
631	13,014	Chief Mtn	Point 13,261	9.8	2,474	Little Squaw Creek	SJ
203	13,579	Chiefs Head Pk	Longs Pk	1.4	719	Isolation Pk	FR
S	13,069	Chiquita, Mt	Ypsilon Mtn	1.0	283	Trail Ridge	FR
370	13,328	Cinnamon Mtn	Point 13,535 B	1.1	308	Handies Pk	SJ
155	13,686	Cirque Mtn	Teakettle Mtn	0.6	546	Mt Sneffels	SJ
404	13,294	"Citadel"	Pettingell Pk	1.0	314	Loveland Pass	FR
198	13,580	Clark Pk	Capitol Pk	1.2	440	Capitol Pk	EL
311	13,414	Cleveland Pk	Tijeras Pk	1.4	434	Crestone Pk	SC
	13,005	"Climber's Point"	"Solitude, Mt"	0.5	225	Vail East	GO
80	13,857	Clinton Pk	Democrat, Mt	2.0	517	Climax	TM
	13,568	"Coffeepot"	Teakettle Mtn	0.4	188	Telluride	SJ
143	13,705	Colony Baldy	Humboldt Pk	1.4	925	Crestone Pk	SC
35	14,073	Columbia, Mt	Harvard, Mt	1.9	893	Mt Harvard	SW
418	13,277	Comanche Pk	Fluted Pk	1.5	497	Horn Pk	SC
504	13,172	Conejos Pk	Summit Pk	8.2	1,912	Platoro	SJ
366	13,334	Coney BM	Bent Pk	1.9	994	Finger Mesa	SJ
	14,060	Conundrum Pk	Castle Pk	0.4	240	Hayden Pk	EL
503	13,176	Copeland Mtn	Alice, Mt	4.1	1,116	Isolation Pk	FR
567	13,100	"Corbett Pk"	Whitehouse Mtn	0.5	320	Ouray	SJ
195	13,588	Cottonwood Pk	Electric Pk A	3.7	1,128	Valley View Hot Spgs	SC
558	13,111	Cow BM	"Darley Mtn"	2.3	531	Wetterhorn Pk	SJ
171	13,656	Coxcomb Pk	Wetterhorn Pk	1.8	796	Wetterhorn Pk	SJ
423	13,270	"Crestolita"	Broken Hand Pk	0.5	490	Crestone Pk	SC
19	14,197	Crestone Needle	Crestone Pk	0.5	457	Crestone Pk	SC
7	14,294	Crestone Pk	Blanca Pk	27.5	4,554	Crestone Pk	SC
	13,569	Crown Mtn	Niagara Pk	0.6	229	Handies Pk	SJ
82	13,852	Crystal Pk	Pacific Pk	0.9	632	Breckenridge	TM
265	13,487	Cuatro Pk	Trinchera Pk	2.2	707	Trinchera Pk	SC
	13,019	Cuba BM	Niagara Pk	3.4	119	Howardsville	SJ
41	14,047	Culebra Pk	Blanca Pk	25.0	4,667	Culebra Pk	SC
555	13,117	"Cupid"	Grizzly Pk D	1.0	377	Grays Pk	FR
192	13,596	Cyclone Mtn	Carbonate Mtn	0.5	336	Saint Elmo	SW
100	13,809	Dallas Pk	Sneffels, Mt	2.0	869	Telluride	SJ

Rank	Elev	Peak Name	Parent	Mile	Rise	Quadrangle	Rg
392	13,300	Daly, Mt	Clark Pk	1.4	800	Capitol Pk	EL
543	13,132	"Darley Mtn"	Point 13,260 A	0.9	512	Handies Pk	SJ
347	13,362	De Anza Pk A	Gibbs Pk	1.1	622	Electric Pk	SC
368	13,333	De Anza Pk B	Mariquita Pk	1.0	473	El Valle Creek	SC
609	13,050	"Dead Man Pk"	Point 13,384	0.8	390	Crestone Pk	SC
123	13,761	Deer Mt	Oklahoma, Mt	1.7	941	Mt Champion	SW
28	14,148	Democrat, Mt	Lincoln, Mt	1.7	768	Climax	TM
	13,140	"Dicker's Peck"	Navajo Pk	0.1	40	Monarch Lake	FR
408	13,290	Dolores Pk	Middle Pk	1.1	710	Dolores Pk	SJ
343	13,370	Dome Mtn	Tower Mtn	1.3	670	Howardsville	SJ
S	13,900	"Drift Pk"	Fletcher Mtn	0.6	280	Copper Mtn	TM
81	13,855	Dyer Mtn	Sherman, Mt	1.2	475	Mt Sherman	TM
481	13,205	Eagle Pk A	Cottonwood Pk	2.0	545	Electric Pk	SC
	13,043	Eagle Pk B	Point 13,100 B	0.4	233	Mt Jackson	SW
307	13,420	Eagles Nest (Pk A)	Powell, Mt	1.2	640	Mt Powell	GO
393	13,300	East Buffalo Pk	West Buffalo Pk	0.9	480	Marmot Pk	TM
	14,260	"East Crestone"	Crestone Pk	0.1	80	Crestone Pk	SC
	14,180	"East La Plata"	La Plata Pk	0.2	80	Mt Elbert	SW
604	13,057	"East Partner Pk" (Pk V)	"Pk X"	1.0	557	Vail East	GO
S	13,382	"East Pole Creek Mtn"	Pole Creek Mtn	0.8	282	Pole Creek Mtn	SJ
	13,333	"East Thorn"	"Silverthorne, Mt"	0.5	233	Willow Lakes	GO
S	13,460	"East Windom"	Windom Pk	0.6	280	Columbine Pass	SJ
	13,309	Echo Mtn	McCauley Mtn	0.5	209	Columbine Pass	SJ
83	13,850	Edwards, Mt	Grays Pk	1.3	470	Grays Pk	FR
S	13,228	Eight, Pk	Nine, Pk	0.4	288	Storm King Pk	SJ
	13,472	Eighteen, Pk	Windom Pk	0.5	212	Columbine Pass	SJ
	14,159	El Diente	Wilson, Mt	0.8	259	Dolores Pk	SJ
394	13,300	"El Punto"	Point 13,340 B	0.6	320	Uncompahgre Pk	SJ
1	14,433	Elbert, Mt	Whitney, Mt	667.0	9,093	Mt Elbert	SW
191	13,598	Electric Pk A	Rito Alto Pk	6.1	938	Electric Pk	SC
406	13,292	Electric Pk B	Arrow Pk	0.6	832	Storm King Pk	SJ
177	13,635	"Electric Pk"	Cathedral Pk	0.9	335	Hayden Pk	EL
225	13,540	Eleven, Pk	Sunlight Pk	0.6	400	Storm King Pk	SJ
42	14,042	Ellingwood Point	Blanca Pk	0.5	342	Blanca Pk	SC
S	13,220	Ellingwood Ridge	La Plata Pk	1.5	280	Mt Elbert	SW
71	13,904	Emerald Pk	Missouri Mtn	1.3	564	Winfield	SW
S	13,140	Emerson Mtn	Amherst Mtn	0.5	280	Columbine Pass	SJ
	13,310	Emery Pk	Point 13,330	0.4	130	Handies Pk	SJ
230	13,538	Emma Burr Mtn	Princeton, Mt	9.6	1,238	Cumberland Pass	SW
196	13,581	Emma, Mt	Gilpin Pk	0.8	561	Telluride	SJ
467	13,218	Engineer Mtn	Point 13,260 A	0.9	438	Handies Pk	SJ
348	13,362	Englemann Pk	Bard Pk	1.8	542	Grays Pk	FR
32	14,083	Eolus, Mt	Wilson, Mt	25.5	3,863	Columbine Pass	SJ
	13,523	Epaulet Mtn	"Epaulie"	0.5	143	Mt Evans	FR
235	13,530	"Epaulie"	Rosalie Pk	1.2	350	Harris Park	FR
	13,630	"Esprit Point"	Shavano, Mt	0.8	250	Maysville	SW
252	13,507	Eureka Mtn	Rito Alto Pk	2.0	807	Rito Alto Pk	SC
544	13,130	Eva, Mt	Parry Pk	0.8	430	Empire	FR
204	13,577	Evans B, Mt	Dyer Mt	1.2	317	Climax	TM
14	14,264	Evans, Mt	Grays Pk	9.8	2,764	Mt Evans	FR
254	13,502	Fairchild Mtn	Ypsilon Mtn	1.2	922	Trail Ridge	FR
472	13,214	Fairview Pk	Henry Mtn	4.6	1,234	Fairview Pk	SW

Rank	Elev	Peak Name	Parent	Mile	Rise	Quadrangle	Rg
494	13,192	"Fancy Pk"	Point 13,768	2.2	372	Mt Jackson	SW
	13,615	Father Dyer Pk	Crystal Pk	0.6	115	Breckenridge	TM
145	13,700	Fifteen, Pk	Turret Pk	0.2	320	Snowdon Pk	SJ
	13,409	Finnback Knob	Horseshoe Mtn	0.6	149	Mt Sherman	TM
557	13,112	Fitzpatrick Pk	Point 13,345	2.1	958	Cumberland Pass	SW
412	13,283	Five, Pk	Four, Pk	0.6	303	Storm King Pk	SJ
59	13,951	Fletcher Mtn	Quandary Pk	1.2	611	Copper Mtn	TM
542	13,132	Flora, Mt	Parry Pk	2.4	686	Empire	FR
	13,076	Florida Mtn	Valois, Mt	0.8	176	Columbine Pass	SJ
216	13,554	Fluted Pk	Adams, Mt	1.2	734	Horn Pk	SC
313	13,410	Four, Pk	Six, Pk	1.2	510	Storm King Pk	SJ
540	13,135	Francisco Pk	Beaubien Pk	1.0	435	El Valle Creek	SC
	13,876	Frasco BM	French Mtn	0.5	256	Mt Massive	SW
63	13,940	French Mtn	Elbert, Mt	2.1	1,080	Mt Massive	SW
	13,761	Fuller Pk	Vermillion Pk	0.5	261	Ophir	SJ
395	13,300	Galena Mtn	Canby Mtn	2.1	360	Howardsville	SJ
116	13,780	Garfield Pk	Grizzly Pk A	0.8	360	Independence Pass	SW
591	13,074	Garfield, Mt	Graystone Pk	1.0	374	Snowdon Pk	SJ
332	13,380	Geissler Mtn East	Twining Pk	1.1	560	Mt Champion	SW
391	13,301	Geissler Mtn West	Geissler Mtn East	0.6	481	Mt Champion	SW
	13,951	Gemini Pk	Sherman, Mt	0.7	171	Mt Sherman	TM
425	13,266	Geneva Pk	Argentine Pk	4.7	926	Montezuma	FR
218	13,553	Gibbs Pk	Rito Alto Pk	4.2	693	Electric Pk	SC
149	13,694	Gilpin Pk	Dallas Pk	1.7	720	Telluride	SJ
S	13,704	Glacier Point	Eolus, Mt	0.5	284	Storm King Pk	SJ
	13,340	Glacier Ridge	Longs Pk	0.5	40	Longs Pk	FR
67	13,913	Gladstone Pk	Wilson, Mt	0.6	733	Mt Wilson	SJ
475	13,209	Gladstone Ridge	Jones Mtn B	2.6	949	Mt Yale	SW
330	13,382	Gold Dust Pk	Jackson, Mt	3.1	922	Mt Jackson	SW
633	13,010	"Golden Bear Pk"	Hagar Mtn	1.2	350	Loveland Pass	FR
117	13,780	Golden Horn	Vermillion Pk	0.4	400	Ophir	SJ
	13,100	Gore Thumb	"Pk L"	0.4	200	Vail East	GO
613	13,041	"Grand Traverse Pk"	"North Traverse Pk"	0.7	301	Willow Lakes	GO
498	13,180	Grand Turk	Sultan Mtn	0.6	404	Silverton	SJ
	13,577	Gravel Mtn	Point 13,688 B	0.4	157	Handies Pk	SJ
	13,430	Gray Needle	Jagged Mtn	0.3	130	Storm King Pk	SJ
190	13,602	Gray Wolf Mtn	Evans, Mt	2.2	582	Mt Evans	FR
9	14,270	Grays Pk	Lincoln, Mt	25.2	2,770	Grays Pk	FR
264	13,489	Graystone Pk	Arrow Pk	0.6	509	Storm King Pk	SJ
	13,049	Green Mtn	"Stony Pass Pk"	0.6	69	Howardsville	SJ
461	13,220	Greenhalgh Mtn	Sheep Mtn A	0.8	400	Howardsville	SJ
206	13,575	Greylock Mtn	Windom Pk	1.2	555	Columbine Pass	SJ
142	13,708	Grizzly Mtn	"North Carbonate"	1.7	568	Saint Elmo	SW
54	13,988	Grizzly Pk A	La Plata Pk	6.7	1,928	Independence Pass	SW
130	13,738	Grizzly Pk B	San Miguel Pk	1.6	758	Ophir	SJ
146	13,700	Grizzly Pk C	Jupiter Mtn	0.7	440	Columbine Pass	SJ
303	13,427	Grizzly Pk D	Torreys Pk	1.5	847	Grays Pk	FR
415	13,281	Grizzly Pk E	Jenkins Mtn	1.9	581	Pieplant	SW
185	13,617	Guardian, The	Silex, Mt	0.6	557	Storm King Pk	SJ
344	13,370	Guyot, Mt	Bald Mtn	2.0	1,324	Boreas Pass	FR
	13,140	Guyselman Mtn (Pk M)	"Pk L"	0.6	240	Mt Powell	GO
462	13,220	Hagar Mtn	Point 13,294	0.5	320	Loveland Pass	FR

Rank	Elev	Peak Name	Parent	Mile	Rise	Quadrangle	Rg
87	13,841	Hagerman Pk	Snowmass Mtn	0.6	341	Snowmass Mtn	EL
213	13,560	Hagues Pk	Longs Pk	16.0	2,420	Trail Ridge	FR
88	13,841	Half Pk	Handies Pk	3.9	1,501	Pole Creek Mtn	SJ
	13,658	Hamilton Pk	Blanca Pk	1.5	278	Blanca Pk	SC
40	14,048	Handies Pk	Uncompahgre Pk	11.2	2,148	Handies Pk	SJ
287	13,454	Hanson Pk	Tower Mtn	3.6	914	Handies Pk	SJ
3	14,420	Harvard, Mt	Elbert, Mt	15.0	2,360	Mt Harvard	SW
471	13,215	"Hassell Pk"	Pettingell Pk	1.5	395	Loveland Pass	FR
536	13,139	Hayden Mtn North	Hayden Mtn South	1.2	519	Ironton	SJ
479	13,206	Hayden Mtn South	"T 8"	1.1	549	Ironton	SJ
	13,561	Hayden Pk	"Electric Pk"	0.8	181	Hayden Pk	EL
312	13,411	"Heisshorn"	Wetterhorn Pk	1.2	471	Wetterhorn Pk	SJ
429	13,262	Heisspitz, The	Four, Pk	0.9	362	Storm King Pk	SJ
	13,164	Helen, Mt	Pk 10	1.3	264	Breckenridge	TM
438	13,254	Henry Mtn	Point 13,345	11.0	1,674	Fairview Pk	SW
359	13,340	Herard, Mt	Cleveland Pk	4.7	2,040	Medano Pass	SC
353	13,350	Hermit Pk	Rito Alto Pk	0.9	330	Rito Alto Pk	SC
451	13,232	Hesperus Mtn	Grizzly Pk B	24.5	2,852	La Plata	SJ
314	13,409	Hilliard Pk	Keefe Pk	0.6	309	Maroon Bells	EL
91	13,831	Holy Cross Ridge	Holy Cross, Mt of the	0.6	331	Mt of the Holy Cross	SW
51	14,005	Holy Cross, Mt of the	Massive, Mt	18.9	2,105	Mt of the Holy Cross	SW
476	13,209	Homestake Pk	Whitney Pk	5.5	1,459	Homestake Reservoir	SW
352	13,352	Hoosier Ridge	Silverheels, Mt	3.3	932	Breckenridge	TM
	13,012	Hope Mtn	Jupiter Mtn	0.9	232	Columbine Pass	SJ
64	13,933	Hope, Mt	La Plata Pk	2.9	873	Mt Elbert	SW
290	13,450	Horn Pk	Fluted Pk	1.3	710	Horn Pk	SC
72	13,898	Horseshoe Mtn	Sherman, Mt	2.8	758	Mt Sherman	TM
607	13,052	Houghton Mtn	Tuttle Mtn	1.5	472	Handies Pk	SJ
584	13,081	"Huerfanito"	Lindsey, Mt	1.1	501	Blanca Pk	SC
93	13,828	"Huerfano Pk"	Lindsey, Mt	1.2	688	Blanca Pk	SC
37	14,064	Humboldt Pk	Crestone Needle	1.4	1,204	Crestone Pk	SC
539	13,136	Hunchback Mtn	White Dome	0.8	356	Storm King Pk	SJ
258	13,497	Hunter Pk	Keefe Pk	1.4	477	Maroon Bells	EL
594	13,071	Hunts Pk	Bushnell Pk	4.3	891	Wellsville	SC
52	14,003	Huron Pk	Missouri Mtn	3.2	1,503	Winfield	SW
	13,447	Hurricane Pk	Hanson Pk	0.8	267	Handies Pk	SJ
60	13,951	Ice Mtn	Huron Pk	2.1	1,011	Winfield	SW
S	13,060	"Igloo Pk"	Point 13,198	0.5	280	Independence Pass	SW
	13,420	Index, The	Animas Mtn	0.2	240	Snowdon Pk	SJ
S	13,831	Iowa Pk	Missouri Mtn	0.6	291	Winfield	SW
	13,500	Iron Nipple	"Huerfano Pk"	0.6	200	Blanca Pk	SC
468	13,218	Irving Pk	Oso, Mt	1.2	638	Columbine Pass	SJ
554	13,118	Isolation Pk	Copeland Mtn	2.2	938	Isolation Pk	FR
337	13,378	Italian Mtn	Star Pk	3.5	1,358	Pearl Pass	EL
163	13,670	Jackson, Mt	Holy Cross, Mt of the	3.2	1,810	Mt Jackson	SW
482	13,205	Jacque Pk	Pacific Pk	4.6	2,065	Copper Mtn	TM
94	13,824	Jagged Mtn	Sunlight Pk	1.4	964	Storm King Pk	SJ
405	13,294	James Pk	Parry Pk	1.5	714	Empire	FR
299	13,432	Jenkins Mtn	Sayres BM	4.0	692	Pieplant	SW
78	13,860	Jones Mtn A	Handies Pk	1.7	520	Handies Pk	SJ
469	13,218	Jones Mtn B	Emma Burr Mtn	3.0	638	Tincup	SW
	13,604	Jones Pk	Point 13,712	0.7	144	Mt Antero	SW

Rank	Elev	Peak Name	Parent	Mile	Rise	Quadrangle	Rg
92	13,830	Jupiter Mtn	Windom Pk	0.6	370	Columbine Pass	SJ
	13,664	"K2"	Capitol Pk	0.5	84	Capitol Pk	EL
232	13,535	"K49"	Deer Mtn	1.2	555	Mt Champion	SW
56	13,980	"Kat Carson"	Kit Carson Mtn	0.2	360	Crestone Pk	SC
246	13,516	Keefe Pk	Point 13,537	1.3	496	Maroon Bells	EL
580	13,085	Keller Mtn	"Valhalla, Mt"	2.1	745	Willow Lakes	GO
509	13,164	Kelso Mtn	Torreys Pk	1.6	784	Grays Pk	FR
S	13,066	Kendall BM	Kendall Mtn	0.7	286	Silverton	SJ
364	13,338	Kendall Mtn	Kendall Pk	0.7	318	Silverton	SJ
289	13,451	Kendall Pk	Canby Mtn	4.1	1,311	Howardsville	SJ
	13,125	Kennedy, Mt	Aztec Mtn	0.6	265	Mtn View Crest	SJ
S	13,220	King Solomon Mtn	Little Giant Pk	0.5	280	Howardsville	SJ
420	13,276	Kiowa Pk	Navajo Pk	1.3	736	Ward	FR
	13,694	"Kismet"	Sneffels, Mt	0.4	194	Mt Sneffels	SJ
23	14,165	Kit Carson Mtn	Crestone Pk	1.3	1,025	Crestone Pk	SC
	13,980	"Kitty Kat Carson"	"Kat Carson"	0.1	80	Crestone Pk	SC
428	13,265	Knife Point	Sunlight Pk	0.8	325	Storm King Pk	SJ
572	13,095	Kreutzer, Mt	Emma Burr Mtn	1.6	355	Tincup	SW
	13,710	La Garita Pk	"Phoenix Pk"	1.9	232	Halfmoon Pass	SJ
273	13,472	La Junta Pk	Wasatch Mtn	0.7	612	Telluride	SJ
5	14,336	La Plata Pk	Elbert, Mt	6.3	2,276	Mt Elbert	SW
95	13,823	"Lackawanna Pk"	Casco Pk	1.8	883	Independence Pass	SW
416	13,281	Lady Washington, Mt	Longs Pk	0.7	301	Longs Pk	FR
339	13,375	Lakes Pk	Cottonwood Pk	2.1	675	Electric Pk	SC
	13,209	Lambertson Pk	Italian Mtn	0.5	229	Pearl Pass	EL
	13,238	Landslide Pk	Geneva Pk	0.4	138	Montezuma	FR
463	13,220	Lavender Pk	Hesperus Mtn	0.5	400	La Plata	SJ
	13,322	Leahy Pk	"Electric Pk"	0.9	142	Hayden Pk	EL
	13,100	"Leaning North Pk"	"Leaning South Pk"	0.5	160	Trinchera Pk	SC
486	13,203	"Leaning South Pk"	Cuatro Pk	1.1	303	Trinchera Pk	SC
484	13,204	Lenawee Mtn	Grizzly Pk D	1.0	344	Grays Pk	FR
237	13,528	Leviathan Pk	Jagged Mtn	0.7	588	Storm King Pk	SJ
8	14,286	Lincoln, Mt	Massive, Mt	22.3	3,866	Alma	TM
43	14,042	Lindsey, Mt	Blanca Pk	2.3	1,542	Blanca Pk	SC
44	14,037	Little Bear Pk	Blanca Pk	1.0	377	Blanca Pk	SC
	13,220	Little Finger	Fifteen, Pk	0.2	120	Snowdon Pk	SJ
310	13,416	Little Giant Pk	Kendall Pk	1.3	556	Howardsville	SJ
530	13,143	Little Horn Pk	Fluted Pk	0.9	323	Horn Pk	SC
556	13,113	Lizard Head	Gladstone Pk	1.9	1,113	Mt Wilson	SJ
546	13,128	Lomo Liso Mtn	Francisco Pk	0.8	308	El Valle Creek	SC
493	13,194	London Mtn	Mosquito Pk	1.7	534	Climax	TM
15	14,255	Longs Pk	Torreys Pk	43.5	2,940	Longs Pk	FR
166	13,661	Lookout Pk	Gilpin Pk	8.6	841	Ophir	SJ
	13,692	Loveland Mtn	Buckskin, Mt	0.8	192	Climax	TM
	13,222	Macomber Pk	Tower Mtn	0.7	122	Howardsville	SJ
354	13,348	Malemute Pk	Conundrum Pk	1.1	368	Hayden Pk	EL
	13,553	Mamma, Mt	Point 13,646	0.5	53	Saint Elmo	SW
426	13,266	Marble Mtn	Milwaukee Pk	1.1	526	Crestone Pk	SC
262	13,490	Marcy, Mt	Point 13,513	1.2	430	Electric Pk	SC
317	13,405	Mariquita Pk	Cuatro Pk	1.4	385	El Valle Creek	SC
24	14,156	Maroon Pk	Castle Pk	8.1	2,336	Maroon Bells	EL
295	13,435	"Mascot Pk"	Yale, Mt	0.8	375	Mt Yale	SW

Rank	Elev	Peak Name	Parent	Mile	Rise	Quadrangle	Rg
	14,300	"Massive Green"	Massive, Mt	0.4	120	Mt Massive	SW
2	14,421	Massive, Mt	Elbert, Mt	5.1	1,961	Mt Massive	SW
193	13,590	Matterhorn Pk	Wetterhorn Pk	0.9	570	Uncompahgre Pk	SJ
	13,335	Maxwell, Mt	Mariquita Pk	0.8	275	El Valle Creek	SC
217	13,554	McCauley Pk	Grizzly Pk C	0.7	454	Columbine Pass	SJ
	13,587	McClellan Mtn	Edwards, Mt	0.8	167	Grays Pk	FR
371	13,327	McHenrys Pk	Chiefs Head Pk	1.2	907	McHenrys Pk	FR
	13,780	McNamee Pk	Clinton Pk	0.5	80	Climax	TM
260	13,496	Mears Pk	"T 0"	1.3	556	Mt Sneffels	SJ
	13,860	Meeker Ridge	Meeker, Mt	0.2	40	Allens Park	FR
68	13,911	Meeker, Mt	Longs Pk	0.7	451	Allens Park	FR
	13,275	Mendota Pk	"T 5"	0.8	175	Telluride	SJ
568	13,100	Middle Mtn A	Point 13,463	1.1	520	Independence Pass	SW
	13,060	Middle Mtn B	Point 13,462 A	0.6	120	Winfield	SW
396	13,300	Middle Pk	Point 13,498	5.4	1,960	Dolores Pk	SJ
242	13,522	Milwaukee Pk	Pico Asilado	0.5	302	Crestone Pk	SC
S	13,468	Miranda Pk	Point 13,565	0.9	288	El Valle Creek	SC
36	14,067	Missouri Mtn	Belford, Mt	1.3	847	Winfield	SW
148	13,695	Monitor Pk	Animas Mtn	0.5	315	Storm King Pk	SJ
524	13,150	Montezuma Pk	Summit Pk	1.6	690	Summit Pk	SJ
345	13,369	Monumental Pk	Aetna, Mt	2.1	1,029	Garfield	SW
115	13,781	Mosquito Pk	Buckskin, Mt	2.3	561	Climax	TM
S	13,192	Moss, Mt	Lavender Pk	0.3	292	La Plata	SJ
305	13,425	Mummy Mtn	Hagues Pk	1.4	485	Estes Park	FR
333	13,380	Music Mtn	Milwaukee Pk	0.9	400	Crestone Pk	SC
315	13,409	Navajo Pk	Apache Pk	0.4	309	Monarch Lake	FR
483	13,205	Nebo, Mt	Point 13,230 A	0.6	505	Storm King Pk	SJ
	13,500	Needle Ridge	Sunlight Pk	0.4	200	Storm King Pk	SJ
101	13,807	Niagara Pk	Jones Mtn A	0.6	587	Handies Pk	SJ
318	13,402	Nine, Pk	Storm King Pk	0.5	582	Storm King Pk	SJ
	13,023	Niwot Ridge	Navajo Pk	0.6	163	Monarch Lake	FR
79	13,860	North Apostle	Ice Mtn	0.4	400	Winfield	SW
255	13,502	North Arapaho Pk	Chiefs Head Pk	15.4	1,665	Monarch Lake	FR
75	13,870	"North Carbonate"	Antero, Mt	2.4	1,050	Saint Elmo	SW
	13,599	"North Crown Mtn"	Niagara Pk	0.6	259	Handies Pk	SJ
	14,039	North Eolus	Eolus, Mt	0.2	179	Storm King Pk	SJ
355	13,346	"North Gold Dust"	Gold Dust Pk	1.3	806	Mt Jackson	SW
S	13,020	"North Irving"	Irving Pk	0.4	280	Columbine Pass	SJ
	14,014	North Maroon Pk	Maroon Pk	0.4	234	Maroon Bells	EL
S	14,340	"North Massive"	Massive, Mt	0.9	280	Mt Massive	SW
	14,020	"North Snowmass"	Snowmass Mtn	0.2	40	Snowmass Mtn	EL
187	13,614	North Star Mtn	Wheeler Mtn	0.9	434	Breckenridge	TM
585	13,079	"North Traverse Pk"	"Valhalla, Mt"	1.3	659	Willow Lakes	GO
589	13,075	North Twilight Pk	Twilight Pk	0.4	335	Snowdon Pk	SJ
	14,260	"Northeast Crestone"	Crestone Pk	0.1	120	Crestone Pk	SC
	14,020	"Northwest Lindsey"	Lindsey, Mt	0.2	40	Blanca Pk	SC
	13,237	Notch Mtn	Point 13,248	0.9	217	Mt of the Holy Cross	SW
107	13,799	"Obstruction Pk"	"Kat Carson"	0.5	339	Crestone Pk	SC
538	13,138	Ogalalla Pk	Copeland Mtn	1.4	718	Isolation Pk	FR
85	13,845	Oklahoma, Mt	Massive, Mt	1.8	745	Mt Champion	SW
616	13,038	"Old Baldy"	North Arapaho Pk	0.9	338	Monarch Lake	FR
194	13,589	One, Pk	White Dome	0.8	409	Storm King Pk	SJ

Rank	Elev	Peak Name	Parent	Mile	Rise	Quadrangle	Rg
106	13,801	Organ Mtn A	San Luis Pk	2.0	694	San Luis Pk	SJ
620	13,032	Organ Mtn B	Amherst Mtn	0.4	452	Columbine Pass	SJ
S	13,432	"Oscar's Pk"	Wasatch Mtn	1.0	292	Telluride	SJ
157	13,684	Oso, Mt	Grizzly Pk C	4.9	1,664	Emerald Lake	SJ
58	13,971	Ouray, Mt	Shavano, Mt	13.5	2,671	Mt Ouray	SW
360	13,340	Owen A, Mt	Point 13,490	2.0	600	Electric Pk	SC
603	13,058	Owen B, Mt	Treasury Mtn	7.5	1,358	Oh Be Joyful	EL
26	14,153	Oxford, Mt	Belford, Mt	1.2	653	Mt Harvard	SW
61	13,950	Pacific Pk	Fletcher Mtn	1.4	570	Breckenridge	TM
259	13,497	Pagoda Mtn	Longs Pk	0.7	397	Isolation Pk	FR
578	13,088	Paiute Pk	Audubon, Mt	0.9	468	Monarch Lake	FR
	13,319	Palmyra Pk	Silver Mtn B	0.5	179	Telluride	SJ
208	13,574	Parnassus, Mt	Bard Pk	1.0	537	Grays Pk	FR
324	13,391	Parry Pk	North Arapaho Pk	12.5	1,720	Empire	FR
349	13,362	Pearl Mtn	Castle Pk	2.5	582	Pearl Pass	EL
	13,270	Pecks Pk	Belford, Mt	1.0	50	Mt Harvard	SW
	13,348	Peerless Mtn	Horseshoe Mtn	0.9	168	Mt Sherman	TM
635	13,006	Pennsylvania Mtn	Evans B, Mt	2.2	699	Climax	TM
550	13,122	Peters Pk	Point 13,322 B	0.4	342	Emerald Lake	SJ
219	13,553	Pettingell Pk	Torreys Pk	7.4	1,563	Loveland Pass	FR
73	13,895	"Phoenix Pk"	San Luis Pk	5.0	1,515	Halfmoon Pass	SJ
188	13,611	Pico Asilado	Crestone Needle	1.7	831	Crestone Pk	SC
57	13,972	Pigeon Pk	Eolus, Mt	1.5	1,152	Snowdon Pk	SJ
547	13,126	Pika Pk	Gold Dust Pk	0.7	506	Mt Jackson	SW
30	14,110	Pikes Pk	Evans, Mt	60.3	5,530	Pikes Pk	FR
131	13,738	Pilot Knob	Golden Horn	0.5	398	Ophir	SJ
178	13,633	Pk 10	Crystal Pk	0.9	373	Breckenridge	TM
492	13,195	Pk 9	Pk 10	0.6	415	Breckenridge	TM
464	13,220	"Pk C"	"Pk G"	1.6	520	Vail East	GO
	13,100	"Pk C Prime"	"Pk C"	0.2	120	Vail East	GO
	13,047	"Pk D"	"Pk G"	1.0	267	Vail East	GO
	13,220	"Pk E"	"Pk G"	0.6	200	Vail East	GO
	13,230	"Pk F"	"Pk G"	0.4	250	Vail East	GO
431	13,260	"Pk G"	Powell, Mt	2.3	1,000	Vail East	GO
	13,100	"Pk H"	"Pk G"	0.4	140	Vail East	GO
473	13,213	"Pk L"	"Pk Q"	1.5	753	Vail East	GO
552	13,121	"Pk N"	"Pk L"	1.2	421	Mt Powell	GO
454	13,230	"Pk Q"	"Pk G"	2.0	730	Vail East	GO
581	13,085	"Pk X"	"Pk Z"	0.8	465	Vail East	GO
442	13,245	"Pk Z"	"Pk G"	4.0	785	Willow Lakes	GO
	13,075	"Pk Z Prime"	"Solitude, Mt"	0.4	215	Vail East	GO
90	13,832	Point 13,832	Redcloud Pk	1.4	812	Redcloud Pk	SJ
99	13,811	Point 13,811	Point 13,832	1.2	551	Redcloud Pk	SJ
109	13,795	Point 13,795	Handies Pk	1.3	495	Redcloud Pk	SJ
118	13,768	Point 13,768	Holy Cross Ridge	0.8	388	Mt of the Holy Cross	SW
121	13,762	Point 13,762	Harvard, Mt	2.8	822	Mt Harvard	SW
133	13,736	Point 13,736	Deer Mtn	1.2	676	Mt Champion	SW
137	13,722	Point 13,722	"Thunder Pyramid"	0.4	302	Maroon Bells	EL
140	13,712	Point 13,712	Shavano, Mt	0.9	332	Mt Antero	SW
S	13,708	Point 13,708	"Animas Forks Mtn"	0.5	288	Handies Pk	SJ
151	13,691	Point 13,691	Point 13,832	2.7	471	Redcloud Pk	SJ
153	13,688	Point 13,688 A	Point 13,832	1.6	428	Redcloud Pk	SJ

Rank	Elev	Peak Name	Parent	Mile	Rise	Quadrangle	Rg
154	13,688	Point 13,688 B	"Animas Forks Mtn"	1.1	388	Handies Pk	SJ
159	13,681	Point 13,681	Silver Mtn A	1.0	501	Uncompahgre Pk	SJ
161	13,674	Point 13,674	Half Pk	1.3	374	Redcloud Pk	SJ
167	13,660	Point 13,660 A	California Pk	1.1	400	Twin Pks	SC
168	13,660	Point 13,660 B	Pole Creek Mtn	1.5	840	Pole Creek Mtn	SJ
S	13,660	Point 13,660 C	"Lackawanna Pk"	0.9	280	Independence Pass	SW
174	13,646	Point 13,646	Grizzly Mtn	1.7	546	Saint Elmo	SW
179	13,631	Point 13,631 A	Garfield Pk	2.2	971	New York Pk	SW
180	13,631	Point 13,631 B	Point 13,722	0.7	331	Maroon Bells	EL
183	13,626	Point 13,626	Princeton, Mt	1.4	486	Mt Yale	SW
186	13,616	Point 13,616	La Plata Pk	1.6	436	Mt Elbert	SW
197	13,581	Point 13,581	Carson Pk	1.5	681	Pole Creek Mtn	SJ
199	13,580	Point 13,580 A	Point 13,581	1.2	360	Pole Creek Mtn	SJ
200	13,580	Point 13,580 B	Adams, Mt	0.5	440	Horn Pk	SC
S	13,580	Point 13,580 C	Harvard, Mt	1.0	280	Mt Harvard	SW
205	13,577	Point 13,577	Point 13,660 A	0.5	317	Blanca Pk	SC
211	13,566	Point 13,566	Point 13,691	1.9	746	Redcloud Pk	SJ
212	13,565	Point 13,565	Culebra Pk	1.4	545	El Valle Creek	SC
S	13,555	Point 13,555	"Huerfano Pk"	1.0	295	Blanca Pk	SC
221	13,550	Point 13,550	"Castleabra"	0.9	530	Gothic	EL
S	13,548	Point 13,548	Mosquito Pk	0.7	288	Climax	TM
222	13,546	Point 13,546	Adams, Mt	0.8	646	Horn Pk	SC
S	13,545	Point 13,545	Twining Pk	0.7	285	Mt Champion	SW
224	13,541	Point 13,541	Point 13,580 B	0.8	361	Crestone Pk	SC
226	13,540	Point 13,540 A	Wilson Pk	1.0	520	Dolores Pk	SJ
227	13,540	Point 13,540 B	Wood Mtn	2.6	520	Redcloud Pk	SJ
231	13,537	Point 13,537	White Rock Mtn	2.5	757	Maroon Bells	EL
233	13,535	Point 13,535	Jones Mtn A	1.5	515	Handies Pk	SJ
234	13,531	Point 13,531	Hope, Mt	1.5	431	Mt Elbert	SW
240	13,524	Point 13,524 A	Carson Pk	1.4	464	Pole Creek Mtn	SJ
241	13,524	Point 13,524 B	Gibbs Pk	3.3	624	Rito Alto Pk	SC
244	13,517	Point 13,517 A	Huron Pk	1.5	457	Winfield	SW
S	13,517	Point 13,517 B	Point 13,580 B	0.4	297	Crestone Pk	SC
248	13,513	Point 13,513	Gibbs Pk	2.4	453	Electric Pk	SC
249	13,510	Point 13,510 A	San Luis Pk	7.8	1,570	Baldy Cinco	SJ
250	13,510	Point 13,510 B	Emma, Mt	5.0	610	Ironton	SJ
253	13,505	Point 13,505	Point 13,631 A	1.3	525	New York Pk	SW
256	13,500	Point 13,500	Twining Pk	0.7	360	Independence Pass	SW
257	13,498	Point 13,498	Point 13,540 A	0.6	358	Dolores Pk	SJ
263	13,490	Point 13,490	Point 13,513	1.0	990	Rito Alto Pk	SC
274	13,472	Point 13,472 A	Ouray, Mt	1.9	1,172	Mt Ouray	SW
S	13,472	Point 13,472 B	Point 13,517 A	0.5	292	Winfield	SW
278	13,463	Point 13,463	Garfield Pk	1.8	563	Independence Pass	SW
279	13,462	Point 13,462 A	Huron Pk	1.1	322	Winfield	SW
280	13,462	Point 13,462 B	Point 13,517 A	1.6	562	Winfield	SW
283	13,460	Point 13,460	Sayers BM	1.4	440	Independence Pass	SW
291	13,450	Point 13,450	Carson Pk	1.2	350	Pole Creek Mtn	SJ
297	13,434	Point 13,434	Kendall Pk	1.2	534	Howardsville	SJ
298	13,433	Point 13,433	Jackson, Mt	0.6	413	Mt Jackson	SW
304	13,427	Point 13,427	Wood Mtn	1.4	407	Handies Pk	SJ
319	13,402	Point 13,402	"Phoenix Pk"	1.7	422	Halfmoon Pass	SJ
321	13,401	Point 13,401	Tijeras Pk	0.9	301	Crestone Pk	SC

Rank	Elev	Peak Name	Parent	Mile	Rise	Quadrangle	Rg
327	13,384	Point 13,384	Cleveland Pk	0.9	364	Crestone Pk	SC
334	13,380	Point 13,380	White Rock Mtn	1.3	480	Gothic	EL
338	13,377	Point 13,377	"Heisshorn"	0.5	357	Wetterhorn Pk	SJ
340	13,374	Point 13,374	Harvard, Mt	1.9	394	Mt Harvard	SW
356	13,345	Point 13,345	Emma Burr Mtn	1.1	445	Cumberland Pass	SW
358	13,342	Point 13,342	Ute Ridge	1.4	726	Rio Grande Pyramid	SJ
361	13,340	Point 13,340 A	"SoSo, Mt"	1.2	440	Emerald Lake	SJ
362	13,340	Point 13,340 B	"Heisshorn"	1.7	745	Uncompahgre Pk	SJ
365	13,336	Point 13,336	Buckskin BM	1.1	636	Maroon Bells	EL
373	13,325	Point 13,325	Storm Pk A	0.5	465	Silverton	SJ
374	13,322	Point 13,322	Jenkins Mtn	2.4	902	Pieplant	SW
377	13,317	Point 13,317	Point 13,626	2.3	737	Saint Elmo	SW
379	13,313	Point 13,313	Baldy Cinco	0.7	413	Baldy Cinco	SJ
380	13,312	Point 13,312 A	Point 13,566	0.8	452	Redcloud Pk	SJ
381	13,312	Point 13,312 B	Pearl Mtn	0.6	412	Pearl Pass	EL
382	13,312	Point 13,312 C	Point 13,463	1.0	452	Pieplant	SW
386	13,310	Point 13,310	Point 13,340 A	0.6	330	Emerald Lake	SJ
388	13,308	Point 13,308	Point 13,342	0.8	606	Rio Grande Pyramid	SJ
390	13,302	Point 13,302	Oso, Mt	1.7	722	Storm King Pk	SJ
397	13,300	Point 13,300 A	Point 13,505	1.4	520	New York Pk	SW
398	13,300	Point 13,300 B	Twining Pk	2.7	600	Mt Champion	SW
399	13,300	Point 13,300 C	Wetterhorn Pk	0.7	440	Wetterhorn Pk	SJ
400	13,300	Point 13,300 D	Point 13,302	0.6	560	Columbine Pass	SJ
S	13,300	Point 13,300 E	Point 13,460	0.6	280	Independence Pass	SW
S	13,300	Point 13,300 F	South Lookout Pk	0.4	280	Ophir	SJ
403	13,295	Point 13,295	Sayers BM	2.7	435	Pieplant	SW
410	13,285	Point 13,285	San Luis Pk	2.5	665	San Luis Pk	SJ
411	13,284	Point 13,284	Point 13,300 B	2.7	424	Mt Champion	SW
413	13,282	Point 13,282	Point 13,300 A	1.1	822	New York Pk	SW
417	13,278	Point 13,278	Rio Grande Pyramid	1.1	633	Weminuche Pass	SJ
430	13,261	Point 13,261	Point 13,278	0.7	321	Weminuche Pass	SJ
432	13,260	Point 13,260 A	Seigal Mtn	2.2	520	Handies Pk	SJ
433	13,260	Point 13,260 B	Precarious Pk	0.8	440	Maroon Bells	EL
434	13,260	Point 13,260 C	Coney BM	1.2	400	Finger Mesa	SJ
437	13,255	Point 13,255	Grizzly Pk E	1.6	555	Winfield	SW
439	13,253	Point 13,253	Point 13,255	2.0	433	Winfield	SW
441	13,248	Point 13,248	Holy Cross Ridge	1.3	308	Mt of the Holy Cross	SW
443	13,244	Point 13,244	Point 13,336	1.1	424	Highland Pk	EL
447	13,235	Point 13,235	Point 13,253	0.9	375	Pieplant	SW
452	13,232	Point 13,232 A	Point 13,260 B	0.4	412	Maroon Bells	EL
453	13,232	Point 13,232 B	Sayres BM	1.7	332	Pieplant	SW
455	13,230	Point 13,230 A	Point 13,308	1.9	770	Rio Grande Pyramid	SJ
S	13,230	Point 13,230 B	Point 13,284	0.7	290	Mt Champion	SW
456	13,229	Point 13,229	Point 13,565	0.6	329	El Valle Creek	SC
459	13,222	Point 13,222 A	Point 13,340 B	0.6	322	Uncompahgre Pk	SJ
460	13,222	Point 13,222 B	Point 13,300 D	0.8	402	Emerald Lake	SJ
470	13,216	Point 13,216	Point 13,380	0.7	316	Maroon Bells	EL
474	13,212	Point 13,212	Point 13,284	0.7	312	Mt Champion	SW
480	13,206	Point 13,206	Point 13,377	0.6	306	Wetterhorn Pk	SJ
489	13,202	Point 13,202	Twining Pk	2.0	422	Mt Champion	SW
490	13,201	Point 13,201	Point 13,300 C	1.3	661	Wetterhorn Pk	SJ
491	13,198	Point 13,198	Grizzly Pk A	2.8	658	Independence Pass	SW

Rank	Elev	Peak Name	Parent	Mile	Rise	Quadrangle	Rg
499	13,180	Point 13,180 A	Point 13,631 B	0.5	320	Maroon Bells	EL
500	13,180	Point 13,180 B	Point 13,691	2.1	524	Redcloud Pk	SJ
S	13,180	Point 13,180 C	Point 13,285	0.5	280	San Luis Pk	SJ
505	13,169	Point 13,169	Point 13,230 A	1.2	989	Rio Grande Pyramid	SJ
510	13,164	Point 13,164	Half Pk	1.3	384	Pole Creek Mtn	SJ
511	13,162	Point 13,162 A	Baldy Cinco	1.3	493	Baldy Cinco	SJ
512	13,162	Point 13,162 B	Point 13,550	0.9	382	Gothic	EL
513	13,159	Point 13,159	Lookout Pk	1.3	379	Ophir	SJ
514	13,158	Point 13,158	Uncompahgre Pk	1.8	378	Uncompahgre Pk	SJ
518	13,155	Point 13,155	Point 13,285	1.7	415	San Luis Pk	SJ
519	13,153	Point 13,153 A	Herard Mtn	0.9	653	Medano Pass	SC
520	13,153	Point 13,153 B	Adams, Mt	0.7	373	Horn Pk	SC
527	13,147	Point 13,147	Monumental Pk	1.4	527	Garfield	SW
528	13,145	Point 13,145 A	La Junta Pk	0.6	325	Telluride	SJ
S	13,145	Point 13,145 B	Point 13,284	1.2	285	Mt Champion	SW
532	13,140	Point 13,140 A	Point 13,255	0.6	320	Winfield	SW
533	13,140	Point 13,140 B	Jenkins Mtn	1.1	320	Pieplant	SW
534	13,140	Point 13,140 C	Truro Pk	0.4	320	New York Pk	SW
S	13,140	Point 13,140 D	"Weminuche Pk"	0.4	280	Emerald Lake	SJ
545	13,130	Point 13,130	Point 13,180 A	0.8	350	Maroon Bells	EL
548	13,123	Point 13,123 A	Point 13,498	1.1	463	Dolores Pk	SJ
549	13,123	Point 13,123 B	Cottonwood Pk	0.8	303	Electric Pk	SC
551	13,122	Point 13,122	Point 13,490	1.2	302	Rito Alto Pk	SC
553	13,121	Point 13,121	Greylock Mtn	0.5	341	Columbine Pass	SJ
559	13,111	Point 13,111	Point 13,510 A	4.6	811	San Luis Pk	SJ
560	13,110	Point 13,110	Point 13,308	1.2	450	Storm King Pk	SJ
561	13,109	Point 13,109	Rhoda, Mt	0.8	329	Howardsville	SJ
563	13,106	Point 13,106	Uncompahgre Pk	2.2	726	Uncompahgre Pk	SJ
565	13,105	Point 13,105	Amherst Mtn	0.9	325	Columbine Pass	SJ
566	13,102	Point 13,102	Monumental Pk	1.7	482	Garfield	SW
569	13,100	Point 13,100 A	Point 13,681	1.8	480	Sheep Mtn	SJ
570	13,100	Point 13,100 B	Pika Pk	2.1	600	Mt Jackson	SW
571	13,100	Point 13,100 C	Point 13,111	1.9	400	Baldy Cinco	SJ
S	13,100	Point 13,100 D	Little Bear Pk	1.0	280	Twin Pks	SC
574	13,093	Point 13,093	Sunshine Mtn	1.4	353	Handies Pk	SJ
575	13,091	Point 13,091	Point 13,106 A	1.8	591	Uncompahgre Pk	SJ
576	13,090	Point 13,090	Point 13,140 C	1.1	350	New York Pk	SW
582	13,085	Point 13,085	Point 13,100 B	1.0	625	Mt Jackson	SW
586	13,078	Point 13,078	Point 13,317	1.4	738	Saint Elmo	SW
590	13,075	Point 13,075	Hanson Pk	1.0	415	Handies Pk	SJ
592	13,074	Point 13,074	Point 13,300 A	1.0	454	New York Pk	SW
595	13,070	Point 13,070	Pomeroy Mtn	0.6	330	Saint Elmo	SW
597	13,069	Point 13,069	Niagara Pk	4.1	329	Howardsville	SJ
598	13,062	Point 13,062 A	Hagerman Pk	2.1	642	Snowmass Mtn	EL
599	13,062	Point 13,062 B	Hermit Pk	1.9	842	Rito Alto Pk	SC
601	13,060	Point 13,060 A	Clark Pk	0.5	320	Capitol Pk	EL
602	13,060	Point 13,060 B	Point 13,062 B	0.4	360	Rito Alto Pk	SC
S	13,060	Point 13,060 C	Peters Pk	0.4	280	Emerald Lake	SJ
605	13,055	Point 13,055	Kreutzer, Mt	1.6	315	Tincup	SW
606	13,054	Point 13,054	Eureka Mtn	1.6	594	Rito Alto Pk	SC
608	13,051	Point 13,051	Silver Mtn A	1.1	351	Uncompahgre Pk	SJ
610	13,050	Point 13,050	Point 13,345	1.5	550	Cumberland Pass	SW

Rank	Elev	Peak Name	Parent	Mile	Rise	Quadrangle	Rg
611	13,046	Point 13,046	Snowdon Pk	0.6	386	Snowdon Pk	SJ
612	13,042	Point 13,042	Twin Sisters East	2.1	942	Silverton	SJ
615	13,039	Point 13,039	Sleeping Sexton	0.9	419	Maroon Bells	EL
618	13,034	Point 13,034	Point 13,111	2.0	654	Baldy Cinco	SJ
621	13,028	Point 13,028	Point 13,060 B	0.7	328	Rito Alto Pk	SC
622	13,026	Point 13,026	Point 13,202	1.7	326	Mt Champion	SW
624	13,020	Point 13,020 A	Point 13,336	0.5	320	Maroon Bells	EL
625	13,020	Point 13,020 B	Pico Asilado	0.7	360	Crestone Pk	SC
S	13,020	Point 13,020 C	Point 13,510 A	0.9	286	Baldy Cinco	SJ
628	13,017	Point 13,017	"Window Pk"	1.0	400	Rio Grande Pyramid	SJ
629	13,016	Point 13,016	Point 13,051	1.5	676	Uncompahgre Pk	SJ
630	13,015	Point 13,015	Point 13,402	1.2	315	Halfmoon Pass	SJ
634	13,010	Point 13,010	Chief Mtn	2.9	1,790	Cimarrona Pk	SJ
636	13,003	Point 13,003	Point 13,026	1.9	503	Mt Champion	SW
637	13,001	Point 13,001	Point 13,202	0.9	501	Mt Champion	SW
	13,180	Point Pun	Graystone Pk	0.6	200	Snowdon Pk	SJ
138	13,716	Pole Creek Mtn	Half Pk	5.2	1,536	Pole Creek Mtn	SJ
522	13,151	Pomeroy Mtn	Grizzly Mtn	2.1	611	Saint Elmo	SW
113	13,786	Potosi Pk	Teakettle Mtn	1.0	806	Ironton	SJ
477	13,208	Powell Pk	McHenrys Pk	0.4	388	McHenrys Pk	FR
201	13,580	Powell, Mt (Pk B)	Jackson, Mt	21.8	3,000	Mt Powell	GO
335	13,380	Precarious Pk	Point 13,631 B	2.1	640	Maroon Bells	EL
529	13,144	Precipice Pk	"U 3"	1.5	484	Wetterhorn Pk	SJ
20	14,197	Princeton, Mt	Antero, Mt	5.2	2,431	Mt Antero	SW
328	13,384	Prize BM	Point 13,631 A	1.6	604	Pieplant	SW
369	13,330	"Proposal Pk"	Hanson Pk	1.9	550	Handies Pk	SJ
	13,980	"Prow, The"	Kit Carson Mtn	0.1	40	Crestone Pk	SC
	13,739	Ptarmigan Pk	Horseshoe Mtn	2.5	279	Mt Sherman	TM
160	13,676	Purgatoire Pk	Vermejo Pk	1.8	849	Culebra Pk	SC
47	14,018	Pyramid Pk	Maroon Pk	2.1	1,518	Maroon Bells	EL
282	13,461	Quail Mtn	Hope, Mt	1.4	921	Mt Elbert	SW
13	14,265	Quandary Pk	Lincoln, Mt	3.2	1,125	Breckenridge	TM
	13,130	"Rain Pk"	"Silverthorne, Mt"	0.6	230	Willow Lakes	GO
70	13,908	Red Mtn A	Culebra Pk	0.7	448	Culebra Pk	SC
	13,500	Red Mtn B	Garfield Pk	0.4	120	Independence Pass	SW
457	13,229	Red Mtn C	Hoosier Ridge	0.7	369	Breckenridge	TM
	13,215	Red Pk A	Hoosier Ridge	0.7	115	Breckenridge	TM
495	13,189	Red Pk B	"Silverthorne, Mt"	1.6	929	Willow Lakes	GO
175	13,642	Redcliff	Coxcomb Pk	0.5	502	Wetterhorn Pk	SJ
46	14,034	Redcloud Pk	Handies Pk	4.9	1,454	Redcloud Pk	SJ
320	13,402	Rhoda, Mt	Point 13,434	0.4	302	Howardsville	SJ
276	13,468	Ridgeway, Mt	Teakettle Mtn	1.0	448	Mt Sneffels	SJ
114	13,783	Rinker Pk	La Plata Pk	1.8	923	Mt Elbert	SW
97	13,821	Rio Grande Pyramid	Jagged Mtn	10.8	1,881	Rio Grande Pyramid	SJ
110	13,794	Rito Alto Pk	Adams, Mt	7.3	1,134	Rito Alto Pk	SC
	13,140	Robeson Pk	Bard Pk	0.9	200	Grays Pk	FR
325	13,391	Rogers Pk	Evans A, Mt	2.4	515	Harris Park	FR
150	13,693	Rolling Mtn	San Miguel Pk	2.3	913	Ophir	SJ
207	13,575	Rosalie Pk	Evans A, Mt	3.0	675	Harris Park	FR
	13,184	Rowe Mtn	Hagues Pk	0.9	44	Trail Ridge	FR
	13,420	Rowe Pk	Hagues Pk	0.4	200	Trail Ridge	FR
419	13,277	Ruby Mtn	Grays Pk	1.2	439	Montezuma	FR

Rank	Elev	Peak Name	Parent	Mile	Rise	Quadrangle	Rg
	13,003	Ruffner Mtn	"S 7"	0.4	23	Sams	SJ
445	13,242	"S 4"	"S 6"	0.8	302	Mt Sneffels	SJ
293	13,441	"S 6"	"T 0"	1.0	381	Mt Sneffels	SJ
466	13,220	"S 7"	Mears Pk	1.0	400	Sams	SJ
440	13,252	"S 8"	Mears Pk	1.6	552	Sams	SJ
541	13,134	"S 9"	"S 8"	0.7	354	Sams	SJ
626	13,020	"S 10"	"S 9"	0.8	360	Sams	SJ
	13,060	Saint Sophia Ridge	Emma, Mt	0.5	160	Telluride	SJ
284	13,460	San Joaquin Ridge	Silver Mtn B	1.3	360	Telluride	SJ
50	14,014	San Luis Pk	Redcloud Pk	27.1	3,116	San Luis Pk	SJ
124	13,752	San Miguel Pk	Vermillion Pk	2.4	1,307	Ophir	SJ
501	13,180	Santa Fe Pk	Geneva Pk	1.3	480	Montezuma	FR
537	13,139	Savage Pk	"Fancy Pk"	2.8	1,153	Mt Jackson	SW
132	13,738	Sayers BM	La Plata Pk	1.9	958	Mt Elbert	SW
421	13,274	Seigal Mtn	"Animas Forks Mtn"	1.0	374	Handies Pk	SJ
158	13,682	Seven, Pk	Six, Pk	0.8	422	Storm King Pk	SJ
	13,132	Sewanee Pk	Point 13,147	0.6	232	Garfield	SW
17	14,229	Shavano, Mt	Antero, Mt	3.8	1,619	Maysville	SW
407	13,292	Sheep Mtn A	Canby Mtn	1.9	632	Howardsville	SJ
	13,188	Sheep Mtn B	San Miguel Pk	1.3	128	Mt Wilson	SJ
506	13,168	Sheep Mtn C	Point 13,681	2.7	592	Sheep Mtn	SJ
596	13,070	Sheep Mtn D	Point 13,105	0.4	370	Columbine Pass	SJ
126	13,748	Sheridan, Mt	Sherman, Mt	1.3	608	Mt Sherman	TM
45	14,036	Sherman, Mt	Democrat, Mt	8.1	896	Mt Sherman	TM
	13,340	Ships Prow	Longs Pk	0.5	40	Longs Pk	FR
308	13,420	"Siberia Pk"	Snowmass Mtn	1.2	760	Snowmass Mtn	EL
181	13,628	Silex, Mt	Storm King Pk	0.8	808	Storm King Pk	SJ
139	13,714	Silver Mtn A	Uncompahgre Pk	2.5	1,054	Uncompahgre Pk	SJ
275	13,470	Silver Mtn B	Wasatch Mtn	2.2	410	Telluride	SJ
96	13,822	Silverheels, Mt	Bross, Mt	5.5	2,283	Alma	TM
351	13,357	"Silverthorne, Mt"	Powell, Mt	10.9	1,097	Willow Lakes	GO
144	13,705	Six, Pk	Jagged Mtn	1.0	685	Storm King Pk	SJ
	13,500	Sixteen, Pk	Fifteen, Pk	0.1	80	Snowdon Pk	SJ
285	13,460	Sleeping Sexton	North Maroon Pk	0.6	440	Maroon Bells	EL
27	14,150	Sneffels, Mt	Wilson, Mt	15.8	3,930	Mt Sneffels	SJ
448	13,234	Sniktau, Mt	Grizzly Pk D	2.4	520	Grays Pk	FR
623	13,024	"Snow Pk"	"Valhalla, Mt"	0.8	484	Willow Lakes	GO
588	13,077	Snowdon Pk	Twilight Pk	3.8	1,337	Snowdon Pk	SJ
31	14,092	Snowmass Mtn	Capitol Pk	2.3	1,152	Snowmass Mtn	EL
	13,620	Snowmass Pk	Hagerman Pk	0.2	120	Snowmass Mtn	EL
577	13,090	"Solitude, Mt"	"Pk Z"	2.0	710	Vail East	GO
309	13,417	"SoSo, Mt"	Oso, Mt	0.8	677	Emerald Lake	SJ
	13,397	South Arapaho Pk	North Arapaho Pk	0.5	97	Monarch Lake	FR
	14,020	"South Bross"	Bross, Mt	0.6	80	Alma	TM
	14,134	"South Elbert"	Elbert, Mt	1.0	234	Mt Elbert	SW
	14,020	"South Little Bear"	Little Bear Pk	0.2	80	Blanca Pk	SC
336	13,380	South Lookout Pk	US Grant Pk	1.2	520	Ophir	SJ
	14,132	"South Massive"	Massive, Mt	0.7	232	Mt Massive	SW
526	13,148	South River Pk	Montezuma Pk	21.3	2,228	South River Pk	SJ
	13,100	South Twilight Pk	Twilight Pk	0.3	200	Snowdon Pk	SJ
	14,110	"South Wilson"	Wilson, Mt	0.3	170	Mt Wilson	SJ
	14,060	"Southeast Longs"	Longs Pk	0.2	240	Longs Pk	FR

Rank	Elev	Peak Name	Parent	Mile	Rise	Quadrangle	Rg
	13,842	Spalding, Mt	Evans, Mt	1.1	262	Mt Evans	FR
	13,123	Spiller Pk	Babcock Pk	0.5	183	La Plata	SJ
306	13,423	Spread Eagle Pk	Point 13,524 B	0.9	443	Electric Pk	SC
444	13,244	Spring Mtn	Venable Pk	0.7	464	Horn Pk	SC
111	13,794	Square Top Mtn	Edwards, Mt	3.4	814	Montezuma	FR
243	13,521	Star Pk	Castle Pk	4.1	816	Pearl Pass	EL
55	13,983	Stewart Pk	San Luis Pk	2.5	883	Stewart Pk	SJ
508	13,165	"Stony Pass Pk"	Canby Mtn	0.7	577	Howardsville	SJ
125	13,752	Storm King Pk	Trinity Pk	1.3	612	Storm King Pk	SJ
266	13,487	Storm Pk A	Tower Mtn	1.4	627	Silverton	SJ
	13,326	Storm Pk B	Longs Pk	0.8	186	Longs Pk	FR
	13,134	Sullivan Mtn	Santa Fe Pk	0.6	274	Montezuma	FR
346	13,368	Sultan Mtn	Twin Sister East	4.6	1,868	Silverton	SJ
401	13,300	Summit Pk	"Phoenix Pk"	40.5	2,760	Summit Pk	SJ
300	13,432	"Sundog"	Sunshine Pk	0.9	332	Redcloud Pk	SJ
39	14,059	Sunlight Pk	Windom Pk	0.5	399	Storm King Pk	SJ
	13,995	"Sunlight Spire"	Sunlight Pk	0.2	215	Storm King Pk	SJ
375	13,321	Sunshine Mtn	Point 13,540 B	2.5	1,421	Handies Pk	SJ
53	14,001	Sunshine Pk	Redcloud Pk	1.3	501	Redcloud Pk	SJ
134	13,735	"T 0"	Dallas Pk	1.4	395	Telluride	SJ
294	13,436	"T 5"	Emma, Mt	1.8	416	Telluride	SJ
350	13,359	"T 7"	Point 13,510 B	1.4	499	Ironton	SJ
378	13,315	"T 8"	"T 7"	0.7	495	Ironton	SJ
270	13,477	"T 10"	Three Needles	0.6	537	Ironton	SJ
251	13,510	"T 11"	Lookout Pk	1.3	452	Telluride	SJ
25	14,155	Tabeguache Pk	Shavano, Mt	0.7	455	Saint Elmo	SW
172	13,651	Taylor Mtn	Aetna, Mt	1.2	631	Garfield	SW
296	13,435	Taylor Pk A	Star Pk	1.3	815	Pearl Pass	EL
521	13,153	Taylor Pk B	Powell Pk	1.0	413	McHenrys Pk	FR
98	13,819	Teakettle Mtn	Sneffels, Mt	1.7	759	Mt Sneffels	SJ
S	13,509	Telluride Pk	Point 13,510 A	0.5	289	Ironton	SJ
S	13,420	Ten, Pk	Jagged Mtn	0.3	280	Storm King Pk	SJ
478	13,208	Teocalli Mtn	Point 13,550	2.4	788	Gothic	EL
	13,213	Thirsty Pk	Lakes Pk	0.8	233	Electric Pk	SC
	13,705	Thirteen, Pk	Monitor Pk	0.2	245	Storm King Pk	SJ
267	13,481	Three Needles	"T 11"	1.0	421	Telluride	SJ
269	13,478	Three, Pk	Trinity Pk East	0.9	498	Storm King Pk	SJ
	13,108	Thunder Mtn	Greylock Mtn	1.0	248	Columbine Pass	SJ
65	13,932	"Thunder Pyramid"	Pyramid Pk	0.6	312	Maroon Bells	EL
	13,300	"Tigger Pk"	Princeton, Mt	1.1	240	Mt Antero	SW
189	13,604	Tijeras Pk	Pico Asilado	1.7	744	Crestone Pk	SC
573	13,095	"Tomboy Pk"	Chicago Pk	0.5	315	Telluride	SJ
11	14,267	Torreys Pk	Grays Pk	0.6	560	Grays Pk	FR
220	13,552	Tower Mtn	Niagara Pk	5.4	1,652	Howardsville	SJ
	13,852	Traver Pk	Clinton Pk	0.7	232	Climax	TM
238	13,528	Treasure Mtn	Hagerman Pk	7.0	2,821	Snowmass Mtn	EL
S	13,701	Treasurevault Mtn	Mosquito Pk	0.4	281	Climax	TM
281	13,462	Treasury Mtn	Treasure Mtn	1.4	522	Snowmass Mtn	EL
376	13,321	Trico Pk	Point 13,510 B	0.9	461	Ironton	SJ
245	13,517	Trinchera Pk	Point 13,565	10.3	977	Trinchera Pk	SC
103	13,805	Trinity Pk	Vestal Pk	1.2	945	Storm King Pk	SJ
128	13,745	Trinity Pk East	Trinity Pk	0.2	405	Storm King Pk	SJ

Rank	Elev	Peak Name	Parent	Mile	Rise	Quadrangle	Rg
120	13,765	Trinity Pk West	Trinity Pk	0.4	385	Storm King Pk	SJ
414	13,282	Truro Pk	Point 13,300 A	1.3	822	New York Pk	SW
450	13,233	Turner Pk	Yale, Mt	3.9	1,173	Tincup	SW
89	13,835	Turret Pk	Pigeon Pk	0.5	735	Snowdon Pk	SJ
487	13,203	Tuttle Mtn	Brown Mtn	1.7	503	Handies Pk	SJ
535	13,140	Twelve, Pk	Monitor Pk	0.5	320	Storm King Pk	SJ
162	13,672	Tweto, Mt	Buckskin, Mt	1.2	412	Climax	TM
515	13,158	Twilight Pk	Pigeon Pk	4.9	2,338	Snowdon Pk	SJ
202	13,580	Twin Pks A	Ellingwood Point	1.6	640	Twin Pks	SC
	13,333	Twin Pks B	Rinker Pk	0.9	233	Mt Elbert	SW
301	13,432	Twin Sister East	Rolling Mtn	2.2	1,332	Ophir	SJ
341	13,374	Twin Sister West	Twin Sister East	0.4	394	Ophir	SJ
632	13,012	Twin Sisters	Bushnell Pk	1.0	552	Bushnell Pk	SC
	13,420	Twin Thumbs	Eleven, Pk	0.2	120	Storm King Pk	SJ
141	13,711	Twining Pk	Point 13,736	2.2	1,251	Mt Champion	SW
271	13,475	Two, Pk	Three, Pk	0.8	535	Storm King Pk	SJ
446	13,241	"U 3"	Redcliff	0.7	461	Wetterhorn Pk	SJ
6	14,309	Uncompahgre Pk	La Plata Pk	84.0	4,249	Uncompahgre Pk	SJ
627	13,020	"Unicorn Pk"	Montezuma Pk	0.6	440	Summit Pk	SJ
	13,036	United States Mtn	Chicago Pk	1.0	176	Ironton	SJ
119	13,767	US Grant Pk	Golden Horn	1.7	747	Ophir	SJ
286	13,455	Ute Ridge	White Dome	4.9	962	Rio Grande Pyramid	SJ
387	13,309	"V 2"	US Grant Pk	0.8	409	Ophir	SJ
239	13,528	"V 3"	US Grant Pk	0.4	388	Ophir	SJ
228	13,540	"V 4"	US Grant Pk	0.4	320	Ophir	SJ
517	13,156	"V 5"	South Lookout Pk	1.3	616	Ophir	SJ
402	13,300	"V 8"	Beattie Pk	0.6	320	Ophir	SJ
435	13,260	"V 9"	Rolling Mtn	1.0	397	Ophir	SJ
272	13,475	"V 10"	Grizzly Pk B	0.7	375	Ophir	SJ
502	13,180	"Valhalla, Mt"	"Silverthorne, Mt"	1.6	760	Willow Lakes	GO
302	13,428	Vallecito Mtn	Leviathan Pk	0.5	568	Storm King Pk	SJ
496	13,185	Valois, Mt	Aztec Mtn	2.1	325	Columbine Pass	SJ
S	13,024	Van Wirt Mtn	Point 13,102	0.7	284	Garfield	SW
367	13,334	Venable Pk	Fluted Pk	2.7	634	Rito Alto Pk	SC
135	13,723	Vermejo Pk	Red Mtn A	1.3	761	Culebra Pk	SC
74	13,894	Vermillion Pk	Gladstone Pk	9.2	3,674	Ophir	SJ
77	13,864	Vestal Pk	Sunlight Pk	4.3	1,124	Storm King Pk	SJ
579	13,088	Virginia Pk	Point 13,140 A	0.8	428	Winfield	SW
389	13,307	Warren, Mt	Rogers Pk	1.1	367	Mt Evans	FR
215	13,555	Wasatch Mtn	Lookout Pk	2.1	495	Telluride	SJ
	13,292	Waverly Mtn	Oxford, Mt	1.1	152	Mt Harvard	SW
465	13,220	"Weminuche Pk"	"SoSo, Mt"	1.8	800	Emerald Lake	SJ
210	13,568	West Apostle	Ice Mtn	0.6	508	Winfield	SW
372	13,326	West Buffalo Pk	Point 13,374	9.7	1,986	Marmot Pk	TM
S	13,741	"West Dallas"	Dallas Pk	0.6	281	Telluride	SJ
	13,047	West Dyer Mtn	Dyer Mtn	0.7	267	Mt Sherman	TM
617	13,035	West Elk Pk	Owen B, Mt	13.9	3,055	West Elk Pk	EL
S	13,740	"West Eolus"	Eolus, Mt	0.3	280	Mtn View Crest	SJ
	14,256	"West Evans"	Evans, Mt	0.3	116	Mt Evans	FR
600	13,062	West Needle Mtn	Twilight Pk	1.0	562	Snowdon Pk	SJ
614	13,041	"West Partner Pk" (Pk U)	"East Partner Pk" (Pk V)	0.9	581	Vail East	GO
184	13,626	West Spanish Pk	Culebra Pk	20.4	3,685	Spanish Pks	SC

Rank	Elev	Peak Name	Parent	Mile	Rise	Quadrangle	Rg
	14,100	"West Wilson"	Wilson, Mt	0.3	120	Mt Wilson	SJ
	13,572	Weston Pk	Horseshoe Mtn	3.6	272	Mt Sherman	TM
49	14,015	Wetterhorn Pk	Uncompahgre Pk	2.8	1,635	Wetterhorn Pk	SJ
587	13,078	Whale Pk	Geneva Pk	4.7	982	Jefferson	FR
152	13,690	Wheeler Mtn	Fletcher Mtn	1.6	310	Copper Mtn	TM
322	13,401	White BM	White Rock Mtn	0.5	381	Gothic	EL
182	13,627	White Dome	Trinity Pk East	2.2	967	Storm King Pk	SJ
	13,684	White Ridge	Sherman, Mt	1.2	184	Mt Sherman	TM
229	13,540	White Rock Mtn	Point 13,550	2.8	800	Gothic	EL
164	13,667	White, Mt	Antero, Mt	1.3	847	Mt Antero	SW
223	13,542	Whitecross Mtn	Handies Pk	1.4	562	Redcloud Pk	SJ
	13,259	Whitehead Pk	Rhoda, Mt	0.4	119	Howardsville	SJ
261	13,492	Whitehouse Mtn	Teakettle Mtn	1.9	592	Ouray	SJ
422	13,271	Whitney Pk	Point 13,768	1.4	691	Mt of the Holy Cross	SW
316	13,408	Wilcox, Mt	Argentine Pk	1.1	548	Montezuma	FR
427	13,266	Wildhorse Pk	Seigal Mtn	4.0	966	Wetterhorn Pk	SJ
331	13,382	Williams Mtn	Twining Pk	4.1	1,682	Mt Champion	SW
562	13,108	Williams Mtn North	Williams Mtn	0.8	408	Mt Champion	SW
383	13,312	Williams Mtn South A	Williams Mtn	1.5	572	Thimble Rock	SW
488	13,203	Williams Mtn South B	Williams Mtn	0.5	423	Mt Champion	SW
619	13,033	Williams Mtn South C	Williams Mtn South A	1.4	493	Thimble Rock	SW
531	13,143	Willoughby Mtn	Point 13,336	1.8	442	Highland Pk	EL
48	14,017	Wilson Pk	Wilson, Mt	1.5	877	Mt Wilson	SJ
16	14,246	Wilson, Mt	Uncompahgre Pk	33.1	4,026	Mt Wilson	SJ
33	14,082	Windom Pk	Eolus, Mt	1.7	1,022	Columbine Pass	SJ
516	13,157	"Window Pk"	Rio Grande Pyramid	0.9	300	Rio Grande Pyramid	SJ
	13,077	Winfield Pk	Virginia Pk	0.7	177	Winfield	SW
	13,041	Wolcott Mtn	"S 6"	0.6	181	Mt Sneffels	SJ
169	13,660	Wood Mtn	Point 13,688 B	0.5	320	Handies Pk	SJ
21	14,196	Yale, Mt	Harvard, Mt	5.6	1,896	Mt Yale	SW
	13,177	Yellow Mtn	Pilot Knob	0.6	197	Ophir	SJ
247	13,514	Ypsilon Mtn	Hagues Pk	2.6	1,116	Trail Ridge	FR

Index

About the Authors

Photo by Andrew Peacock

Photo by Gerry Roach

Gerry Roach is a world-class mountaineer and an accomplished rock climber. After climbing Mount Everest in 1983, he went on to become the second person to climb the highest peak on each of the seven continents in 1985. In 6 decades of mountaineering, Gerry has climbed in dozens of states and countries. He has been on 15 Alaskan expeditions, 10 Andean expeditions and 7 Himalayan expeditions, including first ascents in the kingdom of Bhutan. In 1997, he summited Gasherbrum II in the Karakorum. In 2000, he became the first person to climb North America's 10 highest peaks. He is a member of the American Alpine Club.

Closer to home, Gerry has climbed more than 1,200 named peaks in Colorado, including all the fourteeners, which he completed for the first time in 1975. He finished climbing every named peak in the Indian Peaks Wilderness and Rocky Mountain National Park in 1978. He has also climbed every peak in the Colorado counties of Boulder, Gilpin and Clear Creek, and every named peak in Jefferson County.

Gerry's first book, *Flatiron Classics,* is a guide to the trails and easier rock climbs in the Flatirons above Boulder. His second book, *Rocky Mountain National Park,* is a guide to the classic hikes and climbs in that park. Gerry's guide *Colorado's Indian Peaks* remains the definitive mountaineering guide to that special area. In his best-selling guide *Colorado's Fourteeners,* he shares his intimate knowledge of and love for Colorado's high peaks.

Jennifer Roach is an expert on Colorado's mountains. She has climbed Colorado's 500 highest peaks and all of the state's thirteeners. She has climbed Colorado's mountains for 20 years and knows all about places most of us have never heard of. Jennifer has visited the Lost Creek Wilderness for most of these years and has led many Colorado Mountain Club trips there. She has summited most of the peaks in the Lost Creek Wilderness, between Denver and Colorado Springs, more than once. She is coauthor with Gerry of *Colorado's Lost Creek Wilderness.*

Gerry and Jennifer live in Boulder, Colorado.